SUNDAYS

AND

SEASONS

2003

Augsburg Fortress

SUNDAYS AND SEASONS
2003, Year B

RELATED RESOURCES

Icon: Visual Images for Every Sunday (AFP 0-8066-4077-4)
Worship Planning Calendar, 2003, Year B (AFP 0-8066-4283-1)
Words for Worship, 2003, Year B (AFP 0-8066-4285-8)

ACKNOWLEDGMENTS

Copyright © 2002 Augsburg Fortress. All rights reserved. Except for brief quotations in critical articles or reviews, no part of this book may be reproduced in any manner without prior written permission from the publisher. Write to: Permissions, Augsburg Fortress, Box 1209, Minneapolis, MN 55440-1209.

Scripture quotations are from the New Revised Standard Version Bible © 1989 Division of Christian Education of the National Council of the Churches of Christ in the United States of America. Used by permission.

The prayers (printed in each Sunday/festival section) may be reproduced for one-time, congregational use, provided copies are for local use only and the following copyright notice appears: From Sundays and Seasons, copyright © 2002 Augsburg Fortress.

Annual Materials

Encountering the Gospels of Year B: Karl Gerlach

Seasonal and Weekly Materials

Images of the Season: Gail Ramshaw (Christmas Cycle), Robert Burke (Lent, Three Days), Robert Buckley Farlee (Easter, November), Lyn Langkamer (Summer, Autumn)

Environment and Art for the Season: Johan van Parys (Christmas Cycle), Carlton Gross and the Augsburg Fortress Ecclesiastical Arts staff (Easter Cycle), Deborah Bogaert (Season after Pentecost)

Preaching with the Season and Images for Preaching: David Lechelt (Christmas Cycle), Barbara Berry-Bailey (Lent, Easter), Ronald Roschke (Three Days), Barry Harte (Summer), Erik Strand (Autumn, November)

The Prayers: James Boline

Worship Matters: Linda and Dennis Bushkofsky (Christmas Cycle), John Morris (Easter Cycle), Douglas Ogden (Summer), Nancy Curtis (Autumn, November)

Let the Children Come: Sandra Anderson (Christmas Cycle), Kathy Logan LaDuca (Easter Cycle), David Batchelder (Summer), Carol Detweiler (Autumn, November)

Music Materials

Assembly Song for the Season: Michael Krentz; Mainstream Choral: Jerry Gunderson; Classic Choral: Lorraine Brugh; Children's Choirs: Philip Holzman; Keyboard/Instrumental: Thomas Hamilton; Handbell: Beverly Eiche; Praise Ensemble: Mark Glaeser

Editors

Norma Aamodt-Nelson, Carol Carver, Robert Buckley Farlee, Becky Lowe, Martin A. Seltz, and Eric Vollen

Art and Design

Art: Tanja Butler
Book Design: The Kantor Group, Inc.

Manufactured in the U.S.A.   0-8066-4284-X

1   2   3

Introduction

Advent

Christmas

Epiphany

Lent

The Three Days

Easter

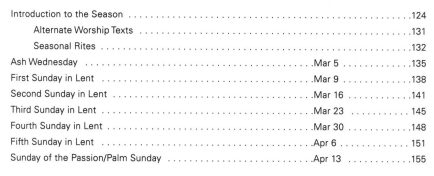

Summer

Autumn

November

Introduction

Many planners and leaders of worship have come

to rely on this resource, and we are glad you find it useful.

We are always looking for ways to improve it, without losing

the elements that have proven their value over the years. In these days when we all feel the many demands on our time, *Sundays and Seasons* is offered not as an invitation to cookie-cutter worship planning, but rather to help users focus on the heart of the week's liturgy and more easily locate appropriate resources.

A VARIETY OF VIEWPOINTS

This book functions on several levels. It can be helpful to pastors who craft sermons, those who formulate the week's liturgies, musicians as they look for the right works to enhance the weekly readings, those who pay particular attention to the visual environment surrounding worship, teachers and others whose focus is on the children in our midst, as well as worship committees and all who simply would like to deepen their understanding of the details of weekly worship. It is built around primary Lutheran worship resources, particularly *Lutheran Book of Worship* and *With One Voice*, but those of other liturgical traditions have found value in it as well.

The various kinds of users who may explore this resource will also find different levels of perspective within. An essay on the gospel texts for year B helps provide an overview to the whole liturgical year. Some general lists and indexes will be helpful throughout the year.

Narrowing the focus a bit, we look at each season of the church year, including the season after Pentecost divided into the sections of summer, autumn, and November. An "Images of the Season" essay sets the stage and provides some insights to stimulate a fresh focus toward worship. Accompanying pieces on Environment and Art, Preaching, Assembly Song, the Shape of Worship, and Music provide practical ideas for that season. For each division of the year, alternate worship texts are provided, and in most cases also some seasonal rites. The alternate texts are not intended necessarily to replace, every week and every instance, the versions given in the

worship books. They are, rather, options to consider as you find them useful in your circumstances.

Finally, each Sunday and major festival is given a variety of resources: Introduction, Images for Preaching, Worship Matters, Let the Children Come, hymn suggestions, musical helps, and more. And brief descriptions are provided for the commemorations and occasions in *Lutheran Book of Worship, Libro de Liturgia y Cántico,* and *This Far by Faith.*

PARTICULAR TO THIS YEAR

A few changes come each year to this resource. This year, at reader request, we have added the appointed verse texts for each Sunday. In the prayers for most weeks, a place is provided to insert the names of those who have died who are important Christian witnesses to your worshiping community. Those may be the coming week's commemorations, or people from your congregation.

One of the strengths of *Sundays and Seasons* is that it brings together a collection of voices and perspectives from many different settings of the church's life. We are grateful again this year for those who contributed to this volume. Karl Gerlach gets us started with a perceptive essay on the gospel readings for the year, what he calls the "Gospel According to Year B," since it combines Mark with John and snippets of Matthew and Luke. Seasonal images are creatively suggested in pieces by Gail Ramshaw, Robert Burke, and Lyn Lyngkamer. Our attention is drawn to the environment for the various seasons in essays by Johan van Parys, Carlton Gross and the Augsburg Fortress Ecclesiastical Arts staff, and Deborah Bogaert. Parish musicians as well as all worship planners will appreciate the well-grounded assembly song ideas from Michael Krentz.

Preachers are always looking for new approaches to the texts for seasons and individual days, and here we are helped by David Lechelt, Barbara Berry-Bailey, Ronald Roschke, Barry Harte, and Erik Strand.

Practical and sometimes provocative thoughts on worship matters come from Linda and Dennis Bushkofsky, John Morris, Douglas Ogden, and Nancy Curtis. Prayers for each week are adapted from ones provided by James Boline. The "Let the Children Come" columns bring us ideas from Sandra Anderson, Kathy Logan LaDuca, David Batchelder, and Carol Detweiler.

Church music recommendations come from contributors well-versed in the practical necessities of that field, including John Helgen (contemporary choral), Jerry Gunderson (mainstream choral), Philip Holzman (children's choral), Lorraine Brugh (classic choral), Thomas Hamilton (keyboard and instrumental), Beverly Eiche (handbell), and Mark Glaeser (praise ensemble).

We are grateful to Dennis Bushkofsky, a former editor of this publication, who contacted and briefed the writers for this year's volume.

RELATED RESOURCES

Sundays and Seasons continues its close association with other Augsburg Fortress lectionary-based resources. *Words for Worship* 2003 contains electronic files of sections within this volume that are intended for group use, in addition to complete lectionary readings and psalms. *Worship Planning Calendar* is closely linked as a workbook counterpart to *Sundays and Seasons*. Users of Life Together lectionary-based curriculum resources will find many supportive connections in this volume.

Tanja Butler's wonderful art throughout this volume is available for use by congregations that purchase the CD-ROM *Icon: Visual Images for Every Sunday*, a three-year set of images for use in designing worship folders and other local materials.

The vast majority of hymns referenced in *Sundays and Seasons* from various published collections are available in *Hymns for Worship*, a CD-ROM with text files and melody music graphics for more than 1,400 hymns. This electronic resource also includes sound reference files, a powerful search engine, and a copyright management tool.

Finally, *Sundays and Seasons* users will want to be watching for resources that will be appearing in the Renewing Worship series, as a new generation of primary worship resources is developed.

FOR THE SAKE OF GOOD WORSHIP

A planning resource like *Sundays and Seasons* is not, of course, an end in itself. It merely seeks to aid those who plan and lead the church's worship. To the extent that it is helpful, please make use of it. It is expected, though, that material needs to be adapted to suit various situations. Where users see something that they think could be improved in general, we appreciate hearing from them. We are, after all, united in our efforts to help the people of God offer up their confession and adoration, supplication and praise.

—Robert Buckley Farlee, general editor

7

Encountering *the* Gospels *of* Year B

"On the day called Sunday," Justin Martyr writes

in his First Apology, "all who live in the cities or country

gather together in one place, and the memoirs of the apostles

or the writings of the prophets are read as long as time permits. Then when the lector has finished, the presider instructs and exhorts to imitate these good things."

We have no way of knowing how these readings were chosen. Nor do we know how long the readings and homily may have been, given the time permitted by workday tasks and the dangers of persecution. We do know that Justin's "memoirs of the apostles" did not include the Fourth Gospel, whose canonical status was controversial in Rome well into the next century, and that Justin himself had a habit of harmonizing material from the other three.

Whether in the second century or the twenty-first, the act of reading in the assembly places a more primitive shape upon the gospels than that of the evangelists, who had taken narrative and teaching traditions and combined them into literary works. Some eighty years before Justin, Jesus stories were not read, but told—anywhere "two or more were gathered," but primarily at the Sunday eucharist or in catechesis preparing for Christian initiation. The author of Mark, the first written gospel, must have listened carefully to what was spoken and prayed there. Yet even after the New Testament canon coalesced some fifty years after Justin was martyred, the dynamic relationship between story and liturgy never stopped. Corporate worship no longer shaped the texts, but still shapes its meaning. As ancient as the church itself, this dynamic tradition encourages congregations to select lectors carefully and train them well, for the liturgy is still where most Christians encounter the gospels. For many, it is the only place.

Simply hearing the lessons read each Sunday without additional study, however, tends to blend the gospels even more than Justin's Synoptic harmonies, especially in lectionary year B. Except for seven Sundays (Baptism of Jesus, Transfiguration, Palm/Passion, and two each in Advent and Lent), it is the year of Mark only in ordinary time. With no birth or childhood nar-

ratives, Mark is silent from Advent 3 through Epiphany, yielding Advent 4 and Christmas to Luke's annunciation and birth story. When Mark does speak in the Christmas cycle, John echoes: about the Baptist (Advent 2, 3) and the calling of the disciples (Epiphany 2, 3). With up to 26 readings to Mark's 29, the Gospel of John takes over for both the Forty (Lent) and Fifty (Easter) Days and interrupts Mark with five continuous readings from John 6, the "Bread of life" commentary on the feeding of the five thousand. The prominence given John is not due just to the relative brevity of Mark— the "Markan Apocalypse" so important to this gospel, for instance, is represented only by two readings—but even more to the shape of the liturgical year. It, too, is the reason for four readings from the other two gospels: from Matthew, the adoration of the magi (the traditional Western Epiphany text) and the Ash Wednesday admonition on fasting (Matt. 6); and from Luke, the ascension and a resurrection appearance from Luke 24 on Easter 3. All these numbers point to a simple liturgical fact: the cycle of "Sundays and seasons" with its rhythm of festival, preparation, and commemoration in three annual lectionaries forms the primary gospel redaction for the assembly.

For those who wish to "instruct and exhort" in harmony with the lectionary, the cumulative levels of harnessing the dynamic between holy words and holy acts are furthered by the design of this book. The first level is the choice of hymns and music that "imitate the good things" of scripture. As the gospel writers before them, the faithful of many times and places cherished these same stories and responded in verse and musical commentary. Many traditional hymns, especially from Germany or the British Isles, continue to inspire instrumental works. Newer supplements add hymns that embody more current understandings of baptism and eucharist as well as offering a sampling from the growing churches of Africa and Asia. Even if your congregation does nothing

8

beyond this selection, a meaningful worship experience is guaranteed almost by accident. The role of music as Luther's "handmaid of the gospel" can be less accidental, however, if homilists take more than a fleeting glance at hymn texts, if only for their wealth of ideas and images for preaching. If a hymn does not yield such treasures, then it likely should not be sung either. Perennial arguments over musical style can also be smoothed when all know that text alone, and neither its melody, age, nor cultural provenance, is most important to the liturgy.

A second level ensures that worshipers hearing "instruction" on Sunday morning are actually instructed— by publicizing seasonal themes and inviting worshipers to listen for them. Again, even if no extra effort is put into applying these themes beyond the choice of hymns, the happy coincidence of biblical text, prayer, and congregational song will take care of the rest.

A third level seeks "to imitate these good things" in acts of corporate worship by allowing gospel texts to generate a plot line for each season, mirroring the dynamic between word and worship that engendered both gospel narratives and their structured proclamation in the liturgical year. The difference here is catechetical, if not culinary: Rather than a haphazard potluck at the table of the word, worshiping in year B becomes a feast on a few dishes well prepared—if not for the tastes, at least for the nourishment of a particular congregation.

The first step is a close reading of "The Gospel according to Year B." When read as if it were an integral book rather than a compilation of pericopes, what themes and images spin out from its various chapters, the liturgical seasons? What speaks particularly to local, national, or global concerns, to special needs of the congregation? The five Sundays of John 6 speak with differing accents to a congregation wishing to deepen its understanding of the eucharist than to one struggling to feed the neighbor, with real or spiritual food.

What voices may be silent in this gospel redaction? If the Feast of the Epiphany is transferred to the second Sunday after Christmas, then Matthew's magi supplant a text that Augustine called one of the most sublime examples of Christian rhetoric, the prologue of John. In that case, one should be sure that it is read at one of the Christmas services. Continue to read each season as if it were the chapter of a book. Listen carefully as the texts speak to you, share your thoughts with other worship leaders, identify the themes to be embodied in this year's worship, publicize them in the congregation, and as the politicians are wont to say, stay "on message" with every choice for the liturgy.

For Advent, you might listen to an older version of the lectionary. As an alternate reading for the first Sunday, *Lutheran Book of Worship* suggests the Palm Sunday gospel, the triumphal entry into Jerusalem from Mark 11. This passage is, of course, jarringly out of place in the historical scheme of things. Yet a layer of meaning usually glossed over on Palm Sunday when the text is usually read, now rises to the surface: Jesus' march into the Holy City becomes the Second Advent and his triumphal reappearance at the end of time. How much more dramatically this text focuses themes of hope and trust than the usual admonition of watching and waiting, simply by proclaiming the reality for which the church watches and waits.

In terms of plot, the seasons of Epiphany and Pentecost reproduce in differing lengths Mark's swift movement to the cross as the definitive and defining revelation of God, represented seasonally by the feasts of the Transfiguration, regarded by some scholars as a "misplaced" resurrection story, and Christ the King, which presents the dialogue between Jesus and Pilate about the "King of the Jews." This basically Lenten shape is augmented in Pentecost by the five-Sunday "mini-season" of John 6, which the fourth evangelist dates to near the Passover. It may be reason enough for Advent in year B to begin with a Holy Week text.

On the surface, the Markan readings for the green seasons seem little more than miracle stories the author pasted together, sometimes enveloping one into another. Yet as Rudolf Bultmann pointed out, the tone of these stories becomes progressively darker, the conflict leading to the cross more pronounced as the action moves toward Jerusalem. All but one of the miracle stories read during Epiphany varies the Markan theme of the "Messianic secret," where Jesus commands both humans and demonic spirits to reveal neither his power nor his true identity. It is only at the cross, in the confession of the centurion, "Surely this was the Son of God," that Mark allows a full epiphany of Jesus.

The Lenten season moves toward that same confession in the reading of the Markan passion narrative, but it does so with three narratives from John. After the story of the temptation and Jesus' prediction of his suffering and death (Mark 8:31-38), the "Gospel according to Year B" moves the Johannine cleansing of the temple into a more Synoptic position and the sign of the serpent in the wilderness closer as well to the cross. Jesus' proclamation that his "hour has come" functions as another Markan passion prediction. The footwashing and the Passion according to John on Maundy Thursday and Good Friday lead to the reading of the Markan resurrection story at the Easter Vigil and the Johannine version on Easter Day.

The Sundays of Easter vary less year to year than the Sundays of any other season but Holy Week. The story of Thomas is always read on the day John dates Jesus' coming among the disciples behind locked doors seven days after the Resurrection, while the Good Shepherd (John 10) on Easter 4 and the High Priestly Prayer (John 17) on Easter 7 only vary as to which section of the text is read. The Gospel according to Year B complements the Thomas story with the meal of broiled fish (Luke 24) and two readings from John 15, the True Vine

and its branches. The Easter season follows no imitative movement toward the Ascension. Rather, it offers the emblematic display of powerful symbols of Christ's presence, continuing among his people even after his ascent to the Father. At the same time, this theme is always balanced with that of absence, grief, and confusion, as indeed the long Johannine discourses before the cross are a long farewell.

This more-than-cursory overview of the seasons of year B is enough to suggest that this second of the lectionary years preserves much of the plot of Mark, even when it uses texts from other gospels to augment its supposed liturgical "deficiencies." Epiphany and Pentecost, even Advent albeit with a slight revision, repeat with varying accents the paschal mystery of the Forty, the Three, and the Fifty Days. Yet this story of the cross, synthesized from a generation of worship and proclamation into the "memoirs of the apostles," is the only story there is, either in the gospels or the worship of the church, "that imitates these good things" of scripture.

Worship Planning Checklist

ADVENT

- Purchase materials needed for the Advent wreath (four candles and enough greens to cover the wreath). Perhaps more than one wreath is desired for your congregation if Sunday school students and other groups gather for worship during the season in locations other than the sanctuary.
- Arrange for the Advent wreath to be set up one or two days before the first Sunday in Advent (December 1 this year).

CHRISTMAS

- Arrange for purchase or donation of a Christmas tree.
- Locate any decorations in storage from previous years for the Christmas tree, the crèche, the chancel, and other interior or exterior areas. Repair or replace decorations as needed.
- Decide on a date and time for Christmas decorating, and solicit volunteer help.
- Prepare extra communion elements and communionware needed for additional worshipers at Christmas services.
- Prepare a sign-up list for those who wish to sponsor additional flowers or poinsettia plants at Christmas.
- Plan for removal of Christmas decorations following the twelve days.
- If handheld candles are used by worshipers on Christmas Eve, determine how many candles and holders can be used from previous seasons and how many new candles and holders will be needed.
- Order special bulletin covers if needed for services on Christmas Eve or Christmas Day.

EPIPHANY

- Determine what (if any) Epiphany decorations are needed.
- If incense is to be used for a service on the festival of the Epiphany, purchase a small quantity of it (along with self-lighting charcoal).
- If the Baptism of Our Lord (January 12) is to be observed as a baptismal festival, publicize the festival through congregational newsletters and bulletins;

arrange for baptismal preparation sessions with parents, sponsors, and candidates; and when the day arrives set out the following:

- Towel (baptismal napkin) for each person baptized
- Baptismal candle for each person baptized
- Shell (if used)
- Oil for anointing (also a lemon wedge and a towel for removing oil from the presiding minister's hands)
- Baptismal garment for each person baptized (if used)
- Fresh water in a ewer (pitcher) or the font

LENT

- If ashes are used on Ash Wednesday, arrange for someone (perhaps one or two altar guild members) to burn palms from the previous Passion Sunday. (Ask members to bring in their own from home if they also saved them.) Or contact a church supply store for a supply of ashes. (A small quantity of ashes mixed with a small amount of olive oil or water will go a long way.)
- Determine whether any Lenten decorations other than Lenten paraments are to be used.
- If crosses or images are draped in purple during the Lenten season, recruit volunteers to do this between the Transfiguration of Our Lord (March 2) and Ash Wednesday (March 5).
- Order enough palm branches to distribute to worshipers on Passion Sunday. (Additional palm branches or plants may be used as decorations that day.) If the long individual palm fronds are used, they will need to be separated ahead of time. Make sure that they are fresh.
- Make sure worshipers know where to gather for a procession with palms liturgy. Prepare signs to direct them. Determine how those with physical

11

disabilities will participate in the procession or be seated ahead of time.

- Reserve leftover palm branches to be burned for ashes next Ash Wednesday.
- Order worship participation leaflets if used for the Ash Wednesday liturgy or Passion Sunday processional liturgy.
- Order additional bulletin covers if needed for any special Lenten services (especially midweek liturgies).

THE THREE DAYS

- Schedule special rehearsals for the liturgies on these days. The liturgies in this week are unique, so all worship leaders, even those involved in previous years, need to prepare for their roles.
- Be sure that altar guild members are well equipped and informed about their tasks for these busy days.
- Locate one or more basin and pitcher sets for the Maundy Thursday liturgy. Towels are also needed for drying the feet of participants.
- Determine how participants will be recruited for the footwashing. Even if all in the congregation are invited, several people should be specifically prepared to participate.
- If the altar and the rest of the chancel are to be stripped on Maundy Thursday, recruit helpers (sacristans/altar guild members, even children) for this task.
- If you ring bells to announce services or chimes to mark times of the day, consider silencing them from the beginning of the Maundy Thursday liturgy until the hymn of praise at the Easter Vigil (or the first celebration of Easter).
- Keeping in mind that all of the liturgies of the Three Days are considered to be as one, do not plan a procession of worship leaders for Good Friday. All worship leaders simply find their own way to their respective places before the service.
- If a rite of procession and veneration of the cross is to be used on Good Friday, find or construct a rough-hewn cross, and determine how it will be placed in the chancel ahead of time or carried in procession.
- Prepare to thoroughly clean the worship space sometime between the Maundy Thursday liturgy and the Easter Vigil.

- If handheld candles are to be used by worshipers at an Easter Vigil, determine how many candles and holders can be used from previous seasons, and how many new candles and holders will need to be purchased.
- Well before the Easter Vigil, purchase a paschal candle (or arrange to make one) that will fit your congregation's stand. When the candle is received or finished, check to be sure it fits the stand snugly yet without being forced into place.
- Prepare materials needed to start a fire at the beginning of the Easter Vigil (kindling, wood, brazier, matches). Also, recruit someone to start and extinguish the fire properly.
- Prior to the Easter Vigil, place the paschal candle stand in the chancel for use throughout the fifty days of Easter.
- Make sure worshipers know where to gather for the service of light at the Easter Vigil. If you plan to gather outside, be sure to make backup plans in case of inclement weather.
- Decide how light will be provided so assisting ministers and lectors can see to read during the Easter Vigil service. Determine what level of light is needed so all members of the congregation can participate during this liturgy. Practice setting lighting levels (at night) with the person who will be responsible for this during the vigil.
- Plan how the readings of the Easter Vigil will be proclaimed. Consider having a different person proclaim each of the readings to enliven the readings for the assembly.
- Prepare extra communion elements and communionware needed for additional worshipers at Holy Week and Easter services.
- Order worship participation leaflets if used for the Maundy Thursday, Good Friday, or Easter Vigil liturgies.
- Order bulletin covers if needed for any Holy Week liturgies.
- It is helpful to prepare printed materials for worship leaders for the Three Days. Consider placing all the texts and musical resources needed by worship leaders into three-ring binders (half-inch binders purchased at office supply stores work well). Highlight speaking parts and instructions for each worship leader in individual copies.

- If the Easter Vigil (or Easter Sunday) is to be observed as a baptismal festival, publicize the festival through congregational newsletters and bulletins; arrange for baptismal preparation sessions with parents, sponsors, and candidates; and when the day arrives set out the following:
  - Towel (baptismal napkin) for each person baptized
  - Baptismal candle for each person baptized
  - Shell (if used)
  - Oil for anointing (also a lemon wedge and a towel for removing oil from the presiding minister's hands)
  - Baptismal garment for each person baptized (if used)
  - Fresh water in a ewer (pitcher) or the font
  - Evergreen branches for sprinkling
- Prepare a sign-up list for people who wish to sponsor Easter lilies or other flowers for Easter Day (and throughout the season of Easter).
- Order extra bulletin covers for additional worshipers on Easter Day.

EASTER

- Determine whether special flowers are to be used on Pentecost. (Some churches order red geraniums to be placed around the church grounds or given away following Pentecost services.)
- If Pentecost is to be observed as a baptismal festival, publicize the festival through congregational newsletters and bulletins; arrange for baptismal preparation sessions with parents, sponsors, and candidates; and when the day arrives set out the following:
  - Towel (baptismal napkin) for each person baptized
  - Baptismal candle for each person baptized
  - Shell (if used)
  - Oil for anointing (also a lemon wedge and a towel for removing oil from the presiding minister's hands)
  - Baptismal garment for each person baptized (if used)
  - Fresh water in a ewer (pitcher) or the font
- On Pentecost, seven votive candles in red glass holders may be lit and placed on or near the altar to recall the gifts of the Spirit.

SUMMER

- If the worship schedule changes, notify local newspapers and change listings on exterior signs and church answering machines.
- Consider ways to make worshipers cooler during warm weather.
- If the congregation worships outside one or more times during the summer, decide how worshipers will know where to gather and how they will be seated.

AUTUMN

- For worship schedule changes, notify local newspapers and change listings on exterior signs and church answering machines.
- If a harvest festival is scheduled, determine what (if any) additional decorations are to be used and who is to do the decorating.
- If one or more food collections are to be received, notify the congregation about them in advance, and arrange to deliver food to the appropriate agency within a day or two after the collection.

NOVEMBER

- Provide a book of remembrance or another way to collect the names of those who have died and who are to be remembered in prayers this month (or only on All Saints Sunday).
- If All Saints is to be observed as a baptismal festival, publicize the festival through congregational newsletters and bulletins; arrange for baptismal preparation sessions with parents, sponsors, and candidates; and when the day arrives set out the following:
  - Towel (baptismal napkin) for each person baptized
  - Baptismal candle for each person baptized
  - Shell (if used)
  - Oil for anointing (also a lemon wedge and a towel for removing oil from the presiding minister's hands)
  - Baptismal garment for each person baptized (if used)
  - Fresh water in a ewer (pitcher) or the font

13

Selected Publishers

AMSI
Contact the Lorenz Corp.

ABINGDON PRESS
201 8th Avenue South
PO Box 801
Nashville TN 37202
800/251-3320 Customer Service
800/836-7802 Fax

AGEHR, INC.
1055 E. Centerville Station Road
Dayton OH 45459
800/878-5459
937/438-0085

ALFRED PUBLISHING CO., INC.
Box 10003
16380 Roscoe Boulevard
Van Nuys CA 91410-0003
800/292-6122 Customer Service
800/632-1928 Fax
818/891-5999 Direct

**AMERICAN LUTHERAN
PUBLICITY BUREAU**
PO Box 327
Delhi NY 13753-0327
607/746-7511 General

ARISTA MUSIC
PO Box 1596
Brooklyn NY 11201

AUGSBURG FORTRESS
PO Box 1209
Minneapolis MN 55440-1209
800/328-4648 Ordering
800/421-0239 Permissions
612/330-3300 General

BECKENHORST PRESS
PO Box 14273
Columbus OH 43214
614/451-6461 General
614/451-6627 Fax

BOOSEY & HAWKES, INC.
35 East Twenty-first Street
New York NY 10010
212/358-5300 General
212/358-5301 Fax

BOSTON MUSIC CO.
215 Stuart Street
Boston MA 02116
617/426-5100 Retail
617/528-6141 Fax

BOURNE COMPANY
5 West 37th Street
New York NY 10018
212/391-4300 General
212/391-4306 Fax

BRENTWOOD-BENSON MUSIC, INC.
741 Cool Springs Blvd
Franklin, TN 37067
800/846-7664 General
615/261-3381 Fax

BROUDE BROTHERS LTD.
141 White Oaks Road
Williamstown MA 01267
413/458-8131

BROADMAN HOLMAN GENEVOX
Customer Accounts Center
127 Ninth Avenue North
Nashville TN 37234
800/251-3225 General
800/296-4036 Fax

C.F. PETERS CORPORATION
Building 36, Atlas Terminal
70-30 80th Street
Glendale NY 11385
718/416-7800 General
718/416-7805 Fax

CARL FISCHER, INC.
Order from local music store

**CHANGING CHURCH FORUM/
PRINCE OF PEACE PUBLISHING**
200 E. Nicollet Boulevard
Burnsville MN 55337
800/874-2044

CHESTER MUSIC
Contact Hal Leonard Corp
Music Dispatch

CHURCH PENSION FUND
Order from: Church Publishing Corp.
445 Fifth Avenue
New York NY 10016
800/242-1918 General
212/779-3392 Fax

CONCORDIA PUBLISHING HOUSE
3558 South Jefferson Avenue
Saint Louis MO 63118
800/325-3040 Customer Service
314/268-1329 Fax
314/268-1000 General

E.C. SCHIRMER MUSIC CO.
138 Ipswich Street
Boston MA 02215
800/777-1919 Ordering
617/236-1935 General
617/236-0261 Fax
614/236-1935

EUROPEAN AMERICAN MUSIC DIST.
Note Service Department
15800 Northwest 48th Avenue
Miami FL 33014
800/628-1528

GIA PUBLICATIONS, INC.
7404 South Mason Avenue
Chicago IL 60638
800/442-1358 General
708/496-3800 General
708/496-3828 Fax

GALAXY COMMUNICATIONS
Contact E.C. Schirmer Music Co

GENEVOX
See Broadman Holman

HINSHAW MUSIC CO, INC.
PO Box 470
Chapel Hill NC 27514-0470
919/933-1691 General
919/967-3399 Fax

HAL LEONARD CORP.
PO Box 13819
7777 West Bluemound Road
Milwaukee WI 53213
414/774-3630 General
800/637-2852 Music Dispatch

HOPE PUBLISHING CO.
380 South Main Place
Carol Stream IL 60188
800/323-1049 General
630/665-3200 General
630/665-2552 Fax

**ICEL (INTERNATIONAL COMMISSION
ON ENGLISH IN THE LITURGY)**
1522 K Street Northwest
Suite 1000
Washington DC 20005-4097
202/347-0800 General

IONIAN ARTS, INC.
PO Box 259
Mercer Island WA 98040-0259
206/236-2210 General

14

THE LITURGICAL CONFERENCE
415 Michigan Avenue Northeast
Suite 65
Washington DC 20017
800/394-0885 Ordering
202/832-6520 General
202/832-6523 Fax

THE LITURGICAL PRESS
St. John's Abbey
PO Box 7500
Collegeville MN 56321-7500
800/858-5450 General
800/445-5899 Fax
320/363-2213 General
320/363-3299 Fax

LITURGY TRAINING PUBLICATIONS
1800 North Hermitage Avenue
Chicago IL 60622-1101
800/933-1800 Ordering
800/933-4779 Customer Service
800/933-7094 Fax

LIVE OAK HOUSE
3211 Plantation Rd.
Austin TX 78745-7424
512/282-3397

THE LORENZ CORPORATION
PO Box 802
Dayton OH 45401-0802
800/444-1144 General

LUDWIG MUSIC PUBLISHING CO.
557 East 140th Street
Cleveland OH 44110-1999
800/851-1150 General
216/851-1150 General
216/851-1958 Fax

MARANATHA!
PO Box 1077
Dana Point, CA 92629
800/245-7664 Retail

MARK FOSTER
Contact Shawnee Press

MASTERS MUSIC PUBLICATIONS
PO Box 810157
Boca Raton FL 33481-0157
561/241-6169 General
561/241-6347 Fax

MORNINGSTAR MUSIC PUBLISHERS
1727 Larkin Williams Road
Fenton MO 63026
800/647-2117 Ordering
314/305-0121 Fax

MUSICA RUSSICA
27 Willow Lane
Madison CT 06443
800/326-3132

NEW GENERATION PUBLISHERS
Box 321
Waverly IA 50677
319/352-4396

NATIONAL MUSIC PUBLISHERS
P.O. Box 4027
Tustin, CA 92781
800/829-1850 General
714/542-0847 Fax

NORTHWESTERN PUBLISHING
HOUSE
1250 North 113th Street
Milwaukee WI 53226-3284
800/662-6093

OREGON CATHOLIC PRESS
5536 Northeast Hassalo
Portland OR 97213
800/547-8992 General
800/462-7329 Fax

OXFORD UNIVERSITY PRESS
2001 Evans Road
Cary NC 27513
800/451-7556 General
919/677-1303 Fax

PARACLETE PRESS
P.O. Box 1568
Orleans, MA 02653
800/451-5006 General
508/255-5705 Fax

PLYMOUTH MUSIC CO.
170 Northeast 33rd Street
Fort Lauderdale FL 33334
954/563-1844 General
954/563-9006 Fax

RANDALL M. EGAN, PUBLISHERS
2024 Kenwood Parkway
Minneapolis MN 55405-2303
612/377-4450 General
*51 Fax

SELAH PUBLISHING CO.
PO Box 3037
58 Pearl Street
Kingston NY 12401-0902
845/338 2816 General
800/852-6172 Ordering
845/338 2991 Fax

SHAWNEE PRESS
PO Box 690
49 Waring Drive
Delaware Water Gap PA 18327-1699
800/962-8584 General
570/476-0550 General
570/476-5247 Fax

THEODORE PRESSER CO.
588 N Gulph Road
King of Prussia PA 19010
610/527-4242 Retail
610/527-7841 Fax

WARNER BROTHERS PUBLICATIONS
15800 Northwest 48th Avenue
Miami FL 33014
800/327-7643 General
305/621-4869 Fax

WESTMINSTER/JOHN KNOX PRESS
100 Witherspoon Street
Louisville KY 40202-1396
800/523-1631 General
800/541-5113 Fax

WORD MUSIC CO.
3319 West End Avenue, Suite 201
Nashville TN 37203
888/324-9673

WORLD LIBRARY PUBLICATIONS
3825 North Willow Road
Schiller Park IL 60176
800/621-5197 General
847/678-0621 General
847/671-5715 Fax

Key *to* Music Publishers

ABI	Abingdon	GAL	Galaxy	MF	Mark Foster		
AFP	Augsburg Fortress	GIA	GIA Publications	MSM	MorningStar Music		
AG	Agape (Hope)	GS	GlorySound	NOV	Novello (Shawnee)		
AGEHR	AGEHR Inc.	Gsch	G. Schirmer	NMP	National Music Publishers		
ALF	Alfred	HAL	Hal Leonard: G. Schirmer	OCP	Oregon Catholic Press		
AMSI	AMSI (Lorenz)	HIN	Hinshaw	OXF	Oxford University Press		
AUR	Aureole	HOP	Hope	PAR	Paraclete		
BEC	Beckenhorst	HWG	H. W. Gray (Warner)	PET	C. F. Peters		
BEL	Belwin (Warner)	INT	Integrity (Word)	PLY	Plymouth		
B&H	Boosey & Hawkes	ION	Ionian Arts	PRE	Presser		
BRN	Bourne	JEF	Jeffers	PVN	Pavane (Intrada)		
CFI	Carl Fischer	KIR	Kirkland House	RME	Randall M. Egan		
CFP	C. F. Peters	KJO	Kjos	SEL	Selah		
CG	Choristers Guild (Lorenz)	LAK	Lake State	SHW	Shawnee		
CHA	Chantry (Augsburg Fortress)	LAW	Lawson-Gould Publishing	SMP	Sacred Music Press (Lorenz)		
CPH	Concordia	LED	Leduc	WAL	Walton		
DUR	Durand (Presser)	LEM	Lemoine (Presser)	WAR	Warner (Plymouth)		
ECS	E. C. Schirmer	LIL	Lillenas (Royal Marketing)	WJK	Westminster John Knox		
FB	Fred Bock Music Co.	LOR	Lorenz	WLP	World Library		
FLA	Flammer (Shawnee)	MAR	Maranatha	WRD	Word Music		
		MAY	Mayhew				

16

Music *for* Worship Key

acc	accompaniment	hc	handchimes	qrt	quartet
bar	baritone	hp	harp	rec	recorder
bng	bongos	hpd	harpsichord	sax	saxophone
bsn	bassoon	hrn	horn	sop	soprano
cant	cantor	inst	instrument	str	strings
ch	chimes	kybd	keyboard	synth	synthesizer
cl	clarinet	M	medium	tamb	tambourine
cong	congregation	MH	medium high	tba	tuba
cont	continuo	ML	medium low	tbn	trombone
cym	cymbal	mxd	mixed	timp	timpani
DB	double or string bass	narr	narrator	trbl	treble
dbl	double	ob	oboe	tri	triangle
desc	descant	oct	octave	tpt	trumpet
div	divisi	opt	optional	U	unison
drm	drum	orch	orchestra	vc	violoncello
eng hrn	English horn	org	organ	vcs	voices
fc	finger cymbals	perc	percussion	vla	viola
fl	flute	picc	piccolo	vln	violin
glock	glockenspiel	pno	piano	ww	woodwind
gtr	guitar	pt	part	xyl	xylophone
hb	handbells	qnt	quintet		

17

Key *to* Hymn *and* Psalm Collections

ASG* *As Sunshine to a Garden: Hymns and Songs of Rusty Edwards.* Mpls: Augsburg Fortress, 1999.

BC *Borning Cry: Worship for a New Generation.* Waverly, IA: New Generation Publishers, 1992.

BL* *Bread of Life: Mass and Songs for the Assembly.* Mpls: Augsburg Fortress, 2000.

CS* *Congregational Song: Proposals for Renewal* (Renewing Worship 1). Evangelical Lutheran Church in America, 2001. Augsburg Fortress.

CW *Christian Worship: A Lutheran Hymnal* (Wisconsin Evangelical Lutheran Synod). Milwaukee: Northwestern Publishing House, 1993.

DH* *Dancing at the Harvest: Songs of Ray Makeever.* Mpls: Augsburg Fortress, 1997.

GC *Gather Comprehensive.* Chicago: GIA Publications, 1994.

GS2* *Global Songs 2: Bread for the Journey.* Mpls: Augsburg Fortress, 1997.

H82 *The Hymnal 1982* (Episcopal). New York: The Church Pension Fund, 1985.

HFW *Hymns for Worship.* Mpls: Augsburg Fortress, 2001.

LBW* *Lutheran Book of Worship.* Mpls: Augsburg; Philadelphia: Board of Publication, LCA, 1978.

LLC* *Libro de Liturgia y Cántico.* Mpls: Augsburg Fortress, 1998.

LS* *LifeSongs.* Mpls: Augsburg Fortress, 1999.

LW *Lutheran Worship* (Lutheran Church–Missouri Synod). St. Louis: Concordia Publishing House, 1982.

NCH *The New Century Hymnal* (United Church of Christ). Cleveland: The Pilgrim Press, 1995.

OBS* *O Blessed Spring: Hymns of Susan Palo Cherwien.* Mpls: Augsburg Fortress, 1997.

PCY *Psalms for the Church Year.* 8 vol. Chicago: GIA Publications.

PH *The Presbyterian Hymnal* (PC-USA). Louisville: Westminster John Knox Press, 1990.

PS *Psalm Songs.* 3 vol. Mpls: Augsburg Fortress, 1998.

PW *Psalter for Worship.* 3 vol. (Cycles A, B, C.) Mpls: Augsburg Fortress.

STP *Singing the Psalms.* 3 vol. Portland: OCP Publications.

TFF* *This Far by Faith.* Mpls: Augsburg Fortress, 1999.

TP *The Psalter: Psalms and the Canticles for Singing.* Louisville: Westminster/John Knox Press.

UMH *The United Methodist Hymnal.* Nashville: The United Methodist Publishing House, 1989.

W3 *Worship: A Hymnal and Service Book for Roman Catholics.* Third ed. Chicago: GIA 1986.

WOV* *With One Voice.* Mpls: Augsburg Fortress, 1995.

W&P* *Worship & Praise.* Mpls: Augsburg Fortress, 1999.

* Indicates resources whose hymns are, at least in part, included in the CD-ROM resource *Hymns for Worship* (Mpls: Augsburg Fortress, 2001).

18

ADVENT

A season pregnant with promise

Images *of the* Season

Advent is like a stump. The growing season is over,

the crops are harvested and the fields are bare. All over

North America trees and bushes are down to their brown

branches, with most of the leaves and all the colorful flowers and fruits gone. In caves and burrows throughout the continent animals hibernate. Dusk comes earlier every day, as if cutting off daylight before our eyes. People sit under sunlamps to treat their depression, because the darkness makes them feel like stumps themselves.

But a stump still has its roots. It always holds the possibility of sending up fresh sprigs from which a new tree will grow. A hibernating bear is not dead, just waiting out the cold, and we can be sure that the bear will emerge, yawning and stretching and hunting again as soon as the weather warms up. Even though the deciduous trees seem, as Charles Dickens said of Jacob Marley, "dead as a doornail," they hold every hope that in some weeks or months green buds will appear.

The lectionary readings for Advent are about our being a stump and yet hoping for new life. We read ancient poems of a subjugated people whose glorious monarchy had been destroyed. Their poets write of their life as a faded leaf, of themselves as withered grass. Yet they are hopeful that a time of blessing will come. They recall that King David was promised an everlasting reign, and they are confident that a new king will be born: God will respond to their deep yearning for blessing, justice, and peace. Yes, people are hungry and tables are bare. But there is the hope that bounty will appear, for a stump does have roots that can sprout anytime. John the Baptist, half-mad with indignation at the desert that he sees in people's lives, promises that something is coming to stir life into dried branches.

Thus Advent is like the winter landscape, appearing bleak and barren, but pregnant with promise. Thus, of course, Advent is like each one of us at some time in our life. Our joys cut down, we feel as if we are a piece of wood that other people are sitting on top of. It seems as if nothing in or around us is still alive. Maybe it is unemployment: will a job ever come through? Maybe we await word from the physicians: will life be worth living

if my beloved is dead? One doesn't get through life without these dry and deathly times.

But we hope. The roots still reach into the soil. We continue trusting that tomorrow, or next week, or next spring, the situation will improve. When I personally am close to despair, my friends and family and neighbors hope for me, reminding me of the promise of new life.

Advent is a time for the Christian community to practice hope. We acknowledge that we are stumps, but that God promises us new growth. So we huddle together in the dark and chill, awaiting the life of God. Even if our roots are dead, we trust that God's grace will awaken our life and send out new shoots. We remind one another to stay awake in case the dawn comes and we miss it. We keep each other company as we anticipate the arrival of the angel, announcing the good news.

North American Advent fits well the season of the earth—the natural calendar—since the year itself is at its stump. But what is particularly dissonant is that Advent is totally out of sync with the North American secular calendar. The secular calendar turns all of December, and increasingly November as well, into a Saturnalia, a month of revels, a continuous party to end the old year and bring in the new. For many people the month is utterly exhausting, with shopping and decorating and baking and concerts and drinking and wrapping. Yet this orgy of celebration is called by the name of Christ, and it is carols about Jesus' birth piped into the malls on December 1 that stimulate us to spend more money. By December 26, Christmas is gone, and Valentine cards appear.

The church need not be an Ebenezer Scrooge, grumping about secular Christmas, bad-mouthing the fun. Cultures commonly celebrate at the winter solstice. But maintaining Advent has profound human benefit, and the church dismisses or truncates this liturgical season to its own loss. Human beings need to acknowledge the stumpiness of life. We all go through times of great need and, finally, death. If you're doing just fine now, then look around, because others, who need what you have, aren't. We all need to practice hope, to try it out for some weeks each year, so that when misery comes, and it will, we know how to call it up in ourselves and within the community. How will we know where hope is, if we never planted it, cultivated it, watered it?

Some Christians do little to observe the liturgical year. At the time of the Reformation, some Protestants abandoned the church year, judging it an unnecessary constraint from church authorities. For several centuries in North America, Christianity spread on the prairie with few resident churches or clergy, and in people's kitchens the liturgical year languished. What resulted was that all these human emotions had to be experienced individually: *I* had to experience guilt by myself; *I* alone had to seek the word of life; *I* had to get ecstatic, if I was the personality-type to get ecstatic, when the Spirit entered me. In religious matters, the individual was isolated from others.

The liturgical year allows a season each year for us all to accompany one another through life. We practice these feelings each year, and best of all, we practice them together. Yes, we are all stumps, you this year, I next, but I also a stump this year because of you. And we all hope for God's life. Come on, you're not dead yet! We'll make it together. Have you heard the news? The wilderness is crowded with people splashing in the river, Mary is pregnant with a new King David, and here are bread and wine, the beginning of the feast.

An increasing number of churches decorate themselves for Advent with blue. Sometimes the color is a deep blue, the sky just before sunrise; sometimes it is a lighter tone, the color of a springtime bird's egg. While the culture inundates the surroundings with Christmas trees and lights and red bows, Advent asks us to keep practicing hope. Remember the poor; stand with the unemployed; visit the mourners. If you dress the virgin Mary in a blue gown, remember that she was not serenely smiling through a normal pregnancy. No: she was hoping, for a husband who would not abandon her, for money to pay the tax, for a place to give birth, for the world to receive whatever was about to spring forth.

Environment *and* Art *for the* Season

As we prepare the worship environment to mark

the change into the Advent season, to what sort of

spiritual realities should we draw people's attention?

What is the season about? The word *Advent* is derived from the Latin phrase *adventus Domini*, meaning "the coming of the Lord." Often, it is understood to refer to the first coming of Jesus. More completely, though, *adventus Domini* refers to the coming of the Lord in the past, today, and especially at the end of time. The season of Advent, therefore, is a season filled with anticipation, not just for the commemoration of the birth of Jesus— the first coming of the Lord—but also anticipation of current, future, and final manifestations.

The readings of Advent illuminate this reality beautifully. The gospel from Mark proclaimed on the first Sunday of Advent invites the listener to be ready. "Be- ware, keep alert; for you do not know when the time will come. . . . Keep awake." This powerful calling presents us, on the one hand, with the invitation to watchfulness and readiness and, on the other hand, contains the awesome promise of the *parousia*, or the *adventus Domini*, or the second coming of the Lord.

A reading from Isaiah on the second Sunday of Advent paints a slightly different and soothing picture of what the eschatological times will bring: "See, the Lord GOD comes with might, and his arm rules for him; his reward is with him, and his recompense before him. He will feed his flock like a shepherd; he will gather the lambs in his arms, and carry them in his bosom, and gently lead the mother sheep." The fear of the eschaton, which the first Sunday of Advent may instill, is now softened with the image of a caring God.

These two complementary texts suggest that the true spirit of Advent lies somewhere between the joy of anticipating Jesus' birth and the awe-inspiring anticipation of Christ's return. The two always go hand in hand. As believers we are invited to take courage in the promise of the past and to prepare for the fulfillment of that promise in the future. The goal, of course, is to become more and more aware of the presence of Christ today.

Thus the incarnation cycle, like every liturgical season and every liturgical gathering, encompasses three time zones: the past, the present, and the future. The incarnation cycle that we celebrate in the here and now places us between the first coming and the second coming. The incarnation cycle comprises commemoration of the past, experience in the present, and anticipation of the future as we recall God's marvelous deeds and prepare for the fulfillment of that which God began with us in Jesus Christ. The Christian who remembers the first coming and awaits the things to come will "stay awake," will "keep watch," will "be on guard," and will be ready for that glorious time when Christ returns and brings this cosmic adventure to completion.

The celebration of the incarnation cycle should focus both on the celebration of the first coming of our Savior with its promise of salvation, and on his second coming in glory, which will bring the fulfillment of that promise. The readings, the environment, the music, and the texts gradually build up to the celebrations of Christmas and Epiphany.

THE ENVIRONMENT FOR THE SEASON

When thinking of the visual surroundings, remember that worship is dynamic and kinetic, and those qualities should be reflected in the environment. A free-hanging suspended Advent wreath, seasonal mobiles, and processional banners all can help to underline the progression of the season. There might be one banner in the procession the first week, two banners the second week, and so forth.

LITURGICAL COLOR

Two color schemes are used for the season of Advent. Since the codification of the liturgical colors in the Roman Catholic church, purple had been the color of the penitential seasons of Advent and Lent. Other Christian denominations, too, followed this custom. As the penitential character of Advent diminished in favor of a spirituality of anticipation and expectation, a desire to differentiate this season from Lent includes the use of liturgical color. Many churches today use blue for the season of Advent, a practice that dates back to some ecclesiastical regions in medieval Europe and now is widely spread among the Lutheran and Anglican churches. Across the denominational borders one might opt for bluish purples, blues, and rose. For a fitting choice of the color palette of this season, just look at the early morning sky on a clear winter morning in northern climes.

THE ADVENT WREATH

The origin of the Advent wreath is somewhat obscure. Some evidence points to pre-Christian Scandinavia, where a wheel was decorated with candles while prayers were offered for the wheel of the earth to be turned so that light and warmth would return. During the Middle Ages Christians adopted this pagan ritual and began to use it in domestic settings. By the year 1500 more formal practices surrounding the Advent wreath had developed.

Its symbols of life and light apply easily to the Christian cosmology in which Christ is both the light that dispels the darkness and the life of the world. The wheel itself, a circle with neither beginning nor end, signifies eternal life. The evergreens too signify eternal life; more specifically: pine, holly, and yew imply immortality; cedar, strength and healing; laurel, victory over suffering; pine cones and nuts, life and resurrection. In its totality, the wreath symbolizes new and eternal life gained through the life, death, and resurrection of Jesus Christ.

The four candles added to the wreath symbolize the four weeks of Advent. According to some traditions, three or four of these candles are blue or purple, in keeping with the liturgical color of Advent. Sometimes, one of the candles—the one lit on *Gaudete* Sunday, the third Sunday of Advent—is rose and invites the people to rejoice because the middle of Advent has been reached. As the emphasis is no longer on the penitential character of Advent, but rather on anticipation and expectation, using white candles has become more popular.

22

Some very (one might say "too") creative communities have a different color for each Sunday of Advent, symbolizing the meaning of that specific Sunday. The problem with this and similar far-fetched schemes is that their meaning is totally lost on the people. Better to keep the focus on the central symbol of the lighted wreath itself.

THE APPEARANCE OF THE WREATH

When building the Advent wreath, make sure that its size is relative to the building. The wreath should be in the shape of a wheel and it should preferably be hanging so that it can turn freely. The best location for the wreath is in the center of the church, above the assembly. Use fresh greens for the wreath and substantial candles. Make provision for the candles to be kept burning once lit.

A practical suggestion: install a (mechanical) pulley in the ceiling of the church. This pulley should be located between the roof and the ceiling so that it remains invisible from the floor of the church. Have a substantial metal frame constructed which will support the greens. Wrap generous amounts of greens around the frame. Add holly and pine cones. Resist the temptation to add ribbons, bows, or any other decorative elements. This is the time to be earthy. In order to be able to keep the candles burning it is best to use lanterns with globes either just above the wreath or else immediately next to the wreath.

RITUAL USE

Because the Advent wreath has become the central symbol of the season, it is good that it be integrated in the celebration of liturgy on each Sunday of Advent. The opening procession may halt beneath the wreath for a blessing and the solemn lighting of one of the candles. After that you can continue the procession while singing the remainder of the song. When everyone is in their place continue with the collect.

ADVENT MOBILES, BANNERS, AND TEMPORARY SCULPTURES

The incarnation cycle, not unlike the paschal cycle, has occasioned beautiful temporary liturgical art. The sanctuary banners of the 1960s initiated creative ways of integrating the entire space in the environment for the season. Ribbons, cloth, cut and folded paper allow for the

entire parish to engage in the preparation of the church. Identify some leaders in your parish; you could even develop an artist-in-residence program to assist in these and other environmental activities. However, it is important to remember that the environment is in service of worship, not the other way around. Also, each season's primary symbols need to be focal. The Advent wreath, as the primary symbol of Advent, should be enhanced by other decorations, not obscured.

THE JESSE TREE

Tree branches and, depending on the size of the church, entire trees such as birch are often brought into the church in order to symbolize the Stem of Jesse or simply death awaiting new life. Some churches hang tiny mirrors in these trees or decorate them with lights, but it is best to leave those trees be. They best communicate their message undecorated. Leave these trees in place throughout the entire incarnation season. As you add evergreens you will create a beautiful dialogue between life and death.

OUTDOOR ENVIRONMENT

Outdoor banners in the colors of the season; wreaths decorated with lights and hung in the arches of the portico; evergreen roping intertwined with lights to decorate light poles; combinations of branches, pine cones, and pods attached to the doors; and so on, all assist in announcing to the world that Christians are celebrating the incarnation. In addition, the spilling out of the seasonal environment into the world emphasizes that liturgy and life or worship and work are one. Worship neither begins nor ends at the doors to the church. Worship happens on both sides of those doors.

WORSHIP AIDS

If you use worship aids other than hymnals, these too should reflect the season. The choice of paper, color of ink, and decorative elements can assist in the illumination of the spirituality of the season.

BEYOND THE TRADITIONAL ADVENT ENVIRONMENT

In addition to the liturgical and biblical symbols that constitute the incarnation cycle, human and cultural realities should be taken into account. For example, during the season of Advent the world celebrates World AIDS Day (December 1) and International Human Rights Day (December 10). It might be beneficial to the community to look outward and see how these celebrations might impact the incarnation observance. For instance, the International Human Rights Day—the day on which the Dalai Lama received the Nobel Prize for Peace—could occasion the use of prayer flags in the liturgical environment, a Buddhist custom brought to this country by refugees from Tibet. Imagine large mobiles, suspended from the ceiling and covered with prayer flags in blues, purple, and rose on which the children have written their intentions. In Tibetan spirituality, every time the flags move it is said that the prayer written on the flags rises to God. Although that interpretation might be stretching our understanding of prayer, the flags can nevertheless function in the same way as banners— as visual reminders of our beliefs and intentions.

Preaching *with the* Season

Advent is the opening season, the season

of beginning and new creation. It is a time of waiting

and anticipation for us and for God. It is a time that is

at first perplexing and fearful, but then filled with great hope and joy. The color of the season is blue for hope. Blue like the sky on a clear and sunny day following snowfall. Blue like the skies of artist John August Swanson, layer upon layer of blue. Advent is a time to uncover these layers of blue and see layers of hope. God is faithful; God has come. God will come again.

The Old Testament readings from Isaiah are a grand invitation to uncover these layers of hope. They are the stories of a people, our ancestors, who have lost their way, their place, and who have a renewed yearning for God and their true home. They are in exile. They are in a dry, wilderness time. The reading from 2 Samuel underscores what we must learn in the wilderness: God continues to build us "a house and a kingdom that will be sure forever" (2 Sam. 7:16). These Old Testament texts offer us many layers of hope to uncover as well as a thoroughgoing witness to the light and future we possess in Jesus Christ.

The gospel invitations to beginning and new creation include Mark's cry of joy at the good news of Jesus Christ given out of the wilderness through John the Baptist, that same prophet seen through the gospel of John's wide-angle lens of light and darkness and the remembrance of all our beginnings in the word, and the annunciation to Mary received with perplexity and fear.

To be sure, fear makes an appearance in the apocalyptic vision of Mark 13 as it does whenever God comes close and offers new life. But fear gives way to renewed assent and songs of joy. Mark's apocalyptic fig tree has tender branches of inexorable faithfulness. God is coming. You can count on it. The new creation does not come forth without birth pangs, but come forth it will. God is faithful and has heard our cry.

Second readings during the season offer encouragement for our waiting and strength for our birthing. I Corinthians 1 proclaims that God is faithful and that we are not lacking in spiritual gifts as we wait. 2 Peter 3 provides divine perspective for our waiting. In I Thessalonians 5 we join in singing "rejoice in the Lord always (and yes, again, I say . . .)." In Romans, we receive God's benediction: we will be "strengthened according to my gospel and the proclamation of Jesus Christ." Again and again throughout the season of Advent we are invited and encouraged to uncover the layers of our true and sure hope, to receive the mystery that is now made known, to follow Paul's lead in making this gospel *my gospel*, and to join the communion of God's people in songs of pure joy.

The shape of the season moves from big, panoramic views like God's coming in Mark's apocalypse and John's cosmic Christ to zoomed-in shots like John the Baptist proclaiming a baptism of repentance, and finally, Mary pondering the angel Gabriel's greeting. Advent offers all the angles in which we may view and reflect upon our life and future. Our communities need them all, because this season highlights exactly that with which we have such trouble: incorporating the coming of God into our daily lives.

We sing "Oh, come, oh, come, Emmanuel," but how does that "God with us" become real in our lives? How do we move from the sentiment to the deep rejoicing? How do we wait and let God come to us, on God's own terms, when we are bombarded with contrary messages? Because we so often fall prey to those enticements, how do we overcome the resulting alienation from God? How do we get past our fears—of loss of control, of an unknown future in God's hands? All of these questions, acknowledged or not, wait for the preacher's treatment, using the lessons at hand.

Call and response is one of the currents that flow through the season. Advent opens with the yearning and cry of a people who are cut off: "O that you would tear open the heavens and come down" (Isa. 64:1). Mark 13 is full of response. We are God's people, and God is faithful. Likewise, on the fourth Sunday in Advent, God calls to Mary (us). The response is at first perplexed and fearful (we can be so crazy about change). Mary's response evolves into faithfulness and joy. She shows such a wonderful openness and patience to God's waiting. God waited for Mary and waits for us too.

Another current is *wilderness and homecoming*. The middle Sundays give two hearings to the cry of John the Baptist, his relationship to Jesus, and his response. Questions of our present wilderness and exile challenge us. Powerful connections to the baptismal river that flows through our wilderness and the light that illumines our darkness offer great hope and incredibly good news.

Images abound in Advent. Linking these together in our preaching opens the text and our response. Robert Farrar Capon, in his book *Fingerprints of God*, is devoted to tracking God through the layers of biblical images. Through the fig tree, the potter and his clay, in the wilderness, in light and dark, and in Mary's womb we see God, ourselves, and each other.

Advent is the opening season, the season of beginning and new creation. We now dare to acknowledge all that clouds in our lives, because soon those clouds will be swept away. For it is the season of the deep, clear blue sky, lightening in the east. Jesus is coming, and we stand on tiptoe to glimpse him.

25

Shape *of* Worship *for the* Season

BASIC SHAPE OF THE EUCHARISTIC RITE

- Confession and Forgiveness: see alternate worship text for Advent in *Sundays and Seasons.* In this and all of the following "alternate worship text" suggestions, it is fine to use the text in place in the worship setting.

GATHERING

- Greeting: see alternate worship text for Advent
- Use the Kyrie
- Omit the hymn of praise

WORD

- Use the Nicene Creed
- The prayers: see alternate forms and responses for Advent

MEAL

- Offertory prayer: see alternate worship form for Advent
- Use the proper preface for Advent
- Eucharistic prayer: in addition to the four main options in *LBW*, see "Eucharistic Prayer A: The Season of Advent" in *WOV* Leaders Edition, p. 65
- Invitation to communion: see alternate worship text for Advent
- Post-communion prayer: see alternate worship text for Advent

SENDING

- Benediction: see alternate worship text for Advent
- Dismissal: see alternate worship text for Advent

OTHER SEASONAL POSSIBILITIES

BLESSING THE ADVENT WREATH

The gathering rite for either the first week or all the weeks in Advent may take the following form of lighting the Advent wreath. (See Environment and Art for the Season for further ideas.) Following the entrance hymn and the greeting, one of the prayers of blessing in the seasonal rites section may be spoken. A candle on the wreath may then be lit during the singing of an Advent hymn, such as "Light one candle to watch for Messiah" (WOV 630). The service then continues with the prayer of the day. On the remaining Sundays in Advent, the number of candles lit before the service would be the total number lit the previous week. One new candle is then lit each week during the service.

Alternatively, candles of the Advent wreath may simply be lit before the service, without any special prayer of blessing. Candles may also be lit during the singing of an entrance hymn, the Kyrie, or the psalm for the day, without any special accompanying prayers or music.

EVENING PRAYER FOR ADVENT

Consider holding an evening prayer service one weeknight each week throughout the Advent season. All the events might take place in a fellowship hall around tables. A possible format for the gatherings:

- Light candles placed at tables as worshipers begin singing a hymn of light ("Joyous light of glory" [*LBW*, p. 143], "O Trinity, O blessed Light" [LBW 275], "O Light whose splendor thrills" [WOV 728] among others). Follow with a table prayer.
- Have a simple meal, perhaps consisting only of soup, bread, and a salad.
- Prepare gifts to be given to homebound people or others in need.
- Close with an abbreviated form of evening prayer:
  - a psalm (especially 141)
  - a short scripture reading (see *LBW*, pp. 179 and 186 for ideas)
  - the Song of Mary (Canticle 6 in *LBW*, or "My soul now magnifies the Lord" [LBW 180], or "My soul proclaims your greatness" [WOV 730])
  - brief prayers of intercession, perhaps from the people gathered
  - the Lord's Prayer
  - dismissal
- Other possibilities for musical settings of evening prayer include *Joyous Light Evening Prayer* (Ray Makeever), *Stay with Us, Lord* (David Cherwien), and *Holden Evening Prayer* (Marty Haugen).

Try to focus in these gatherings on things that people of all ages can do together, so that families are brought together during this time of year.

LECTIONARY OPPORTUNITY FOR HEALING SERVICES

- Third Sunday in Advent (first reading)

Assembly Song *for the* Season

Hope, expectation, judgment, repentance,

peace, waiting, patience, and preparation are all words

for the Advent season. What music best expresses

this season, best captures the spirit of its message? Gregorian chant might be uniquely suited to Advent; its timeless quality relates well to this season so concerned with God's time, *kairos*, as opposed to clock time, *chronos*. The flowing chant tune of "Oh, come, oh, come, Emmanuel" (LBW 34) is surely one reason it is one of the most loved of Advent hymns. Look for opportunities to use some chant melodies in this Advent's celebrations, and help people learn to wait by saving the Christmas music for Christmas.

GATHERING

- To put Advent in proper perspective, use "Lo! He comes with clouds descending" (LBW 27) as the entrance hymn on the first Sunday in Advent; then use it as the sending hymn on the fourth Sunday.
- Omit the hymn of praise during this season (save it for Christmas), and highlight the Kyrie, using either a litany form (with its prayer for peace) or the chant melody "Kyrie" found at WOV 604. Let the assembly repeat each line of the melody after a cantor, making a six-fold Kyrie (omit the final line); use handbells with pitches D, G, A (and E) to accompany the singing.

WORD

- Use the chant "Alleluia" found at WOV 611a for the gospel acclamation. Use bells (G, A, D) to give the pitch to the assembly for the alleluias, have the choir or cantor sing the proper verse (the tone is found in the accompaniment edition of *WOV*; the text is given at each Sunday in this resource), and then use the bells again to support the assembly as they repeat the alleluias.

- On the fourth Sunday in Advent, use the Magnificat (Luke 1:47-55) for the psalm. Have the choir sing one of the many fine choral arrangements of this text that are readily available, or use "My soul does magnify the Lord" (TFF 168), "My soul now magnifies the Lord" (LBW 180), or "My soul proclaims your greatness" (WOV 730) for the assembly.

MEAL

- Two possibilities for seasonal offertory hymns are "People, look east" (WOV 626) and "Fling wide the door" (LBW 32). The former helps people relate their preparations at home to setting the table for the eucharist; the latter asks Jesus to come and live in the hearts of people. Use of a triangle would heighten the dance-like character of both these tunes.
- For the "Lamb of God" at the distribution, use the chant "Agnus Dei" at WOV 620. It could be sung first by the choir in Latin, and then by the assembly in English.

SENDING

- Use a single song for the post-communion as the table is cleared (instead of both a post-communion canticle and a sending hymn). "Blessed be the God of Israel" (WOV 725) is based on the Benedictus, one of the three Lukan canticles associated with Advent, Christmas, and Epiphany. Other seasonal choices include "Surely it is God who saves me" (WOV 635), "O day of peace" (WOV 762), "On Jordan's stormy banks" (TFF 49), and "Give thanks" (W&P 41), which echoes the text of the Magnificat (the psalm for the fourth Sunday in Advent).

27

Music *for the* Season

VERSE AND OFFERTORY

Cherwien, David. *Verses for the Sundays in Advent.* U, org, opt hb.
MSM 80-001.

Gospel Acclamations. Cant, choir, cong, inst.   MAY 0862096324.

Haas, David. *Advent/Christmas Gospel Acclamations.* 2 pt, org, gtr, solo
inst.   OCP 8732GC.

Hillert, Richard. *Verses and Offertory Sentences, part 1: Advent through Christ-mas.* U, kybd.   CPH 97-5509.

Krentz, Michael. *Alleluia Verses for Advent.* SAB, org.   AFP 0800647041.

Schiavone, J. *Gospel Acclamation Verses for the Sundays of Advent.*   GIA G-2110.

Wetzler, Robert. *Verses and Offertories: Advent 1—Baptism of Our Lord.*
SATB, kybd.   AFP 0800648994.

CHORAL

Bach, J.S. "Savior of the Nations, Come" in *Bach for All Seasons.* SATB,
kybd.   AFP 080065854X.

Ellingboe, Bradley. "Soul, Adorn Yourself with Gladness." SATB.
AFP 0800658477.

Haugen, Kyle. "Lost in the Night." SAB, pno.   AFP 0880659244.

Holst, Gustav. "Let All Mortal Flesh Keep Silence." SATB, org, opt
orch.   GAL S& B2309.

Janzen, Janet L. "Thou Shalt Know Him When He Comes." SATB,
kybd, opt tpt.   MSM 50-0021.

Jean, Martin. "Advent Hymn." SATB.   AFP 0800656628.

Jennings, Carolyn. "Climb to the Top of the Highest Mountain."
SATB, children's choir/solo, kybd.   KJO C-8118.

Ley, Henry G. "Come, Thou Long Expected Jesus" in *The Oxford Easy
Anthem Book.* SATB, org.   OXF.

Lovelace, Austin. "The Comings of the Lord." SAB, kybd.
CPH 98-3210.

Manz, Paul. "E'en So, Lord Jesus, Quickly Come." SATB.
MSM 50-0001.

Powell, Robert J. "Adam Lay Ybounden." SATB, org.
AFP 0800659104.

Schalk, Carl. "As the Dark Awaits the Dawn." SATB, org.
AFP 0800658450.

Shute, Linda Cable. "Come, Jesus, Come Morning Star." SATB, org.
AFP 0800659163.

Sirett, Mark G. "Thou Shalt Know Him." SATB.   AFP 0800655206.

Thoburn, Crawford R. "The Linden Tree." SATB, kybd.
AFP 0800652134.

Walker, David. "The Hills Are Bare at Bethlehem." U/2 pt, Orff inst.
AFP 6000118457.

CHILDREN'S CHOIRS

Christopherson, Dorothy. "Come, Lord Jesus. We Are Waiting."
U, cong, 3 oct hb, sop glock, kybd.   CG CGA592.

Clyde, Arthur. "Advent Candle Song." U, opt cong, kybd, fl/C inst.
AFP 0800646436.

Hopson, Hal H. "Advent Joy." U, kybd.   CG CGA870.

Schalk, Carl. "Light the Candle." U, org.   MSM 50-0006.

KEYBOARD/INSTRUMENTAL

Augsburg Organ Library: Advent. Org.   AFP 0800658957.

Guilmant, Alexandre. "March Upon Handel's 'Lift Up Your Heads.'"
Org.   SCH 11311.

Heiller, Anton. "Nun komm der Heiden Heiland." Org.
Ludwig Doblinger Pub 02-375.

Oliver, Curt. *Advent Keyboard Seasons.* Pno/kybd.   AFP 0800655788.

Uehlein, Christopher. *A Blue Cloud Abbey Christmas Organ Book.* Org.
AFP 0800659791.

Wasson, Laura. *A Christmas Season Tapestry for Piano.* Pno.
AFP 080065725X.

HANDBELL

Afdahl, Lee J. "Prepare the Royal Highway." 3–5 oct. L2+.
AFP 080065577X.

Hopson, Hal H. "Advent Carol" *(Veni, Emmanuel).* 3–5 oct.
CG CGB154.

Prichard, R./arr. Barbara Kinyon. "Come Thou Long Expected
Jesus." 2 oct.   JEF MHP1689.

Rogers, Sharon Elery. "Advent Bells." 2 oct.   MSM 30-001.

Vivaldi, Antonio/arr. Paul Kinney. "Vivaldi Concerto." 3–5 oct.
CG CGB228.

PRAISE ENSEMBLE

Besig, Don. "Emmanuel Is Coming!" SATB, kybd.   FLA A7401.

Drennan, Patti. "Every Valley." SATB, kybd, op solo, fl.
ALF 18379. SAB.   ALF 18380.

Robinson, Marc A. "Prepare Ye." SATB, kybd, perc.   KJO Ed8830.

28

Alternate Worship Texts

CONFESSION AND FORGIVENESS

In the name of the Father, and of the ✛ Son,
and of the Holy Spirit.
Amen

As we await the fullness of Christ's coming,
let us acknowledge our sins and failures before God.

Silence for reflection and self-examination.

Our indifference toward your coming,
we confess to you, Lord.
Our desire to control time and seasons,
we confess to you, Lord.
Our failure to be alert to signs of your presence in our midst,
we confess to you, Lord.
Our lack of concern for those who come after us,
we confess to you, Lord.
Our injustices toward people you came to save,
we confess to you, Lord.

In the mercy of almighty God,
I declare to you the forgiveness of your sins,
and the grace to know joy in the Savior's coming.
Amen

GREETING

May the One who was, and who is, and who is to come,
be with you in grace and peace.
And also with you.

PRAYERS

Walking in the light of the coming Savior,
let us pray for the church, the world,
and all who await the dawn of God's justice.

A brief silence.

Each petition ends:
We pray to the Lord:
show us your light.

Concluding petition:
Show us your light, O God,
and bring us to the day of our redemption,
through Jesus Christ our Lord.
Amen

OFFERTORY PRAYER

Gracious God,
we come to your table
with gifts of heart and hand.
Fill us with your love
so that our lives
may bear the fruit of your Word,
Jesus Christ our Savior. Amen

INVITATION TO COMMUNION

The door to God's banquet hall is open.
Enter into the joy of this feast.

POST-COMMUNION PRAYER

O God, in this meal
we have been given a foretaste
of the feast that is to come.
Help us always to be alert
to your gifts in our midst;
through Jesus Christ our Lord.
Amen

BLESSING

May the holy and living God ✛ bless you
in darkness and in light,
in fasting and in feasting,
in sadness and in joy.
Amen

DISMISSAL

Go in peace.
Let everyone know the hope that fills you.
Thanks be to God.

29

Seasonal Rites

Blessing of the Advent Wreath

FIRST SUNDAY IN ADVENT

We praise you, O God, for this evergreen crown
that marks our days of preparation for Christ's advent.
As we light the first candle on this wreath,
rouse us from sleep, that we may be ready to greet our Lord
when he comes with all the saints and angels.
Enlighten us with your grace,
and prepare our hearts to welcome him with joy.
Grant this through Christ our Lord,
whose coming is certain and whose day draws near.
Amen

Light the first candle.

SECOND SUNDAY IN ADVENT

We praise you, O God, for this circle of light
that marks our days of preparation for Christ's advent.
As we light the candles on this wreath,
kindle within us the fire of your Spirit,
that we may be light shining in the darkness.
Enlighten us with your grace,
that we may welcome others as you have welcomed us.
Grant this through Christ our Lord,
whose coming is certain and whose day draws near.
Amen

Light the second candle.

THIRD SUNDAY IN ADVENT

We praise you, O God, for this victory wreath
that marks our days of preparation for Christ's advent.
As we light the candles on this wreath,
strengthen our hearts as we await the Lord's coming in glory.
Enlighten us with your grace,
that we may serve our neighbors in need.
Grant this through Christ our Lord,
whose coming is certain and whose day draws near.
Amen

Light the third candle.

FOURTH SUNDAY IN ADVENT

We praise you, O God, for this wheel of time
that marks our days of preparation for Christ's advent.
As we light the candles on this wreath,
open our eyes to see your presence
in the lowly ones of this earth.
Enlighten us with your grace,
that we may sing of your advent among us
in the Word made flesh.
Grant this through Christ our Lord,
whose coming is certain and whose day draws near.
Amen

Light the fourth candle.

Lessons and Carols for Advent (Based on the O Antiphons)

The O Antiphons are a set of medieval refrains originally used before and after the singing of the Magnificat. They were in use already in the eighth century. Each of them invokes the Messiah under a different title derived from the Old Testament. This title is then amplified, and followed by an appeal to "come" and save us in a particular way. Around the twelfth century, they were collected into a Latin verse hymn, which was later translated by John Mason Neale, finally becoming the beloved Advent hymn "Oh, come, oh, come, Emmanuel" (LBW 34). (The version in LBW omits two of the original seven stanzas, which are included here, in the version from Congregational Song: Proposals for Renewal, *Augsburg Fortress, 2001. Revised wording for the other stanzas is also available in that resource.) These antiphons form the structure of this service.*

ENTRANCE HYMN
Fling wide the door   LBW 32

DIALOGUE
Blessed is the king who comes in the name of the Lord.
Peace in heaven, and glory in the highest heaven!
I will hear what the Lord God has to say—
A voice that speaks for peace.
Peace for all faithful people
And those who turn to him in their hearts.
God's help is near for those who fear him,
That his glory may dwell in our land.
Blessed is the king who comes in the name of the Lord.
Peace in heaven, and glory in the highest heaven!

OPENING PRAYER
The Lord be with you.
And also with you.
Let us pray.
Gracious God, through the ages you have sent your promise to your people in many ways, through many voices. But in these last days, your Son has come to bring it among us in person. Through your Spirit, prepare our hearts to recognize him in his many forms, and to receive him as our Lord and Savior.
Amen

LESSONS AND CAROLS
Antiphon   *spoken or chanted*
> O Wisdom,
> proceeding from the mouth of the Most High,
> pervading and permeating all creation,
> mightily ordering all things:
> Come and teach us the way of prudence.

O Wisdom, Word of God   tune: LBW 34
> O Wisdom, Word of God most high,
> embracing all things far and nigh:
> in strength and beauty come and stay;
> teach us your will and guide our way.
> Rejoice! Rejoice! Emmanuel
> shall come to you, O Israel.

From *Congregational Song: Proposals for Renewal* © 2001 Augsburg Fortress.

Lesson: Isaiah 40:3-5
Carol: Prepare the royal highway   LBW 26

Antiphon
> O Adonai,
> and ruler of the house of Israel,
> who appeared to Moses in the burning bush
> and gave him the Law on Sinai:
> Come with an outstretched arm and redeem us.

Oh, come, oh, come, great Lord of might   LBW 34, stanza 2

Lesson: Exodus 6:2-7a
Carol: My Lord, what a morning   WOV 627

Antiphon
> O Root of Jesse,
> standing as an ensign before the peoples,
> before whom all kings are mute,
> to whom the nations will do homage:
> Come quickly to deliver us.

Oh come, strong Branch of Jesse   LBW 34, stanza 3

Lesson: Isaiah 11:1-5, 10
Carol: Come, thou long-expected Jesus   LBW 30

Antiphon

O Key of David and scepter of the house of Israel,
you open and no one can close,
you close and no one can open:
Come and rescue the prisoners
who are in darkness and the shadow of death.

Oh, come, O Key of David   LBW 34, stanza 5

Lesson: Isaiah 42:6-9
Carol: Hark, the glad sound!   LBW 35

Antiphon

O Dayspring,
splendor of light everlasting:
Come and enlighten those who sit in darkness
and in the shadow of death.

Oh, come, blest Dayspring   LBW 34, stanza 4

Lesson: Isaiah 9:1-3a
Carol: Awake, awake, and greet the new morn   WOV 633

Antiphon

O King of the nations,
the ruler they long for,
the cornerstone uniting all people:
Come and save us all,
whom you formed out of clay.

O Ruler of the nations, come   tune: LBW 34
O Ruler of the nations, come,
O Cornerstone that binds in one:
refresh the hearts that long for you;
restore the broken, make us new.
Rejoice! Rejoice! Emmanuel
shall come to you, O Israel.
From *Congregational Song: Proposals for Renewal* © 2001 Augsburg Fortress.

Lesson: Ephesians 2:12-18
Carol: The King shall come   LBW 33 (stanzas 1, 2, 5)

Antiphon

O Emmanuel,
our king and our lawgiver,
the anointed of the nations and their Savior:
Come and save us, Lord our God.

Oh, come, oh, come, Emmanuel   LBW 34, stanza 1

Lesson: Isaiah 7:13-15
Carol: All earth is hopeful   WOV 629

RESPONSIVE PRAYER

Our world stumbles blindly toward chaos—
Come and be our Wisdom.
What we imagine to be strength is really weakness—
Come and be our mighty Lord.
We yearn for a standard to look up to—
Come and be our Root of Jesse.
We languish in prisons of mind and spirit—
Come and be our Key of David.
The darkness grows thick around us—
Come and be our Light of day.
We are scattered, lacking a sure leader—
Come and be our King of peace.
We need to know that God is with us—
Come and be our Emmanuel,
that we may rejoice in you. Amen

THE LORD'S PRAYER

BLESSING AND DISMISSAL

Let us bless the Lord.
Thanks be to God.
In our Savior Christ, God is with us.
Almighty God, Father, ✛ Son, and Holy Spirit,
bless you now and forever.
Amen

SENDING HYMN

I want to walk as a child of the light   WOV 649

32

December 1, 2002

First Sunday in Advent

INTRODUCTION

The days of Advent point the people of God toward the three comings of the Lord Jesus. He came among us at Bethlehem. He comes among us now in the scriptures, the waters of baptism, the eucharistic meal, and the community of faith. He will come again in glory to judge the living and the dead. Keep awake, for his coming is certain and his day draws near.

PRAYER OF THE DAY

Stir up your power, O Lord, and come. Protect us by your strength and save us from the threatening dangers of our sins, for you live and reign with the Father and the Holy Spirit, one God, now and forever.

VERSE

Alleluia. Show us your mercy, O LORD, and grant us your salvation. Alleluia. (Ps. 85:7)

READINGS

Isaiah 64:1-9

This communal lament comes from a people who have had their hopes and dreams shattered. The great visions of a restored Jerusalem and a renewed people of God, spoken of in Isaiah 40–55, have not been realized. Instead, the people experience ruin, conflict, and famine. This lament calls God to account—to be the God who has brought deliverance in the past.

Psalm 80:1-7, 16-18 (Psalm 80:1-7, 17-19 [NRSV])

Show us the light of your countenance, and we shall be saved. (Ps. 80:7)

1 Corinthians 1:3-9

Paul's first letter to the Corinthians addresses many problems that arose in the early church. Still, he sets these problems within the context of thanksgiving for the grace and faithfulness of God.

Mark 13:24-37

In today's reading, Jesus encourages his followers to look forward to the day when he returns in power and glory to end all suffering.

COLOR Blue *or* Purple

THE PRAYERS

Walking in the light of the coming Savior, let us pray for the church, the world, and all who await the dawn of God's justice.

A BRIEF SILENCE.

Your people long for the light of your presence, O God. Enlighten your church with servants who yearn to lead your people in love. We pray to the Lord:

show us your light.

The world longs for the light of your presence, O God. Illumine your creatures with care for one another and all creation, that righteousness and peace may prevail in our land and among the nations. We pray to the Lord:

show us your light.

The peoples of the earth long for the light of justice and truth, O God. Shed your soothing light on those who are sick and suffering, homeless and unemployed, lonely and forgotten *(especially)*. We pray to the Lord:

show us your light.

This household of faith longs for the light of hope and healing, O God. Send the brightness of your mercy to all who worship here this day, that our darkness might be banished and our burdens lightened. We pray to the Lord:

show us your light.

The whole company of heaven lives in the joy of your endless light. May we with *(names, and)* all the faithful departed one day behold you in the light of your unveiled glory. We pray to the Lord:

show us your light.

HERE OTHER INTERCESSIONS MAY BE OFFERED.

Show us your light, O God, and bring us to see the day of our redemption, through Jesus Christ our Lord.

Amen

IMAGES FOR PREACHING

O that you would tear open the heavens and come down. Could there be a more direct request for this opening Sunday of this opening season? It is not the curtain rising on the first act; rather, it is our deepest longing that God would tear the curtain in two and tabernacle with us. Come and be with us. Show your power. Make it unmistakable!

33

Against the backdrop of many future and awesome displays of God's power including mountains quaking, darkened sun and moon, and nations trembling, we are invited to reflect upon the tender branches of a fig tree. The putting forth of its leaves is a sign of the inexorable coming forth of figs. The Son of Man *will* come with great power and glory. God will demonstrate holy might. The powers in the heavens will be shaken, earthly powers laid low, and we will know, unmistakably, that we are the clay and that God is the potter. But in the midst of this unrelenting word of God's righteousness is a tender word of mercy and hope. *We are the work of God's hands. Heaven and earth will pass away but God's words will not. We are not lacking in any spiritual gift as we await the coming of our Lord. God is faithful.*

On the calendar, we are opposite the greening and promise of summer fruit and busy with our own attempts to brighten our darkness and fulfill our deepest yearnings. How welcome, then, God's word that keeps coming—a word that spares nothing in directness or promise; a word aimed at opening our hearts and showing us that God hears our cry.

WORSHIP MATTERS

This Sunday's first reading from Isaiah 64 reminds us of our need for confession and forgiveness: "We have all become like one who is unclean, and all our righteous deeds are like a filthy cloth" (v. 6a).

Many congregations provide regular opportunities for confession and forgiveness in their worship life. They need not all be experienced in the same way throughout the year, though. Some seasons seem especially appropriate for confessional liturgies. Lent is the season most commonly viewed as a period for confession, but the season of Advent, with its emphasis on preparation before the festival of Christmas, also lends itself well to this rite. Congregations that limit their use of orders for confession and forgiveness might at least include them throughout this season, possibly using the form in Alternate Worship Texts in this resource.

LET THE CHILDREN COME

On this first Sunday in Advent, invite children to gather around the Advent wreath as an older child lights the first candle. Send the children back to their families with lengths of blue ribbon while everyone sings "Light one candle to watch for Messiah" (WOV 630). The sanctuary is dressed in blue as we prepare for Christ's coming. The children may tie this ribbon around a doorknob in their home as a reminder to carry preparations for Jesus' birth into their daily lives.

HYMNS FOR WORSHIP
GATHERING
Wake, awake, for night is flying   LBW 31, CS 82
Awake, awake, and greet the new morn   WOV 633
A story for all people   W&P 2

HYMN OF THE DAY
O Savior, rend the heavens wide   LBW 38

ALTERNATE HYMN OF THE DAY
Lo! He comes with clouds descending   LBW 27
My Lord, what a morning   WOV 627, TFF 40

COMMUNION
Soul, adorn yourself with gladness   LBW 224
Now in this banquet   W&P 104
As the grains of wheat   WOV 705

SENDING
O God, our help in ages past   LBW 320
Soon and very soon   WOV 744, TFF 38, W&P 128

ADDITIONAL HYMNS AND SONGS
Come now, O Prince of Peace   GS2 50
As the dark awaits the dawn   OBS 46
Watchman, tell us of the night   H82 640
He who began a good work   W&P 56
Let justice roll like a river   W&P 85

MUSIC FOR THE DAY
PSALMODY
Callahan, Mary David. PW B.
Furlong, Sue. "God of Hosts, Bring Us Back" in PS 1.
Haugen, Marty. "Psalm 80/85" in *Gather*. GIA.
Hopson, Hal H. "Psalm 80" in *Eighteen Psalms for the Church Year.* HOP HH3941.
Marcus, Mary. "First Sunday in Advent" in *Psalm Antiphons-1.* U, hb, cong. MSM 80-721.
Smith, Tim. "Lord, Make Us Turn to You" in STP 1.

34

CHORAL

Bach, J. S. "Zion Hears the Watchmen Singing" in *Bach for All Seasons*. SATB.

Brahms, Johannes. "O Savior Rend the Heavens Wide." op. 74, no. 2. (O Heiland, reiß die Himmel auf). SATB. GSCH HL 50300310.

Carter, John and Mary Kay Beall. "Blessed Are They Who Walk in the Pathways of Peace." SAB, pno.   AFP 080067510X.

Cherwien, David. "O Savior, Rend the Heavens Wide." 2 pt mxd. CPH 98-3209.

Hopp, Roy. "From the Apple in the Garden." AFP 0800674138. SATB, org.   AFP 0800675150.

Keesecker, Thomas. "Hark! A Thrilling Voice Is Sounding." SATB, pno.   CPH 98-3228.

Schalk, Carl. "As the Dark Awaits the Dawn." SATB, kybd. AFP 0800658450.

Sirett, Mark. "Thou Shalt Know Him." SATB.   AFP 0800655206. SSAA.   AFP 0800675304.

Thomas, André. "Keep Your Lamps." SATB, conga drm. HIN HMC-577.

CHILDREN'S CHOIRS

Ellingboe, Bradley. "We Light the Advent Candles." U, kybd, Orff/opt inst.   AFP 0800674243.

Hopson, Hal, arr. "Dance and Sing, for the Lord Will Be with Us." U/2 pt, kybd, opt tamb.   CG CGA749.

Sleeth, Natalie. "O Come, O Come, Emmanuel." U with desc, kybd. CG CGA273.

KEYBOARD/INSTRUMENTAL

Burkhardt, Michael. "Soon and Very Soon" in *As Though the Whole Creation Cried*. Org.   MSM 10-555.

Koetsier, Jan. " 'Wake, Awake,' Partita for Trombone and Organ." Tbn, org.   Hnssler-Verlag HE 13.057.

Osterland, Karl. "Fanfare and Trio on 'Helmsley' " in *I Wonder as I Wander*. Org.   AFP 0800657225.

Various composers. "O Heiland, reiß die Himmel auf" in *Augsburg Organ Library: Advent*. Org.   AFP 0800658957.

Walcha, Helmut. "Macht hoch die Tür" in *Chorale Preludes I*. Org. PET 4850.

Wold, Wayne. "Suite on 'Wake, Awake' " in *Light One Candle*. Org. AFP 800655745.

HANDBELL

McFadden, Jane. "Rejoice, Rejoice, Believers." 2–3 oct. AFP 6000001177.

Moklebust, Cathy. "Savior of the Nations, Come." 2–3 oct, L2. AGEHR 3031705-725.

Organ, Anne Krentz. "Three Advent Settings." (Tif in veldele). 3 oct. AFP 080067491X.

PRAISE ENSEMBLE

Chapman, Steven Curtis. "O Come, O Come Emmanuel." SATB, pno.   WRD 080689407277.

Smith, Michael W. and Stephen Curtis Chapman/arr. Allen. "Our God Is with Us." SATB, pno, orch. Genevox GVX 0-7673-9676-6.

Walker, Tommy. "Lift Up Your Heads" in *I Will Sing Songbook*. INT.

Tuesday, December 3

FRANCIS XAVIER, MISSIONARY TO ASIA, 1552

Francis Xavier was born in the Basque region of northern Spain. Francis's native Basque language is unrelated to any other, and Francis admitted that learning languages was difficult for him. Despite this obstacle he became a missionary to India, Southeast Asia, Japan, and the Philippines. At each point he learned the local language and, like Martin Luther, wrote catechisms for the instruction of new converts. Another obstacle Francis overcame to accomplish his mission work was a propensity to seasickness. All his travels to the Far East were by boat. Together with Ignatius Loyola and five others, Francis formed the Society of Jesus (Jesuits). Francis spoke out against the Spanish and Portuguese colonists when he discovered their oppression of the indigenous people to whom he was sent as a missionary.

Pray for churches and missionaries in Asia, spiritual heirs to Francis Xavier. Consider singing "Lord your hands have formed" (WOV 727, Philippine traditional) to honor the work of Francis.

Friday, December 6

NICHOLAS, BISHOP OF MYRA, C. 342

Though Nicholas is one of the church's most beloved saints, little is known about his life. In the fourth century he was a bishop in what is now Turkey. Legends that surround Nicholas tell of his love for God and neighbor, especially the poor. One famous story tells of Nicholas secretly giving bags of gold to the three daughters of a father who was going to sell them into prostitution because he could not provide dowries for them. Nicholas has become a symbol of anonymous gift giving.

In some countries gifts are given on this day, and may include a visit from Nicholas himself. One of the ways Nicholas can be remembered is to have the congregation or families within it gather to prepare gifts that will be given anonymously as a way to remind us of the tradition of giving gifts as a sign of God's love given freely to all.

Saturday, December 7

AMBROSE, BISHOP OF MILAN, 397

Ambrose was a governor of northern Italy and a catechumen when he was elected bishop of Milan. He was baptized, ordained, and consecrated a bishop all on the same day. While bishop he gave away his wealth and lived in simplicity. He was a famous preacher and is largely responsible for the conversion of St. Augustine.

He is also well known for writing hymns. On one occasion, Ambrose led people in a hymn he wrote while the church in which they were secluded was threatened by attack from Gothic soldiers. The soldiers turned away, unwilling to attack a congregation that was singing a hymn. Ambrose's hymn "Savior of the nations, come" (LBW 28) could be sung during these first weeks in Advent when the apocalyptic readings on Sundays encourage believers to stand firm in their faith.

36

December 8, 2002

Second Sunday in Advent

INTRODUCTION

John, the Advent prophet, stands by the waters of baptism and calls the church to see that "our God is here." In baptism God makes us sisters and brothers of the Lord Jesus. God clothes us with the Holy Spirit, a fire to warm what is cold within us and to kindle our hearts with love. Fed by word and meal, we go forth ourselves to prepare the way of the Lord by proclaiming the good tidings that Christ is coming.

PRAYER OF THE DAY

Stir up our hearts, O Lord, to prepare the way for your only Son. By his coming give us strength in our conflicts and shed light on our path through the darkness of this world; through your Son, Jesus Christ our Lord, who lives and reigns with you and the Holy Spirit, one God, now and forever.

VERSE

Alleluia. Prepare the way of the Lord, make his paths straight; all flesh shall see the salvation of our God. Alleluia. (Luke 3:4, 6)

READINGS

Isaiah 40:1-11

In grand, flowing, poetic lines, the prophet known as Second Isaiah announces that the exile of God's people in Babylon is over. The Lord will deliver Israel in an exodus more magnificent than the exodus from Egypt. This word can be trusted, because the only enduring reality in life is the word of the Lord.

Psalm 85:1-2, 8-13

Righteousness and peace shall go before the LORD. (Ps. 85:13)

2 Peter 3:8-15a

The Second Letter of Peter is written to Christians who believed that Jesus would return very soon and were perplexed by the seeming delay. The author reminds the readers that the certainty of God's promise is more important than the timing.

Mark 1:1-8

The gospel of Mark does not begin with a story of Jesus' birth but with the voice of one crying out in the wilderness: Prepare the way of the Lord.

COLOR Blue *or* Purple

THE PRAYERS

Walking in the light of the coming Savior, let us pray for the church, the world, and all who await the dawn of God's justice.
A BRIEF SILENCE.

O God, your tender voice of love reaches all who sit in deepest gloom. Speak to all people throughout the world, lifting those who live among dark valleys of division and despair. We pray to the Lord:
show us your light.

Your strong voice of assurance gives hope in the midst of the changes and chances of life. Guide your church, O God, as it seeks to speak words of faith to a world seeking stability and comfort. We pray to the Lord:
show us your light.

Your welcoming voice of authority breaks through the silence to give strength and hope. Grant that bishops, pastors, diaconal ministers, associates in ministry, and all who serve in positions of leadership in the church will be guided by your voice, so that together we may carry your word to those who await its coming. We pray to the Lord:
show us your light.

Your soothing voice of comfort brings balm to the broken spirit. Lift up the hearts of all whose courage falters, whose heads are bowed down in sickness or addiction, and whose ears are unable to hear a word of hope in this holy season *(especially)*. We pray to the Lord:
show us your light.

Your eternal voice of glory rings through the courts of heaven. Give us voices to praise your name with *(names, and)* all who have gone before us, whose voices join with ours in the endless song of praise in your light-filled presence.
HERE OTHER INTERCESSIONS MAY BE OFFERED.

Show us your light, O God, and bring us to see the day of our redemption, through Jesus Christ our Lord.
Amen

IMAGES FOR PREACHING

The beginning of the good news of Jesus Christ, the Son of God. How ironic that good news begins in the wilderness. That it begins in the rough and uneven places. That it begins with the ancient cry of a displaced, homeless people. That it begins for us in the ditches of life, in those times when we are thrown off our well-worn paths of self-this and self-that. That it begins with acknowledgment of a still deeper need: to name our sin and to be named *child of God.*

The good news of Jesus Christ begins in the "wildness" of John the baptizer, who was clothed with camel's hair and who ate locusts and wild honey. From this starting point of apparent disinterest in other priorities, John exhorted people to acknowledge and turn to God. But he also said it would take more than our repentance to put us on a straight path home—it would take the one who baptizes with the Holy Spirit. Mark 1 moves quickly from John the messenger to Jesus, Son of God and Savior. It is *God's* acknowledgment and initiative—and that is very good news for us.

In a world where "bad news" sells and gets most of the press, the meaning of "good news" may become diminished. Richard I. Deibert says, "The word 'Gospel' is more accurately translated 'glad tidings' and carries the emotional content of a cry of joy. Think of it this way, you have chosen to study *the Cry of Joy about Jesus Christ, the Son of God,* according to Mark" (*Interpretation Bible Studies: Mark*, Knoxville, Tenn.: Geneva Press, 1999, p. 2).

We find this joy in the straight path of the Lord, in being connected to one another in Jesus Christ. Joy is God's baptismal river flowing through our wilderness. Joy is being clothed in white and dining on bread and wine. Joy is coming home.

WORSHIP MATTERS

Today's second reading reminds us of the Lord's patience with us. As worship leaders and worship planners meet, do we practice the gift of patience with one another?

Worship is important to us, and we may want to bring about a swift change in how our congregation worships. But group process and change in congregations takes time to evolve. If a vision or a goal is important to us (such as weekly communion or a richer experience of the season of Advent), it may be necessary for us to be patient with others. Most people simply need to live

37

with something for awhile before they can determine whether they want to have it as a regular feature in their lives. Incremental change may be a better way of reaching the goal.

LET THE CHILDREN COME

In advance of this Sunday, invite the congregation to wear blue to celebrate the second Sunday in Advent. When the children see a sea of blue, they will sense that this waiting and watching is important work of the congregation. Carry this work into the community by placing an evergreen tree in the worship space, or in the narthex. Bring gifts of blue to share with people in need of such offerings, as well as blue ornaments to decorate the tree. Gifts could include items such as blue striped mittens, blue boxes of macaroni and cheese, a bright blue ball. Continue to collect gifts throughout the remainder of Advent. Have families deliver the gifts several days before Christmas.

HYMNS FOR WORSHIP

GATHERING

Comfort, comfort now my people   LBW 29
People, look east   WOV 626

HYMN OF THE DAY

All earth is hopeful/Toda la tierra   WOV 629, TFF 47

ALTERNATE HYMN OF THE DAY

Prepare the royal highway   LBW 26
A story for all people   W&P 2

COMMUNION

Spirit song   TFF 105, W&P 130
O God, our help in ages past   LBW 320
Now in this banquet   W&P 104

SENDING

Hark, the glad sound!   LBW 35
Blessed be the God of Israel   WOV 725

ADDITIONAL HYMNS AND SONGS

Come to be our hope, O Jesus   GS2 18
Wild and lone the prophet's voice   PH 409
On Jordan's stormy banks I stand   TFF 49
The King of glory   W&P 136

MUSIC FOR THE DAY

PSALMODY

Callahan, Mary David.   PW B.

Christopherson, Dorothy. "The Lord Is My Salvation." U, fl, opt perc.   AFP 0800651278.

Harbor, Rawn. "O Lord, Let Us See Your Kindness."   TFF 8.

Haugen, Marty. "Psalm 85: Let Us See Your Kindness" in PCY.

MacAller, Dominic. "Let Us See Your Kindness" in STP 4.

Makeever, Ray. "Dancing at the Harvest."   DH 40.

Marcus, Mary. "Second Sunday in Advent" in *Psalm Antiphons-1.* U, hb.   MSM 80-721.

Smith, Alan. "Let Us See, O Lord, Your Mercy" in PS I.

CHORAL

Handel, G. F. "And the Glory of the Lord" in *Messiah.* SATB, org.   NOV 07 0137.

Helgen, John. "Prepare the Royal Highway." SATB, pno.   AFP 0800674227.

Jennings, Carolyn. "Climb to the Top of the Highest Mountain." SATB, opt children's choir.   Curtis C8118.

Keesecker, Thomas. "All Earth Is Hopeful." U, 2–3 pt trbl, pno.   AFP 0800657411.

Robinson, Marc. "Prepare Ye." SATB, solo, perc, kybd.   KJO 8830.

Taulé, Alberto, arr. Jerry Gunderson. "All the Earth Is Waiting." SSA.   CPH 98-3233.

Walter, Johann. "Rise Up! Rise Up!" in *Chantry Choirbook.* SATB.   AFP 0800657772.

CHILDREN'S CHOIRS

Shafferman, Jean Anne, arr. "Shine, Candle, Shine!" in *Treasures New and Old.* U, kybd.   Alfred Music 11689.

Wold, Wayne. "Every Valley, Every Mountain" in *Three Songs for Advent.* U, kybd.   AFP 0800652959.

KEYBOARD/INSTRUMENTAL

Burkhardt, Michael. "Variations on 'Puer Nobis.'" Org.   MSM 10-005.

Cherwien, David. "Taulé" in *O God, Beyond All Praising.* Org.   AFP 0800657241.

Leavitt, John. "Hark the Glad Sound" in *Hymn Preludes for the Church Year.* Org.   AFP 800650328.

Mann, Adrian. "Puer Nobis" in *Arise and Rejoice!* Kybd, inst.   AFP 0800674960.

Miller, Aaron David. "Puer Nobis" in *Augsburg Organ Library: Advent.* Org.   AFP 0800658957.

Porter, Rachel Trelstad. "Taulé" in *Praise, My Soul.* Pno.   AFP 0800659511.

38

HANDBELL

Honoré, Jeffrey. "Two for Advent." 2–3 oct.   AFP 0800658930.

Moklebust, Cathy. "People Look East." 3–5 oct.   AFP 0800656660.

Organ, Anne Krentz. "Three Advent Settings (Besançon)." 3 oct.
    AFP 080067491X.

PRAISE ENSEMBLE

Helgen, John. "Prepare the Royal Highway." SATB, pno.
    AFP 0800674227.

Shaw, Kirby. "Comfort Ye My People." 3 pt, pno.   HAL 08721079.

Van Gilder, Joe/arr. Tommy Walker. "Prepare Ye the Way." SATB,
    pno.   MAR/WRD 0 80689 82527 9.

Wednesday, December 11

LARS OLSEN SKREFSRUD, MISSIONARY TO INDIA, 1910

Lars Olsen Skrefsrud was born in Norway in 1840.
When he was nineteen years old, he and some friends
robbed a bank. In prison he began to read religious
books. Visits with a pastor who came to the prison re-
vived Skrefsrud's earlier desire to become a pastor. In
1863 he began work among the Santals of northern
India. His work among them included providing a written language, translating the gospels and the Small Catechism, and writing hymns in that language. He also
taught agriculture and carpentry methods to raise the
Santal's standard of living. The Christian community he
founded there continues to flourish.

Consider ways in which Skrefsrud's life echoes the
prophetic work of Isaiah and John the Baptist who prepared the way of the Lord. In what ways can a congregation's proclamation of the gospel and its work for justice
point the way to the coming Christ?

Thursday, December 12

OUR LADY OF GUADALUPE

Many Mexican and Mexican-American Christians, as
well as many others of Central and South America, commemorate Mary, mother of our Lord on this day. In a
famous painting found on the cloak of Juan Diego, a
sixteenth-century Mexican Christian, Mary is depicted
as an indigenous native, head bowed in prayer, and pregnant with the word of God. As a sign of the blending of
the Aztec and European culture, as a sign of God's identification with the poor and powerless, and as an evangelical sign of the coming of the gospel to the new world,
Our Lady of Guadalupe can be a powerful symbol of
Advent longing for the Word of God among the poor in
this hemisphere. Images for preaching on this day might
arise from Revelation 12, Luke 1:39-56, or Luther's
Commentary on the Magnificat.

Saturday, December 14

JOHN OF THE CROSS, RENEWER OF THE CHURCH, 1591
TERESA OF AVILA, RENEWER OF THE CHURCH, 1582

John and Teresa were both members of the Carmelite religious order. John met Teresa when she was working to
reform the Carmelite Order and return it to a stricter
observance of its rules, from which she believed its
members had departed. John followed Teresa's lead and
encouraged others to follow her reform. He was imprisoned when he encountered opposition to the reform.
Both John and Teresa's writings reflect a deep interest in
mystical thought and meditation. Their emphasis on
contemplation can guide us in our Advent worship as we
watch for the coming Christ.

Both John and Teresa believed that authentic prayer
leads to greater love of neighbor and service to those in
need. Teresa wrote, "Christ has no body now but yours . . .
yours are the eyes through which he looks in compassion
on the world." In one of John's poems, *The Spiritual
Canticle*, he cried, "Oh that my griefs would end! Come,
grant me thy fruition full and free!"

December 15, 2002

Third Sunday in Advent

INTRODUCTION

The ancient name for this day is *Gaudete*, or "Rejoice Sunday," inspired by the opening words of the second reading, "Rejoice always." In the midst of our preparations and longings we rejoice that the faithful one who brings good news to the oppressed and brokenhearted is already in our midst, helping us hold fast to what is good. With John the Baptist we point the way to the coming light that brings great joy to all the world.

PRAYER OF THE DAY

Almighty God, you once called John the Baptist to give witness to the coming of your Son and to prepare his way. Grant us, your people, the wisdom to see your purpose today and the openness to hear your will, that we may witness to Christ's coming and so prepare his way; through Jesus Christ our Lord, who lives and reigns with you and the Holy Spirit, one God, now and forever.
or
Lord, hear our prayers and come to us, bringing light into the darkness of our hearts; for you live and reign with the Father and the Holy Spirit, one God, now and forever.

VERSE

Alleluia. See, I am sending my messenger ahead of you, who will prepare your way before you. Alleluia. (Matt. 11:10)

READINGS

Isaiah 61:1-4, 8-11

The people returned to Jerusalem from their exile in Babylon as the prophet had said. What they now face, however, is unforeseen hardship and oppression. Through the prophet, the Lord announces the good news of impending healing, restoration, and transformation. This good news of joy is both unexpected and inexplicable.

Psalm 126

The Lord has done great things for us. (Ps. 126:4)

or Luke 1:47-55

The Lord has lifted up the lowly. (Luke 1:52)

1 Thessalonians 5:16-24

First Thessalonians is believed to be the earliest of Paul's letters. He concludes his first epistle with joyful admonitions and blessings grounded in the hope of Christ's coming.

John 1:6-8, 19-28

John's gospel describes Jesus as the "light of the world." John the Baptist is presented as a witness to Jesus, as one who directs attention away from himself to Christ, the true light.

COLOR Blue *or* Purple

THE PRAYERS

Walking in the light of the coming Savior, let us pray for the church, the world, and all who await the dawn of God's justice.

A BRIEF SILENCE.

O God, who by your Spirit prepares the way, make us ready to receive the Light of lights, and enable us to continue our Advent waiting with courage. We pray to the Lord:

show us your light.

Anoint the whole church with your Spirit so that we may proclaim your freedom where we see captivity and oppression. We pray to the Lord:

show us your light.

Make us sensitive to the needs of the whole human family, the unemployed, the homeless, and all who are ill or who are grieving losses in this season of celebration (*especially*). We pray to the Lord:

show us your light.

Give us strength to cry out into the wilderness of our world that in Jesus you have come to bind up, to heal, and to forgive. We pray to the Lord:

show us your light.

United with those who have gone before us in the communion of saints, may we with (*names,* and) all the blessed dead walk in the light of your eternal presence now and forever. We pray to the Lord:

show us your light.

HERE OTHER INTERCESSIONS MAY BE OFFERED.

Show us your light, O God, and bring us to see the day of our redemption, through Jesus Christ our Lord. **Amen**

IMAGES FOR PREACHING

As the winter solstice draws near, daylight decreases, yet light remains a vital element of our life. Besides making do with artificial light, we crave the "real thing" in natural and reflected forms. As skiers and mountain climbers can testify, sunlight reflected off snow is intense. After a new snowfall on a clear and sunny day, the brightness can blind you. It's not the sun itself, but you can't miss the power source behind the reflection. Likewise, John the Baptist was not the light of the Son, but his reflection of the light was vibrant and life-giving. John the Baptist came *so that all might believe through him.* Such an invitation and reflection is for us to offer as well.

Moving to the Gospel of John for this third Sunday in Advent allows us to take out the wide-angle lens once again. We are reminded that our story began in the Word. We are reminded that creation, that life itself, is God's great ongoing relational act. It's the Word *with* God, John's witness testifying to Jesus' light, gathered people created in the image of the communal God.

Life and our journey are a great mixture of light and darkness. The diminishment of natural light prompts a consequent, interior response. Do we huddle? Do we contract? If we have courage and honesty, we may admit that we like the darkness because it helps us hide—from each other and from ourselves. Attractive as that obscurity can be, though, what if light enters our darkness? Vulnerability, yes, but now we are vulnerable to a loving and creative God, and with that comes a new beginning, a confident, hope-filled awareness. It is the light of Christ shining through John and through you and me! *This is God's planting: comfort for those who mourn, a mantle of praise instead of a faint spirit.* To comfort, to praise: we get to reflect that light, each day, in our flesh.

WORSHIP MATTERS

This Sunday's reading from Isaiah 61 provides us with eloquent words about our hope that is able to comfort those who mourn. In what ways does your congregation reach out to those who mourn in your midst?

Offering some kind of grief ministry (perhaps a support group that regularly listens to one another's stories, shares scripture readings, and prays for one another) can be an important extension of the liturgy of Christian burial. Extending eucharistic visits to those who grieve may also be important ways to minister in your community, especially at this time of the year when families often experience losses most acutely.

LET THE CHILDREN COME

Make hospitality the focus for this Sunday. Hospitality means welcoming everyone, getting them comfortably settled in, and helping them to feel that they belong to the church family. To help your youngest ones feel welcomed, encourage the congregation to pass the peace today by making a point of greeting the children around them. Have the children practice the refrain from "Oh, come, oh, come, Emmanuel" (LBW 34) so they can confidently sing along with the big people next Sunday. Make a variety of small Christmas ornaments in Sunday school or in an Advent workshop. Save the decorations for the fourth Sunday in Advent.

HYMNS FOR WORSHIP
GATHERING
Rejoice, rejoice, believers   LBW 25
I want to walk as a child of the light   WOV 649

HYMN OF THE DAY
Hark! A thrilling voice is sounding   LBW 37, CS 35

ALTERNATE HYMN OF THE DAY
Creator of the stars of night   CS 22
Night of silence   W&P 101

COMMUNION
Now we join in celebration   LBW 203
What feast of love   WOV 701
Emmanuel   TFF 45, W&P 36

SENDING
Joy to the world   LBW 39
The Spirit sends us forth to serve   WOV 723

41

ADDITIONAL HYMNS AND SONGS

Sweet coming for which we long   OBS 79

Blest be the King whose coming   H82 74

Lift up your heads   W&P 88

Lost in the night   LBW 394

MUSIC FOR THE DAY

PSALMODY

Callahan, Mary David.   PW B.

Mahnke, Allan. "Psalm 126" in *Seventeen Psalms for Cantor and Congregation*. CPH 97-6093.

Roff, Joseph. *Psalms for the Cantor, vol. III.* WLP 2504.

Smith, Alan. "The Lord Has Done Great Things" in PS 1.

Stewart, Roy James. "The Lord Has Done Great Things" in PCY V.

CHORAL

Clarke, Richard/arr. Jeffrey Honoré. "Advent Song: Lead Us from Darkness." SATB, solo, cong, kybd, 4 hb, opt fl.   GIA G-3902.

Hopp, Roy. "And a Little Child Shall Lead Them." SATB. org, opt cong.   AFP 0800674006.

How, Martin. "Advent Message." U.   OXF W.161.

Jean, Martin. "Advent Hymn." SATB.   AFP 0800656628.

Manz, Paul. "E'en So Lord Jesus, Quickly Come." SATB.   MSM 50-0001.

Schaefer, Martin J. "A Canticle for Advent." SAB, kybd, opt cong.   AFP 0800657446.

CHILDREN'S CHOIRS

Eggert, John. "Hosanna Now through Advent." U, kybd, C inst.   AFP 0800674146.

Lindh, Jody. "An Advent Carol." U, kybd.   CG CGA648.

Sleeth, Natalie. "Only a Baby Came" in *Laudamus*. 2 pt, kybd.   Hinshaw HMB126.

KEYBOARD/INSTRUMENTAL

Cherwien, David. "Freuen wir uns all in ein" in *Hymn Preludes and Free Accompaniments, vol. 21*. Org.   AFP 0800648838.

Cotter, Jeanne. "Let All Mortal Flesh Keep Silence" in *After the Rain*. Pno.   GIA G-3390.

Sedio, Mark. "Rejoice, Rejoice Believers" in *Let Us Talents and Tongues Employ*. Org.   AFP 800655729.

Various. "Merton" in *Augsburg Organ Library: Advent*. Org.   AFP 0800658957.

Young, Jeremy. "Creator alme siderum" in *Gathering Music for Advent*. Kybd, 2 inst.   AFP 0800656588.

HANDBELL

Lamb, Linda. "People, Look East." 2–3 oct.   JEF MHP2139.

Stephenson, Valerie. "Potpourri for Bells or Chimes." 2–3 oct.   AGEHR 8600120-725.

PRAISE ENSEMBLE

Larson, Lloyd. "Soon He Will Come." SATB, pno.   Richmond Music Press MI-415.

Robinson, Marc. "Prepare Ye." SATB, perc, opt pno.   KJO 8830.

Traditional. "The King of Glory"   W&P 136.

Monday, December 16

LAS POSADAS

Las Posadas, "lodgings," is celebrated in homes of Mexican heritage and is becoming a popular parish practice as well. Families or groups of people wander through the neighborhood to mark the journey of Mary and Joseph to Bethlehem. They knock on doors, asking to come in, but a rude voice says that there is no room. The visitors either respond that Mary is about to give birth to the king of heaven, or they sing an Advent carol foretelling his birth. Eventually the door is opened, and everyone is welcomed into a great party of traditional Mexican holiday food and singing.

The traditional songs of this celebration are included in *Libro de Liturgia y Cántico* (284–86). Prepare a special package or offering for a shelter or halfway house. Las Posadas can be a strong reminder of Christ's humble birth among the poor and the importance of extending hospitality.

Saturday, December 21

ST. THOMAS, APOSTLE

Thomas is perhaps best remembered as "Doubting Thomas." But alongside this doubt, the Gospel of John shows Thomas as fiercely loyal: "Let us also go, that we may die with him" (John 11:16). And John's gospel shows Thomas moving from doubt to deep faith. Thomas makes one of the strongest confessions of faith in the New Testament, "My Lord and my God!" (John 20:28). From this confession of faith, ancient stories tell of Thomas's missionary work to India where Christian communities were flourishing a thousand years before the arrival of sixteenth-century missionaries.

Though we hear about Thomas each year on the second Sunday of Easter, Thomas can also serve as an Advent saint. He watched for the risen Christ and looked for the signs of Christ's incarnation. Advent is that same watch for us. We look for the coming of Christ in our lives, his risen presence in the sacraments, and his incarnation soon to be celebrated at Christmas.

December 22, 2002

Fourth Sunday in Advent

INTRODUCTION

With Mary, the church hears these words: Do not be afraid, you have found favor with God. You, the people of God. You, the baptized Christian. In an anxious and uncertain world, you need not be fearful, the Lord is with you. With these words of consolation, we also hear Mary's response: I am the servant of the Lord. Baptized into the Lord's death and resurrection, and strengthened by his body and blood, we are sent into the world to witness to God's favor for all creation.

PRAYER OF THE DAY

Stir up your power, O Lord, and come. Take away the hindrance of our sins and make us ready for the celebration of your birth, that we may receive you in joy and serve you always; for you live and reign with the Father and the Holy Spirit, now and forever.

VERSE

Alleluia. The virgin shall conceive and bear a son, and they shall name him Emmanuel. Alleluia. (Matt. 1:23)

READINGS

2 Samuel 7:1-11, 16

Instead of David building a house (temple) for the Lord, the Lord promises to establish David's house (dynasty) forever. Centuries later, after the Babylonian exile, no king sat on the throne. Even then, however, the people of Israel remembered this promise and continued to hope for a king, the messiah, the Lord's anointed.

Canticle: Luke 1:47-55

The Lord has lifted up the lowly. (Luke 1:52)

or Psalm 89:1-4, 19-26

Your love, O Lord, forever will I sing. (Ps. 89:1)

Romans 16:25-27

These final words from Paul's letter to the Romans offer a doxology, or prayer of praise to God, whose wisdom and strength are the basis for hope in the gospel.

Luke 1:26-38

In this annunciation, Luke makes clear that God comes with good news for ordinary people (Mary) from little-known places (Nazareth). This king will not be born to royalty in a palace, but to common folk in a stall. Here Luke highlights the role of the Spirit, a special emphasis in his gospel.

COLOR Blue or Purple

THE PRAYERS

Walking in the light of the coming Savior, let us pray for the church, the world, and all who await the dawn of God's justice.

A BRIEF SILENCE.

O Root of Jesse, through the house of David you came to flower as the world's Prince of peace. Grant safety for those who travel in the coming days, that we might all find ourselves at home in your peaceful presence. We pray to the Lord:

show us your light.

O Key of David, your humble rule opens all that is closed. Grant wisdom and compassion to all who guide the nations of the world. Lead them in peaceful ways so your saving justice will be made known among all people. We pray to the Lord:

43

show us your light.

O Dayspring from on high, illumine with your healing presence those who are grieving losses and suffering from anxiety or illness in this season (*especially*). Give to all in need an assurance of your nearness to them in the midst of their pain. We pray to the Lord:

show us your light.

O Ruler of the nations, you call all people of the world to the light of your love. Help the people of your church, and especially this congregation, to be faithful proclaimers of this message of hope. We pray to the Lord:

show us your light.

O Immanuel, your abiding presence with us dispels our darkness and transforms it into light and life. May we, with (*names,* and) all those who have fallen asleep peacefully in you, at length be brought to the bright courts of heaven and into endless day. We pray to the Lord:

show us your light.

HERE OTHER INTERCESSIONS MAY BE OFFERED.

Show us your light, O God, and bring us to see the day of our redemption, through Jesus Christ our Lord.

Amen

IMAGES FOR PREACHING

Mary ponders the greeting of the Lord with perplexity and fear. So would we. It is not the sort of salutation we come across in our holiday cards, but a markedly different message. Conceiving and bearing the Son of the Most High? The Holy One setting up a tent, this close? Within me? Mary's first response is not the leap of prenatal John or the loud joyful cry of Elizabeth. Confronted with an angel bearing this sort of word, we too would ask, What is happening to me? What is happening to my world?

The prophet Nathan receives the word that it is the *Lord* that will make *us* a house. Who is David, or who are we, to build God a house? God isn't the sort to settle down that way; God is the mover. Having moved his people from Egypt, from slavery to freedom, from darkness to light, from death to new creation, God continues to build us *a house and a kingdom that will be sure forever.*

God finally comes close, comes among us, but in a way different from any we could imagine. At last God chooses a house, and it is Mary's womb. The virgin's heart beats quickly in fear and in anticipation, that she will have an intimate part in the fulfillment of humanity's deepest yearning. And it is God's anticipation as well.

Touch your heart and trace the quickening beat within. Imagine young Mary, her fear and then the quickening of her heart. Such a mystery, that an obscure Jewish maiden should become pregnant in this way. Then imagine a beautiful rose, opening petal by petal to reveal yet a greater mystery: Within the humanity of Mary, *God is here.* Mary assents and then sings her joy. Jesus, Son of the Most High, is coming. Soon, the birth; and soon, we will join the song of Mary and the heavenly host.

WORSHIP MATTERS

People who worship outdoors or in rented community spaces know that fundamentally it is not necessary to have dedicated facilities in which to worship. Most congregations do not live willingly in this kind of a situation for long, though. Like David in today's first reading, we feel the need to construct spaces dedicated for our praise of God.

Two resources that may be beneficial for congregations considering construction of new buildings or renovation of old spaces for worship are *Where We Worship* (both a study book and leader/process guide published by Augsburg Fortress) and *Environment and Art Letter* (a periodical published by Liturgy Training Publications). Both resources give numerous visual examples of spaces that are fitting vehicles for the worship of God, while allowing for significant human interactions.

LET THE CHILDREN COME

Mary sang joyfully in response to the angel Gabriel's message that she would be the mother of the Messiah. The congregation can join in Mary's joyful preparation as you sing "Oh, come, oh, come, Emmanuel" (LBW 34), keeping in mind that the children have learned the refrain. Let the children help transform the Advent wreath into a Christmas wreath. This activity could include some suggestions from Environment and Art for the Season (Christmas). At the conclusion of the service invite the children to bring their ornaments and gather around the wreath. Extinguish the candles. If the wreath is a suitable size and design, it could be moved to a vertical position before the children redecorate it. Display it in your sanctuary or narthex as a visual transition from the anticipation of Advent to the joyful day of Christ's birth.

HYMNS FOR WORSHIP

GATHERING

Oh, come, oh, come, Emmanuel   LBW 34, CS 55

Light one candle to watch for Messiah   WOV 630

HYMN OF THE DAY

Savior of the nations, come   LBW 28, CS 65

ALTERNATE HYMN OF THE DAY

Sing of Mary, pure and lowly   WOV 634
Canticle of the turning   W&P 26

COMMUNION

Of the Father's love begotten   LBW 42
Eat this bread (Taizé)   TFF 125, WOV 709

SENDING

Come, thou long-expected Jesus   LBW 30, CS 21
People, look east   WOV 626

ADDITIONAL HYMNS AND SONGS

Nova, nova   H82 266
Tell out, my soul   H82 437/8
King of kings   W&P 80

MUSIC FOR THE DAY
PSALMODY

Callahan, Mary David.   PW B.
Mahnke, Allan. "Psalm 89" in *Seventeen Psalms for Cantor and Congregation.* Cant, cong.   CPH.
Ogden, David. "I Will Sing" in PS 1.
Ridge, R. D. "Forever Will I Sing" in STP 3.
Trapp, Lynn. "Four Psalm Settings." U, cong, opt SATB, org.   MSM 80-701.
Weber, Paul. "I Will Sing the Story of Your Love." SATB, kybd.   AFP 0800657004.
Whitaker, Howard. "I Will Sing of Mercies." SATB.   AFP 0800649680.

CHORAL

Bach, J. S. "Savior of the Nations, Come" in *Bach for All Seasons.* SATB, org.   AFP 080065854X.
Baker, Richard. "My Soul Doth Magnify the Lord." SATB.   RME.
Benson, Robert. "Gabriel's Message." SATB, kybd.   AFP 0800675134.
Brahms, Johannes. "A Dove Flew Down from Heaven" in *Chantry Choirbook.* SATB.
Ferguson, John. "Advent Processional on 'Savior of the Nations, Come.' " SATB.   AFP 080065238X.

Jennings, Carolyn. "A New Magnificat." SATB, org, SA solos, opt cong.   AFP 080065255X. Also in *The Augsburg Choirbook.* AFP 0800656784.
Laster, James. "Sing of Mary, Pure and Lowly." SATB, org.   AFP 0800674235.
McIntyre, John Samuel. "Advent Procession on 'Savior of the Nations, Come.' " SATB, hb, ch, fc, org.   AFP 0800654579.
Prower, Anthony. "Gabriel's Message." SSA, org.   CPH 98-3634.
Schroeder, Hermann. "The Angel Gabriel." SATB.   CPH 98-2381.
Schütz, Heinrich/arr. Robert Buckley Farlee. "My Soul Exalts Your Name, O Lord." SATB, kybd.   AFP 080067524X.

CHILDREN'S CHOIRS

Algonzin, Charlotte. "How Will We Know Him?" U, kybd, opt fl.   CG CGA634.
Bedford, Michael. "Nova, Nova!" U, kybd, opt fl, tamb.   CG CGA838.
Sleeth, Natalie. "Light One Candle" in *Sunday Songbook.* U, kybd.   Hinshaw HMB102.

KEYBOARD/INSTRUMENTAL

Albright, William. "Nun komm, der Heiden Heiland" in *A New Liturgical Year,* ed. John Ferguson. Org.   AFP 0800656717.
Bach, J. S. "Nun komm, der Heiden Heiland." Various ed. Org.
Glick, Sara. "Raquel" in *Piano Arrangements for Worship: Advent, Christmas, Epiphany.* Kybd.   AFP 0800659783.
Powell, Robert J. "Postlude on 'Veni, Emmanuel' " in *Sent Forth: Short Postludes for the Day.* Org.   AFP 0800654889.
Sedio, Mark. "The Angel Gabriel from Heaven Came" in *Let Us Talents and Tongues Employ.* Org.   AFP 0800655729.

HANDBELL

Edwards, Dan. "Joy to the World." 2–3 oct.   AGEHR 5957659-705.
Hussey, William. "Let All Mortal Flesh Keep Silence." 3–5 oct.   MSM 30-804.
Wagner, Douglas. "Advent Bell Carol." 2 oct, SATB, kybd.   JEF WB BSC-00260.

PRAISE ENSEMBLE

Grant, Amy and Chris Eaton/arr. Roger Emerson. "Breath of Heaven (Mary's Song)." SATB, pno.   HAL 08595535.
Grant, Amy and Michael W. Smith/arr. Bob Krogstad. "No Eye Had Seen." SATB, kybd.   WRD 301 0727 16X.

45

CHRISTMAS

The coming of God's light in human form

Images *of the* Season

At Christmas, all the trees of the wood sing

for joy. Spruces, pines, cedars, and firs liven up the short

daylight with their many shades of green. In front yards

and town squares evergreens are strung with hundreds of lights, and countless homes and stores, offices and church buildings bring trees indoors and decorate them up with paper stars, colored balls, lights, and ribbons. If we could find a moment of quiet on Christmas Day, we could hear all these trees singing.

The solstice has come and gone. On or about December 21, the earth turned and now each day brings us more minutes of light. In ancient times this period was filled with great celebrations: all would not die; the sun has been reborn; let's decorate our cold bleak houses with evergreens, light the candles, and let the party begin! The increasing darkness in the Northern Hemisphere is reversed: light is alive after all. And because light is restored, the evergreen trees seem to sing that we all would survive.

Thus it was that the fourth-century Christians recognized the similarity between the solstice, the return of natural light, and the nativity of the Lord—the coming of God's light in human form. The winter solstice provided the perfect metaphor for the incarnation. The world is a dark place, growing darker and darker. Any thoughtful person questions whether the end is approaching. But in the birth of Jesus, God enters the dying world. Death turns around. The light shines, and the darkness cannot overcome it. And so on Christmas Day, Christians pray the psalm in which all the trees of the wood sing for joy.

On Christmas Eve, when we read the Lukan birth narrative, the prayer of the day praises the light come into the dark night. On Christmas Day we read the Johannine prologue, in which what is born among us at Christmas is the very light with which God created the world. The readings and prayers appointed for Christmas Day praise this light. John's "In the beginning" echoes Genesis 1, for the annual winter solstice reminds us of both the first creation of the world and of its recreation in Christ. And here is an interesting note: the prayer for

Christmas Day is the same prayer appointed for the first reading at the Easter Vigil. So we are reminded that the light of the incarnation, which is the light of creation, is also the light of Christ bursting forth brilliantly at the resurrection.

Even to a people who understand the movement of the planets around the sun, the solstice is a wonderful gift. Like a surprise, the increasing light makes us smile. The trees are singing with the promise that spring will come. Christmas is a time of joyous surprise as we receive God's gifts of life yet again. The darkness has not overwhelmed us. And yet the gift of Christ comes to us together: the bread and wine, the body and blood of Christ, are given *for you;* that is, for *all* of you. In a simple, almost hidden way, we receive God's gift of life.

This joy of this subtle surprise contrasts with the dominant mood of letdown that North American culture experiences during the Twelve Days of Christmas. Crisis centers report these days to be a time of great family turmoil, of most suicide attempts, of deepest personal loneliness. Santa Claus promised us perpetual happiness, a mythic family gathering, mounds of toys, all of our heart's desires. But we must admit it didn't happen. Heaven didn't establish itself in my living room this year. We got sick on the eggnog.

Christian Christmas is different from secular Christmas. Christian Christmas begins, rather than concludes, on the evening of December 24. It lasts twelve days, rather than twelve hours. It celebrates the light of Christ in a world that remains in most ways exceedingly dark. It seeks to discover the gift that God is, rather than being disappointed that God didn't come through with what we wanted: a perfect plum pudding or the precise present I dropped so many hints about. Christian Christmas is the beginning of joy, not the end of it. Secular Christmas suggests that a roly-poly man drops down from the sky to give us everything on our list. Of course we are disappointed. Christian Christmas gives us the life of the

Trinity: the Creator of light, Christ our light, and the shining Spirit, the God who means to make of us the light that the dark world seeks.

We see the difference between secular Christmas and Christian Christmas in the saints' observances that fall in the Twelve Days. While everyone lines up at the mall to return rejected Christmas presents, the church observes the life and death of Stephen, the first martyr; John, the writer whose visionary poem of the birth of light connects the nativity with the creation of the first light; the Holy Innocents, the boy babies of Bethlehem killed out of King Herod's fear; and the Name of Jesus, the day to remember that in the incarnation God becomes an embodied person just like one of us. With the saints we sing the angelic song, "Glory to God in the highest," and with the martyrs we pray, "Receive our prayer."

Because secular Christmas is for so many people a painful time, a season of disappointment and loneliness, it is important for the church's Christmas to be other. Let it be among us a time of telling the truth in love. Let it be a time for sharing in the gift of Christ's body and blood. Let us remind one another that, all evidence to the contrary notwithstanding, God is born among us and light has come. Let us receive the gift, and be gift to one another. And let us walk away from the piped-in music long enough to hear all the trees of the wood singing for joy.

Environment *and* Art *for the* Season

The word *Christmas,* derived from *Cristes maesse,*

really means the "celebration of Christ" or "Christ's feast."

It implies that at Christmas the Christians celebrate

the fullness of the mystery of Christ, and not just his birth. Therefore, merely to equate Christmas with a birthday party is entirely inappropriate.

In the same way as Advent is a meditation on and the anticipation of Christ's coming in the past, the present, and the future, Christmas celebrates Christ's birth in this world, yesterday, today, and tomorrow.

In preparation for the fulfillment of the promise we may want to contemplate the Orthodox image of the *Theotokos,* the God-bearer, the mother of God. As we ponder the mystery of the Virgin bearing the divine child, we are called to mystically share in that privilege and be *Theotokoi* ourselves, God-bearers, Christ-bearers to one another. The incarnation cycle is a time to learn what it means to be pregnant with the love of God and to bear the promise of salvation to one another.

THE ENVIRONMENT OF CHRISTMAS

The liturgical color of Christmas is white, not red or green or a combination of the two. White of course may always be enhanced with silver and gold or derivative colors. It is important to remember that liturgical vestments as well as paraments derive their meaning from their shape and their color and not from the secondary symbols, which on occasion are applied. Secondary symbols hide primary symbols; we would be well advised to concentrate on primary symbols.

THE MANGER

HISTORICAL ROOTS AND THEOLOGICAL INTERPRETATION

Although Saint Francis is often credited with the popularization of the Christmas manger, the custom of erecting some form of a manger far predates this saint. The Basilica of Saint Mary Major in Rome already had a chapel of the crib by the fifth century with a representation of the scene of Jesus' birth as described in the gospels and visualized by artists. The custom of reenacting the birth of Jesus with live mangers has its origin in eleventh-century Christmas plays.

What Saint Francis did was to interpret this custom in a theological manner. To see the child in the crib allowed him to meditate on the mystery of God becoming human: to see with human eyes, to hear with human ears, to love and to feel the pain of the heart as well as bodily pain.

The baby in the crib and the suffering servant on the cross were two images that never left Francis's mind and became important to the spirituality of the people across Europe: God became human, suffered, and died for the salvation of the world

After the death of Francis, crib-making became popular throughout Europe and eventually throughout the world. Christmas scenes, mangers, crèches now bear the cultural and ethnic marks of many different peoples.

THE APPEARANCE OF THE MANGER

It is important to remember that any element of the liturgical environment should serve worship, rather than allow worship to become an occasion to showcase environment. Any environment that draws attention to itself away from the celebration is inappropriate for worship. Thus, if a church decides to erect a manger, it should be done in such a way that it does not obstruct, obscure, or detract from worship. It might be best to erect the manger outside or in a place suitable for visitation and meditation on the mystery the crib may inspire, away from the central worship area.

Selecting a manger set may be an occasion to reach beyond one's own cultural and ethnic barriers. Saint Francis would undoubtedly have preferred live animals and lifesize images; however, today it might be more practical and eye-opening to have a manger made in Africa, Asia, or South America or any place that would assist the congregation in understanding the importance of the incarnation of God into the entirety of the human family for the salvation of the whole world.

THE RITUAL USE OF THE MANGER

Though few worshiping communities ritually engage the manger in the celebration of Christmas, some virtue may be found in doing so. One would, of course, not want to duplicate some of the medieval (and, unfortunately, contemporary) customs where during the liturgy the image of the baby Jesus slides down from heaven on a wire and lands in the crib. Still, one might consider a procession during one of the Christmas services to the crib where a prayer and a blessing might be spoken.

THE CHRISTMAS TREE
HISTORICAL ROOTS AND THEOLOGICAL INTERPRETATION

Some sources report that ancient Romans decorated trees with small pieces of polished metal during Saturnalia, a winter festival in honor of the god of agriculture, Saturnus.

During the Middle Ages, on the eve of Christmas—which is the day on which Adam and Eve were commemorated with mystical plays—an evergreen was decorated with apples, symbolizing the tree of paradise.

It is believed that Martin Luther was the first to introduce a tree decorated with candles into the home. He is said to have been inspired by the star-filled sky he encountered during a walk through the woods on a clear winter night.

By the nineteenth century the custom of decorating a tree in the homes of Christians had become popular in the Western Hemisphere. Today, some 35 million Christmas trees are sold yearly in the United States alone.

THE APPEARANCE OF THE CHRISTMAS TREE

Placed either outside or inside the church, a lit Christmas tree is a wonderful symbol of the tree of life and light, the tree of paradise. It brings joy to people's hearts as they indulge in feelings of nostalgia, and it invites them to look toward the future when the promise of eternal life and undying light will be fulfilled.

The tree or trees should be chosen to match the dimensions of the church. Rather than placing them in the chancel alone, consider placing them throughout the church, emphasizing that the entire people of God celebrate, not just the ministers.

Trees, if at all possible, should be real so that they touch all the human senses, including smell. Environment committees should show restraint in the decoration of the trees. A Christmas tree for the use of the church should not be made to look like its competition in the local mall, or even in our homes. Simplicity and dignity are two wonderful virtues to be exercised when engaging in any type of environment for worship.

As is the case with all liturgical decor, the Christmas tree should not obscure or hinder the visual and acoustical celebration of the liturgy. Make sure, for example, that the trees do not hide the music ministers. One may want to gradually add Christmas trees and evergreens to the liturgical environment throughout the incarnation cycle, starting on the second Sunday of Advent and ending with Epiphany.

THE CHRISTMAS WREATH

As a way of emphasizing the unity of the season, the wreath used to indicate the time of preparation and anticipation by marking every Sunday of Advent may be retained throughout the rest of the incarnation cycle. Make sure that the greens are still fresh. If necessary, replace them with new greens. You may want to add some color to the wreath by incorporating poinsettias in the wreath. If you used blue or purple candles for the Advent wreath you may want to replace them with white candles for the Christmas season and keep them lit throughout the season. No ritual use is prescribed for the Christmas wreath, and therefore it does not make any sense to continue the practice of beginning the liturgy beneath the wreath. However, a community may consider the possibility of proclaiming the gospel during the Christmas season under the Christmas wreath, in the midst of the assembly.

FLOWERS FOR CHRISTMAS

The poinsettia is undoubtedly the premier flower at Christmas. Certain flowers are associated with certain liturgical seasons, not unlike music and colors.

The origin of the custom of using poinsettias for Christmas lies in seventeenth-century Mexico. According to a legend, a boy by the name of Pablo was on his way to the parish church to visit the nativity set. As he got closer he realized he had no gifts for the baby Jesus, which was the custom. Hurriedly he picked some branches along the roadside and placed these by the crib. As his friends mocked the poor selection of gift, the green branches sprouted brilliant red star-shaped flowers.

The red of the flowers symbolizes the love of God for the world, sealed in the red blood of Jesus spilled for the salvation of the world on the cross. Poinsettias therefore point to the manger as holding the promise of death, albeit salvific death. For this same reason, some nativity sets picture the crib where the baby Jesus is laid in the shape of a tomb or a coffin.

Environment committees are often tempted to use more flowers, rather than fewer. Thus, in many churches, one finds a chancel filled with poinsettias and ministers trying to gracefully (or not) maneuver around them during services. Worship is better served with creative placement of fewer poinsettias throughout the entire church. Not only will it facilitate movement around the liturgical furnishings, it will also emphasize the fact that the entire worship space is the sanctuary where the body of Christ celebrates.

BEYOND THE TRADITIONAL
CHRISTMAS ENVIRONMENT

Different nations, cultural and ethnic groups observe vastly different customs to mark Christmas. It is always beneficial for us to look beyond ourselves and to learn about other cultures. A broader view not only enriches our local celebrations, but might also help in breaking down any barriers that exist.

Although Christmas is not generally observed as a religious holiday in Japan, the custom to decorate trees at that time does exist. The Japanese use origami cranes for that purpose. Because the crane is a symbol of life, the tree decorated with cranes becomes a tree of life. Imagine mobiles suspended from the ceiling, covered with 1,000 cranes folded by the children of the parish. Or, in lieu of cranes, the children may be invited to fold origami stars and decorate them tastefully with silver and gold glitter (something even the smallest children can do). These too can be made into giant mobiles. In either and all cases, do exercise restraint. It is easy to go overboard. Always practice simple elegance.

Preaching *with the* Season

It's Christmas! As children, we waited so long

for that announcement. How could the time from Thanksgiving

to Christmas ever be that long? Whether we are young

or old, ready or not, Christmas does come. It is the beginning of God's great gospel initiative on our behalf. Jesus was and Jesus *is* born unto us. The incarnation of God forms the fullness of time and the fulfillment of all creation's yearning. The time of delivery is the time of our deliverance.

Our seasons and styles of waiting differ. Our wait may be right at the surface or hidden deep within. We may yearn for large-scale transformations of the world or simple gifts of new life in our daily patterns. Whatever we look for, finally each year, Christmas is announced. God tends to our waiting and God fulfills our yearning. Because Jesus *was* born unto us, we no longer wait. Gertrud Mueller Nelson says it well:

> *Hodie Christus natus est.* Today Christ is born to us. The word *hodie* means something special to me. It is eternal and it is now. The world's constant baiting of us with progress and a better future prevents us from living as best as we can in the now for the creation of the future. Rather, we want to live ahead of ourselves in a future we don't even have in reality, disconnected from the heritage of our past traditions and robbed of our full presence in today. (Even heaven is consigned to the "better deal" ahead that we have no role in creating right now.) The other danger is that we leave the mysteries of the incarnation trapped in history, which relegates the incarnation to an event long past, its sacred action dead and irrelevant to the life we are living. The mythic reality tells us that what was true continues to be true, and we no longer have to wait for God's presence amongst us. (*To Dance with God,* Mahwah, N.J.: Paulist Press, 1986, p. 98)

The waiting of all our Advents is over. God is here. The yearning of all our seasons is fulfilled. God seeks us out, God breaks into our darkness. Jesus is born! The light shines brightly over the manger and we see that we are the children of God.

Though the preacher may want to save the full exposition on baptism as related to Christ for the feast of the Baptism of Our Lord, an opportunity lies within these liturgies to make the point for people who might not often hear it. The incarnation is truly a marvelous event, but it is our baptism into that same divine-human reality that makes it all worthwhile for us. At Christmas, Christ becomes the *child* of God. With our baptism, we become children *of God.* We are siblings of Jesus both because he was born among us, but also because we were born again into God's family.

A wonderful correlation flows between the seasons of the church year and our liturgy. If Advent is "call and response" or invocation, Christmas is "gathering." It is God's gathering of us to be God's children. It is our being gathered, enlightened to be light for the world, renewed to offer new creation, and freed to offer a greater hope to a world that walks in darkness.

The seasonal triptych of Advent–Christmas–Epiphany is a tightly woven invocation, gathering, and sending into a new creation, offering the fulfillment of our deepest longing and God's hope for us. Christmas is the center picture of this triptych. The incarnation of God is at the center of our journey and our hope. Here is the manger. Here is the child carrying the light. Here we see that we are children of God. God's tabernacling with us is our true homecoming. Currier and Ives marketing and cultural promptings for an "old fashioned Christmas" give way to the recognition and meeting of our true needs.

The Day itself is a triptych observance of Eve, Dawn, and Day. At night, break of day, and in full sun, our sight and the world are transformed. Each liturgy creates its own character, which will be reflected in the preaching. Luke's narrative, so well known, is full of the earthy touches that help people to relate to it. The difficulty is to walk the line between genuine emotion and mere sentimentality. John's gospel, on the other hand, is lofty, exalted—and so the challenge becomes making the connections between it and the hearers while being true

52

to the vision of the Word made flesh. Yes, sometimes we despair at finding something new to say, yet we are inspired by the incarnation itself—the same old miracle, ever new.

In exuberant songs, in quiet pondering, and in joyous gathering at the table, God's light, *Jesus*, flows and fills all our hours and days. The light must flow forth from the manger. So the light of the Savior becomes the light of the day, becomes the light of the season, and the triptych of one becomes the twelve of a season of new creation: God is born to us, God is born to the world.

Opposition does come. We remember Stephen, the Holy Innocents, and the sword poised at the heart of Mary during the Twelve Days. The embrace of these stories speaks powerfully to the injustices and darkness of our present day. They also direct us to the cross of God's persistent embrace in Jesus. The opposition will not stop the light from shining.

On the second Sunday after Christmas, we hear again the beginning of John's gospel and our new beginning. Jesus is the light and our life. And in Jesus, God gathers a great company, offering the world a kingdom of peace. *Glory to God in the highest!*

Shape *of* Worship *for the* Season

BASIC SHAPE OF THE EUCHARISTIC RITE

- Confession and Forgiveness: see alternate worship text for Christmas in *Sundays and Seasons* as an option to the form in the liturgy setting

GATHERING

- Greeting: see alternate worship text for Christmas
- Use the Kyrie, particularly for the most festive liturgies during this season
- Use the hymn of praise ("Glory to God")

WORD

- Use the Nicene Creed
- The prayers: see alternate forms and responses for Christmas

MEAL

- Offertory prayer: see alternate worship text for Christmas
- Use the proper preface for Christmas
- Eucharistic prayer: in addition to the four main options in *LBW*, see "Eucharistic Prayer B: The Season of Christmas" in *WOV* Leaders Edition, p. 66
- Invitation to communion: see alternate worship text for Christmas
- Post-communion prayer: see alternate worship text for Christmas

SENDING

- Benediction: see alternate worship text for Christmas
- Dismissal: see alternate worship text for Christmas

OTHER SEASONAL POSSIBILITIES
PROCLAMATION OF THE BIRTH OF CHRIST

The services on Christmas Eve may begin with the proclamation of the birth of Christ (see text in the seasonal rites section), taken from the ancient martyrology. The proclamation should be understood as the announcement of the incarnation within human history rather than a literal counting of years. The lights may be turned down, and, following a period of silence, the proclamation may be read or sung on one note by a leader standing at the entrance to the church. Following the proclamation, the lights are turned on as the entrance hymn is begun.

CANDLE LIGHTING OPTIONS
FOR CHRISTMAS EVE
OPTION 1

- The liturgy may begin with a service of light as at evening prayer. The congregation may face the

53

entrance to the church, and handheld candles may be lit. As the procession passes during the Christmas versicles, all turn to face forward.

- Christmas versicles *LBW*, p. 175
- Hymn of light (LBW 45, 56, or WOV 638)
- Thanksgiving for light (see *LBW*, p. 144)
- The service may then continue with the greeting, followed by the hymn of praise and the prayer of the day.

OPTION 2

- Light handheld candles at the reading of the gospel. A hymn, such as "The first Noel" (LBW 56) or "Angels, from the realms of glory" (LBW 50), may be sung as handheld candles are lit. The gospel may be read from the midst of the people. "Silent night, holy

night!" (LBW 65) may be sung following the gospel, after which handheld candles are extinguished.

OPTION 3

- Light handheld candles at the close of the service. Following the post-communion canticle (or at a service without communion, following the offering and the prayers), handheld candles are lit. Instrumental or choral music may accompany the candle lighting.
- Hymn: "Silent night, holy night!" (LBW 65:1–2; or another hymn of light, as listed in option 1)
- Reading from John 1:1-14. A gospel procession may move to the midst of the assembly.
- LBW 65:3 (or the final stanza of another hymn of light)
- Benediction and dismissal

54

Assembly Song *for the* Season

After the waiting and watching of the Advent season,

Christmas calls for a full celebration, a celebration that lasts

twelve days, not just for December 24 and 25. For all Christmas

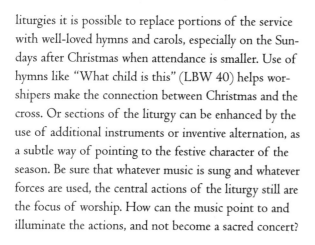

liturgies it is possible to replace portions of the service with well-loved hymns and carols, especially on the Sundays after Christmas when attendance is smaller. Use of hymns like "What child is this" (LBW 40) helps worshipers make the connection between Christmas and the cross. Or sections of the liturgy can be enhanced by the use of additional instruments or inventive alternation, as a subtle way of pointing to the festive character of the season. Be sure that whatever music is sung and whatever forces are used, the central actions of the liturgy still are the focus of worship. How can the music point to and illuminate the actions, and not become a sacred concert?

GATHERING

- Worshipers often arrive early for Christmas services; have an extended period of music as they gather. Use familiar (and new) hymns and carols, and include the choirs and instrumentalists as well. It can also be a

time to sing more of those beloved carols, including some that may not be in the hymnal. In this way all are able to use their gifts to praise the Christ, the light of the world.
- Use the litany form of the Kyrie, with the prayer for peace echoing the song of the angels.
- At some liturgies, you might replace the "Glory to God in the highest" with a "Gloria hymn" for the hymn of praise: "Angels we have heard on high" (LBW 71), "Hark! The herald angels sing" (LBW 60), " 'Twas in the moon of wintertime" (LBW 72), or "Gloria en las alturas" (LLC 297). At another service, use the Glory to God from the worship setting, but adorn it with handbell chords or ostinatos.

WORD

- For the gospel acclamation, continue to use the "Alleluia" (WOV 611a) from Advent, especially on

Christmas Eve. "Let our gladness have no end" (LBW 57) or "He came down" (TFF 37) serve well when the Gospel is from John 1.

- Introducing new Christmas hymns is especially tricky, because people are so fond of the traditional hymns they know. The Word portion of the service might be the best time to teach a new song (another possibility would be in the extended gathering music). Although we want to be wary of subtracting from the rite on festivals, it's fine to insert an additional response to a reading. "Before the marvel of this night" (WOV 636), "Holy child within the manger" (WOV 638), and "Peace came to earth" (WOV 641) are all worthy of attention.

MEAL

- "Let all mortal flesh keep silence" (LBW 198), which originated as an offertory text, makes a good choice for a seasonal offertory song. With an introduction of appropriate length (and possibly with interludes between stanzas) it can serve as the music both while the money offerings are received and the gifts of the people are presented at the altar. Other offertory possibilities are "What child is this" (LBW 40), "Angels, from the realms of glory" (LBW 50), and "All is ready now" (W&P 4).

- As an initial communion song, in place of "Lamb of God," sing "Gloria" (WOV 640). Have the choir lead it as a round, and use the instrumental enhancements available in *Music from Taizé* Instrumental Edition from GIA Publications.

SENDING

- Songs for sending include "Go, tell it on the mountain" (TFF 52, LBW 70), which works especially well on the Sundays after Christmas, and "Good Christian friends, rejoice" (LBW 55). If you used "From heaven above" (LBW 51) as the hymn of the day on Christmas Eve, consider using selected stanzas (perhaps 1, 2, 3, 13, and especially 14) on the second Sunday after Christmas to help tie the season together.

55

Music *for the* Season

VERSE AND OFFERTORY

Boehnke, Paul. *Festive Verse Settings for Christmas, Epiphany and Transfiguration.* SATB, opt kybd.   MSM 80-100.

Haas, David. *Advent/Christmas Gospel Acclamations.* 2 pt, org, gtr, solo inst.   OCP 8732GC.

Hillert, Richard. *Verses and Offertory Sentences I: Advent through Christmas.* U.   CPH 97-5501.

Schiavone, J. *Gospel Acclamation Verses for the Christmas Season.*   GIA G-2111.

Wetzler, Robert. *Verses and Offertories: Advent 1–Baptism of Our Lord.* SATB, kybd.   AFP 0800648994.

CHORAL

Bach, J. S. "From Heaven Above to Earth I Come" in *Bach for All Seasons.* SATB.   AFP 080065854X.

Brooks, Barrington. "Betelehemu" (Nigerian Carol). SATB, drm. LAW 52744.

Caracciolo, Stephen. "Hush! My Dear, Lie Still and Slumber." SATB. LOR 15/1491R.

Carnahan, Craig. "The Christ Child Lay on Mary's Lap." SATB, pno/harp.   AFP 0800659260.

Hobby, Robert. "It Came upon the Midnight Clear." SATB, kybd. CPH 98-3460.

Kadidlo, Philip. "In the Bleak Midwinter." SATB, pno. AFP 0800674162.

Leavitt, John. "The Virgin Mary Had a Baby Boy." SATB, opt perc. AFP 080064686X.

Niedmann, Peter. "Wexford Carol." SATB, org.   AFP 0800659279.

Schalk, Carl. "Where Shepherds Lately Knelt." SATB. AFP 0800646525.

Shepperd, Mark. "Shepherd, Play Your Pipes Tonight." SATB, kybd, ob.   AFP 0800655826.

Shute, Linda Cable. "Glory in the Highest/Gloria en las alturas." SATB, pno, opt perc.   AFP 088065918X.

Sirett, Mark G. "What Sweeter Music." SATB.   AFP 0800659287.

CHILDREN'S CHOIRS

Bedford, Michael. " 'Twas in the Moon of Wintertime." 2 pt trbl, kybd, sop rec/fl, Orff inst.   AFP 0800674316.

Collins, Dori Erwin. "Hurry to the Stable." U, kybd. AFP 0800674154.

Grotenhuis, Dale. "Infant Holy, Infant Lowly." 2 pt, kybd, fl. MSM 50-1402.

Linder, Jane. "A Christmas Lullaby." U, kybd, opt fl.   CG CGA857.

McRae, Shirley. " 'Twas in the Moon of Wintertime" in *Let Us Praise God.* U, Orff inst, perc.   AFP 11-7208.

Pote, Allen. "Hurry to Bethlehem." U/2 pt, pno.   CG CGA858.

Wetzler, Robert. "Still, Still, Still." U, org, opt fl.   AFP 0800645219.

KEYBOARD/INSTRUMENTAL

Callahan, Charles. *Christmas Fantasy.* Org duet.   MSM 10-130.

Carlson, J. Bert. *Carols from Many Lands.* Pno.   AFP 0800659767.

Fiess, Stephen. "Variations on 'Twas in the Moon of Wintertime.' " MSM 10-122. Org.

Lau, Robert. "Alleluias" in *Portraits of Bethlehem.*   FLA HF-5212. Org.

Lind, Robert. *On December Five and Twenty!* Org.   AFP 0800653351.

Mann, Adrian. *'Tis the Season: Preludes for Treble Instrument and Keyboard.* Kybd, inst.   AFP 0800659848.

Moore, David W. *Three Carols for Piano and Solo Instrument.* Pno, inst. AFP 0800659082.

Pelz, Walter. "Variations on 'From Heaven Above.' " Org. AFP 080064798X.

HANDBELL

Buckwalter, Karen. "Sing We Now of Christmas." 3–5 oct, org, L3. AGEHR 8056632-705.

Dobrinski, Cynthia. "Angels We Have Heard on High." 3–5 oct, org, tpt, timp.   AGEHR 8600074-705

Sherman, Arnold. "O Little Town of Bethlehem." 3–4 oct. MSM 30-103.

Tucker, Margaret. "Swedish Christmas Medley." 3–5 oct. L3. AFP 0800659953.

Young, Philip M. "Four Christmas Lullabies for Handbells." 3–5 oct, L3.   AFP 0800657349.

Young, Philip. "Sussex Carol." 4–5 oct.   BEC HB38.

PRAISE ENSEMBLE

Cloninger, Claire and Paul Baloche. "You Are Emmanuel" in *The Ultimate Youth Choir Book.* SATB, kybd.   WRD 0 80689 33017 9.

Grant, Amy and Chris Eaton. "Breath of Heaven (Mary's Song)." SATB, kybd.   HAL 08595535.

Mason, Babbie and Donna Douglas/arr. Jack Schrader. "King Jesus Is His Name." SATB, kybd.   HOP GC 953.

Alternate Worship Texts

CONFESSION AND FORGIVENESS

In the name of the Father, and of the ✛ Son,
and of the Holy Spirit.
Amen

Beholding the miracle born in human flesh,
let us approach the God of grace
to confess our human sin and weakness.

Silence for reflection and self-examination.

God of grace,
we confess before you
that we have wandered from your presence
to seek the false security
of other gods around us.
We often look for you
in strongholds of power and wealth,
and do not see your presence
among the ordinary places of our world.
Forgive us, O Lord, and
redirect us to forms of service
that fulfill your desire for us. Amen

Out of God's great mercy, Jesus Christ took on our humanity,
and from that same love made flesh
we are given forgiveness of all our sins.
Amen

GREETING

The grace of the child born for us,
and the joy of the son given to us
be with you all.
And also with you.

PRAYERS

Rejoicing in God's gift of gentle grace, let us pray for the church,
the world, and all on whom the light of Christ shines.

A brief silence.

Each petition ends:
God of grace,
hear our prayer.

Concluding petition:
Hear our prayers, gracious God,
and bathe us always in the light of your Word made flesh,
Jesus Christ our Lord.
Amen

OFFERTORY PRAYER

God of time and eternity,
you have given your only Son,
born of Mary, to save and redeem us.
Receive now these gifts that we bring,
and let the works of our hands
proclaim the news of your redeeming love
in Jesus Christ our Lord. Amen

INVITATION TO COMMUNION

In this holy sacrament God makes a home with us.
Let us approach in wonder at all that God has done.

POST-COMMUNION PRAYER

In this meal, O God,
you have come to us anew,
and we are renewed in soul and body.
Strengthen us in our calling to serve you,
and help us proclaim the news of your redeeming love
to all who are in need.
We ask this through Christ our Lord.
Amen

BLESSING

May you glory in the birth of the Son of God,
and may the blessing of almighty God,
the Father, ✛ the Son, and the Holy Spirit
be among you and remain with you forever.
Amen

DISMISSAL

Go in the peace of God's gift of love.
Thanks be to God.

57

Seasonal Rites

Blessing of the Nativity Scene

This blessing may be used after the sermon or after the communion of the people on Christmas Eve.

O Lord our God, with Mary and Joseph, angels and shepherds, and the animals in the stable, we gather around your Son, born for us. Bless us with your holy presence, and inspire us to help those who have no place to dwell. Be with us that we might share Christ's love with all the world, for he is our light and salvation. Glory in heaven and peace on earth, now and forever.
Amen

Proclamation of the Birth of Christ

58

Today, the twenty-fifth day of December,
unknown ages from the time when God created the heavens
and the earth and then formed man
and woman in his own image.

Several thousand years after the flood,
when God made the rainbow shine forth
as a sign of the covenant.
Twenty-one centuries from the time of Abraham and Sarah;
thirteen centuries after Moses led the people of Israel out of
    Egypt.

Eleven hundred years from the time of Ruth and the Judges;
one thousand years from the anointing of David as king;
in the sixty-fifth week according to the prophecy of Daniel.

In the one hundred and ninety-fourth Olympiad;
the seven hundred and fifty-second year from the foundation
of the city of Rome.

The forty-second year of the reign of Octavian Augustus;
the whole world being at peace,
Jesus Christ, the eternal God and Son of the eternal Father,
desiring to sanctify the world by his most merciful coming,
being conceived by the Holy Spirit,
and nine months having passed since his conception,
was born in Bethlehem of Judea of the Virgin Mary.

Today is the nativity of our Lord Jesus Christ according to the
    flesh.

Lessons and Carols for Christmas

This service may be used during the twelve days of Christmas.

ENTRANCE HYMN

Oh, come, all ye faithful   LBW 45
Once in royal David's city   WOV 643
Jesus, the Light of the world   TFF 59

DIALOG

The people who walked in darkness have seen a great light.
The light shines in the darkness,
and the darkness has not overcome it.
Those who dwelt in the land of deep darkness,
on them light has shined.
We have beheld Christ's glory,
glory as of the only Son from the Father.
To us a child is born, to us a Son is given.
In him was life, and the life was the light of all people.

OPENING PRAYER

The Lord be with you.
And also with you.
Let us pray.
Almighty God, you have filled us with the new light of the Word who became flesh and lived among us. Let the light of our faith shine in all we do; through your Son, Jesus Christ our Lord, who lives and reigns with you and the Holy Spirit, one God, now and forever.
Amen

LESSONS AND CAROLS

First Reading: Isaiah 9:2-7
Lo, how a rose is growing   LBW 58
Emmanuel   TFF 45, W&P 36
Lo, how a rose e'er blooming   HFW

Second Reading: Micah 5:2-5a
O little town of Bethlehem   LBW 41, HFW (FOREST GREEN)
There's a star in the East   WOV 645, TFF 58

Third Reading: Luke 1:26-35, 38
What child is this   LBW 40
Sing of Mary, pure and lowly   WOV 634
Jesus, what a wonderful child   TFF 51

Fourth Reading: Luke 2:1-7
Away in a manger   LBW 67, WOV 644
I wonder as I wander   WOV 642, TFF 50
The virgin Mary had a baby boy   TFF 53

Fifth Reading: Luke 2:8-16
Infant holy, infant lowly   LBW 44
Before the marvel of this night   WOV 636
Mary had a baby   TFF 55

Sixth Reading: Luke 2:21-36
In his temple now behold him   LBW 184; HFS (REGENT SQUARE)
That boy-child of Mary   TFF 54

Seventh Reading: Matthew 2:1-11
The first Noel   LBW 56
We three kings of Orient are   WOV 646
Sister Mary   TFF 60

Eighth Reading: Matthew 2:13-18
Oh, sleep now, holy baby   WOV 639
Oh, Mary, gentle poor Mary (María, pobre María)   LLC 310

Ninth Reading: John 1:1-14
Of the Father's love begotten   LBW 42
Let our gladness have no end   LBW 57
He came down   TFF 37

RESPONSIVE PRAYER

Glory to God in the highest,
and peace to God's people on earth.
Blessed are you, Prince of peace.
You rule the earth with truth and justice.
Send your gift of peace to all nations of the world.
Blessed are you, Son of Mary. You share our humanity.
Have mercy on the sick, the dying,
and all who suffer this day.
Blessed are you, Son of God.
You dwell among us as the Word made flesh.
Reveal yourself to us in word and sacrament
that we may bear your light to all the world.

THE LORD'S PRAYER

BLESSING AND DISMISSAL

Let us bless the Lord.
Thanks be to God.
May you be filled with the wonder of Mary, the obedience of
Joseph, the joy of the angels, the eagerness of the shepherds,
the determination of the magi, and the peace of the Christ child.
Almighty God, Father, ✝ Son, and Holy Spirit bless you now and
forever.
Amen

SENDING HYMN

Hark! The herald angels sing   LBW 60
Jesus, the Light of the world   TFF 59

59

December 24, 2002

The Nativity of Our Lord
Christmas Eve (I)

INTRODUCTION

At darkest night we gather to celebrate the great light of our salvation. More than the celebration of a birth, Christmas marks the mystery of the incarnation—God sharing our humanity. In this liturgy Christ is present among us—as the word of hope and peace proclaimed to us, and as the word made flesh in communion. With the heavenly host we sing, "Glory to God in the highest heaven," and like the shepherds we return to our homes, workplaces, and communities to tell of the wonders we have seen and heard.

PRAYER OF THE DAY

Almighty God, you made this holy night shine with the brightness of the true Light. Grant that here on earth we may walk in the light of Jesus' presence and in the last day wake to the brightness of his glory; through your only Son, Jesus Christ our Lord, who lives and reigns with you and the Holy Spirit, one God, now and forever.

VERSE

Alleluia. To you is born this day a Savior, who is the Messiah, the Lord. Alleluia. (Luke 2:11)

READINGS

Isaiah 9:2-7

Originally, this poem was written to celebrate either the birth or the coronation of a new Davidic king. After the fall of Jerusalem, this poem came to be viewed as an expression of the hope that eventually God would raise up a new ruler who would possess the qualities described in the text.

Psalm 96

Let the heavens rejoice and the earth be glad. (Ps. 96:11)

Titus 2:11-14

The brief letter to Titus is concerned with matters regarding church leadership. Here the letter cites an early confession of faith as an example of sound Christian doctrine.

Luke 2:1-14 [15-20]

Luke tells the story of Jesus' birth with reference to rulers of the world because this birth has significance for the whole earth, and conveys a divine offer of peace.

COLOR White

THE PRAYERS

Rejoicing in God's gift of gentle grace, let us pray for the church, the world, and all on whom the light of Christ shines.

A BRIEF SILENCE.

Wonderful Counselor, you increase our joy as the church gathers on this holy night to sing of your presence among us. May the story of salvation live in the hearts of all who sing of its wonders. God of grace,
hear our prayer.

Mighty God, you broke the yoke of sin's burden through the birth of your Son. Comfort those whose burdens distract them from the deeper peace of this holy night and grant them a restful mind. God of grace,
hear our prayer.

Everlasting Father, uphold all who are in sorrow or in need of your divine goodness and mercy *(especially)*. We remember with thanksgiving *(names, and)* all who have died and who now rest in your peaceful light. God of grace,
hear our prayer.

Prince of Peace, may your reign be known in all places of violence and unrest, and grant resolution to conflicts throughout the world. God of grace,
hear our prayer.

HERE OTHER INTERCESSIONS MAY BE OFFERED.

Hear our prayers, gracious God, and bathe us always in the light of your Word made flesh, Jesus Christ our Lord.
Amen

IMAGES FOR PREACHING

The time came to deliver her child. . . . In the dark of a stable, light came streaming forth. For the people who walked in darkness, the light came. For us, the light comes and we can see. The time of delivery is the time of our deliverance, as from a dark dungeon; God's taking on of human flesh is our emancipation, the sloughing of our shackles, our being created anew. It is the birth of hope where no such luminescence formerly was permitted.

60

So the stars shine this night, at least figuratively. And our eyes and hearts are directed toward them. We join Abraham in hearing God's cosmic invitation to count all the stars and know the scope of God's love for us. Tonight's brightness, though—this warmth, this hope—comes not from the distant past of a galaxy, nor from the distant future of a promise. All this light emanates from the one who was promised and now is: *Savior, Messiah, Lord!*

The time came to deliver her child. . . . The time is now. Newly delivered children turn their world upon its head *now.* Because of the first Christmas we don't have to wait any longer. Heaven is not some faraway place. God is not removed or distant. God is here; Christ is born to us. The terrified shepherds and singing angels give testimony to the same reality: God takes on our flesh this night. Our exuberant songs allow our bodies to take wing even when our minds would slow us down and ask, "How can this be?" The light, unexpectedly, comes to us from a lowly manger. With Mary we ponder what—on earth—it all could mean. With the shepherds we tremble at the awe of God acting in this dramatic fashion, for us. Finally, we too must glorify and praise God, and find how we might pass this light to others in darkness. For the light in this night is Immanuel. *God is with us!*

WORSHIP MATTERS

Words from Titus this evening remind us that God's salvation is for all. It is a crucial message for worshipers to hear, and it is also a crucial message for worship leaders to remember for this festival.

Many preachers and regular worshipers may feel as if Christmas is a time to scold infrequent worshipers about their laxity. Resist the urge. This day is a time to celebrate everyone's presence (much as families may also be doing these days with the return of those they haven't seen for a while). Words and gestures of gracious welcome are the order of the day. After all, that's what God has already done for us!

LET THE CHILDREN COME

Have a crèche scene procession as Mary, Joseph (carrying an empty manger), a donkey, cows, a horse, and other stable animals gather in the stable. Sing "Away in a manger" (LBW 67 or WOV 644) while the crèche scene is forming in front of the congregation. We are watching and waiting for God to send us the greatest gift of all—

Jesus! In thanksgiving, we respond by giving our gifts to others. During the offering, have the children process up to the crèche and place their offerings of nonperishable food in large baskets or boxes near the crèche scene. Consider donating these gifts to a food bank or to families in need of such offerings in January, after the abundance of the holiday season has passed.

HYMNS FOR WORSHIP
GATHERING

Oh, come, all ye faithful   LBW 45
Once in royal David's city   WOV 643

HYMN OF THE DAY

From heaven above   LBW 51*, CS 30
* *If a shorter version of the hymn is desired, one option would be to sing stanzas 1, 2, 8, 12, 13, 14.*

ALTERNATE HYMN OF THE DAY

Before the marvel of this night   WOV 636
A stable lamp is lighted   LBW 74, CS 4

COMMUNION

What child is this   LBW 40
Silent night, holy night!   LBW 65
Jesus, name above all names   TFF 268, W&P 77

SENDING

Hark! The herald angels sing   LBW 60
Peace came to earth   WOV 641

ADDITIONAL HYMNS AND SONGS

Gloria en las alturas/Glory in the highest   LLC 297
Hush, little Jesus boy   TFF 56
Still, still, still   PH 47
All is ready now   W&P 4

MUSIC FOR THE DAY
PSALMODY

Christopherson, Dorothy. "The Lord Is King." U, opt cong, kybd. AFP 0800650611.

Haas, David and Marty Haugen. "Psalm 96: Proclaim to All the Nations" in GC.

Harbor, Rawn. "Let the Heavens Rejoice and the Earth Be Glad." TFF 10.

Hobby, Robert.   PW B.

61

Hurd, David. "Psalm 96." SATB/U, opt cong.   AFP 0800649818.

Jenkins, Stephen. "A Christmas Psalm." SATB/U, cong, org.
MSM 80-102.

Ollis, Peter. "Today a Saviour Has Been Born" in PS 1.

CHORAL

Bach, J. S. "From Heaven Above to Earth I Come" in *Bach for All Seasons*. SATB, kybd.   AFP 080065854X.

Benson, Robert. "The Snow Lay on the Ground." SATB. org.
AFP 0800674294.

Burkhardt, Michael. "From Heaven Above to Earth I Come." SATB, solo/U trb, kybd, 2 trbl inst, str qt.   MSM 50-1040. Inst pts. MSM 50-1040A.

Cool, Jayne Southwick. "Gentle Mary Laid Her Child." 2 pt mxd, pno.   AFP 0800675142.

Handel, G. F. "For Unto Us a Child Is Born." SATB.   NOV 07 0137.

Heim, Bret. "Under the Feeble Stable Light." SATB, fl, org, opt hp.
CPH 98-3444.

Kadidlo, Phil. "In the Bleak Midwinter." SATB, pno.
AFP 0800674162.

Schalk, Carl. "Before the Marvel of This Night." SATB, org.
AFP 0800646037.

Schalk, Carl. "Cradle Hymn." SATB, fl, org.   AFP 080067412X.

Schroeder, Hermann. "In Bethlehem a Wonder." SATB, fl, vln/ob.
CPH 98-2063.

CHILDREN'S CHOIRS

Bedford, Michael. " 'Twas in the Moon of Wintertime." U/2 pt trbl, kybd, opt fl, hand drm.   AFP 0800674316.

Collins, Dori Erwin. "Hurry to the Stable." U, kybd.
AFP 0800674154.

Lau, Robert. "In Bethlehem Town." U, opt 2 pt, kybd, opt C inst.
KIR/LOR 10/1304K.

Rutter, John. "Angels' Carol." 2 pt, hp/pno.   HIN HMC986.

KEYBOARD/INSTRUMENTAL

Ashdown, Franklin. "Triptych on an English Noel." Org.
AFP 0800675002.

Cotter, Jeanne. "Silent Night" in *Winter Grace: Music for Christmas and Wintertime*. Pno, C inst, vc/bsn.   GIA G-3371.

Langlais, Jean. "La Nativité" in *Poemes Evangelique*. Org.
Herelle p 32.359.

Mann, Adrian. "Irby" in *'Tis the Season: Preludes for Treble Instrument and Keyboard*. Kybd, C/B-flat inst.   AFP 0800659848.

Pepping, Ernst. "Vom Himmel hoch" in *A New Liturgical Year*, ed. John Ferguson. Org.   AFP 0800656717.

Young, Jeremy. "Before the Marvel of This Night" in *Pianoforte Christmas*. Pno.   AFP 0800655702.

HANDBELL

Afdahl, Lee J. "Once in Royal David's City." 3–5 oct, opt hc, fc.
AFP 0800658892.

Honoré, Jeffrey. "Silent Night." 3–5 oct, opt SATB, cong, fl, gtr, org.
CPH 97-6901.

Moklebust, Cathy. "Still, Still, Still." 2–3 oct, L2, opt hc.   AGEHR CGB 201.

Page, Anna Laura. "Mary Had a Baby." 3–5 oct, L2+, opt hc.
AGEHR 08056509-705.

PRAISE ENSEMBLE

Angerman, David and Joseph M. Martin. "Sing! Shout! Jubilate!"
SATB, acc.   FLA A7134.

Estes, Jerry. "Hark! The Herald Angels Sing." 3 pt mxd, pno.
Lavirt Music HT9701.

Gorieb, Sy and Tim Hosman. "A King Is Born" in *Hosanna! Music Songbook 8*. INT.

Gruber, Franz/arr. Robinson. "Silent Night." SATB, acc. Also available in SAB.   Sparkle SV9830.

Hanson, Handt/arr. Paul Murakami. "Like a Rose in Winter." SAB, kybd, opt cong.   AFP 0800675339.

Landis, Keith. "Name of All Majesty" in *Renew*. HOP.

Lindh, Jody W. "Come, Let Us Sing." U, kybd.   CG CGA-478.

Sterling, Robert. "Away in a Manger." SATB, orch.
WRD 301095316X.

December 25, 2002

The Nativity of Our Lord
Christmas Dawn (II)

INTRODUCTION

The liturgy proclaims, "To you is born this day a Savior!" The scriptures announce the presence of God among the people of the earth. At the table we meet the child born of Mary, our crucified and risen Lord. Through baptism we become children of the true Light. We go forth to proclaim the news of great joy: God is with us.

PRAYER OF THE DAY

Almighty God, you have made yourself known in your Son, Jesus, redeemer of the world. We pray that his birth as a human child will set us free from the old slavery of our sin; through Jesus Christ our Lord, who lives and reigns with you and the Holy Spirit, one God, now and forever.

VERSE

Alleluia. The LORD said to me, You are my son; this day have I begotten you. Alleluia. (Ps. 2:7)

READINGS

Isaiah 62:6-12
Salvation will come to the holy city of Jerusalem.
Psalm 97
Light has sprung up for the righteous. (Ps. 97:11)
Titus 3:4-7
Because of Jesus' earthly appearance, we know we are saved by the grace of God.
Luke 2:[1-7] 8-20
A song from angels and news announcing Jesus' birth come first to shepherds living in the fields outside Bethlehem.

COLOR White

THE PRAYERS

Rejoicing in God's gift of gentle grace, let us pray for the church, the world, and all on whom the light of Christ shines.
A BRIEF SILENCE.

Kind and loving God, we bless you for the wondrous appearance of your Son who became human to dwell among us. On this blessed morning that celebrates his birth, may Christ be born in us today. God of grace,
hear our prayer.
Saving God, you proclaim to the ends of the earth the salvation that is for all people. Bless all servants of your church who tell again the story of your wondrous love. God of grace,
hear our prayer.
O Light of the world, you entered the creation to become one with it. Cure the warring madness of the nations, that peace may prevail on the earth you have made. God of grace,
hear our prayer.
Holy and redeeming one, you never forsake us but always seek us out. In the quiet of this Christmas dawn, remind all who suffer *(especially)* of your tender love that guards and guides us until our life's end. God of grace,
hear our prayer.
God of hope and comfort, you promise an eternal dawn to those who love your appearing. Keep us united with those who have died and who now rest in your holy wings *(especially)*. God of grace,
hear our prayer.
HERE OTHER INTERCESSIONS MAY BE OFFERED.
Hear our prayers, gracious God, and bathe us always in the light of your Word made flesh, Jesus Christ our Lord.
Amen

IMAGES FOR PREACHING

A new day breaks upon us. Already, our robust late-night celebrations announced that our salvation has come; God has broken into our nights and days, God has sought us out. The quiet of early morning belies such a cosmic break. But oh, how we need this quiet. Perhaps it is the time Mary's pondering finds resonance within us. Perhaps Christmas Dawn is our breathing in with all of creation the incredible cry of joy at the birth of our Lord Jesus Christ.

63

The morning air is fresh, full of God's oxygen. Breathe in and breathe out and again more deeply. The dawn of a new humanity came and comes to us. Isaiah's sentinels and Luke's shepherds knew. They had seen the coming of the Lord. We too have seen and offer our sentinel experience to the world. Christmas dawn offers the quiet realization that God truly has broken into our lives. A gracious new path—a *gospel* path—of God's initiative is offered. We are beckoned to follow and break with our tired, old ways of seeing God and each other. God's forgiveness begets confession and release, hope and renewed energy. God's incarnation begets an incredible openness, a newness, and an invitation to live our lives as God's gracious gift.

During this season, many work hard to find the joy of Christmas. Yet too often, all our efforts end up short of our expectations. The hubbub of gift exchange leaves us short of breath and frustrated with our attempts to fill the emptiness inside.

The joy of Christmas is not our initiative, but God's. God seeks us and God comes to dwell in our flesh. Christmas dawn invites reflective assent that God makes our journey a gift, unearned and indeed unearnable. The celebration now includes the keen acknowledgment and gratitude that comes with pondering in our hearts God's miraculous initiative. Breathe deeply. It's a new day.

WORSHIP MATTERS

Especially for those who prepare and lead worship, happening upon a miracle while we are engaged in our responsibilities may seem farthest from our minds. Like the shepherds who returned glorifying and praising God for what they had seen in Bethlehem, we also have the opportunity to encounter a miracle each time that we gather for worship. Indeed we believe that Christ is in our midst whenever two or three are gathered, and whenever God's word and sacraments are shared.

These days of heightened activity preoccupy worship leaders with matters far removed from the miracle of the incarnation. Yet God is no less present with us now than God was present with all who gathered around the manger in Bethlehem. Though we may only get around to celebrating Jesus' birth once a year, the real miracle is that he is always with us.

LET THE CHILDREN COME

Assemble the people involved in the crèche scene from the Christmas Eve service. Add a real baby or a doll in the manger and several shepherds. Have them in place before the joyful prelude of Christmas hymns. During the prelude, invite children to peek in the manger to see baby Jesus. Remind everyone that our rejoicing and gift giving at Christmas is to celebrate the birth of God's son, Jesus. Children may continue to bring gifts of nonperishable food items to place near the crèche scene.

HYMNS FOR WORSHIP
GATHERING

O day full of grace   LBW 161
Come rejoicing, praises voicing   LBW 66

HYMN OF THE DAY

Go tell it on the mountain   LBW 70, TFF 52

ALTERNATE HYMN OF THE DAY

Good Christian friends, rejoice   LBW 55
In the bleak midwinter   CS 44

COMMUNION

Away in a manger   LBW 67, WOV 644
What feast of love   WOV 701

SENDING

Go tell it on the mountain   LBW 70, TFF 52
There's a star in the East   WOV 645, TFF 58
Hear the angels   W&P 57

ADDITIONAL HYMNS AND SONGS

For all people Christ was born   DH 52
Break forth, O beauteous heavenly light   H82 91
Christians, awake, salute the happy morn   H82 106
The trees of the field   W&P 138
Jesus, the Light of the world   TFF 59

MUSIC FOR THE DAY
PSALMODY

Beckett, Debbie. "This Day New Light Will Shine" in PS 1.
Guimont, Michel. "Psalm 97: The Lord Is King" in GC.
Hobby, Robert.   PW B.

Hopson, Hal H. "Psalm 97" in *Psalm Refrains and Tones for the Common Lectionary.* U, cong.   HOP 425.

Hopson, Hal H. "Psalm 97" in TP.

Marcus, Mary. "The Nativity of Our Lord/Christmas Day" in *Psalm Antiphons-2.*   MSM 80-722.

CHORAL

Albrecht, Mark. "Come Rejoicing, Praises Voicing." SAB, kybd, opt inst.   AFP 0800674073.

Fedak, Alfred. "The Shepherds Were Not Waiting." SATB, kybd, opt ob or fl.   AFP 0800675290.

Mathias, William. "Hodie Christus natus est." SATB.   OXF A400.

Rutter, John. "Shepherd's Pipe Carol." SATB.   OXF W76.

Scott, K. Lee. "He Is Born." SATB.   MSM-50-1000.

CHILDREN'S CHOIRS

Bedford, Michael. "Hodie Christus natus est." U/2 pt, kybd. CG CGA421.

Mitchell, Tom, arr. "Hydom, Hydom." U, kybd.   CG CGA787.

KEYBOARD/INSTRUMENTAL

Albrecht, Timothy. "Go Tell It" in *Grace Notes, vol. 1.* Org. AFP 0800652886.

Carlson, J. Bert. "Go Tell It" in *Carols from Many Lands.* Kybd. AFP 0800659767.

Kerr, J. Wayne. "Rocking" in *Sing We Now of Christmas.* Org. AFP 0800675029.

Lochstampfor, Mark. "Greensleeves" in *Four Carols for Christmas.* Org. AFP 0800674979.

Uehlein, Christopher. "Dance Prelude on 'Bring a Torch, Jeannette, Isabella'" in *Augsburg Organ Library: Christmas.* Org. AFP 080065935X.

Vaughan Williams, Ralph. "Greensleeves" in *The Oxford Book of Wedding Music.* Org.   OXF.

HANDBELL

Dobrinski, Cynthia. "Joy to the World." 3–5 oct, L3, opt tpt, timp. AGEHR 3266830-705.

Mathis, William H. "Wir hatten gebauet" in *Three Favorite German Carols.* 4–5 oct, opt hc.   AFP 0800675936.

Moklebust, Cathy. "Jesus, Jesus, Rest Your Head." 2–3 oct, L1. AGEHR 80564383-705.

Morris, Hart. "On This Day Earth Shall Ring." 3–5 oct, opt perc. CPH 97-6681.

PRAISE ENSEMBLE

Carter, John. "Dancing into the Promise." 3 pt mxd, pno. SOM AD2056.

Catherwood, David. "Child in the Manger." SAB, acc, fl.   ALF 7958.

Estes, Jerry. "Angels We Have Heard on High." SAB, pno. Lavirt Music HT9501.

Founds, Rick and Bill Batstone. "We Praise You for Your Glory" in *Maranatha! Music Praise Chorus Book, 3rd ed.* MAR.

Keaggy, Cheri. "There Is Joy in the Lord" in *Maranatha! Music Praise Chorus Book, 3rd ed.* MAR.

Martin, Gilbert M. "The Jesus Gift." SATB, pno.   HIN HMC-235.

65

December 25, 2002

The Nativity of Our Lord
Christmas Day (III)

INTRODUCTION

Since the beginning of time, the coming of light has been a sign of life and hope. The sun and the stars transform the darkness into an inhabitable space. On the festival of the Lord's nativity, the church gathers to celebrate the light of God's grace present in Christ. In the holy bath of baptism, he enlightens and claims us as sisters and brothers. In the holy word of scripture, Christ speaks to us of God's love for each human being. In the holy eucharistic meal, he gives us the bread of eternal life. From this festive liturgy we go forth to be lightbearers in the ordinary rhythms of daily life.

PRARYER OF THE DAY

Almighty God, you wonderfully created and yet more wonderfully restored the dignity of human nature. In your mercy, let us share the divine life of Jesus Christ who came to share our humanity, and who now lives and reigns with you and the Holy Spirit, one God, now and forever.

VERSE

Alleluia. When the fullness of time had come, God sent his Son. Alleluia. (Gal. 4:4)

READINGS

Isaiah 52:7-10

In chapters 40–55, the prophet announces that the Lord will soon end the exile of God's people in Babylon. In today's reading, the prophet again announces this victory. Note that he is so certain this victory will take place that he announces his message in the past tense, as though it has already happened.

Psalm 98

All the ends of the earth have seen the victory of our God. (Ps. 98:4)

Hebrews 1:1-4 [5-12]

The opening words of this stately epistle present Jesus as the ultimate message of God to us, as the one who perfectly reveals God's glory and being.

John 1:1-14

The prologue to the Gospel of John describes Jesus as the creative Word of God made flesh, God's true presence among us, the one whose very existence reveals God as "full of grace and truth."

COLOR White

THE PRAYERS

Rejoicing in God's gift of gentle grace, let us pray for the church, the world, and all on whom the light of Christ shines.

A BRIEF SILENCE.

Let us pray that we, being anointed with the oil of gladness, may celebrate the birth of our Savior with joy and thanksgiving. God of grace,

hear our prayer.

For bishops, pastors, and all the people of your church who speak the glories of the Word made flesh, that they may proclaim your reign of love. God of grace,

hear our prayer.

For the peoples of all nations, whose eyes are straining to see peace and salvation. May they be governed by good rulers who are led by your wisdom and justice. God of grace,

hear our prayer.

For those in need, whose minds and bodies cry out for hope and healing (*especially*), that they may know your mercy and lovingkindness. God of grace,

hear our prayer.

For those who travel during these holy days, that their journeys may be safe and their homecomings full of joy. God of grace,

hear our prayer.

HERE OTHER INTERCESSIONS MAY BE OFFERED.

We give thanks for our beloved dead (*especially*), with whom we remain united in your eternal communion of saints. God of grace,

hear our prayer.

Hear our prayers, gracious God, and bathe us always in the light of your Word made flesh, Jesus Christ our Lord.

Amen

IMAGES FOR PREACHING

In the manger, upon the city walls, and now upon the mountains, peace, good news, and salvation are announced. Through Sundays and seasons, high feasts and ordinary time, Christmas Eve, Christmas Dawn, and now Christmas Day, we join all of creation in singing praise and thanks to God. We go to the very beginning and then we are brought to this very present time. The cosmic Christ who brought all things into being has come to make us children of God.

In infancy, childhood, and adolescence, Jesus, *life itself*, shines on us. In adulthood, early, middle, and later years, the light still shines. In illness or health, life or death, the light still shines because the light is Jesus and Jesus is joined to us and we to him: God enfleshed and we the children of God. Water drawn from the wellspring of life flows with the blood from Christ's pierced side upon the hill and into our valleys, offering godly faith, hope, and love. Into this water, so teeming with life, we are dipped, washed, and made anew. We go to the beginning and a new beginning is brought to us. The circle of life is whole and inviting. We are born children of God.

Let us now celebrate the mass of Christ. Let us cup our hands together as a manger of new life; let us, like John, testify to the light; let us receive Jesus' body and blood as God has received ours. Jesus Christ is born today and we are born children of God.

WORSHIP MATTERS

For all of its seemingly magical qualities, the bedrock solid truth to this day is that Jesus became real to us as the divine word. Isaiah 52 focuses our attention on the announcement of good news, while the Gospel according to John speaks eloquently about the Word that became flesh. Once all the glitter, twinkling lights, and wrapping papers are removed, what remains of this holiday is the Word. Of course it's not just any word.

Does your worshiping assembly treat the reading and preaching of God's word with the care and respect that it deserves? Lectors who are poorly prepared because they have not read through the texts even a few times before the service will not indicate by their actions how significant the readings are. (Please note that there is a difference between occasional mistakes and simple poor preparation.) If we treat the scriptures with the care and reverence they deserve, hearers will give them greater attention as well.

LET THE CHILDREN COME

Bring little bells to ring to celebrate this joyful day. Announce a refrain from a hymn when the bells will be played. Store the bells with parents for the remainder of the worship service. Children may lead the congregation in singing a Christmas hymn they learned earlier. Send the children home with candy canes, a sweet reminder of the shepherds who first received the joyful news of the Christ Child's birth.

HYMNS FOR WORSHIP

GATHERING
Oh, come, all ye faithful   LBW 45
Once again my heart rejoices   LBW 46
All my heart this night rejoices   CS 9

HYMN OF THE DAY
Hark! The herald angels sing   LBW 60

ALTERNATE HYMN OF THE DAY
Let all together praise our God   LBW 47
Cold December flies away   LBW 53

COMMUNION
Of the Father's love begotten   LBW 42
The hills are bare at Bethlehem   LBW 61

SENDING
Let all together praise our God   LBW 47
Angels, from the realms of glory   LBW 50

ADDITIONAL HYMNS AND SONGS
Gentle Mary laid her child   PH 27
Word of God, come down on earth   WOV 633
How lovely on the mountains   TFF 99
What have we to offer   W&P 156
The virgin Mary had a baby boy   TFF 53

MUSIC FOR THE DAY

PSALMODY
Beall, Mary Kay. "Psalm 98" in *Sing Out! A Children's Psalter*. U, kybd. WLP.

Grotenhuis, Dale. "New Songs of Celebration/Ps 98." SATB, org, brass, cong.   SEL 241-098.

Haugen, Marty/arr. David Haas. "All the Ends of the Earth: Psalm 98." U/SATB, cant/choir, cong, opt gtr.   GIA G-2703.

67

Hobby, Robert. PW B.

Hurd, David. "Cantate Domino: Psalm 98." SATB.
    AFP 0800650468.

Johnson, Alan. "All the Ends of the Earth" in PS I.

Joy to the world LBW 39

Lau, Robert. "Sing to the Lord a New Song." SATB.
    AFP 080064963X.

Pelz, Walter L. "Psalm 98 Complete Score." SATB, cong, 2 tpt, 2 tbn.
    AFP 0800649389.

Shute, Linda Cable. "Forever Will I Sing/Psalm 98." SATB, kybd,
    opt hb, cong. AFP 0800674103.

CHORAL

Distler, Hugo. "Lo, How a Rose" in *Chantry Choirbook*. SATB.

Holst, Gustav. "Christmas Day." SATB. NOV 1001-33.

Roberts, Paul. "The Word Became Flesh." Also in *Augsburg Choirbook*
    AFP 0800656784. SATB, fl. AFP 0800657659.

Shute, Linda Cable. "Forever Will I Sing." SATB, kybd, opt hb, cong.
    AFP 0800674103.

Thomas, Andre. "African Noel." SATB (div), perc. LAW 52747.

Vangeloff, Nicholas. "Go Tell It on the Mountain." SATB.
    HOP SP 804.

Willcocks, David. "Hark! The Herald Angels Sing" in *100 Carols for
    Choirs*. SATB, org. OXF 0193532271.

CHILDREN'S CHOIRS

Eddleman, David, arr. "A la nanita nana" (Murm'ring a Lullaby).
    2 pt, kybd. CFI CM8303.

Kemp, Helen, arr. "Welcome, Dearest Jesus." U, sop/alto glock, alto
    metallophone/hb, fc, kybd. CG CGA531.

KEYBOARD/INSTRUMENTAL

Cherwien, David. "Of the Father's Love Begotten" in *Gotta Toccata*.
    Org. AFP 0800658752.

Kolander, Keith. "Lo desembre congelat" in *Augsburg Organ Library:
    Christmas*. Org. AFP 080065935X.

Pachelbel, Johann. "Vom Himmel hoch" in *Selected Organ Works, vol 2*.
    Org. KAL 3761.

Uehlein, Christopher. "Mendelssohn" in *A Blue Cloud Abbey Christmas
    Organ Book*. Org. AFP 0800659791.

Wasson, Laura E. "Adeste fideles" in *A Christmas Season Tapestry*. Pno.
    AFP 080065725X.

HANDBELL

Chepponis, James. "Christmastime Alleluia." Cant, cong, acc, opt
    SATB, gtr, C inst, hb. GIA G-4453.

Krentz, Michael E. "Angels We Have Heard on High." 3 oct.
    AFP 0800655699.

McChesney, Kevin. "Angel Glory." 3–5 oct. AFP 0800653955.

Rogers, Sharon Elery. "Infant Holy in a Manger." 2–3 oct.
    AFP 0800674871.

PRAISE ENSEMBLE

Angerman, David and Joseph M. Martin. "Sing! Shout! Jubilate!"
    SATB, acc. FLA A7134.

Dearman, Kirk. "Above All Else" in *Songs for Praise and Worship*. WRD.

Smith, Byron J. "Worthy to Be Praised." SATB, pno. LAW 52654.

Smith, Leonard E. "Our God Reigns" in *Songs for Praise and Worship*.
    WRD.

Ylvisaker, John. "Great Is Our God" in *Borning Cry*. NGP.

Ziegenhals, Harriet. "Oh, Sing to the Lord." U/2 pt, kybd, perc.
    CG CGA640.

Thursday, December 26

ST. STEPHEN, DEACON AND MARTYR

St. Stephen was a deacon and the first martyr of the church. He was one of those seven upon whom the apostles laid hands after they had been chosen to serve widows and others in need. Later, Stephen's preaching angered the temple authorities, and they ordered him to be put to death by stoning.

The Christmas song "Good King Wenceslas" takes place on the feast of Stephen. The king sees a peasant gathering wood near the forest and sends his page to invite the peasant to a feast. The song, with its theme of charity to the poor, can be a way to remember St. Stephen who cared for widows and those in need. Congregations and families within them can be invited to include gifts to charitable organizations during these days of Christmas in honor of St. Stephen.

Friday, December 27

ST. JOHN, APOSTLE AND EVANGELIST

John, the son of Zebedee, was a fisherman and one of the twelve. John, his brother James, and Peter were the three who witnessed the light of the transfiguration. John and James once made known their desire to hold positions of power in the kingdom of God. Jesus' response showed them that service to others was the sign of God's reign in the world. Though authorship of the gospel and the three epistles bearing his name has often been attributed to the apostle John, this tradition cannot be proven from scriptural evidence.

John is a saint for Christmas through his proclamation that the word became flesh and dwelt among us, that the light of God shines in the darkness, and that we are called to love one another as Christ has loved us. According to an early story about John, his enemies once tried to murder him with poisoned wine. On this day, many Christians in Europe will toast one another with the words: I drink to the love of John.

Saturday, December 28

THE HOLY INNOCENTS, MARTYRS

In a culture where Christmas is overcommercialized and sentimentalized, the commemoration of The Holy Innocents, Martyrs, on the fourth day of Christmas must come as something of a shock. How could the birth of a baby be the occasion for the death of anyone? Yet these martyrs were the children of Bethlehem, two years old and younger, who were killed by Herod who worried that his reign was threatened by the birth of a new king. St. Augustine called these innocents "buds, killed by the frost of persecution the moment they showed themselves." Those linked to Jesus through their youth and innocence encounter the same hostility Jesus encounters later in his ministry.

Remembering all innocent victims and taking up the words of the prayer of the day, which pray God to "frustrate the designs of evil tyrants and establish your rule of justice, love, and peace" can mark this commemoration.

69

December 29, 2002

First Sunday after Christmas

INTRODUCTION

With Simeon and Anna, the church proclaims that salvation has come to the people of God in Christ Jesus. "The splendor of the Lord is over heaven and earth"— Christ is present in the world for all people in all conditions of life. In, with, and through Jesus, the Christian community welcomes all people to the scriptures, the baptismal bath, and the holy supper.

PRAYER OF THE DAY

Almighty God, you have made yourself known in your Son, Jesus, redeemer of the world. We pray that his birth as a human child will set us free from the old slavery of our sin; through Jesus Christ our Lord, who lives and reigns with you and the Holy Spirit, one God, now and forever.

or

Almighty God, you wonderfully created and yet more wonderfully restored the dignity of human nature. In your mercy, let us share the divine life of Jesus Christ who came to share our humanity, and who now lives and reigns with you and the Holy Spirit, one God, now and forever.

VERSE

Alleluia. Let the peace of Christ rule in your hearts. Alleluia. (Col. 3:15)

READINGS

Isaiah 61:10—62:3

The people who returned to Jerusalem and Judah after the exile were greatly disappointed. The prophet's promises about the glories of the renewed Jerusalem and the wonderful life the people would experience were not fulfilled. Nevertheless, the prophet declares with certainty that the Lord's salvation will fully come to pass.

Psalm 148

The splendor of the LORD is over earth and heaven. (Ps. 148:13)

Galatians 4:4-7

Paul proclaims the ultimate significance of the nativity: Jesus was born the Son of God so that, because of him, we all may be God's children.

Luke 2:22-40

Luke's narrative continues with stories that emphasize Jesus' connection to Judaism. His family is devout in its observance of the law, and Jesus himself is recognized as one who will bring glory to Israel.

COLOR White

THE PRAYERS

Rejoicing in God's gift of gentle grace, let us pray for the church, the world, and all on whom the light of Christ shines.

A BRIEF SILENCE.

O God, you clothe us with the garments of salvation and cover us with the robe of righteousness. Grant unity to your church as we claim the common clothing that is ours through baptism into Christ. God of grace,
hear our prayer.

O God, your glory is seen by the nations, and your wonders shall be known by all people. Rescue all who are trampled by war and violence, and bring an end to bloodshed and hatred in the world you have made. God of grace,
hear our prayer.

O God, in your presence is healing and wholeness. Touch the lives of all who are sick and sorrowful *(especially)*, that they may know the comfort and consolation of your Holy Spirit. God of grace,
hear our prayer.

O God, you are the hope of every generation. We give you thanks for the elders in our midst who point us to your faithfulness. Remind them of your steadfast and unchanging love. God of grace,
hear our prayer.

O God, in you we grow in strength and wisdom. Deepen the nurturing love of all fathers, mothers, and guardians of children, a love that is rooted in your fatherly goodness and motherly care. God of grace,
hear our prayer.

HERE OTHER INTERCESSIONS MAY BE OFFERED.

O God, you are the life of the world to come. We commend to your eternal care our beloved dead *(especially)*. Keep us united with them always in the communion of saints. God of grace,
hear our prayer.

Hear our prayers, gracious God, and bathe us always in the light of your Word made flesh, Jesus Christ our Lord.
Amen

IMAGES FOR PREACHING

Simeon's words to Mary must have made her quake: "This child is destined for the falling and the rising of many in Israel, and to be a sign that will be opposed so that the inner thoughts of many will be revealed—and a sword will pierce your own soul, too" (Luke 2:34b-35).

Was it not enough that shepherds had already reported the heavenly message that this one, her firstborn, would be Savior, Messiah, and Lord? Mary was dutiful in her response; she followed the law and the message of the angels. She observed a week of ceremonial uncleanliness and her son was circumcised and named Jesus ("he who saves"). After thirty-three more days of blood purification (Lev. 12:4), Jesus is brought by his parents to Jerusalem for presentation. Did Mary hope for some shelter from the wild prophecies of angels and shepherds? She didn't receive that in the temple. She heard again cosmic words about her little one and the sword was again poised at her heart.

Simeon's words to Mary accompany the feast days of St. Stephen and Holy Innocents during the twelve days of Christmas. Opposition to the birth of Jesus is immediate, strong, and persistent. The illumination of Jesus reveals God and humanity.

Clearly, the parameters of our relating to God and one another have changed. No longer is it our seeking shelter in the law; now, almighty God comes to dwell, to tabernacle with us.

Jesus will also take a forty-days journey. Wilderness times and temporary shelters are part of our journey. Opposition without and within us is painful. We know that sword. But we also believe Simeon's words that Jesus is our salvation. Simeon and Anna speak *good news*: God's tabernacling is in human hearts, embracing light and darkness, trust and opposition, falling and rising. Jesus is born to us. Jesus is our eternal home and peace.

WORSHIP MATTERS

Today Isaiah 61 speaks of being clothed with garments of salvation. For the Christian this allusion leads to the white robe given to the souls in Revelation 6:11. It is one reason why a white garment is often associated with baptism. In a real sense, then, the white alb that is the basic clothing of worship leaders is the garment for all believers.

If these basic garments are symbolic of our salvation, they deserve to be properly cared for: regularly laundered, rips in seams mended, whole albs replaced when they are too badly worn.

Beyond their significance and the history of their use, worship vestments can be an economical investment for worship leaders. Good quality albs may provide years (even decades) of service. They will be "in style" for a longer period of time than almost any other kind of clothing. In addition, albs and other vestments help focus attention away from the person wearing them to the actual celebration of worship.

LET THE CHILDREN COME

The challenge of these next two Sundays is to continue the joyful celebration of Christmas. The gifts have been unwrapped. The Christmas tree at home looks naked without its abundance of brightly colored boxes at its feet. During the prelude, have the children (pair older and younger ones) randomly tie three-foot lengths of white, gold, and silver ribbons around the sides of pews or the backs of chairs. Let children lead the congregation in the refrain from a Christmas hymn they have prepared. A possibility might be "Go tell it on the mountain" (LBW 70, TFF 52). Keep the Christmas ribbons up until next week.

HYMNS FOR WORSHIP
GATHERING

Angels from the realms of glory   LBW 50
Angels we have heard on high   LBW 71
Holy Child within the manger   WOV 638

HYMN OF THE DAY

What child is this   LBW 40

ALTERNATE HYMN OF THE DAY

Peace came to earth   WOV 641
In a lowly manger born   LBW 417

COMMUNION

Come with us, O blessed Jesus   LBW 219, HFW
I wonder as I wander   WOV 642

SENDING

O Lord, now let your servant   LBW 339
Oh, sleep now, holy baby   WOV 639

ADDITIONAL HYMNS AND SONGS

O Zion, open wide thy gates   H82 257
Ahora, Señor/At last, Lord   LLC 247
Let there be praise   W&P 87

MUSIC FOR THE DAY
PSALMODY

Bell, John L. "Glory to God Above!" in *Psalms of Patience, Protest and Praise.*   Iona/GIA G-4047.

Hobby, Robert. PW B.

Hopson, Hal H. "Psalm 148" in *Psalm Refrains and Tones for the Common Lectionary.* U, cong.   HOP 425.

Marcus, Mary. "First Sunday after Christmas" in *Psalm Antiphons-2.*   MSM 80-722.

Ogden, David. "Let All Creation Sing" in PS 1.

Praise the Lord! O heavens   LBW 540

Praise the Lord of heaven!   LBW 541

Vaughan Williams, Ralph. "Psalm 148" in UMH.

CHORAL

Bell, John L. "Nunc Dimittis." SATB, solo.   GIA G-5161.

Britten, Benjamin. "This Little Babe." SATB, hp/pno.   B&H OCTB1830.

Desamours, Emile. "Noèl Ayisyen" SATB.   MF 582.

Hopson, Hal H. "The Song of Simeon." SATB (div), opt acc.   MSM 50-7032.

Scholz, Robert. "Nunc dimittis." SSATB, kybd, opt full orch.   AFP 6000001223. Orch pts.   AFP 6000001215.

71

CHILDREN'S CHOIRS

Horman, John. "Angel Song" in *We Come to Praise Him*. U, kybd.
    CG CGC5.

Sleeth, Natalie. "Sing Noel" in *Sunday Songbook*. U, kybd.
    HIN HMB102.

KEYBOARD/INSTRUMENTAL

Buys, Ann. "Go Tell It on the Mountain" in *Fourteen American Spirituals and Hymns*. Pno.   GIA G-5322.

Cherwien, David. "A la ru" in *Eight for Eighty-Eight*. Pno, opt inst.
    AFP 0800657322.

Jordan, Alice. "Procession on 'Once in Royal David's City' " in *Hymns of Grateful Praise*. Org.   Broadman 4570-43.

Osterland, Karl. "A la ru" in *I Wonder as I Wander*. Org.
    AFP 0800657225.

Porter, Rachel Trelstad. "Greensleeves" in *Praise, My Soul*. Pno.
    AFP 0800659511.

HANDBELL

Afdahl, Lee J. "A la ru" in *Three Spanish Carols for Handbells*. 2–3 oct.
    AFP 0800658108.

Manz, Paul/arr. Martha Lynn Thompson. "Now Sing We, Now Rejoice." 3–5 oct, solo inst/hc.   MSM 30-116.

Mathis, William H. "Three Favorite German Carols." 4–6 oct, opt hc.
    AFP 0800674936.

McChesney, Kevin. "Carol of the Bells." 3 oct.
    AGEHR 1834142-705.

Tucker, Margaret R. "A Swedish Christmas Medley: Son of Jul."
    3–5 oct.   AFP 0800659953.

PRAISE ENSEMBLE

Hopson, Hal H. "Glory to God." SATB, kybd.   HOP MA500.

Liebergen, Patrick M. "At Christmas Time All Christians Sing."
    SATB, kybd, fl.   ALF 7895.

McHugh, Phill/arr Mauldin. "God and God Alone." SAB, orch.
    Benson Company OT-1084.

Ray, Mel. "Arise and Sing" in *Songs for Praise and Worship*.   WRD.

Wednesday, January I

THE NAME OF JESUS

The observance of the octave (eighth day) of Christmas has roots in the sixth century. Until the recent past Lutheran calendars called this day "The Circumcision and Name of Jesus." The emphasis on circumcision is the older emphasis. Every Jewish boy was circumcised and formally named on the eighth day of his life. Already in his youth, Jesus bears the mark of a covenant that he makes new through the shedding of his blood, now and on the cross. That covenant, like Jesus' name, is a gift to us and marks us as children of God. Baptized into Christ we begin this new year in Jesus' name. Sustained by the gift of his body and blood we will find that this year, too, we will be sustained by the gift of Christ's body and the new covenant in Christ's blood.

Thursday, January 2

JOHANN KONRAD WILHELM LOEHE, PASTOR, 1872

Loehe was a pastor in nineteenth-century Germany. From the small town of Neuendettelsau he sent pastors to North America, Australia, New Guinea, Brazil, and the Ukraine. His work for a clear confessional basis within the Bavarian church sometimes led to conflict with the ecclesiastical bureaucracy. Loehe's chief concern was that a parish finds its life in the eucharist, and from that source evangelism and social ministries would flow. Many Lutheran congregations in Michigan, Ohio, and Iowa were either founded or influenced by missionaries sent by Loehe, and the chapel at Wartburg Theological Seminary is named in his honor.

Loehe's vision to see the eucharist at the center of parish life can lead us on to think about ways that the incarnate presence of Christ sends us out on a life of ministry and mission.

January 5, 2003

Second Sunday after Christmas

INTRODUCTION

As the twelve days of Christmas come to an end, we continue to sing and be radiant over the goodness of God. We celebrate the light that the darkness has not overcome, Jesus Christ our Lord. That light is made known to us in the incarnation, God sharing our humanity in the Word made flesh. In communion, the Word is made flesh in us as well, that we may go forth from worship to share the light of Christ in our daily lives.

Kaj Munk is remembered today as a twentieth-century martyr. He was a Danish pastor who spoke forcefully against the Nazis as being anti-Christian, and was killed by the Gestapo in 1944.

PRAYER OF THE DAY

Almighty God, you have filled us with the new light of the Word who became flesh and lived among us. Let the light of our faith shine in all that we do; through your Son, Jesus Christ our Lord, who lives and reigns with you and the Holy Spirit, one God, now and forever.

VERSE

Alleluia. All the ends of the earth have seen the victory of our God. Alleluia. (Ps. 98:4)

READINGS

Jeremiah 31:7-14

Like the prophets who announce homecoming and salvation in the book of Isaiah, Jeremiah announces the wondrous homecoming of God's people from exile. Once again the Lord enters in human history to fulfill the covenantal promise made during the exodus from Egypt so long ago: "I will be your God, and you will be my people."

or Sirach 24:1-12

In this passage from the book also known as Ecclesiasticus, Wisdom begins to tell her history. She is in some ways a parallel to the Word in John 1; although more identified with the law of Moses, she is all-present, yet dwelling in a special way among the chosen people.

Psalm 147:13-21 (Psalm 147:12-20 [NRSV])

Worship the Lord, O Jerusalem; praise your God, O Zion. (Ps. 147:13)

or Wisdom of Solomon 10:15-21

We sing, O Lord, to your holy name; we praise with one accord your defending hand. (Wis. 10:20)

Ephesians 1:3-14

The Letter to the Ephesians addresses the church concerning God's plans and purpose for the world. It begins with a prayer thanking God for the blessings that already belong to us in Christ and for the yet more glorious future that awaits us.

John 1:[1-9] 10-18

John's gospel presents Jesus as the full embodiment of God's grace and truth, as the one who reveals God's love for the whole creation.

COLOR White

THE PRAYERS

Rejoicing in God's gift of gentle grace, let us pray for the church, the world, and all on whom the light of Christ shines.

A BRIEF SILENCE.

Let us pray that in this new year all who have been baptized into Christ Jesus will resolve to testify to his light with renewed zeal. God of grace,

hear our prayer.

Let us pray that in this new year nation shall not rise up against nation, and that mutual understanding and a spirit of righteousness will prevail over all peoples of the earth. God of grace,

hear our prayer.

Let us pray that in this new year God's healing and comforting Spirit will be known among all the children of the earth (*especially*), so that they may rejoice once again in healing and wholeness. God of grace,

hear our prayer.

Let us pray for all students and young people, that they may be supported by their families and faith communities as they learn and grow. God of grace,

73

hear our prayer.

HERE OTHER INTERCESSIONS MAY BE OFFERED.

Let us pray for grace to entrust our faithful departed to God's never-failing care, which sustained them in their pilgrimage on earth and which continues to hold them in communion with us, with Kaj Munk *(other names)*, and with all the saints in light. God of grace,

hear our prayer.

Hear our prayers, gracious God, and bathe us always in the light of your Word made flesh, Jesus Christ our Lord. **Amen**

IMAGES FOR PREACHING

And the Word became flesh and lived among us.... Christmas is our homecoming; it is God's great gathering time. The Lord exhorts us (Jer. 31:7-14) to "sing aloud with gladness." God is going to "gather them from the farthest parts of the earth, among them the blind and the lame, those with child and those in labor, together; a great company, they shall return here." In Immanuel, God's gathering of the great company continues. The remnant of Israel broadens to Gentile and Jew, and the tribe of Jacob expands to the tribe of Jesus. "From his fullness we have all received, grace upon grace" (John 1:16). The invitation has been made and continues to be offered *in our flesh* to be children of God.

John August Swanson beautifully pictures God's great gathering in Jesus in his serigraph *Peaceable Kingdom*. No homogeneity here: it's lion and lamb, fox and fowl together, with all the great diversity and color of creation. At the center is a child holding the light: Jesus! It is an incredible creation (and humanity) that God gathers and restores in his incarnation. Both Jeremiah and John testify to this vision. Christmas is the gathering of *the great company*; Christmas is the deeper acknowledgment that "All things came into being through him, and without him not one thing came into being" (John 1:3). We are gathered, restored, renewed, made whole, born again *in Jesus*.

God's Christmas gathering and our homecoming are our destiny. God's desire and initiative for his firstborn and for all of his children are inexorably interwoven. The one who was "destined for the falling and rising of many in Israel"(Luke 2:34) is the one in whom we are destined "for adoption as his children"(Eph. 1:5). So, we come to the manger once again and are renewed for God's sending. We join the joyful cry of a new creation.

WORSHIP MATTERS

Jeremiah 31 speaks of people throughout the earth gathering in God's presence on Mount Zion. Such an image is, in a sense, our vision each time we worship.

Though none of us serves in a congregation that literally would be the gathering place for all peoples of the earth, how might our worship be different if we believed that our weekly assemblies were miniaturized versions of the vision from Jeremiah? Would our gatherings be more racially, ethnically, linguistically, and economically diverse? What are the barriers to the full participation of your immediate community in your congregation's worship? How might you seek to eliminate some of those barriers in the coming year?

LET THE CHILDREN COME

To keep the joyfulness of the Christmas season alive, suggest the greeting "the Christmas peace of God to you" (or simply "Christmas peace") during the passing of the peace. Here's one way you can help children make the transition from Christmas to Epiphany: During the recessional, have children untie and collect the white, silver, and gold ribbons used to decorate the sanctuary. Staple the ribbons to a large gold star, which will lead the procession on the Epiphany of Our Lord.

HYMNS FOR WORSHIP

GATHERING

Joy to the world   LBW 39
Word of God, come down on earth   WOV 716

HYMN OF THE DAY

Let our gladness have no end   LBW 57

ALTERNATE HYMN OF THE DAY

From east to west   LBW 64
Praise to you, O Christ, our Savior   WOV 614, W&P 118

COMMUNION

Of the Father's love begotten   LBW 42
What feast of love   WOV 701

SENDING

The first Noel   LBW 56
Lord, dismiss us with your blessing   LBW 259

ADDITIONAL HYMNS AND SONGS

All is ready now   W&P 4
Between the times   DH 103
On this day earth shall ring   H82 92
Sing we now of Christmas   UMH 237
There is a Redeemer   W&P 140

MUSIC FOR THE DAY
PSALMODY

Bell, John L. "Sing to God with Joy" in *Psalms of Patience, Protest and Praise.* Iona/GIA G-4047.

Folkening, John. "Psalm 147" in *Six Psalm Settings with Antiphons.* SATB/cong, opt kybd.   MSM 80-700.

Hobby, Robert.   PW B.

Hopson, Hal H. "Psalm 147" in *Psalm Refrains and Tones for the Common Lectionary.* U, cong.   HOP 425.

Marcus, Mary. "Second Sunday after Christmas" in *Psalm Antiphons-2.* U, cong, hb/org.   MSM 80-722.

Phillips, J. Gerald. *Psalms for the Cantor, vol. III.*   WLP 2504.

Polyblank, Christopher. "Praise the Lord" in PS 3.

CHORAL

Bell, John L. "Before the World Began." SATB, ob.   GIA G-4381.

Eccard, Johann. "Raise a Song, Let Praise Abound" in *Chantry Choirbook.* SATTB.   AFP 0800657772

Kosche, Kenneth. "Let Our Gladness Have No End." SATB, hb.   CPH 98-3139.

Zimmermann, Heinz W. "And the Word Became Flesh." SATB.   CPH 97-2177.

CHILDREN'S CHOIRS

Artman, Ruth. "Let Us Dance and Sing." 2 pt, kybd, opt hb, fl, perc.   HIN HMC833.

Ramseth, Betty Ann. "Alleluia! Christ Is Born!" U/2 pt, kybd.   CG CGA294.

KEYBOARD/INSTRUMENTAL

Carlson, J. Bert. "Snowy Flakes" in *Carols from Many Lands.* Pno.   AFP 0800659767.

Cherwien, David. "Divinum mysterium" in *Gotta Toccata.* Org.   AFP 0800658752.

Leavitt, John. "Let Our Gladness Have No End" in *Hymn Preludes for the Church Year.* Org.   AFP 0800650328.

Milford, Robin. "On Christmas Night" in *Augsburg Organ Library: Christmas.* Org.   AFP 080065935X.

Wasson, Laura. "The First Nowell" in *A Christmas Season Tapestry.* Pno.   AFP 080065725X.

HANDBELL

Helman, Michael. "Rise Up, Shepherd." 2–3 oct.   AFP 0800653753.

Herbek, R. "Christmas Chorales" (Medley: "Sleepers Awake"; "Break Forth, O Beauteous Light"; and "O Morning Star"). 3–5 oct.   JEF MGNHBO155.

Nelson, Susan T. "Divinum mysterium" in *Plainchant Meditation and Morning Suite.* 3 oct.   AFP 080065546X.

Rogers, Sharon Elery. "The Snow Lay on the Ground." 2 oct.   MSM 30-114.

PRAISE ENSEMBLE

Card, Michael. "The Word" in *Find Us Faithful.* Sparrow Corp.

Harrah, Walt. "The Lord Is My Light" in *Maranatha! Music Praise Chorus Book, 3rd ed.*   MAR.

Haugen, Marty. "He Came Down." SATB, children, solo, gtr, pno, perc.   GIA G-3808.

Pote, Allen. "A Song of Joy." SATB, pno.   HOP AP450.

Tunney, Dick and Melodie Tunney/arr. Larson. "Seekers of Your Heart." SATB, orch.   GS A-6292.

Sunday, January 5

KAJ MUNK, MARTYR, 1944

Munk (his first name is pronounced KY), a Danish Lutheran pastor and playwright, was an outspoken critic of the Nazis who occupied Denmark during the Second World War. His plays frequently highlighted the eventual victory of the Christian faith despite the church's weak and ineffective witness. The Nazis feared Munk because his sermons and articles helped to strengthen the Danish resistance movement. In one of his sermons for New Year's Day he wrote, "The cross characterizes the flags of the North [Nordic countries]. . . . Lead us, thou cross in our flag, lead us into that Nordic struggle where shackled Norway and bleeding Finland fight against an idea which is directly opposed to all our ideals" (*Four Sermons*, trans. J. M. Jensen. Blair, Nebr.: Lutheran Publishing House, 1944).

Munk's life and death invite us to ponder the power of the gospel in the midst of social and political conflicts. Offer prayers for those who face persecution and for those who resist and challenge tyranny.

75

EPIPHANY

God is revealed, and all is new

Images *of the* Season

Depending on where in North America you live,

it may happen to you during January and February once,

or many times: When you go to bed at night all the trees

and bushes are naked brown, bare branches and stalks, but in the morning every single twig glistens with ice. Each evergreen needle wears a stunning cloak of ice. As you look at this once-drab scene now transformed into another world, you wonder: How can such small twigs hold so much ice? How can our yard, which appeared so dead, be so miraculously transfigured? But look quickly, right now: the sun will soon melt all the shimmering magic away. Perhaps as the sun begins its shining, we can glimpse minute rainbows on some of the branches.

The icy cover changes how we live. Some of us are glad to walk slowly, to creep the car carefully along, for we want time to see the spectacular sight. Power lines are down, schools are closed, the church meeting postponed. The ice, which is nothing more than quite cold water, has realigned everything.

Each gospel narrative in the Epiphany season is like another ice storm, transforming the scene with amazing water and with shimmering light. The season begins with the magi traveling across the miles and presenting royal gifts to a newborn. Mary and Joseph look outside and are astonished to see on their doorstep an entourage of sages—surely more than three, probably wise women as well—altering their lives. In the sky is a star so brilliant that one can follow its movement. The season moves from the magi honoring an infant to the disciples witnessing the transfiguration. In both stories only a few people are alert enough to see the transformation that Christ brings to the world.

The infant grows up and is baptized by John, and the heavens open and a dove descends: the sky itself breaks open. Early Christians said that on that surprising day all the waters of the earth were renewed and all the monsters who lurked in the seas were defeated. Some fishermen recognize something new, and abandon their nets. The crowd sees only Jesus of Nazareth, but a madman glimpses the glory of God manifested before him, and the evil demon escapes as quickly as it can. Those

bound by fever, leprosy, and paralysis see a bright light shining in Christ, and their restraints melt away. God is revealed, and all is new.

Like the ice that melts by midmorning, these transformations do not radiate a perpetual glow hour after hour, day after day. You have to be in the right place at the right time to see them. You have to help one another remember them, and be there next week to glimpse them again, trusting through the dark and barren time that such enlightenment is possible once more. Yes, in that dazzling vision, the glorious Christ meets with Moses and Elijah, two visionaries who had actually seen God; but too quickly the scene is over, and we see only an ordinary person standing there alone. Our baptisms are over, and it seems like the same persons there, the same hungry baby, the same adults with their problems still there. Baptism affords no continuous halo. We wear albs for an hour, but then we take them off, and for the rest of the week it seems like the same old gang, in jeans or work clothes or suits.

And what is going on outside the liturgy during January and February? The wind is cold, sometimes bitter. People who describe life on the prairie say that the weather is trying to kill you. It is dark, and people stay indoors. Nothing much happens these weeks. Concerts get cancelled. City folk, who pretend that their buildings will keep them safe, complain at having to wear mufflers and mittens, or they freeze because they refuse to. Valentines wallpaper the stores in red, trying to liven things up. On February 15, the red hearts disappear, and pastel Easter bunnies begin hopping around the mall, spreading through these nastiest weeks of the year their pagan hope that springtime will come.

In great contrast, the church calls this time Epiphany and practices enlightenment. Together we glimpse a glory of God that others are not seeing. It is a season to admit that God's splendor is not like that of a Hollywood production, all enthusiastic action to

78

amuse the couch potato in each of us. Rather, Epiphany is assembling each week on bleak Sundays because we have faith that God will diamond-coat the trees. The demon within us will flee before the shining light, and at least for an hour we will see in each other's faces a kind of luminous spirit. Did you see the heavens open? No? Well, I did, trust me. God is here, transforming the world.

Epiphany is a good time for catechesis. North America followed the pattern that with the fields too frozen for cultivation, winter was the time for education.

School went on when farming didn't. But whether we work in the fields or go to the lake during the summer, we buckle down to study in the winter. Perhaps we can examine all the light imagery in the liturgy, or sing all the Epiphany and morning hymns, or a have a discussion on where we see God's light illumining our dark world. It's a good time to sit together in a warm room and help one another see.

Don't forget, however, to keep one eye to the window. The frost is on the panes, the field is wearing an alb, and the branches don a silver cope overnight.

Environment *and* Art *for the* Season

The word *epiphany* is the English version

of the Greek *epiphaneia*, meaning appearance, revelation,

manifestation. The origin of the feast, which was

79

traditionally celebrated on January 6, may be traced to the church in the East and is apparently an older celebration of the mystery of the incarnation than December 25. When December 25 was adopted as the celebration of the birth of Jesus, the feast of the Epiphany changed focus to the Baptism of the Lord in the East and the visitation by the magi in the West. In the East the feast is known as the *Theophany*, or the "revelation of God."

Today, the churches of the West celebrate the Epiphany of Our Lord as the culmination and the climax of the incarnation cycle. On this day of superlatives the church celebrates the manifestation of the baby born in Bethlehem as the Son of God. After the shepherds, the magi were the first to encounter Jesus and reveal him as the King of kings. In addition to that, Christ is revealed in the words of Simeon, in the words coming from heaven during the baptism of Jesus by John in the river Jordan, and through the first miracle of water turned into wine at the wedding feast of Cana. Though Jesus' baptism has since been separated into its own festival, each one of these revelations has been related to the Epiphany throughout the ages in different church communities. Therefore, although the emphasis in the West

is on the epiphany to the magi, the celebration of the Epiphany embraces all epiphanic experiences, even those that may be happening today.

The ethos of this celebration is one of great solemnity and festivity. If at all possible, rather than declining, the solemnity of the celebration of the incarnation should increase from the solemnity of Christmas until the Epiphany and culminate in a celebration of celebrations.

Based on the gospels, the symbols of this feast are a guiding star; gold, frankincense and myrrh; water; a dove; and wine, in addition to all the symbols with which the church has marked the entire incarnation cycle.

A cultural setback to the success of this feast is that the people experience Christmas day as the highlight of the season, and once this day passes, the season is over. In liturgical terms, however, the season is just beginning and the climax is the feast of the Epiphany.

THE ENVIRONMENT OF EPIPHANY

The environment for Christmas, which has gradually been building since the first Sunday of Advent, needs to be kept up through the feast of Epiphany. Plants need to be kept alive; greens may have to be replaced; the liturgical vestments and paraments are maintained. In short, the sound, the smell, the sight, the taste, the touch of the incarnation cycle does not weaken until the day of Epiphany is past.

As a matter of fact, the liturgy on this day (or the day it is celebrated) ought to be extra festive. In her diary detailing the liturgical celebration in Jerusalem, Egeria—a fifth-century nun—writes most glowingly about the "excesses" of Epiphany. Even today, lights should be burning bright during this feast of the manifestation of the Lord. Communities that make use of incense are to bring out their most expensive incense today. At the table of the Lord, wine should flow abundantly.

On the first Sunday after the Epiphany, the Baptism of Our Lord, a water rite at the beginning of the service both sets the theme for the day and reminds all present of their own baptism. See *Holy Baptism and Related Rites* (Augsburg Fortress, 2002) for a provisional rite for the remembrance of baptism.

LITURGICAL COLOR

On the feast of Epiphany and the Sunday following, the liturgical color for the vestments, the paraments, banners, hangings, booklets, and so forth is white. Any enrichment of this color with silver and gold is appropriate. Epiphany—the celebration of the revelation of the divinity of the child born in Bethlehem—is the high point and culmination of the incarnation cycle. Rich and brilliant textiles are especially appropriate this day. Later on in the season, the color changes to green as we begin the stories of Jesus' ministry. For churches that celebrate the Presentation of Our Lord on February 2, however, the color reverts to white for this isolated piece of the incarnation cycle. And of course, as the season and the cycle end with the glory of the Transfiguration, we adorn the church with white once more before the solemnity of Lent.

EXTRA CANDLES AND LIGHT

On the feast of the Epiphany when Christ is revealed as the light of the world, as well as on the Presentation (often called Candlemas in Anglican churches) and Transfiguration, the environment should be bathed in light. If your church has extra candelabras or room for

votive lights, place them freely throughout the church and light them for the liturgy.

Some cultures follow a custom of using lanterns during the Christmas season. In the Philippines, for example, these lanterns are in the shape of a star and made out of bamboo sticks, covered with colorful rice paper. Ukrainians and Poles have a similar custom. On Epiphany, it could be wonderful to involve children in the processions carrying such lanterns. Consider investing in glass lanterns that could safely be carried by children. If you customarily proclaim the gospel under the wreath during the Christmas season, children carrying lanterns might accompany this procession on Epiphany.

Another option is to give everyone lighted candles during the gospel acclamation to be held during the proclamation of the gospel.

THE BAPTISMAL FONT

On the feast of the Baptism of Our Lord, you will want to emphasize the importance of baptism, baptismal water, and the place of baptism. If you have a large font, the liturgy could begin there with a blessing. After that the assembly might be invited to refresh themselves at the waters of salvation while an appropriate song is sung. As everyone reaches their usual place, the song is concluded and the collect is prayed.

If your church does not have a permanent font, you may want to place the temporary font in a prominent location on this feast day and draw attention to the importance of baptism during worship.

EVERGREENS

If worship and its environment are indeed "progressive" and if the Epiphany of Our Lord is the climax of the incarnation cycle, then it is the time to pull out all the stops. In terms of the evergreens, rather than put them all in place by Christmas, Epiphany is the day when the last one should be added, completing the environment for the incarnation cycle.

EPIPHANY WREATH

The wreath that marked every Sunday of Advent with the lighting of a candle and held red poinsettias for Christmas now becomes the Epiphany wreath. Make sure that the greens are still reasonably fresh. If necessary replace at least part of the greens. Because light and brightness are integral to this celebration, you might want to replace the red poinsettias with white ones or at least add some white ones to the red. At the risk of going overboard, you may consider weaving some gold and silver ribbons through the wreath. Make sure the candles are still lit and visible. After the day of Epiphany, though, it will be time to take down the wreath; the original greens will be getting quite dry.

FLOWERS FOR EPIPHANY

In addition to the red poinsettias that graced the Christmas environment white poinsettias or other white flowers may enhance the brilliance of the day of Epiphany. Make sure that any dead flowers are removed from the church.

THE MANGER

As the churches in the West celebrate the arrival of the magi on Epiphany, many churches in different cultures have customs that surround the magi. The domestic custom of placing the magi at a distance from the manger and day after day allowing them to get closer to the holy family has resulted in a similar church custom where the magi are placed away from the manger and "travel a great distance" to arrive at the crèche on Epiphany.

HANGING BANNERS AND MOBILES

The colors of these banners—which may be made out of ribbons, cloth, papers, or a combination of all these elements—began in Advent as blues and purples and pinks. As the cycle progressed, white, silver, and gold were added. Now that the fullness of the season has been reached, nearly all the blue, purple, and pink has been removed in favor of silver and gold. Some blue, purple, and pink remain in order to keep the unity of the season.

AS THE SEASON PROGRESSES

The Sundays after the Baptism of Our Lord are really not part of the incarnation cycle, but a transitional "ordinary time" (except, of course, for the festivals within). It is appropriate, then, to reduce the amount of festive adornment, without going to the extent of Lent's severity. A few hangings could remain (greens might join blues and a little silver), and if dormant trees were used beginning in Advent, those could certainly be kept in place. When the Presentation and Transfiguration come around, additional decoration is desirable.

81

Preaching *with the* Season

The season of Epiphany is the season of light.

Light is the ancient symbol for the season. The season begins

with the magi following the star they observed rising

in the East. It culminates in a fantastic light show of Jesus' transfiguration. The glory of God shines in and through Jesus Christ.

The light also shines in us. The question of being in the light of God, of being right with God and neighbor is taken up immediately at the Baptism of Our Lord. On that day the incarnational reality appears to us again. God breaks into our lives, and removes all barriers. God's Spirit descends upon Jesus at his baptism and God says, "You are my Son, the Beloved; with you I am well pleased" (Mark 1:11). The promise of Christmas Eve is

fulfilled. The favor of God is poured out upon humanity through Jesus.

We are dipped into the Light when we are baptized. In the Eastern Orthodox Church, Epiphany is the day to receive new members through baptism who are called *il-luminandi*—the illuminated ones. The Epiphany of Our Lord and the Baptism of Our Lord are a tightly woven couplet responding to the question of how we will participate in the Light. We join Jesus in the waters of our baptism. We believe that the Spirit descends upon us and that God declares us to be God's beloved children.

The next couplet of the season are two tellings of the calling of the first disciples, one from John and the other from Mark. John gives us that wonderful evangelical and eucharistic rhythm: Jesus finds Philip, Philip finds Nathanael, and so on down the line until finally it is we who are found and united with Christ. Mark gives us the call to "fish for people." We see in this story that God is casting his net in Jesus. Happily, many are caught in the net of God's love.

The couplet of the calling of the disciples (and our calling) builds upon the first couplet of light and baptism. The calling to "fish for people" flows from our baptism in Christ. Fishing for people is our baptismal vocation. As we respond to this calling and live out our baptism in Christ, the light of Christ becomes brighter to us and those around us.

The Presentation of Our Lord is at the center of the season. Just as we catch our "green" stride, we are invited to take a step back, take out the Christmas white once again and anchor ourselves in the unveiling of God's presentation. Mary and Joseph presented Jesus at Jerusalem; God would present Jesus at the cross for the redemption of the world. Jesus' day of presentation redirects us to see that our days are gifts of God and offerings of redemption for the world.

The latter half of the season is an ascent to the Transfiguration of Our Lord. Ascent to our baptismal calling and weekly sending into the world make us hungry to see the Author of this growing light and transformation in our world. We want to see more deeply and confidently. We follow exuberantly.

Four healing stories take us to the Epiphany peak and to the fullness of God present in Jesus Christ. They flow consecutively from Mark 1:21 to Mark 2:12. Each story offers a different hue of light. Jesus shows the way with a magnificent palette.

To follow Jesus, to be in the Light, is to be healed, to be made whole. Jesus' healings result in physical signs of his presence. People are cured of leprosy or rise from fever to serve. Jesus invites us to look still deeper and to see the spiritual and communal core of his mission.

The first story is the exorcism of an unclean spirit. The emancipated man is now free to receive the Holy Spirit. The second story is the theme of restoration to service and who God created us to be. The third is restoration to community: whether beggar or "puffed up," God invites us to a wider embrace. Finally, we see the lowering of the paralytic by four friends. Jesus is deeply moved by their faith. Here the deeper spiritual and communal healing is most tightly woven. *We have never seen anything like it!* It is deep ownership of Jesus' teaching and healing ministry. These four friends are an icon of Immanuel and his vision for a restored humanity.

We come to the mountaintop and the fullness of God's revelation in Jesus Christ. The opposition and doubts, woven through the narrative of the season, are pushed to the edge of this searing white experience. The cloud cover comes and again God speaks, "This is my Son, the Beloved; listen to him!" (Mark 9:8). It is a mighty exhortation for life in the valley and a wonderful promise for all who dream and see visions of the children of God.

82

Shape *of* Worship *for the* Season

BASIC SHAPE OF THE EUCHARISTIC RITE

- Confession and Forgiveness: see alternate worship text for Epiphany in *Sundays and Seasons* as an option to the form in the liturgy setting.

GATHERING

- Greeting: see alternate worship text for Epiphany
- Consider omitting the Kyrie on the "green" Sundays after the Epiphany, but use the Kyrie on the festivals of the Epiphany, the Baptism of Our Lord, and the Transfiguration of Our Lord, as well as the Presentation of Our Lord, if it is observed.
- Use the hymn of praise throughout Epiphany ("Glory to God")

WORD

- Use the Nicene Creed for festival days and Sundays in this season; use the Apostles' Creed for the Sundays after the Epiphany
- The prayers: see alternate forms and responses for Epiphany

BAPTISM

- Consider having a baptismal festival on the Baptism of Our Lord (January 12)

MEAL

- Offertory prayer: see alternate worship text for Epiphany
- Use the proper preface for Epiphany
- Eucharistic prayer: in addition to the four main options in *LBW*, see "Eucharistic Prayer C: The Season of Epiphany," *WOV* Leaders Edition, p. 67

- Invitation to communion: see alternate worship text for Epiphany
- Post-communion prayer: see alternate worship text for Epiphany

SENDING

- Benediction: see alternate worship text for Epiphany
- Dismissal: see alternate worship text for Epiphany

OTHER SEASONAL POSSIBILITIES

- The festival of the Epiphany of Our Lord (January 6) is a fitting occasion to use incense. *Worship Wordbook* (pp. 103–104), *Manual on the Liturgy* (pp. 279–82), and *Altar Guild and Sacristy Handbook* (p. 81) are three possible resources to consult for instructions on using incense.
- Because of the words from Simeon's song "a light for revelation to the Gentiles, and for glory to your people Israel," some communities observe the tradition of blessing candles for the use of the congregation on the festival of the Presentation of Our Lord (February 2). In England, the day is often called Candlemas for this reason. Such a blessing could be done in conjunction with the offertory. See the order in Seasonal Rites.

83

Assembly Song *for the* Season

"A light to reveal you to the nations and the glory

of your people Israel." The Epiphany season works out the meaning

of these words in readings that talk of Jesus' calling

his disciples and healing many who were sick. Using "Holy Communion: All Times and Places" (setting 6) from *WOV,* with its suggestions for liturgical songs from around the globe, is a fitting way to celebrate Jesus, the light of the whole world.

Besides Epiphany itself, three festivals occur during the season this year: the Baptism of Our Lord, the Presentation of Our Lord (February 2), and the Transfiguration of Our Lord. Can music be a connecting thread between these festivals, lifting them out of the ordinary Sundays?

GATHERING

- Epiphany offers a good opportunity to use hymns and songs that use light imagery. Many can be found in the morning sections of our hymnbooks. Others are in the Epiphany sections. *Hymns for Worship* lists 46 hymns containing the theme of light.
- Sing "O Morning Star, how fair and bright!" (LBW 76) as the entrance hymn on the Epiphany of Our Lord, and again on the Presentation and Transfiguration.
- Use "Glory to God" as the hymn of praise consistently through the season, in a well-known setting that can be elaborated with instruments on the festival days. Alternatively, "Glory to God, we give you thanks" (WOV 787) from Great Britain and "All glory be to God on high" (LBW 166) from Germany offer metrical versions of this canticle.

WORD

- Use the first phrase of "Glory to God, we give you thanks" (WOV 787) as a seasonal psalm refrain; sing the verses to *LBW* tones 1 or 3 (transposed to D major), or tone 8. If the season is too long for a single refrain to remain "fresh," use the assisting minister's line from "Glory to God in the highest" from *LBW* setting 2 on the festivals or as a change of pace in February.
- Use the proper verses on the three festival days,

chanted by the choir or cantor to *LBW* tone 1 or 3 (in D major), and framed by the assembly singing two alleluias set to the final musical phrase of "O Morning Star, how fair and bright!" (LBW 76).
- Other possibilities for the gospel acclamation include "Glory to God, glory in the highest" (WOV 788) from Peru and "The people who walked in darkness" (LBW 8) from North America.

MEAL

- For the offertory procession, particularly early in the season, use a song that calls to mind the procession of the magi: "As with gladness men of old," stanzas 1, 2, and 3 (LBW 82) or "Hail to the Lord's anointed," stanzas 1 and 4 (LBW 87). Another possibility from Nicaragua is "Now we offer/Te ofrecemos" (WOV 761); if sung in their entirety the latter two are long enough to cover both the reception of monetary offerings and the presentation of gifts at the altar.
- For the distribution, use one of the many settings of "Lamb of God" in the service music sections of *WOV, TFF,* or *LLC* (bilingual texts are found at 239 and 240).

SENDING

- "Lord, now you let your servant go in peace," known as the Song of Simeon or Nunc dimittis, is taken from Luke 2 and is read this year on the Presentation of Our Lord. It makes a fitting song to conclude the eucharistic meal. On the three festival days the sending could be elaborated by including both this canticle and a sending hymn. On the Transfiguration of Our Lord, use "Alleluia, song of gladness" (WOV 654), as the church says "farewell" to the alleluia that does not reappear until Easter.
- Other seasonal sending songs include "O Lord, now let your servant" (LBW 339), "Arise, your light has come!" (WOV 652), and "We are marching in the light of God" (WOV 650, W&P 148, TFF 63).

84

Music *for the* Season

VERSE AND OFFERTORY

Boehnke, Paul. *Festive Verse Settings for Christmas, Epiphany and Transfiguration.*
SATB, opt kybd. MSM 80-100.

Cherwien, David. *Verses for the Epiphany Season.* U, opt hb, org.
MSM 80-200.

Johnson, David N. *Verses and Offertories for Epiphany 2 through*
Transfiguration. U, kybd. AFP 0800649028.

Verses and Offertory Sentences, Part II: Epiphany through Transfiguration.
CPH 97-5502.

CHORAL

Bach, J. S./arr. Hal H. Hopson. "The Only Son from Heaven."
SATB, kybd. AFP 0800647092.

Bengtson, Bruce. "Behold My Servant." SATB, org, opt cong.
AFP 0880659120.

Busarow, Donald. "O Morning Star, How Fair and Bright." SAB,
cong, trbl inst, org. CPH 98-2819.

Christiansen, F. Melius. "Beautiful Savior." SATB.
AFP 0800652584.

Erickson, Richard. "I Want to Walk as a Child of the Light." SATB,
org. AFP 0800658396.

Ferguson, John. "Jesus! Name of Wondrous Love" in *St. John Passion.*
SATB, org. AFP 0800658582.

Forsberg, Charles. "Fairest Lord Jesus." SATB, pno.
AFP 0800656962.

Helgen, John. "Brighter Than the Sun." SATB, kybd.
AFP 0800659155.

Kosche, Kenneth T. "Rejoice and Be Merry." SATB. MSM 50-1080.

Larkin, Michael. "Jesus! Name of Wondrous Love." SATB, kybd.
CPH 98-3560.

Martinson, Joel. "Arise, Shine." SATB, org. AFP 0800652401.

Schalk, Carl. "All the Ends of the Earth." SATB, org. CPH 98-3546.

Soper, Scott. "Children of the Light." SATB, kybd, opt gtr, opt cong.
GIA G-4616.

Tallis, Thomas. "O nata lux." SATTB. OXF 43.228.

Willan, Healey. "Arise, Shine." SATB, org. CPH 98-1508.

CHILDREN'S CHOIRS

Bågenfelt, Susanne. "There's a Light in the World." U, opt 2 pt, kybd.
AFP 0800674286.

Davis, Katherine. "Who Was the Man." U, kybd. CG CGA110.

Farrell, Bernadette. "Share the Light." 2 pt, kybd, gtr, opt inst.
OCP 11307CC.

Kemp, Helen. "Set the Sun Dancing!" U, kybd, opt 3–4 oct hb.
CG CGA780.

Schram, Ruth, arr. "This Little Light of Mine." WAR SV98127.

KEYBOARD/INSTRUMENTAL

Behnke, John A. "Partita on 'I Want to Walk as a Child of the
Light.'" Org. CPH 97-6595.

Burkhardt, Michael. "Partita on 'O Morning Star, How Fair and
Bright.'" Org. MSM 10-202.

Linker, Janet. *Three Epiphany Pieces.* Org. AFP 0800658221.

Michel, Johannes Matthias. "Afro-Cuban" (In dir ist Freude) in *Organ,*
Timbrel and Dance. Org. CPH 97-6805.

Pelz, Walter. "Deo Gracias" in *Hymn Settings for Organ and Brass.*
AFP 0800650697.

Sedio, Mark. *Dancing in the Light of God.* Pno. AFP 0800656547.

Wold, Wayne L. "Suite on 'Bright and Glorious Is the Sky.'" Org.
AFP 0800659023.

HANDBELL

Angerman, David. "I'm Gonna Let It Shine." 2–3 oct, LI.
AGEHR 5551106-725.

Kinyon, Barbara. "Brightest and Best (of the Stars)." 2–3 oct.
JEF MCO976709.

Moklebust, Cathy. "Meditation on 'Beautiful Savior.'" 3–5 oct.
CG CGB175.

Rogers, Sharon Elery. "As with Gladness." (Medley). 2–3 oct.
JEF MAMHB31.

Tucker, Sondra. "I Want to Walk as a Child of the Light." 3–5 oct.
L2. AFP 0800658868.

PRAISE ENSEMBLE

Kendrick, Graham. "Shine, Jesus, Shine!" SATB, kybd.
HOP GC 937.

Smith, Michael W. and Deborah D. Smith. "Shine on Us." SATB, kybd.
WRD 301 0876 165. Choraltrax. WRD 301 7547 086.
Orch. WRD 301 0593 252.

Williams, J. Paul and Joseph M. Martin. "Arise! Shine!" SATB, kybd.
GS A 7063. Cass. GS MC 5189. Orch. GS LB 5360.

85

Alternate Worship Texts

CONFESSION AND FORGIVENESS

In the name of the Father, and of the ✛ Son,
and of the Holy Spirit.
Amen

As God's beloved daughters and sons,
let us call to mind our need for reconciliation
with God and one another.

Silence for reflection and self-examination.

God of the nations,
in baptism you anoint us
to be your holy people in the world,
yet we have not been faithful to you.
We have not loved and accepted one another.
We have not reached out
to those who are poor, hungry, or lost.
Forgive us, and fill us with your light,
that we may delight in your goodness
and serve you with joy,
through Jesus Christ our Lord. Amen

In Christ the grace and mercy of God are revealed;
in Christ your sins are forgiven.
Walk, then, as children of the light.
Amen

GREETING

The grace of God that extends to all nations in Christ Jesus
through the work of the Holy Spirit be with you all.
And also with you.

PRAYERS

Let us pray that the radiance of Christ will illumine the church,
the nations, and all who seek the light.

A brief silence.

Each petition ends:
Lord, in your mercy,
hear our prayer.

Concluding petition:
Hear our spoken and silent prayers, O God of light,
and reveal yourself to us, through your Son,
Jesus Christ our Lord.
Amen

OFFERTORY PRAYER

Merciful God,
as you have blessed us with many gifts,
so receive now these offerings of ourselves,
our time, and our possessions.
Through this meal unite us as your body,
that we may be a light to all nations;
for the sake of him who gave himself for us,
Jesus Christ our Lord. Amen

INVITATION TO COMMUNION

The gifts of God for the people of God.

POST-COMMUNION PRAYER

God of glory,
in this sacrament you unite us in the body of your Son.
May we who have been guests at this table
grow in love for one another,
that through us your light may shine in all the world,
through Jesus Christ our Lord.
Amen

BLESSING

May God, who lightens all our paths,
accompany you on your journey this day and always.
The Lord bless you and keep you.
The Lord's face shine on you with grace and mercy.
The Lord look upon you with favor and ✛ give you peace.
Amen

DISMISSAL

Go in peace to spread the light of Christ.
Thanks be to God.

Seasonal Rites

Blessing of the Home at Epiphany

Matthew writes that when the magi saw the shining star stop overhead, they were filled with joy. "On entering the house, they saw the child with Mary his mother" (2:10-11). In the home, Christ is met in family and friends, in visitors and strangers. In the home, faith is shared, nurtured, and put into action. In the home, Christ is welcome.

Twelfth Night (January 5) or another day during the season of Epiphany offers an occasion for gathering with friends and family members for a blessing of the home, using the following as a model. Someone may lead the greeting and blessing, while another person may read the scripture passage. Following an eastern European tradition, a visual blessing may be inscribed with white chalk above the main door; for example, 20 + C M B + 03. The numbers change with each new year. The three letters stand for either the ancient Latin blessing Christe mansionem benedica, which means "Christ, bless this house," or the legendary names of the magi (Caspar, Melchior, and Balthasar).

GREETING

May peace be to this house and to all who enter here. By wisdom a house is built and through understanding it is established; through knowledge its rooms are filled with rare and beautiful treasures.

See Proverbs 24:3-4.

READING

As we prepare to ask God's blessing on this household, let us listen to the words of scripture.

In the beginning was the Word, and the Word was with God, and the Word was God. He was in the beginning with God. All things came into being through him, and without him not one thing came into being. What has come into being in him was life, and the life was the light of all people. The Word became flesh and lived among us, and we have seen his glory, the glory as of a father's only son, full of grace and truth. From his fullness we have all received, grace upon grace.

See John 1:1-4, 14, 16.

INSCRIPTION

This inscription may be made with chalk above the entrance:

20 + C M B + 03
    The magi of old, known as
C Caspar,
M Melchior, and
B Balthasar
    followed the star of God's Son who came to dwell among us
20 two thousand
03 and three years ago.
+ Christ, bless this house,
+ and remain with us throughout the new year.

PRAYER

O God, you revealed your Son to all people by the shining light of a star. We pray that you bless this home and all who live here with your gracious presence. May your love be our inspiration, your wisdom our guide, your truth our light, and your peace our benediction; through Christ our Lord. Amen

Then everyone may walk from room to room, blessing the house with incense or by sprinkling with water, perhaps using a branch from the Christmas tree.

Adapted from *Come, Lord Jesus: Devotions for the Home* (Augsburg Fortress, 1996).

Ecumenical Service during the Week of Prayer for Christian Unity

CONFESSION AND FORGIVENESS

We gather as the people of God
to offer our repentance and praise,
to pray for the unity of the church
and the renewal of our common life.
Trusting in God's mercy and compassion,
let us ask for the forgiveness of our sins.

Silence for reflection and self-examination.

Lord Jesus, you came to reconcile us
to one another and to the Father:
Lord, have mercy on us.
Lord, have mercy on us.

87

Lord Jesus, you heal the wounds
of pride and intolerance.
Christ, have mercy on us.
Christ, have mercy on us.

Lord Jesus, you pardon the sinner
and welcome the repentant.
Lord, have mercy on us.
Lord, have mercy on us.

May almighty God grant us pardon and peace,
strengthen us in faith,
and make us witnesses to Christ's love.
Amen

HYMN OF PRAISE

PRAYER OF THE DAY

God our Father, your Son Jesus prayed that his followers might
be one. Make all Christians one with him as he is one with you,
so that in peace and concord we may carry to the world the
message of your love; through your Son, Jesus Christ our Lord,
who lives and reigns with you and the Holy Spirit, one God, now
and forever.
Amen

READINGS

Isaiah 2:2-4
Psalm 133
Ephesians 4:1-6
John 17:15-23

SERMON

HYMN OF THE DAY

THANKSGIVING FOR BAPTISM

*The people remain standing after the hymn as the minister(s)
gather at the font. After the prayer, the people may be sprinkled
with water from the font. Or at the conclusion of the service,
they may be invited to dip their hands in the font and trace the
sign of the cross over themselves.*

The Lord be with you.
And also with you.
Let us give thanks to the Lord our God.
It is right to give our thanks and praise.

Holy God and mighty Lord, we give you thanks,
for you nourish and sustain us and all living things
with the gift of water.
In the beginning your Spirit moved over the waters,
and you created heaven and earth.
By the waters of the flood you saved Noah and his family.
You led Israel through the sea out of slavery
into the promised land.
In the waters of the Jordan
your Son was baptized by John and anointed with the Spirit.
By the baptism of his death and resurrection
your Son set us free from sin and death
and opened the way to everlasting life.

We give you thanks, O God,
that you have given us new life in the water of baptism.
Buried with Christ in his death,
you raise us to share in his resurrection
by the power of the Holy Spirit.
May all who have passed through the water of baptism
continue in the risen life of our Savior.
To you be all honor and glory, now and forever.
Amen

CONFESSION OF FAITH

There is one Lord, one faith, and one baptism.
United in Christ, let us confess the faith we hold in common.

The people recite the Apostles' Creed.

THE PRAYERS

At the conclusion, the people pray the Lord's Prayer.

GREETING OF PEACE

The Lord Jesus prayed for the unity of his disciples.
We look for the day when the church will shine forth
in unity at his holy supper.
The peace of the Lord be with you always.
And also with you.

The people exchange a sign of Christ's peace.

BLESSING AND DISMISSAL

SENDING HYMN

Blessing of the Candles

*On the feast of the Presentation of Our Lord (Candlemas),
February 2, some traditions dedicate the candles to be used in
worship during the following year. The candles may be brought
forward with the offertory procession, or they may be placed on
a table near the altar prior to the service. This prayer is said by
the presiding minister before the offertory prayer.*

Let us pray.
Blessed are you,
O Lord our God, ruler of the universe.
You have enriched our lives with every good and perfect gift;
you have commanded us to show your splendor to our children
and to praise you with lives of love, justice, and joy.
Accept these candles which we offer in thanksgiving;
may they be to us a sign of Christ,
the Light of the world,
the light no darkness can overcome.
Bring us all at length to your perfect kingdom,
where you live and reign with the Son and the Holy Spirit,
now and forever.
Amen

89

January 6, 2003

The Epiphany of Our Lord

INTRODUCTION

In the East three great epiphanies are celebrated on this day: the magi's adoration of the Christ child, Jesus' baptism in the Jordan River, and his first miracle in which he changes water into wine. Epiphany celebrates Christ being made known, or made "manifest," to all nations.

The sacraments are for us the great epiphany of God's grace in which we behold the mystery of God among us. The magi offered gifts of gold, frankincense, and myrrh. Having seen the light of Christ, we offer the gift of ourselves, our time, and our possessions—that others may also know the epiphany of God's mercy and love.

PRAYER OF THE DAY

Lord God, on this day you revealed your Son to the nations by the leading of a star. Lead us now by faith to know your presence in our lives, and bring us at last to the full vision of your glory, through your Son, Jesus Christ our Lord, who lives and reigns with you and the Holy Spirit, one God, now and forever.

VERSE

Alleluia. We observed his star in the East, and have come to pay him homage. Alleluia. (Matt. 2:2)

READINGS

Isaiah 60:1-6

Isaiah promises that God's salvation, light, and glory will shine out to all nations, and people shall come bearing gifts to the place of that light, the restored Jerusalem.

Psalm 72:1-7, 10-14

All kings shall bow down before him. (Ps. 72:11)

Ephesians 3:1-12

Paul understands the secret purpose of Christ: In the "rich variety" of God's wisdom, the "boundless riches" of Christ are given to Jews and Gentiles alike.

Matthew 2:1-12

The spiritual quest of all human beings is mirrored in the journey of the magi. They find and adore the Christ child, the fulfillment of their hope, the epiphany and glory of God.

COLOR White

THE PRAYERS

Let us pray that the radiance of Christ will illumine the church, the nations, and all who seek the light.

A BRIEF SILENCE.

God of light, break through the shadows that cover our hearts with the full radiance of your life-giving word and sacraments. Lord, in your mercy,

hear our prayer.

Shine on your holy church, that beholding your glory it may radiantly proclaim your praise. Lord, in your mercy,

hear our prayer.

Lead the nations to your light, and reveal to their leaders the new dawn of your justice and truth, that violence and war may give way to peace and goodwill. Lord, in your mercy,

hear our prayer.

Illumine those who struggle in sickness and in sorrow *(especially)*, that the warmth of your healing presence will remind them that they are not alone. Lord, in your mercy,

hear our prayer.

Enlighten all who seek your face and yearn to be led into the light of your truth and wisdom. Lord, in your mercy,

hear our prayer.

HERE OTHER INTERCESSIONS MAY BE OFFERED.

Remind us always that we are surrounded by a great cloud of witnesses—all your saints in light. Keep us united with those who have gone before us *(especially)*, and bring us with them to your light. Lord, in your mercy,

hear our prayer.

Hear our spoken and silent prayers, O God of light, and reveal yourself to us, through your Son, Jesus Christ our Lord.

Amen

IMAGES FOR PREACHING

We observed his star at its rising. . . . We observed his star in the east. Each day the sun's power is revealed at break of day in the east. Light is the ancient Epiphany symbol. For Jews or Christians to be "in the light" is to be right

90

with God, to be alive in God. Christians have long called Jesus the light of the world. It is Jesus who brings us into right relation with God and one another. What was hidden was made known to all the nations. Jesus is humanity's great star, illuminating God's wide embrace and salvation for all. Jesus is the bright path for the magi and for you and me.

Our world is full of stars: movie stars, athletic stars, music stars. The world comes to their door and they burn brightly for a time. But what of this star, Jesus, who appears as a helpless baby? Is it not ironic that these wise men from the East would pay this little one homage? The magi came because they believed the stars. In some sense, the world and the heavens stopped over Jesus; this birth had cosmic import. Herod trembled and the powerful ones of the world with him, while for the downtrodden, hope was reborn.

The magi are wonderfully colorful characters in this story. They represent the magnificence of this world and the diversity of its peoples streaming to the source.

They came bearing gifts offered in homage and for burial, joining those who would later bring myrrh to his tomb. They worshiped God's love, from birth to death, poured out for the world.

And more: the epiphany of our Lord prefigured his resurrection. The star rising in the east looked to Jesus rising on the third day. The Light of the world continues to shine brightly; the darkness cannot overcome him.

WORSHIP MATTERS

Even though they may not seem very grand, our offertory processions can be signs of honoring God in much the same way that the gifts of the magi honored Jesus. We believe that the physical things we offer in our worship—monetary gifts, bread, and wine—are transformed by God to be channels of divine grace and love.

Are we presenting the best of ourselves in the way that the magi apparently did? Is the bread we offer the finest bread from our kitchens and tables? Is the wine what we might provide for a truly festive meal? Are the monetary offerings symbolic of the importance that we attach to God and to God's place in our lives? Stewardship and worship are indeed connected.

LET THE CHILDREN COME

Stars and wise men bring wonder and mystery into the world of children. On this festival day involve the children in a meandering procession led by a large golden star, perhaps adorned with ribbons from last Sunday. Wind around the pews or seats in your worship space. The children following the star may carry streamers of many colors to symbolize the magi traveling from countries afar who followed the star to find Jesus, the new king. Drape the streamers over three golden boxes to illustrate the gifts the magi brought to show their reverence for the new King. During the procession, introduce "We are marching in the light of God" (WOV 650). Consider using this hymn as the sending hymn throughout the season of Epiphany, the season of light.

HYMNS FOR WORSHIP
GATHERING
As with gladness men of old   LBW 82
We three kings of Orient are   WOV 646

HYMN OF THE DAY
Brightest and best of the stars of the morning   LBW 84

ALTERNATE HYMN OF THE DAY
O Morning Star, how fair and bright!   LBW 76
There's a light in the world   ASG 41

COMMUNION
Beautiful Savior   LBW 518
Come and taste   W&P 30

SENDING
Angels, from the realms of glory   LBW 50
Jesus shall reign   LBW 530
Sister Mary   TFF 60

ADDITIONAL HYMNS AND SONGS
The people who in darkness walked   H82 125/6
What star is this   H82 124
All hail King Jesus!   W&P 3
Shine, Jesus, shine   WOV 651, TFF 64, W&P 123

MUSIC FOR THE DAY
PSALMODY

Hail to the Lord's anointed   LBW 87

Hobby, Robert.   PW B.

Hughes, Howard. "Psalm 72" in TP.

Jesus shall reign   LBW 530

Joncas, Michael. "Psalm 72: Every Nation on Earth" in *Gather*.   GIA.

Marcus, Mary. "The Epiphany of Our Lord" in *Psalm Antiphons-3*. U, cong, hb/org.   MSM 80-723.

Ogden, David. "In His Days" in PS I.

CHORAL

Bach, J. S. "The Only Son from Heaven" in *Bach for All Seasons*. SATB, kybd.   AFP 080065854X. Inst pts.   AFP 0800659546.

Held, Wilbur. "When Christ's Appearing Was Made Known" in *To God Will I Sing*. MH voice.   AFP 0800674332. ML voice. AFP 0800674340.

Mendelssohn, Felix. "There Shall a Star Come Out of Jacob" in *Chantry Choirbook*. SATB, org.   AFP 0800657772.

Morris, Sally. "One Gift the Magi Bore." SATB, kybd.   GIA G-5035.

Shute, Linda. "The Magi Who to Bethlehem Did Go." SATB, pno, opt perc.   AFP 0800658361.

CHILDREN'S CHOIRS

Bågenfelt, Susanne. "There's a Light in the World." U, kybd, opt inst. AFP 0800674286.

Christopherson, Dorothy. "The Night of the Star." U, opt desc, pno, fl, perc.   AFP 0800657543.

Miller, Jeff. "Star Shine Bright." U, kybd, opt C inst.   CG CGA759.

KEYBOARD/INSTRUMENTAL

Drischner, Max. "Wie schön leuchtet der Morgenstern" in *Augsburg Organ Library: Epiphany*. Org.   AFP 0800659341.

Duruflé, Maurice. "Prélude sur l'Introït de l'Épiphanie" in *Augsburg Organ Library: Epiphany*. Org.   AFP 0800659341.

Koetsier, Jan. "Partita for English Horn and Organ: V: Andante Sostenuto" (Wie schön leuchtet). Eng hrn, org. Amsterdam: Donemus Publishing.

Leupold, Anton Wilhelm. "Marsch der heiligen drei Koenige" in *Augsburg Organ Library: Epiphany*. Org.   AFP 0800659341.

Linker, Janet. "Morning Star" in *Three Epiphany Pieces*. Org. AFP 0800658221.

Moore, David W. "We Three Kings" in *Three Carols for Piano and Solo Instrument*. Pno, C/B-flat inst.   AFP 0800659082.

HANDBELL

Helman, Michael. "Three Kings of Orient" in *Rise Up, Shepherd*. 2–3 oct.   AFP 0800655753.

Ivey, Robert. "We Three Kings." 3 oct.   JEF TP49442007.

Kinyon, Barbara. "What Star Is This That Beams So Bright" (Puer nobis). 2 oct.   JEF MCG B111.

PRAISE ENSEMBLE

Damazio, Sharon. "We Are Your Church" in *Hosanna! Music Songbook vol. 7*.   INT HMSB07.

Goreib, Sy and Rick Riso. "The Light of Life" in *God Is Able*.   INT.

Jolly, Todd. "Rise and Shine." SAB, kybd.   PVN P1025.

Kendrick, Graham. "Shine, Jesus, Shine" in *Shine Jesus Shine Songbook*. SATB, kybd.   Alleluia Community Ministries, Inc. 00957.

O'Brien, Chris and Margaret Davis. "Arise, Shine" in *The Maranatha! Singers I: See the Lord*.   MAR.

Thursday, January 9

ADRIAN OF CANTERBURY, TEACHER, C. 710

African by birth, Adrian (or Hadrian) worked with Theodore, archbishop of Canterbury, in developing the church in England, particularly through his direction of an influential school where many church leaders were instructed.

The growing awareness of the multicultural life of the church leads many to discover surprises in the church's history; for example, that an African missionary such as Adrian would have been influential in the development of the church in England, a church sometimes perceived only as Western and European in its history. Within parish groups, use the example of Adrian to explore the cross-cultural influence within the ancient church.

January 12, 2003

The Baptism of Our Lord
First Sunday after the Epiphany

INTRODUCTION

In the waters of baptism, we are joined to the Son in whom the Father is well pleased. The font is our Jordan where the Holy Spirit comes to us, strengthening and enlightening us for service in the world. On this great baptismal day, the church prays that all who are reborn as daughters and sons of God will continue to grow in faith, hope, and love.

PRAYER OF THE DAY

Father in heaven, at the baptism of Jesus in the River Jordan you proclaimed him your beloved Son and anointed him with the Holy Spirit. Make all who are baptized into Christ faithful in their calling to be your children and inheritors with him of everlasting life; through your Son, Jesus Christ our Lord, who lives and reigns with you and the Holy Spirit, one God, now and forever.

VERSE

Alleluia. You are my Son, the Beloved; with you I am well pleased. Alleluia. (Mark 1:11)

READINGS

Genesis 1:1-5

To a people experiencing the chaos of defeat, devastation, and exile, these familiar words bring great comfort. Out of chaos, God brings order. Creation by command demonstrates God's absolute sovereignty, which is not shared with any other gods. Notice the sequence of "evening" and "morning"—the Jewish day begins with sunset.

Psalm 29

The voice of the LORD is upon the waters. (Ps. 29:3)

Acts 19:1-7

Just as the Holy Spirit came upon Jesus at his baptism, so early Christians recognized that the Holy Spirit would come to them when they were baptized in Jesus' name.

Mark 1:4-11

Mark's gospel reports the story of Jesus' baptism with some irony: the one on whom the Spirit descends is himself the one who will baptize others with the Holy Spirit.

COLOR White

THE PRAYERS

Let us pray that the radiance of Christ will illumine the church, the nations, and all who seek the light.

A BRIEF SILENCE.

Holy God, strengthen and unite your one holy church in its common baptismal life, that your Holy Spirit may empower all the baptized to be light-filled witnesses of the gospel. Lord, in your mercy,

hear our prayer.

Lord of the nations, protect all who live in regions where the darkness of war and bloodshed threatens to overpower the light of reconciliation. Lord, in your mercy,

hear our prayer.

God of mercy, make us attentive to your Spirit, who calls us to welcome all into community. Hold the sick among us in your healing hand *(especially)*, that they might be restored to wholeness. Lord, in your mercy,

hear our prayer.

Spirit of God, descend upon those who are baptized this day and make them powerful proclaimers of your love. Bless those who are inquiring into the faith, that they too may come closer to your light. Lord, in your mercy,

hear our prayer.

HERE OTHER INTERCESSIONS MAY BE OFFERED.

Holy God, your radiance unites us and our beloved dead *(especially)*. Keep us united with them until that day when we all stand before your unveiled glory. Lord, in your mercy,

hear our prayer.

Hear our spoken and silent prayers, O God of light, and reveal yourself to us, through your Son, Jesus Christ our Lord.

Amen

IMAGES FOR PREACHING

Water is the most basic element of life. The world's surface, and our bodies, are primarily water. Before we are born, we live in a watery womb. We cannot live long without water. Is it any surprise that God would take this primary stuff and infuse it with the Holy Spirit? In the

93

beginning the Spirit breathed over the waters bringing forth life. In Mark's gospel, Jesus rises up out of his baptismal waters and sees the heavens torn apart and the Spirit descending upon him. The moment brings new life for humanity, and tears apart the barrier our sin erected between God and humanity. The Holy of Holies is no longer sequestered behind a temple curtain or in the highest realm of heaven. It is all broken open in the baptism of Jesus. It is the first day of new creation, of new life for all of us.

The new creation spreads and grows through the Holy Spirit. Paul's question, "Into what then were you baptized?" is a relational one. This joining together in the Holy Spirit, this baptism, is God's act by which we are joined together in Jesus Christ. It is the peace the angels sang of at the nativity of our Lord, "peace among those whom [God] favors!" (Luke 2:14b). At Jesus' baptism, God speaks this word of life: "You are my Son, the Beloved; with you I am well pleased" (Mark 1:11). The favor of God is bestowed upon Jesus and, in turn, upon us through the Holy Spirit's presence at our baptism. Through us, God's peace is made known and offered to the world.

The first day of a new creation is given in the baptism of our Lord. The heavens are torn apart and the nations have access to God. The basic element of life, water, is now filled with the Holy Spirit.

WORSHIP MATTERS

Considering how important the symbol of light is throughout our scriptures and worship texts, it is amazing how poorly lit many of our worship spaces are. In former centuries churches often were dark because too many windows weakened the walls, and candles or oil lamps provided little illumination. But most of our worship spaces can benefit from more recent technologies.

Lighting—whether natural, ambient, or direct—is a significant aspect of interior design. How it is used in the worship environment has important consequences and communicates a message, intended or not. Is lighting sufficient in order for worshipers to read a worship folder or book without eye strain? Are primary liturgical centers highlighted (altar, ambo/pulpit, font)? Does the practice of spotlighting the pulpit while dimming all other lights elevate the sermon above all other worship elements, or cause the preacher to lose eye contact with the congregation?

LET THE CHILDREN COME

Children enjoy playing with water. Water sounds may be featured during this major baptismal festival. Invite the children to gather around the font to share in the baptisms you celebrate today. Consider adjusting the placement of your font (near the entrance to the sanctuary) or the pathways the people take on their way to the altar for the Eucharist so they pass by the font. Invite the congregation to dip their fingers in the font and mark their foreheads with the sign of the cross as a renewal of their own baptisms.

HYMNS FOR WORSHIP
GATHERING

Songs of thankfulness and praise   LBW 90
When long before time   WOV 799
Morning has broken   W&P 98

HYMN OF THE DAY

When Jesus came to Jordan   WOV 647

ALTERNATE HYMN OF THE DAY

From God the Father, virgin-born   LBW 83, CS 29
When long before time   WOV 799

COMMUNION

Spirit of God, descend upon my heart   LBW 486
Baptized in water   WOV 693
Waterlife   W&P 145

SENDING

Let all things now living   LBW 557
Go, my children, with my blessing   WOV 721, TFF 161

ADDITIONAL HYMNS AND SONGS

Christ, when for us you were baptized   H82 121
Crashing waters at creation   NCH 326
Wade in the water   TFF 114

MUSIC FOR THE DAY
PSALMODY

Busarow, Donald. "It Is a Good Thing to Give Thanks." SATB, cong, hb.   CPH 98-3126.

Hobby, Robert.   PW B.

Hopson, Hal H. "Psalm 29."   TP.

Marshall, Jane. "Psalm 29" in *Psalms Together II.* U.   CG CGC-21.

Smith, Geoffrey Boulton. "Give Strength to Your People, Lord."   PS 1.

CHORAL

Biery, James. "The Waters of Life." SATB, org.   AFP 0800657683.

Hanson, Handt/arr. Phil Kadidlo. "Waterlife." SAB, kybd, opt sax, cong.   AFP 0800674413.

Helgen, John. "Brighter Than the Sun." SATB, pno.   AFP 0800659155.

Helman, Michael. "Christ, When for Us You Were Baptized." SAB, kybd.   AFP 0800674057.

Neswick, Bruce. "Epiphany Carol." U, org.   AFP 0800653912. Also in *The Augsburg Choirbook.*   AFP 0800656784.

Uhl, Dan. "This Is My Beloved Son" in *The Augsburg Choirbook.* SATB, org.   AFP 0800656784.

CHILDREN'S CHOIRS

Callahan, Charles. "The Baptism of Our Lord." U, opt desc, org.   MSM 50-2003.

Ferguson, John. "Jesus, My Lord and God." U, org.   AFP 0800646193.

KEYBOARD/INSTRUMENTAL

Fruhauf, Ennis. "King's Lynn" in *Augsburg Organ Library: Epiphany.* Org.   AFP 0800659341.

Hyslop, Scott M. "When Jesus Came to Jordan" in *Six Chorale Fantasias.* Inst, pno.   AFP 0800656601.

Kallman, Daniel. "Children of the Heavenly Father" in *Three Hymns.* 2 vln, pno.   MSM 20-971.

Mann, Adrian. "Salzburg" in *'Tis the Season: Preludes for Treble Instrument and Keyboard.* Pno, C/B-flat inst.   AFP 0800659848.

Organ, Anne Krentz. "Salzburg" in *Come to Us, Creative Spirit.* Pno.   AFP 080065904X.

HANDBELL

Lamb, Linda R. "I Am Thine, O Lord." 3–5 oct.   ALF API9636.

Larson, Katherine Jordahl. "Beautiful Savior." 3–4 oct.   AFP 0800653963.

Moklebust, Cathy. "Let All Things Now Living." 3–5 oct.   CG CGB170.

Tucker, Sondra. "Wade in the Water." 3–5 oct.   HOP 2074.

PRAISE ENSEMBLE

Leck, Henry H. "Siyahamba" in *South African Suite.* SAB.   PLY HL-400.

Makeever, Ray. "In the Water."   DH.

Park, Andy. "The River Is Here" in *Hosanna! Music Songbook 11.* INT.

Runyan, William M./arr. Vaclav Nelhybel. "Great Is Thy Faithfulness." SATB, kybd.   HOP VN109.

Wimber, John. "Spirit Song" in *Songs for Praise and Worship.*   WRD.

Monday, January 13

GEORGE FOX, RENEWER OF SOCIETY, 1691

Fox severed his ties among family and friends in search of enlightenment. He found no comfort in the traditional church, and he became an itinerant preacher. His preaching emphasized the abiding inward light given by God to believers as the real source of comfort and authority. His preaching led to the establishment of preaching bands of women and men known as the "Publishers of the Truth." In time, these preachers established local communities that came to be known as the Society of Friends, or Quakers. During visits to the Caribbean and North America, Fox witnessed the evil of the slave trade and he founded the abolitionist movement in England.

Quakers are known for the long period of silence in their meetings. Consider growing into the practice of silence in worship. Be mindful of the ways that silence breaks the hectic pace of life and leads us to attend to the wisdom of God in spoken word and through service to others.

Tuesday, January 14

EIVIND JOSEF BERGGRAV, BISHOP OF OSLO, 1959

In 1937, Berggrav was elected bishop of Oslo and primate of Norway. In 1940, he was asked to negotiate with the Nazi regime in order to ascertain its intentions regarding the social and religious life of the Norwegian people. Rejecting any compromise with the occupation forces, he left the negotiations and demanded that the Nazis recognize the rights of the Jews and the autonomy of the church. Deprived of his episcopal title in 1943, he was placed under arrest, only to escape and remain in hiding in Oslo until the end of the war.

During the season of Epiphany the life of Berggrav is another witness to the light of Christ. His life raises questions for believers today about the readiness to risk title, power, and prestige to speak for victims of injustice and seek truth in the midst of evils that face us in the world.

95

Wednesday, January 15

MARTIN LUTHER KING JR., RENEWER OF SOCIETY,
MARTYR, 1968

Martin Luther King Jr. is remembered as an American prophet of justice among races and nations, a Christian whose faith undergirded his advocacy of vigorous yet nonviolent action for racial equality. A pastor of churches in Montgomery, Alabama, and Atlanta, Georgia, his witness was taken to the streets in such other places as Birmingham, Alabama, where he was arrested and jailed while protesting against segregation. He preached nonviolence and demanded that love be returned for hate. Awarded the Nobel Peace Prize in 1964, he was killed by an assassin on April 4, 1968.

Congregations may choose to remember King by singing "We shall overcome" (TFF 213) or "Holy God, you raise up prophets" (TFF 299).

96

Friday, January 17

ANTONY OF EGYPT, RENEWER OF THE CHURCH, C. 356

Antony was born in Qemen-al-Arous, Upper Egypt, and was one of the earliest Egyptian desert fathers. Born to Christian parents from whom he inherited a large estate, he took personally Jesus' message to sell all that you have, give to the poor, and follow Christ. After making arrangements to provide for the care of his sister, he gave away his inheritance and became a hermit. Later, he became the head of a group of monks that lived in a cluster of huts and devoted themselves to communal prayer, worship, and manual labor under Antony's direction. The money they earned from their work was distributed as alms. Antony and his monks also preached and counseled those who sought them out.

Antony and the desert fathers serve as a reminder that certain times and circumstances call Christians to stand apart from the surrounding culture and renounce the world in service to Christ.

Saturday, January 18

THE CONFESSION OF ST. PETER
WEEK OF PRAYER FOR CHRISTIAN UNITY BEGINS

The Week of Prayer for Christian Unity is framed by two commemorations, today's Confession of St. Peter and next week's Conversion of St. Paul. Both are remembered together on June 29, but these two days give us an opportunity to focus on key events in each of their lives. Today we remember that Peter was led by God's grace to acknowledge Jesus as "the Christ, the Son of the living God" (Matt. 16:16).

This confession is the common confession that unites us with Peter and with all Christians of every time and place. During these weeks of Epiphany, with their emphasis on mission, consider an ecumenical worship service with neighboring congregations to embody the unity we share in our confession of Christ, a unity granted us in our one baptism, a unity we yearn to embody more fully. The hymn "We all are one in mission" (WOV 755) could be sung at this service.

January 19, 2003

Second Sunday after the Epiphany

INTRODUCTION

In the weeks of Epiphany, the church focuses on its mission in the world. Like Samuel we seek to hear God's voice as we pray: "Speak, your servant is listening." In baptism God calls us to be servants who go forth with a simple mission: invite others to come and see. Having seen God's great epiphany in Christ Jesus, we now graciously invite others to see Christ who is with us in the word, the waters of rebirth, and the holy supper.

The Week of Prayer for Christian Unity, which began yesterday, continues until next Saturday. Today the church commemorates Henry, a twelfth-century bishop of Uppsala, Sweden, who was martyred while on a missionary trip to Finland. Tomorrow the United States remembers Dr. Martin Luther King Jr.

PRAYER OF THE DAY

Lord God, you showed your glory and led many to faith by the works of your Son. As he brought gladness and healing to his people, grant us these same gifts and lead us also to perfect faith in him, Jesus Christ our Lord.

VERSE

Alleluia. The LORD said to me: You are my servant in whom I will be glorified. Alleluia. (Isa. 49:3)

READINGS

1 Samuel 3:1-10 [11-20]

Today's reading recounts the transition from the leadership of Eli the priest to Samuel. At a time when visions and auditions were rare and unexpected, the Lord comes to Samuel and calls him to speak the divine word.

Psalm 139:1-5, 12-17 (Psalm 139:1-6, 13-18 [NRSV])

You have searched me out and known me. (Ps. 139:1)

1 Corinthians 6:12-20

Some recent converts in the Corinthian church believed that God was interested only in what was spiritual so that what they did with their bodies did not matter. Paul's response affirms God's concern for the entire person.

John 1:43-51

In John's gospel, Jesus' ministry begins with the call of disciples, who then bring others to Jesus. Philip's friend Nathanael moves from skepticism to faith when he accepts the invitation to "Come and see."

COLOR Green

THE PRAYERS

Let us pray that the radiance of Christ will illumine the church, the nations, and all who seek the light.

A BRIEF SILENCE.

Let us pray for the church, that it might have a sense of urgency in its proclamation, and that the world may know of God's love for the whole creation. Lord, in your mercy,

hear our prayer.

Let us pray for all bishops, pastors, associates in ministry, deaconesses, and diaconal ministers, that they might hear the word of God and have courage for their tasks of proclamation and service. Lord, in your mercy,

hear our prayer.

Let us pray for all who seek to find the common ground between peoples of the world who are divided by nation, race, religion, or any other walls. Lord, in your mercy,

hear our prayer.

Let us pray for all in need, those who are facing illness, those who are grieving losses, those who are unemployed, those to whom death draws near *(especially)*. Lord, in your mercy,

hear our prayer.

Let us pray for all who are teachers in our parish and community, that they might responsibly lead and nurture us in ways of wisdom, knowledge, and the fear of the Lord. Lord, in your mercy,

hear our prayer.

HERE OTHER INTERCESSIONS MAY BE OFFERED.

Let us pray in thanksgiving for the lives of all who have died, for Bishop Henry of Uppsala *(other names)*, and especially those most dear to us, that we will be kept united with them while we live and when we die. Lord, in your mercy,

hear our prayer.

97

Hear our spoken and silent prayers, O God of light, and reveal yourself to us, through your Son, Jesus Christ our Lord.

Amen

IMAGES FOR PREACHING

The Kingdom grew and spread; the Epiphany light shined brighter. Jesus' birth was only the beginning of the Word taking flesh. Here it continues: Jesus finds Philip, Philip finds Nathanael, and Philip says, "We have found him about whom Moses in the law and also the prophets wrote, Jesus son of Joseph from Nazareth" (John 1:45). In short, we have found Jesus!

How do we find Jesus today? It's still the work of the Holy Spirit. God continues to seek us. And the encounter is still so wonderfully incarnational. God seeks us in our flesh. The Holy Spirit is at work in us. The light breaks in and God's Spirit bears fruit. We see. We see God at work in us and the world. We have found God. The rhythm of life beats in these encounters: Jesus finds Philip, Philip finds Nathanael, and finally we too say, We have found Jesus!

The spreading light is relational: one by one God invites people into a new covenant, a covenant made with the body and blood of Jesus. *This is my body, this is my blood,* and we say, Thanks be to God! The eucharistic rhythms offer a powerful witness to the world and a beacon to our communities.

Once again we come to the gate of heaven and earth and discover it wide open. Like deceitful Jacob who dreamed of angels ascending and descending from heaven, we are recipients of divine grace, undeserved love: in Jesus Christ God comes to dwell with us. Already we share in the "angels of God ascending and descending upon the Son of Man" (John 1:51).

It is the second Sunday after the Epiphany of our Lord and the light grows as we receive it from the church and reach out to share it with others.

WORSHIP MATTERS

Occurring this year during the Week of Prayer for Christian Unity, the U.S. observance of Martin Luther King Jr. Day (January 20) may present an opportunity for many congregations to schedule some kind of ecumenical worship. Those who have the day off from school or from work may be interested in participating in a re-gional or citywide celebration that brings together many different congregations and community groups. If such a gathering event is not happening in your community, why not start one? Demonstrate your unity while at the same time remembering one of the twentieth century's most powerful witnesses to the faith.

LET THE CHILDREN COME

Beginning this Sunday, the church wears mostly green up to the Transfiguration of Our Lord, when the bright white paraments return. Epiphany green can be like the green traffic signal, encouraging us to go and tell others about Jesus. In this Week of Prayer for Christian Unity, celebrate the "little epiphany" that Jesus is God's gift to people around the world. Introduce a hymn from another culture. Have children, scattered throughout the congregation, play rhythm instruments. Consider singing "We are marching in the light of God" (WOV 650) as the sending hymn.

HYMNS FOR WORSHIP

GATHERING

Thy strong word   LBW 233

All my hope on God is founded   WOV 782

HYMN OF THE DAY

The Son of God, our Christ   LBW 434

ALTERNATE HYMN OF THE DAY

I, the Lord of sea and sky   WOV 752, TFF 230

The summons   W&P 137

COMMUNION

Dear Lord and Father of mankind   LBW 506

This is my body   TFF 121, WOV 707

SENDING

O Jesus, I have promised   LBW 503

We are marching in the light of God   TFF 63, WOV 650, W&P 148

ADDITIONAL HYMNS AND SONGS

Come, labor on   H82 541

Whom shall I send?   UMH 582

I can hear my Savior calling   TFF 146

The Lord is my light   TFF 61

Come to the mountain   W&P 32

MUSIC FOR THE DAY

PSALMODY

Farrell, Bernadette. "O God, You Search Me."   PS 3.

Hopson, Hal H.   PW B.

Lisicky, Paul. "Psalm 139: Filling Me with Joy" in *Gather Comprehensive*. GIA.

Mahnke, Allan. "Psalm 139" in *17 Psalms for Cantor and Congregation*. Cong, cant.   CPH 97-6093.

Marshall, Jane. "A Psalm of Praise." SATB.   AFP 11-4673.

Wondrous are your ways, O God   LBW 311

CHORAL

Bell, John L. "Will You Come and Follow Me." SATB.   GIA G-4384.

Schulz-Widmar, Russell. "O Gracious Light." SATB.   GIA G-2825.

Schutte, Daniel L./arr. Ovid Young. "Here I Am, Lord." SATB, pno. AFP 0800656059.

Sensmeier, Randall. "When Jesus Came from Nazareth." 2 pt mxd, opt fl, vc, kybd.   GIA G-5137.

Sweelinck, Jan Pieterszoon. "Sing to the Lord, New Songs Be Raising" in *Chantry Choirbook*. SATB.   AFP 0800657772.

CHILDREN'S CHOIRS

Pote, Allen. "Psalm 139." SATB, pno.   CG CGA610.

Schram, Ruth, arr. "This Little Light of Mine." 2 pt, kybd, opt gtr, drm.   StudioPR SV98127.

KEYBOARD/INSTRUMENTAL

Biery, James. "Salzburg" in *Augsburg Organ Library: Epiphany*. Org. AFP 0800659341.

Honoré, Jeffrey. "Shine, Jesus, Shine." Pno.   CPH 97-6698.

Kerr, J. Wayne. "Ebenezer" in *Christ Is Alive!* Org.   AFP 0800658027.

Organ, Anne Krentz. "He Comes to Us as One Unknown" in *Come to Us, Creative Spirit*. Pno.   AFP 080065904X.

Sedio, Mark. "Repton" in *How Blessed This Place*. Org.   AFP 0800658035.

HANDBELL

Afdahl, Lee J. "Repton" in *Dear Lord—Lead On*. 3–5 oct. AFP 080065630X.

Kinyon, Barbara. "O Jesus, I Have Promised." 5–6 oct.   JEF MBEHB91.

Sherman, Arnold. "Here I Am, Lord." 3–5 oct.   AG 2140.

PRAISE ENSEMBLE

Butler, Terry. "Cry of My Heart" in *Maranatha! Music Praise Chorus Book, 3rd ed.*   MAR.

Knapp, Phoebe P./arr. V. Whaley and C. Clevenger. "Blessed Assurance." SATB, pno.   PLY SHS9705.

LeBlanc, Lenny. "Come and See" in *Maranatha! Music Praise Chorus Book, 3rd ed.*   MAR.

Makeever, Ray. "When You Call."   DATH.

Pote, Allen. "Psalm 139." SATB, pno.   CG CGA610.

Schutte, Dan/arr. Mark Hayes. "Here I Am, Lord." SATB, orch. GS A7101.

Sunday, January 19

HENRY, BISHOP OF UPPSALA, MISSIONARY TO FINLAND, MARTYR, 1156

Henry, an Englishman, became bishop of Uppsala, Sweden, in 1152, and is regarded as the patron of Finland. He traveled to Finland with the king of Sweden on a mission trip and remained there to organize the church. He was murdered in Finland by a man whom he had rebuked and who was disciplined by the church. Henry's burial place became a center of pilgrimage. His popularity as a saint is strong in both Sweden and Finland.

Today is an appropriate day to celebrate the Finnish presence in the Lutheran church. Consider singing "Lost in the night" (LBW 394), which uses a Finnish folk tune. During Epiphany we celebrate the light of Christ revealed to the nations, and martyrs such as Henry continue to reveal that light through their witness to faith.

99

Saturday, January 25

THE CONVERSION OF SAINT PAUL
WEEK OF PRAYER FOR CHRISTIAN UNITY ENDS

Today the Week of Prayer for Christian Unity comes to an end. The church remembers how a man of Tarsus named Saul, a former persecutor of the early Christian church, was led by God's grace to become one of its chief preachers. The risen Christ appeared to Paul on the road to Damascus and called him to proclaim the gospel. The narratives describing Paul's conversion in the Acts of the Apostles, Galatians, and I Corinthians inspire this commemoration, which was first celebrated among the Christians of Gaul.

The entire Week of Prayer for Christian Unity gives us a chance to consider our calling in light of Paul's words in Galatians that all are one in Christ. The hymn "Bind us together" (WOV 748) can be used to pray that Christ will continue to hold us in our baptismal unity.

January 26, 2003

Third Sunday after the Epiphany

INTRODUCTION

In today's gospel reading, Jesus uses the common experience of fishing and turns it upside down. Each baptized Christian, born in God's gracious sea, is called to fish for people. We are given the net of God's mercy and the gift of the Holy Spirit's presence as we go forth and invite others to join us in our communal journey of discipleship.

Timothy, Titus, and Silas, three missionary companions of the apostle Paul, are remembered today by the church.

PRAYER OF THE DAY

Almighty God, you sent your Son to proclaim your kingdom and to teach with authority. Anoint us with the power of your Spirit, that we, too, may bring good news to the afflicted, bind up the brokenhearted, and proclaim liberty to the captive; through your Son, Jesus Christ our Lord.

VERSE

Alleluia. Jesus went throughout Galilee, teaching, proclaiming the good news, and curing every disease. Alleluia. (Matt. 4:23)

READINGS

Jonah 3:1-5, 10

Unlike other prophetic books that focus on the prophet's message, this book focuses on the prophet himself. The book of Jonah is really a comedy starring a reluctant prophet who is given a one-sentence message: Nineveh will be destroyed in forty days. The point of the story is to get the reader to wrestle with the question: "On whom should God have mercy?"

Psalm 62:6-14 (Psalm 62:5-12 [NRSV])

In God is my safety and my honor. (Ps. 62:8)

1 Corinthians 7:29-31

In his letters to the Corinthians, Paul addresses many problems experienced by those who want faith to shape daily life. Here he insists that our future hope in Christ ought to affect the way we conduct ourselves in the present.

Mark 1:14-20

Before Jesus calls his first disciples, he proclaims a message that becomes known as the gospel or good news from God. God is ready to rule our lives. Those who recognize this good news will respond with repentance and faith.

COLOR Green

THE PRAYERS

Let us pray that the radiance of Christ will illumine the church, the nations, and all who seek the light.
A BRIEF SILENCE.

Unite all Christians of the world, that petty differences and profound divisions alike would be reconciled as we strengthen our baptismal bonds. Lord, in your mercy,
hear our prayer.

Even as Jesus taught his disciples to fish for people, may we who follow in your way always strive to care for all people without reserve. Lord, in your mercy,
hear our prayer.

Bless the cities of our world with honest leaders and responsible citizens. Give urban dwellers patience and delight as they live and work among many people. Lord, in your mercy,
hear our prayer.

Gently watch over those who are ill *(especially)*. Give your strength and patience, courage and healing. Lord, in your mercy,
hear our prayer.

Energize the ministries of outreach in this congregation so that many will hear your message of hope and forgiveness. Raise up new workers to help us tend to our tasks of service and proclamation. Lord, in your mercy,
hear our prayer.

HERE OTHER INTERCESSIONS MAY BE OFFERED.

Give us a sense of continuity and community with those who have died and now rest from their labors, including Timothy, Titus, and Silas *(other names)*. Comfort all those who mourn the loss of a loved one. Lord, in your mercy,
hear our prayer.

100

Hear our spoken and silent prayers, O God of light, and reveal yourself to us, through your Son, Jesus Christ our Lord. **Amen**

IMAGES FOR PREACHING

Any fan of the movies knows that many trailers, or "coming attractions," are works of art in themselves. They can deliver a powerful punch in just a few minutes. In fact, for some highly anticipated movies, people have been known to pay just to see the trailer, then leave. Expertly made as the trailers are, though, they don't take the place of the film they promote. In most cases, the movie itself delivers far more than can even be hinted at in a short preview.

In the perspective of the gospels, John the baptizer was the preview of the Christ. A powerful preacher in his own right, he proclaimed repentance and preparation. Now, though, the real thing appeared. Jesus came, like John preaching repentance, but more: the time is fulfilled, the kingdom of God is near.

So arresting is the imagery of fishermen now called to fish for people that we often skip over Jesus' arrival on the scene. But just as the protagonist's first appearance in a film can be a dramatic moment, so this epiphany has its own import. Jesus comes to Galilee, the backwater of Judea, his home territory. He proclaims the good news of God—at this point still a somewhat fuzzy concept, at least to his hearers. Yet he calls them, and us, to believe that this good news is present in him.

And then Jesus starts to gather the church from among the common people. Follow me, he says. Without that invitation, those fishermen could not have followed. That was protocol then: one didn't follow a rabbi unless one was invited. And that is reality now: we do not become followers of Christ, fishers of people, on our own whim. It is only possible because the Spirit calls us, gathers us, enlightens us. With that invitation secured, the plot begins to move, and we are more than viewers—we are actors!

WORSHIP MATTERS

For practical considerations, congregations often delegate their evangelism and worship efforts to different committees (or even to different staff members), but worship and outreach share a genuine connection. Principle 51 from *The Use of the Means of Grace*, the Evangelical Lutheran Church in America's statement on the practice of word and sacrament, states: "In every gathering of Christians around the proclaimed Word and the holy sacraments, God acts to empower the Church for mission."

That same statement, in a background paragraph, says: "This Supper forms the Church, as a community, to bear witness in the world. Our need to be nourished and sustained in this mission is one principal reason for the frequent celebration of the sacrament" (background 54a).

LET THE CHILDREN COME

Jesus' ministry was filled with surprises. Four fishermen dropped their nets and followed Jesus, without knowing their destination. Surprise! Now the fishermen would be fishing for people. When you pass the peace today, have the congregation do something unexpected. Join hands in rows of chairs or pews. The security of holding hands will help children, and adults, sense that in the midst of surprises we can trust Jesus to lead us. Holding hands is also a tactile way to show that we are one family in Christ.

HYMNS FOR WORSHIP

GATHERING

God, whose almighty word   LBW 400
Each morning brings us   WOV 800

HYMN OF THE DAY

You have come down to the lakeshore   WOV 784, LLC 560

ALTERNATE HYMN OF THE DAY

They cast their nets   LBW 449, CS 80
My chosen one   BL S8

COMMUNION

Come, my way, my truth, my life   LBW 513
Come, let us eat   LBW 214, TFF 119

SENDING

Go, my children, with my blessing   WOV 721, TFF 161
Let us talents and tongues employ   WOV 754, TFF 232
Go in peace and serve the Lord   W&P 46

ADDITIONAL HYMNS AND SONGS

This bread that we break   DH 30
You walk along the shoreline   NCH 504
This little light of mine   TFF 65
Go, make disciples   W&P 47

MUSIC FOR THE DAY
PSALMODY

Haas, David/arr. Jeanne Cotter. "In God Alone" in PCY III.

Hopson, Hal H.   PW B.

Marcus, Mary. "Third Sunday after the Epiphany" in *Psalm Antiphons, vol. 3.* U, opt hb.   MSM 80-723.

CHORAL

Clausen, René. "Prayer of St. Francis." SATB, kybd.   MF 2087.

Erickson, Richard. "I Want to Walk as a Child of the Light." SATB, org.   AFP 0800658396.

Hayes, Mark. "Let the Word Go Forth." SATB, kybd.
AFP 0800674189.

Hovland, Egil. "The Glory of the Father." SATB.   Walton W2973.

Schrader, Jack. "Order My Steps (In Your Word)." SATB, pno.
HOP C-5083.

Telemann, G. P. "O Praise the Lord, All Ye Nations." SATB.
CPH 974838.

CHILDREN'S CHOIRS

Althouse, Jay. "Gather Us In." 2 pt, kybd.   Alfred 18323.

Pote, Allen. "Sing a Song of Praise." U, org, opt fl.   CG CGA182.

KEYBOARD/INSTRUMENTAL

Brahms, Johannes. "Intermezzo." op. 118, no. 2. Pno.
Various editions.

Farlee, Robert Buckley. "Pescador de hombres" in *Many and Great.* Org.
AFP 0800658949.

Sedio, Mark. "Pescador de hombres" in *A Global Piano Tour.* Pno.
AFP 0800658191.

HANDBELL

Afdahl, Lee J. "You Have Come Down to the Lakeshore" in *Two Spanish Tunes for Handbells.* 3–5 oct, opt perc and handchimes.
AFP 0800657381.

Bettcher, Peggy. "Shine, Jesus, Shine." 2–3 oct, L2.
AGEHR 3181757-725.

PRAISE ENSEMBLE

Althouse, Jay. "Come Follow Me." SAB, acc.   ALF 4255.
Also available. SATB.   ALF 4254. 2 pt.   ALF 4256.

Barbour, John, and Anne Barbour. "I Will Follow" in *Maranatha! Music Praise Chorus Book, 3rd ed.*   MAR.

Chapman, Steven Curtis/arr. Marty Hamby. "For the Sake of the Call" in *Men of God Arise!* SATB, children, acc.   RM SPBK4006.

Kendrick, Graham. "Shine, Jesus, Shine" in *Shine Jesus Shine Songbook.*
SATB, acc.   Alleluia Community Ministries, Inc. 00957.

Kendrick, Graham. "We Declare That the Kingdom of God Is Here" in *Come & Worship.*   INT.

Makeever, Ray. "Rest in God Alone."   DH.

Sunday, January 26
TIMOTHY, TITUS, AND SILAS

Following the celebration of the conversion of Paul, we remember his companions. Today, we remember Timothy, Titus, and Silas. They were missionary coworkers with Paul. Timothy accompanied Paul on his second missionary journey and was commissioned by Paul to go to Ephesus where he served as bishop and overseer of the church. Titus was a traveling companion of Paul, accompanied him on the trip to the council of Jerusalem, and became the first bishop of Crete. Silas traveled with Paul through Asia Minor and Greece and was imprisoned with him at Philippi where they were delivered by an earthquake.

This festival invites the church to remember Christian leaders, bishops, pastors, and teachers—both men and women—who have been influential in the lives of individual members as gospel signs of the light of Epiphany.

Monday, January 27
LYDIA, DORCAS, AND PHOEBE

Today we remember three women in the early church who were companions in Paul's ministry. Lydia was Paul's first convert at Philippi in Macedonia. She was a merchant of purple-dyed goods, and because purple dye was extremely expensive, it is likely that Lydia was a woman of some wealth. Lydia and her household were baptized by Paul and for a time her home was a base for Paul's missionary work. Dorcas is remembered for her charitable works, particularly making clothing for needy widows. Phoebe was a *diakonos*, a deacon in the church at Cenchreae, near Corinth. Paul praises her as one who, through her service, looked after many people.

Today provides an opportunity for congregations to reflect the ministry of women, ordained and lay, wealthy and poor, who have given of themselves in service to the church and to the ministry of the gospel in their congregations.

February 2, 2003

The Presentation of Our Lord

INTRODUCTION

Joseph and Mary may have thought they were simply fulfilling the law (as written in Lev. 12) that said a woman should offer a sacrifice after the birth of a child in order to be ritually cleansed, but through the prophecy of Simeon and Anna, a witness was made that the baby they presented in the temple was no ordinary child, but rather the longed-for Messiah. Now we find that Christ is our temple, the place of God's mercy, and at the same time all the baptized faithful are a temple, a dwelling place for God.

PRAYER OF THE DAY

Blessed are you, O Lord our God, for you have sent us your salvation. Inspire us by your Holy Spirit to see with our own eyes him who is the glory of Israel and the light for all nations, your Son, Jesus Christ our Lord.

VERSE

Alleluia. My eyes have seen your salvation. Alleluia. (Luke 2:30)

READINGS

Malachi 3:1-4

This reading concludes a larger section (2:17—3:5) in which the prophet speaks of the coming of the God of justice. Malachi looks for that day when the wondrous power of God will purify the priestly descendents of Levi who minister in the temple at Jerusalem.

Psalm 84

How dear to me is your dwelling, O Lord. (Ps. 84:1)

or Psalm 24:7-10

Lift up your heads, O gates, and the King of glory shall come in. (Ps. 24:7)

Hebrews 2:14-18

Jesus shared human nature fully so that his death might be for all humans a liberation from slavery to death's power. Here the writer uses the image of priestly service in the temple as a way of describing the life and saving death of the Lord Jesus. He is the high priest who offers his life on behalf of his brothers and sisters.

Luke 2:22-40

This story is a study in contrasts: the infant Jesus with the aged prophets; the joy of birth with the ominous words of Simeon to Mary; the faithful fulfilling of the law with the presentation of the one who will release its hold over us. Through it all, we see the light of God's salvation revealed to the world.

COLOR White

THE PRAYERS

Let us pray that the radiance of Christ will illumine the church, the nations, and all who seek the light.

A BRIEF SILENCE.

For the church, that beholding the light revealed to the nations, we may glorify God and reflect that light to others. Lord, in your mercy,

hear our prayer.

For the natural resources of creation, the environment, and all living creatures, that all would be preserved from abuse and neglect. Lord, in your mercy,

hear our prayer.

For those who have no voice in our society, for immigrants and refugees, for those in exile or being held captive, and for all others who are stifled in speech and expression; Lord, in your mercy,

hear our prayer.

For those in this congregation who struggle in relationships, and for those whose spirits contend with forces that wish them harm; for those whose bodies are weak and in need of God's healing strength *(especially)*; Lord, in your mercy,

hear our prayer.

For the aged among us, that like Anna and Simeon their voices may be strong in witness to Christ, and that we may hear them. Lord, in your mercy,

hear our prayer.

HERE OTHER INTERCESSIONS MAY BE OFFERED.

Remembering those servants who have gone in peace, we pray that with them we may at length fully see your salvation in that place where sorrow or pain are no more. Lord, in your mercy,

hear our prayer.

Hear our spoken and silent prayers, O God of light, and

103

reveal yourself to us, through your Son, Jesus Christ our Lord.

Amen

IMAGES FOR PREACHING

They brought him up to Jerusalem to present him to the Lord.... Who would have thought on that day of destiny how this going up to Jerusalem and presentation would be fulfilled on the cross? Simeon speaks the words of falling and rising and Anna declares Jesus the one in whom we have our redemption. Mary and Joseph make their sacrifice of two birds. But what cost the ultimate redemption of humanity would take. The presentation of Jesus in Jerusalem becomes God's presentation for the life of the world. By law, Mary and Joseph offer their firstborn to the Lord; by amazing grace, God offers his firstborn so that we might all be the children of God.

We are reminded this day that it is God's presentation that accomplishes the world's redemption. We are imprisoned in a darkness that we cannot escape. God's presentation and sacrifice in Jerusalem for the love of the world embraces the very heart of human darkness and reveals the light for revelation and glory.

The readings for today keenly illuminate the spiritual gymnastics of the human heart. We can get terribly focused on *our* presentation, our offering, our sacrifice, and our purity. Our response is important and it does make a difference, but our response flows from that ultimate presentation of God at the cross. Hebrews 2:14-15 gets to the core: "Since, therefore, the children share flesh and blood, Jesus himself likewise shared the same things, so that through death he might destroy the one who has the power of death, that is, the devil, and free those who all their lives were held in slavery by the fear of death." We are free, and Simeon and Anna go in peace.

WORSHIP MATTERS

One significant contribution of Lutheran liturgy to the wider church is the use of the Song of Simeon (Nunc dimittis) as a post-communion canticle. Some of us may have sung this song for years following communion without considering why.

During the eucharist we are permitted to hold Christ in our hands just as Simeon and Anna did. So we are able to sing along with them. Our eyes have just seen the Lord's salvation too. The Song of Simeon is a bibli-

cal song of profound joy. It is worth holding onto this gem, especially in the weeks after Christmas and Epiphany. If you have not discovered a joyful setting of this canticle for your congregation, try singing "Now, Lord, you let your servant go in peace" (WOV 624), or a hymn that alludes to the Song of Simeon, "All earth is hopeful (WOV 629, TFF 47).

LET THE CHILDREN COME

Flickering candles are fascinating to young children. They are mesmerized by the flames—on a birthday cake or on the altar. Candlelight marks the passage of time in our secular lives. The light of the paschal candle marks the new lives we have in the resurrected Lord. Simeon and Anna's faces light up in the presence of the Christ child. Simeon praises God in a simple song, declaring that Jesus is "a light for revelation to the Gentiles and for glory to your people Israel" (Luke 2:32). While singing Simeon's song (LBW 339 or 349), have children distribute little unlit candles (birthday candles) to the congregation. Invite families to set aside a time at home to burn their candles and say a prayer, giving thanks for God's gift of Jesus.

HYMNS FOR WORSHIP
GATHERING

Of the Father's love begotten   LBW 42

Our Father, by whose name   LBW 357

HYMN OF THE DAY

In his temple now behold him   CS 42, LBW 184

ALTERNATE HYMN OF THE DAY

O Lord, now let your servant   LBW 339

I want to walk as a child of the light   WOV 649

COMMUNION

What child is this   LBW 40

SENDING

Lord, dismiss us with your blessing   LBW 259

Take the name of Jesus with you   TFF 159

ADDITIONAL HYMNS AND SONGS

In peace and joy I now depart   CS 43

Oh, love, how deep   LBW 88

MUSIC FOR THE DAY

PSALMODY

Haas, David. "How Lovely." PCY 9.

Joncas, Michael. "Psalm 84: How Lovely Is Your Dwelling Place." STP I.

Lift up your heads, O gates WOV 631

Pavlechko, Thomas. PW C.

Porter, Tom. "Happy Are They Who Dwell in Your House." Cong, choir, kybd, gtr, inst. GIA G-3026.

CHORAL

Bell, John L. "Nunc Dimittis." SATB, solo. GIA G-5161.

Brahms, Johannes. "How Lovely Is Thy Dwelling Place" in *Chantry Choirbook*. SATB. AFP 0800657772.

Courtney, Craig. "Sanctus." SSATBB. LOR 10/2499R.

Hopson, Hal. "Song of Simeon." SATB (div), opt acc. MSM 50-7032.

Vaughan Williams, Ralph. "O How Amiable." SATB. OXF 45.056.

CHILDREN'S CHOIRS

Bedford, Michael. "Light of the World" from *Singing the Seasons*. U, kybd, opt 2 oct hb. CG CGA854.

Kemp, Helen, arr. "Welcome, Dearest Jesus." U, sop/alto glock, alto metallophone/hb, fc, kybd. CG CGA531.

KEYBOARD/INSTRUMENTAL

Cherwien, David. "Kuortane" in *Organ Plus One*. Org, opt inst. AFP 0800656180.

Organ, Anne Krentz. "Houston" in *Woven Together*. Pno, inst. AFP 0800658167.

Wold, Wayne L. "Houston" in *Child of the Light*. Org. AFP 0800657993.

HANDBELL

Rogers, Sharon Elery. "I Love to Tell the Story." 3–5 oct. ALF 18559.

Smith, Douglas Floyd. "Thy Dwelling Place." 3–5 oct, opt hc, hp/kybd. AGEHR. AG35175.

Tucker, Sondra K. "I Want to Walk as a Child of the Light." 3–5 oct. AFP 0800658868.

PRAISE ENSEMBLE

McHugh, Phill/arr. Mauldin. "God and God Alone." SAB, orch. Benson Company OT-1084.

Ray, Mel. "Arise and Sing" in *Songs for Praise and Worship*. WRD.

105

February 2, 2003

Fourth Sunday after the Epiphany

INTRODUCTION

In the scriptures the word is announced through prophets who speak for God, and later through Jesus who teaches with authority. The church continues to proclaim the gospel of God's great love for humankind. We gather around Christ, the Word made flesh, to hear that God is gracious and full of compassion. It is the authority of the gospel that enables us to announce a prophetic word of judgment and mercy to the world in which we live.

PRAYER OF THE DAY

O God, you know that we cannot withstand the dangers that surround us. Strengthen us in body and spirit so that, with your help, we may be able to overcome the weakness that our sin has brought upon us; through Jesus Christ, your Son our Lord.

VERSE

Alleluia. The Spirit of the Lord is upon me, because he has anointed me to bring good news to the poor. Alleluia. (Luke 4:18)

READINGS

Deuteronomy 18:15-20

Today's reading, part of a longer discussion of prophecy in Deuteronomy 18, stands within a still broader context: an updating of the law for the Israelite community as the people wait to enter the promised land. Here Moses assures the people that God will continue to guide them through prophets who will proclaim the divine word.

Psalm 111

The fear of the Lord is the beginning of wisdom. (Ps. 111:10)

1 Corinthians 8:1-13

God's people are set free by Jesus' death and resurrection. Customary restrictions no longer apply. Notice, though, that those for whom Christ died find this freedom has limits. The gospel compels us to care about each other.

Mark 1:21-28

The story has barely begun, and already the battle is joined. Jesus sides with humanity against every force that would bring death and disease. These forces recognize Jesus and know what his power means for them. This battle, however, is only the first fight. The war will go on much longer.

COLOR Green

THE PRAYERS

Let us pray that the radiance of Christ will illumine the church, the nations, and all who seek the light.
A BRIEF SILENCE.

For the church of Christ, that God will raise up prophetic voices to proclaim God's living word without reserve. Lord, in your mercy,
hear our prayer.

For the natural resources of creation, the environment, and all living creatures, that all would be preserved from abuse and neglect. Lord, in your mercy,
hear our prayer.

For those who have no voice in our society, for immigrants and refugees, for those in exile or being held captive, and for all others who are stifled in speech and expression; Lord, in your mercy,
hear our prayer.

For those in this congregation who struggle in relationships, and for those whose spirits contend with forces that wish them harm; for those whose bodies are weak and in need of God's healing strength *(especially)*; Lord, in your mercy,
hear our prayer.
HERE OTHER INTERCESSIONS MAY BE OFFERED.

Remembering *(names, and)* those who have died, we pray that with them we may at length find rest in your gracious and eternal presence where sorrow or pain will be no more. Lord, in your mercy,
hear our prayer.

Hear our spoken and silent prayers, O God of light, and reveal yourself to us, through your Son, Jesus Christ our Lord.
Amen

IMAGES FOR PREACHING

"What is this?" the world began to ask. Who is this person of authority?

We join Simon and Andrew, James and John and follow Jesus this sabbath to the synagogue at Capernaum. There Jesus taught and there the people saw his authority. The master fisherman cast his net that day in the synagogue and caught, of all things, a possessed man. The unclean spirit who inhabited the man knew who Jesus was—the holy enemy—and gave witness to him. But mere knowledge is insufficient. We who follow Jesus need to be inhabited by Christ's Spirit in order to be children of God. Christ needs to have authority over us. And so Jesus silenced the unclean spirit and cast him out of the man. The world began to notice, and to wonder, because of events like the healing of the man with the unclean spirit. The Author of all that "was, is, and will be" was being made manifest.

True authority is hard to come by. Order can be coerced, orders can be enforced, but authority—the power that comes from within, by virtue of who the person is—seldom is encountered. It is much more common for us to be influenced by, even inhabited by, spirits whose power comes from our own sinful desires. We allow them to possess us, displacing the image of God with which we were created.

How blessed we are, then, when we come face to face with Christ's authority, when his love casts out our fear, our greed, our hatred. The words from Christmas still echo in our ears: "Cast out our sin, and enter in, be born in us today. . . . Oh, come to us, abide with us, our Lord Immanuel!" (LBW 41).

WORSHIP MATTERS

Do you expect to receive people into your worship services who do not have years of worshiping experience behind them? How we receive newcomers may communicate (or fail to communicate) much about our beliefs in God.

Rather than watering everything down, it is possible to make it easier for people to enter into the centuries-old traditions that Christians have established. Worship folders, carefully prepared for the first-time visitor, can be an aid to everyone. Do not assume that everyone knows what an *LBW* is (while most people will be able to understand the "green book"). Sermons can be founded

106

on good theological insights without trotting Greek words into the pulpit. If you need to, employ a genuine outsider to go through bulletins and other church publications to identify any coded terms or phrases. You might be surprised!

LET THE CHILDREN COME

Who is Jesus? In the Gospel of Mark we meet Jesus the teacher. In another "little epiphany" we see that Jesus not only teaches through words, but through actions. This Sunday consider a buddy system, pairing high school students with third and fourth graders. High school students sit with their buddies throughout the worship service, leading the younger ones through the order of worship. Meet with the high school students prior to the worship service to explain their teaching responsibilities.

HYMNS FOR WORSHIP

GATHERING

Let the whole creation cry   LBW 242
When in our music God is glorified   WOV 802, LBW 555

HYMN OF THE DAY

Rise, shine, you people!   LBW 393

ALTERNATE HYMN OF THE DAY

There is a balm in Gilead   TFF 185, WOV 737
Word of God, come down on earth   WOV 716

COMMUNION

Whatever God ordains is right   LBW 446
Healer of our every ill   WOV 738
Christ, have mercy on us all   DH 26
Here is bread   W&P 58

SENDING

Give to our God immortal praise!   LBW 520
My Lord of light   WOV 796

ADDITIONAL HYMNS AND SONGS

The right hand of God   GS2 22
God, you have given us power   H82 584
Satan, we're going to tear your kingdom down   TFF 207
I will sing of the mercies of the Lord   W&P 74

MUSIC FOR THE DAY

PSALMODY

Cherwien, David. "I Will Give Thanks to the Lord." U, desc.
    CPH 98-2930.
Hopson, Hal H. "Psalm 111" in *Psalm Refrains and Tones for the Common Lectionary.* U, cong, kybd.   HOP 425.
Hopson, Hal H.   PW B.
Marshall, Jane. "Psalm 111."   UMH.
Nelson, Ronald. "I Will Give Thanks." SATB, U.   AFP 0800647424.

CHORAL

Bach, J. S. "Bring Low Our Ancient Adam" in *Bach for All Seasons.* SATB, kybd.   AFP 080065854X. Inst pts.   AFP 0800659546.
Farlee, Robert Buckley. "Holy God." SATB, org, opt cong.
    AFP 0800675207.
Hobby, Robert. "O God of Light." SATB, brass qnt.   MSM 60-8002A.
Mendelssohn, Felix. "On God Alone My Hope I Build" in *Chantry Choirbook.* SATB.   AFP 0800657772.
Shephard, Richard. "The Secret of Christ." SATB.   GIA G-4186.
Wood, Dale. "Rise, Shine!" SATB, org.   AFP 0800655923.
    Also in *The Augsburg Choirbook.*   0800656784.
Young, Gordon. "O For a Thousand Tongues to Sing." SATB, kybd.
    FLA A-6382.

CHILDREN'S CHOIRS

Collins, Dori Erwin. "God Will Always Be with Me." U, kybd, opt fl.
    AFP 0800675193.
Kemp, Helen. "Look Around." U/2 pt, kybd.   CG CGA823.
Ziegenhals, Harriet. "Oh, Sing to the Lord" (Cantad al Señor).
    U/2 pt, kybd, opt maracas.   CG CGA640.

KEYBOARD/INSTRUMENTAL

Cherwien, David. "Toccata and Fugue on 'Rise, Shine, You People.'"
    Org.   AFP 080065403X.
Frahm, Frederick. "Liebster Jesu, wir sind hier" in *Augsburg Organ Library: Epiphany.* Org.   AFP 0800659341.
Nicholson, Paul. "There Is a Balm in Gilead." Org, 2 inst.
    AFP 0800656202.
Oliver, Curt. "Liebster Jesu, wir sind hier" in *Built on a Rock.* Pno.
    AFP 080065496X.

HANDBELL

Buckwalter, Karen. "Prayer for Healing." 3–5 oct.   AGEHR AG35174.
Cota, Sanders. "O For a Thousand Tongues to Sing." 3–5 oct.   AG 2114.
Linker, Janet. "Rise, Shine, You People!" 3–5 oct, org, opt tpt.
    AFP 0800655052.

107

Young, Philip. "There Is a Balm in Gilead." 3–4 oct.
AFP 0800653572.

PRAISE ENSEMBLE

Collins, Jamie Owens. "The Battle Belongs to the Lord" in *Songs for Praise and Worship.* WRD.

Davis, Greg and Greg Fisher/arr. John Innes. "Honor the Lord." SATB, kybd. HOP WT1522.

Haugen, Marty. "He Came Down." SATB, children, solo, gtr, pno, perc. GIA G-3808.

Hendricks, J. "The Mighty One of Israel" in *Come & Worship.* INT.

Pethel, Stan. "He Is Exalted" (with "O For a Thousand Tongues to Sing") in *The Sunday Celebration Choir Kit.* 2 pt mxd, kybd. WAR 08741317.

Sunday, February 2

THE PRESENTATION OF OUR LORD

See pages 103–105.

Monday, February 3

ANSGAR, ARCHBISHOP OF HAMBURG,
MISSIONARY TO DENMARK AND SWEDEN, 865

A traditional emphasis during the weeks of Epiphany has been the mission of the church. Ansgar is a monk who led a mission to Denmark and then later to Sweden where he built the first church. His work ran into difficulties with the rulers of the day and he was forced to withdraw into Germany where he served as a bishop in Hamburg. Despite his difficulties in Sweden, he persisted in his mission work and later helped consecrate Gothbert as the first bishop of Sweden. Ansgar also had a deep love for the poor. He would wash their feet and serve them food provided by the parish.

Ansgar is particularly honored by Scandinavian Lutherans. The Church of Sweden honors him as an apostle. His persistence in mission and his care for the poor invite congregations to reflect on their own ministry of bearing the light of Christ during the days of Epiphany.

Wednesday, February 5

THE MARTYRS OF JAPAN, 1597

In the sixteenth century, Jesuit missionaries, followed by Franciscans, introduced the Christian faith in Japan. But a promising beginning to those missions—perhaps as many as 300,000 Christians by the end of the sixteenth century—met complications from competition between the missionary groups, political difficulty between Spain and Portugal, and factions within the government of Japan. Christianity was suppressed. By 1630, Christianity was driven underground.

Today we commemorate the first martyrs of Japan, twenty-six missionaries and converts, who were killed by crucifixion. Two hundred and fifty years later when Christian missionaries returned to Japan, they found a community of Japanese Christians that had survived underground. The Martyrs of Japan are a somber reminder of the cost of Christianity and discipleship. Their witness invites us to pray for the church's own witness to the gospel and encourages us to trust that the church is sustained in times of persecution.

February 9, 2003

Fifth Sunday after the Epiphany

INTRODUCTION

In today's gospel Jesus cures the sick, proclaims the gospel, and casts out demons. His ministry reveals God's compassionate heart in which the lowly are lifted up and the brokenhearted are healed. As we gather around Christ present in word and meal, we are given strength to wait for the Lord in the midst of our suffering. Living as the body of Christ, our very lives are signs of God's gracious intent for humankind.

PRAYER OF THE DAY

Almighty God, you sent your only Son as the Word of life for our eyes to see and our ears to hear. Help us to believe with joy what the Scriptures proclaim, through Jesus Christ our Lord.

VERSE

Alleluia. Jesus said: I am the light of the world. Whoever follows me will never walk in darkness but will have the light of life. Alleluia. (John 8:12)

READINGS

Isaiah 40:21-31

The Judeans in exile have a reason to be hopeful: the One who will bring them to freedom is the God who created the world and gives strength to those who are weary.

Psalm 147:1-12, 21c (Psalm 147:1-11, 20c [NRSV])

The LORD heals the brokenhearted. (Ps. 147:3)

1 Corinthians 9:16-23

Paul continues his careful argument about the freedom of God's people. In Christ we are free, he says, not to injure one another, but to help. Using his own work as an example, Paul argues that we are not so much free from each other as free for each other.

Mark 1:29-39

Everywhere Jesus goes, many people expect him to set them free from oppression. Everywhere he goes, he heals them, and sets them free. Disease, devils, and death are running for their lives. The forces that diminish human life are rendered powerless by Jesus.

COLOR Green

THE PRAYERS

Let us pray that the radiance of Christ will illumine the church, the nations, and all who seek the light.

A BRIEF SILENCE.

O God of the weary and faint, grant strength to your people, that the church would radiate the healing wholeness that is the birthright of all creation. Lord, in your mercy,

hear our prayer.

O God of all, you bring rulers and those in authority to justice in your light. Show your wise and all-loving face to the leaders of the nations, that they may govern fairly and rule wisely. Lord, in your mercy,

hear our prayer.

O God of healing, guide medical researchers who search for cures to illnesses that are chronic or fatal. Comfort and cure those among us who are sick with various diseases *(especially)*. Lord, in your mercy,

hear our prayer.

O God of the weak and the strong, bless the ministries of all parish nurses, hospitals, and homes for the elderly with a spirit of compassion and mercy. Lord, in your mercy,

hear our prayer.

HERE OTHER INTERCESSIONS MAY BE OFFERED.

O God of life and death, knowing that the faithful departed *(including)* are in your hands, we commend ourselves to those same hands of steadfast faithfulness and love. Lord, in your mercy,

hear our prayer.

Hear our spoken and silent prayers, O God of light, and reveal yourself to us, through your Son, Jesus Christ our Lord.

Amen

IMAGES FOR PREACHING

Have you not known? Have you not heard? Have you not understood who it is that we worship? Have you not encountered the mighty deeds of God, whose hands

109

created and still preserve us and our world? Have you not shared in wonderment at the mysteries of life and death, healing and wholeness?

Have you not heard of the young married woman, mother of two children, who died of cancer? Have you not heard of how she, after her first round of chemotherapy, gave thanks to God for the blessing of cancer? Yes, she spoke of the people she had met and how she had been deepened in Jesus Christ and how she would not have traded the journey for anything. Have you not heard of how she knew the peace of God before she died? She saw visions of Jesus and she saw her family laughing again in the future. And she fervently wished that her extended family and friends could see, feel, and taste the peace of God. Outwardly, it looked like cancer had won. To the world, many prayers for healing look unanswered. But to all who knew her, prayers for healing were answered. The greatest healing was known; the peace of God that surpasses our understanding was given.

Have you not heard how Jesus came to Simon's mother-in-law who was in bed with fever? Have you not heard of how he took her by the hand and lifted her up? Jesus raised her up. She was restored and she began to serve.

The whole city gathered around the door. Many were drawn by the physical signs of healing. Many more have come to know the deepest healing, the peace of God poured out in Jesus Christ. This is the message Jesus came to proclaim.

WORSHIP MATTERS

Congregations offer various opportunities for a ministry of healing. Some provide monthly or weekly services of healing. Others provide prayer stations for healing during the distribution of communion. Although prayers with the laying on of hands for healing may be a relatively recent phenomenon within Lutheran and many other mainline denominations, it is an ancient biblical tradition.

Anecdotal reports from terminally ill people suggest that they receive less care and physical contact than do other people. Congregations can offer people with illness something that fills a genuine void—touch. Even if you are uncomfortable introducing the practice of laying on of hands, most people will appreciate the holding of a

hand during prayer. Such a simple gesture may be profoundly important in someone's life.

LET THE CHILDREN COME

Who is Jesus? Jesus is a healer. Today's text is one in a series of healing stories from the Gospel of Mark. Jesus healed out of compassion for the people. Today, we can bring our troubles to Jesus in prayer. At an appropriate time, have parents help children write down one thing that is troubling them. During the prayers, set aside one petition for parents to softly read their children's prayers in unison. After a few moments the pastor says something like, "Lord, in your mercy," and everyone responds: "hear our prayer."

HYMNS FOR WORSHIP
GATHERING

O Christ, the healer, we have come   LBW 360
Great God, your love has called us   WOV 666
I was glad   W&P 68

HYMN OF THE DAY

Hope of the world   LBW 493

ALTERNATE HYMN OF THE DAY

Your hand, O Lord, in days of old   LBW 431
You who dwell in the shelter of the Lord   WOV 779, W&P 110

COMMUNION

Here, O my Lord, I see thee   LBW 211
I am the Bread of life   WOV 702

SENDING

I love to tell the story   LBW 390, TFF 228
Praise to you, O God of mercy   WOV 790, W&P 119
May you run and not be weary   W&P 97

ADDITIONAL HYMNS AND SONGS

Can we by searching find out God   H82 476
Silence! Frenzied, unclean spirit   NCH 176
God has smiled on me   TFF 190
Beauty for brokenness   W&P 17

110

MUSIC FOR THE DAY

PSALMODY

Hopson, Hal H.   PW B.

Polyblank, Christopher. "Praise the Lord" in PS 3.

CHORAL

Goudimel, Claude. "As the Deer, for Water Yearning" in *Chantry Choirbook*. SATB.   AFP 0800657772.

Hopson, Hal. "We Are Singing for the Lord Is Our Light." U/SATB, pno, opt cong.   HOP C5060

Nelson, Eric. "How Can I Keep from Singing." SATB.   AFP 0800675177.

Tcimpidis, David. "Hail to the Lord's Anointed." SATB, org.   GIA G-3182.

Thompson, Randall. "Have Ye Not Known." SATB.   E C Schirmer 1035.

Zimmermann, Heinz Werner. "The Lord Is My Light." SATB.   CPH 98-2174.

CHILDREN'S CHOIRS

Handel, G. F./arr. Robert Powell. "Then Will I Jehovah's Praise." U, kybd.   CG CGA220.

Schoenfeld, William. "The Prayer of St. Patrick." U, kybd.   CG CGA462.

KEYBOARD/INSTRUMENTAL

Albrecht, Mark. "On Eagle's Wings" in *Timeless Tunes for Flute and Piano*. Pno, C/B-flat inst.   AFP 0800659074.

Diemer, Emma Lou. "Hankey" in *A New Liturgical Year*, ed. John Ferguson. Org.   AFP 0800656717.

Osterland, Karl. "Houston" in *Lift One Voice*. Org.   AFP 0800659007.

Peeters, Flor. "Scherzo" in *Suite Modale*, op. 43. Org.   LEM.

Wasson, Laura E. "Hankey" and "On Eagle's Wings" in *A Piano Tapestry, vol. 2*. Pno.   AFP 0800658183.

HANDBELL

Honoré, Jeffrey. "On Eagle's Wings." 3–5 oct.   CPH 97-6429.

McChesney, Kevin. "When We Are Living." 3–5 oct, opt hc.   AFP 0800655079.

Starks, Howard F. "Praise to the Lord, the Almighty." 3–6 oct.   JEF MRW8130.

PRAISE ENSEMBLE

Allen, Tricia and Martin J. Nystrom. "We Will Wait" in *Hosanna Music Songbook, vol. 7*.   INT. HMSB07.

Fragar, Russell. "All the Power You Need" in *Hosanna! Music Songbook 11*. INT.

Joncas, Michael/arr. Mark Hayes. "On Eagle's Wings." SATB. acc.   ALF 16104.

Manzo, Laura. "They Shall Soar Like Eagles." SATB, kybd, fl. Fred Bock Music Co. BG2109. Also available: 2 pt.   BG2078. SAB.   BG2023.

Pote, Allen. "A Song of Joy." SATB, pno.   HOP AP450.

Friday, February 14

CYRIL, MONK, 869; METHODIUS, BISHOP, 885; MISSIONARIES TO THE SLAVS

These two brothers from a noble family in Thessalonika in northeastern Greece were priests and missionaries. After some early initial missionary work by Cyril among the Arabs, the brothers retired to a monastery. They were later sent to work among the Slavs, the missionary work for which they are most known. Since Slavonic had no written form at the time, the brothers established a written language with the Greek alphabet as its basis. They translated the scriptures and the liturgy using this Cyrillic alphabet. The Czechs, Serbs, Croats, Slovaks, and Bulgars regard the brothers as the founders of Slavic literature. The brothers' work in preaching and worshiping in the language of the people are honored by Christians in both East and West.

February 16, 2003

Sixth Sunday after the Epiphany
Proper 1

INTRODUCTION

Today's readings include two stories of lepers cleansed of their disease. Naaman washes in the Jordan River, and Jesus stretches out his hand and touches a leper. In the waters of baptism we are cleansed of our sin, and throughout our lives we continue to be nourished by the healing power of the eucharistic meal. With our words and deeds we touch others with God's compassion and love.

PRAYER OF THE DAY

Lord God, mercifully receive the prayers of your people. Help us to see and understand the things we ought to do, and give us grace and power to do them; through your Son, Jesus Christ our Lord.

VERSE

Alleluia. Lord, to whom shall we go? You have the words of eternal life. Alleluia. (John 6:68)

READINGS

2 Kings 5:1-14

Elisha tells Naaman, a Syrian general, to immerse himself in the Jordan River where he is cleansed of his leprosy, revealing not the magic of certain water but the power of Israel's God.

Psalm 30

My God, I cried out to you, and you restored me to health. (Ps. 30:2)

1 Corinthians 9:24-27

Paul uses two athletic images—the runner and the boxer—to call us to a life of discipline in which self-control is for the sake of a higher good, in this case the good of all God's people.

Mark 1:40-45

Jesus cures a leper and asks him to tell no one but a priest, in accordance with Levitical law. Though Jesus performs miracles, his identity as Messiah will not be understood until the cross.

COLOR Green

THE PRAYERS

Let us pray that the radiance of Christ will illumine the church, the nations, and all who seek the light.

A BRIEF SILENCE.

That the preaching and teaching of the church would be done so freely that many will be awakened to faith and become fervent proclaimers of your word of unfailing love. Lord, in your mercy,

hear our prayer.

That the work of health organizations would extend to all areas of the world where your children struggle with disease and disability. Lord, in your mercy,

hear our prayer.

That those who are living with terminal illness and other diseases (*especially*) will find compassionate care from loving people whom you call to vocations of healing service. Lord, in your mercy,

hear our prayer.

That those who are candidates for baptism might be nurtured by faithful mentors and supportive faith communities. Lord, in your mercy,

hear our prayer.

HERE OTHER INTERCESSIONS MAY BE OFFERED.

That those who have died (*especially*) will surround us in the great cloud of witnesses as we continue on our earthly pilgrimage. Lord, in your mercy,

hear our prayer.

Hear our spoken and silent prayers, O God of light, and reveal yourself to us, through your Son, Jesus Christ our Lord.

Amen

IMAGES FOR PREACHING

Jesus did not hesitate to cross the religious boundaries of his day. Unclean, excommunicated, a person with leprosy came to Jesus. He knew who Jesus was: "If you choose, you can make me clean" (Mark 1:40). The departing of the leprosy was the unveiling of yet a greater act of restoration for the man and all of humanity. Jesus revels in getting his hands dirty. His insistence would lead him to the cross; God's choice would bring healing and wholeness to a broken world.

Great Naaman, mighty general and favored one of the king of Aram, suffered from leprosy. He heard of Israel's prophet and he went, "taking with him ten talents of silver, six thousand shekels of gold, and ten sets of garments. He brought the letter to the king of Israel, which read, 'When this letter reaches you, know that I have sent to you my servant Naaman, that you may cure him of his leprosy'" (2 Kings 5:5b-6). What a different position Naaman was in than the poor beggar of Mark's gospel. Naaman had heard of a good opportunity and he brought all of his resources to bear; Naaman came to buy the goods. He anticipated an audience with Israel's holy man and a show of spiritual intervention. He received neither. He received, rather, a messenger and a simple message: *Go and wash in the river.*

We too have been washed in the river of life, the river of God's forgiveness, the river of restoration. In unexpected ways, Jesus comes to those who are "clean" or unclean, the mighty and the low, the favored and the unfavored, and offers a simple word: "I do choose. Be made clean!" (Mark 1:41). "Glory to God in the highest heaven, and on earth peace among those whom he favors" (Luke 2:14). The star shines brightly.

WORSHIP MATTERS

"If the prophet had commanded you to do something difficult, would you not have done it?" (2 Kings 5:13).

How many times do we refrain from doing something in worship with our congregations simply because it may be difficult for them? If liturgy is indeed the people's work, then we ought not feel bad about making people work when they come to worship. Forgiveness is hard work. Being transformed to the will of God is hard work. The scriptures were not written by us at all—that's why listening to them is frequently hard work.

Encouraging our assemblies to learn a new tune or to experience a different form of worship is not impossible given an appropriate amount of preparation and careful introduction. If we anticipate what the challenges might be, and not present too many at once, most congregations will be glad for the opportunity to stretch a bit.

LET THE CHILDREN COME

The leper in the text from Mark could not contain his surprise and joy when Jesus healed him. The leper "went out and began to proclaim it freely and to spread the word..." (Mark 1:45). In this season of light and revela-

tion, give the children an incentive for spreading the word. Include in the worship bulletin a large star outline. Children may color it in or fill it with names of people with whom they can share the story of Jesus. Cut out the star and use it as a pattern for making star cookies at home. Share the cookies and the story.

HYMNS FOR WORSHIP
GATHERING
Evening and morning   LBW 465
O God beyond all praising   WOV 797
Lord, I lift your name on high   W&P 90

HYMN OF THE DAY
O Christ the healer, we have come   LBW 360

ALTERNATE HYMN OF THE DAY
O God, whose will is life and good   LBW 435
Healer of our every ill   WOV 738

COMMUNION
Lord Jesus, think on me   LBW 309
Thy holy wings   WOV 741

SENDING
Oh, that the Lord would guide my ways   LBW 480
Hallelujah! We sing your praises   WOV 722, TFF 158
Go ye therefore   W&P 49

ADDITIONAL HYMNS AND SONGS
Come, let us join our friends above   UMH 709
From God Christ's deity came forth   H82 443
I've just come from the fountain   TFF 111, WOV 696
Create in me a clean heart   W&P 35

MUSIC FOR THE DAY
PSALMODY
Hopson, Hal H.   PW B.
Inwood, Paul. "I Will Praise You, Lord" in *RitualSong*. GIA.
Smith, Alan. "I Will Praise You" in PS 2.

CHORAL
Bach, J. S. "Jesu, Joy—My Joy Forever" in *Bach for All Seasons*. SATB, kybd.   AFP 080065854X. Inst pts.   AFP 0800659546.
Bisbee, B. Wayne. "God of Peace." 2 pt mxd/equal vcs, kybd.   AFP 0800675126.

113

Cherwien, David. "I've Just Come from the Fountain." 2 pt, pno.
AMSI 832.

Mendelssohn, Felix. "For the Lord Will Lead" in *To God Will I Sing*.
MH voice. AFP 0800674332. ML voice. AFP 0800674340.

Sheppard, Mark. "Balm in Gilead." SATB, kybd. AFP 0800657918.

Wood, Dale. "Arise, My Soul, Arise!" SATB. SMP S-181.

Zimmermann, H. W. "Praise the Lord." SATB. CPH 98-2176.

CHILDREN'S CHOIRS

Page, Sue Ellen. "Jesus' Hands Were Kind Hands." U, fl, kybd.
CG CGA485.

Wetzler, Robert. "Jesus." U/2 pt, kybd. Carl Fischer CM7825.

KEYBOARD/INSTRUMENTAL

Albrecht, Mark. "Thaxted" in *Timeless Tunes for Flute and Piano*. Pno,
C/B-flat inst. AFP 0800659074.

Bisbee, B. Wayne. "Salzburg" in *From the Serene to the Whimsical*. Org.
AFP 0800654412.

Farlee, Robert Buckley. "Thaxted" in *Gaudeamus!* Org.
AFP 0800655389.

Honoré, Jeffrey. "Healer of Our Every Ill" in *Contemporary Hymn Settings for Organ*. Org. AFP 0800674782.

Wood, Dale. "Distress" in *Preludes and Postludes, vol. 3*. Org.
AFP 0800648560.

HANDBELL

Afdahl, Lee J. "Thaxted." 3–5 oct, opt brass, timp.
AFP 0800658140.

Ingram, Barbara. "There Is a Balm in Gilead." 3–5 oct, opt fl.
JEF RO 3014.

Thompson, Martha Lynn. "Thy Holy Wings." 3–5 oct, opt hc, windchimes, narr. ALF 19005.

PRAISE ENSEMBLE

Elliott, John G. "Mourning into Dancing" in *I Call You to Praise*.
SATB, orch. Elliott SB-004/1762-79434-7.

Espinosa, Eddie. "Change My Heart, O God." *The Celebration Hymnal*.
MAR.

Founds, Rick. "I Will Not Be Shaken" in *Praise Hymns & Choruses*,
4th ed. MAR.

Pethel, Stan. "He Is Exalted" (with "O For a Thousand Tongues to
Sing") in *The Sunday Celebration Choir Kit*. 2 pt mxd, acc.
WAR 08741317.

Tuesday, February 18
MARTIN LUTHER, RENEWER OF THE CHURCH, 1546

For those in the habit of remembering the work of Martin Luther on Reformation Day, this commemoration may seem out of place. But it is a custom to remember saints on the day of their death, their "heavenly birthday." On this day Luther died at the age of 62. For a time, he was an Augustinian monk, but it is his work as a biblical scholar, translator of the Bible, reformer of the liturgy, theologian, educator, and father of German vernacular literature, that holds him in our remembrance. In Luther's own judgment, the greatest of all of his works was his catechism written to instruct people in the basics of faith. And it was his baptism that sustained him in his trials as a reformer.

If a congregation has catechumens who will be baptized at the Easter Vigil, they might receive the catechism during the Enrollment of Candidates on the first Sunday in Lent (March 9). If there are no catechumens, a congregation might study the catechism during Lent to renew its own baptismal faith.

Thursday, February 20
RASMUS JENSEN, THE FIRST LUTHERAN PASTOR IN NORTH AMERICA, 1620

Jensen came to North America in 1619 with an expedition sent by King Christian IV of Denmark and Norway. The expedition took possession of the Hudson Bay area, naming it Nova Dania. Within months of their arrival, most of the members of the expedition died, including Jensen. After this expedition, much Danish missionary activity was concentrated in India and the Virgin Islands.

Today would be an appropriate time to give thanks for the church in Canada, which flourished even after its early struggles. It would also be an opportunity to pray for missionaries who face difficulty in their tasks.

February 23, 2003

Seventh Sunday after the Epiphany
Proper 2

INTRODUCTION

Though we often proclaim God's faithfulness in ages past, God continues to do new things in our midst. In baptism God provides water in the wilderness, and in the Lord's supper God gives us food and drink for sustenance. The crosses placed on our brows in baptism are the seal of the Spirit's presence in our lives, and by the authority of Christ each pastor proclaims that we are forgiven. Healed and restored, we pray that God's healing and forgiveness would be made known in our daily lives.

Today is the commemoration of Polycarp, an influential early Christian bishop who was martyred in A.D. 156, as well as of Bartholomaeus Ziegenbalg, an eighteenth-century missionary who helped bring Christianity to the Tamil people on the southeast coast of India.

PRAYER OF THE DAY

Lord God, we ask you to keep your family, the Church, always faithful to you, that all who lean on the hope of your promises may gain strength from the power of your love; through your Son, Jesus Christ our Lord.
or
God of compassion, keep before us the love you have revealed in your Son, who prayed even for his enemies; in our words and deeds help us to be like him through whom we pray, Jesus Christ our Lord.

VERSE

Alleluia. Sanctify us in the truth; your word is truth. Alleluia. (John 17:17)

READINGS

Isaiah 43:18-25

Addressing the Jewish exiles in Babylon, the prophet announces that God is sending refreshing water. God will remove their transgressions and forget their sins.

Psalm 41

Heal me, for I have sinned against you. (Ps. 41:4)

2 Corinthians 1:18-22

When some in the Corinthian community perceive Paul as someone who is unreliable, he defends himself by af-

firming the "yes" of God's promises and the Spirit as the seal of that pledge.

Mark 2:1-12

Jesus' power over sin and disease is revealed in his healing of a paralytic. Behind the story is a controversy over whether the Messiah has the authority to forgive sin.

COLOR Green

THE PRAYERS

Let us pray that the radiance of Christ will illumine the church, the nations, and all who seek the light.
A BRIEF SILENCE.

God of guidance, give us the faith to trust your promises given in Christ, and the courage to act on that faith, on behalf of others as well as ourselves. Lord, in your mercy,
hear our prayer.

God of creation, give faith in your continual work to your whole church, that we might trust you for the new things you long to give us. Lord, in your mercy,
hear our prayer.

God of forgiveness, give to the leaders of the nations a strong sense of your merciful justice, that they may govern your people wisely. Lord, in your mercy,
hear our prayer.

God of healing, show yourself to those who are suffering, grant comfort to those who are sick *(especially)*, and may all find hope in your never-failing promises. Lord, in your mercy,
hear our prayer.

God of love, bless those who contemplate life-long commitments of friendship, marriage, and parenthood. May they learn ways of trust and forgiveness as they look to you. Lord, in your mercy,
hear our prayer.

HERE OTHER INTERCESSIONS MAY BE OFFERED.

O God, you lead all saints to their home in your eternal light. Reunite us with Polycarp, Bartholomaeus Ziegenbalg, *(other names)* and all who have served you, when you shall finally call us all to be in your presence. Lord, in your mercy,
hear our prayer.

115

Hear our spoken and silent prayers, O God of light, and reveal yourself to us, through your Son, Jesus Christ our Lord.
Amen

IMAGES FOR PREACHING

We have never seen anything like it! We are almost to the top of the mount of transfiguration. Our climb brings vision and it is God's vision of us: *Your sins are forgiven.* With the Spirit's help, the vision takes on the quality of faith: *we believe it.* From that point, it moves out into mission: we desire to free others with this word from God's heart. The incarnation of God becomes our new life.

Jesus bids us to follow him and fish for people. In this movement toward each other and toward God, we experience the casting of God and the gathering net of new life. How moved Jesus must have been by the four friends who lowered the paralyzed man to him. *They believed.* They had been caught in the net of God's love. They knew how God had moved toward them.

God is doing a new thing in Jesus. It is the new covenant. It is our "way in the wilderness and rivers in the desert" (Isa. 43:19b). In Jesus, "every one of God's promises is a 'Yes'" (2 Cor. 1:20). Yes, yes, yes! The cry of love and life resounds in heaven and on earth. God dug through our tiered cosmology of self-righteousness and fear to bring humility, confidence, and joy. The incarnation is God's great affirmation of life. Our journey with Immanuel is God's faith, hope, and love taking root in our lives.

They believed. Yes! They believed.

WORSHIP MATTERS

What wonderful words are presented in today's first reading from Isaiah 43: "I will not remember your sins." This message is the joy that all Christians are allowed to announce, particularly those ordained to word and sacrament ministry.

Prayers of confession may be included within the congregation's prayers at any time, particularly as they may relate to the readings and preaching on a given day. Orders for confession and forgiveness may be used prior to the service, or following the prayers and prior to the sharing of peace in the communion liturgy. Then the gift of peace may be understood as an aspect of forgiveness and reconciliation with one another.

Seasonal forms for confession and forgiveness in this volume may encourage congregations to explore the use of this worship element in a variety of ways throughout the year.

LET THE CHILDREN COME

One theme in the text from Mark is the strong friendship of five friends and their deep faith in Jesus. This Sunday, encourage the children to bring a friend to worship. Next Sunday the "alleluias" will be put away until Easter. Have the children make a white and gold "Alleluia" banner. Instead of burying the banner, prepare a purple storage box. Decorate with Lenten symbols such as crosses and crowns of thorns. Teach a closing hymn with alleluias that the children may sing while they process with the banner. These preparations may be done today in Sunday school (with their friends) or as a family activity after worship.

HYMNS FOR WORSHIP
GATHERING

Praise the Lord, O heavens   LBW 540
O God beyond all praising   WOV 797
Jesus, we want to meet   TFF 145

HYMN OF THE DAY

My soul, now praise your maker!   LBW 519

ALTERNATE HYMN OF THE DAY

Praise, my soul, the King of heaven   LBW 549, CS 59
There's a wideness in God's mercy   LBW 290, CS 76, 77

COMMUNION

I lay my sins on Jesus   LBW 305
Taste and see   TFF 126

SENDING

Lord, take my hand and lead me   LBW 333
My life flows on in endless song   WOV 781

ADDITIONAL HYMNS AND SONGS

Depth of mercy   UMH 355
I call on thee, Lord Jesus Christ   H82 634
Lead me, guide me   TFF 70, W&P 84
Rejoice in the mission   W&P 120

116

MUSIC FOR THE DAY

PSALMODY

Carroll, J. Robert. "Lord, Heal My Soul" in *RitualSong*.   GIA.

Hopson, Hal H.   PW B.

CHORAL

Britten, Benjamin. "Jubilate Deo." SATB.   Oxford S551.

Fleming, Larry. "Humble Service." SATB.   AFP 0800646223.

Hampton, Keith. "He's Got the Whole World." SATB.
AFP 0800659600.

Hopp, Roy. "God of Grace and God of Laughter." SATB, pno/hrp,
ob/C inst.   AFP 0800659570.

Mathis, William and Donald D. Livingston. "Come Down, O Love
Divine." SATB, org.   AFP 0800675355.

Powell, Robert J. "The Great Creator of the Worlds." SATB, org.
AFP 0800657470.

White, David Ashley. "There's a Wideness in God's Mercy." SATB,
org.   SEL 420-243.

CHILDREN'S CHOIRS

Davis, Katherine. "Who Was the Man?" U, kybd.   CG CGA110.

Shepherd, John. "A Living Faith." U/2 pt, kybd.   CG CGA580.

KEYBOARD/INSTRUMENTAL

Albrecht, Mark. "Here I Am, Lord" in *Timeless Tunes for Piano and Solo
Instrument, vol. 3*. Kybd, C/B-flat inst.   AFP 0800675037.

Bach, J.S. "In dir ist Freude" in *Orgelbüchlein*. Org.   CPH 97-5774.

Farlee, Robert Buckley. "Praise, My Soul" in *Augsburg Organ Library:
Epiphany*. Org.   AFP 0800659341.

Rendler, Elaine. "Spiritual Offerings" in *Keyboard Praise, vol. 2*. Kybd.
OCP 9081GC.

HANDBELL

Buckwalter, Karen. "Prayer for Healing." 3–5 oct.   AGEHR AG35174.

Kastner, Michael. "Balm in Gilead." 3–5 oct, opt hc.   JEF FBBG0957.

Morris, Hart. "I Must Tell Jesus." 3–5 oct, L4.
AGEHR 5957816-725.

Tucker, Sondra K. "There's a Wideness in God's Mercy." 3–5 oct.
AFP 0800674901.

PRAISE ENSEMBLE

Bullock, Geoff. "Jesus, Jesus" in *Hosanna! Music Songbook 11*.   INT.

Burkhardt, Michael. "Go, My Children, with My Blessing." U, 2–3 pt,
pno.   MSM 50-9416.

Honoré, Jeffrey. "How Can I Keep from Singing." SATB, pno.
CG CGA-567.

Sutton "Your Mercy Flows" in *Songs for Praise and Worship*.   WRD.

Ylvisaker, John. "Blest in the Land" in *Borning Cry*.   NGP.

Sunday, February 23

POLYCARP, BISHOP OF SMYRNA, MARTYR, 156

Polycarp was bishop of Smyrna and a link between the apostolic age and the church at the end of the second century. He is said to have been known by John, the author of Revelation. In turn he was known by Iranaeus, bishop of Lyon in France, and Ignatius of Antioch. At the age of eighty-six he was martyred for his faith. When urged to save his life and renounce his faith, Polycarp replied, "Eighty-six years I have served him, and he never did me any wrong. How can I blaspheme my king who saved me?" The magistrate who made the offer was reluctant to kill a gentle old man, but he had no choice. Polycarp was burned at the stake.

In preaching on the upcoming Transfiguration Sunday, one might use the example of Polycarp to underscore what Paul is saying in 2 Corinthians: "Therefore, since it is by God's mercy that we are engaged in this ministry, we do not lose heart."

BARTHOLOMAEUS ZIEGENBALG, MISSIONARY TO INDIA, 1719

Bartholomaeus Ziegenbalg was a missionary to the Tamils of Tranquebar on the southeast coast of India. The first convert to Christianity was baptized about ten months after Ziegenbalg began preaching. His missionary work was opposed both by the local Hindus and also by Danish authorities in that same area. Ziegenbalg was imprisoned for his work on a charge of converting the natives. The Copenhagen Mission Society that opposed him wanted an indigenous church that did not reflect European patterns or show concern for matters other than the gospel. Ziegenbalg, in contrast, argued that concern for the welfare of others is a matter of the gospel. Today, the Tamil Evangelical Lutheran Church carries on his work.

With Ash Wednesday a week away, consider Isaiah 58:1-12 for the first reading, "Is not this the fast that I choose . . . to share your bread with the hungry." Ziegenbalg's missionary work can lead us into Lent with the reminder that we are called to live in service to others.

117

Monday, February 24

ST. MATTHIAS, APOSTLE

After Christ's ascension, the apostles met in Jerusalem to choose a replacement for Judas. Matthias was chosen over Joseph Justus by the casting of lots. Little is known about Matthias and little is reported about him in the account of his election in Acts 1:15-26. Matthias traveled among the disciples from the time of Jesus' baptism until his ascension. His task, after he was enrolled among the eleven remaining disciples, was to bear witness to the resurrection.

Tuesday, February 25

ELIZABETH FEDDE, DEACONESS, 1921

Fedde was born in Norway and trained as a deaconess. In 1882, at the age of 32, she was asked to come to New York to minister to the poor and to Norwegian seamen. Her influence was wide ranging, and she established the Deaconess House in Brooklyn and the Deaconess House and Hospital of the Lutheran Free Church in Minneapolis. She returned home to Norway in 1895 and died there.

Fedde was an example of selfless service to those in need. How does your congregation reach out to those who are sick, in need, or forgotten? Perhaps ways to reach out that have been overlooked can easily be incorporated in your congregation's ministry.

Saturday, March 1

GEORGE HERBERT, PRIEST, 1633

As a student at Trinity College, Cambridge, George Herbert excelled in languages and music. He went to college with the intention of becoming a priest, but his scholarship attracted the attention of King James I. Herbert served in parliament for two years. After the death of King James and at the urging of a friend, Herbert's interest in ordained ministry was renewed. He was ordained a priest in 1630 and served the little parish of St. Andrew Bremerton until his death. He was noted for unfailing care for his parishioners, bringing the sacraments to them when they were ill, and providing food and clothing for those in need.

Herbert was also a poet and hymnwriter. One of his hymns, "Come, my way, my truth, my life" (LBW 513) invites an intimate encounter with Christ through a feast that "mends in length" and could be included as a communion hymn on Transfiguration Sunday.

March 2, 2003

The Transfiguration of Our Lord
Last Sunday after the Epiphany

INTRODUCTION

This Epiphany festival concludes the season suffused with the image of light. In Advent the church prays for the light of God's justice in the world. At Christmas we celebrate this light in Christ, and throughout the weeks of Epiphany we welcome this gracious light in the diverse cultures of the world. From the mountain of transfiguring light, Christ goes forth to Jerusalem and leads us to the passover from death to life. Here we find the meaning of his birth and baptism: he was born to die, so that in our death, we might be born to eternal life.

Today the church calls to mind the ministry of John and Charles Wesley, renewers of the church. They wished to lead a revival of the Church of England in the eighteenth century, but their work resulted, after their deaths, in the founding of the Methodist denomination. Charles is also known for the many fine hymns he wrote.

PRAYER OF THE DAY

Almighty God, on the mountain you showed your glory in the transfiguration of your Son. Give us the vision to see beyond the turmoil of our world and to behold the king in all his glory; through your Son, Jesus Christ our Lord, who lives and reigns with you and the Holy Spirit, one God, now and forever.

or

O God, in the transfiguration of your Son you confirmed the mysteries of the faith by the witness of Moses and Elijah, and in the voice from the bright cloud you foreshadowed our adoption as your children. Make us with the king heirs of your glory, and bring us to enjoy its fullness, through Jesus Christ our Lord, who lives and reigns with you and the Holy Spirit, one God, now and forever.

VERSE

Alleluia. You are the fairest of men; grace flows from your lips. Alleluia. (Ps. 45:2)

READINGS

2 Kings 2:1-12

Today's reading centers on the transfer of power and authority from the prophet Elijah to Elisha. Their travels, which retrace the path of Joshua back to Moab (the place where Moses died), and the parting of the waters demonstrate that Elisha and Elijah are legitimate successors of the great lawgiver Moses.

Psalm 50:1-6

Out of Zion, perfect in beauty, God shines forth in glory. (Ps. 50:2)

2 Corinthians 4:3-6

The epiphany, or revelation of God, at Jesus' transfiguration is renewed in every believer's life when the light of Christ shines in the heart to reveal God's glory.

Mark 9:2-9

Mark's gospel presents the transfiguration as a preview of what would become apparent to Jesus' followers after he rose from the dead. Confused disciples are given a vision of God's glory manifest in the beloved Son.

COLOR White

THE PRAYERS

Let us pray that the radiance of Christ will illumine the church, the nations, and all who seek the light.

A BRIEF SILENCE.

God of grace, your people long to see a glimpse of your face and to hear your voice speak plainly. Bless your church with faithful bishops, pastors, and other leaders who will direct people to your saving glory. Lord, in your mercy,
hear our prayer.

God of awe and mystery, show yourself plainly to all who seek spiritual direction, that their search would be complete as they behold the wonders of your love. Lord, in your mercy,
hear our prayer.

God of all nations, manifest your glory in providing relief and assistance to people suffering from natural disasters and major crises. Lord, in your mercy,
hear our prayer.

God of wellness and health, look in mercy upon those who suffer from illness and infirmity, from depression and grief *(especially)*. Show them the light of your face. Lord, in your mercy,
hear our prayer.

119

HERE OTHER INTERCESSIONS MAY BE OFFERED.

God of continuity, teach us to value our days, and keep us in communion with John Wesley, Charles Wesley *(other names),* and all those we love whose earthly lives have come to an end. Lord, in your mercy,

hear our prayer.

Hear our spoken and silent prayers, O God of light, and reveal yourself to us, through your Son, Jesus Christ our Lord.

Amen

IMAGES FOR PREACHING

At the transfiguration of Jesus we remember a blazing chariot, a burning bush, and the glory of God on Mt. Sinai. Jesus is the center, but Elijah and Moses are present along with Peter, James, and John. Jesus was unveiled to them and to us. Divine fire coursed through him, causing his clothes to become dazzling white. The very glory of God lit up the day.

We also recognize, on that high mountain, our inordinate desire to put God in "God's place." It's much safer to have a God light years away or enclosed in the tabernacle. The disciples were terrified, and building a shelter, a place, was the one thing that occurred to Peter. Like David wanting to build a house for God, the disciples weren't sure they could stand to know God that intimately. It would be safer to work through religious institutions, or even better, once again to relate to Jesus as teacher and friend.

We also know, when we leave the mount of transfiguration, how quickly the doubt again rushes in. *Was God really that present? That close? How could it be?* They walked down that Epiphany peak to James and John's vying for power, Peter's denial, and our cries of "crucify him, crucify him." Doubt and opposition are woven into this journey of faith and hope. Yet God gives us the light to shine out of our darkness.

An African legend is told of a man who despairs of the suffering of humanity, wonders where God is, and goes on a journey. He climbs the mountain of "God is in his place." He meets someone coming down and they have a conversation about his journey. Questions are asked but the man's mind is not changed. He reaches the top of the mountain and asks where God is. He is told that God has gone down into the valley to be with the people. He had met God on the way up. We have met God on the mountain, and in Jesus God now accompanies us to the valley.

WORSHIP MATTERS

"For we do not proclaim ourselves; we proclaim Jesus Christ as Lord and ourselves as your slaves for Jesus' sake" (2 Cor. 4:5). Today's second reading reminds us that the center of our worship, and indeed of our whole life of faith, is none other than Christ himself. Even though we do well to prepare as best as we are humanly able in order to lead our congregations, the center of worship is not on our own abilities or excellence (or any lack thereof).

It is a simple and perhaps often mentioned truth, yet in many ways we may be in danger of forgetting the statement's implications. It is common for many worshiping assemblies to applaud a choir anthem or other musical offering. Is it God who is being applauded or are we moving the focus from God to those who seek to serve God? How can we encourage our worshipers to understand the entire liturgy as an act glorifying God?

LET THE CHILDREN COME

The transfiguration is the final burst of light before the darkness of Lent descends. Sing joyous hymns filled with light, such as "Shine, Jesus, shine" (WOV 651). Prominently display the Alleluia banner the children made last Sunday. During the announcements teach the congregation the meaning of the burying of the alleluias during Lent. Have children sing the hymn they learned last Sunday as they recess with the Alleluia banner. Place it in the purple storage box in the narthex.

HYMNS FOR WORSHIP

GATHERING

Holy majesty, before you   LBW 247

Alleluia, song of gladness   WOV 654

HYMN OF THE DAY

Oh, wondrous type! Oh, vision fair   LBW 80

ALTERNATE HYMN OF THE DAY

How good, Lord, to be here   LBW 89

Come to the mountain   W&P 32

COMMUNION

Beautiful Savior   LBW 518

Thine the amen, thine the praise   WOV 801

120

SENDING

In thee is gladness   LBW 552
Shine, Jesus, shine   WOV 651

ADDITIONAL HYMNS AND SONGS

Eternal light shine in my heart   H82 465/6
Swiftly pass the clouds of glory   PH 73
The Lord is my light   TFF 61
We see the Lord   W&P 153

MUSIC FOR THE DAY

PSALMODY

Bell, John L. "Let the Giving of Thanks" in *Psalms of Patience, Protest and Praise.* Iona/GIA G-4047.

Dean, Stephen. "I Will Show God's Salvation."   PS 3.

Folkening, John. "Six Psalm Settings with Antiphons." SATB, cong, opt kybd.   MSM 80-700.

Hobby, Robert.   PW B.

Hopson, Hal H. "Psalm 50."   TP.

CHORAL

Bouman, Paul. "Christ upon the Mountain Peak." SATB. CPH 98-2856.

Cherwien, David. "Beautiful Savior." SATB, org, cong, opt fl. AFP 0800675088.

Hampton, Keith. "My God Is an Awesome God." SATB, pno. AFP 0800659171.

Helman, Michael. "Go Up to the Mountain of God." SATB, pno, opt fl.   AFP 0800658353.

Martinson, Joel. "Transfiguration." U, desc, opt cong, org. PAR PPM09511.

Schalk, Carl. "Jesus, Take Us to the Mountain." SATB.   MSM 50-2601.

Wolff, Drummond. "Oh, Wondrous Type! Oh, Vision Fair." SATB, tpt, org, opt cong.   CPH 98-2690.

CHILDREN'S CHOIRS

Bridges, David. "O Splendor of God's Glory Bright." U, 2 oct hb, kybd.   CPH 98-2956.

DeVinney, Richard. "We Come to Praise Him" in *We Come to Praise Him.* U, kybd.   CG CGA5.

KEYBOARD/INSTRUMENTAL

Hamilton, Gregory. "Schönster Herr Jesu" in *Augsburg Organ Library: Epiphany.* Org.   AFP 0800659341.

Miller, Aaron David. "Deo gracias" in *Augsburg Organ Library: Epiphany.* Org.   AFP 0800659341.

Mulet, Henri. "Carillon-Sortie."   BEL MS 474. Also in *French Masterworks for Organ.*   WAR FE 09431.

Sedio, Mark. "Toccata on 'Christ, Whose Glory Fills the Skies' " in *Organ Tapestries, vol. 1.* Org.   CPH 97-6812.

HANDBELL

Behnke, John. "When Morning Gilds the Skies." 3–6 oct. AFP 0800674863.

Keller, Michael R. "Transfiguration." 5–7 oct.   AGEHR AG57002.

Page, Anna Laura. "Fairest Lord Jesus." 2–3 oct, L1. AGEHR 1905751-725.

Thompson, Martha Lynn. "Climbin' Up the Mountain." 3–5 oct, L2. AGEHR 5957691-725.

PRAISE ENSEMBLE

Baloche, Paul. "Guiding Light" in *Hosanna! Music Songbook 7.*   INT.

Fettke, Tom. "Beautiful Savior." SATB, pno.   WRD 3010638167.

Smith, Michael W. and Debbie Smith. "Shine on Us" in *My Utmost for His Highest.*   WRD.

Starke, Stephen P. "Greet the Rising Sun" in *Hymnal Supplement 98.* CPH.

Sunday, March 2

JOHN WESLEY, 1791; CHARLES WESLEY, 1788; RENEWERS OF THE CHURCH

The Wesleys were leaders of a revival in the Church of England. Their spiritual discipline of frequent communion, fasting, and advocacy for the poor earned them the name "Methodists." The Wesleys were missionaries in the American colony of Georgia for a time but returned to England discouraged. Following a conversion experience while reading Luther's *Preface to the Epistle to the Romans,* John was perhaps the greatest force in eighteenth-century revival. Their desire was that the Methodist Societies would be a movement for renewal in the Church of England, but after their deaths the societies developed a separate status.

Charles wrote more than 600 hymns, twelve of which are in *Lutheran Book of Worship* and one in *With One Voice.* Two of Charles's hymns are especially appropriate for Transfiguration: "Christ, whose glory fills the skies" (LBW 265) and "Love divine, all loves excelling" (LBW 315).

LENT

We encounter God who makes

and keeps covenant with us

Images *of the* Season

Particular images belong to each of the church's

seasons and are filtered through the experience of how

we observed those seasons in the past. The filters through

which we experience the church's seasons include our age, the kind of congregation in which we experience the seasons, how involved our family was/is in the worship life of the parish, and the ways in which pastors, musicians, and other leaders of worship attempted to interpret past seasons to us.

Lent's "theme" changed significantly during the past half-century. Anyone 45 years old or older may well recall observing the first five weeks of Lent focusing on the passion and death of Jesus. Lent was a dark and somber time. Hymns were almost all penitential and mournful, creating a funereal mood. A passion narrative gathered from all the gospels (and faithful to none of them) was invariably read at midweek services. Though we were told that the Sundays during Lent were "in" but not "of" the season, it was hard to separate the severity of midweek from what could have been a more uplifting Sunday observance. Holy Week, in this model, became a weeklong funeral observance for Jesus.

Thankfully, the past quarter-century provided a fresh emphasis in the observance of Lent. This season now returns us to the basics of faith formation. Lent now offers primarily a time for baptismal preparation—a time for a retreat, if you will. Retreats are designed to help people look within themselves, guided by scripture (and a retreat leader), and to ask basic questions about spiritual relationships.

Lent is the time when candidates for baptism receive final shaping that will end in their incorporation into Christ's body at the Vigil of Easter. Whether or not your congregation will be blessed with new baptisms at the Vigil, the whole church joins in on a virtual retreat, to support the candidates' final preparations—but also to prepare, individually, to renew and reaffirm their own baptismal covenant at the Vigil. (It is true, of course, that Lent has tremendous value also for congregations who do not make use of the Easter Vigil, but historically and pastorally, that is still the goal toward which Lent leans.)

Retreats provide opportunity for a retreat leader to instruct. Those on retreat react to the leader's presentation and probe its meaning with others on the retreat. Retreats provide quiet time for personal reflection on our own condition before God—time to remove the distractions of our everyday routine, to immerse ourselves in the written word, to engage in prayer, and to focus on what really makes us tick.

Think of Lent as a time to ask questions like "Who am I?" and "Who is God?" and "What is the relationship between God and me?" and "What is the church's task in this relationship?" Each of these retreat questions helps to prepare the candidate for baptism *and* the whole congregation for the Great Three Days and the celebration of the Easter season. Our Lenten retreat will be informed by the lessons appointed for Sunday. Our retreat leader will be anyone involved in the leadership of worship during the season.

Lent speaks of my own guilt and continuing sin, and of my need to be cleansed, purged, washed. I complain when things don't go my way, or when I lack what I perceive to be the necessities of life. A disobedient creature, I am unable to save myself. Darkness appeals to me more than light. Though I seldom fully admit it, I need the reestablishment of God's gracious authority in my life.

At the same time, I learn of my restoration to spiritual health and that I am an ambassador of good news. Lent's first day calls me to a life of almsgiving, prayer, and fasting. Those Lenten disciplines are intended to propel the disciple to acts of mercy, not to get God's attention (Ash Wednesday). Discipleship is a matter of denying self, taking up the cross, and following Jesus (second Sunday in Lent).

The God we encounter during Lent is a covenant maker, promising never to destroy humankind with water (while using water to save life), putting a bow in the sky as a self-reminder never to be involved in wholesale destruction again (first Sunday in Lent). God acts on behalf of the chosen people, bringing them out of slavery and giving them the Decalogue—the framework of relationship between God and human beings (third Sunday in Lent).

When people complain, God sends swift punishment that causes death, but then just as quickly raises up the means by which death can be avoided—a bronze serpent in the desert, and ultimately the Christ on the cross. God seeks not the world's destruction but its salvation (fourth Sunday in Lent). That salvation (life) can only happen if the suffering and death of the innocent one—God's own Son—happens first. After the obedient death on the cross, Jesus is exalted by God and praised by all creation as all creatures bow their knee (Sunday of the Passion).

God is honored as Creator and giver of the law. As nature shows God's glory, so the law is the sweet guide to life with God. As God's people are restored to spiritual health, they are led to praise God and to serve their neighbors (third Sunday in Lent).

Lent teaches us the importance of faith and trust. Though well beyond the age of procreating, Abraham receives the gift of God's promise in faith (second Sunday in Lent). The Servant suffers the indignities of op-

pressors but is vindicated by the Lord God. The message of the cross sounds foolish, but in its foolish sounding words, God saves those who are perishing.

Retreats are meant to be done in the company of other people. Thus, we make our Lenten retreat in the company of the community of faith where we live and work. Experienced retreaters who have made this Lenten retreat before share a responsibility to encourage and support those who are retreating for the first time. Experienced retreaters help to provide the welcoming environment in which God can create new and honest hearts in us, cleanse us and make us strong, renew us by the Holy Spirit, lead the erring back so that they can embrace the truth of God's word and hold it fast, and make us instruments of God's redeeming love.

Then, when our retreat ends in the darkness of the Easter Vigil, we are prepared both to welcome the candidates for baptism into the family of God and to reaffirm our own baptismal promises so that God's holy people will be able to walk through the wilderness of this world to the glory of the world to come, proclaim God's reign of love, share in Christ's obedience and in the ultimate glorious victory of Christ's resurrection.

Environment *and* Art *for the* Season

When entering the church on Ash Wednesday,

many worshipers will be struck by the major change since

the last celebration. Gone are the festive hangings

and flowers. A stark but welcoming simplicity greets the congregation. As somber as it is, Ash Wednesday is not really a time of mourning. Instead it marks the beginning of a period of special discipline. It is also a time for spiritual cleansing and redirection, which should be evident somehow in the liturgical environment.

EXTERIOR ENVIRONMENT

As throughout the year, make good use of exterior signs to identify worship times, announce special services, and to welcome visitors. Consider the use of large purple

banners affixed near major entrances to indicate the liturgical season. The placement of large crosses on the church lawn is better left until later in the season—more appropriately for Passion Sunday and Holy Week.

INTERIOR ENVIRONMENT

The narthex should be a place of welcome in any season. In its function as a preparatory space for worship, it should give some indication of the mood or central focal points throughout Lent. Artwork in the narthex could relate to the central themes of the season. Even though

Lent is seen increasingly as a time set aside for baptismal preparation and renewal, the focus on the cross is not lost, particularly in year B. Images tying together baptism and the cross would be appropriate. Use money from memorial gifts and other undesignated funds to commission lasting pieces of religious art from local artists. Works that will be part of a congregation's permanent collection may have the opportunity to tell the gospel story for a generation or more to come.

Arrangements of dried branches, rather than flowers, could be used to decorate gathering and other spaces during this season. For a more restrained version of floral decoration, use natural elements from the surrounding landscape, such as forsythia branches or pussy willows. Whatever is done for decoration, keep things simple throughout the forty days of Lent.

Consider the season of Lent as a time to "cleanse the house." Have paraments, banners, any flags, and other decorations removed for cleaning and to be made ready for Easter. Polish silver and brass worship appointments and communionware. Ceramic communion vessels, or anything with a duller appearance might be considered for use in this season instead. It is a good time to remove clutter and other extraneous materials from rooms, hallways, and closets. As a season for spiritual cleansing, let it also be a time for cleansing the church's house of everything that no longer serves a purpose.

Many churches have the tradition of covering any crosses in the worship space with purple voile. Others use unbleached linen. Still others extend the tradition to cover all crosses and all pictures in the building with the voile or linen.

For Ash Wednesday, paraments and vestments are typically black with little or no symbolism (alternatively they may be purple for the beginning of Lent). Austerity is the key word for Ash Wednesday. Paraments can be coarse, woven pieces in black or dark gray, reminding us of the dust of the ashes. Many use unbleached linen.

Purple is the color for Lent. It represents the penitential nature of the season, as we begin with confession and end with absolution at the Maundy Thursday service. We celebrate the forty days and all the Sundays in Lent with restraint. In this season, especially, it is appropriate to omit symbolism entirely, having simple unadorned fabrics as symbols in themselves.

A generous amount of palms will normally be required for the procession on Passsion (Palm) Sunday. Even though many congregations may continue to use purple paraments and vestments, the color scarlet is more symbolic of Holy Week, reminding us of the color of blood.

Preaching *with the* Season

For better or for worse, it seems the Lenten piety

of downcast eyes, fallen countenances, and silent departures

in half-lighted sanctuaries for midweek worship has been

replaced with intense eye contact for midweek Bible study, smiles and stimulating conversation at midweek soup suppers, and well-lighted spaces for dialogue sermons or Lenten dramas. Many of these changes are welcome, as is the renewed emphasis on Lent's baptismal roots. Lest the pendulum swing too far away from the past, though, it is good to remember that in addition Lent is still, and will always be, a time of reflection on Christ's journey to Calvary. Not that this reflection is limited to Lent, but we cannot ignore the lectionary road signs at this time in the church year.

Perhaps two attitudes predominate as we approach our Lenten journey with an eye on the cross. In one we see it as a time to grieve that God came among us, only to die and rise *because of me and sinners like me*. (Yes, we must admit in our misery that he did rise—but in order

126

to rise, he had to die by way of a gruesome, agonizing death, taking on our sins.) An air of egoism dwells in this attitude, hinting that the incarnation was "our fault" rather than God's merciful action. We hopefully find ourselves drawn to the flip side of this attitude, in which Lent becomes a time of reflection on and rejoicing in the truth that the divine self-revelation came to die and rise for us all, even me. What wondrous love!

We preachers do well to acknowledge the darker, almost morbid side of Lenten piety, even as we try to lead worshipers beyond that fixation. The cross needs to have a central place, yet we cannot pretend that we don't know how the story ends. We just recently came out of a mission-oriented season in which we sang how we "love to tell the story," so of course we know the ending! And so, one image for the season of Lent is that of a favorite scene in a play or chapter in a book, one that we can never pick up too often. Whether it makes us cry or laugh or think or rethink, anytime is always a good time to be Lent. Anytime is always a good time to "do" Lent, because Easter always follows Lent and as Easter people, enjoying the fruits of the resurrection, we want Christ. "Give [us] Jesus." Any time of the day, the church year, at any point in his life, incarnation or otherwise, give us Jesus.

The Lenten journey begins with an ash "rubbing" of the cross we received in baptism. It was always there, but now during Lent that cross is somewhat easier for others to see, and somewhat more intense for us to feel. For some, centuries-old practices of intensive forty-day rituals may make that cross seem harder to bear. But those who would be followers of Christ are commanded to "take up your cross."

Lent is a time in which we experience the community in Christ in a way that is not experienced in the happiness of Christmas and Easter. It is a time in which we receive a wake-up call to return to the Lord and to look deep within, and repent, and in our exposure understand that we are not alone in our journey. It is a time in which we feel the full range of emotions as people of God. How we express those emotions differs from place to place, but wherever we may be scattered throughout the world, we are on the road to Calvary—with Jesus and with one another.

In our struggles with evil, we encounter help along the way via divine messengers of various sorts, supporting us and helping to reveal God's will for our lives. We are surrounded by the forgiven sinners who comprise the church: gathered believers baptized into Christ's death and resurrection, called, enlightened, and sanctified by the Spirit. However much we might wish that Jesus' death for us was not necessary, we can only be grateful that it was offered for our salvation.

Our preaching need not take sides in some struggle between a baptismal emphasis for Lent and a cross and passion one. The two work hand in hand. We feel the weight of our sins, which Christ took on; we confess and repent, turning around; we daily return to the baptismal waters in which we are joined to Christ's death; we hear and cling to the words of forgiveness; and rise, still with Christ, and rejoice—all in the season of Lent. Yes, we experience moments of concern and near despair along the path that leads to and through the cross. But we do not lose heart, because we know how the story ends.

127

Shape *of* Worship *for the* Season

BASIC SHAPE OF THE EUCHARISTIC RITE

- Confession and Forgiveness: see alternate worship text for Lent in *Sundays and Seasons* as an option to the form in the liturgy setting.

GATHERING

- Greeting: see alternate worship text for Lent
- Use the Kyrie during Lent
- Omit the hymn of praise during Lent

WORD

- For dramatic readings based on lectionary passages, use *Scripture Out Loud!* (AFP 0806639644) for Ash Wednesday and the fourth Sunday in Lent
- For contemporary dramas based on lectionary passages, use *Can These Bones Live?* (AFP 0806639652) for Ash Wednesday, the fifth Sunday in Lent, and Passion Sunday
- Use the Nicene Creed
- The prayers: see the prayers for Ash Wednesday and each Sunday

MEAL

- Offertory Prayer: see alternate worship text for Lent
- Use the proper preface for Lent
- Use the proper preface for Passion beginning with Passion Sunday
- Eucharistic prayer: in addition to four main options in *LBW*, see "Eucharistic Prayer D: The Season of Lent" in *WOV* Leaders Edition, p. 68
- Invitation to communion: see alternate worship text for Lent
- Post-communion prayer: see alternate worship text for Lent

SENDING

- Benediction: see alternate worship text for Lent
- Dismissal: see alternate worship text for Lent

OTHER SEASONAL POSSIBILITIES

- Ash Wednesday liturgy: see *LBW* Ministers Edition, pp. 129–31; congregational leaflets available from Augsburg Fortress (AFP 080660574X)
- Enrollment of Candidates for Baptism (for first Sunday in Lent): see *Welcome to Christ: Lutheran Rites for the Catechumenate*, pp. 18–21
- Midweek Lenten worship: see order for evening prayer services in seasonal rites section
- Blessing of Candidates for Baptism (for third, fourth, and fifth Sundays in Lent): see *Welcome to Christ: Lutheran Rites for the Catechumenate*, pp. 22–34
- Procession with Palms liturgy for Passion Sunday: see *LBW* Ministers Edition, pp. 134–35; congregational leaflets available from Augsburg Fortress (AFP 0806605766)
- Blessing of oil: This could be done as a synod or other group of congregations wishing to celebrate this order; see Dedication of Worship Furnishings in *Occasional Services*, pp. 176–77

Assembly Song *for the* Season

"Guide now the people of your Church, that,

following our Savior, we may walk through the wilderness

of this world toward the glory of the world to come"

(prayer of the day, first Sunday in Lent). This season invites us on a journey, a journey that is a return. We return to the grace of baptism, as new catechumens prepare for baptism at the Easter Vigil. We return to the church, our ark that carries us through the flood. And we return home, to God, who is gracious and merciful, slow to anger, and abounding in steadfast love.

Lent is not an extended Holy Week, and each Sunday in Lent is a celebration of the resurrection. Still, it is good to "fast the ears," just as many people keep a Lenten fast for their stomachs. Musical practices include keeping more silence, simplifying (and softening) accompaniments to the assembly's song, omitting the hymn of praise, and not singing the word *alleluia*. Some congregations do without the postlude during this season. Reduce or eliminate percussion and other instruments (especially brass), saving their more festive sounds until Easter.

GATHERING

- Use the Litany (*LBW*, p. 168), following or in place of the Order for Confession and Forgiveness, for the only entrance music on the first Sunday in Lent. Have the procession move through the church, stopping at various stations. Or place several singers in the corners of the church to sing the leader parts, and surround the people with this prayer. Use bells to keep the pitch and add solemnity.
- On the other Sundays, highlight the Kyrie. Sing a different Kyrie each week: "Your heart, O God, is grieved" (LBW 96) and the settings in the service music portions of *WOV, LLC,* and *TFF* are possibilities.
- Or use a familiar Kyrie from *LBW* setting 1 or 2, but sing it unaccompanied with a single bell to give the pitch.

WORD

- Have the people sing "Return to the Lord your God" for the gospel acclamation on Ash Wednesday; it can be used for the whole season.
- "The word of God is source and seed" (WOV 658, based on the gospel for the fifth Sunday in Lent) is another possibility for a seasonal acclamation. Its use would remind the assembly that every Sunday is a "little Easter," even in Lent.
- Introduce the prayers by singing "O Lord, hear my prayer" (WOV 772) or "Lord, listen to your children praying" (WOV 775, TFF 247) several times. Keep the music quiet and reflective.

MEAL

- "Create in me" is the appointed offertory for Ash Wednesday; it works well throughout the season. Use the setting at WOV 732, especially if the choir and/or people enjoy singing in harmony. Or a setting is found at the end of all three communion settings in *LBW*. Another possible seasonal offertory hymn is "Alas! And did my Savior bleed" (LBW 98).
- Sing "Holy, holy, holy Lord" during the great thanksgiving, but save the loudest stops on the organ or embellishing instruments for Easter.
- Begin the distribution with "O Christ, thou Lamb of God" (LBW 103), sung unaccompanied if possible. Keep more silence during communion than normal.

SENDING

- Keep the sending simple, with either a post-communion canticle ("Lord, now you let your servant go in peace") or a hymn, not both. Appropriate seasonal hymns include "I want Jesus to walk with me" (WOV 660), "Take the name of Jesus with you" (TFF 159), and "Praise and thanks and adoration" (LBW 470).

129

Music *for the* Season

VERSE AND OFFERTORY

Busarow, Donald. *Verses and Offertories, Part III—Ash Wednesday through Maundy Thursday.* SATB, org. CPH 97-5503.

Cherwien, David. *Verses for the Sundays in Lent.* U/2 pt, org. MSM 80-300.

Farlee, Robert Buckley. *Verses and Offertories for Lent.* U/SATB. AFP 0800649494.

Gospel Acclamations. Cant, choir, cong, inst. MAY 0862096324.

Schiavone, J. *Gospel Acclamation Verses for the Sundays of Lent.* GIA G-2160.

Schramm, Charles. *Verses for the Lenten Season.* SATB, opt org. MSM 80-301.

CHORAL

Bach, J. S. "Jesu meine Freude" in *Bach for All Seasons.* SATB, opt kybd. AFP 080065854X.

Christiansen, Paul. "Wondrous Love." SATB. AFP 0800652665.

Farrant, Richard. "Lord, for Thy Tender Mercy's Sake" in *The Parish Choir Book.* SATB. CPH CHI137.

Ferguson, John. "Ah, Holy Jesus." SATB, org, opt cong. AFP 0800654528.

Gilpin, Greg. "Kyrie." SATB, pno. SHW A-2076.

Goudimel, Claude. "As the Deer, for Water Yearning" in *Chantry Choirbook.* SATB. AFP 0800657772.

Hampton, Keith. "Give Me Jesus." SATB, sop solo. AFP 0800659554.

Hopson, Hal H. "A Lenten Walk" in *The Augsburg Choirbook.* 2 pt mxd, org, opt timp, opt hb. AFP 0800656784.

Hopson, Hal H. "O Lord, Hear Me." SAB, pno. LOR 10/2152LA.

Oldroyd, George. "Prayer to Jesus." SATB, org. OXF A 73.

Pasquet, Jean. "Create in Me a Clean Heart." SAB, kybd. AFP 600010121X.

Schiavone, John. "Wilt Thou Forgive?" SATB. CPH 98-2119.

Willcocks, Jonathan. "O Holy Jesus (Prayer of St. Richard of Chichester)." SATB, org. SMP 10/1937S.

CHILDREN'S CHOIRS

Bedford, Michael. "Jesus to the Wilderness" in *Singing the Seasons.* U, kybd, opt 2 oct hb. CG CGA854.

Bedford, Michael. *Seven Songs for the Church Year.* U, opt hb. CG CGA 693.

Farrell, Bernadette. "Share the Light." 2 pt, kybd, gtr, opt inst. OCP 11307CC.

Hopson, Hal H. "I Want Jesus to Walk with Me." 2 pt trbl/mxd, kybd. CG CGA701.

Jennings, Carolyn. "Ah, Holy Jesus." SA, cont, vc. AFP 0800645154.

KEYBOARD/INSTRUMENTAL

Albinoni, Tomaso. "Adagio in G Minor" in *Organ Music for Funerals and Memorial Services, book 2.* Org. AFP 0800647858.

Augsburg Organ Library: Lent. Org. AFP 0800658973.

Ferguson, John. *Thy Holy Wings.* Org. AFP 0800647955.

Jordan, Alice. "Aria." Ob/fl, org. MSM 20-972.

Miller, Aaron David. *Triptych for Lent and Easter.* Org. AFP 0800659457.

Mozart, W. A. "Adagio in C." Org/eng hrn. CPH 97-5429.

Nicholson, Paul. "Were You There." Inst, org. AFP 0800654080.

Young, Jeremy. *At the Foot of the Cross.* Pno. AFP 0800655397.

HANDBELL

Curtis, Cynthia. "Jesus, Keep Me Near the Cross." 3 oct. National Music Pub HB485.

Dobrinski, Cynthia. "Were You There." 3–5 oct. JEF HP1551.

Linker, Janet/arr. Jane McFadden. "Come to Calvary's Holy Mountain." 3–5 oct, org. CG B190.

McElveen, Paul. "Lenten Meditation." 2–3 oct. CPH 97-6257.

Nelson, Susan T. "Plainchant Meditation and Morning Suite." 3 oct. AFP 080065546X.

Parry, Joseph/arr. J. Linker. "Reflection on 'Aberystwyth'" 3–5 oct. CPH 97-6759.

PRAISE ENSEMBLE

Espinosa, Eddie. "Change My Heart, O God." SATB, kybd. MAR 301 0813 163.

Larson, Lloyd. "A Lenten Prayer (O Lord throughout These Forty Days)." SATB, kybd. LOR 10/1794L.

Nockels, Nathan and Christy Nockels. "My Heart, Your Home" in *Extravagant Grace Songbook.* SAT[B], kybd. INT 16737.

Zschech, Darlene/arr. Jay Rouse. "The Potter's Hand" in *Hillsongs Choral Collection Songbook.* Hillsongs.

130

Alternate Worship Texts

CONFESSION AND FORGIVENESS
In the name of the Father, and of the ✛ Son,
and of the Holy Spirit.
Amen

Trusting in the promise of God's covenant with us,
let us be bold to confess our sin.

Silence for reflection and self-examination.

Most faithful God,
we confess that we have failed
to be faithful in our promises to you
and to walk in the way of Christ.
We neglect to serve others;
we turn from the good you created in us,
and in so doing we allow evil to increase.
We look to you for mercy and healing.
Strengthen our faith, increase our hope,
and guide us in the path of humble service. Amen

All who turn to God in repentance
find their sin forgiven
for the sake of Jesus Christ, our Savior.
Deny yourselves, then,
take up your cross, and follow him.
Amen

GREETING
The grace and mercy of God,
who in Christ bears our burdens and saves us from sin,
be with you all.
And also with you.

PRAYERS
As we journey through this season of repentance and renewal,
let us turn to God who mercifully gives us new life.

A brief silence.

Each petition ends:
Hear us, O God;
your mercy is great.

Concluding petition:
Merciful God, hear our cry when we call to you;
renew and uphold us with your Spirit,
through Jesus Christ our Lord.
Amen

OFFERTORY PRAYER
Compassionate God,
we offer you these gifts
as signs of our time and labor.
Receive the offering of our lives,
and feed us with your grace,
that, even in the midst of death,
all creation might feast on your unending life
in Jesus Christ our Lord. Amen

INVITATION TO COMMUNION
This is the Lamb of God who takes away the sin of the world.
Happy are those who are called to his supper.
Lord, I am not worthy to receive you,
but only say the word and I shall be healed.

POST-COMMUNION PRAYER
God of our pilgrimage,
in this meal you nourish us
with the gifts of faith and hope.
Sustain us on our journey
that, refreshed by your grace,
we may reach the promised land,
the Easter feast of victory
in Jesus Christ our Lord.
Amen

BLESSING
The blessing of God's eternal love,
the courage to follow the way of the cross,
and the guidance of the Spirit in the desert places of our world,
✛ be among you and remain with you forever.
Amen

DISMISSAL
Go in peace. Proclaim God's love for all.
Thanks be to God.

131

Seasonal Rites

Midweek Evening Prayer for Lent

This flexible order of evening prayer may be celebrated as a midweek service during Lent. It is an adaptable form of vespers with readings and music that highlight the Lenten journey from ashes to the baptismal font of Easter.

OVERVIEW: MIDWEEK BAPTISMAL THEMES FROM THE SUNDAY READINGS FOR LENT, YEAR B

FIRST WEEK
Genesis 9:8-17 and 1 Peter 3:18-22
Saved in the waters of the flood

SECOND WEEK
Mark 8:31-38
Baptized into the way of the cross

THIRD WEEK
1 Corinthians 1:18-25
Marked with the cross of Christ

FOURTH WEEK
Ephesians 2:1-10
Blessed with grace and created for good works

FIFTH WEEK
John 12:20-33
Buried with Christ like seed in the earth

SERVICE OF LIGHT

A lit vesper candle may be carried in procession during the following versicles and placed in its stand in front of the assembly.

These versicles may be sung to the tones given in Evening Prayer, LBW, *p. 142.*

Behold, now is the accept- | able time;
now is the day of sal- | vation.
Turn us again, O God of | our salvation,
that the light of your face may shine on | us.
May your justice shine | like the sun;
and may the poor be lifted | up.

HYMN OF LIGHT

One of the following hymns may be sung.
Dearest Jesus, at your word   LBW 248
O Light whose splendor thrills   WOV 728
Christ, mighty Savior   WOV 729
I heard the voice of Jesus say   TFF 62

THANKSGIVING FOR LIGHT

This is set to music in LBW, *p. 144.*
The Lord be with you.
And also with you.
Let us give thanks to the Lord our God.
It is right to give our thanks and praise.
Blessed are you, O Lord our God, king of the universe,
who led your people Israel by a pillar of cloud by day
and a pillar of fire by night:
Enlighten our darkness by the light of your Christ;
may his Word be a lamp to our feet and a light to our path;
for you are merciful, and you love your whole creation,
and we, your creatures, glorify you, Father, Son, and Holy Spirit.
Amen

PSALMODY

The first psalm may be Psalm 141, as printed in LBW, *pp. 145–46; other settings can be found at* LBW 5, TFF 18, W&P 86.

An additional psalm or canticle may be used for each of the weeks during Lent (see settings in Psalter for Worship*):*

FIRST WEEK
Psalm 46

SECOND WEEK
Psalm 13

THIRD WEEK
Psalm 29

FOURTH WEEK
Psalm 84

FIFTH WEEK
Psalm 42

132

HYMN

Possibilities for hymns related to the readings for each of the weeks follow.

FIRST WEEK
Thy holy wings   WOV 741
Oh, happy day when we shall stand   LBW 351
'Tis the old ship of Zion   TFF 199

SECOND WEEK
"Come, follow me," the Savior spake   LBW 455
This is the Spirit's entry now   LBW 195
I want Jesus to walk with me   WOV 660, TFF 66

THIRD WEEK
Nature with open volume stands   LBW 119
Baptized in water   WOV 693
Beneath the cross of Jesus   LBW 107

FOURTH WEEK
Wash, O God, our sons and daughters   WOV 697
Only by grace   W&P 112
Jesus, refuge of the weary   LBW 93

FIFTH WEEK
O Sun of justice   WOV 659
The word of God is source and seed   WOV 658
On my heart imprint your image   LBW 102

OTHER HYMN OPTIONS INCLUDE:
We were baptized in Christ Jesus   WOV 698
O blessed spring   WOV 695
All who believe and are baptized   LBW 194

READINGS FOR EACH OF THE WEEKS OF LENT
FIRST WEEK
Genesis 9:8-17 and 1 Peter 3:18-22

SECOND WEEK
Mark 8:31-38

THIRD WEEK
1 Corinthians 1:18-25

FOURTH WEEK
Ephesians 2:1-10

FIFTH WEEK
John 12:20-33

A homily or meditation may follow the reading.

Silence is kept by all.

The silence concludes:

Long ago, in many and various ways,
God spoke to our ancestors by the prophets;
but in these last days God has spoken to us by the Son.

133

GOSPEL CANTICLE
My soul now magnifies the Lord   LBW 180
My soul proclaims your greatness   WOV 730
My soul does magnify the Lord   TFF 168

LITANY

The music for the litany in LBW, p. 148, may be used with the following.

In peace, let us pray to the Lord.
Lord, have mercy.
For the peace from above, let us pray to the Lord.
Lord, have mercy.
For the peace of the whole world,
for the well-being of the church of God,
and for the unity of all, let us pray to the Lord.
Lord, have mercy.
For those who are preparing for the Easter sacraments,
let us pray to the Lord.
Lord, have mercy.
For the baptized people of God and for their varied ministries,
let us pray to the Lord.
Lord, have mercy.
For those who are poor, hungry, homeless, or sick,
let us pray to the Lord.
Lord, have mercy.
Help, save, comfort, and defend us, gracious Lord.

Silence is kept by all.

Rejoicing in the fellowship of all the saints,
let us commend ourselves, one another,
and our whole life to Christ, our Lord.
To you, O Lord.

PRAYER OF THE DAY

From the previous Sunday if a service is held during the week.

THE LORD'S PRAYER

BLESSING

For a musical setting, see LBW, p. 152.

Let us bless the Lord.
Thanks be to God.

The almighty and merciful Lord,
the Father, the Son, and the Holy Spirit,
bless and preserve us.
Amen

134

Service of the Word for Healing in Lent

An order for Service of the Word for Healing is presented in the seasonal materials for autumn. It may also be adapted for use during Lent in the following ways:

DIALOG

Behold, now is the acceptable time;
now is the day of salvation.
Return to the Lord, your God,
who is gracious and merciful, slow to anger,
and abounding in steadfast love.
God forgives you all your sins
and heals all your infirmities.
God redeems your life from the grave
and crowns you with mercy and lovingkindness.
God satisfies you with good things,
and your youth is renewed like an eagle's.
Bless the Lord, O my soul,
and all that is within me bless God's holy name.

FIRST READING: Isaiah 53:3-5
PSALM: Psalm 138
GOSPEL: Matthew 8:1-3, 5-8, 13-17

THE PRAYERS

HYMNS

Either of these hymns may be used when the Service of the Word for Healing occurs during Lent:
Jesus, refuge of the weary   LBW 93
In the cross of Christ I glory   LBW 104

March 5, 2003

Ash Wednesday

INTRODUCTION

Christians gather on Ash Wednesday to mark the beginning of Lent's baptismal preparation for Easter. On this day, the people of God receive an ashen cross on the forehead (a gesture rooted in baptism), hear the solemn proclamation to keep a fast in preparation for Easter's feast, and contemplate anew the ongoing meaning of baptismal initiation into the Lord's death and resurrection. While marked with the ashes of human mortality, the church hears God's promise of forgiveness and tastes God's mercy in the bread of life and the cup of salvation. From this solemn liturgy, the church goes forth on its journey to the great baptismal feast of Easter.

PRAYER OF THE DAY

Almighty and ever-living God, you hate nothing you have made and you forgive the sins of all who are penitent. Create in us new and honest hearts, so that, truly repenting of our sins, we may obtain from you, the God of all mercy, full pardon and forgiveness; through your Son, Jesus Christ our Lord, who lives and reigns with you and the Holy Spirit, one God, now and forever.

VERSE

Return to the LORD, your God, who is gracious and merciful, slow to anger, and abounding in steadfast love. (Joel 2:13)

READINGS

Joel 2:1-2, 12-17

The context of this reading is a liturgy of communal lamentation. The prophet has called the temple community to mourn a devastating plague of the past and to announce a day of darkness, the day of the Lord. The community is called to repent, to return to God who is gracious and merciful.

or Isaiah 58:1-12

God chooses a fast that is not merely outward, but one that gives evidence of repentance through works of mercy.

Psalm 51:1-18 (Psalm 51:1-17 [NRSV])

Have mercy on me, O God, according to your loving-kindness. (Ps. 51:1)

2 Corinthians 5:20b—6:10

Out of love for humankind, the sinless one experienced sin and suffering so that the redemptive power of God could penetrate the darkest, most forbidding, and tragic depths of human experience. No aspect of human life is ignored by the presence of God's grace. With faith in this redemption, Paul announces that this day is a day of God's grace, an acceptable time to turn toward God's mercy.

Matthew 6:1-6, 16-21

In this passage Matthew sets forth a vision of genuine righteousness illustrated by three basic acts of Jewish devotion: almsgiving, prayer, and fasting. Jesus does not denounce the acts—in the New Testament they are signs of singular devotion to God—rather, he criticizes those who perform them in order to have a sense of self-satisfaction or to gain public approval. Care for those who are poor, intense prayer, and fasting with a joyous countenance are signs of loving dedication to God.

COLOR Black *or* Purple

THE PRAYERS

As we journey through this season of repentance and renewal, let us turn to God who mercifully gives us new life.
A BRIEF SILENCE.

O God, you call your people to turn from sin and to live in the joy and freedom of forgiveness. Give endurance to all the baptized who seek to practice the disciplines of Lent. Hear us, O God;
your mercy is great.

O God, you call all people to work together for the common good. Assist the leaders of the nations to remove all obstacles that would deter the reconciling efforts of peacemakers. Hear us, O God;
your mercy is great.

O God, grant compassion to all who minister in the healing arts: medical professionals, healing practitioners,

135

and all caregivers. Show your mercy to those who are ill (*especially*) and bring them peace of mind and heart. Hear us, O God;

your mercy is great.

O God, you call your people to turn from sin to live for you alone. Guide all who are preparing for baptism, that the forty days of Lent would bring them to the waters of life. Hear us, O God;

your mercy is great.

HERE OTHER INTERCESSIONS MAY BE OFFERED.

O God, you call your people to be with you in endless light. Bless the memory of our faithful departed, and keep us ever one with them in the communion of saints. Hear us, O God;

your mercy is great.

Merciful God, hear our cry when we call to you; renew and uphold us with your Spirit, through Jesus Christ our Lord.

Amen

136

IMAGES FOR PREACHING

We are jolted from an Epiphany image of quiet stillness, that of the candle shining in the darkness. Lest sleep be our death, the glaring sound of the trumpet reveille serves a three-fold purpose: (1) an alarm of the coming of the day of the Lord, (2) a "heads-up" preceding the command to return to the Lord, and (3) an aural metaphor of how the practice of "showtime piety" appears to God—gauche, inappropriate, and unacceptable.

In our society, regardless of the style of music, the trumpet is a much celebrated instrument; in the church, piety is celebrated as the instrument by which we express our devotion and allegiance to Christ. In these lessons, we see what happens when a good thing goes awry. And so it can be with our Lenten practices. We see the difference in the holy response called for in Joel (fasting, assembly of young and old), and the mockery that giving, prayer, and fasting have become in the time of Matthew. In the twenty-first century, we walk a fine line between the two.

Rather than the outward show of piety (e.g., giving for the sake of being praised by members; silver-tongued, sanitized prayer for the sake of mesmerizing the visitors; or obvious, anorexic-like fasting), a more appropriate response to the wake-up trumpet sound would be an inward look at the reasons why we do the things we do. Do we do them for love of Christ or love of praise? This kind of soul searching will result in a troubled spirit, a broken and contrite heart, which transform the very same acts of "showtime piety" to gifts of devotion and allegiance that are well-pleasing in God's sight.

WORSHIP MATTERS

The awful truth is rubbed into our foreheads on this day in the sign of an ashen cross. The truth of our mortality, the truth of our sin, the truth of our disobedience is placed there for everyone to see. Christ's death forms us and reforms us during this season, but this death was hardly beautiful or neat or clean. It was dirty and awful like the ashes we receive. And yet through this tragic, painful, ugly death, amazingly we gain life.

Traditionally, ashes are made by burning the palms from the previous Passion Sunday. You can order ashes from any number of church providers, but burning them with the help of confirmation students provides a powerful symbol to begin this day. Once the palms are burned you may want to sift the ashes, then place them in a small bowl and add a little olive oil or water. During the liturgy the ministers mark foreheads with the words, "Remember that you are dust, and to dust you shall return."

LET THE CHILDREN COME

The sign of the cross on our foreheads in baptism marks us as children of God.

The sign of the cross on our forehead in ashes reminds us of our death with Christ. The cross on Easter reminds us of the resurrection of Christ. If children can see the palms from last Passion Sunday or smell the smoke as they are burned, they will remember more easily. The ashes remind us of Jesus and his death for us. They remind us of how much God loves us. He died and rose again to save us from the power of sin and death.

HYMNS FOR WORSHIP
GATHERING

Just as I am, without one plea   LBW 296
Softly and tenderly Jesus is calling   WOV 734, TFF 155

HYMN OF THE DAY

Savior, when in dust to you   LBW 91

ALTERNATE HYMN OF THE DAY

When in the hour of deepest need   LBW 303
You are mine   W&P 158

COMMUNION

Lord, Jesus think on me   LBW 309
Create in me a clean heart   WOV 732
We remember you   W&P 152

SENDING

Abide with us, our Savior   LBW 263
Christ, mighty Savior   WOV 729, CS 19
Stay with us   WOV 743

ADDITIONAL HYMNS AND SONGS

Wilt thou forgive   H82 140, 141
Out of the depths I call   H82 666
What can wash away my sin?   TFF 69
In deepest night   OBS 63

MUSIC FOR THE DAY
PSALMODY

Cooney, Rory. "Psalm 51: Create Me Again." U/2 pt, cong, opt inst.
GIA G-3975.
Hopson, Hal H. "Psalm 51" in *Ten Psalms*. SATB, cong.
HOP HH 3930.
Hurd, Bob. "Create in Me" in STP 1.
Marshall, Jane. "Psalm 51" in *Psalms Together II*. U.   CG CGC-21.
Rees, Elizabeth. "O Lord, You Love Sincerity of Heart" in PS 2.
Schwarz, May.   PW B.
Wellicome, Paul. "I Will Leave This Place" in PS 2.

CHORAL

Bach, J.S. "Bring Low Our Ancient Adam" in *Bach for All Seasons*.
SATB, kybd. AFP 080065854X.   Inst pts. AFP 0800659546.
Brahms, Johannes. "Create in Me, O God." SATBB.   Gsch 7504.
Haas, David. "Dust and Ashes." 2 pt, opt gtr, kybd.   GIA G-3655.
Hopson, Hal H. "A Psalm of Confession." SATB, opt solo.
AFP 080065952X.
Muskrat, Bruce. "Create in Me." SATB.   CPH 98-2311.
Schalk, Carl. "Have Mercy On Me, O God." SATB.
AFP 0800657845.
Telemann, G.P. "Make Me Pure, O Sacred Spirit" in *To God Will I Sing*.
MH voice.   AFP 0800674332. ML voice.
AFP 0800674340.

CHILDREN'S CHOIRS

Cooney, Rory. "Psalm 51: Create Me Again." U/2 pt, cong, opt inst.
GIA G-3975.
Hopson, Hal H. "I Want Jesus to Walk with Me." 2 pt, kybd.
CG CGA701.
Marshall, Jane. "Create in Me, O God." U antiphonal, kybd.
CG CGA750.

KEYBOARD/INSTRUMENTAL

Keesecker, Thomas. "I Want Jesus to Walk with Me" in *Come Away to the Skies*. Pno.   AFP 0800656555.
Miller, Aaron David. "Aberystwyth" in *Improvisations for the Church Year*.
Org.   AFP 0800674812.
Organ, Anne Krentz. "Aberystwyth" in *Christ, Mighty Savior*. Kybd.
AFP 0800656806.
Thomas, Paul Lindsley. "Variation on the Welsh Hymn Tune 'Aberystwyth.'" Org.   OXF 93-112.

HANDBELL

Afdahl, Lee J. "Psalm 51." 3–5 oct, opt marimba/kybd.
AFP 0800675061.
Espinosa, Eddie and Patricia Cota. "Change My Heart, O God."
3–5 oct, opt hc.   AG 2136.
Wood, W. "Jesus, Lover of My Soul." 2–3 oct.   JEF MNAHB405.

PRAISE ENSEMBLE

Camp, Steve and Carman Licciardello. "Revive Us, O Lord" in *Songs for Praise and Worship*. WRD.
Espinosa, Eddie and Bob Kilpatrick/arr. John F. Wilson. "Change My Heart/Lord, Be Glorified." SATB, kybd.   HOP GC992.
Makeever, Ray. "Be Merciful, O God" in DH.
Nelson, Jeff. "Purify My Heart" in *Raise the Standard Worship Team Book*.
3 pt.   MAR 3010124368.
Paris, Twila. "Lamb of God" in *Songs for Praise and Worship*.   WRD.

Friday, March 7

PERPETUA AND HER COMPANIONS,
MARTYRS AT CARTHAGE, 202

In the year 202 the emperor Septimius Severus forbade conversions to Christianity. Perpetua, a noblewoman, Felicity, a slave, and other companions were all catechumens at Carthage in North Africa. They were imprisoned and sentenced to death. Perpetua's father, who was not a Christian, visited her in prison and begged to

137

lay aside her Christian convictions in order to spare her life and spare the family from scorn. Perpetua responded and told her father, "We know that we are not placed in our own power but in that of God."

During the weeks of Lent, congregations that do not have catechumens can pray for those who do as they approach their own death and rebirth in the waters of baptism at the Easter Vigil, and are clothed with the new life of Christ.

THOMAS AQUINAS, TEACHER, 1274

Thomas Aquinas was a brilliant and creative theologian of the thirteenth century. He was first and foremost a student of the Bible and profoundly concerned with the theologi-

cal formation of the church's ordained ministers. As a member of the Order of Preachers (Dominicans), he worked to correlate scripture with the philosophy of Aristotle, which was having a renaissance in Aquinas's day. Some students of Aristotle's philosophy found in it an alternative to Christianity. But Aquinas immersed himself in the thought of Aristotle and worked to explain Christian beliefs in the philosophical culture of the day. The contemporary worship cultural studies done by the Lutheran World Federation resonate with Aquinas's method.

Aquinas was also a hymnwriter. His hymn "Thee we adore, O hidden Savior" (LBW 199) is traditionally sung on Maundy Thursday and might also be sung this Sunday as a communion hymn.

March 9, 2003

First Sunday in Lent

INTRODUCTION

Jesus joins the church in the wilderness for forty days as we contemplate the meaning of our baptism into his death and resurrection. We are with Noah in the ark, Israel in the desert, and Elijah on rocky Mount Horeb for a time of prayer, fasting, and preparation. We make this journey together as a people brought into existence by God's mercy. We hear this covenant proclaimed in the word of God and share this promise in the body and blood of Christ.

PRAYER OF THE DAY

Lord God, you led your ancient people through the wilderness and brought them to the promised land. Guide now the people of your church, that, following our Savior, we may walk through the wilderness of this world toward the glory of the world to come; through your Son, Jesus Christ our Lord, who lives and reigns with you and the Holy Spirit, one God, now and forever.
or
Lord God, our strength, the battle of good and evil rages within and around us, and our ancient foe tempts us with his deceits and empty promises. Keep us steadfast

in your Word and, when we fall, raise us again and restore us through your Son, Jesus Christ our Lord, who lives and reigns with you and the Holy Spirit, one God, now and forever.

VERSE

One does not live by bread alone, but by every word that comes from the mouth of God. (Matt. 4:4)

READINGS

Genesis 9:8-17

Today's reading centers on the conclusion to the flood story. The Lord destroys the earth by flood, except for Noah, his family, and the animals on the ark. Yet, divine destruction, because of human sinfulness, gives way to divine commitment. As in the first creation (Gen. 1), God blesses the human community and establishes a covenant with all creatures.

Psalm 25:1-9 (Psalm 25:1-10 [NRSV])

Your paths are love and faithfulness to those who keep your covenant. (Ps. 25:9)

1 Peter 3:18-22

In this reading, the author emphasizes God's saving

action on behalf of Noah, his family, and the creatures. This saving presence continues to be manifested through Christ in the act of baptism.

Mark 1:9-15

The Spirit that comes upon Jesus at his baptism sustains him when he is tested by Satan so that he might proclaim the gospel of God's reign.

COLOR Purple

THE PRAYERS

As we journey through this season of repentance and renewal, let us turn to God who mercifully gives us new life.
A BRIEF SILENCE.

O God of promise, strengthen all the baptized in the covenant you made with us in baptism, and empower us to speak your promises in the wilderness of this world. Hear us, O God;
your mercy is great.

O God of voice and word, speak tenderly to the world that you made, that the nations may know your loving presence, and their leaders your guiding wisdom. Hear us, O God;
your mercy is great.

O God of patience and kindness, remember those who approach death, and strengthen those who keep watch with them. Heal those who are sick (*especially*) and assure them of your abiding presence. Hear us, O God;
your mercy is great.

O God of our relationships, bless those preparing for baptism. Give holy guidance to those who mentor them and to congregations who will receive them. Hear us, O God;
your mercy is great.
HERE OTHER INTERCESSIONS MAY BE OFFERED.

O God of all eternity, keep our blessed dead in your eternal embrace until, with (*names,* and) all your saints, we are reunited with them by your grace. Hear us, O God;
your mercy is great.

Merciful God, hear our cry when we call to you; renew and uphold us with your Spirit, through Jesus Christ our Lord.
Amen

IMAGES FOR PREACHING

In baptism we are sealed by the Holy Spirit and marked by the cross. On Ash Wednesday, we receive an ash "rubbing" of that cross, and here the Spirit of God in the form of a dove gives us a different function of those holy wings. This holy bird swoops down, like a dive-bomber, wings extended not to gather us underneath, but rather to scatter us. It is a challenging image but in a flash in Mark the bird acts more like a hawk than a dove. However frightening, it is the same Spirit present in baptism that now drives us into the desolate places where demons dwell and the tempter lurks.

But even in those desolate places, though scattered, we are not alone. We are but one part of God's creation. See the promise made to Noah in Genesis? It was between Noah and every living creature with him. It seems Noah and Jesus have animals as well as humans as companions on their journeys. Even when it seems we are alone, we are not. In the desolate times and places in our life, we will find temptations that appear to be blessings as well as the unlikeliest companions and divine messengers.

Like Jesus himself who was not recognized as having been sent by God, we may fail to recognize those sent to us on our journey. Are we looking for love or respect in the wrong places? Are we discounting Christ's presence in too many faces? The evil one comes wrapped in some very nice packaging. Lent's trumpet sounds so that we might wake up lest we fail to recognize our messengers when they are sent to us.

WORSHIP MATTERS

Be sure to mind your prepositions during the Lenten season. All of the Lenten Sundays are Sundays "in" Lent, not "of" Lent. Each Sunday of the church year is always a day of resurrection, so even during the more somber and muted season of Lent, we still gather on Sunday to acknowledge, celebrate, and give thanks for Christ's victory over the forces of evil, death, and darkness.

One simple way to remember the focus of our Sunday celebration during the Lenten season is to teach our congregations to make the sign of the cross. The tracing of the cross on our bodies is a visible reminder of the promises that are always ours. While we may gather during these forty days (plus Sundays) for repentance, reflection, and renewal, we find ourselves constantly surrounded by the life-giving water of promise, marked with the cross of Christ forever.

139

LET THE CHILDREN COME

This first Sunday in Lent is a good time to remind the congregation of the new church season. The new season is visible in the sanctuary in the change in color of the paraments to purple. It may be heard in changes in the liturgy, in eucharistic prayers, psalm tones, and the absence of Alleluias. If practical, you could have a family process with the purple paraments. It is also a time of preparation for baptism and, in many places, confirmation. Link this preparation to Jesus' time of preparation. A mention during the service of those who are involved in preparation and what they are doing will make it more real.

HYMNS FOR WORSHIP

GATHERING

If you but trust in God to guide you   LBW 453
Many and great, O God, are your works   WOV 794
I want Jesus to walk with me   WOV 660, TFF 66

HYMN OF THE DAY

Lord, keep us steadfast in your Word   LBW 230

ALTERNATE HYMN OF THE DAY

Lord of our life   LBW 366
Thy holy wings   WOV 741

COMMUNION

Draw near and take the body of the Lord   LBW 226
This is my body   WOV 707, TFF 121

SENDING

A mighty fortress is our God   LBW 228, 229; CS 1, 2
Shalom   WOV 724

ADDITIONAL HYMNS AND SONGS

Kind Maker of the world   H82 152
Mark how the Lamb of God's self-offering   NCH 167
Yield not to temptation   TFF 195
Amazing love   W&P 8
Out in the wilderness   W&P 115

MUSIC FOR THE DAY

SERVICE MUSIC

The Great Litany (*LBW*, p. 168) is especially suited for the gathering rite on the first Sunday in Lent, when it may be sung in a slow extended procession, replacing confession/forgiveness, entrance hymn, and Kyrie. Establishing a flowing and insistent cadence is key to the effective use of this ancient sung prayer.

PSALMODY

Brugh, Lorraine.   PW B.

Haas, David/arr. Jeanne Cotter. "Remember Your Mercies" or "Teach Me Your Ways" in PCY.

Hallock, Peter/arr. Carl Crosier. "Psalm 25" in *The Ionian Psalter.* ION.

Hurd, Bob. "To You, O God, I Lift Up My Soul" in STP 2.

Mahnke, Allan. "Psalm 25" in *Seventeen Psalms for Cantor and Congregation.* CPH 97-6093.

Ogden, David. "Here I Am" in PS 3.

Wellicome, Paul. "Remember Your Mercy, Lord" in PS 1.

CHORAL

Busarow, Donald. "Lord, Keep Us Steadfast in Your Word." 2 pt mxd, kybd, inst.   CPH 98-2602.

Hampton, Keith. "Give Me Jesus." SATB, opt solo.   AFP 0800659554.

Hopson, Hal H. "A Lenten Walk." 2 pt mxd, org, opt solo, opt timp, hb.   AFP 080065448X.

Parker, Alice "Take Me to the Water." SAATB.   GIA G-4238.

Parker, Alice, arr. "We Will March Thro' the Valley." SSATB, solo.   GIA G-4242.

Pelz, Walter L. "Show Me Thy Ways." SATB, ob, gtr/kybd.   AFP 0800645421.

Wesley, Samuel Sebastian. "O Lord My God" in *The New Church Anthem Book.* SATB.   OXF 0193531097.

CHILDREN'S CHOIRS

Hobby, Robert. "Thy Holy Wings/I Lift My Soul." MSM 50-9453. U, fl, pno.

Powell, Robert. "A Lenten Prayer." CG CGA159. U, fl, org.

KEYBOARD/INSTRUMENTAL

Buxtehude, Dieterich. "Erhalt uns, Herr" in *Orgelwerke.* Org. Various editions.

Carlson, J. Bert. "Erhalt uns, Herr" in *Blessed Assurance: Hymn Preludes for Organ.* Org.   AFP 0800674774.

Sedio, Mark. "Thy Holy Wings" in *Dancing in the Light of God.* Pno.   AFP 0800656547.

Walcha, Helmut. "Ein feste Burg" in *A New Liturgical Year,* ed. John Ferguson. Org.   AFP 0800656717.

Webster, Richard. "Bred dina vida vingar" in *Augsburg Organ Library: Lent.* Org. AFP 0800658973.

HANDBELL

Edwards, Dan R. "Meditation." 2–3 oct. JEF MCGB220.

McFadden, Jane. "Bred dina vida vingar" in *Two More Swedish Melodies.* 3–4 oct, opt hc. AFP 0800657357.

Thompson, Martha Lynn. "Thy Holy Wings." 3–5 oct. ALF AP19005.

PRAISE ENSEMBLE

Haugen, Marty. "Tree of Life" (Lenten verses) in *Gather.* GIA.

Honoré, Jeffrey. "How Can I Keep from Singing." SATB, pno. CG CGA-567.

Joncas, Michael/arr. Mark Hayes. "On Eagle's Wings." SATB, acc. ALF 16104.

Lowry, Nancy. "Wellspring" in *Maranatha! Music Praise Chorus Book,* 3rd ed. MAR.

Makeever, Ray. "In the Water" in DH.

March 16, 2003

Second Sunday in Lent

INTRODUCTION

The readiness of Abraham and Sarah, and the eagerness of Jesus to do God's will are models for contemporary disciples in the church. Baptized into Christ's death and resurrection, we are called to live a distinctive style of life shaped by faith in God's mercy. As followers of Christ, we take up our cross and stand with all those who suffer in our midst. Our Lenten journey always takes us to the cross, the heart of God's love for the world.

PRAYER OF THE DAY

Eternal God, it is your glory always to have mercy. Bring back all who have erred and strayed from your ways; lead them again to embrace in faith the truth of your Word and to hold it fast; through Jesus Christ your Son our Lord, who lives and reigns with you and the Holy Spirit, one God, now and forever.

Wednesday, March 12

GREGORY THE GREAT, BISHOP OF ROME, 604

Gregory was born into a politically influential family. At one time he held political office and at another time he lived as a monk, all before he was elected to the papacy. Gregory's work was extensive. He influenced public worship through the establishment of a lectionary and prayers to correlate with the readings. He established a school to train church musicians, and Gregorian chant is named in his honor. He wrote a treatise underscoring what is required of a parish pastor serving a congregation. He sent missionaries to preach to the Anglo-Saxons who had invaded England. And at one time he organized distribution of grain during a shortage of food in Rome.

Gregory's life serves as an example of the link between liturgy and social justice. His Lenten hymn, "O Christ, our king, creator, Lord" (LBW 101) sings of God's grace flowing out from the cross to all creation.

VERSE

God so loved the world that he gave his only Son, so that everyone who believes in him may not perish but may have eternal life. (John 3:16)

READINGS

Genesis 17:1-7, 15-16

In today's reading, the writer connects the covenant made with Abraham and Sarah to the "everlasting" covenant made with Noah. The relationship between God and Abraham's descendants is as sure as the relationship between God and the seasons and times of the year. The name changes further emphasize the firmness of God's promise.

Psalm 22:22-30 (Psalm 22:23-31 [NRSV])

All the ends of the earth shall remember and turn to the LORD. (Ps. 22:26)

Romans 4:13-25

Paul is trying to persuade the Roman Christians that people are made right with God through faith rather than by works of the law. Abraham became the ancestor of God's chosen people not by keeping the law but by trusting God to keep his promises.

Mark 8:31-38

After Peter confesses his belief that Jesus is the Messiah, Jesus tells his disciples for the first time what is to come. Peter's response indicates that he does not yet understand the way of the cross that Jesus will travel.

COLOR Purple

THE PRAYERS

As we journey through this season of repentance and renewal, let us turn to God who mercifully gives us new life.
A BRIEF SILENCE.

God Almighty, the promises you give to us rest on your grace, not on our deeds. Like Abraham and Sarah, help us to trust in your word and believe in your faithfulness. Hear us, O God;
your mercy is great.

O God, you have given birth to a multitude of nations. Guide their leaders with peacemaking hearts and lead them always in honesty and justice. Hear us, O God;
your mercy is great.

Bless all who serve those who are unemployed or homeless. Strengthen those who care for the sick *(especially)*, that they might see your work in their lives. Hear us, O God;
your mercy is great.

Guide all who lead in the worship of this congregation—musicians and artists, lectors and ushers, assisting ministers and altar guilds—that by their ministry we will be enabled to set our minds on holy things. Hear us, O God;
your mercy is great.
HERE OTHER INTERCESSIONS MAY BE OFFERED.

Challenge us, O God, to see beyond ourselves and to know that we are surrounded always by a great cloud of witnesses, including *(names, and)* all our dearly departed. Hear us, O God;
your mercy is great.

Merciful God, hear our cry when we call to you; renew and uphold us with your Spirit, through Jesus Christ our Lord.
Amen

IMAGES FOR PREACHING

In last week's gospel reading we heard God make a promise to Noah, and now this week, we hear a promise made to Abraham. But we also hear the "promise" of Jesus that he must suffer, be rejected and disrespected, and then killed. It is a promise he makes to himself and to his followers. Peter obviously does not understand or does not hear the promise to rise again after three days, or else he would not have attempted to set him straight. Suffering, rejection, and death he clearly understands. Rising after death he clearly does not understand, and therefore he does not even question it. Maybe if this promise were made to someone in these times, he simply would ask for clarification of this *rising thing*. "Is this a medical procedure, or what?" one would ask.

Jesus lists the conditions of discipleship for us, and it seems the only thing that is a certainty is the promise that Jesus will undergo great suffering, be rejected, killed, and after three days rise. Jesus kept all his promises and now the conditions of discipleship for his followers mirror what Jesus himself had to endure—deny one's self, be rejected, lose one's life. The temptation here is to seek the crown of human glory rather than pursue the cross of Christ, but that false glory is the work of Satan. We hear the echoes of the temptations in the wilderness. And we hear another promise: that those ashamed of Jesus and his words will be treated with equal shame when he comes in glory.

WORSHIP MATTERS

Lent is a time of gestation. Something is being born among us—a promise, a new hope, a renewed commitment.

For Abraham and Sarah the promise was literally a time of gestation—offspring to be born, generations to follow, an everlasting covenant.

As worship planners and leaders, it is good for us every so often to ask the question, "What is being born among us?" or "How are we keeping God's promises alive and furthering them in what we do and say in our public worship?" Take some time during this Lenten season in your parish to assess your worship life. Do we speak the whole language of covenant and promise in this place? Are the primary bearers of covenant—word and sacrament—visible and accessible in our congregation? How are we passing on God's covenant to those who will follow us in this place?

LET THE CHILDREN COME

God made a covenant with Abraham and Sarah that from them would come great nations. They are given new names as a sign of that promise. In baptism parents and sponsors (and the congregation) promise to bring children to worship and to teach them the Ten Commandments, the creed, and the Lord's Prayer, which help them grow in their faith. Children can recognize and honor the elders—especially those who help teach them about their faith—by sending a note of thanks for their example and support.

HYMNS FOR WORSHIP

GATHERING

How firm a foundation   LBW 507
Our Father, we have wandered   WOV 733

HYMN OF THE DAY

I want Jesus to walk with me   WOV 660, TFF 66

ALTERNATE HYMN OF THE DAY

"Come, follow me," the Savior spake   LBW 455
Lead me, guide me   W&P 84, TFF 70

COMMUNION

Let us ever walk with Jesus   LBW 487
As the sun with longer journey   WOV 655
Come and taste   W&P 30

SENDING

O God, my faithful God   LBW 504
All my hope on God is founded   WOV 782
Step by step   W&P 132

ADDITIONAL HYMNS AND SONGS

Bread for the journey   GS2 40
All to Jesus I surrender   TFF 235
Father, I adore you   W&P 37
Some folk would rather have houses   TFF 236

MUSIC FOR THE DAY

PSALMODY

Brugh, Lorraine. PW B.
Haugen, Marty. "Psalm 22: My God, My God" in GC.
Harbor, Rawn. "My God, My God." TFF 2.
Hopson, Hal H. "Psalm 22" in Eighteen Psalms for the Church Year.
U/SATB.   HOP HH3941.

Manion, Tim. "My God, My God" in STP 1.
Sarum plainsong. "Lord, Why Have You Forsaken Me" in PH.
Schiavone, John. "My God, My God" in STP 3.
Smith, Alan. "My God, My God" in PS 2.

CHORAL

Distler, Hugo. "A Lamb Goes Uncomplaining Forth" in Chantry Choirbook. SATB.   AFP 0800657772.
Farrant, Richard. "Lord, for Thy Tender Mercy's Sake" in The New Church Anthem Book. SATB.   OXF 0193531097.
Gehring, Philip. "The God of Abraham Praise." SATB, org, 2 tpt.   MSM 50-7008.
Neswick, Bruce. "Hearken to My Voice, O Lord" in The Augsburg Choirbook. 2 pt, kybd.   AFP 0800656784.
Schalk, Carl. "All the Ends of the Earth." SATB, org.   CPH 98-3546.
Smith, Lani. "Take Up Your Cross." SATB, kybd.   LOR 1783L.
Trinkley, Bruce. "I Want Jesus to Walk with Me." SATB, pno.   AFP 0800657051.

CHILDREN'S CHOIRS

Bell, John L. "The Love of God Comes Close." U, kybd.   GIA G5049.
Hassell, Michael. "Is There Anybody Here Who Loves My Jesus?" 2 pt, kybd.   AFP 0800674596.
Sleeth, Natalie. "Part of the Plan" from Sunday Songbook. U/opt div.   HIN HMB-102.

KEYBOARD/INSTRUMENTAL

Billingham, Richard. "Sojourner" in Seven Reflections on African American Spirituals. Org.   AFP 0800656229.
Cherwien, David. "Sojourner" in Groundings: Five New Organ Settings. Org.   AFP 0800659805.
Glick, Sara. "Sojourner" in Piano Arrangements for Worship. Pno, opt perc, inst.   AFP 0800658809.
Mann, Adrian. "Sojourner" in Arise and Rejoice! Kybd, C/B-flat inst.   AFP 0800674960.
Manz, Paul. "Lord, Whose Love in Humble Service" in Three Hymns for Flute, Oboe and Organ. Fl, ob, org.   MSM 20-871.
Peeters, Flor. "Adagio" in Suite Modale. op. 43. Org.   LEM.

HANDBELL

McFadden, Jane. "Day by Day." Two More Swedish Melodies. 3–4 oct, opt 2–4 oct, hc.   AFP 0800657357.
Moklebust, Cathy. "Kyrie." 2–4 oct.   AFP 0800647777.
Zabel, Albert. "Adagio in G Minor." 5 oct, org.   JEF MSPHP-5395.

143

PRAISE ENSEMBLE

Boltz, Ray. "Take Up Your Cross" in *The Ray Boltz Anthology*. Diadem Music.

Goebel-Komala, Felix. "Psalm of Hope." SATB, cant, cong, kybd, gtr, timp. GIA G-4403.

Paris, Twila/arr. Torrans. "We Bow Down." SAB, kybd. Songpower ZJP7006.

Rodgers, Dawn and Eric Wyse. "Wonderful, Merciful Savior" in *Songs for Praise and Worship*. WRD.

Monday, March 17

PATRICK, BISHOP, MISSIONARY TO IRELAND, 461

At sixteen, Patrick was kidnapped by Irish pirates and sold into slavery in Ireland. He himself admitted that up to this point he cared little for God. He escaped after six years, returned to his family in southwest Britain, and began to prepare for ordained ministry. He later returned to Ireland, this time to serve as a bishop and missionary. He made his base in the north of Ireland and from there made many missionary journeys with much success. In his autobiography he denounced the slave trade, perhaps from his own experience as a slave.

Patrick's famous baptismal hymn to the Trinity "I bind unto myself today" (LBW 188) can be used as a meditation on Lent's call to return to our baptism.

Wednesday, March 19

JOSEPH, GUARDIAN OF OUR LORD

The gospels are silent about much of Joseph's life. We know that he was a carpenter or builder by trade. The Gospel of Luke shows him acting in accordance with both civil and religious law by returning to Bethlehem for the census and by presenting the child Jesus in the temple on the fortieth day after his birth. The Gospel of Matthew tells of Joseph's trust in God who led him through visionary dreams. Because Joseph is not mentioned after the story of a young Jesus teaching in the temple, it is assumed that he died before Jesus reached adulthood.

Congregations might consider a Sicilian tradition to commemorate Joseph that combines the three Lenten disciplines of fasting, almsgiving, and prayer. The poor are invited to a festive buffet called "St. Joseph's Table." Lenten prayers and songs interrupt the course of the meal. What other ways can a congregation's almsgiving and charity be increased during Lent?

Saturday, March 22

JONATHAN EDWARDS, TEACHER, MISSIONARY TO THE AMERICAN INDIANS, 1758

Edwards was a minister in Connecticut and has been described as the greatest of the New England Puritan preachers. One of Edwards's most notable sermons found its way into contemporary anthologies of literature. In this sermon, "Sinners in the hands of an angry God," he spoke at length about hell. Throughout the rest of his works and his preaching, however, he had more to say about God's love than God's wrath. His personal experience of conversion came when he felt overwhelmed with a sense of God's majesty and grandeur rather than a fear of hell. Edwards served a Puritan congregation, where he believed that only those who had been fully converted ought to receive communion; his congregation thought otherwise. Edwards left that congregation and carried out mission work among the Housatonic Indians of Massachusetts. He became president of the College of New Jersey, later to be known as Princeton.

March 23, 2003

Third Sunday in Lent

INTRODUCTION

In our society, even churches can become like market-places, and congregations can be characterized chiefly as consumers. The drive to satisfy every taste and opinion can distract the church from its center: Jesus Christ among us in the regular celebration of word and sacrament. In the word of God and the eucharistic meal, the temple of Christ's body is strengthened for its witness in daily life.

PRAYER OF THE DAY

Eternal Lord, your kingdom has broken into our troubled world through the life, death, and resurrection of your Son. Help us to hear your Word and obey it, so that we become instruments of your redeeming love; through your Son, Jesus Christ our Lord, who lives and reigns with you and the Holy Spirit, one God, now and forever.

VERSE

Jesus humbled himself and became obedient to the point of death—even death on a cross. (Phil. 2:8)

READINGS

Exodus 20:1-17

This covenant is the third one the church hears in this cycle of readings. After escaping from slavery, the Israelites come to Mount Sinai where God instructs them how to live together in community. The Ten Commandments recognize that God is the creator of all things. Flowing from God, the life of the community flourishes when marked by the basic building blocks recounted in today's reading: honesty, trust, fidelity, and respect for life, family, and property.

Psalm 19

The commandment of the LORD gives light to the eyes. (Ps. 19:8)

1 Corinthians 1:18-25

Paul's preaching about the salvation God offers through the cross was met with suspicion. How can victory come out of death? Some thought this message was nonsense. But Paul announces that God's wisdom overturns common expectations about who God is and where God intends to be.

John 2:13-22

Jesus attacks the commercialization of religion by driving merchants out of the temple. When challenged, he responds mysteriously, with the first prediction of his own death and resurrection. In the midst of a seemingly stable religious center, Jesus suggests that the center itself has changed.

COLOR Purple

THE PRAYERS

As we journey through this season of repentance and renewal, let us turn to God who mercifully gives us new life.
A BRIEF SILENCE.
We pray that the whole church on earth would be united in its love for the commands of God and in its embrace of the whole creation. Hear us, O God;
your mercy is great.
We pray that the wisdom of the world will be overtaken by God's foolishness, and that human strength will be overshadowed by God's weakness. Hear us, O God;
your mercy is great.
We pray for those suffering from addictions and all who are ill *(especially)*, that destructive life patterns and disease will be driven out by the healing presence of Christ. Hear us, O God;
your mercy is great.
We pray for all who are entering the community of faith through baptism, that their journey will bring them to the font of forgiveness and to the table of truth. Hear us, O God;
your mercy is great.
HERE OTHER INTERCESSIONS MAY BE OFFERED.
We pray in thanksgiving for *(names, and all)* the faithful departed, whose lives continue to bear witness to the light of Christ in which they now abide eternally. Hear us, O God;
your mercy is great.
Merciful God, hear our cry when we call to you; renew and uphold us with your Spirit, through Jesus Christ our Lord.
Amen

145

IMAGES FOR PREACHING

People hear what they want to hear. And unless corrected, they distort it more and more as time and events progress. Jesus of Nazareth was, of course, more than just a temple reformer. But in today's gospel, that was what he was trying to do: not undercut Judaism, certainly not bring down the temple, just bring its policies back in line with what they should have been. He said it himself, "I have not come to abolish the law and the prophets." And whether this reformation was misunderstood or understood and contested, Jesus' testimony about his identity and power was misunderstood as a sort of terrorist threat to destroy the temple, which later was used against him in his trial before Pilate. His own disciples did not remember what he said or understand its meaning until after he was raised from the dead.

For those who believe, anything we say can be used against Jesus by those who are not believers. We are called to invite people to share with us in a relationship with Christ, and the gospel of Jesus' death is good news to those who believe. But though the same words are spoken, those who do not accept Jesus as the Christ hear a different message. St. Paul testifies to it, "The message about the cross is foolishness to those who are perishing...." It is only through the gift of faith, created by the Holy Spirit though the hearing of the word, that the killing letter becomes the saving words. Only through the drinking in of the Spirit can one be empowered for transformation from resistance into enlightenment. It is up to us, the ones in Christ, to lead them to that water.

WORSHIP MATTERS

Most of us who lead public worship are uncomfortable with too much quiet time. If a pause occurs during the worship service, it is only because it is marked as such in the bulletin or because someone forgot where he or she was in the service.

But today's first reading reminds us to keep sabbath and to keep it holy. We need to clean up and clear away much of the busy-ness and debris that works its way into our worship life. Worship is meant to have a rhythm to it. Part of that rhythm includes significant space within the liturgy for silence and reflection.

LET THE CHILDREN COME

Today the Ten Commandments form part of the first reading. Parents and sponsors in baptism promise to teach children the commandments. Now is a good time to not only repeat them in the Old Testament but to reflect on their meaning as spelled out in Luther's Small Catechism. Children like rules, and because of their stage of development they often respond more easily to rules than to more complex ethical judgments. In a society that often ridicules the law and rules as foolishness it is important to reflect on the meaning and the goodness of the "rules" God gave Moses.

HYMNS FOR WORSHIP
GATHERING

Oh, for a thousand tongues to sing   LBW 559

Christ is made the sure foundation   WOV 747

HYMN OF THE DAY

God of grace and God of glory   LBW 415

ALTERNATE HYMN OF THE DAY

Lord Christ, when first you came to earth   LBW 421

God, the sculptor of the mountains   TFF 222

COMMUNION

Thee we adore, O hidden Savior   LBW 199

You satisfy the hungry heart   WOV 711

SENDING

I love your kingdom, Lord   LBW 368

The Spirit sends us forth to serve   WOV 723

Lead me, guide me   W&P 84, TFF 70

ADDITIONAL HYMNS AND SONGS

God, you have given us power   H82 584

How deep the silence of the soul   NCH 509

Jesus, keep me near the cross   TFF 73

We are called   W&P 147

When I survey the wondrous cross   TFF 79

MUSIC FOR THE DAY
PSALMODY

Bell, John L. "May the Words of My Mouth" in *Psalms of Patience, Protest and Praise.* U.   Iona/GIA G-4047.

Brugh, Lorraine.   PW B.

Dohms, Ann Celeen. *Sing Out! A Children's Psalter.* U/kybd. WLP/S. Paluch Co.

Hruby, Dolores. *Seasonal Psalms for Children.*   WLP 7102.

Inwood, Paul. "You, Lord, Have the Message" in STP 2.

Joncas, Michael. "Lord, You Have the Words" in STP I.

Ogden, David. "You, Lord, Have the Message of Eternal Life" in PS 2.

CHORAL

Bertalot, John. "Amazing Grace." SATB, org.   AFP 0800649141. Also in *The Augsburg Choirbook*.   AFP 0800656784.

Fleming, Larry. "Give Me Jesus." SATB.   AFP 0800645278. Also in *The Augsburg Choirbook*.   AFP 0800656784.

Kosche, Kenneth. "Come, Let Us Fix Our Eyes on Jesus." 2 pt, kybd, opt C inst, opt vc/bsn.   CPH 98-3198. Inst pts.   98-3231

Schalk, Carl. "Lord, It Belongs Not to My Care." SATB.   AFP 0800645901.

Schütz, Heinrich. "Praise to You, Lord Jesus" in *Chantry Choirbook*. SATB.   AFP 0800657772.

Shute, Linda Cable. "You Satisfy the Hungry Heart." SATB, org.   AFP 0800674693.

Willcocks, Jonathan. "O Holy Jesus." SATB, kybd.   SMP 10/1937S.

CHILDREN'S CHOIRS

Bach, J. S./arr. Michael Burkhardt. "The Heavens Declare Thy Glory." U, 2 trbl inst, opt bass inst.   MSM 50-7503.

Erickson, John. "We Come with Joy." U, org.   CG CGA554.

Young, Jeremy. "The Seed Song." 2 pt, kybd.   AFP 0800674685.

KEYBOARD/INSTRUMENTAL

Cherwien, David. "Toccata on 'In the Cross of Christ I Glory'" in *Augsburg Organ Library: Lent*. Org.   AFP 0800658973.

Organ, Anne Krentz. "Cwm Rhondda" in *Piano Reflections for the Church Year*. Pno.   AFP 080067474X.

Peeters, Flor. "Koraal" in *Suite Modale*, op. 43. Org.   LEM 23673 HL.

HANDBELL

Kinyon, Barbara. "Two Meditations on the Cross." 2–3 oct.   JEF MHP1545.

McChesney, Kevin. "Jesus, Keep Me Near the Cross." 3 oct, opt hc.   JEF JHS9251.

Nelson, Susan T. "Elegy." 3 oct, opt sop sax, solo ringer/inst, pno.   AFP 080065434X.

PRAISE ENSEMBLE

Altrogge, Mark. "You Are My God" in *Hosanna! Music Songbook 7*.   INT.

Harris, Ron. "On Our Side" in *Hosanna! Music Songbook 7*.   INT.

Klein, Laurie/arr. Jack Schrader. "I Love You, Lord." SATB, pno.   HOP GC936.

Kreutz, Robert E./arr. John Ferguson. "Gift of Finest Wheat." SATB, cong, org.   GIA G-3089.

Starke, Stephen P. "Greet the Rising Sun" in *Hymnal Supplement 98*. CPH.

Monday, March 24

OSCAR ARNULFO ROMERO,
BISHOP OF EL SALVADOR, MARTYR, 1980

Romero is remembered for his advocacy on behalf of the poor in El Salvador, though it was not a characteristic of his early priesthood. After being appointed as bishop he preached against the political repression in his country. He and other priests and church workers were considered traitors for their bold stand for justice, especially defending the rights of the poor. After several years of threats to his life, Romero was assassinated while presiding at the eucharist. During the 1980s thousands died in El Salvador during political unrest.

Romero is remembered as a martyr who gave his life on behalf of the powerless in his country. Our Lenten journey of conversion calls us to be bold in our witness to Christ, to work on behalf of the powerless, and speak on behalf of justice and equality for all people created in the image of God.

Tuesday, March 25

THE ANNUNCIATION OF OUR LORD

Nine months before Christmas we celebrate the annunciation. In Luke we hear how the angel Gabriel announced to Mary that she would give birth to the Son of God and she responded, "Here am I, the servant of the Lord." Ancient scholars believed that March 25 was also the day on which creation began, and was the date of Jesus' death on the cross. Thus from the sixth to eighth centuries, March 25 was observed as New Year's Day in much of Christian Europe.

Set within Lent, Mary's openness to the will of God is an example of faithful discipleship and leads us to consider the work of God in our own lives. Consider singing "The angel Gabriel" (WOV 632) or, as a canticle after communion, sing a setting of the Magnificat, such as the paraphrase "My soul proclaims your greatness" (WOV 730).

147

Saturday, March 29

HANS NIELSEN HAUGE,
RENEWER OF THE CHURCH, 1824

Hans Nielsen Hauge was a layperson who began preaching about "the living faith" in Norway and Denmark after a mystical experience that he believed called him to share the assurance of salvation with others. At the time, itinerant preaching and religious gatherings held without the supervision of a pastor were illegal, and Hauge was arrested several times. He also faced great personal suffering: his first wife died and three of his four children died in infancy.

Some might remember Hauge during Lent by singing the Norwegian hymn "My heart is longing" (LBW 326), with its devotional response to the death of Christ.

March 30, 2003

Fourth Sunday in Lent

INTRODUCTION

In today's gospel reading, Jesus compares himself to the serpent in the wilderness. He is lifted up on the cross so that all who hold to him will be healed. God sent the Son, not to condemn, but to save the world. We who have heard the words of love and mercy in today's scriptures go forth to speak with forgiveness rather than condemnation. Our baptism calls us to a life of good works, not to point to ourselves but to the immeasurable riches of God's grace made known to all the world in Christ our Lord.

PRAYER OF THE DAY

God of all mercy, by your power to heal and to forgive, graciously cleanse us from all sin and make us strong; through your Son, Jesus Christ our Lord, who lives and reigns with you and the Holy Spirit, one God, now and forever.

VERSE

Just as Moses lifted up the serpent in the wilderness, so must the Son of Man be lifted up, that whoever believes in him may have eternal life. (John 3:14-15)

READINGS

Numbers 21:4-9

Throughout the Hebrew scriptures, the time of Israel's wandering in the desert is seen as a period of testing. Though God delivers the people from slavery and provides for all their needs on the journey, they whine and grumble. They fail to see the gift of salvation in the exodus. Yet God's anger is not the final word. God continues to lead the people toward the land promised to their ancestors.

Psalm 107:1-3, 17-22

The LORD delivered them from their distress. (Ps. 107:19)

Ephesians 2:1-10

God raised us up to new life while we yet belonged to powers of evil. If such was our past, we now live with Christ and will spend eternity discovering the breadth of God's goodness.

John 3:14-21

To explain the salvation of God to the religious leader Nicodemus, Jesus refers to the scripture passage quoted in today's first reading. Just as those who looked upon the bronze serpent were healed, so people will be saved when they behold Christ lifted up on the cross.

COLOR Purple

THE PRAYERS

As we journey through this season of repentance and renewal, let us turn to God who mercifully gives us new life.
A BRIEF SILENCE.

Let us pray for patience on our journey through these Lenten forty days. Give strength to all servants of the church who lead people on the way of the cross. Hear us, O God;
your mercy is great.

148

Let us pray for a way of life centered in works of justice and peace for people of all races and nationalities. Hear us, O God;

your mercy is great.

Let us pray for farmers and all who prepare the soil for planting, that the seeds they sow may lead to a bountiful harvest. Hear us, O God;

your mercy is great.

Let us pray for those who are sick, for those who have suffered natural disasters, and for all who cry out to you (*especially*). Hear us, O God;

your mercy is great.

Let us pray for all preparing to affirm their faith, for those preparing for baptism and communion, and for all who seek to deepen their spiritual awareness, that their faith would be strengthened in this season. Hear us, O God;

your mercy is great.

HERE OTHER INTERCESSIONS MAY BE OFFERED.

Let us pray in thanksgiving for the members of this congregation who have died, and all the blessed dead who now live in the light of your eternal love. Hear us, O God;

your mercy is great.

Merciful God, hear our cry when we call to you; renew and uphold us with your Spirit, through Jesus Christ our Lord.

Amen

IMAGES FOR PREACHING

All three readings—the account of the serpent in the wilderness from Numbers, Jesus' recounting of that account, and Paul's proclamation to the Ephesians—work hand in hand to provide clear images of and references to God's grace and resurrection. The cross, like the serpent, has the power to destroy, yet paradoxically it also has the power to restore. The same judge who holds the authority to sentence us to death after death because of who we are, trespassers and evildoers, has the mercy to grant us life after life because of unconditional love for us through our faith in Christ. It is the same document that can be read two different ways. The lens through which the pronouncement is read is faith. Life is pronounced, for those who believe and thereby accept God's grace; death, for those who do not believe and cannot accept it.

Why would one choose death over life? Because the prince of this world and the ways of this world are seductive and appear to provide a shortcut, an easier route than the way that leads to Calvary. We know that temptation, and as we traverse desolate valleys on our journey, scripture reminds us of others in salvation history who traveled in the wilderness and judgment they faced in their rebellion.

But God has always been rich in mercy, even before the gift of Jesus Christ. And God continues to be merciful, because whoever believes in Jesus in whatever time and in whatever place will not be condemned, but will have eternal life. Psalm 107 responds to this good news with a loud Amen: "Give thanks to the LORD, for he is good, and his mercy endures forever."

WORSHIP MATTERS

How do those who lead worship in your parish prepare for their task? Many of us, lay and clergy, often run from place to place on Sunday mornings. From adult education class to conversations in the hallway to last-minute instructions to the altar guild, we are often just catching our breath before launching into the liturgy.

But we might set a different kind of tone and example for our public prayer life. Encourage one another to pray before leading worship. Gather in a quiet spot for prayer. Ask for God's blessing upon the lector, the preacher, the cantor, the choir, the ushers, the greeters, the altar guild, the acolytes, the organist, and all those who participate in the life of worship. As today's second reading reminds us, we are not saved, not even made better in God's eyes by all of our "running around" and all the things we do to make worship life "perfect." Even the leaders of the Sunday morning assembly are saved by grace, "not the results of works."

LET THE CHILDREN COME

Jesus Christ was lifted up on the cross, becoming our savior and redeemer. Through his death on the cross we receive eternal life. A cross should be prominently displayed in the sanctuary where everyone can see it. Children can be taught to bow as the cross passes in procession or as they approach the altar. They can be taught to make the sign of the cross during prayer to remind them that they were claimed by Christ in their baptism.

149

HYMNS FOR WORSHIP

GATHERING

Give to our God immortal praise!   LBW 520
The Word of God is source and seed   WOV 658

HYMN OF THE DAY

What wondrous love is this   LBW 385

ALTERNATE HYMN OF THE DAY

God loved the world   CS 33, LBW 292
By grace we have been saved   W&P 25

COMMUNION

Come, my way, my truth, my life   LBW 513
Eat this bread   WOV 709, TFF 125

SENDING

My God, how wonderful thou art   LBW 524
Bind us together   WOV 748, TFF 217, W&P 18

150

ADDITIONAL HYMNS AND SONGS

How can we sinners know   UMH 372
O love that casts out fear   H82 700
That priceless grace   TFF 68
There is a Redeemer   W&P 140

MUSIC FOR THE DAY

PSALMODY

Brugh, Lorraine.   PW B.
Hopson, Hal H.   TP.
Stewart, Roy James. "Give Thanks to the Lord" in *Choral Refrains from Psalms for the Church Year*, vol. 5.   GIA G-3746-A.

CHORAL

Christiansen, Paul. "Wondrous Love." SATB.   AFP 0800652665.
Distler, Hugo. "For God So Loved the World" in *Chantry Choirbook*. SAB.   AFP 0800657772.
Martinson, Joel. "God So Loved the World." SA, org.   CPH 98-3098.
Scholz, Robert. "What Wondrous Love." SATB, div.   MSM 50-9017.
Schulz-Widmar, Russell. "We Are Not Our Own." SATB.   AFP 0800657810.
Traditional/arr. Bob Chilcott. "Steal Away." SATB.   OXF X403.

CHILDREN'S CHOIRS

Carter, John/arr. Mary K. Beall. "How Excellent Is Your Name." 2 pt, kybd.   AFP 0800674553.

Johnson, Ralph. "As Moses Lifted Up." U, fl, org.   CG CGA440.
Shafferman, Jean Anne. "A Lenten Lesson." U/2 pt, opt hb, kybd.   ALF 4216.

KEYBOARD/INSTRUMENTAL

Alain, Jehan. "Choral Dorien" in *Augsburg Organ Library: Lent*. Org.   AFP 0800658973.
Cotter, Jeanne. "What Wondrous Love Is This" in *After the Rain*. Pno.   GIA G-3390.
Nicholson, Paul. "Wondrous Love." Org, tpt.   AFP 0800654099.
Pinkston, Daniel S. "Wondrous Love" in *Three Hymns for Clarinet and Piano*. Cl, pno.   MSM 20-761.
Thomas, David Evan. "Wondrous Love" in *Early American Tunes for Organ*. Org.   AFP 0800674804.

HANDBELL

Honoré, Jeffrey. "Amazing Grace." 3–5 oct.   CPH 97-6915.
McChesney, Kevin. "Beach Spring." 2–3 oct.   AFP 080065885X.

PRAISE ENSEMBLE

Altrogge, Mark. "How Great Is Your Love" in *Hosanna! Music Book* 7. INT.
Lloyd, Kit. "John 3:16" in *Praise Chorus Book*.   MAR 3100002377.
Lojeski, Ed. "Amazing Grace." SATB, pno, gtr, perc.   HAL 08300531.
Mohr, Jon and Randall Dennis. "More Than Anything" in *Point of Grace Songbook*. 3 pt, kybd.   WRD 3010294492.

Monday, March 31

JOHN DONNE, PRIEST, 1631

This priest of the Church of England is commemorated for his poetry and spiritual writing. Most of his poetry was written before his ordination and is sacred and secular, intellectual and sensuous. He saw in his wife Anne—a marriage that resulted in his imprisonment—glimpses of the glory of God and a human revelation of divine love. In 1615 he was ordained and seven years later he was named Dean of St. Paul's Cathedral in London. By that time his reputation as a preacher was firmly in place.

In his poem, "Good Friday, 1613. Riding westward" he speaks of Jesus' death on the cross: "Who sees God's face, that is self life, must die; What a death were it then to see God die?"

Friday, April 4

BENEDICT THE AFRICAN, CONFESSOR, 1589

Born a slave on the island of Sicily, Benedict first lived as a hermit and labored as a plowman after he was freed. When the bishop of Rome ordered all hermits to attach themselves to a religious community, Benedict joined the Franciscans where he served as a cook. Although he was illiterate, his fame as a confessor brought many visitors to the humble and holy cook, and he was eventually named superior of the community. A patron saint of African Americans, Benedict is remembered for his patience and understanding when confronted with racial prejudice and taunts.

Use the story of Benedict's ministry as a confessor to revisit Martin Luther's notion of the spiritual importance of mutual consolation of one another.

April 6, 2003

Fifth Sunday in Lent

INTRODUCTION

In today's gospel reading, Jesus speaks of grain dying in the earth as an image of his death and resurrection. Christ is the seed fallen to earth that yields the harvest of life, health, and salvation. Christ is the one who accompanies us in our baptismal death and raises us to life with him. Christ is the grain of wheat that we share in the breaking of the bread. Christ's Spirit strengthens us in lives of fruitful service to those who hunger and thirst for life.

Two great artists whose works often opened up churchly themes are commemorated today: Albrecht Dürer, who died April 6, 1528, and Michelangelo Buonarroti (known generally by his given name), who died in 1564.

PRAYER OF THE DAY

Almighty God, our redeemer, in our weakness we have failed to be your messengers of forgiveness and hope in the world. Renew us by your Holy Spirit, that we may follow your commands and proclaim your reign of love; through your Son, Jesus Christ our Lord, who lives and reigns with you and the Holy Spirit, one God, now and forever.

VERSE

The Son of Man came not to be served but to serve, and to give his life a ransom for many. (Mark 10:45)

READINGS

Jeremiah 31:31-34

The Judeans in Babylon blamed their exile on their ancestors who had broken the covenant established at Sinai. Here the prophet looks to a day when the people can no longer make such a complaint. There will be no need to teach the law because God will write the holy law in their hearts.

Psalm 51:1-13 (Psalm 51:1-12 [NRSV])

Create in me a clean heart, O God. (Ps. 51:11)

or Psalm 119:9-16

I treasure your promise in my heart. (Ps. 119:11)

Hebrews 5:5-10

The Bible often speaks of Jesus as the "lamb of God" who takes away the sin of the world. This reading from Hebrews expands upon this image with another: Jesus is also the high priest whose suffering became the gracious gift of salvation.

John 12:20-33

Jesus entered Jerusalem for the last time to celebrate the Passover festival. Here Jesus' words about seeds planted in the ground turn the disaster of his death into the promise of a harvest in which everyone will be gathered.

COLOR Purple

THE PRAYERS

As we journey through this season of repentance and renewal, let us turn to God who mercifully gives us new life.

151

A BRIEF SILENCE.

God of love, give us faith that we may hold ever tighter to you even as we loosen our grip on the comforts and securities of this world, that at the end, your Son may draw us to himself. Hear us, O God;
your mercy is great.

God of eternal beckoning, may the world and all its inhabitants be brought into your open arms of grace and to abundant life. Hear us, O God;
your mercy is great.

God of healing, may those who are sick and distressed be given a glimpse of your mercy *(especially)*, that they may find you in the midst of their pain and hardship. Hear us, O God;
your mercy is great.

God of gathering, you promise to be with us wherever two or three come together. Watch over the ministry of this congregation as we seek to be faithful in this community. Hear us, O God;
your mercy is great.

HERE OTHER INTERCESSIONS MAY BE OFFERED.

God of all time, you hold your servants Albrecht Dürer and Michelangelo Buonarroti, together with all our departed brothers and sisters, in your eternal safekeeping. Grant that we may all one day awaken to see you face to face. Hear us, O God;
your mercy is great.

Merciful God, hear our cry when we call to you; renew and uphold us with your Spirit, through Jesus Christ our Lord.
Amen

IMAGES FOR PREACHING

When the unbelievers come to faith, you *know* the kingdom is at hand. With every conversion to Christianity, with every baptism into the body of Christ, with each new reception into the Lord's family, Jesus is glorified; not our congregations, not our pastors, not even our denomination, but Jesus is glorified. In this world, during Lent and any other time of the year when it is so hard to be faithful to what Christ would have us do, Jesus is glorified when we resist the temptation to hate and perpetuate injustice. We see signs of the kingdom breaking in when peoples who decades ago would not live within the same municipal boundaries struggle to understand one another through Bible study and worship.

Jesus was lifted up not as a politician, but as sacrifice for sin and a model of the godly life. With the Gentiles seeking him out, it is time to move into the next phase of his incarnation—his passion—so that even more may come to believe, and subsequently have life.

As this chapter in our well-loved book ends and leads us to Holy Week and the Three Days, we hear Jesus restating his conditions for following him, and we are reminded that we *must* follow him. For lectionary purposes, these are Jesus' last words to us before he faces trial and death. They are, for many, his last words before the passion—the last thing some will hear him say because they will desert him before he is crucified. The last words of a loved one are powerful words. They shape our lives after that person has left us. We *must* follow so that others may follow, and in that Jesus is glorified.

WORSHIP MATTERS

The word *lent* comes from a word that literally means "spring." This fifth Sunday in Lent is the first Sunday in April, and for those of us in the Northern Hemisphere, if spring is not already upon us, there should at least be some hints of it in the air. But in the church we will still be trying to maintain some Lenten decorum. T. S. Eliot writes in *The Wasteland* about April being the cruelest month of all with memory and desire stirring our dull roots. Keeping Lent becomes more difficult as winter loses its grip on us.

But keep the fast. It is these months when, as Eliot reminds us, deep memories are stirred and we need to be connected to the abiding things of life all the more.

LET THE CHILDREN COME

The seed that dies brings new life. It's spring and most areas show signs of new life: trees budding, flowers growing and blooming. Bring some of the signs of new green life into the sanctuary. (Save the flowers for Easter.) Plants need water, sun and warmth to grow. To grow spiritually we need the baptismal water, the light of the risen Christ, and the warmth of the Holy Spirit.

Remind parents that next Sunday is the start of the holiest week of the church season, the basis for our faith. To begin to understand the joy of the resurrection it is important for children to walk to Calvary and participate in the events of the week.

152

HYMNS FOR WORSHIP

GATHERING

Now the green blade rises   LBW 148
Restore in us, O God   WOV 662

HYMN OF THE DAY

The Word of God is source and seed   WOV 658

ALTERNATE HYMN OF THE DAY

My faith looks up to thee   LBW 479
Amazing love   W&P 8

COMMUNION

My heart is longing to praise my Savior   LBW 326
As the grains of wheat   WOV 705
Seed, scattered and sown   W&P 121

SENDING

We sing the praise of him who died   LBW 344
O Christ the same   WOV 778
Step by step   W&P 132

ADDITIONAL HYMNS AND SONGS

I shall walk in the presence of God   GS2 26
Rich in promise   OBS 108
Lead us, heavenly Father   H82 559
How to reach the masses   TFF 227
Create in me a clean heart   W&P

MUSIC FOR THE DAY

PSALMODY

Brugh, Lorraine.   PW B.
Cooney, Rory. "Psalm 119: Happy Are Those Who Follow" in GC. U.
Hallock, Peter/arr. Carl Crosier. "Psalm 119" in *The Ionian Psalter*.
    ION.
Walker, Christopher. "Teach Me, O God" in PS 3.
Webb, Richard. "Thy Word."   W&P 143.

CHORAL

Albrecht, Mark. "Lamb of God." SATB, pno.   AFP 6000001290.
Bach, J. S. "Jesus, My Sweet Pleasure" in *Bach for All Seasons*. SATB,
    kybd.   AFP 080065854X.
Christiansen, F. Melius. "Lamb of God." SATB.   AFP 0800652592.
Hogan, Moses, arr. "Lord, I Want to Be a Christian." SATB.
    HAL 08703140.

Joncas, Michael. "Be Merciful, O Lord." SAB/U, kybd, opt 2 C inst,
    cong.   GIA G-3433.
Wesley, Samuel Sebastian. "Wash Me Thoroughly" in *The New Church
    Anthem Book*.   OXF 0193531097.

CHILDREN'S CHOIRS

How, Martin. "Lenten Litany." U, opt solos, kybd.   B&H 6080.
Marshall, Jane. "Dear Lord, Lead Me Day by Day." U, kybd, opt fl.
    CG CGA637.
Young, Jeremy. "The Seed Song." U, opt 2 pt, kybd, opt gtr.
    AFP 0800674685.

KEYBOARD/INSTRUMENTAL

Albrecht, Mark. "Sweet Hour of Prayer" in *Two on a Bench, vol. 2*. Pno
    duet.   AFP 0800674731.
Gervais, Pam. "Sweet Hour of Prayer" in *It Is Well with My Soul*. Pno.
    AFP 0800674766.
Hailstork, Adolphus. "Adagio and Fugue in F Minor." Org.
    MSM 10-915.
Osterland, Karl. "Gaudeamus Domino" in *Lift One Voice*. Org.
    AFP 0800659007.
Petersen, Lynn L. "I Want Jesus to Walk with Me" in *Spiritual Sounds
    for Trombone and Organ*. Tbn, org.   CPH 97- 6887.

HANDBELL

Lohr, A. "Jesus, the Very Thought of Thee." 3–5 oct.
    JEF MSF089391.
McFadden, Jane. "The Londonderry Air" (text, "O Christ, the
    Same"). 2–3 oct, opt inst/hc.   AFP 0800656296.
Young, Philip M. "There Is a Balm in Gilead." 3–4 oct.
    AFP 0800653572.

PRAISE ENSEMBLE

Altrogge, Mark. "Thank You for the Cross" in *Hosanna! Music Book*.
    INT.
Espinosa, Eddie and Bob Kilpatrick/arr. John Wilson. "Change My
    Heart/Lord, Be Glorified." SATB, kybd.   HOP GC992.
Grant, Amy/arr. Michael Smith. "Thy Word."   W&P 144.
Harlan, Benjamin. "Open Thou Mine Eyes." SATB, kybd.
    GS A-6722.
Merkel, Steve. "More of You" in *Let Your Glory, Fall Choral Collection*.
    INT.
Nelson, Jeff. "Purify My Heart" in *Raise the Standard Worship Team Book*.
    3 pt, kybd.   MAR 3010124368.

153

Sunday, April 6

ALBRECHT DÜRER, PAINTER, 1528;
MICHELANGELO BUONARROTI, ARTIST, 1564

These two great artists revealed through their work the mystery of salvation and the wonder of creation. Dürer's work reflected the apocalyptic spirit of his time in which famine, plague, and social and religious upheaval were common. He was sympathetic to the reform work of Luther but remained Roman Catholic. At Dürer's death, Luther wrote to a friend, "Affection bids us mourn for one who was the best." Michelangelo was a sculptor, painter, poet, and architect. His works such as the carving of the Pieta and the statue of David reveal both the tenderness and the grandeur of humanity.

With Passion Sunday one week away, give some consideration to the ways in which the art of these two people might highlight the church's celebration of the mystery of Christ's passion.

154

Wednesday, April 9

DIETRICH BONHOEFFER, TEACHER, 1945

Bonhoeffer was a German theologian who, at the age of 25, became a lecturer in systematic theology at the University of Berlin. In 1933, and with Hitler's rise to power, Bonhoeffer became a leading spokesman for the confessing church, a resistance movement against the Nazis. He was arrested in 1943. He was linked to a failed attempt on Hitler's life and sent to Buchenwald, then later to Schoenberg prison. After leading a worship service on April 8, 1945, at Schoenberg, he was taken away to be hanged the next day. His last words as he left were, "This is the end, but for me the beginning of life."

A hymn written by Bonhoeffer shortly before his death includes the line, "By gracious powers so wonderfully sheltered, and confidently waiting come what may, we know that God is with us night and morning, and never fails to greet us each new day" (WOV 736). Bonhoeffer's courage is a bold witness to the paschal mystery of Christ's dying and rising of the upcoming three days.

Thursday, April 10

MIKAEL AGRICOLA, BISHOP OF TURKU, 1557

Agricola was consecrated as the bishop of Turku in 1554 without papal approval. As a result, he began a reform of the Finnish church along Lutheran lines. He translated the New Testament, the prayerbook, hymns, and the mass into Finnish, and through this work set the rules of orthography that are the basis of modern Finnish spelling. His thoroughgoing work is particularly remarkable in that he accomplished it in only three years. He died suddenly on a return trip from negotiating a treaty with the Russians.

During these final days of the Lenten journey the Finnish hymn, "Lord, as a pilgrim" (LBW 485), can be sung at parish gatherings. Its emphasis on God's faithful presence through the offenses and suffering of life can lead us to the foot of the cross.

April 13, 2003

Sunday of the Passion
Palm Sunday

INTRODUCTION

On this day the church continues its procession with our crucified and risen Lord. He is in our midst as we hear of his life-giving death and as we share his body and blood. At the beginning of this great week, the passion gospel sets forth the central mystery of the Christian faith: Christ emptied himself in death so that we might know God's mercy and love for all creation.

READINGS FOR PROCESSION WITH PALMS

Mark 11:1-11

or John 12:12-16

Psalm 118:1-2, 19-29

Blessed is he who comes in the name of the LORD. (Ps. 118:26)

PRAYER OF THE DAY

Almighty God, you sent your Son, our Savior Jesus Christ, to take our flesh upon him and to suffer death on the cross. Grant that we may share in his obedience to your will and in the glorious victory of his resurrection; through your Son, Jesus Christ our Lord, who lives and reigns with you and the Holy Spirit, one God, now and forever.

VERSE

The hour has come for the Son of Man to be glorified. (John 12:23)

READINGS FOR LITURGY OF THE PASSION

Isaiah 50:4-9a

The image of the servant of the Lord is one of the notable motifs in Isaiah 40–55. Today's reading is a description of the mission of the servant. When early Christians read this text they heard in this servant of God the voice of Jesus. Thus, the reading was associated with the Lord's passion. The servant does not strike back at his detractors but trusts in God's steadfast love.

Psalm 31:9-16

Into your hands, O LORD, I commend my spirit. (Ps. 31:5)

Philippians 2:5-11

Paul quotes from an early Christian hymn that describes Jesus' death on the cross as the primary model for Christians of obedience and unselfishness.

Mark 14:1—15:47

The passion story in Mark's gospel presents Jesus as one who dies abandoned by all. He shows himself to be the true Son of God by giving his life for those who have forsaken him.

or Mark 15:1-39 [40-47]

COLOR Scarlet *or* Purple

THE PRAYERS

155

As we journey through this season of repentance and renewal, let us turn to God who mercifully gives us new life.
A BRIEF SILENCE.

O God, your Son endured triumphs and terrors in his return to Jerusalem. Give endurance to all your people in this holy week, and give us courage to enter fully into its life and mystery. Hear us, O God;
your mercy is great.

O God, may the gentle rule of Jesus as the prince of peace be a reality in every nation of the earth. Hear us, O God;
your mercy is great.

O God, may your grace sustain all who face religious persecution, abuse, or discrimination of any kind. Bless those who are sick and sorrowing with your comforting presence *(especially)*. Hear us, O God;
your mercy is great.

O God, guide those who are preparing to receive the grace of baptism at the conclusion of this week, that they may be prepared to enter fully into the Christian faith. Hear us, O God;
your mercy is great.

HERE OTHER INTERCESSIONS MAY BE OFFERED.

O God, your days are without number and your love is without limit. Keep us in communion with *(names, and all)* those who have entered into your endless joy, and bring us with them into the fullness of light. Hear us, O God;
your mercy is great.

Merciful God, hear our cry when we call to you; renew and uphold us with your Spirit, through Jesus Christ our Lord.
Amen

IMAGES FOR PREACHING

"Hosanna!" on Sunday, "Crucify him" on Friday. This sentence spans a range of passion, the magnitude of the feelings of the people to whom Jesus came and for whom Jesus died, and we get them all on Palm/Passion Sunday.

In the processional gospel we hear the loud "hosannas," we feel the exhilaration of the crowd, we smell the pungent stench of the colt. Our feet are tired from walking along in sandals rather than sneakers with good arch supports. We duck palm branches, lest one catch us in the eye. But from where the twenty-first century believer sits, we see a Jesus who is not buying into this "hosanna" business. Unlike the partying Jesus at the wedding at Cana in Galilee, we get no indication that Jesus is feeling what the crowd is feeling. Those who do not know the story (and even now, "some have never heard" the old, old story) will discover in the appointed gospel reading that Jesus knows better. Jesus knows that this temporal glory is short-lived.

And so our passions intensify as our journey moves step by step, closer and closer to Golgotha (Place of the Skull), the place of Jesus' execution, the place where we confront our own complicity. (*" 'Twas I, Lord Jesus, I it was denied thee; I crucified thee."*)

The Passion gospel reading gives a "variety pack" of all the images and emotions of Holy Week: disappointment, betrayal, fear, pain, guilt. During the Three Days we unpack those images one by one. We must travel through them to get to the other images on the other side: the confusion, joy, and gratitude of the empty tomb.

WORSHIP MATTERS

Passion Sunday is a day of transition. We move from Jesus' triumphal entry into Jerusalem, complete with palm branches and shouting, to the tragic events of Holy Week, culminating at the foot of the cross.

Make the same transition within your liturgy on this day. First of all, plan hymns and music for the first part of the liturgy that reflect the more buoyant nature of the

exuberant crowds that met Jesus as he rode into the capital city. Then focus the latter half of the liturgy (much of which should happen naturally with the reading of the Passion) on the more meditative and reflective nature of the crucifixion. Finally, move. As the liturgy moves, the congregation should also move. Begin this liturgy outside or in a hallway or gathering area and then move to the sanctuary. The physical movement of the congregation should help to point them ritually in the direction of Christ's passion.

Don't forget to save some of the palms for next year's Ash Wednesday liturgy!

LET THE CHILDREN COME

This Sunday is one full of possibilities for children. The service begins with a procession of the blessed palms. Allow children to be part of the procession as we sing "to whom the lips of children made sweet hosannas ring." Younger children can carry a palm branch or frond while older children can pass palms to members of the congregation.

During the reading of the Passion, members of the congregation may be used to acting out the Passion. Children are a welcome part of the crowd that followed the action. Either in the arms or on the shoulders of an adult, children shout "Hosanna" and "Crucify him" and sense the emotions of the Passion.

HYMNS FOR WORSHIP
GATHERING

At the name of Jesus   LBW 179
Lift up your heads, O gates   WOV 631
Lift up your heads   W&P 88

HYMN OF THE DAY

A lamb goes uncomplaining forth   LBW 105

ALTERNATE HYMN OF THE DAY

When I survey the wondrous cross   CS 88, LBW 482, TFF 79
There is a Redeemer   W&P 140

COMMUNION

My song is love unknown   LBW 94, WOV 661
Lamb of God   W&P 82

SENDING

O sacred head, now wounded   LBW 116, 117
There in God's garden   WOV 668

ADDITIONAL HYMNS AND SONGS

Hosanna! Come and deliver   DH 59
Stricken, smitten, and afflicted   LW 116
Calvary   TFF 85

MUSIC FOR THE DAY

SERVICE MUSIC

Music for the procession with palms needs careful planning in light of space and movement factors. An assembly in a winding single file procession will be unable to sing together easily. The refrain to "All glory, laud, and honor" (LBW 108) or "Lift up your heads, O gates" (WOV 631) might be sung by all, with stanzas sung by strategically placed cantors.

PSALMODY

Bell, John L. "In You, O Lord, I Found Refuge" in *Psalms of Patience, Protest and Praise.* U/choir.   GIA G-4047.

Cooney, Rory. "I Place My Life" in *Choral Refrains from Psalms for the Church Year, vol. 4.* U/SATB.   GIA G-3612-A.

DeBruyn, Randall. "Father, I Put My Life in Your Hands" in STP 4.

Farlee, Robert Buckley.   PW B.

Haas, David. "I Put My Life in Your Hands/Pongo Mi Vida." U/SATB, cong, inst.   GIA G-3949.

Plainchant/arr. G. Boulton Smith. "Father, into Your Hands."   PS 2

Schiavone, John. "Father, I Put My Life in Your Hands."   STP 1

CHORAL

Bell, John L. "O The Lamb." SATB, pno.   GIA G-4533.

Benson, Robert. "Ride On, Ride On in Majesty." SATB, org, opt cong.   AFP 0800674634.

Bruckner, Anton. "Christus factus est." SATB.   Summy Birchard.

Carter, John. "Blessed Is He Who Comes in the Name of the Lord!" SATB, U children, pno/org.   AFP 0800674510.

Cooney, Rory. "Palm Sunday Processional." SATB, cant, kybd, opt brass/str, cong.   GIA G-5012.

Farlee, Robert Buckley. "Solemn Reproaches of the Cross." Solo, SATB, pno.   AFP 0800674723.

Gesius, Bartholomaeus. "Sing Hosanna to the Son of David" in *Chantry Choirbook.* SATB.   AFP 0800657772.

Johnson, David N., arr. "O Dearest Lord, Thy Sacred Head." SATB, fl.   AFP 0800645790.

CHILDREN'S CHOIRS

Carter, John. "Blessed Is He Who Comes in the Name of the Lord!" SATB, U children/solo, pno/org.   AFP 0800674510.

Taranto, Steven. "Into Jerusalem." U, kybd, Orff inst.   CG CGA735.

Yarrington, John. "O Thou, Eternal Christ, Ride On." 2 pt, org, hb, snare drm.   AFP 0800673042.

KEYBOARD/INSTRUMENTAL

Albrecht, Mark. "Valet will ich dir geben" in *Festive Processionals.* Org, tpt.   AFP 0800657975.

Diemer, Emma Lou. "Valet will ich dir geben" in *Augsburg Organ Library: Lent.* Org.   AFP 0800658973.

Leavitt, John. "My Song Is Love Unknown." Org, inst.   AFP 080065689X.

Organ, Anne Krentz. "Shades Mountain" in *Woven Together.* Kybd, inst.   AFP 0800658167.

Reger, Max. "Benedictus," op. 59, no. 9. Org.   PET 3114.

Reger, Max. "O Sacred Head, Now Wounded." Org, vln, ob.   CPH 97-6255.

HANDBELL

Afdahl, Lee J. "Gethsemane." 3–5 oct.   AFP 080065367X.

Moklebust, Cathy. "My Song Is Love Unknown." 3–5 oct.   CG CGB203.

Kinyon, Barbara. "Hosanna, Loud Hosanna." 2–3 oct.   JEF MHP1488.

McChesney, Kevin. "Hosanna, Loud Hosanna." 3–4 oct, L2.   AGEHR 1811116-725.

PRAISE ENSEMBLE

Choplin, Pepper. "Jazz Hosanna." SATB, acc, tamb.   FB BG2303.

Dempsey, Larry. "Glory to the King" in *Renew.*   HOP.

Jabusch, Willard. "The King of Glory" in *The Other Song Book.* Fellowship Publications.

Kendrick, Graham. "Welcome the King" in *Hosanna! Music Songbook, vol. 12.*   INT. 12906.

Pote, Allen. "Hosanna." SATB, kybd, gtr.   CG CGA596.

Smith, Michael W. and Deborah D. Smith/arr. Bill Wolaver. "Hosanna." SATB, kybd.   WRD 3010268165.

157

April 14, 2003

MONDAY IN HOLY WEEK

INTRODUCTION

Monday, Tuesday, and Wednesday in Holy Week focus on the events of the last week of Jesus' earthly life. Rather than trying to "walk where Jesus walked," the church uses these days to view Christ more particularly in our lives today. Jesus comes to us in our day through the reading of scripture, through preaching, through the water of baptism, through the bread and wine of communion, and through the prayers.

Be open to the surprising ways in which Christ is made known to you this week. Also look for opportunities to share the gift of his life with others.

This week concludes with the Three Days: Maundy Thursday, Good Friday, and the Resurrection of Our Lord.

PRAYER OF THE DAY

O God, your Son chose the path that led to pain before joy and the cross before glory. Plant his cross in our hearts, so that in its power and love we may come at last to joy and glory; through your Son, Jesus Christ our Lord.

VERSE (MONDAY, TUESDAY, AND WEDNESDAY)

May I never boast of anything except the cross of our Lord Jesus Christ. (Gal. 6:14)

READINGS

Isaiah 42:1-9
  The servant brings forth justice.
Psalm 36:5-11
  Your people take refuge under the shadow of your wings. (Ps. 36:7)
Hebrews 9:11-15
  The blood of Christ redeems for eternal life.
John 12:1-11
  Mary anoints the feet of Jesus with costly perfume.

COLOR Scarlet *or* Purple (Monday, Tuesday, and Wednesday)

April 15, 2003

TUESDAY IN HOLY WEEK

PRAYER OF THE DAY

Lord Jesus, you have called us to follow you. Grant that our love may not grow cold in your service, and that we may not fail or deny you in the hour of trial.

READINGS

Isaiah 49:1-7
  The servant brings salvation to earth's ends.
Psalm 71:1-14
  From my mother's womb you have been my strength. (Ps. 71:6)
1 Corinthians 1:18-31
  The cross of Christ reveals God's power and wisdom.
John 12:20-36
  The hour comes for the Son of Man to be glorified.

April 16, 2003

WEDNESDAY IN HOLY WEEK

PRAYER OF THE DAY

Almighty God, your Son our Savior suffered at human hands and endured the shame of the cross. Grant that we may walk in the way of his cross and find it the way of life and peace; through your Son, Jesus Christ our Lord.

READINGS

Isaiah 50:4-9a
  The servant is vindicated by God.
Psalm 70
  Be pleased, O God, to deliver me. (Ps. 70:1)
Hebrews 12:1-3
  Look to Jesus, who endured the cross and sits at the right hand of God.
John 13:21-32
  Judas, who is later to betray Jesus, departs from the last supper.

THE THREE DAYS

The church's family gathers around its center

Images *of the* Season

At the fulcrum of the entire church year is the *Triduum*—

the Great Three Days—the span of time in which the salvation

of the world is the focus of the church's contemplation.

During the three days that stretch from Maundy Thursday through Easter Day, the whole history of salvation comes into its clearest focus as we watch the agent of God's redeeming activity—Jesus the Christ—bring to completion all of the divine promises from Eden's garden through the formative events of the Torah and on to his own passion and triumph.

But the church does more than simply *watch* during these three days. The church *participates* in the drama that unfolds before our eyes as Jesus eats a meal with friends, prays that another way might yet be found to accomplish the Father's will, submits to arrest by state officials, offers no defense to charges brought by false witnesses, and finally is nailed to a cross, where the Holy One of God offers up his spirit into the hands of the one who sent him.

The church knows the outcome of the story. The story does not change from year to year. For at the end of the Great Three Days, Jesus breaks the bonds of death, crosses over from death to life, grabs hold of all who are united to him by baptism and drags them out of the fierce clutches of the great enemy Death into the shining bright light of new life.

Think of the Three Days as a reunion of the church's family around specific images made real once again to pass on the story of God's salvation in Jesus the Christ.

The family gathers around a *cross* that gives life.

The cross was intended by the Roman government as a means of cruel punishment for hardened criminals. On this cross, though, hangs the salvation of the whole world. This cross and its message is total foolishness to the one who is unspiritual. The cross is a stumbling block to those who want to save themselves. But for the family that gathers during these Three Days, the cross is the throne for the Lamb. More than a piece of jewelry, the cross is the sign of triumph, the noblest tree of all, symbol of the world's redemption for its "burden makes us free" (LBW 118:4).

The family gathers around a *meal* that sustains spiritual life.

Whether it is Sunday dinner at the family table, a night out at a favorite restaurant, a banquet to commemorate some special occasion, or a burger and fries at a fast-food convenience stop, eating is essential to human beings. We can go for long stretches without food, but finally the body needs to receive nourishment.

When God's people Israel were about to be set free from Egyptian bondage, God provided a meal to sustain them on their journey out of Egypt and as a remembrance of God's mighty act of deliverance. In the context of that Passover meal, Jesus provides a new meal for the church for regular sustenance on the journey through the valleys and peaks and wilderness of life in this world. Though the bread and wine are not meant to give physical strength, Christ's body and blood that come with those physical means do give forgiveness, life, and salvation to all who believe.

The family gathers around *words* that tell the story of salvation.

Words—spoken, written, or signed—are essential to communication. How frustrated we become when we cannot find the proper word to express an idea, a feeling, a mood. What a disappointment when we cannot adequately describe a scene from nature because "words just don't do it justice."

Because of the inadequacy of our own words during the Three Days, we must turn to the pages of scripture to listen to the heart of the story of salvation. The Gospel of John tells of Jesus' new commandment to love one another (13:1-17, 31b-35) on Maundy Thursday. Isaiah's powerful image of the Suffering Servant (Isaiah 52:13—53:12) and John's passion narrative (18:1—19:42) speak of suffering and death as part of God's plan of salvation. Then, at the Great Vigil of Easter, the family turns once more to the pages of scripture—God's own word. We turn as many as twelve times to those

160

words: to hear the story of creation and God's destruction of that creation through the waters of the flood... to hear how God tests Abraham, delivers Israel through the waters of the Red Sea, and offers salvation freely to all... to listen to descriptions of new hearts and new spirits created in people and new life breathed into dry and lifeless bones by the breath of the spirit. The words tell how God's heart is changed when people respond to God's call to repentance. The words sing the praise of God through the law delivered through Moses and tell of the trust of three young men who do not bend to what is false. Words, words, and more words—words that bring to life again the story of salvation, because they are God's words that are trustworthy and true.

The family gathers around *fire* that dispels darkness.

Fire is fascinating both to young and old alike. Sitting in front of a roaring fireplace with a loved one gives rise to a sense of security and safety. Sitting on a log around a campfire, singing camp songs, kindles a sense of happy community. Standing at a distance and watching a burning building elicits a sense of anxiety.

At the conclusion of Maundy Thursday's liturgy, all candles are extinguished. Two nights later the family gathers around a new fire, from which the paschal candle is lit.

The single light of the paschal candle breaks the darkness of this night of vigil. As the family prepares to enter to place of gathering for vigil, light from the single candle spreads to individual candles. The light grows, dispelling not only darkness but fear as well. In the reflection of that light, faces of family members become more clear. The joy of this night of vigil becomes more apparent.

The family gathers around *water* that washes clean.

Water quenches thirst and refreshes the body. Water causes seeds to sprout and grow. Water destroys life and property when it goes beyond its appointed boundaries. Water provides a means for transportation.

All of Holy Lent points to the ritual bath at the Vigil, when candidates are plunged in the waters of baptism and are joined to the death and resurrection of the one who passes over from death to life, Jesus the Victor. The water of the font, together with the ritual words, brings about a new relationship between creature and Creator, a relationship of cleansing and new birth and community. Washed of all sin, we stand before God in clothing of innocence and purity.

Having gathered as family to retell the story of salvation, the church is now ready to break forth in great joy to celebrate the paschal feast for a week of weeks.

161

Environment *and* Art *for the* Season

Maundy Thursday marks the first day of the

Three Days. It is the most sacred and important

time of year, for it celebrates the paschal mystery

of the death and resurrection of our Lord. Maundy Thursday, in particular, observes the commandment to love one another, together with the institution of the last supper.

EXTERIOR ENVIRONMENT

Because these days are important to so many people, even for persons who may not worship regularly, it is essential that persons responsible for the placement of outdoor signs listing times of services do so carefully. Try drawing attention to just the main days and service times, or refresh the signs each day by removing information from prior days' celebrations that is no longer needed.

Any exterior signs of Lenten observances may be removed by Saturday of Holy Week. If a cross was used as an exterior symbol during Holy Week, consider draping it in white and gold fabrics for the Easter celebration. Church grounds should look the best they can for this festival. All of nature joins in the glories of the resurrection. Even the bees that provided the substance for the paschal candle get into the act (see the Easter proclamation in *LBW* Ministers Edition, pp. 143–46).

INTERIOR ENVIRONMENT

If the congregation uses scarlet paraments for Holy Week, their use is continued through Maundy Thursday. In lieu of scarlet paraments, white may be considered for Maundy Thursday, but probably a white different from the white used for the most festive occasions of Easter and Christmas. Even if real bread is not used at other times of the year, its use on Maundy Thursday helps to underscore the meal aspect of communion on this day.

Another key element of the Maundy Thursday liturgy is footwashing, which focuses on the servanthood of Christ. The footwashing is accomplished with a ceramic bowl and pitcher, a chair and towel for each participant, and a towel and apron for the presiding minister. A practical consideration is to fill the basin with hot water so that by the time it is used it is still warm. The presiding minister removes chasuble and stole during the footwashing.

Yet another highlight of this service is the stripping of the altar, which is symbolic of Jesus' humiliation at the hands of the soldiers on Good Friday. Everything should be removed in an orderly, respectful manner, with vessels, candles, and ornaments removed to the sacristy first, followed by paraments, linens, and other furnishings. Many (if not all) altar guild members may be recruited for duty on this evening in order to empty the worship space of its adornments.

The Three Days continues with Good Friday. The altar is bare, as well as the entire worship space—no flowers or paraments. Visually this day is centered on the cross. A rough-hewn cross may be placed before the altar prior to the service, or it may be carried into the space at the appropriate time in the Good Friday liturgy (see *LBW* Ministers Edition, p. 142). It may be flanked on each side by tall candles that are set on the floor (for a diagram of this see *Manual on the Liturgy*, p. 324). Provision may be made for kneeling in front of the cross, whether in the form of a special kneeler or loose cushions.

The Vigil of Easter stands at the climax of the Three Days, as well as the entire liturgical year itself. It is the beginning of the great fifty days of Easter rejoicing, drawing to a close the Lenten period of fasting and special discipline. Paraments, banners, and flowers reappear. The finest white or gold set of paraments that the parish can afford should be used for this festival.

A large fire is typically built in an outside grill or brazier for the first lighting of the paschal candle. The procession begins with the paschal candle (or if incense is used, with a thurifer carrying the burning incense). It is preferable for the entire congregation to be involved in the procession, carrying candles with flame that is passed from the paschal candle.

The baptismal font should be filled with water prior to Easter Vigil. Font covers should be removed, making the font available for all (ideally such availability would be the case throughout the year). Even if no one is baptized at this service, the font is nonetheless an important focal point for the liturgy.

A new paschal (Easter) candle, which leads the procession into the worship space this evening, is purchased or made especially for this service. (If the paschal candle is made or purchased unadorned, instructions for decorating it are provided in *Manual on the Liturgy*, pp. 326–27). Have the stand for the paschal candle in place near the altar prior to the service. The base of the stand may be decorated with flowers. Throughout the year the paschal candle proclaims the light of Christ that calls, leads, and guides the faithful on their earthly pilgrimage. (After the Easter season the paschal candle and its stand are ordinarily placed near the baptismal font.) An evergreen bough may be placed near the baptismal font for use by the presiding minister in sprinkling the congregation during the renewal of baptismal vows.

It almost goes without saying that everything is at its whitest and brightest for this evening, as well as for the entirety of the Easter season that follows. A cantor or an assisting minister sings in the Easter proclamation: "This is the night in which all who believe in Christ are rescued from evil and the gloom of sin, are renewed in grace, and are restored to holiness."

The Resurrection of Our Lord (Easter Sunday) continues the festive celebration begun in the Easter Vigil. The worship area and its attendant areas should continue to sparkle on Easter Day. If anything, the environment should be even more splendid than for the Easter Vigil. In the use of banners and other decorations, do try to make a distinction between symbols that speak of Christ's victory and the common spring-oriented ones (such as baby chicks). The egg as symbol calls for careful consideration. It can function as a symbol of resurrection, but that meaning might need to be explained in order to lift it from the sea of commercialism.

Preaching *with the* Season

The Three Days are the heart of the matter—

the pivot around which the entire liturgical year revolves.

It is more than a remembrance of the story of our salvation.

It is the drama itself, told again, with the faithful as key actors in the play. The church knows very well that Jesus died once for all and that his resurrection is an accomplished fact. And yet, even with that theological truth well established, the drama of the Three Days has a profound capacity for bringing the story of salvation into our experience. It is something more than a series of important Bible stories to be retold and remembered again; they are to be lived.

The key to finding a fruitful approach to these days is to think of our actions sacramentally. Baptism is the sacrament of initiation, and it is the focus of the church's Easter celebration in the Vigil. Baptism is the action by which we are incorporated into the story of Jesus: buried with Christ to rise with him. Baptism makes Jesus' story our own: his death is our death so that our death might now be in him. His resurrection is our victory—here and now—over sin, death, and Satan, as well as a foretaste of the final victory we will experience at the end of all our stories.

Likewise, this season also revolves around the eucharist. Jesus structures his words and behaviors at that meal in a way that draws us into the action. "For you," Jesus says over the bread. The meal is not meant merely as a symbol of some deeper theological truth. We are to be involved in the action itself. "Here," says Jesus, "take, eat, drink." The good news is to be taken into us and we, too, are drawn into the action at the table. It is our guilt and our forgiveness that are the subject matter for the meal. "Is it I, Lord? Is it I?" Yes, it is. We cannot hold the action of the eucharist off at arm's length; it is not eucharist that way. No, the meal becomes the meal only when we consume it, take it into ourselves. So, too, these stories of the Triduum are not merely a recounting of a once-upon-a-time. Yes, Christ died once for all. Yes, the sacrifice is complete in itself. But we are drawn into it, dissolved with Christ in baptismal waters, filled with his own flesh and blood in eucharistic bread and wine.

The goal of our celebration is to take up the story and make our way through it again. Our aim, really, is to let the story take possession of us, work its way into our hearts and minds so that from there it may flow through our bloodstream to our hands and feet and mouths. The church found ways of reliving the story for nearly twenty centuries now, and along the way the faithful acquired some useful tools to help make it happen. Twenty-first-century cyberjunkies imagine they invented something new in virtual reality. The church has been practicing it and living it for two millennia. And as our recent technologies are discovering, so the church already knew, that for virtual reality to be effective it really has to be multimedia, involving, if possible, the whole human sensorium. These days offer us a dazzling array of experiences to hear and see, touch and taste and smell. As Saint Augustine said, sacraments are *visible words.* A good Triduum brings the drama of salvation into the experience of the faithful by making it accessible to our senses.

These days present a major challenge to the preacher. In one sense it is the sheer weight of the entire "great and holy week" that makes the task of proclamation feel so consequential, so difficult as to be almost overwhelming. If the scope of God's soteriological project is so immense, how can we ever find the words to express it? But the challenge of proclamation in this week is both more simple and, at the same time, more profound. Quite practically, it is not always clear where or when a sermon should happen in the liturgies of Holy Week. The week began with the lengthy reading of the passion according to Matthew, and there is hardly a way (or time) to top that!

Maundy Thursday seems a little more amenable to preaching. It is almost a "regular" eucharist, and so the homily feels at home here. The preacher, more than likely, will have a job for this liturgy.

Good Friday presents another challenge for the preacher. The Good Friday liturgy in *Lutheran Book of Worship* does not require preaching. And again, we are invited to hear the entire passion from beginning to end, this

163

time from John. Other liturgical traditions are available to congregations for this day. The tenebrae liturgy can easily be adapted to preaching; sometimes it is combined with meditations on the "Seven Last Words" of Jesus, an artificial (and therefore, perhaps less helpful) conflation of Jesus' saying on the cross from all four gospels. Other liturgies focus on the stations of the cross with corresponding homiletic reflection.

The Easter Vigil also makes it possible to forgo preaching in any traditional sense. The twelve (or fewer) readings could stand on their own, and a psalm followed by silence is the mandated response to hearing the word.

So here it is, the Three Days, the center of the church's life, and does the church mean to suggest that the preacher ought to be almost totally silent? Hardly! But what I would like to suggest is that, contained within the church's historic liturgical traditions, there lies a deep wisdom and a radical invitation for us to reconsider what the task of proclamation is all about. The idea is both simple and profound: *The church's proclamation of salvation in these liturgies takes place within the liturgical actions themselves.* Our definition of proclamation does not have to be limited to what takes place in a ten-minute monologue by a pastor standing in a pulpit. The Three Days encourage us to stretch our homiletic imagination in order to see that sermons are found in long stories well told, bowls of water and dirty feet, broken bread and poured wine, stripped altars, silent darkness, and flint-struck fire. Perhaps the preacher will do her work the best this week not by writing homilies but by paying attention to how stories are read, how furniture is arranged, how movements are made, how feet get washed and candles are lit. Each action is a sermon. Each liturgical antiquity is an invitation for us to expand our homiletic consciousness. But even more, each action becomes a powerful tool for doing the very thing God wants done in baptism and eucharist: to make the gospel real, experienced, and lived inside us and between us and through us into the world. Considered from this perspective, the liturgies of the Three Days provide unique opportunities to unfold the drama of our salvation in powerful ways.

The Triduum is really a single liturgy involving the drama of redemption stretching from Thursday evening into the brightness of Easter. The Maundy Thursday eucharist begins with a final confession of sin and re-

ceiving of absolution—delayed or anticipated for forty days—giving the faithful an opportunity to repent and amend their lives. The homily may be shifted to the beginning of the liturgy, giving the preacher an opportunity to close what began on Ash Wednesday. The rite of footwashing deepens the significance of all Jesus' actions this night and gives Maundy Thursday its name (in Latin, *mandatum*, the new command). Peter's reticence at having his feet washed curiously mirrors that of many moderns: we do not want other people to see our dirty feet! But Peter, and all of us, need to be clear that we need to be washed. Although we want to hold the bad news off and apply it to other people, it has to do with us: our treachery, our unworthiness, our vulnerability to temptation and denial and falling away. We need this night!

The liturgy of Good Friday is the celebration of the triumph of Jesus' cross. The reading of the full Passion, this time according to John, is a wonderful way to keep the feast, for in this telling of the tale Jesus, even as he is crucified, is the king lifted high upon his throne, drawing all humanity to himself. Again, a minimalist "staging" of the story might allow the faithful to enter the action more deeply, just as long as the staging does not get in the way of the story itself. Worship planners might also think about the ways in which the cross is visually brought before the people. It can be carried in procession as a "rough-hewn cross," or the more ornate and permanent cross in the sanctuary might be unveiled after its forty-day hiding. The service ends quietly. Provision might be made for worshipers to have an opportunity to kneel before the cross and meditate before they leave in silence.

The Triduum comes to a dramatic climax at the Easter Vigil. Here worship planners will want to give the greatest attention to how symbol and setting might become powerful proclamations of the good news of Jesus' resurrection. A fire struck from flint—sparks of light that can only be seen in the dark—is a dramatic incarnation of the life that comes out of Jesus' death. The spark hits a small clump of dried grass and needs some breath (spirit! *pneuma! ruach!*) to make it burst into flame. The paschal candle lifted into the darkness proclaims that the light of Christ conquers sin and death. The growing multiplication of flames mirrors the growing of the body of Christ as more and more saints

164

are taken into the mystery. (It also finally makes clear why it is we give candles to those who are baptized.) The long story stretches out before us from creation through flood and election and prophets' warnings until at last we are brought to the brink of the celebration and the new day dawns above us. Each step along the way we receive the word and take it to heart. Each person's quiet meditations in the silence may speak more eloquently than preached words could possibly achieve, surrounded as we are this night with so much symbol, so many images swirling around our heads: servant bees making wax, the light of the candle reaching to the stars and toward the cosmic Christ risen above all creation, drawing us upward, pulling us into the spiral of the new day and the life to come! Alleluia! Christ is risen indeed! Alleluia!

Shape *of* Worship *for the* Season

BASIC SHAPE OF THE MAUNDY THURSDAY LITURGY

- See Maundy Thursday liturgy in *LBW* Ministers Edition, pp. 137–38; also available as a congregational leaflet from Augsburg Fortress (AFP 0806605758)

GATHERING

- The sermon may begin the liturgy
- An order for corporate confession and forgiveness may be used (*LBW*, pp. 193–94)
- The peace follows the order for confession and forgiveness

WORD

- The washing of feet may follow the reading of the gospel
- For a dramatic reading based on the gospel use *Scripture Out Loud!* (AFP 0806639644)
- For a contemporary drama based on the second reading, use *Can These Bones Live?* (AFP 0806639652)
- No creed is used on Maundy Thursday
- The prayers: see the prayers for Maundy Thursday in *Sundays and Seasons*

MEAL

- Offertory prayer: see alternate worship text for the Three Days in *Sundays and Seasons* as an option to the ones provided in the liturgy setting
- Use the proper preface for Passion
- Eucharistic prayer: in addition to the four main options in *LBW*, see "Eucharistic Prayer D: The Season of Lent" in *WOV* Leaders Edition, p. 68

- Invitation to communion: see alternate worship text for the Three Days
- Post-communion prayer: see alternate worship text for the Three Days
- No post-communion canticle
- Stripping of the altar, accompanied by singing of Psalm 22, follows post-communion prayer
- No benediction on Maundy Thursday
- No dismissal on Maundy Thursday

BASIC SHAPE OF THE GOOD FRIDAY LITURGY

- See Good Friday liturgy in *LBW* Ministers Edition, pp. 139–43; also available as a congregational leaflet from Augsburg Fortress (AFP 0806605774)

WORD

- The Passion according to St. John is read; a version involving readers and congregation may be used (AFP 0806605707)
- For a reading based of the passion interspersed with choral music, use *St. John Passion* (AFP 0800658582) or a similar setting
- The bidding prayer for Good Friday may be used (*LBW* Ministers Edition, pp. 139–42)
- Adoration of the Crucified may be used (*LBW* Ministers Edition, p. 142)
- No communion for Good Friday

165

- No benediction for Good Friday
- No dismissal for Good Friday

BASIC SHAPE OF THE RITE FOR THE EASTER VIGIL

- See Vigil of Easter in *LBW* Ministers Edition, pp. 143–53; *WOV* Leaders Edition, pp. 88–89; *Vigil of Easter—Music Edition* (AFP 0806605782); also see congregational leaflet from Augsburg Fortress (AFP 0806605790)

LIGHT

- The service of light may begin outside at the lighting of a new fire
- The congregation processes into the darkened nave following the lighted paschal candle
- A cantor sings the Easter proclamation (Exsultet)

WORD

166

- Twelve readings appointed for the Easter Vigil (each of which may be followed by a sung response and a prayer) are listed in *WOV* Leaders Edition, pp. 88–89. All or some of them may be used, but the first and fourth should always be read.
- Psalm responses to the readings may be found in *Psalter for Worship* Year C
- Canticle of the Sun (CS 8, LBW 527) may conclude the service of readings as an alternative to the Song of the Three Young Men
- For dramatic readings based on two of the appointed passages, see *Scripture Out Loud!* (AFP 0806639644)
- For contemporary dramas based on five of the passages, see *Can These Bones Live?* (AFP 0806639652)

BAPTISM

- If no candidates will be baptized, a congregational renewal of baptism may be used; notes for this portion of the liturgy are printed in *LBW* Ministers Edition, p. 152

MEAL

- During the movement from font to the place of the meal, a litany may be sung. Options include the Litany of the Saints in the seasonal rites section (a setting may be found in *Welcome to Christ: Lutheran Rites for the Catechumenate* [AFP 0806633956], pp. 70–71),

the Litany in *Manual on the Liturgy: Lutheran Book of Worship*, pp. 336–37, or the Kyrie from Settings One, Two, or Three in *LBW.*
- The hymn of praise (traditionally "Glory to God") is sung
- During the hymn of praise, lights may be turned on, accompanied by the ringing of bells
- The prayers: see the prayers for Vigil of Easter in *Sundays and Seasons*
- Offertory prayer: see alternate worship text for the Three Days
- Use the proper preface for Easter
- Eucharistic prayer: in addition to four main options in *LBW*, see "Eucharistic Prayer E: The Season of Easter" in *WOV* Leaders Edition, p. 69
- Invitation to communion: see alternate worship text for the Three Days
- Post-communion prayer: see alternate worship text for the Three Days
- Benediction: see alternate worship text for the Three Days
- Dismissal: see alternate worship text for the Three Days

BASIC SHAPE OF THE RITE FOR EASTER DAY

- Confession and Forgiveness: see alternate worship text for the Easter season

GATHERING

- Greeting: see alternate worship text for the Three Days
- Use the Kyrie
- Use the hymn of praise ("This is the feast of victory")

WORD

- For a dramatic reading based on the Easter gospel from John, use *Scripture Out Loud!* (AFP 0806639644)
- Use the Nicene Creed
- The prayers: see the prayers for Easter Day in *Sundays and Seasons*

MEAL

- Offertory prayer: see alternate worship text for the Three Days
- Use the proper preface for Easter

- Eucharistic prayer: in addition to four main options in *LBW*, see "Eucharistic Prayer E: The Season of Easter" in *WOV* Leaders Edition, p. 69
- Invitation to communion: see alternate worship text for the Three Days
- Post-communion prayer: see alternate worship text for the Three Days

SENDING

- Benediction: see alternate worship text for the Three Days
- Dismissal: see alternate worship text for the Three Days

OTHER SEASONAL POSSIBILITIES
PASCHAL VESPERS

- If you are able to gather for worship on Easter Evening, a festival form of evening prayer may be desired. Although it is printed as a part of morning prayer, consider appending the paschal blessing to evening prayer (*LBW*, pp. 138–41) anytime in the Easter season. See notes for this order in *LBW* Ministers Edition, p. 16, and *Manual on the Liturgy*, pp. 294–95. A hymn, such as "We know that Christ is raised" (LBW 189), "I bind unto myself today" (LBW 188), or "O blessed spring" (WOV 695), may replace the canticle "Te Deum," which is customarily associated with morning prayer.

Assembly Song *for the* Season

Into these three short days the church places

its central teachings and actions. Powerful stories retell

God's savings deeds for all people. Powerful actions invite

the assembly into those stories to receive again God's mercy and grace. Let the music of the assembly be simple rather than complex; let it aid the focus and flow of the action. Such music will also be powerful.

MAUNDY THURSDAY

- Keep the choral involvement on this day and Good Friday simple, giving priority to supporting the song of the whole assembly. Simplicity will also allow the choirs to prepare for festive music for the Festival of the Resurrection.
- During the laying on of hands for individual absolution and the footwashing, use a Taizé ostinato chorale: "O Lord, hear my prayer" (WOV 772) or "Ubi caritas et amor" (WOV 665).
- "What shall I render to the Lord" (from the psalm for the day) is appropriate for the offertory.
- During the distribution of communion sing some classic hymns on the Lord's Supper, such as "Soul, adorn yourself with gladness" (LBW 224) and

"Thee we adore, O hidden Savior" (LBW 199). "Ubi caritas et amor" (CS 92) is also appropriate.
- Have a solo voice sing or read Psalm 22 during the stripping of the altar, so the people can focus on the action of preparing for Good Friday.

GOOD FRIDAY

- The assembly's song this day should be simple and unadorned, unaccompanied if possible. Allow ample time for the silent reflection.
- If the choir takes part in this liturgy, let them sing the Passion according to St. John; settings for various voicings are available from music publishers. GIA Publications, Inc., also has the Passion set to chant for three singers.
- Conclude the service with "Sing, my tongue" (LBW 118). The cross of Jesus is our triumph.

EASTER VIGIL

- Pacing is especially important at the Easter Vigil,

167

because the service is long with many actions and much music. Begin simply for the musical responses during the Service of Readings, using chant settings from *Music for the Vigil of Easter* (AFP) or *Psalter for Worship, Cycle B* (AFP).

- Musical resources for the liturgy of baptism are found in *Welcome to Christ: Lutheran Rites for the Catechumenate* (AFP). They include a baptismal song, "Springs of water, bless the Lord," and "A Litany of the Saints."

- Use "Glory to God" as the hymn of praise to welcome Easter. Ring bells during the singing—tower bells if available, or randomly ring as many handbells as are in the appropriate key. Decorate the church for Easter as the hymn is sung; sing an additional hymn such as "Christ the Lord is ris'n today; Alleluia!" (LBW 128) if more music is needed for this transition.

- The liturgy of the meal should be joyful. Use music from the full range of the church's song. "This is the feast" may be used at the offertory; "I bind unto myself today" (LBW 188) is a hymn that can serve there as well. "I'm going on a journey" (TFF 115) is a baptismal song that could be used during the distribution of communion. Keep the sending simple, using either "Thank the Lord" as the post-commu-

168

nion canticle, "We know that Christ is raised" (LBW 189), or another Easter hymn.

FESTIVAL OF THE RESURRECTION

- This "queen of feasts" should be celebrated fully, using all the resources of the assembly in decoration, action, and song. Use Luther's classic hymn of the day, "Christ Jesus lay in death's strong bands" (LBW 134). It is a powerful statement of the Easter gospel, and could be sung on succeeding Sundays at the distribution. Alternate the interior stanzas between high and low voices, and let the choir sing a stanza in harmony.

- Be sure that the great thanksgiving is the high point of the celebration. Make the Sanctus equal to the big hymns of the service in its treatment; ring handbells randomly or use the zimbelstern on the organ; use brass if available.

- Begin the distribution music with "Celtic Alleluia" (WOV 613), sung three times accompanied by bells (A, B, D, and E, with perhaps a C-sharp replacing the D on the final chord).

- Use both "Thank the Lord" as the table is cleared and a full Easter hymn as the cross leads the people back to the world to share the news that "Christ is risen. He is risen indeed. Alleluia!"

Music *for the* Season

See the Easter section for additional music appropriate for the Resurrection of Our Lord.

CHORAL

Byrd, William. *The Passion According to St. John.* SAB, solos.   CPH 97-486.

Elgar, Edward. "Ave verum corpus" in *The New Church Anthem Book.* SATB, opt sop solo, kybd.   OXF 0193531097. Octavo. HWG GCMR 00039.

Ferguson, John. "Ah, Holy Jesus." SATB, org, opt cong. AFP 0800654528.

Ferguson, John. *St. John Passion.* SATB, org.   AFP 0800658582.

Haas, David. "Song of the Lord's Command." U, desc, cant, cong, gtr/kybd, C inst.   GIA G-4682.

Johnson, David N. "Saw Ye My Savior?" SATB, org, opt fl. AFP 6000098189.

Mozart, W. A. "Agnus Dei." SATB, org/pno.   CFI CM8174.

Mozart, W. A. "Ave verum corpus" in *Chantry Choirbook.* SATB. AFP 0800657772.

Nelson, Ronald A. *Three Pieces for Lent and Easter* ("Surely He Hath Borne Our Griefs," "Christ Hath Humbled Himself," "When I Awake"). SAB/SATB, org.   AFP 11- 2196.

Organ, Anne Krentz. "Love One Another." SATB.   AFP 0800659643.

Proulx, Richard. "You, Lord, We Praise." 2 pt mxd, 5 hb. CPH 98-3448.

Scott, K. Lee. "The Tree of Life." SATB, org.   MSM 50-3000.

Van, Jeffrey. "Lamb of God." SATB.   AFP 0800649958.

Victoria, Tomás Luis de. *The Passion According to St. John.* SATB, solos. CPH 97-5430.

Williams, David H. "What Wondrous Love Is This." 2 pt mxd, org. AMSI 205.

Yarrington, John. "O Savior of the World." SATB, org. AFP 0800673158.

CHILDREN'S CHOIRS

Anderson, Norma. "The Walk to Calvary." U, kybd.   CG CGA739.

Bouman, Paul. "Behold the Lamb of God." 2 pt, kybd.   CPH 98-1088.

Linder, Jane. "Christ Is Risen." U, kybd, opt hb.   CG CGA767.

Pooler, Marie. "Wondrous Love" in *Unison and Two-Part Anthems.* U/2 pt, kybd.   AFP 0800648919.

Purcell, Henry/arr. Dolores Hruby. "Celebrate This Happy, Holy Day." U, kybd, C inst.   CG CGA-587.

Schalk, Carl. "Where Charity and Love Prevail." 2 pt, ob, kybd. CPH 98-2701.

KEYBOARD/INSTRUMENTAL

Albrecht, Mark. *Early American Hymns and Tunes for Flute and Piano.* Pno, solo inst.   AFP 0800656911.

Augsburg Organ Library: Lent. Org.   AFP 0800658973.

Elmore, Robert. "Chorale Prelude on 'Herzliebster Jesu' " in *Sonata for Organ.* Org.   FLA HF-5107.

Gelineau, Joseph. *Four Moments of Prayer.* Fl.   GIA 3313.

Manz, Paul. "Toccata on 'At the Lamb's High Feast We Sing.' " Org.   MSM 10-423.

Nicholson, Paul. "Were You There?" Org, fl.   AFP 0800654080.

Sedio, Mark. *Music for the Paschal Season.* Org.   AFP 0800656237.

HANDBELL

Ingram, Barbara. "Thine Is the Glory." 2–3 oct.   JEF MR0 0502.

Sherman, Arnold B. "Song of Joy." 3–4 oct, L2+.   AG 1422. 5 oct, L3.   AGI425.

Sherman, Arnold. "He Never Said a Mumbalin' Word." 3–5 oct.   HOP 1844.

Wagner, Douglas. "Agnus Dei." 3 oct.   AGI452.

Zabel, Albert. "The Strife Is O'er." 3–5 oct.   AFP 080065806X.

PRAISE ENSEMBLE

Evans, Darrell and Chris Springer. "Redeemer, Savior, Friend" in *The Smithton Outpouring Songbook.* SAT[B], kybd.   INT 15727.

Haugen, Marty. "Tree of Life." SATB, kybd.   GIA G-2944.

Kendrick, Graham/arr. Wilson. "Amazing Love." SATB, kybd. HOP C 5043.

Martin, Joseph M. "Behold the King." SATB, kybd.   FLA A 7340.

Morgan, Reuben. "My Redeemer Lives" in *Shout to the Lord 2000 Songbook.* SAT[B], kybd.   INT 14247.

Rodgers, Dawn and Eric Wyse. "Wonderful, Merciful, Savior" in *Extravagant Grace Songbook.* SAT[B], kybd.   INT 16737.

Alternate Worship Texts

GREETING (EASTER DAY)
Alleluia! Christ is risen.
Christ is risen indeed. Alleluia!

The grace of our risen Savior,
the love of God,
and the communion of the Holy Spirit
be with you all.
And also with you.

OFFERTORY PRAYER (MAUNDY THURSDAY)
God of glory,
receive these gifts and the offering of our lives.
As Jesus offered himself for all people,
draw us to serve in the midst of this world,
that all creation may be brought from bondage to freedom,
from darkness to light,
and from death to life;
through Jesus Christ our Lord. Amen

OFFERTORY PRAYER (EASTER VIGIL/DAY)
To you, O Giver of life,
we offer our thanks, our praise,
and these gifts from your living world.
As you give new life to us,
so may we live always in you
for the sake of Jesus Christ, our risen Lord.
Amen

INVITATION TO COMMUNION
(MAUNDY THURSDAY)
Come to the supper of the Lord.
Share in the bread and cup of salvation.

INVITATION TO COMMUNION (EASTER VIGIL/DAY)
Christ our Passover is sacrificed for us.
Therefore let us keep the feast. Alleluia!

POST-COMMUNION PRAYER (MAUNDY THURSDAY)
Lord God, in a wonderful sacrament
you have left us a memorial of your suffering and death.
May this sacrament of your body and blood
so work in us that the way we live
will proclaim the redemption you have brought;
for you live and reign with the Father and the Holy Spirit,
one God, now and forever.
Amen

POST-COMMUNION PRAYER (EASTER VIGIL/DAY)
Eternal God,
through baptism into the death and resurrection of Christ
you welcome us to this table
and nourish us with the food and drink of the promised land.
Now send us forth into the world,
that we may be witnesses to your glory
made known to us in Jesus Christ, our risen Lord.
Amen

BLESSING (EASTER VIGIL/DAY)
Alleluia! Christ is risen.
Christ is risen indeed. Alleluia!

Almighty God, Father, ✙ Son, and Holy Spirit
bless you and raise you to newness of life,
now and forever.
Amen

DISMISSAL (EASTER VIGIL/DAY)
Go in peace. Serve the risen Christ.
Thanks be to God. Alleluia, alleluia!

170

Seasonal Rites

Litany of the Saints

This may be used in the Easter Vigil as the transition from the Service of Holy Baptism to the Service of Holy Communion. A musical setting is available in Welcome to Christ: Lutheran Rites for the Catechumenate *(Augsburg Fortress, 1997), p. 70.*

Lord, have mercy.
Lord, have mercy.
Christ, have mercy.
Christ, have mercy.
Lord, have mercy.
Lord, have mercy.

Be gracious to us.
Hear us, O God.
Deliver your people.
Hear us, O God.

You loved us before the world was made:
Hear us, O God.
You rescued the people of your promise:
Hear us, O God.
You spoke through your prophets:
Hear us, O God.
You gave your only Son for the life of the world:
Hear us, O God.

For us and for our salvation he came down from heaven:
Great is your love.
And was born of the virgin Mary:
Great is your love.
Who by his cross and suffering has redeemed the world:
Great is your love.
And has washed us from our sins:
Great is your love.
Who on the third day rose from the dead:
Great is your love.
And has given us the victory:
Great is your love.
Who ascended on high:
Great is your love.
And intercedes for us at the right hand of God:
Great is your love.

For the gift of the Holy Spirit:
Thanks be to God.
For the one, holy, catholic, and apostolic church:
Thanks be to God.
For the great cloud of witnesses into which we are baptized:
Thanks be to God.

For Sarah and Abraham, Isaac and Rebekah:
Thanks be to God.
For Gideon and Deborah, David and Esther:
Thanks be to God.
For Moses and Isaiah, Jeremiah and Daniel:
Thanks be to God.
For Miriam and Rahab, Abigail and Ruth:
Thanks be to God.
For Mary, mother of our Lord:
Thanks be to God.
For John, who baptized in the Jordan:
Thanks be to God.
For Mary Magdalene and Joanna, Mary and Martha:
Thanks be to God.
For James and John, Peter and Andrew:
Thanks be to God.
For Paul and Apollos, Stephen and Phoebe:
Thanks be to God.
Other names may be added
For all holy men and women, our mothers and fathers in faith:
Thanks be to God.
For the noble band of the prophets:
Thanks be to God.
For the glorious company of the apostles:
Thanks be to God.
For the white-robed army of martyrs:
Thanks be to God.
For the cherubim and seraphim, Michael and the holy angels:
Thanks be to God.

Be gracious to us.
Hear us, O God.
Deliver your people.
Hear us, O God.

171

Give new life to these chosen ones by the grace of baptism:
Hear us, O God.
Strengthen all who bear the sign of the cross:
Hear us, O God.
Clothe us in compassion and love:
Hear us, O God.
Bring us with all your saints to the river of life:
Hear us, O God.

Lord, have mercy.
Lord, have mercy.
Christ, have mercy.
Christ, have mercy.
Lord, have mercy.
Lord, have mercy.

April 17, 2003

Maundy Thursday

INTRODUCTION

On this day the Christian community gathers to share in the holy supper Christ gave the church to reveal his unfailing love for the human family. In the actions of this liturgy, Christ demonstrates this love by speaking his faithful word, washing our feet, and giving us his body and blood. From this gathering we are sent to continue these actions in daily life: to serve those in need, to offer mercy, to feed those who are hungry.

This first liturgy of the Three Days has no ending; it continues with the worship of Good Friday and concludes with the Vigil of Easter. Together the Three Days proclaim the mystery of our faith: Christ has died. Christ is risen. Christ will come again.

PRAYER OF THE DAY

Holy God, source of all love, on the night of his betrayal, Jesus gave his disciples a new commandment: To love one another as he had loved them. By your Holy Spirit write this commandment in our hearts; through your Son, Jesus Christ our Lord, who lives and reigns with you and the Holy Spirit, one God, now and forever.
or
Lord God, in a wonderful Sacrament you have left us a memorial of your suffering and death. May this Sacrament of your body and blood so work in us that the way we live will proclaim the redemption you have brought; for you live and reign with the Father and the Holy Spirit, one God, now and forever.

VERSE

As often as you eat this bread and drink the cup, you proclaim the Lord's death until he comes. (1 Cor. 11:26)

READINGS

Exodus 12:1-4 [5-10] 11-14

Israel remembered its deliverance from slavery in Egypt by celebrating the festival of Passover. This festival featured the slaughter, preparation, and consumption of the Passover lamb, whose blood was used to protect God's people from the threat of death. The early church de-scribed the Lord's supper using imagery from the Passover, especially in portraying Jesus as the lamb who delivers God's people from sin and death.

Psalm 116:1, 10-17 (Psalm 116:1-2, 12-19 [NRSV])
Omit "Hallelujah"

I will take the cup of salvation and call on the name of the Lord. (Ps. 116:11)

1 Corinthians 11:23-26

The only story from the life of Jesus that Paul recounts in detail is this report of the last supper. His words to the Christians at Corinth are reflected today in the liturgies of churches throughout the world.

John 13:1-17, 31b-35

The story of the last supper in John's gospel recalls a remarkable event not mentioned elsewhere. Jesus performs the duty of a slave, washing the feet of his disciples and urging them to do the same for each other.

COLOR Scarlet *or* White

THE PRAYERS

As we enter into the mystery of our salvation during these great three days, let us pray for new life in the church, and new hope for the world and all who are in need.

A BRIEF SILENCE.

For the church, that it would proclaim the love of Christ by demonstrating in word and deed its love for one another and its care for the earth. Lord, in your mercy,
hear our prayer.

For the world, that its strife and tensions would be eased by leaders blessed with your wisdom's counsel. Lord, in your mercy,
hear our prayer.

For all who are in need, that the followers of Christ would serve those who are suffering, learning from Christ's example as a servant of all. Lord, in your mercy,
hear our prayer.

For all members of this congregational community, and especially those preparing for baptism, that these three days might be a living experience of the body of Christ

173

who promises to meet us always in the bread and wine of the holy supper. Lord, in your mercy,
hear our prayer.
HERE OTHER INTERCESSIONS MAY BE OFFERED.

For the faithful departed, with whom we are united in a holy communion, that our voices may join with theirs in the unending hymn of heaven. Lord, in your mercy,
hear our prayer.
We offer you these prayers, O God, in the shadow of the cross, in the hope of the paschal feast to come, and in the name of Jesus Christ who endured the cross and grave.
Amen

IMAGES FOR PREACHING

The disciples gathered around that supper table could hardly have missed the sense that it was an unusual night, filled with import. Of course, Passover time was upon them, and they would have been well aware of that night being different from all other nights. But even within that context, this night was extraordinary.

They were used to Jesus violating the norms of religious and social convention, so when he began to take on a servant's role, it would have caught them by surprise, but they wouldn't have been shocked. But when he began actually to touch their feet, to wash the dust and smell from them, that clearly got through to them in a way that no words possibly could. Peter spoke for them all, as was often the case, in objecting to this unseemly display. It is clear, though, that his objections were based in love for his Lord, because when he was presented with the alternative of having no share with Christ, he offered his whole body for washing.

In a gospel filled with signs, this sign was one of the last, and most profound. Nothing—not even our precious dignity and self-image—dare stand between us and our service to and love for our fellow humans. If the disciples still didn't fully understand the centrality of this self-giving message in Jesus' good news, they would soon see his own love demonstrated to its ultimate degree. Now, though, the amazing evening continued with prediction of a betrayal by one of them, with the suggestion of Peter's denial, with a profound last address. If John's record even approaches the actual events of that night, it must have left the disciples deeply shaken. Yet Jesus himself frames the events of that night, and the days to come, with the only possible summary: "Just as I have loved you, so also you should love one another."

WORSHIP MATTERS

Think of the next three days as one day. Think of the next three liturgies as one great liturgy. Some parishes make this connection more obvious by simply printing one worship folder for Maundy Thursday, Good Friday, and the Easter Vigil. It is a wonderful way to say in print that these three days, while separate on the calendar, are essentially of one piece.

If you have never attempted footwashing in your congregation, perhaps this year is the time to try it. Footwashing provides an illustration of Christ's commandment that we love one another as he has loved us.

Several stations may be used for the footwashing. After the ministers wash each other's feet, members of the worshiping community come forward, remove their shoes and socks, and sit in a chair. Water is simply poured over the feet from a pitcher into a basin. The feet are then dried with a cloth.

LET THE CHILDREN COME

Nothing can give worship more personal meaning than participating in the liturgy and drama of the day. If footwashing is offered to all who choose to participate, it should include children. If a few are selected a child can be in the group. Children should be prepared ahead of time to maintain the solemnity and to help them understand the concept of serving others.

All children, whether they receive communion or not, can be welcomed at the Lord's table and given a blessing. Be sure they know that God's gift through this sacrament is for them.

HYMNS FOR WORSHIP
GATHERING

O Jesus, joy of loving hearts   LBW 356
Great God, your love has called us   WOV 666

HYMN OF THE DAY

Where charity and love prevail   LBW 126

ALTERNATE HYMN OF THE DAY

Thee we adore, O hidden Savior   LBW 199
A new commandment   WOV 664

174

COMMUNION

Jesu, Jesu, fill us with your love   WOV 765, TFF 83

Ubi caritas et amor   WOV 665

Where true charity and love abide   CS 90

Broken in love   W&P 24

ADDITIONAL HYMNS AND SONGS

An upper room did our Lord prepare   PH 94

Now to your table spread   PH 515

Taste and see   TFF 126

Now in this banquet   W&P 104

Where true charity and love abide   CS 92

MUSIC FOR THE DAY

PSALM 116

Brown, Teresa. "The Blessing Cup" in PS 2.

Daigle, Gary/arr. Rory Cooney. "I Will Walk in the Presence of God" in *Choral Refrains from Psalms for the Church Year, vol. 4*. U. GIA G-3612-A.

Farlee, Robert Buckley.   PW B.

Glynn, John. "Lord, How Can I Repay" in PS 2.

Mahnke, Allan. *Seventeen Psalms for Cantor and Congregation*. U/SATB, cong.   CPH 97-6093.

Roberts, Leon C. "I Will Call upon the Name of the Lord."   TFF 14.

Schalk, Carl. "Now I Will Walk at Your Side" in *Sing Out! A Children's Psalter*. U/2 pt.   WLP 7191.

CHORAL

Duruflé, Maurice "Ubi caritas." SATB.   DUR 312-41253.

Jasterse, Greg. "Abide with Me." SATB.   AFP 0800674707.

Mozart, W. A. "Ave verum corpus" in *Chantry Choirbook*. SATB, org. AFP 0800657772.

Organ, Anne Krentz. "Love One Another." SATB. AFP 0800659643.

Proulx, Richard. "God Is Love." SATB, cant, cong, org, ob. GIA G-4853.

Proulx, Richard "Ubi caritas." SATB.   GIA G-1983.

CHILDREN'S CHOIRS

Hopson, Hal H., arr. "Fill Us with Your Love." U/2 pt, kybd. AG HH3923.

Kemp, Helen. "A Lenten Love Song." U, kybd.   CG CGA486.

KEYBOARD/INSTRUMENTAL

Biery, Marilyn. "Ubi caritas" in *Augsburg Organ Library: Lent*. Org. AFP 0800658973.

Cotter, Jeanne. "Eat This Bread" in *After the Rain*. Pno.   GIA G-3390.

Langlais, Jean. "Meditation: Communion" (based on "Ubi caritas") in *Suite Medievale*. Org.   Salabert Editions.

Messiaen, Olivier. "Le Banquet Celeste." Org.   Durand ed.

Organ, Anne Krentz. "Adoro te devote" in *Christ, Mighty Savior: Piano Reflections*. Pno.   AFP 0800656806.

HANDBELL

Afdahl, Lee J. "Gethsemane." 3–5 oct.   AFP 080065367X.

Redhead, Richard/arr. David Angerman. "Go to Dark Gethsemane." 2–3 oct.   CPH 97-6780.

Semmann, Barbara. "Processionals for the Time of Lent." 5 oct. CPH 97-6524.

PRAISE ENSEMBLE

Foley, John B./arr. Schrader "One Bread, One Body." 3 pt mxd, pno. HOP A709.

Makeever, Ray. "Take Off Your Shoes" in DH.

Martin, Joseph. "He Loved Them to the End." SATB, acc. GS A-6768.

Paris, Twila/arr. Rhodes. "Lamb of God." SATB, orch. WRD 301092416x.

Webb, Richard. "In Remembrance of Me" (The Lord's Prayer). Faith Inkubators.

April 18, 2003

Good Friday

INTRODUCTION

On this day the church gathers to hear the proclamation of the passion, to pray for the life of the world, and to meditate on the life-giving cross. The ancient title for this day—the triumph of the cross—reminds us that the church gathers to offer thanksgiving for the wood of the tree on which hung our salvation.

PRAYER OF THE DAY

Almighty God, we ask you to look with mercy on your family, for whom our Lord Jesus Christ was willing to be betrayed and to be given over to the hands of sinners and to suffer death on the cross; who now lives and reigns with you and the Holy Spirit, one God, forever and ever.
or

Lord Jesus, you carried our sins in your own body on the tree so that we might have life. May we and all who remember this day find new life in you now and in the world to come, where you live and reign with the Father and the Holy Spirit, now and forever.

READINGS

Isaiah 52:13—53:12

Today's reading reinterprets the common idea that suffering is God's punishment for sin: "You get what you deserve." What is new is the idea that the innocent sufferer brings benefits for the community. The suffering and death of the servant serve God's purposes: the redemption of God's people.

Psalm 22

My God, my God, why have you forsaken me? (Ps. 22:1)

Hebrews 10:16-25 *or* Hebrews 4:14-16; 5:7-9

The writer to the Hebrews uses the Hebrew scriptures to understand the meaning of Christ's death on the cross. Like a great priest, Jesus offered his own blood as a sacrifice for our sins so that now we can worship God with confidence and hope.

John 18:1—19:42

On Good Friday, the story of Jesus' passion—from his arrest to his burial—is read in its entirety from the Gospel of John.

THE PRAYERS

On Good Friday, the church's ancient Bidding Prayer is said or sung. See *LBW,* Ministers Edition, pp. 139–42; or *Book of Common Worship,* pp. 283–86.

IMAGES FOR PREACHING

The symbolism of the cross is complex. The Egyptian ankh, a cross with a looped upper arm, signifies the sun, the sky, and the earth, or perhaps a person (the circle representing the head; the horizontal, the arms; and the upright, the body). Placed in the center of the cosmos, the cross becomes the bridge or ladder by which the soul may reach God. In medieval allegory, the cross often appears as a Y-shaped tree, derived from the tree of life. In the cross, north, south, east, and west come together. And the cross is where opposites meet: the positive and the negative, the superior and the inferior, life and death.

This meeting of opposites is found throughout scripture. It is by the work of the cross that the first become last and the last first (Mark 10:31). The tiniest mustard seed becomes the greatest tree (Matt. 13:31-32). Those who mourn are comforted, and the meek inherit the earth (Matt. 5:4-5). The powerful are brought down from their thrones, and the lowly are lifted up; the hungry are filled with good things, and the rich are sent away empty (Luke 1:52-53). The Son of God is beaten like a criminal (John 19:1).

By the cross of Christ comes new life. By Jesus' death, we are made whole; by his bruises, we are healed; out of his dark anguish comes light (Isa. 53:5, 11). The righteous one, hanged with the transgressors, bore our iniquities and made us righteous (vv. 11, 12), and now our all-knowing God says, "I will remember their sins no more" (Heb. 10:17).

WORSHIP MATTERS

Sometimes the unexpected happens, such as, perhaps, the electricity going out just prior to a Good Friday liturgy. Turn the unexpected into a blessing: use candles for the readings and sing the hymns either with piano or a cappella.

While a tenebrae service may provide some dramatic flair, the Good Friday liturgy found in *Lutheran Book of*

Worship Ministers Edition allows for a simple but moving worship service. Especially when used over a number of years, it allows the perspective of John's gospel—the triumph on the cross—to take center stage. Teach your congregation the Bidding Prayer found within this service; it is an ancient and riveting litany prayed from the foot of the cross.

LET THE CHILDREN COME

A rough-hewn wood cross carried in procession as a litany is chanted or spoken will help illustrate the solemnity of the service, and is only one of many dramatic touches that make the Three Days naturally appealing to younger worshipers. Many children will appreciate the tactile gesture of touching the cross in individual prayer at the end. Children can be taught the simple words of the first verse of "Were you there" (LBW 92).

HYMNS FOR WORSHIP

GATHERING

The liturgy begins in silence on Good Friday.

HYMN OF THE DAY

There in God's garden   WOV 668

ALTERNATE HYMN OF THE DAY

Were you there   LBW 92, TFF 81
Nature with open volume stands   LBW 119

ADDITIONAL HYMNS AND SONGS

Strange King   DH 61
When we are tempted to deny your Son   PH 86
They crucified my Lord   TFF 80
Amazing love   W&P 8
At the foot of the cross   W&P 11

MUSIC FOR THE DAY

PSALM 22

Farlee, Robert Buckley.   PW B.
Harbor, Rawn. "My God, My God."   TFF 2.

CHORAL

Casals, Pablo. "O vos omnes." SATB.   Tetra AB128.
Farlee, Robert Buckley. "Solemn Reproaches of the Cross." Solo, SATB, pno.   AFP 0800674723.
Fleming, Larry L. "Sing and Ponder." SATB.   AFP 0800653491.

Kadidlo, Phil. "Go to Dark Gethsemane." SATB, pno.   AFP 0800674529.
Leighton, Kenneth. "Solus ad victimam" in *The New Church Anthem Book.* SATB, org.   OXF 0193531097.
Proulx, Richard. "Were You There" in *The Augsburg Choirbook.* SATB.   AFP 0800656784.
Roesch, Robert. "Behold, Behold My Savior's Grief." SA(T)B, kybd.   AFP 0800674502.
Schütz, Heinrich. "Praise to You, Lord Jesus" in *Chantry Choirbook.* SATB.   AFP 0800657772.

CHILDREN'S CHOIRS

Christopherson, Dorothy. "There Was a Man." U, pno, ob.   AFP 0800657047.
Jennings, Carolyn, "Ah, Holy Jesus." SA.   AFP 0800645154.

KEYBOARD/INSTRUMENTAL

Bach, J. S. "Herzlich tut mich verlangen." BWV 727. Org. Various editions.
Berthier, Jacques. "My Soul Is Sad" in *Liturgical Meditations.* Fl. GIA 3133.
Diemer, Emma Lou. "Were You There" in *Augsburg Organ Library: Lent.* Org.   AFP 0800658973.
Farlee, Robert Buckley. "Shades Mountain" in *Many and Great.* Org. AFP 0800658949.
Langlais, Jean. "My Soul Longeth to Depart in Peace" (O Sacred Head) in *Neuf Pieces.* Org.   S. Bornemann/HWG SB 5337.

HANDBELL

Larson, Katherine Jordahl. "Tallis' Canon and Were You There." 3–4 oct.   AFP 080065191X.
Mathis, William. "Beneath the Cross of Jesus." 3 oct. SMP 20/1173 S.
Sherman, Arnold. "O Sacred Head, Now Wounded." 3–5 oct. HOP 1732.

PRAISE ENSEMBLE

Barbour and Skidmore "The Holy Heart" in *Maranatha! Music Praise Chorus Book, 3rd ed.*   MAR.
Goebel-Komala, Felix. "Psalm of Hope." SATB, cant, cong, gtr, kybd, timp.   GIA G-4403.
Paris, Twila. "Lamb of God" in *Songs for Praise and Worship.*   WRD.
Rouse, Jay and Randy Vader/arr. Camp Kirkland. "Behold Calvary's Lamb." SATB, orch.   Sparrow Corp. AO8189.
Schram, Ruth Elaine. "Not My Will but Thine." SATB, acc, ob. FLA A6603.

177

April 19, 2003

The Resurrection of Our Lord
Vigil of Easter

INTRODUCTION

This liturgy's Easter Proclamation announces, "This is the night in which all who believe in Christ are rescued from evil and the gloom of sin, are renewed in grace, and are restored to holiness." It is the very foundation of our Christian faith, and it is what makes this vigil the crowning moment of the church's year. This night the church celebrates the presence of the risen Lord as he brings us to new life in baptism, gives us his body and blood, speaks his word of promise, and comes to us in the Christian community.

PRAYER OF THE DAY

O God, who made this most holy night to shine with the glory of the Lord's resurrection: Stir up in your Church that Spirit of adoption which is given to us in Baptism, that we, being renewed both in body and mind, may worship you in sincerity and truth; through Jesus Christ our Lord, who lives and reigns with you, in the unity of the Holy Spirit, one God, now and forever.

VERSE

Alleluia. Christ being raised from the dead will never die again; death has no more dominion over him. Alleluia. Let us sing to the Lord who has triumphed gloriously. Alleluia. (Rom. 6:9; Exod. 15:1)

READINGS

Creation: Genesis 1:1—2:4a
Response: Psalm 136:1-9, 23-36
God's mercy endures forever. (Ps. 136:1b)
The Flood: Genesis 7:1-5, 11-18; 8:6-18; 9:8-13
Response: Psalm 46
The Lord of hosts is with us; the God of Jacob is our stronghold. (Ps. 46:4)
The Testing of Abraham: Genesis 22:1-18
Response: Psalm 16
You will show me the path of life. (Ps. 16:11)
Israel's Deliverance at the Red Sea: Exodus 14:10-31; 15:20-21
Response: Exodus 15:1b-13, 17-18
I will sing to the Lord who has triumphed gloriously. (Exod. 15:1)

Salvation Freely Offered to All: Isaiah 55:1-11
Response: Isaiah 12:2-6
With joy you will draw water from the wells of salvation. (Isa. 12:3)
The Wisdom of God: Proverbs 8:1-8, 19-21; 9:4b-6 or Baruch 3:9-15, 32—4:4
Response: Psalm 19
The statutes of the Lord are just and rejoice the heart. (Ps. 19:8)
A New Heart and a New Spirit: Ezekiel 36:24-28
Response: Psalm 42 and Psalm 43
My soul is athirst for the living God. (Ps. 42:2)
The Valley of the Dry Bones: Ezekiel 37:1-14
Response: Psalm 143
Revive me, O Lord, for your name's sake. (Ps. 143:11)
The Gathering of God's People: Zephaniah 3:14-20
Response: Psalm 98
Lift up your voice, rejoice and sing. (Ps. 98:5)
The Call of Jonah: Jonah 3:1-10
Response: Jonah 2:1-3 [4-6] 7-9
Deliverance belongs to the Lord. (Jonah 2:9)
The Song of Moses: Deuteronomy 31:19-30
Response: Deuteronomy 32:1-4, 7, 36a, 43a
The Lord will give his people justice. (Deut. 32:36)
The Fiery Furnace: Daniel 3:1-29
Response: Song of the Three Young Men 35-65
Sing praise to the Lord and highly exalt him forever. (Song of the Three Young Men 35b)

NEW TESTAMENT READING

Romans 6:3-11
Christians are baptized into the death of Christ, and are also joined to Christ's resurrection.
Response: Psalm 114
Tremble, O earth, at the presence of the Lord. (Ps. 114:7)

GOSPEL

Mark 16:1-8
The resurrection of Jesus is announced, and the response is one of terror and amazement.

COLOR White *or* Gold

THE PRAYERS

As we celebrate the joy of the resurrection, let us pray for new life in the church, and new hope for the world and all who are in need.

A BRIEF SILENCE.

On this holy night, let us pray for the church, that it would be strengthened to proclaim the message of freedom and new life in the resurrection of Jesus Christ from death. Lord, in your mercy,

hear our prayer.

On this holy night, let us pray for the world, that the redeeming word of the crucified and risen Christ will reach its farthest corners and every inhabitant. Lord, in your mercy,

hear our prayer.

On this holy night, let us pray for all who are in the darkness of despair or depression, for all who are suffering from chronic pain, and for all who await your healing and life-giving touch in their lives *(especially).* Lord, in your mercy,

hear our prayer.

On this holy night, let us pray for the newly baptized and for all who have renewed their baptism, that the power of Christ's resurrection will send them out to proclaim the gospel of their salvation. Lord, in your mercy,

hear our prayer.

HERE OTHER INTERCESSIONS MAY BE OFFERED.

On this holy night, let us pray for those who have been standing in sorrow at the graves of loved ones, that they might be comforted with the blessed hope of everlasting life with all who share in Christ's resurrection. Lord, in your mercy,

hear our prayer.

Gracious God, hear our prayers and receive them for the sake of the crucified and risen one, our Savior Jesus Christ.

Amen

IMAGES FOR PREACHING

The consistent witness of scripture is that God has adopted us—chosen to bring us into the family of God—and cared for us.

God said, "Let us make humankind in our image," and then God gave the man and the woman dominion over everything that lives on the earth.

God called Abram to take Sarai and all his family to the land of Canaan, and there God made of them a great nation.

God led Moses and the children of Israel safely out of Egypt and through the Red Sea to the promised land.

When God's children strayed, God sent prophets to call them home and to create for them a vision of restoration. God even promised to put new hearts in the people.

We learn from the Bible—our family history—how to be members of this family: God made us responsible for creation and God calls us to radical obedience—to feed the hungry, welcome the stranger, clothe the naked, visit the imprisoned, and care for the widow and orphan.

And we learn from the Bible what God has done for us: God sent Jesus. The long-promised Messiah became one of us; preached, taught, and healed among us; was crucified, died, and was buried. And then he rose from death. By Jesus' resurrection, God gives us the greatest gift of all: eternal life in Christ Jesus.

God adopted us as sons and daughters. The rite of Holy Baptism is the act of adoption. Paul said, "Therefore, we have been buried with him by baptism into death, so that, just as Christ was raised by him from the dead by the glory of the Father, so we too might walk in newness of life" (Rom. 6:4).

WORSHIP MATTERS

Like the liturgy of Passion Sunday, the Vigil of Easter is designed to move. Begin outside by lighting the Paschal candle with a new fire, and then move to a darkened room where the congregation can huddle together to hear the ancient stories of faith proclaimed once more. Move then to yet a third place for baptism, a place where all can gather around the font to welcome and celebrate those now washed into the life and death of Christ. And then finally, follow the paschal candle one more time to the table to share the Easter meal and fill the space with the good news of resurrection. Be sure to make provisions for those whose mobility is limited.

LET THE CHILDREN COME

The lighting of the new fire, the distribution of candles during the service of light—older children, too, can participate in these parts of the liturgy, under the watchful eye of parents. Have the children gather at the baptismal

179

font for baptisms or the renewal of baptismal vows where they can see and hear and be reminded of their own baptisms. Children who are old enough may participate as readers.

HYMNS FOR WORSHIP

HYMN OF THE DAY

Our Paschal Lamb, that sets us free   WOV 679, HFW

ALTERNATE HYMN OF THE DAY

Come, you faithful, raise the strain   LBW 132
Shout for joy loud and long   WOV 793

COMMUNION

Come, let us eat   LBW 214
I am the Bread of life   WOV 702
The trumpets sound, the angels sing   W&P 139

SENDING

Now all the vault of heaven resounds   LBW 143
We know that Christ is raised   LBW 189

ADDITIONAL HYMNS AND SONGS

Awake, O sleeper!   DH 63
O Love of God, how strong   H82 455, 456
We praise thee, O God   TFF 100
Come and see   W&P 29

MUSIC FOR THE DAY

AROUND THE GREAT FIRE

Berthier, Jacques. "Within Our Darkest Night" in *Songs and Prayers from Taizé*.   GIA.
Biery, James. "Easter Sequence." U/brass qrt/org.   MSM 80-404.
Schutte, Dan. "Holy Darkness." Cong, kybd, gtr, vln, vla, vc, hrn.   OCP 9906CC

AROUND THE LIGHT OF CHRIST

Batastini, Robert. "Exsultet" (Easter Proclamation). U chant.   GIA G-2351.
"Rejoice Now, All Heavenly Choirs" in *Music for the Vigil of Easter*. Cant, cong.   AFP 0806605790.
Tamblyn, Bill. "Lumen Christi." Presider, cant, SATB, org, perc.   OCP 7235CC.
"The Exsultet" in TP.

AROUND THE READINGS

Reponses to all readings in PW C.
Trapp, Lynn. "Responses for the Triduum." Cant, cong, kybd, opt solo/C inst.   MSM 80-305.

FIRST READING

Carmona. "A Canticle of Creation." U/cant, desc, org, trt.   OCP 9973.
Erickson, Richard. "When Long Before Time." SATB, org.   AFP 0800656768.
Hopson, Hal H. "O Praise the Lord Who Made All Beauty." U, kybd.   CG CGA 143.
Smith, Alan. "God's Love Is Forever!" in PS 2.

SECOND READING

Cherwien, David. "God Is Our Refuge and Strength." U, org.   MSM 80-800.
Harbor, Rawn. "The Lord of Hosts Is with Us."   TFF 6.
Rock of my salvation   W&P 161

THIRD READING

Inwood, Paul. "Centre of My Life" in PS 2.
Trinkley, Bruce. "I Want Jesus to Walk with Me." SATB, pno.   AFP 0800657071.

FOURTH READING

Barker, Michael. "Miriam's Song." U, kybd, opt tamb.   CG CGA 740.
Cherwien, David. "Go Down, Moses." U, kybd.   Evangel/AMSI (Lorenz).
Daw, Carl, Jr. "Metrical Canticles 25 and 26" in *To Sing God's Praise*. Cong, kybd.   HOP 921.
Gibbons, John. "Canticle of Moses" in PS 2.

FIFTH READING

DeLong, Richard. "Seek Ye the Lord" in *Five Sacred Songs*. Solo, kybd.   ECS 4759.
Lindh, Jody. "Behold, God Is My Salvation." U/2 pt, org.   CPH 98-3193.
Rusbridge, Barbara. "Sing a Song to the Lord" in PS 1.
Surely it is God who saves me   WOV 635

SIXTH READING

Cox, Joe. "Psalm 19" in *Psalms for the People of God*. Cant, choir, cong, kybd.   SMP 45/1037S.
Ogden, David. "You, Lord, Have the Message of Eternal Life" in PS 2.

SEVENTH READING

As pants the hart for cooling streams   LBW 452
As the deer   W&P 9
Howells, Herbert. "Like as the Hart." SATB, org.   OXF 42.066.
Hurd, Bob. "As the Deer Longs" in PS 2.

180

EIGHTH READING

Great is the Lord   W&P 53

Show me the way   DH 45

NINTH READING

Johnson, Alan. "All the Ends of the Earth" in PS I.

Jothen, Michael. "O Sing Ye!" U, kybd.   BEC BP1128.

Martinson, Joel. "Psalm 98." SATB, cong, trt, org.   CPH 98-3225.

TENTH READING

I, the Lord of sea and sky   WOV 752, TFF 230

TWELFTH READING

Daw, Carl, Jr. "Metrical Canticles 13 and 14" in *To Sing God's Praise.* Cong, kybd.   HOP 921.

Proulx, Richard. "Song of the Three Children." U, opt 2 pt, cant, cong, perc, org.   GIA G-1863.

AROUND THE FONT

"A Litany of the Saints" and "Springs of water, bless the Lord" in *Welcome to Christ: Lutheran Rites for the Catechumenate.* AFP 0806633956.

Cherwien, David and Susan Cherwien. "Life Tree." SAB, org, opt fl.   CPH 98-3190.

Cooney, Rory/arr. Gary Daigle. "Glory to God/Sprinkling Rite." Choir, cong, gtr, kybd, fl.   GIA G-4020.

Farlee, Robert Buckley. "O Blessed Spring." SATB, ob, org, opt cong.   AFP 0800654242.

Keesecker, Thomas. "Washed Anew." SAB/SATB, opt 2 oct hb, opt cong.   AFP 6000001355.

Palmer, Nicholas. "Cleanse Us, O Lord: Sprinkling Rite." Cant, SATB, cong, gtr, org, opt inst.   GIA G-4064.

Taylor-Howell, Susan. "You Have Put on Christ." U/3 pt, opt Orff inst.   CG CGA 325.

Trapp, Lynn. "Music for the Rite of Sprinkling." SATB, org.   MSM 80-901.

You have put on Christ   WOV 694

PSALM 114

Farlee, Robert Buckley.   PW C.

Hopson, Hal H. *Psalm Refrains and Tones.*   HOP 425.

The Psalter—Psalms and Canticles for Singing.   WJK.

CHORAL

Bach, J. S. "Lord Jesus Christ, God's Only Son" in *Bach for All Seasons.* SATB, kybd.   AFP 080065854X.

Inst pts.   AFP 0800659546.

Connolly, Michael. "Where, O Death Is Your Victory?" SATB, pno, 2 ww.   GIA G-4772.

Erickson, Richard. "Come Away to the Skies." SATB, fl, fc.   AFP 0800656776. Also in *The Augsburg Choirbook.*   AFP 0800656784.

Hopson, Hal H. "For as the Rain and Snow." SATB.   AFP 080065868X.

Jennings, Kenneth. "All You Works of the Lord" in *The Augsburg Choirbook.* SATB, org.   AFP 0800656784.

Proulx, Richard. "Our Paschal Lamb, That Sets Us Free." SATB, org.   AFP 0800656113.

CHILDREN'S CHOIRS

Beebe, Hank. "Roll the Stone Away." 2 pt, kybd.   HAL 08596566.

Kemp, Helen. "God's Great Lights." U, antiphonal kybd, opt cong.   CPH 98-3072.

KEYBOARD/INSTRUMENTAL

Glick, Sara. "Mannion" *in Piano Arrangements for Worship.* Pno, opt inst.   AFP 0800658809.

Helman, Michael. "Palestrina" in *Three for Easter.* Org.   AFP 0800674790.

Martinson, Joel. "Miriam's Dance." Org.   CPH 97-6490.

Peeters, Flor. "Scherzo" in *Suite Modale,* op. 43. Org.   LEM 23673 HL.

HANDBELL

Boersma, Barbara. "Dry Bones." 3–5 oct.   NMP169.

Rogers, Sharon Elery. "Come All Christians." 2–3 oct.   JEF MDPDBI029621.

Zabel, Albert. "The Strife Is O'er, the Battle Done." 3–5 oct.   AFP 080065806X.

PRAISE ENSEMBLE

Klein, Laurie/arr. Jack Schrader. "I Love You, Lord." SATB, pno.   HOP GC936.

Nystrom, Martin/arr. Christopher. "As the Deer." SATB, acc, fl.   WAR 08740834.

Paris, Twila. "We Bow Down" in *Songs For Praise and Worship.*   WRD.

Smith, Byron J. "Worthy to Be Praised." SATB, pno.   LAW 52654.

Ylvisaker, John. "Great Is Our God." in *Borning Cry.*   NGP.

Ziegenhals, Harriet. "Oh, Sing to the Lord." U/2 pt, kybd, perc.   CG CGA640.

181

April 20, 2003

The Resurrection of Our Lord
Easter Day

INTRODUCTION

The story of Mary Magdalene is the church's story. We hear the voice of the risen Lord in the scriptures. We receive his body and blood in the holy supper. We encounter him in our brothers and sisters and in all those in need who look for salvation. We are charged to go forth in daily life and proclaim with our words and deeds that we have seen the Lord. It is the day of resurrection, the day the Lord has made. Let us be glad and rejoice.

PRAYER OF THE DAY

O God, you gave your only Son to suffer death on the cross for our redemption, and by his glorious resurrection you delivered us from the power of death. Make us die every day to sin, so that we may live with him forever in the joy of the resurrection; through Jesus Christ our Lord, who lives and reigns with you and the Holy Spirit, one God, now and forever.

or

Almighty God, through your only Son you overcame death and opened for us the gate of everlasting life. Give us your continual help; put good desires into our minds and bring them to full effect; through Jesus Christ our Lord, who lives and reigns with you and the Holy Spirit, one God, now and forever.

VERSE

Alleluia. Christ being raised from the dead will never die again; death no longer has dominion over him. Alleluia. On this day the Lord has acted; we will rejoice and be glad in it. Alleluia. (Rom. 6:9; Ps. 118:24)

READINGS

Acts 10:34-43

Peter's sermon, delivered at the home of Cornelius, a Roman army officer, is a summary of the essential message of Christianity: Everyone who believes in Jesus, whose life, death, and resurrection fulfilled the words of the prophets, receives forgiveness of sins through his name.

or Isaiah 25:6-9

In the face of desolation, the people of God are promised that the Lord will make a new appearance marked by joy and feasting, and by the abolishment of death itself.

Psalm 118:1-2, 14-24

On this day the Lord has acted; we will rejoice and be glad in it. (Ps. 118:24)

1 Corinthians 15:1-11

Paul discusses many things in his letters to the Corinthians, but in these verses he tells them what he thinks is most important of all: the good news that Jesus has been raised from the dead.

or Acts 10:34-43

See above.

John 20:1-18

This morning began with confusion: the stone was moved and the tomb was empty. Disciples arrive, then angels, and finally Jesus himself. Out of the confusion, hope emerges, and a weeping woman becomes the first to confess her faith in the risen Lord.

or Mark 16:1-8

The resurrection of Jesus is announced, and the response is one of terror and amazement.

COLOR White *or* Gold

THE PRAYERS

Standing in the glorious light of the resurrection, let us pray for the church, the world, and all who wait for the Spirit's revealing power.

A BRIEF SILENCE.

O God, as the church celebrates Jesus' glorious resurrection from the dead, may we be made bold in the witness of Christ's resurrection through all that we say and do. We pray to the Lord:

Lord, hear our prayer.

We praise you, O God, for destroying the shroud of sin cast over all peoples, and for saving the world by the resurrection of your Son. We pray to the Lord:

Lord, hear our prayer.

Gracious God, in the midst of her weeping Mary Magdalene was met at the tomb by the risen Christ. Meet all who weep this day with the comfort of your

182

care, and touch the sick (especially) with your joy and peace. We pray to the Lord:

Lord, hear our prayer.

Merciful God, we are your forgiven people graced with the gift of new life in Christ. Empower the newly baptized to emerge from the font as faithful disciples and bold proclaimers of the gospel. We pray to the Lord:

Lord, hear our prayer.

HERE OTHER INTERCESSIONS MAY BE OFFERED.

Even as you raised your Son from the dead on the third day, we pray that you will hold our beloved dead in your eternal rest until the day when you raise us all to share the marriage feast of the Lamb with you forever. We pray to the Lord:

Lord, hear our prayer.

Gracious God, hear our prayers and receive them for the sake of the crucified and risen one, our Savior Jesus Christ.

Amen

IMAGES FOR PREACHING

One might think that this event would be the final word, this resurrection of Jesus. He had completed his work, death had done its worst, and now behold! He lives! In a sense, of course, that thought is correct: nothing more is needed, except to trust in this witness of the empty tomb. That "except," however, is a major stumbling block for many, and even those who were present and saw the physical signs of the resurrection were confused and alarmed. We have the benefit of thousands of years of interpretation to help us accept Christ's resurrection as fact, but are hampered by a worldview that resists such illogical claims, as well as by plain old lack of faith.

Even when we can set aside our reservations and believe that Christ is risen, though, still we find that this resurrection is not the end of the matter. As we will be discovering throughout the seven weeks of Easter, the message of the resurrection carries with it an inherent need to be told. In both John and Mark, the shocked witnesses (viewers) at the empty tomb are told that they need to be witnesses (forth-tellers) as well. "Go and say" (John); "Go, tell" (Mark).

This "further agenda" is modeled well by Paul in the reading from I Corinthians. He reminds his readers that he passed on to them what he himself first received, probably from Ananias (Acts 9). And he implies the hope that those Corinthians, having received the good news of the resurrection, will not keep it to themselves.

There really is no last word to Christ's life, and we must not let the resounding song die out among us. It's fine to sing alleluias in our churches on this joyful day, as long as then we go and announce the news to all who will hear.

WORSHIP MATTERS

Pull out all the stops for this first day of fifty days of rejoicing. Think about what you can do to enhance the liturgy, the space, and the whole atmosphere of worship to mark this day of new life and celebration. The liturgy has been described as an accordion. Some days the accordion is pushed all the way in from both sides and the sound is somewhat hushed and diminished, but then on other days the accordion is pulled all the way open and the band is playing and people are dancing and children are laughing and even those watching are clapping along to the rhythm of the song. Easter Day is one of these latter days in which it might be difficult to distinguish the proper liturgy of the church from a carnival.

LET THE CHILDREN COME

The use of special music that is joyous and festive as well as trumpets to emphasize the tone of the music catch children's attention. Songs with alleluias such as "Jesus Christ is risen today" and others with simple alleluia refrains allow even the nonreader to participate. Bright flowers and banners add to the joyful mood. Children and families can be encouraged to sit on aisles and up front so that they can see in an often crowded church.

HYMNS FOR WORSHIP

GATHERING

Christ is risen! Alleluia   LBW 131

Alleluia! Jesus is risen!   WOV 674

HYMN OF THE DAY

Christ Jesus lay in death's strong bands   LBW 134

ALTERNATE HYMN OF THE DAY

Christ is risen! Shout hosanna!   CS 16, WOV 672

I will sing, I will sing   W&P 73

COMMUNION

At the Lamb's high feast we sing   LBW 210

Alleluia, alleluia, give thanks   WOV 671

183

SENDING

Thine is the glory   LBW 145
No longer strangers   W&P 102

ADDITIONAL HYMNS AND SONGS

Morning breaks upon the tomb   CW 159
On earth has dawned this day of days   H82 201
They crucified my Savior   TFF 90
The trumpets sound, the angels sing   W&P 139

MUSIC FOR THE DAY

SERVICE MUSIC

Consider one of the following embellished versions of the liturgy as a way of elevating the musical acclamations for this day:

Cherwien, David. *Alternatives Within* (*LBW,* settings 1 and 2). Org, opt inst.   AFP 0800654870.

Farlee, Robert Buckley. *Great and Promised Feast.* Org, SATB, brass, opt. hb.   AFP 0800659309.

Ferguson, John. *Festival Setting of the Communion Liturgy* (*LBW,* setting 2). Full score. Org, SATB, opt brass.   CPH 98-2994.

Hillert, Richard. *Festival Setting of the Communion Liturgy* (LBW , setting 1). Full score. CPH 97-5939. Choral desc.   CPH 97-2755. Hb. U, desc, org, brass, ob, timp, 3 oct hb.   CPH 97-5958.

PSALMODY

Chepponis, James J. "Eastertime Psalm." Cant, cong, opt choir, opt tpts/hb.   GIA G-3907.

Farlee, Robert Buckley.   PW B.

Gieseke, Thomas. "Psalm 118." U.   CPH 98-2754.

Hommerding, Alan J. "This Is the Day" in *Sing Out! A Children's Psalter.* U.   WLP 7191.

Hruby, Dolores M. "Psalm 118" in *Seasonal Psalms for Children.* U, opt Orff inst.   WLP 7102.

Roberts, Leon C. "The Lord Is My Strength."   TFF 15.

Trapp, Lynn. "This Is the Day." SATB, cong, cant, opt tpt, org.   MSM 80-403.

CHORAL

Benson, Robert. "Good Christians All, Rejoice and Sing." SATB, org, brass qrt.   AFP 0800659597.

Clausen, René. "At the Name of Jesus." SATB (div), org, opt tpt/tbn/tba.   MF MF-2052.

Fleming, Larry. "Lord of the Dance." SATB.   AFP 0800655354.

Larkin, Michael. "A Glorious New Day." SATB, kybd.   AFP 0800674480.

Mathias, William. "Alleluia! Christ Is Risen." SATB, brass, org, perc.   OXF 42.479. Inst pt.   OXF 42.479-70.

Mendelssohn, Felix. "Jesus Christ, My Sure Defense—Alleluia" in *Chantry Choirbook.* SATB.   AFP 0800657772.

Powell, Robert. "That Easter Day." SATB, pno.   AFP 0800674669.

Telemann, G. P. "Hallelujah" in *To God Will I Sing.* MH voice.   AFP 0800674332. ML voice.   AFP 080067434X.

CHILDREN'S CHOIRS

Nagy, Russell. "Christ Is Risen! Alleluia!" U, kybd, inst pts. High Street Music JH524.

Page, Anna Laura. "A New Song." 2 pt, kybd, opt fl.   AFP 0800674499.

Wold, Wayne. "The Whole World Sings Alleluia." U, kybd.   CG CGA708.

KEYBOARD/INSTRUMENTAL

Folkening, John. "Two Brass Fanfares." Brass qrt.   AFP 0800674944.

Gigout, Eugene. "Grand Choeur Dialogue." Org, brass qnt. Denver Brass Publications CAN00126. Also for organ alone in *French Masterworks for Organ.*   WAR FE 09431.

Giomo, Carla. "An Easter Fanfare." Org, brass qrt.   GIA 5351.

Webster, Richard. "Paschal Suite for Organ and Trumpet." Org, tpt.   AFP 080065692X.

HANDBELL

Afdahl, Lee J. "Jesus Christ Is Risen Today." 3–5 oct.   AFP 0800659899.

Kerkorian, Greg. "Alleluia. The Strife is O'er." 2–3 oct.   JEF MJHS9166.

Larson, K. J. "Easter Resonance." (Medley). 2–3 oct.   JEF MC0976624.

Nelson, Susan. "Easter Alleluia" (O Filii et Filiae). 3–5 oct, opt h, perc, solo inst.   JEF MCGB216.

PRAISE ENSEMBLE

Batstone, Billy. "Glory to the Lamb" in *Maranatha! Music Praise Chorus Book, 3rd ed.*   MAR.

Garrett, Les. "This Is the Day" in *All God's People Sing.*   CPH.

Herring, Anne/arr. Wilson. "Easter Song." SATB, pno, hb.   HOP F958.

Rouse, Jay and Randy Vader/arr. Camp Kirkland. "No Cross, No Crown." SATB, orch.   Sparrow Corp AO8215.

Schrader, Jack. "Easter Anthem." SATB, kybd.   HOP A609.

184

April 20, 2003

The Resurrection of Our Lord
Easter Evening

INTRODUCTION

Easter is a feast. And what feasting can be shared from the scriptures this evening! The news of God's salvation, brought to the world in the death and resurrection of Christ, is worthy of the grandest of celebrations. The gospel from Luke 24 may remind us that the meal we receive in the sacrament of communion is a share in Christ's death and resurrection. Like the disciples who met with the Lord on the evening of his resurrection, Christ's words and his supper burn in us as well.

PRAYER OF THE DAY

Almighty God, you give us the joy of celebrating our Lord's resurrection. Give us also the joys of life in your service, and bring us at last to the full joy of life eternal; through your Son, Jesus Christ our Lord, who lives and reigns with you and the Holy Spirit, one God, now and forever.

VERSE

Alleluia. Christ being raised from the dead will never die again; death no longer has dominion over him. Alleluia. Beginning with Moses and all the prophets, Jesus interpreted the things about himself in all the scriptures. Alleluia. (Rom. 6:9; Luke 24:27)

READINGS

Isaiah 25:6-9

God prepares a splendid feast on the holy mountain. All peoples will toast God's salvation.

Psalm 114

Hallelujah. (Ps. 114:1)

1 Corinthians 5:6b-8

Christ clears out the old yeast in all people, making ready for the purity of the new.

Luke 24:13-49

The resurrected Christ makes himself known to two of the disciples in the breaking of bread. Only upon receiving the bread do the disciples make the connection to the words Christ spoke to them earlier on the road.

COLOR White

THE PRAYERS

Standing in the glorious light of the resurrection, let us pray for the church, the world, and all who wait for the Spirit's revealing power.

A BRIEF SILENCE.

That the newly baptized and all who renew their baptismal vows may walk in newness of life, we pray to the Lord:

Lord, hear our prayer.

That the light of Easter guide all who work for justice and peace in our world, we pray to the Lord:

Lord, hear our prayer.

That the healing power of the resurrection give hope to all who are unloved and forgotten, poor and hungry, hospitalized and sick *(especially)*, we pray to the Lord:

Lord, hear our prayer.

That you free us from prejudice, so we may show no partiality as we share the good news of the resurrection, we pray to the Lord:

Lord, hear our prayer.

That you open our eyes to recognize you in this eucharist and in the suffering and joy of daily life, we pray to the Lord:

Lord, hear our prayer.

HERE OTHER INTERCESSIONS MAY BE OFFERED.

That as we remember all our beloved dead, you would unite our voices with theirs until we join them at the great and promised feast, we pray to the Lord:

Lord, hear our prayer.

Gracious God, hear our prayers and receive them for the sake of the crucified and risen one, our Savior Jesus Christ.

Amen

IMAGES FOR PREACHING

Many of us have played the game known at times as "Telephone," in which the participants sit in a circle and whisper a message down the line until it comes back to the person who started it. That person then announces to the group the differences between how it began and how it ended up. In this evening's gospel, Jesus seems to be taking part in a variation on this game. He had just risen from the dead that morning, yet already—even among his dedicated followers—the confusion and distortion were setting in. The news was being relayed, but problems immediately surfaced with some of the key points. Jesus was described as "a prophet mighty in word and deed"—fine as far as it goes, but that isn't far enough. Cleopas and company knew he had been crucified, "but [as if the two were unconnected] we had hoped that he was the one to redeem Israel." Then they describe the women's witness to the empty tomb and the angels' message of the resurrection, but they cannot take that crucial step of faith to believe and proclaim the good news.

We too have garbled things pretty badly. We have confused scientific, empirical reality with the reality of faith, and have accepted and passed along as truth the opinion that the two cannot coexist. Perhaps we have even added some static, arising from our own lack of faith.

How wonderful, then, that Christ—the risen Christ—steps in to set things right, to return us to the original and life-giving message: this suffering and then entering into glory—was it not necessary? And then, because at best, words can be twisted and misunderstood, how gracious that Christ opens not just our ears, but our other senses as well through the sacraments. At last the glorious message comes to us directly from the one who breaks the bread: "The Lord has risen indeed!"

WORSHIP MATTERS

Break the bread in your community this Easter evening, and allow your hearts to burn within you from the presence of Christ. In fact, allow Christ's presence to burn within the hearts of all the faithful throughout the Easter season. Easter is the perfect time to introduce the weekly celebration of communion into your congregation. If your parish does not currently celebrate communion each week, plan on introducing the weekly celebration during the Sundays of Easter. However, before you simply spring this change on the people, share with worship committees, clergy, and church councils the opportunity to focus the community around the table during this time of resurrection. Gently teaching people about the joys of a weekly celebration of communion and allowing them to experience this grace will bring new life to your community.

LET THE CHILDREN COME

Along with the addition of the alleluias, children can be encouraged to hear the words in Luke 24, "He took bread, blessed and broke it, and gave it to them." Point out that these words were spoken Maundy Thursday and are words they will hear again every time eucharist is offered. Every Sunday becomes a "little Easter."

HYMNS FOR WORSHIP
SUGGESTED HYMNS

Come, you faithful, raise the strain   LBW 132
That Easter day with joy was bright   LBW 154
Abide with us, our Savior   LBW 263
Stay with us   WOV 743

ADDITIONAL HYMNS AND SONGS

As I walked home to Emmaus   LLC 362
O Thou who this mysterious bread   UMH 613
Open our eyes, Lord   TFF 98
We will glorify   W&P

HYMN OF THE DAY

Abide with us, our Savior   LBW 263

MUSIC FOR THE DAY
SERVICE MUSIC

For a musical setting of the eucharistic liturgy especially suited to evening and to the Easter cycle of the church year, consider *Stay with Us, Lord*, with music by David Cherwien and hymn texts by Susan Palo Cherwien (full music edition, AFP 0800674839; congregational part, AFP 0800674847).

CHORAL

Farlee, Robert Buckley. "We Are a Garden Walled Around" in *To God Will I Sing*. MH voice.   AFP 0800674332. ML voice.   AFP 080067434X.

Hovland, Egil. "Stay with Us." SATB, kybd.   AFP 0800658825.

Pelz, Walter. "Stay with Us." SAB, org.   CPH 98-3073.

KEYBOARD/INSTRUMENTAL

Biery, James. "Dunlap's Creek" in *Augsburg Organ Library: Easter*. Org.   AFP 0800659368.

Ferguson, John. "In Quiet Joy." Org.   MSM 10-422.

Keesecker, Thomas. "Come Away to the Skies" in *Come Away to the Skies, A Collection for Piano*. Pno.   AFP 0800656555.

Kolander, Keith. "Three Arias for Piano and Solo Instrument." Pno,
inst.   AFP 0800658175.

HANDBELL

Waldrop, Tammy. "The Resurrection and the Book." 2–3 oct hb/hc,
narr.   JEF MRO3211.

Young, Philip M. "Good Christian Friends, Rejoice and Sing."
2–3 oct.   AFP 080065627X.

Saturday, April 19

OLAVUS PETRI, PRIEST, 1552;
LAURENTIUS PETRI, ARCHBISHOP OF UPPSALA, 1573;
RENEWERS OF THE CHURCH

These two brothers are commemorated for their introduction of the Lutheran movement to the Church of
Sweden after studying at the University of Wittenberg.
They returned home and, through the support of King
Gustavus Vasa, began their work. Olavus published a catechism, hymnal, and a Swedish version of the mass. He
resisted attempts by the king to gain royal control of the
church. Laurentius was a professor at the university in
Uppsala. When the king wanted to abolish the ministry
of bishops, Laurentius persuaded him otherwise and the
historic episcopate continues in Sweden to this day. Together the brothers published a complete Bible in
Swedish and a revised liturgy in 1541.

This commemoration is perhaps best observed during the week after Easter, during which the Church of
Sweden can be remembered in prayer. The Easter hymn
"Praise the Savior, now and ever" (LBW 155) uses a
Swedish folk tune and can be sung to commemorate the
contributions of the Petris and the Swedish church to
our worship life.

Monday, April 21

ANSELM, ARCHBISHOP OF CANTERBURY, 1109

This eleventh-century Benedictine monk stands out as one
of the greatest theologians between Augustine and Thomas
Aquinas. He is counted among the medieval mystics who
emphasized the maternal aspects of God. Of Jesus Anselm
says, "In sickness you nurse us and with pure milk you feed
us." He is perhaps best known for his theory of atonement,

the "satisfaction" theory. In this theory he argued that
human rebellion against God demands a payment but because humanity is fallen, it is incapable of making that satisfaction. Therefore God takes on human nature in Jesus
Christ in order to make the perfect payment for sin.

Tuesday, April 22

DAY OF CREATION (DÍA DE LA CREACIÓN)

This day calls us to attend to the glories of creation that
surround us. Especially in the Northern Hemisphere,
creation springs green again after the death of winter,
and we are mindful of our stewardship of the earth as
our God-given home. The great hymn of Francis of Assisi, "All creatures of our God and King" (LBW 527)
might be sung today both for its Easter alleluias and its
rejoicing in the gift of creation. "Dear mother earth,
who day by day unfolds rich blessings on our way, oh,
praise him! Alleluia! The fruits and flow'rs that verdant
grow, let them his praise abundant show. Oh, praise him!
Oh, praise him! Alleluia, alleluia, alleluia!" Indeed, all
creation sings the praise of its creator.

187

Wednesday, April 23

TOYOHIKO KAGAWA, RENEWER OF SOCIETY, 1960

Toyohiko Kagawa was born in 1888 in Kobe, Japan. Orphaned early, he was disowned by his remaining extended
family when he became a Christian. Kagawa wrote,
spoke, and worked at length on ways to employ Christian principles in the ordering of society. His vocation to
help the poor led him to live among them. He established schools, hospitals, and churches. He also worked
for peace and established the Anti-War League. He was
arrested for his efforts to reconcile Japan and China after
the Japanese attack of 1940.

In celebration of his witness, recognize those people
in your parish who work on behalf of the poor and oppressed and who, through their work, reveal the peace of
Christ that is a gift of the resurrection.

Friday, April 25

ST. MARK, EVANGELIST

Though Mark himself was not an apostle, it is likely that he was a member of one of the early Christian communities. The gospel attributed to him is brief and direct. It is considered by many to be the earliest gospel. Tradition has it that Mark went to preach in Alexandria, Egypt, where he was martyred.

Mark's story of the resurrection ends with women at the tomb who say nothing to anyone because of their fear. Though their witness faltered, the good news of the resurrection, the good news of these fifty days, reaches out to include us.

EASTER

We are sent forth as witnesses to the resurrection

Images *of the* Season

Easter is, in our usual way of thinking, the great

festival of unalloyed joy, of final triumph. Christ has won the victory

over death, and now no clouds remain to block the sun.

Our Savior is triumphant, and we who have been baptized into his death now also share in his everlasting life—so our voices should be filled with nothing but exuberant alleluias.

That's all true, and yet. . . . It is noteworthy that the gospels for this season don't really exhibit an immediate, unfettered outburst of ecstasy at the news of the risen One. Indeed, if we began our Easter celebrations with the resurrection tale from Mark, the reaction of the first witnesses to Christ's rising is one more of fear than of festivity: "So they went out and fled from the tomb, for terror and amazement had seized them; and they said nothing to anyone, for they were afraid." That hymn text seems to be missing from our canon, the one that goes "Christ is arisen! Say nothing at all / For fear and amazement has us in its thrall."

That fearful reaction to what is supposedly good news is found several times in the gospels early in this season. The disciples are locked into a room in fear. In Luke's account, the congregation of the disciples, upon first seeing their risen Lord, is startled and terrified. That response comes up often enough that maybe we should pay closer attention to it.

Easter, for all the joy it brings us each year, is old hat to most of us. We've been through the paschal cycle enough times that though we are still gripped by the awe of Christ's passion, we aren't surprised or amazed at the news of his rising from death. We respond with alleluias because we have been conditioned to do so—but maybe that isn't the most natural reaction. After all, it is the creator of life overturning the fundamental rules of the game. As we have come to expect, life begins, continues, and ends: That is the way the world works. True, life may not be all happiness, and death causes us grief, but it also is predictable in its overall shape; we know what to expect, and that is a comfort.

But if we can't rely on death to keep its end of the bargain, then what does that mean for the rest of our existence? What is life, anyway, if it cannot be defined, fenced in, by its opposite, death? And, what's worse, what are those who are new to this whole "Easter" phenomenon to think when the eyes of faith see realities that conflict with those experienced by their earthbound, empirical eyes? Grandma died believing in Christ, who (we now hear) conquered death. And if death were no longer in charge, and Grandma suddenly reappeared among us, alive again, wouldn't we be terrified?

It isn't that we, or those first disciples, fail to believe in the resurrection. Rather, those stories of fear demonstrate the truth that such a dramatic departure from what we thought was enduring reality takes some getting used to. We may have sung lots of alleluias on Easter Day, but we need to live awhile with the concept that Christ is alive in our lives.

Fortunately, Easter is not a "one-shot" festival. That week of weeks gives us time to adapt to this startling new truth. And we see that transition reflected in the gospels. After the shock and amazement of the early Sundays, we hear words meant to soothe and encourage us. The shepherd has not run away in the face of the wolf, but has stayed, giving up his life in order to take it up again— that helps give us some context to the resurrection. Christ is the vine, and so we recognize ourselves as part of a living, fruit-bearing organism, one that may be pruned but, we now see, will not die. And the readings keep getting more confident, more at home with this new, post-resurrection order. Christ calls us not servants, but friends. Friends! If we are friends with the Risen One, imagine what we can do! And yes, basking in the power that Jesus has prayed upon us, finally we need not imagine our mission, because it is spread before us as the Spirit of the victorious Christ comes upon us, and we are sent forth— no longer fearful but growing each day into our new identities as witnesses to the resurrection.

Looking back from the vantage point of Pentecost, those early fears seem a bit silly, maybe not worthy of

190

us—which may be why those of us who have been around the liturgical-year block a few times tend to dismiss fear as a legitimate response to the resurrection. Give us trumpets and lilies as Easter images, not trembling bodies huddled behind locked doors. But in a perverse way, by insisting only and always on the triumphal view of Easter, we may be in danger of covering over its reality. Flowers and flourishes are great fun and entirely appropriate for this great festival, but they won't get us far in the world outside the church doors, where people still react in fear to the notion that their working reality, not always pleasant but at least somewhat predictable, is being replaced by something new and unknown. What's more, if we are using Easter alleluias merely to drown out (temporarily) our own groans of pain and whimpers of fear, then are we really any better off?

Perhaps it is not such a bad idea to respect the fear and hesitance that we and others feel upon encountering Christ risen from the dead. Yes, resurrection changes everything, and some of those changes may be hard to bear. If we have been living as though death had the final word in life, love, work, and all the rest, and have

developed some intricate coping mechanisms only to have that whole structure ripped away by this new Easter worldview, "alleluia" may not be the first response that comes to mind. Not if we are really honest with ourselves.

What if, instead, we join those cowering behind those barred doors, and start not with a shout but with a murmur: "Did you hear? Could it be true?" Give the idea some time to sink in. Talk about what it might mean for us. Take a taste of the risen Lord sacramentally present with us, and see that it is good. Let him come to us in his gentle way, allowing our trust levels gradually to grow. We share in all this process with the other fearful ones in our community, both within and without the community of faith. And as the weeks of Easter progress, instead of the alleluias wearily fading away, they actually increase with our Spirit-born confidence. Then, on that glorious Day of Pentecost, we accompany all the others who confronted these paschal mysteries, our fears taken in and transformed, and we are sent out as witnesses not only to *the* resurrection, but indeed to *our* resurrection!

191

Environment *and* Art *for the* Season

The Easter season is the queen of feasts. It lasts

for a "week of weeks." Note that the Sundays within these

fifty days are Sundays *of* Easter, not merely a device

for counting the days between Easter Sunday and Pentecost. Even though spring officially arrived during Lent, its true essence may not appear until sometime during this season. This time of year brims with festivity. Graduations, Mother's Day, weddings, and the beginning of the summer vacation season on Memorial Day weekend (or Victoria Day in Canada), all lend an air of exuberance during this time of year. But amidst all of these more secular pursuits, the church tells its story of the resurrection. Let our festivity in this season primarily be in praise of the joy of Easter.

EXTERIOR ENVIRONMENT

Outdoor plantings are frequent signs of the earth's renewal during this season, especially in northern climes. The church can use this natural annual return of another growing season to proclaim new life through the resurrection. In urban areas where parks and lawns may be limited, churches often have at least a small lawn, or just enough open space for window boxes and placing large pots directly on the sidewalk. Take advantage of these spaces to brighten up the neighborhood and to proclaim the joy in new growth. "Now the green blade rises," proclaims the spirited Easter carol. Congregations having larger exterior spaces might consider using them in special ways to proclaim the joy of creation and God's care of the earth.

INTERIOR ENVIRONMENT

In the narthex and other gathering spaces during this season, consider placing containers of spring flowering bulbs. Decorate walls with brightly colored banners or artwork appropriate to this season. Scenes from the various gospels of this season may provide inspiration for visual artwork used during these weeks: Jesus' appearance to Thomas (John 20), Jesus eating fish with the disciples (Luke 24), Jesus as the good shepherd (John 10), and the ascension (Luke 24), among others.

The use of banners in the worship space beginning with Easter Day is very appropriate. If alleluia was "buried" prior to Lent, be sure to bring it back now.

White paraments, white flowers, and continued use of a lit paschal candle through to Pentecost Day, will help to proclaim the special significance of this joyous season.

The paschal cycle comes to a close on the day of Pentecost, with the celebration of the Spirit's sending to the church. Paraments for this occasion are red. Flowers are traditionally red as well, along with members of the congregation being encouraged to dress in red clothing. This great festival celebrates of the outpouring of the Holy Spirit on the church. All the festivity appropriate to Easter or Christmas is appropriate on this occasion as well.

The final impression on the day of Pentecost is one of explosive expansion. We go beyond the walls of our church. We extend the boundaries of our witness. A grand procession out of church to a nearby park, with banners flying and instruments sounding, would be a wonderful expression of the church's joy.

192

Preaching *with the* Season

It is the season of both the church year and the

calendar year when we talk of planting, new life, and growth.

Those things that were earlier planted and slept in the earth

now come forth. The church looks forward to and rejoices in the use of these images as much as one takes pleasure in viewing a field of blooming crocuses. We know what to expect every year at a certain time, and we delight at the first signs that our expectations are being fulfilled, whether it is the first green shoot of a bulb we hoped we planted deep enough or the return of the long awaited bird's song. It is in the absence of the familiar images that we lose our direction. New life imagery is our Easter compass and we should never grow tired using it in preaching, because the church never grows tired of hearing it used.

One of the most vivid images for Easter, one which practically writes its own sermon, has already been given to us by Jesus in the gospel for the last Sunday in Lent. "Unless a grain of wheat falls into the earth and dies, it remains just a single grain; but if it dies, it bears much fruit." The death and resurrection of the incarnate

Christ tell us and indeed demonstrate for us the life cycle of those who believe and are baptized.

This vision of new life and what that new life entails is given to us throughout the gospel readings in the Easter season—the reaction to the empty tomb, the doubt of Thomas and others, the assurance of the Good Shepherd's guidance. Once the church is convinced that Jesus really is who he claimed, and is even given physical proof ("Do you have anything here to eat?"), the lectionary allows us to revisit those things the Lord said when we disciples were only vaguely aware of what Jesus meant. Only after witnessing Jesus' life, death, and resurrection do we begin to get a glimpse of the big picture, a picture that we will see completely in our own resurrection. And in our daily struggle to be faithful followers, we experience death and rebirth—many mini-resurrections, so to speak.

The horticultural, agricultural imagery Jesus uses withstands the test of time. It was helpful in proclamation in his time and it still works in our time, despite our increasing urbanity. In his words to comfort his disciples he explains that death is not the end. The grain that dies produces wheat. We know that wheat then becomes bread. And though the "I am" saying in the Easter season is "I am the good shepherd," we clearly remember Jesus also saying, "I am the bread of life." Jesus is that on which we feed, both literally in the Lord's supper and spiritually in the course of our faith journey.

We are responsible for distributing that bread to the hungry multitudes who have not tasted and seen the goodness of the Lord. And Jesus' analogy of branches spreading out from the one true vine, the good branches producing good fruit, reinforces the believer's role in the spreading of the good news. This message is clearly articulated on Ascension Day in Jesus' words as he withdrew from them and was taken into the heavens, "repentance and forgiveness of sins is to be proclaimed in [the Messiah's] name to all nations, beginning from Jerusalem."

Liturgically speaking, the color used for the Sundays in Easter is celebrative white. However, because the color green is a prominent image in the lessons, some homiletical effort might be made to connect the colors of the calendar season to the colors we "see" in the lessons, thus connecting the Sunday images to images in daily life. Not only can we sing of "the green blade rising from the buried grain," but also talk about the "green faith," the immature faith that is subject to fears and doubts; the brown of dead branches, the orange of the fire in which they burn. What colors are in the altar flowers? Do they reflect the colors in the texts?

All of God's creation is at hand to assist us in proclaiming that Christ is risen. Let those who have eyes, see.

PENTECOST

The Day of Pentecost officially brings an end to the Easter Season, and it ends on such a high note that the following Sunday, Trinity Sunday, could almost seem anticlimactic. After having been put on alert by Jesus to wait for the Advocate, the Spirit of truth will come and clothe Jesus' disciples with power from on high, the natural progression demands that we celebrate all the Trinity in unity. But the *dunamis* of Pentecost is so explosive that even though we have been put on alert, we are still not ready for what the Holy Spirit gives us when it comes.

Now with an understanding of the work of each person of the Trinity we live out the salvation story; creatures of our God and King, redeemed by the blood of Jesus the Lamb who was slain and rose to a glorious resurrection in which we share, and guided and guarded by the Spirit of God that we are never alone in our mission to build and be the Church of Christ.

Shape *of* Worship *for the* Season

BASIC SHAPE OF THE EUCHARISTIC RITE

- Confession and Forgiveness: see alternate worship text for Easter in *Sundays and Seasons* as an option to the text in the liturgy setting.
- Or, use Confession and Forgiveness with sprinkling from the seasonal rites section

GATHERING

- Greeting: see alternate worship text for Easter
- Use the Kyrie throughout Easter
- As the hymn of praise, use "This is the feast of victory"

WORD

- For dramatic readings based on lectionary passages, use *Scripture Out Loud!* (AFP 0806639644) for the second and third Sundays of Easter and Pentecost Day
- For contemporary dramas based on lectionary passages, use *Can These Bones Live?* (AFP 0806639652)

193

for the second and fourth Sundays of Easter and Pentecost Day
- Use the Nicene Creed
- The prayers: see the prayers in the Easter section of *Sundays and Seasons*

BAPTISM

- Consider observing Pentecost Day (June 8) as a baptismal festival

MEAL

- Offertory prayer: see alternate worship text for Easter
- Use the proper preface for Easter; use the proper preface for Pentecost on Pentecost Day
- Eucharistic Prayer: in addition to four main options in *LBW,* see "Eucharistic Prayer E: The Season of Easter" in *WOV* Leaders Edition, p. 69; and "Eucharistic Prayer F: The Day of Pentecost" in *WOV* Leaders Edition, p. 70
- Invitation to communion: see alternate worship text for Easter
- Post-communion prayer: see alternate worship text for Easter

SENDING

- Benediction: see alternate worship text for Easter
- Dismissal: see alternate worship text for Easter

OTHER SEASONAL POSSIBILITIES
ROGATION BLESSING

- See seasonal rites section; may be used to conclude worship on the sixth Sunday of Easter (traditionally, rogation days are the Monday, Tuesday, and Wednesday before Ascension Day) or at another time when such a blessing is appropriate

VIGIL OF PENTECOST

- A celebration for this evening could be modeled on the Easter Vigil, but using these elements:
  - Service of Light (from *LBW,* pp. 142–44)
  - Service of Word (eucharistic rite, from the prayer of the day through the hymn of the day)
  - Service of Baptismal Affirmation (from *LBW,* pp. 199–201, with the congregation gathering around the font, space permitting; water may be sprinkled from the font during the recitation of the creed)
  - Service of Communion (from the offering through the dismissal)

Assembly Song *for the* Season

Easter is a feast of feasts, a week of weeks

for singing alleluias with full-throated voice. The familiar

stories of Jesus' resurrection and post-resurrection

appearances sound out anew, and are literally new for many listeners. The fifty days of Easter are no time to grow tired of singing, no time to hold back in our music. But it can also be a time for quieter reflective music, even silence—music or silence that allows the assembly to hear Jesus speaking as Mary heard him in the garden, quietly calling her name. Not everything should be "higher, louder, faster" even as we celebrate the feast of victory for our God.

GATHERING

- Sing a strong, familiar Easter hymn as the entrance hymn on all the Sundays of this season. On the festival of the Ascension and the seventh Sunday of Easter, this could be an Ascension hymn; on Pentecost sing a hymn invoking the presence of the Holy Spirit.
- Use both the Kyrie and hymn of praise ("This is the feast") throughout the season. If you used more elab-

194

orate liturgical settings on Easter Day, continue them through Pentecost.

WORD

- Use "alleluias" for seasonal psalm refrains. The refrains to LBW hymns 135, 139, and 144; and the final three "alleluias" from LBW 143 offer good possibilities.
- Use more "alleluias" for the gospel acclamation—the service music sections of *WOV, TFF,* and *LLC* offer many possibilities. Use percussion if appropriate. Sing the chosen setting both before and after the gospel, especially if there is a procession, or have the choir chant the proper verse in between two singings. Alternatively, have the choir sing one of the published settings of the alleluia verses for the Easter season.
- On Pentecost, use the sequence hymn "Come, Holy Ghost, our souls inspire" (LBW 472) following the gospel acclamation. It is especially powerful sung unaccompanied, with perhaps a few handbells rung randomly to keep the assembly on pitch.
- Highlight the hymn of the day with choral stanzas or descants, alternation between men/women or left

side/right side, and full and creative use of organ and instruments.

MEAL

- "He is arisen! Glorious Word!" (LBW 138) and "This joyful Eastertide" (LBW 149 or WOV 676) are good choices for seasonal offertory hymns. If a more elaborate offertory procession is held, use "At the Lamb's high feast we sing" (LBW 210) or "Our Paschal Lamb, that sets us free" (WOV 679).
- Continue to give the "Holy, holy, holy Lord" (Sanctus) sufficient weight throughout the season.
- Continue the "Celtic Alleluia" (WOV 613) to begin the distribution music. During the meal is a good time for some quieter music, such as "Here is bread" (W&P 58) or "Alleluia, alleluia, give thanks" (WOV 671).

SENDING

- This season is one in which both a post-communion canticle ("Thank the Lord"/"Thankful hearts") and sending hymn are appropriate. Let the cross of Christ lead the way back out into the world, as it leads the way into worship during the entrance hymn.

195

Music *for the* Season

VERSE AND OFFERTORY

Cherwien, David. *Verses for the Sundays of Easter.* U, org.   MSM 80-400.

Farrell, Bernadette. "Eastertide Gospel Acclamation."   OCP 7172CC.

Gospel Acclamations. Cant, choir, cong, inst.   MAY 0862096324.

Pelz, Walter L. *Verses and Offertories: Easter–The Holy Trinity.* SATB, org.
   AFP 0800649044.

Schalk, Carl. *Verses and Offertory Sentences: Part IV, Easter Day through Easter 7.*
   CPH 97-5504.

Willan, Healey/arr. Gunther. *Verses for the Easter Season.* SATB, kybd.
   CPH 98-3057.

CHORAL

Collins, Dori Erwin. "Offering." SATB, U, pno, fl, opt hb.
   AFP 0800659694.

Fleming, Larry. "Lord of the Dance." SATB.   AFP 0800655354.

Hassler, Hans L. "Cantate Domino" in *Chantry Choirbook.* SATB.
   AFP 0800657772.

Haugen, Marty. "Halle, Halle, Halle." SATB, cant, opt. cong, perc,
   kybd.   GIA G-3961.

Helman, Michael. "We Walk by Faith." SATB, pno, opt fl, hb.
   AFP 0800659759.

Hopp, Roy. "God of Grace and God of Laughter." SATB, ob,
   hp/pno.   AFP 0800659570.

Jennings, Kenneth. "With a Voice of Singing." SATB.
   AFP 0800645669.

Jordan, Alice. "See the Land, Her Easter Keeping." SATB, org.
   RME EC92-107.

Kosche, Kenneth T. "It Is a Good Thing." SATB.   AFP 0800659635.

Pelz, Walter. "Crown Him with Many Crowns." SATB, cong, org,
   3 tpt.   AFP 080064803X.

Schalk, Carl. "Thine the Amen." SATB, org, opt cong.
   AFP 0800646126.

St. Thomas More Group. *Easter Mysteries.* SATB, kybd, gtr, inst.
   OCP 9858GC.

CHILDREN'S CHOIRS

Bedford, Michael. "Ring the News!" from *Singing the Seasons.* U, kybd,
   opt 2 oct hb.   CG CGA854.

Cherwien, David, arr. "O Holy Spirit Enter In." U/2 pt/SATB, org.
   CPH 983484.

Proulx, Richard. "Easter Carol." U/2 pt, fl, kybd.   GIA G-4465.

Ramseth, Betty Ann and Melinda Ramseth Hoiland. *A Child's World.*
   U, Orff inst, opt gtr.   AFP 0800653173.

Rathman, Dawn. "Go Forth." U, kybd, gtr.   CPH 98-3332.

Running, Joseph. "An Easter Carol." U, kybd.   MSM 50-4751.

KEYBOARD/INSTRUMENTAL

Albrecht, Mark. *Festive Processionals.* Org, tpt.   AFP 0800657985.

Augsburg Organ Library: Easter. Org.   AFP 0800659368.

Callahan, Charles. "An Easter Prelude for Flute and Organ." Org, fl.
   MSM 20-460.

Dengler, Lee. *Easter Piano Variations* (Lyra Davidica, Christ ist erstanden,
   Vruechten). Pno.   CPH 97-6776.

Manz, Paul. *Improvisations for the Easter Season.* Org.   MSM 10-402.

Roberts, Myron J. *Prelude and Trumpetings.* Org.   HWG G.B. 298.

Rutter, John. "Variations on an Easter Theme." Org duet.
   OXF 0-19-375715.

Webster, Richard. "Paschal Suite for Organ and Trumpet." Org, tpt.
   AFP 080065692X.

HANDBELL

Moklebust, Cathy. "Lift High the Cross." 3–5 oct, org, cong, opt
   brass qrt.   CG CGB 193.

Sleeth, Natalie/arr. Martha Lynn Thompson. "Hymn of Promise."
   3–5 oct, 2 pt vcs, opt hc.   AG 1519.

Thompson, Martha Lynn. "The Morning Trumpet." 3–5 oct.
   HOP 1937.

VanKley, J. "Beautiful Savior." 3–5 oct.   JEF RW8117.

Young, Philip. "Good Christians, Rejoice and Sing." 2–3 oct.
   AFP 080065627X.

PRAISE ENSEMBLE

Founds, Rick/arr. Gary Rhodes. "Lord, I Lift Your Name on High."
   SATB, kybd.   WRD 301 0805 160.

Pethel, Stan. "Celebrate the Victory." SATB, kybd.   LOR 10/2334LA.

Pote, Allen. "On the Third Day." SATB, kybd, hb.   HOP F1000.
   Brass.   F1000B.

196

Alternate Worship Texts

CONFESSION AND FORGIVENESS

In the name of the Father, and of the ✛ Son,
and of the Holy Spirit.
Amen

By our baptism into the death and resurrection of Christ,
God raised us to new life.
Let us confess to God our sins
and all that waits for resurrection in our lives.

Silence for reflection and self-examination.

God of love,
we find it hard to believe the witness of the resurrection:
we resist your unfailing love for us and for others,
and we turn our backs on the gift of new life,
choosing instead the old way of sin,
the way that takes us away from you
and leads us back toward death.
Free us from this power of sin,
guide us by your Spirit,
and help us in our weakness,
that we may live as your children,
restored to new and everlasting life. Amen

By God's grace you are forgiven and born anew.
May you be strengthened daily with the power
to walk in God's light and love.
Amen

GREETING

Alleluia! Christ is risen!
Christ is risen indeed. Alleluia!

The grace of our risen Savior, the love of God,
and the communion of the Holy Spirit be with you all.
And also with you.

PRAYERS

Standing in the glorious light of the resurrection,
let us pray for the church, the world,
and all who wait for the Spirit's revealing power.

A brief silence.

Each petition ends:
We pray to the Lord:
Lord, hear our prayer.

Concluding petition:
Gracious God, hear our prayers and receive them
for the sake of the crucified and risen one,
our Savior Jesus Christ.
Amen

OFFERTORY PRAYER

Living God,
in Christ's resurrection
you raised up new life for the world.
Receive what we offer,
that others might know that life
through the gifts you give us
to use and to share. Amen

INVITATION TO COMMUNION

This is the feast of victory for our God. Alleluia!

POST-COMMUNION PRAYER

O God of love,
you bind us to yourself in this sacrament,
and strengthen us through this meal
for service to the world.
Guide us by your Spirit
that we may forever witness to the name
of Jesus Christ, the Lord of life.
Amen

BLESSING

May almighty God ✛ bless you,
renew the risen life of Christ within you,
and bring forth in you the fruits of the Holy Spirit.
Amen

DISMISSAL

Alleluia! Go and tell the news that Christ is risen.
Christ is risen indeed. Alleluia!

197

Seasonal Rites

Confession and Forgiveness with Sprinkling

The order may be used before the entrance hymn or in conjunc-tion with the entrance hymn (in procession). People are invited to turn and face the baptismal font or the place where the sprin-kling bowl is located. All stand.

St. Paul writes, "As many of you as were baptized into Christ have clothed yourselves with Christ" (Gal. 3:27). As we are clothed with Christ, we are clothed with God's mercy. Standing under that mercy, we freely confess that we have sinned and fallen short of the glory of God.

Silence for reflection and self-examination.

In the waters of Holy Baptism
God liberated us from sin and death,
joining us to the death and resurrection
of our Lord Jesus Christ.
Our life in Christ is marked
by a constant return to our baptism.
We daily die to sin and rise to newness of life.

THANKSGIVING OVER THE WATER
Gracious God,
from age to age
you made water a sign of your presence among us.
In the beginning your Spirit brooded over the waters,
calling forth life that was good.
You led the people of Israel safely through the Red Sea
and into the land of promise.
In the waters of the Jordan,
you proclaimed Jesus Beloved,
the One upon whom your favor rests.

By water and the Spirit
you adopted us as your daughters and sons,
making us heirs of the promise,
and laborers for the Reign of God.
In the sprinkling of this water,
remind us of our baptism.

Shower us with your Spirit ✛,
so that we may experience anew
your forgiveness,
your grace,
and your love.
Amen

An ordained minister sprinkles the people with water, in silence or during the entrance hymn (in procession). The singing of Psalm 51 in Lent and Psalm 117 in Easter, with an appropriate antiphon, may be used in place of the entrance hymn. After the sprinkling, the liturgy of Holy Communion continues with the greeting (Kyrie or hymn of praise), and prayer of the day.

Rogation Blessing

PRAYER FOR SEEDS
Hold seeds aloft.
Creating God, you have given seed to the sower and bread to the people. Nourish, protect, and bless the seeds which your people have sown in hope. By your loving and bountiful giving, may they bring forth their fruit in due season, through Jesus Christ our Lord. Amen

PRAYER FOR THE SOIL
Hold soil aloft.
Giver of life, we give you thanks that in the richness of the soil, nature awakens to your call of spring. We praise you for the smell of freshly tilled earth, the beauty of a cleanly cut furrow, and a well-plowed field. We ask that you help us to be good stewards of this land. In the name of the one who gives us new life, Jesus Christ our Lord. Amen

PRAYER FOR WATER AND RAIN
Hold water aloft.
Sustaining God, we receive the fruits of the earth from you. We give you thanks for the smell of the earth after rain, for its wel-come cooling, and its necessary hydration for the land. We ask that the rain come as often as it is needed so that the crops may flourish and the coming harvest be indeed bountiful. Amen

April 27, 2003

Second Sunday of Easter

INTRODUCTION

In the waters of baptism, God raises us up in Jesus and gives us life that endures. Though we do not see him in the flesh, he continues to reveal himself to us in the breaking of the bread, our foretaste of the feast to come. Day by day, we pray that God would strengthen our faith, so that we who have not seen Christ Jesus may truly confess him as our Lord and God.

PRAYER OF THE DAY

Almighty God, with joy we celebrate the festival of our Lord's resurrection. Graciously help us to show the power of the resurrection in all that we say and do; through your Son, Jesus Christ our Lord, who lives and reigns with you and the Holy Spirit, one God, now and forever.

VERSE

Alleluia. Christ being raised from the dead will never die again; death no longer has dominion over him. Alleluia. Blessed are those who have not seen and yet have come to believe. Alleluia. (Rom. 6:9; John 20:29)

READINGS

Acts 4:32-35

In today's reading, the church glimpses the life of the first Christian community. Here the author of Acts describes the social dimension of Christian life. Animated by the Spirit of the risen Lord, the body of Christ cares for those in need and holds all things in common.

Psalm 133

How good and pleasant it is to live together in unity. (Ps. 133:1)

1 John 1:1—2:2

This letter of John begins with poetic testimony to Jesus as the word of life. Through him we have firsthand experience of God and know for certain that God loves us and forgives us our sin.

John 20:19-31

The story of Easter continues as the risen Lord appears to his disciples. His words to Thomas offer a blessing to all who entrust themselves in faith to the risen Lord.

COLOR White

THE PRAYERS

Standing in the glorious light of the resurrection, let us pray for the church, the world, and all who wait for the Spirit's revealing power.

A BRIEF SILENCE.

Let us pray that God's gifts of word and sacraments would bring deeper unity among those who celebrate Christ's Easter victory. We pray to the Lord:

Lord, hear our prayer.

Let us pray that the joy of the resurrection would create a world in which those in need will not be forsaken and the resources of all people will be distributed fairly and honestly. We pray to the Lord:

Lord, hear our prayer.

Let us pray that the joy of the resurrection would bestow grace upon all who, like Thomas, are full of doubts and questions, that they might be given a trusting and believing heart. We pray to the Lord:

Lord, hear our prayer.

Let us pray that the joy of the resurrection would bring complete healing to those who struggle with illness *(especially)*. May all who are in pain be touched with the peace from God. We pray to the Lord:

Lord, hear our prayer.

Let us pray that the joy of the resurrection would sustain all who have been newly baptized and those who have renewed their baptism. May inquirers continue to be drawn to the joy of this faith community. We pray to the Lord:

Lord, hear our prayer.

HERE OTHER INTERCESSIONS MAY BE OFFERED.

Let us pray that the joy of the resurrection would cross the boundaries of time and eternity, so that all who are in grief may know the hope of the new creation. We pray to the Lord:

Lord, hear our prayer.

Gracious God, hear our prayers and receive them for the sake of the crucified and risen one, our Savior Jesus Christ.

Amen

199

IMAGES FOR PREACHING

We could lump all followers of Christ into two categories: those who believe, and those who do not believe, who doubt. It seems that simple, but at any given time in our faith journey we are both kinds. That mixed identity is, oddly, part of being disciples.

Was Thomas the "bad guy," that is, the only faithless doubter? Or was he only articulating what the other disciples did not have the courage to say aloud when Jesus appeared to them? The text does not tell us they required proof. Maybe Jesus anticipated their requirement and showed them before they asked.

All three synoptic gospels remember Jesus saying, "Many will come in my name, and say 'I am he!' " (Mark 13:6). Perhaps Thomas, recalling those words, simply asked for some identification, something that would let him know it was really Jesus, his Lord and his God. It is not a bad example for all of us to follow before we go running after someone or something that is actually the seducer dressed in deceptive clothing.

We who live in the light of the resurrection still seek signs of the presence of the Lord, especially when dealing with loss or the troubles and trials of life that surround us, making us prisoners of fear and doubt and confusion. It is then that we are most vulnerable and can easily be led astray. The disciple who believes that the light shines in the darkness is also aware of the dangers that lurk in that darkness, and will question, "Where are you, Lord? Can I see some I.D.?"

The risen Christ is indeed with us. In that recognition and in the understanding of through whom and in what circumstances the Lord appears to us, we too are able to confess: "My Lord and my God."

WORSHIP MATTERS

The Greek word for resurrection literally means to "stand up." It has been the tradition of many churches, therefore, to honor our Lord's resurrection by not kneeling for prayer, to receive communion, or for any reason during the Easter season, but to always "stand up." As Christ has been raised from the dead, so too we stand arisen, demonstrating the resurrection with our bodies.

The posture of resurrection might also reach to other areas of our worship. As we with Thomas confess Jesus as "our Lord and our God," we are able to worship in ways that raise up all of God's people, to use words that lift up those who are bent down by life's heavy load,

to sing the song of the whole world—standing with the many and varied churches of the continents.

LET THE CHILDREN COME

Sharing Jesus' peace with one another as a liturgical act can be seen to have its origins in the gospel. It should be modeled by the liturgical leaders who can make an effort to greet children as well as adults and parents who can greet children appropriately. The congregation may be encouraged to use names, especially in greeting children. It may be helpful to remind people that it is a time to show Christian care for others and not a time for small talk.

HYMNS FOR WORSHIP
GATHERING

The strife is o'er, the battle done   LBW 135
Christ is risen! Shout hosanna!   WOV 672, CS 16
Christ has arisen, alleluia   WOV 678, TFF 96

HYMN OF THE DAY

O sons and daughters of the King   LBW 139

ALTERNATE HYMN OF THE DAY

Thine is the glory   LBW 145
We walk by faith and not by sight   WOV 675

COMMUNION

Now we join in celebration   LBW 203
Dona nobis pacem   WOV 774

SENDING

On our way rejoicing   LBW 260
We are marching in the light of God   WOV 650, TFF 63, W&P 148
God be with you   W&P 50

ADDITIONAL HYMNS AND SONGS

Day of arising   OBS 54, CS 24
Eternal light, shine in my heart   H82 465, 466
These things did Thomas count as real   NCH 54
Come and see   W&P 29

MUSIC FOR THE DAY
PSALMODY

Hopson, Hal H. "Psalm 133" in TP.
Miren qué bueno/Behold, how pleasant   GS2 21

Mirad cuán bueno/Behold, how good and delightful   LLC 475
Young, Jeremy.   PW B.

CHORAL

Bouman, Paul. "God Is Light." SATB, org.   AFP 0800653254.

Crüger, Johann. "Awake, My Heart, with Gladness" in *Chantry Choirbook*. SATB, 2 C inst.   AFP 0800657772.

Gehring, Philip. "O Sons and Daughters." SATB, 2 trp, 2 tbn.
   CPH 97-6077.

Helman, Michael. "We Walk by Faith." SATB, pno, opt 4 oct hb, fl.
   AFP 0800659759.

Hillert, Richard. "O Sons and Daughters of the King." SAB, cong,
   opt tpt, org.   CPH 98-3117.

Pelz, Walter. "Peace I Leave with You." SATB.   AFP 0800645650.

Proulx, Richard. "Easter Carol." 2 pt, fl, kybd.   GIA G-4465. Fl pt.
   GIA G-4465INST.

Roberts, William Bradley. "In All These You Welcomed Me." U, org,
   opt ob/inst.   AFP 6000001207.

CHILDREN'S CHOIRS

Cool, Jayne Southwick. "I'm a Disciple, Too!" U, opt 2 pt, kybd.
   AFP 080067457X.

Sherman, Arnold. "An Upper Room." U, kybd.   AMSI 505.

Sleeth, Natalie. "Hymn of Promise." 2 pt, kybd.   HOP A580.

KEYBOARD/INSTRUMENTAL

Farnam, Lynnwood. "Toccata on 'O filii et filiae.'" Org.
   PRE 25819-6.

Held, Wilbur. "O filii et filiae" in *Augsburg Organ Library: Easter*. Org.
   AFP 0800659368.

Helman, Michael. "O filii et filiae" in *Three for Easter: Festive Hymn Settings for Organ*. Org.   AFP 0800674790.

Porter, Emily Maxson. "Judas Maccabaeus" in *Augsburg Organ Library: Easter*. Org.   AFP 0800659368.

Uhl, Dan. "Christ Is Risen! Alleluia!" (Morgenlied) in *Easter Suite*.
   Org, tpt, opt timp.   AFP 0800655419.

HANDBELL

Geschke, Susan. "This Day of Gladness." 2–3 oct.   JEF MCGB208.

Maggs, Charles. "Siyahamba." (*We Are Marching in the Light of God*).
   3 oct.   JEF GE GP1034.

Nelson, Susan. "Easter Alleluia." (O filii et filiae). 3–5 oct, opt hc,
   perc, solo inst.   JEF MCGB216.

Organ, Anne Krentz. "Earth and All Stars" (Alleluia! Jesus Is Risen).
   3 oct, opt hc.   AFP 0800658086.

PRAISE ENSEMBLE

Grant, Amy and Wes King. "Salt and Light" in *Songs from the Loft*.
   WRD.

Harris, Margaret J. "I Will Praise Him" in *Hosanna! Music Songbook vol. 6*.
   INT HMSB06.

Pote, Allen. "Many Gifts, One Spirit." SAB, kybd.
   Coral Key Music 392-41417. SATB.   392-41388.
   SSA.   392-41466.

Smith, Gary Alan. "Peace I Leave with You." SATB, pno.
   ABI 02742-X.

Zschech, Darlene. "Walking in the Light" in *God Is in the House*.
   MAR.

Tuesday, April 29

CATHERINE OF SIENA, TEACHER

Catherine of Siena was a member of the Order of Preachers (Dominicans) and among Roman Catholics she is the first woman to receive the title "Doctor of the Church." She was a contemplative and is known for her mystical visions of Jesus. This gift of mysticism apparently extended back into her childhood, much to the dismay of her parents who wanted her to be like other children. Catherine was a humanitarian who worked to alleviate the suffering of the poor and imprisoned. She was also a renewer of church and society and advised both popes and any uncertain persons who told her their problems.

Thursday, May 1

ST. PHILIP AND ST. JAMES, APOSTLES

Philip was one of the first disciples of Jesus, who after following Jesus invited Nathanael to "come and see." According to tradition, he preached in Asia Minor and died as a martyr in Phrygia. James, the son of Alphaeus is called "the Less" to distinguish him from another apostle named James, commemorated July 25. Philip and James are commemorated together because the remains of these two saints were placed in the Church of the Apostles in Rome on this day in 561.

   Their invitation to "come and see" is at the heart of the catechumenate. During these fifty days of Easter how can your community invite others to come and see the new life of Christ?

Friday, May 2

ATHANASIUS, BISHOP OF ALEXANDRIA, 373

Athanasius attended the Council of Nicea in 325 as a deacon and secretary to the bishop of Alexandria. At the council, and when he himself served as bishop of Alexandria, he defended the full divinity of Christ against the Arian position held by emperors, magistrates, and theologians. Because of his defense of the divinity of Christ he was considered a troublemaker and was banished from Alexandria on five separate occasions. As bishop, one of his paschal letters to surrounding bishops gives a list for books that should be considered canonical scripture. He lists the twenty-seven New Testament books that are recognized today.

Athanasius is an appropriate saint for Easter. His name means "deathless one" though he himself lived in threat of death because of his theological stand. We are made in God's likeness, Athanasius affirmed. By the resurrection we are remade in the likeness of the Son who conquered death.

May 4, 2003

Third Sunday of Easter

INTRODUCTION

The church gathers in the power of the risen Lord. Here in this assembly made holy by its consecration in baptism, Christ opens the scriptures and reveals himself to us. Gathered at his table as the bread is broken, we see that his life has been broken for us, so that our broken lives might be healed. From the table of the word and the table of the eucharist, Christ feeds us with his love and abundant mercy.

The church today remembers Monica, the mother of Augustine, who helped to shape the faith of that significant church father.

PRAYER OF THE DAY

O God, by the humiliation of your Son you lifted up this fallen world, rescuing us from the hopelessness of death. Grant your faithful people a share in the joys that are eternal; through your Son, Jesus Christ our Lord, who lives and reigns with you and the Holy Spirit, one God, now and forever.

VERSE

Alleluia. Christ being raised from the dead will never die again; death no longer has dominion over him. Alleluia. Our hearts burn within us while he opens to us the scriptures. Alleluia. (Rom. 6:9; Luke 24:32)

READINGS

Acts 3:12-19

Peter testifies to the Easter faith, proclaiming that Christ's resurrection fulfills the promises of God and brings blessing even to those who killed him.

Psalm 4

The LORD does wonders for the faithful. (Ps. 4:3)

1 John 3:1-7

The First Letter of John encourages Christians to abide in Christ so that God's love will be found in them. The baptized are children of God in Christ. To be a child of God is to have a mission: to offer God's love in a world of conflict.

Luke 24:36b-48

In this account of an appearance after his resurrection, Jesus opens the minds of the disciples to understand him as Messiah. Jesus convinces the disciples that he has been raised, and sends them on a mission to proclaim the message of repentance and forgiveness.

COLOR White

THE PRAYERS

Standing in the glorious light of the resurrection, let us pray for the church, the world, and all who wait for the Spirit's revealing power.

A BRIEF SILENCE.

God of peace, your presence calms our fears and terrors. Give all the baptized such a boldness in faith and proclamation that many will have their minds opened to understand and experience your love. We pray to the Lord:
Lord, hear our prayer.

God of life, grant your wisdom to all who are in positions of power and authority across the world as they guide the peoples of all nations. We pray to the Lord:
Lord, hear our prayer.

God of compassion, grant to all who are facing surgery or medical treatments a generous measure of peace in mind and heart. Touch the sick with your tenderness *(especially)*, that they may be reassured of your love. We pray to the Lord:
Lord, hear our prayer.

God of strength, empower the youth ministry of this congregation and of the whole church, that young people will hear and be kept firmly in the joy and freedom of the gospel. We pray to the Lord:
Lord, hear our prayer.

HERE OTHER INTERCESSIONS MAY BE OFFERED.

God of comfort, you promise that one day we shall see you as you are. Until that day, keep us united in the communion of saints with Monica *(other names)*, and all who have died and who rest peacefully in you. We pray to the Lord:
Lord, hear our prayer.

Gracious God, hear our prayers and receive them for the sake of the crucified and risen one, our Savior Jesus Christ.
Amen

IMAGES FOR PREACHING

This appearance is at least the fourth of the risen Jesus in three Sundays, two having been told last week. Keeping in mind Jesus' predictions of his return while he was still with the disciples, this fourth telling of the resurrection should be entitled "I told you so!" As a matter of fact, Jesus says just that, "These are my words that I spoke to you while I was still with you" (implied: words that you neither understood nor heeded). If anyone in the congregation has been listening, or even if someone missed a Sunday, or was away on vacation, no one could miss the fact that "Christ is risen; he is risen indeed!"

But this week's gospel reading gives us better insight into the emotional state of the other disciples while taking the heat off Thomas. These disciples in Luke, too, were "startled," "terrified," and "frightened." And "doubts arose" in *their* hearts, as well. They, too, required physical proof. Though they did not the place their fingers in the marks of the nails, Jesus did have to eat food to prove that he was real and not simply an apparition. Luke even tells us it was a broiled piece of fish, in case any latter-day hearers need that specificity.

So, contrary to what was said last week, maybe there is only one kind of disciple in this world: those who unwittingly follow Jesus; who hear what he says, but do not understand what he means; and who, only after struggling and loss, call to remembrance the saving words of restoration. It is only when we reach that point that we can truly be witnesses of those things and tell our stories that others may come to be disciples.

WORSHIP MATTERS

For God's word to be heard, it must be read clearly and carefully, but good reading also requires good listening.

Encourage worshipers to read the lessons prior to arriving at church, and invite them to listen closely as the scripture is read once again on Sunday morning. Include tips for reading so that worshipers will better prepare themselves for worship. For example, in the Easter season the first reading is always from the Acts of the Apostles, and this lectionary year B, the second reading is from the First Letter of John.

Those prepared to hear God's word may find themselves to be more fertile soil for the word to take root and grow.

LET THE CHILDREN COME

Jesus welcomes people and cares for them. Children come to know the risen Jesus through the liturgy—singing about him, being fed by him at his table, being healed and refreshed by him through prayer and worship, and by caring for others through their offerings, the sign of peace, and prayers. Jesus' presence in the liturgy reveals who he is to the children.

HYMNS FOR WORSHIP
GATHERING

Now all the vault of heaven resounds   LBW 143
This joyful Eastertide   LBW 149, WOV 676

203

HYMN OF THE DAY

The strife is o'er, the battle done   LBW 135

ALTERNATE HYMN OF THE DAY

Alleluia! Jesus is risen!   WOV 674, TFF 91
Alleluia, alleluia, give thanks   WOV 671

COMMUNION

Come, let us eat   LBW 214, TFF 119
Stay with us   WOV 743
Come to the table   W&P 33
Now the body broken   DH 31

SENDING

Around you, O Lord Jesus   LBW 496
Let us talents and tongues employ   WOV 754, TFF 232

ADDITIONAL HYMNS AND SONGS

Blessing be and glory   OBS 50
Awake, my soul   H82 546
Forth in the peace of Christ we go   W3 627
Behold, what manner of love   TFF 218
Come and taste   W&P 30

MUSIC FOR THE DAY

PSALMODY

Haugen, Marty. "Psalm 4: Let Your Face Shine upon Us" in GC.
Schütz, Heinrich. "Psalm 4: Oh, Hear When I Cry to Thee" in *Ten More Psalms from the "Becker Psalter."* CPH 97-4880.
Young, Jeremy.   PW B.

CHORAL

Bobb, Barry. "God's Creative Dream." SATB, pno.   AFP 0800674715.
Farlee, Robert Buckley. "Christ Is Living" (Cristo Vive). SATB, org, perc, gtr.   AFP 0800652479.
Gerike, Henry. "The Strife Is O'er, the Battle Done." SATB, tpt, kybd.   CPH 98-2446.
Mendelssohn, Felix. "See What Love." SATB, kybd.   AFP 0800645618.
Pelz, Walter. "Stay with Us." SAB, org.   CPH 98-3073.
Philips, Peter. "Surgens Jesus" in *The New Church Anthem Book.* SSATB, org.   OXF 0193531097.
Shute, Linda Cable. "This Joyful Eastertide." 2 pt mxd, desc, 5 oct hb, perc, kybd.   AFP 0800656083.
Ulrich, Jerry. "Heleluyan." SATBB.   ABI 50290X.

CHILDREN'S CHOIRS

Jothen, Michael. "We Are Children of Our God." U/2 pt, kybd, opt fl, opt 3–4 oct hb, opt cong.   CG CGA731.
Pearson, Brian and Sherry Pearson. "Life Together." U, opt 2 pt, kybd, opt perc.   AFP 0800674197.
Rathman, Dawn. "Go Forth." U, kybd, gtr.   CPH 98-3332.

KEYBOARD/INSTRUMENTAL

Cherwien, David. "This Joyful Eastertide" in *Amazing Grace: Four for Piano.* Pno.   AFP 0800659031.
Helman, Michael. "Victory (Palestrina)" in *Augsburg Organ Library: Easter.* Org.   AFP 0800659368.
Honoré, Jeffrey. "Alleluia No. 1" in *Contemporary Hymn Preludes for Organ.* Org.   AFP 0800674782.
Vogt, Emanuel. "Mfurahini, Haleluya" in *Augsburg Organ Library: Easter.* Org.   AFP 0800659368.
Walcha, Helmut. "Mit Freuden zart" in *Chorale Preludes II.* Org.   PET 4871.
Wasson, Laura E. "Alleluia No. 1" in *A Piano Tapestry, vol. 2.* Pno.   AFP 0800658183.

HANDBELL

Bock, Almon C. III "The Strife Is O'er." 2 oct.   AFP 0800653688.
Geschke, Susan. "A Joyous Alleluia." 3 oct.   CG CGB226.
Rogers, Sharon Elery. "An Easter Festival." 2–3 oct.   JEF MLC-201090L.
Zabel, Albert. "The Strife Is O'er." 3–5 oct.   AFP 080065806X.

PRAISE ENSEMBLE

Althouse, Jay. "Someone Is There." SATB, acc.   GS A-6306.
Butler, Randy and Terry. "At the Cross" in *Fifteen Best Loved Worship Classics from Vineyard Music, Change My Heart, O God, vol 2.* Vineyard Publications.
Espinosa, Eddie. "Change My Heart, O God" in *Songs for Praise and Worship.* WRD.
Hanson, Handt. "Come Touch" in *Spirit Touching Spirit.* Prince of Peace Publishing.
Lowery, Robert/arr. John A. Schreiner. "Here Is Love" in *Favorite Hymns of Promise Keepers.* 3 pt, kybd.   MAR 3010133367.
Smith, Gary Alan. "Peace I Leave with You." SATB, pno.   ABI 02742-X.

Sunday, May 4

MONICA, MOTHER OF AUGUSTINE, 387

Monica was married to a pagan husband who was ill-tempered and unfaithful. She rejoiced greatly when both her husband and his mother became Christian. But it is because she is the mother of Augustine that she is best known. Monica had been a disciple of Ambrose and eventually Augustine came under his influence. Almost everything we know about Monica comes from Augustine's *Confessions*, his autobiography. She died far from her home but said to her son, "Do not fret because I am buried far from our home in Africa. Nothing is far from God, and I have no fear that God will not know where to find me, when Christ comes to raise me to life at the end of the world." Her dying wish was that her son remember her at the altar of the Lord wherever he was.

Monica's life bore witness to the vital role that parents play in the faith formation of their children. Consider how the church supports parents in that task.

Thursday, May 8

VICTOR THE MOOR, MARTYR, 303

Known also as Victor Maurus, this native of the African country of Mauritania was a Christian from his youth. He served as a soldier in the Praetorian Guard. Under the persecution of Maximian, Victor died for his faith at Milan. Few details are known about his life but many churches in the diocese of Milan are dedicated to him.

205

May 11, 2003

Fourth Sunday of Easter

INTRODUCTION

Like our Good Shepherd who holds all people in love, the church is called to lead those who thirst to living waters. At the banquet table set before us, the shepherd who lays down his life for the lost gives himself to us. Here is a great promise: Christ leads us through the shadows and valleys of life. He will neither abandon nor forget us. He is with us, now and forever.

PRAYER OF THE DAY

God of all power, you called from death our Lord Jesus, the great shepherd of the sheep. Send us as shepherds to rescue the lost, to heal the injured, and to feed one another with knowledge and understanding; through your Son, Jesus Christ our Lord, who lives and reigns with you and the Holy Spirit, one God, now and forever.

or

Almighty God, you show the light of your truth to those in darkness, to lead them into the way of righteousness. Give strength to all who are joined in the family of the Church, so that they will resolutely reject what erodes their faith and firmly follow what faith requires; through your Son, Jesus Christ our Lord, who lives and reigns with you and the Holy Spirit, one God, now and forever.

VERSE

Alleluia. Christ being raised from the dead will never die again; death no longer has dominion over him. Alleluia. I am the good shepherd. I know my own and my own know me. Alleluia. (Rom. 6:9; John 10:14)

READINGS

Acts 4:5-12

Peter and John are arrested when the healing of a lame man becomes an occasion for preaching in public about Jesus. When questioned by religious leaders, Peter attributes the healing to the power of the risen Christ.

Psalm 23

The Lord is my shepherd; I shall not be in want. (Ps. 23:1)

1 John 3:16-24

The First Letter of John speaks of the great gift of God's love bestowed on all people in Christ. Here John notes that love is a social gift, something to be shared.

John 10:11-18

In language that recalls the twenty-third psalm, Jesus describes himself as the shepherd who cares for his sheep. He is willing to die for them, and he is able to overcome death for them.

COLOR White

THE PRAYERS

Standing in the glorious light of the resurrection, let us pray for the church, the world, and all who wait for the Spirit's revealing power.

A BRIEF SILENCE.

Watchful God, give to your church faithful bishops and pastors who will shepherd their synods and congregations with vision and compassion. We pray to the Lord:
Lord, hear our prayer.

Abundant God, help the people of the world to find ways to share their resources and thus to care for one another in their need. We pray to the Lord:
Lord, hear our prayer.

Knowing God, assure all who are sick *(especially)* that you will not forsake them, and that you are present with them in their pain and discomfort. We pray to the Lord:
Lord, hear our prayer.

Saving God, bless all mothers who honor you by making your love known to the families in their care. We pray to the Lord:
Lord, hear our prayer.

HERE OTHER INTERCESSIONS MAY BE OFFERED.

Abiding God, sustain the dying and those who watch with them, comfort those who grieve *(especially)*, and keep us united with *(names,* and with*)* all our brothers and sisters who have died in your arms. We pray to the Lord:
Lord, hear our prayer.

Gracious God, hear our prayers and receive them for the sake of the crucified and risen one, our Savior Jesus Christ.
Amen

IMAGES FOR PREACHING

As the Western world becomes increasingly secular, and as religious diversity takes an ever more prominent place,
it becomes more and more difficult to imagine that at any time soon will "every tongue confess that Jesus Christ is Lord" (Phil. 2:11). But Jesus promises it: "one flock, one shepherd" . . . one day.

So often pastors are likened to the good shepherd, bishops have shepherd's staves as a sign of office, congregations are referred to as "the flock." But here Jesus says, "*I am* the good shepherd." It would seem that pastors and bishops, in a sense, merely lead sheep; we are not in the habit of laying down our lives for our parishioners. It may happen on occasion, but not because it is in the letter of call.

Questions and speculation and even affirmations arise about who "the other sheep who are not of this fold" are. Since we do not have more explanation from Jesus, these guesses will continue. A more important lesson for us from Jesus' words is that we ought to maintain an exclusive focus on Christ, who is the good shepherd, and that we as members of the shepherd's flock should not move farther away from Christ by denying those who want to come into the fold. All those who hear and answer the voice of Jesus are called. In hearing God's word, they are enlightened, and in their baptism they are sanctified. They, too, are the church: members of the flock who are known by Jesus.

One day, according to God's promise, all whom we recognize as part of the great communion of saints will be joined to yet more sheep from other folds. Until that blessed day, we listen carefully to our shepherd's voice and give praise to the one who laid down his life in order to take it up again.

WORSHIP MATTERS

This Sunday is a perfect time to emphasize the place of the psalter in worship. Most people know Psalm 23 as well as any portion of scripture. Use their familiarity with this psalm to introduce the psalter (the biblical collection of psalms) as a regular part of your worship service.

Psalms can be sung or read responsively. Psalms can be read as one of the scripture readings. Many hymns are based on psalm text, and almost all the psalms have been set to music at one time or another. The psalms were the ancient hymnbook of the Jewish people and cover the whole range of human emotions and experiences. Bring them alive once again in your parish as you sing praises, wrestle with tragedy, or ask for God's blessings.

LET THE CHILDREN COME

The shepherd image is frequently used in church school, from the Christmas pageant with the shepherds to the parable of the lost sheep. This Sunday especially, Jesus is referred to as the good shepherd. Children will enjoy hymns that reflect this identification. They can also join in Psalm 23 today, if done in an appropriate way—perhaps spoken with an antiphon or in the form of a simple hymn.

HYMNS FOR WORSHIP

GATHERING

Good Christian friends, rejoice and sing!   LBW 144
When in our music God is glorified   WOV 802
Morning has broken   W&P 98

HYMN OF THE DAY

The Lord's my shepherd   LBW 451

ALTERNATE HYMN OF THE DAY

Have no fear, little flock   LBW 476
Be bold, be strong   W&P 15

COMMUNION

He leadeth me   LBW 501, TFF 151
You satisfy the hungry heart   WOV 711

SENDING

With God as our friend   LBW 371
All my hope on God is founded   WOV 782

ADDITIONAL HYMNS AND SONGS

Awake, O sleeper!   DH 63
Alleluia, alleluia! Hearts and voices   H82 191
Jesus, our mighty Lord   H82 478
Savior, like a shepherd lead us   TFF 254
Step by step   W&P

MUSIC FOR THE DAY

PSALMODY

Cherwien, David. "Psalm 23: The Lord Is My Shepherd." U, cong, org.   MSM 80-840.
Christopherson, Dorothy. "The Lord Is My Shepherd." U, hb, kybd, opt sign language.   AFP 6000109016.
Glynn, John. "My Shepherd Is the Lord" in PS 2.
Haugen, Marty. "Shepherd Me, O God." SATB, cong, kybd, C inst, opt glock, str.   GIA G-2950.

Niedmann, Peter. "My Shepherd Will Supply My Need." U, kybd, opt desc.   SEL 410-822,
Ollis, Peter. "The Lord Is My Shepherd" in PS 2.
Roberts, Leon C. "The Lord Is My Shepherd." TFF 3.
Smith, T. R. "The Lord Is My Shepherd" in STP 4.
The Lord's my shepherd   LBW 451
The King of love my shepherd is   LBW 456
Young, Jeremy. PW B.

CHORAL

Bach, J. S./arr. Julia Morgan. "Sheep May Safely Graze." SATB, 2 fl, kybd.   BEC BP1369.
Ellingboe, Bradley. "Jesus, Good Shepherd." SATB, kybd/harp.   AFP 0800658272.
Haugen, Marty. "Shepherd Me, O God." SATB, cant, cong, opt str/ww, kybd.   GIA G-2950.
Johnson, Carolyn. "Have No Fear, Little Flock." SATB, kybd.   AFP 0800674545.
Kosche, Kenneth. "The Lord's My Shepherd." SATB, org, opt cong, opt str.   MSM 60-9018.
Leavitt, John. "The Lord Is My Shepherd." SATB.   CPH 98-3594.
Schütz, Heinrich. "O Lord, I Trust Your Shepherd Care" in *Chantry Choirbook*. SATB, cont.   AFP 0800657772.

CHILDREN'S CHOIRS

Lau, Robert. "Jesus, Like a Shepherd Lead Us." U, kybd.   Jenson 423-10022.
Roberts, William Bradley. "Savior, Like a Shepherd Lead." U, kybd, opt fl/C inst.   AFP 0800646983.
Sleeth, Natalie. "God Bless Families." U, kybd.   CG CGA298.

KEYBOARD/INSTRUMENTAL

Cherwien, David. "Bicentennial" in *Organ Plus One*. Org, inst.   AFP 0800656180.
Harbach, Barbara. "Crimond" in *Augsburg Organ Library: Easter*. Org.   AFP 0800659368.
Howells, Herbert. "Psalm 23" in *Three Psalm Preludes for Organ, Set 1*.   NOV 59 0353 10.
Porter, Emily Maxson. "He Leadeth Me" in *For All the Faithful*. Org.   AFP 0800659422.
Powell, Robert J. "St. Columba" in *Eight Hymn Tunes*. Fl, ob, org.   CPH 97-5652.
Sedio, Mark. "Little Flock" in *Music for the Paschal Season*. Org.   AFP 0800656237.

207

HANDBELL

Behnke, John A. "I Know That My Redeemer Lives." 2–3 oct.
JEF MC0983197.

Helman, Michael. "Gift of Finest Wheat." 3–5 oct, opt hc.
AFP 0800657365.

McChesney, Kevin. "The King of Love My Shepherd Is." 3–5 oct.
JEF MLC201199L.

Tucker, Sondra. "My Shepherd Will Supply My Need." 2–3 oct.
JEF MLSHB95049.

PRAISE ENSEMBLE

Barbour, Anne and John Barbour. "Greater Love" in *Maranatha! Music Praise Chorus Book, 3rd ed.*   MAR.

Bradbury, William. "Savior Like a Shepherd Lead Us." in *Praise Worship Songbook, vol 3.*   INT.

Kingsley, Gershon/arr. Eric Knight. "Shepherd Me, Lord." SAB, gtr, pno, perc. Also available: SA/TB, SSA, SATB.   BRN 115735.

Nystrom, Marty. "Shepherd of My Soul" in *Maranatha! Music Praise Chorus Book, 3rd ed.*   MAR.

Pote, Allen. "The Lord Is My Shepherd." SATB, pno.   CG CGA-551.

208

Wednesday, May 14

PACHOMIUS, RENEWER OF THE CHURCH, 346

Pachomius was born in Egypt about 290. He became a Christian during his service as a soldier. In 320 he went to live as a hermit in Upper Egypt, where other hermits lived nearby. Pachomius organized them into a religious community in which the members prayed together and held their goods in common. His rule for monasteries influenced both eastern and western monasticism, through the Rule of Basil and the Rule of Benedict respectively.

The Egyptian (Coptic) church may be unfamiliar to many western Christians. Use the commemoration of Pachomius to teach about the Egyptian church at parish gatherings this week.

May 18, 2003

Fifth Sunday of Easter

INTRODUCTION

Like vines that grow from a single strong root, we are grafted into Christ at baptism and nourished on his life with the eucharist. Christ feeds our hunger and satisfies our thirst with his word and sacraments and encourages us so that we might become fruitful in service to others. Today Christ calls the church to remember the source of our faith, hope, and love.

Today the church commemorates Erik, king of Sweden from 1150 to 1160 and martyr.

PRAYER OF THE DAY

O God, form the minds of your faithful people into a single will. Make us love what you command and desire what you promise, that, amid all the changes of this world, our hearts may be fixed where true joy is found; through your Son, Jesus Christ our Lord, who lives and reigns with you and the Holy Spirit, one God, now and forever.

VERSE

Alleluia. Christ being raised from the dead will never die again; death no longer has dominion over him. Alleluia. Jesus said, I am the way, and the truth, and the life. Alleluia. (Rom. 6:9; John 14:6)

READINGS

Acts 8:26-40

Philip and Stephen were among the first deacons chosen for service in the early church. After Stephen was martyred, Philip and the rest were scattered but continued to preach. In this encounter, reflection on scripture leads to baptism into the body of Christ.

Psalm 22:24-30 (Psalm 22:25-31 [NRSV])

All the ends of the earth shall remember and turn to the LORD. (Ps. 22:26)

1 John 4:7-21

This letter is a commentary on Jesus' command to "love one another." Love is the mark of God's abiding presence, because God is love. Love gives itself away in service to those in need.

John 15:1-8

On the night of his arrest, Jesus taught his disciples about the relationship they would have with him. Those who abide in his word and love would bear fruit, for apart from him, they could do nothing.

COLOR White

THE PRAYERS

Standing in the glorious light of the resurrection, let us pray for the church, the world, and all who wait for the Spirit's revealing power.

A BRIEF SILENCE.

Let us pray for the church, that it may remain true to the vine from which it grows, and may bear fruits of worship, mission, and service. We pray to the Lord:

Lord, hear our prayer.

Let us pray for this congregation, that its ministries of education and learning would be deepened by teachers who are impassioned by God's word and eager to impart its joys and promises to their students. We pray to the Lord:

Lord, hear our prayer.

Let us pray for the world God has created, that where war paralyzes people with fear and chaos, peace and unity will be restored. We pray to the Lord:

Lord, hear our prayer.

Let us pray for those who wait patiently for cures and for medications yet undeveloped. May strength be given to all who live in chronic pain or sickness that they will never be forsaken (*especially*). We pray to the Lord:

Lord, hear our prayer.

Let us pray for vibrant and fruitful congregational life rooted in the word of God and the sacraments of God's love. May we make disciples who will join us in bearing fruit for the reign of God. We pray to the Lord:

Lord, hear our prayer.

HERE OTHER INTERCESSIONS MAY BE OFFERED.

Let us pray with thanksgiving for Erik (for *names*) and all who rest in the sure and certain hope of the resurrection. We pray to the Lord:

Lord, hear our prayer.

Gracious God, hear our prayers and receive them for the sake of the crucified and risen one, our Savior Jesus Christ.

Amen

IMAGES FOR PREACHING

As the pastoral candidate entered the room, he smiled and speedily scanned each call committee member from crown to heel. They, in turn, scanned right back. As he took his seat, pleasantries were exchanged, including some superficial chatter about the upcoming Super Bowl. Pastor Devereaux crossed his legs just as Mrs. Mendoza fired off the first question, "Pastor, how would you describe hell?"

The answer to that question is embedded in today's gospel reading. Many people have burning fire as their image for hell, but that is at best an incomplete picture. Jesus says he is the vine and we are the branches. We know that a branch cannot survive on its own after it has been cut off; its only fate is death. (According to the text the vinegrower does not transplant it, or re-root it in water; whether there are any such options, we must leave to God's gracious wisdom.) If we stay true to the words of Jesus, the dead do not, cannot, will not do anything, which is why Jesus says, "apart from me you can do nothing." The spiritually dead do nothing that counts for anything. And so, after the branches die, they are not good for anything except to be disposed of, thrown into the fire. Hell is not the fire, hell is being cut off from God.

"Abide in me," says Jesus. Now that you are here, stay. It is an imperative that implies we do have a choice. It is a word to those who call themselves followers of God. Hell is not where we are sent, it is where we choose to go, if we do not abide in Christ, but rather cut ourselves off from the true vine.

WORSHIP MATTERS

Baptism connects us to Christ forever. Spend some time recovering the baptismal images and symbols already in your sanctuary on this fifth Sunday of Easter. Rich images to be explored fill the scripture lessons this week; tie them to the life-giving waters of promise in your congregation.

209

If your font can be moved, move it to the middle of the front aisle this week. Do portions of the liturgy (confession, children's sermon, creed, prayers) directly from the font. Make sure the font contains clean, clear, life-giving water. Place some fresh flowers or plants at its base. Make the baptismal area a place of life this week, so that people see the streams of living water that flow from it.

LET THE CHILDREN COME

Children often find scripture and Jesus' teachings and the church hard to understand, just like the Ethiopian official did. It is important to find places and times to help make connections that they can understand—through hymns, through solid scriptural teaching and preaching to the adults who are called, like Philip, to interpret scripture. Clear simple preaching with good illustrations helps to engage not only children but also adults, teachers and parents who teach the children.

HYMNS FOR WORSHIP

GATHERING

Beautiful Savior   LBW 518

O God beyond all praising   WOV 797

HYMN OF THE DAY

O blessed spring   WOV 695, CS 52

ALTERNATE HYMN OF THE DAY

Joyful, joyful we adore thee   LBW 551

You are mine   W&P 158

COMMUNION

Ubi caritas et amor   WOV 665, CS 92

Jesu, Jesu, fill us with your love   WOV 765, TFF 83

Broken in love   W&P 24

SENDING

My God, how wonderful thou art   LBW 524

Hallelujah! We sing your praises   WOV 722, TFF 158

ADDITIONAL HYMNS AND SONGS

We will go with God   GS2 10

God, bless your church with strength!   PH 418

I've just come from the fountain   WOV 696, TFF 111

We bring the sacrifice of praise   W&P 150

MUSIC FOR THE DAY

PSALMODY

Brugh, Lorraine.   PW B.

Harbor, Rawn. "My God, My God."   TFF 2.

Young, Jeremy.   PW B.

CHORAL

Basler, Paul. "Alleluia." SATB, hrn, perc.   PLY PJMS-116.

Buxtehude, Dietrich. "Everything You Do" in *Chantry Choirbook*. SATB, org.   AFP 0800657772.

Cherwien, David. "Life Tree." SAB, org, opt fl, opt cong.   CPH 98-3190.

Farlee, Robert Buckley. "O Blessed Spring." SATB, ob/vln/cl, org, opt cong.   AFP 0800654242. And in *The Augsburg Choirbook*.   AFP 0800656784.

Haan, Raymond. "I Am the Vine." SATB, org.   HWG GCMR 3473.

Hopson, Hal H. "Praise the Lord." SAB, kybd.   AFP 0800674626.

Rutter, John. "Christ the Lord Is Risen Again." SATB.   OXF 42.362.

CHILDREN'S CHOIRS

Christopherson, Dorothy. "God's Great Love." U, opt desc, kybd, perc.   AFP 0800652207.

Hopson, Hal. "Love One Another." U/2 pt, kybd.   CG CGA741.

Jothen, Michael. "You Are the Branches." U, 2–3 pt trbl/mxd vcs, kybd, opt cong, gtr, bass gtr, 3 oct hb, perc.   CG CGA755.

Wold, Wayne L. "Build New Bridges." U/2 pt, kybd.   AFP 0800657438.

KEYBOARD/INSTRUMENTAL

Albrecht, Mark. "O Waly Waly" in *Three for Piano and Sax*. Pno, sax/C inst.   AFP 0800657977.

Biery, James. "Berglund" in *Tree of Life*. Org.   AFP 0800655370.

Cherwien, David. "We Know That Christ Is Raised" in *Gotta Toccata*. Org.   AFP 0800658752.

Farlee, Robert Buckley. "Berglund" in *Gaudeamus!* Org.   AFP 0800655389.

Organ, Anne Krentz. "Berglund" in *On Eagle's Wings*. Pno.   AFP 0800655524.

Uhl, Dan. "Alleluia! Jesus Is Risen!" (Earth and All Stars) in *Easter Suite*. Org, tpt, opt timp.   AFP 0800655419.

HANDBELL

Behnke, John. "O Waly Waly." 2–3 oct, opt fl.   AFP 0800657403.

Shepard, Timothy. "Earth and All Stars." 3–5 oct.   JEF BC HHB37.

PRAISE ENSEMBLE

Beall, Mary Kay. "Come to the Feast." 2 pt mxd, kybd. HOP PP151.

Dearman, Kirk and Deby Dearman. "Instruments of Your Peace" in *Hosanna! Music Songbook 11.*   INT.

Jothen, Michael. "You Are the Branches." U, 2-3 pt, kybd, gtr, hb, perc.   CG CGA755.

Rouse, Jay. "I Will Abide." SATB, orch.   Sparrow AO8200.

Walker, Tommy. "No Greater Love" in *The Maranatha! Singers, I See the Lord, vol. 1.*   MAR.

Sunday, May 18

ERIK, KING OF SWEDEN, MARTYR, 1160

Erik, long considered the patron saint of Sweden, ruled there from 1150 to 1160. He is honored for efforts to bring peace to the nearby pagan kingdoms and for his crusades to spread the Christian faith in Scandinavia. He established a protected Christian mission in Finland that was led by Henry of Uppsala. As king, Erik was noted for his desire to establish fair laws and courts and for his concern for the poor and sick. Erik was killed by a Danish army that approached him at worship on the day after the Ascension. He is reported to have said to them, "Let us at least finish the sacrifice. The rest of the feast I shall keep elsewhere." As he left worship he was killed.

The commemoration of Erik could be the beginning of a discussion on the relationship between civil rule and the place of faith in the public sphere.

Monday, May 19

DUNSTAN, ARCHBISHOP OF CANTERBURY, 988

By Dunstan's time, Viking invaders had wiped out English monasticism. Dunstan played an important role in its restoration. He was commissioned by King Edmund to reestablish monastic life at Glastonbury, which became a center for monasticism and learning. He was exiled by a later king, Edwy, whom he had publicly rebuked. After Edwy's death Dunstan was made Archbishop of Canterbury and carried out a reform of church and state. He corrected abuses by the clergy, encouraged laity in their devotional life, and was committed to concerns of justice. He was also well known as a musician and for his painting and metal work.

Wednesday, May 21

JOHN ELIOT, MISSIONARY
TO THE AMERICAN INDIANS, 1690

John Eliot was born in England and his first career was as a schoolteacher. In 1631 he came to New England to preach to the Puritan settlers. In New England he developed an interest in the Algonkian Indians and learned their language and customs. He published a catechism in 1654 and in 1658 translated the scriptures in Algonkian, the first complete Bible printed in the colonies. Eliot also established towns for Indians who had converted to Christianity. These towns were away from Puritan colonies and were established so that the Algonkians could preserve their own culture and live according to their own laws. Eliot also trained indigenous leaders to serve as missionaries to their own people.

As we pray for greater respect and justice for indigenous peoples, use this commemoration as an opportunity to learn of various American Indian and Native Alaskan tribal spiritualities and traditions.

211

Friday, May 23

LUDWIG NOMMENSEN,
MISSIONARY TO SUMATRA, 1918

Ludwig Ingwer Nommensen was born in Schleswig-Holstein. In the early 1860s he went to Sumatra to serve as a Lutheran missionary. His work was among the Batak people, who had previously not seen Christian missionaries. Though he encountered some initial difficulties, the missions began to succeed following the conversion of several tribal chiefs. Nommensen worked to make the church as local as possible. He translated the scriptures into Batak while honoring much of the native culture, and did not seek to replace it with a European one. At the time of World War II all missionaries were driven out, and the Batak people took over leadership of their own church.

Saturday, May 24

NICOLAUS COPERNICUS, 1543;
LEONHARD EULER, 1783; TEACHERS

Scientists such as Copernicus and Euler invite us to ponder the mysteries of the universe and the grandeur of God's creation. Copernicus is an example of a renaissance person. He formally studied astronomy, mathematics, Greek, Plato, law, medicine, and canon law. He also had interests in theology, poetry, and the natural and social sciences. Copernicus is chiefly remembered for his work as an astronomer and his idea that the sun, not the earth, is the center of the solar system. Euler is regarded as one of the founders of the science of pure mathematics and made important contributions to mechanics, hydrodynamics, astronomy, optics, and acoustics.

Include Psalm 8 in a devotional reading today. It praises God for the wonder of creation and at the same time ponders the mystery of God's care for all people and is a fitting commemoration for the work of Copernicus and Euler.

May 25, 2003

Sixth Sunday of Easter

INTRODUCTION

The church is called to be an apostolic community that dwells in the new commandment of Christ. The challenge of the gospel is not to love others as others love us, but to love others as Jesus Christ loves us. He sees our failings and fears with utter clarity, yet offers us the gentle gifts of forgiveness and healing. Here we find ground for hope: we are made friends of God in baptism.

PRAYER OF THE DAY

O God, from whom all good things come: Lead us by the inspiration of your Spirit to think those things which are right, and by your goodness help us to do them; through your Son, Jesus Christ our Lord, who lives and reigns with you and the Holy Spirit, one God, now and forever.

VERSE

Alleluia. Christ being raised from the dead will never die again; death no longer has dominion over him. Alleluia. Those who love me will keep my word, and my Father will love them, and we will come to them and make our home with them. Alleluia. (Rom 6:9; John 14:23)

READINGS

Acts 10:44-48

Jesus is raised from the dead as Lord of all creation. The risen Christ comes to all persons regardless of their condition in life. In today's reading, a Roman army officer welcomes Peter's witness to Christ. The Holy Spirit descends on these Roman "outsiders," causing amazement among the witnesses.

Psalm 98

Shout with joy to the LORD, all you lands. (Ps. 98:5)

1 John 5:1-6

John calls upon Christians to love God and to love one another. Toward the end of this text, John says exactly what this faithfulness means: we love God when we obey God's commandments.

John 15:9-17

On the night of his arrest, Jesus delivers a final testimony to his disciples to help them in the days ahead. Here, he repeats the most important of all his commands, that they love one another.

COLOR White

THE PRAYERS

Standing in the glorious light of the resurrection, let us pray for the church, the world, and all who wait for the Spirit's revealing power.

A BRIEF SILENCE.

Gracious God, nurture your church in its ministries of pastoral care and leadership. Challenge us to be con-

cerned for the needs of others. We pray to the Lord:
Lord, hear our prayer.
Gracious God, in the risen Christ you befriended the world. Guide those who provide safety and protection through military and other forms of public service, and bless all communities with a deep desire to serve the common good. We pray to the Lord:
Lord, hear our prayer.
Gracious God, help us to hear your call to come to the aid of people who are alone and despairing, forgotten and lonely, sick and low in spirit (*especially*). We pray to the Lord:
Lord, hear our prayer.
Gracious God, bless the efforts of this congregation to help people discover places where lasting spiritual friendships are formed. We pray to the Lord:
Lord, hear our prayer.
HERE OTHER INTERCESSIONS MAY BE OFFERED.
Gracious God, bless the memory of all who died for the cause of peace, and bring us with all the saints to that world where our joy will be complete and you will be our all in all. We pray to the Lord:
Lord, hear our prayer.
Gracious God, hear our prayers and receive them for the sake of the crucified and risen one, our Savior Jesus Christ.
Amen

IMAGES FOR PREACHING

Some who are getting on in years will recall a popular song that stated "Love is all you need." Though it sounds like hyperbole, in today's gospel Jesus seems to indicate that it is not far from the truth.

After all, if everyone in the world truly loved one another in the sense that Jesus meant it, there would be no wars, no hungry people, no homeless people, no divorce, no abused people, children or adults. There would be no greed, no violence. We would finally all just get along. The problem, of course, is that we are sinful human beings—we are not perfect and therefore, neither is our love. Only Jesus loved with a perfect love and we strive toward that model of selfless love.

Someone once said that the entire story of salvation history can be summed up in one word: love—God's love for us through Jesus Christ. But it goes beyond even salvation. Jesus cites the ability to love as he loves as a requirement to be called his friends. Does that mean we

cannot sing "What a friend we have in Jesus" if we do not love? It appears to be the case. The sentence structure is conditional: "You are my friends *if* you do what I command you. And this is my commandment, that you love one another." One is still permitted to serve, but until you love, you cannot be a friend.

Jesus also connects that ability to love with the fullness of joy. Often people talk about the joy of being saved. But unless we love one another, that joy is not complete. And in that complete joy, we bear fruit that lasts.

The ultimate purpose of Jesus' commands, then, is not to save us, but rather to bring us to love—or are those the same thing?

WORSHIP MATTERS

The same commandment that Christ gave to us on Maundy Thursday appears again in a somewhat different context. Is it easier to love in the midst of celebration or sorrow? Is the commandment better heard when we are standing on the top of a mountain or at the foot of the cross? Christ asks us to love at both times, in both moments.

Planning for worship is about learning to love the community that you serve. Lasting, meaningful worship is not imposed upon a congregation by a planning team that thinks it knows best. Worship that matters is born out of a community that is in love with each other and the risen Lord. Worship then becomes not a matter of "getting one's way" but of expressing the song and praise of those gathered to love one another as Christ has loved.

LET THE CHILDREN COME

Psalm 98 is a joyful psalm that reminds us we are in the Easter season and celebrating Jesus' resurrection. Are we still singing alleluias? "Earth and all stars!" (LBW 558) is a hymn based on this psalm. It is not easy for children to sing but with the use of simple instruments like tambourines and cymbals children are able to "sing" along.

HYMNS FOR WORSHIP
GATHERING

Love divine, all loves excelling   LBW 315
Lord, you give the great commission   WOV 756
Lord, this day we've come to worship   TFF 137

213

HYMN OF THE DAY

Now all the vault of heaven resounds   LBW 143

ALTERNATE HYMN OF THE DAY

Great God, your love has called us   WOV 666

Jesu, Jesu, fill us with your love   WOV 765, TFF 83

COMMUNION

For the bread which you have broken   LBW 200, CS 28

Ubi caritas et amor   WOV 665, CS 92

SENDING

O Zion, haste   LBW 397

Blessed assurance   WOV 699, TFF 118

Behold, what manner of love   TFF 218

ADDITIONAL HYMNS AND SONGS

With all your heart   DH 95

O thou who camest from above   H82 704

I heard an old, old story   TFF 97

As the deer   W&P 9

MUSIC FOR THE DAY

PSALMODY

Beall, Mary Kay. *Sing Out! A Children's Psalter.* WLP. U, kybd.

Haas, David/arr. Marty Haugen. "Psalm 98: All the Ends of the Earth." U/SATB, cong.   GIA G-2703.

Hopson, Hal H. "Psalm 98" in *Ten Psalms.* U/SATB, cong.   HOP HH 3930.

Johnson, Alan. "All the Ends of the Earth" in PS I.

Smith, T. R. "The Lord Has Revealed" in STP 4.

Young, Jeremy. PW B.

CHORAL

Bach, J. S. "Alleluia" in *Bach for All Seasons.* SATB, opt kybd.   AFP 080065854X.

Hobby, Robert A. "Now All the Vault of Heaven Resounds." SAB, org, 2 tpt, opt hb, cong.   AFP 0800658655.

Hopson, Hal H. "Sing Aloud to God." SATB, org, opt tpt.   AFP 0800674642.

Kallman, Daniel. "Charity and Love." SATB, org, fl, cl, opt hb.   KJO J15.

Manuel, Ralph. "Alleluia." SATB.   HIN HMC-927.

Tallis, Thomas. "If Ye Love Me." SATB.   OXF TCM69.

Wolff, Drummond. "Now All the Vault of Heaven Resounds." SATB, org, 2 tpt, 2 tb.   CPH 98-2785.

Young, Carlton. "Fill Us with Your Love." SATB, kybd.   AG 7256.

CHILDREN'S CHOIRS

Bedford, Michael. "Cantate Domino." U/2 pt, kybd.   CG CGA689.

Cool, Jayne Southwick. "The Life, the Truth, the Way." U/2 pt, pno.   AFP 0800674677.

Rutter, John. "All Things Bright and Beautiful." 2 pt, kybd.   HIN HMC663.

KEYBOARD/INSTRUMENTAL

Althouse, Jay. "All Creatures of Our God and King" in *The Sacred Trumpet Soloist.* Tpt, kybd.   ALF 18923.

Carter, John. "Lasst uns erfreuen" in *Contemplative Folk Tunes for Piano.* Pno.   AFP 0800659775.

Cherwien, David. "Hyfrydol" in *Groundings: Five New Organ Settings.* Org.   AFP 0800659805.

Dahl, David P. "Lasst uns erfreuen" in *Hymn Interpretations for Organ.* Org.   AFP 0806658248.

Honoré, Jeffrey. "Hyfrydol" in *Classic Embellishments.* Org, opt inst.   AFP 0800658728.

Leavitt, John. "Joyous Day." Org.   HWG GSTC01112.

Miller, Aaron David. "Lasst uns erfreuen" in *Improvisations for Organ.* Org.   AFP 0800674812.

Sedio, Mark. "Chereponi" in *Dancing in the Light of God.* Pno.   AFP 0800656547.

HANDBELL

Helman, Michael. "Jesu, Jesu, Fill Us with Your Love." 3–5 oct, opt hc.   AFP 0800658876.

McChesney, Kevin. "Jesu, Jesu, Fill Us with Your Love." 2–3 oct.   AFP 0800658116.

Stephenson, Valerie W. "All Creatures of Our God and King." 3–6 oct.   CPH 97-6868.

Tucker, Sonya. "Meditation on Hyfrydol." 3 oct.   CG CGB182.

PRAISE ENSEMBLE

Angerman, David and Joseph M. Martin. "Sing! Shout! Jubilate!" SATB, acc.   FLA A7134.

Kallman, Daniel. "What a Friend We Have in Jesus." SATB, pno.   MSM 50-9065.

Smith, Byron. J. "Worthy to Be Praised." SATB, pno.   LAW 52654.

Ylvisaker, John. "Great Is Our God" in *Borning Cry.*   NGP.

Ziegenhals, Harriet. "Oh, Sing to the Lord." U/2 pt, kybd, perc.   CG CGA640.

Tuesday, May 27

JOHN CALVIN, RENEWER OF THE CHURCH, 1564

John Calvin began his studies in theology at the University of Paris when he was fourteen. In his mid-twenties he experienced a conversion that led him to embrace the views of the reformation. His theological ideas are systematically laid out in his *Institutes of the Christian Religion.* He is also well known for his commentaries on scripture. He was a preacher in Geneva, was banished once, and then later returned to reform the city with a rigid, theocratic discipline.

Calvin is considered the father of the Reformed churches. In today's gospel, as Jesus prays that all his followers may be one, hold up the ecumenical agreements that Lutherans in the United States and Canada share with churches of the Reformed tradition as an example of the unity we share in Christ.

May 29, 2003

The Ascension of Our Lord

INTRODUCTION

The risen Lord enters the invisible presence of God in order to be present in all times and places to the church and to the world. Where shall we find the risen and ascended Lord today? In his word and his bread, in his people and his washing with water and the Spirit, and in all who cry out for mercy.

Today the church commemorates Jiři Tranovský, hymnwriter, who died in 1637.

PRAYER OF THE DAY

Almighty God, your only Son was taken up into heaven and in power intercedes for us. May we also come into your presence and live forever in your glory; through your Son, Jesus Christ our Lord, who lives and reigns with you and the Holy Spirit, one God, now and forever.

VERSE

Alleluia. Christ being raised from the dead will never die again; death no longer has dominion over him. Alleluia. I am with you always, to the end of the age. Alleluia. (Rom. 6:9; Matt. 28:20)

READINGS

Acts 1:1-11

Before he is lifted into heaven, Jesus promises that the missionary work of the disciples will spread out from Jerusalem to all the world. His words provide an outline for the book of Acts.

Psalm 47

God has gone up with a shout. (Ps. 47:5)

or Psalm 93

Ever since the world began, your throne has been established. (Ps. 93:3)

Ephesians 1:15-23

After giving thanks for the faith of the Ephesians, Paul prays that they might also see the power of God, who in the ascension enthroned Christ as head of the church, his body.

Luke 24:44-53

At the time of his ascension, Jesus leaves the disciples with the promise of the Holy Spirit and an instruction that they should await the Spirit's descent.

COLOR White

THE PRAYERS

Standing in the glorious light of the resurrection, let us pray for the church, the world, and all who wait for the Spirit's revealing power.

A BRIEF SILENCE.

Let us pray for eyes to see and ears to hear, that by baptism into Christ our minds would be open to understand God's word and recognize God's activity in our midst. Lord, in your mercy,

215

hear our prayer.

Let us pray for love toward all the saints and toward all the world, that a spirit of wisdom and revelation will be given to all authorities and those in power. Lord, in your mercy,

hear our prayer.

Let us pray for hearts of compassion that are moved to action toward those who are troubled, lonely, fearful, and in need of your healing touch (*especially*). Lord, in your mercy,

hear our prayer.

Let us pray for those waiting for their calling to be revealed to them, that they may find a fulfilling vocation in this world. Lord, in your mercy,

hear our prayer.

Let us give thanks for Jiři Tranovský and all who gave a faithful witness to the gospel and were faithful servants unto death. Lord, in your mercy,

hear our prayer.

216 *HERE OTHER INTERCESSIONS MAY BE OFFERED.*

Let us pray for the grieving, that we may be signs of God's presence with them in their loss, and that the hope of the resurrection will keep them united with their beloved departed. Lord, in your mercy,

hear our prayer.

Gracious God, hear our prayers and receive them for the sake of the crucified and risen one, our Savior Jesus Christ.

Amen

IMAGES FOR PREACHING

No words are more memorable than final words. Jesus told his disciples over and over who he was, and what would happen to him and to them. The details of his lengthy farewell (in John) may well have been lost on them in the panic and fear of the crucifixion. But they found forgiveness and joy in his resurrection, and now before he "withdraws" he reminds them one last time of what scripture had been saying all along: that he, the Messiah, was to suffer and to rise from the dead on the third day. It happened just as he said. Now they, as witnesses, are to proclaim repentance and forgiveness to all people starting right where they are, in Jerusalem.

Jesus must have talked repeatedly in sermons and parables to get his followers to understand what he was all about and what their mission would be, in light of all

they had gone through with Jesus and because of Jesus. But even as he was carried up, and even though they were continually in the temple blessing God, we do not get the sense from the text that the disciples are ready for what is about to happen and what is about to come to them on the day of Pentecost.

A powerful healing and a heads-up come to us simultaneously in this text and where it falls in the church year. How many times have we heard who Jesus is, what we are to do? And how many times have we been baffled and confused at what Jesus is doing after he told us countless times. Yet even in our cluelessness, we are blessed. And as we too are continually blessing God, who knows what awaits us?

WORSHIP MATTERS

The Ascension of Our Lord is a wonderful day to gather with other churches to celebrate the reign and glory of our risen Lord. Arrange with three or four other local congregations to celebrate the ministries that you share and to support those joint ministries. Worshiping with our sisters and brothers in Christ helps link us all to this one holy, catholic and apostolic church and provides us with a vision of the church beyond the boundaries of our local congregations.

The power and promise of Christ's resurrection and ascension remind all us that the breadth and depth of God's love is always wider and more inclusive than we would have planned for or can ever imagine.

LET THE CHILDREN COME

The disciples knew Jesus was present with them even after his ascension. We can point out to children the places in the liturgy where we can sense Jesus still present among us: in the gathering, speaking, feeding, healing, baptizing. Jesus is indeed among us and we are joyful. This joy can be expressed in hymns and greetings and joy-filled prayers.

HYMNS FOR WORSHIP
GATHERING

Crown him with many crowns   LBW 170
Glory to God, we give you thanks   WOV 787

HYMN OF THE DAY

O Christ, our hope   LBW 300

ALTERNATE HYMN OF THE DAY

Look, the sight is glorious   LBW 156
Clap your hands! Shout for joy!   ASG 6

COMMUNION

Now the silence   LBW 205
Eat this bread   WOV 709, TFF 125
We will glorify   W&P 154

SENDING

Beautiful Savior   LBW 518
Come away to the skies   WOV 669

ADDITIONAL HYMNS AND SONGS

On Christ's ascension I now build   LW 150
How lovely on the mountains   TFF 99
Majesty   W&P 94

MUSIC FOR THE DAY

PSALMODY

Beckstrand, William. PW B.

Bell, John L. "Psalm 47: Clap Your Hands All You Nations" in *Psalms of Patience, Protest and Praise.* U/SATB.   GIA G-4047.

Brown, Teresa. "God Goes Up" in PS 2.

Chepponis, James J. "Eastertime Psalm: Psalms for Easter, Ascension, and Pentecost." Cant, cong, opt choir, opt tpt, hb.   GIA G-3907.

Hughes, Howard. "Psalm 47: God Mounts His Throne and God Is King." Cant, cong, acc.   GIA G-2029.

Inwood, Paul. "A Blare of Trumpets" in PS 2.

Sterk, Valerie Stegink. "Psalm for Ascension." SATB, org, children, cong, tamb.   SEL 241-047.

CHORAL

Benson, Robert. "O Lord Most High, Eternal King." SATB, org.   AFP 0800674200.

Billings, William. "Rejoice Ye Shining Worlds." SATB.   CPH 98-3281.

Chepponis, James. "You Shall Be My Witnesses." 2 pt, cant, cong, kybd, opt fl.   GIA G-2543.

Erickson, Richard. "Come Away to the Skies." SATB, fl, fc.   AFP 0800656776.

Farlee, Robert Buckley. "The Lightener of the Stars" in *To God Will I Sing.* MH voice.   AFP 0800674332.
ML voice.   AFP 080067434X.

Mendelssohn, Felix. "Above All Praise" in *The New Church Anthem Book.* SATB, org.   OXF 0193531097.

Olson, Howard. "He's Ascended into Heaven" in *Set Free.* SATB.   AFP 0806600454.

Pelz, Walter. "Crown Him with Many Crowns." SATB, cong, org, 3 tpt.   AFP 080064803X.

Riegel, Friedrich Samuel. "See God to Heaven Ascending" in *Chantry Choirbook.* SATB.   AFP 0800657772.

Vaughan Williams, Ralph. "O Clap Your Hands." SATB (div), org, 3 tpt, 3 tbn, tba, timp.   GAL 1.5000.

CHILDREN'S CHOIRS

Artman, Ruth, arr. "Little Jewels." 2 pt, kybd, 2 oct hb.   BEC BP1315.

Carter, John. "How Excellent Is Your Name." 2 pt, kybd.   AFP 0800674553.

Helman, Michael. "Jesus, We Want to Meet." U, 3 oct hb, perc.   AFP 0800655885.

KEYBOARD/INSTRUMENTAL

Alain, Jehan. "Trois Mouvements: Andante." Fl, org.   LED.

Organ, Anne Krentz. "Diademata" in *Piano Reflections for the Church Year.* Pno, opt inst.   AFP 080067474X.

Preston, Simon. "Alleluyas" in *Modern Organ Music, book 1.* Org.   OXF.

Sedio, Mark. "Middlebury" in *Two on a Bench.* Pno duet.   AFP 0800659090.

Thomas, David Evan. "Middlebury" in *Augsburg Organ Library: Easter.* Org.   AFP 0800659368.

Wold, Wayne L. "Bryn Calfaria" in *A November to Remember.* Org.   AFP 080068983X.

HANDBELL

Afdahl, Lee J. "And All Shall Clap Their Hands." 3–5 oct.   AFP 0800675053.

Kinyon, Barbara. "Daystar." 2–3 oct.   JEF MHP1930.

Larson, Katherine Jordahl. "Beautiful Savior." 3–4 oct.   AFP 0800653963.

Leavitt, John. "A Grand Processional." 3 oct.   AFP 6000001193.

Tucker, Sondra. "Come Away to the Skies." 3–5 oct.   CPH 97-6739.

PRAISE ENSEMBLE

Barrett, Michael. "Truly God Is Good" in *Two S.A.B. Praise Anthems.* SAB, acc.   GS D-5450.

Davis, Greg and Greg Fischer/arr. Innes. "Honor the Lord." SATB, pno.   HOP WT1522.

Liles, Dwight. "Clap Your Hands" in *Spirit Touching Spirit* Prince of Peace Publishing.

Smith, Tim. "Our God Is Lifted Up" in *Songs for Praise and Worship.* WRD.

217

Thursday, May 29

JIRI TRANOVSKY, HYMNWRITER, 1637

Tranovský is considered the "Luther of the Slavs" and the father of Slovak hymnody. Trained at the University of Wittenberg in the early seventeenth century, Tranovský was ordained in 1616 and spent his life preaching and teaching in Prague, Silesia, and finally Slovakia. He produced a translation of the Augsburg Confession and published his hymn collection *Cithara Sanctorum* (Lyre of the Saints), the foundation of Slovak Lutheran hymnody.

Use the commemoration to pray for the Slovak church and to give thanks for the gifts of church musicians. Sing Tranovský's Easter hymn, "Make songs of joy" (LBW 150) at parish gatherings today.

June 1, 2003

218

Seventh Sunday of Easter

INTRODUCTION

This past Thursday the church celebrated the Ascension of Our Lord. Today's gospel includes the words of Jesus' high priestly prayer the night before his death. Though he is absent from us, Christ gives the church his word and sacraments so that we may be one in him, and united in his service to all who seek God. Even as Jesus' followers waited for the promised Holy Spirit, we pray during these days before Pentecost that the Spirit would renew the lives of all who profess faith in Christ.

Today the church commemorates Justin Martyr, killed in the second century for teaching Christianity.

PRAYER OF THE DAY

Almighty and eternal God, your Son our Savior is with you in eternal glory. Give us faith to see that, true to his promise, he is among us still, and will be with us to the end of time; who lives and reigns with you and the Holy Spirit, one God, now and forever.

or

God, our creator and redeemer, your Son Jesus prayed that his followers might be one. Make all Christians one with him as he is one with you, so that in peace and con-

Saturday, May 31

THE VISITATION

The Visitation marks the occasion of Mary visiting her cousin Elizabeth. Elizabeth greeted Mary with the words, "Blessed are you among women," and Mary responded with her famous song, the Magnificat. Luke tells us that even John the Baptist rejoiced and leapt in his mother's womb when Elizabeth heard Mary's greeting. Today we are shown two women: one too old to have a child bears the last prophet of the old covenant, and the other, still quite young, bears the incarnate Word and the new covenant.

In what ways does the church bear the good news of Christ to others and remain faithful to God's call?

cord we may carry to the world the message of your love; through Jesus Christ our Lord, who lives and reigns with you and the Holy Spirit, one God, now and forever.

VERSE

Alleluia. Christ being raised from the dead will never die again; death no longer has dominion over him. Alleluia. I will not leave you orphaned; I am coming to you. Alleluia. (Rom. 6:9; John 14:18)

READINGS

Acts 1:15-17, 21-26

The image of Israel's twelve tribes is mirrored in the twelve apostles of Jesus. They signify the Lord's mission to his people, to all others who welcome him, and to the new community of the church, a light to the nations. In this reading, the early church selects Matthias to fill the vacancy among the twelve caused by the death of Judas Iscariot.

Psalm 1

The LORD knows the way of the righteous. (Ps. 1:6)

1 John 5:9-13

On this Sunday of the Easter season, the second reading offers a final witness to the risen Christ. John points to the continuing presence of God's Son in the lives of those who believe.

John 17:6-19

In this reading the church hears Jesus' words on the night before his death. This gospel reports the words of Jesus' prayer, a prayer for his disciples and for all who would believe in him through their words.

COLOR White

THE PRAYERS

Standing in the glorious light of the resurrection, let us pray for the church, the world, and all who wait for the Spirit's revealing power.

A BRIEF SILENCE.

God of truth, sanctify your church in the truth, and bless our seminaries and theological schools with instructors who are faithful to your word. Lord, in your mercy,

hear our prayer.

Holy One, protect people in every land who face imminent danger and violence. Send peacemakers and mediators to assist the leaders of nations at war. Lord, in your mercy,

hear our prayer.

Living God, you know the hearts of all your children. Touch those who are in need of healing *(especially)*, that they may sense your nearness. Lord, in your mercy,

hear our prayer.

Merciful One, watch over the children of our congregational community, and grant parents and guardians wisdom as they oversee the growth of their children. Lord, in your mercy,

hear our prayer.

HERE OTHER INTERCESSIONS MAY BE OFFERED.

Kind and compassionate God, bless the dying and those who keep watch with them. Keep us united with Justin (with *names*) and all those who have gone before us in the communion of saints. Lord, in your mercy,

hear our prayer.

Gracious God, hear our prayers and receive them for the sake of the crucified and risen one, our Savior Jesus Christ.

Amen

IMAGES FOR PREACHING

The placement here of Jesus' prayer for his disciples just before his crucifixion may seem incongruent, but it is a

wonderful blessing and reminder to have this prayer "bookend" us into and out of Easter, as we approach Pentecost.

This intimate one-way conversation from Son to Father gives us the image that Jesus had of his followers then and the image he has of us now. Although gospel writers, commentators, and seminary professors depict Jesus' disciples as clueless and bumbling, we hear Jesus affirm them ("they know in truth that I came from you"), lift them up ("they do not belong to the world"), and tell us they were worthy companions on his journey ("they have kept your word").

This prayer of Jesus is also about his followers today—it is not just limited to his first century disciples. We still need protection from the evil one, and sanctification for the work we do in the world. In our struggle to preach Christ crucified in a society so blinded by material wealth at any cost and so enamored with creature comforts, it is this kind of prayer on our behalf that invokes the Holy Spirit. When we hear Jesus pray this prayer for us, it is a foretaste of the feast of Pentecost, a sampling of the clothing of power from on high. Indeed, to know that Christ prayed for "me" gives us strength when we thought we were spent, success when we thought we were failures, and vision to see transformation where we thought none was possible.

WORSHIP MATTERS

One short of the number linked to the twelve tribes of Israel, the eleven disciples gather together to select one, Matthias, to add to their ranks.

How do we fill our ranks in the church? Although no number is prescribed for average worship attendance, how do we attract new people to hear the wonderful Easter message? How do we fulfill the mission of the gospel?

Worship often seems to be at odds with evangelism, but evangelism is simply the natural by-product of worship. When worship truly "happens," the gospel is preached, the sacraments are administered, and in some manner, the church grows.

Like that very early church, we need to make sure that our ministry is full and cared for. The worship life of the church must always be given the good intentions and hard work of those who care about its future.

219

LET THE CHILDREN COME

Jesus prays for his disciples. Praying for Jesus' disciples is important and that prayer can continue in the prayers of the church as worship leaders pray for groups of disciples such as church school teachers, church leaders, missionaries, and Christians faced with hardship throughout the world. Groups of children can also be named. Ask God to keep them safe as Jesus did.

HYMNS FOR WORSHIP

GATHERING

Lord of light   LBW 405

Here in this place (Gather us in)   WOV 718

Majesty   W&P 94

HYMN OF THE DAY

Christ is made the sure foundation   WOV 747, LBW 367

ALTERNATE HYMN OF THE DAY

We worship you, O God of might   LBW 432

I shall not be moved   TFF 147

COMMUNION

O Master, let me walk with you   LBW 492

Draw us in the Spirit's tether   WOV 703

SENDING

Rejoice, O pilgrim throng   LBW 553

The Spirit sends us forth to serve   WOV 723

ADDITIONAL HYMNS AND SONGS

In you, O Lord, I put my trust   CW 448

God of mercy, God of grace   H82 538

Lord, I want to be a Christian   TFF 234

Blessing, honor and glory   W&P 21

MUSIC FOR THE DAY

PSALMODY

Bell, John L. "Psalm I: Happy Is the One" in *Psalms of Patience, Protest and Praise*. U/SATB.   GIA G-4047.

Hallock, Peter/arr. Carl Crosier. *The Ionian Psalter*. ION.

Harbor, Rawn. "Happy Are They." TFF 1.

Howard, Julie. *Sing for Joy: Psalm Settings for God's Children*. Liturgical Press 8146-2078-7.

Schenbachler, Tim. "Happy Are They" in STP 2.

Young, Jeremy. PW B.

CHORAL

Davies, H. Walford. "God Be in My Head" in *The New Church Anthem Book*. SATB, kybd.   OXF 0193531097.

Ferguson, John. "Come, Labor On." SATB, org.   MSM-50-6502.

Handel, G. F. "All My Spirit Longs to Savor" in *Chantry Choirbook*. SATB, kybd.   AFP 0800657772.

O'Brien, Francis Patrick. "Your Wonderful Love." SAB, cant, cong, gtr, kybd.   GIA G-4520.

Pelz, Walter. "Peace I Leave With You" in *Augsburg Choirbook*. SATB. AFP 0800656784.

Schalk, Carl. "Christ Is Made the Sure Foundation." SATB, org, brass qrt, cong.   MSM 60-9003.

Thompson, Randall. "Alleluia." SATB.   ECS 1786.

CHILDREN'S CHOIRS

Ferguson, John. "Jesus, My Lord and God." U, org. AFP 0800646193.

Ziegenhals, Harriet. "You Shall Have a Song." 2 pt, kybd, opt fl. HOP A577.

KEYBOARD/INSTRUMENTAL

Biery, James. "Union Seminary" in *Tree of Life*. Org. AFP 0800655370.

Lemmens, Nicolas Jacques. "Fanfare." Org.   HWG GSOC 68.

Osterland, Karl. "Union Seminary" in *Lift One Voice*. Org. AFP 0800659007.

Pelz, Walter. "Oh, Love, How Deep." Org.   CPH 97-5675.

Proulx, Richard. "Westminster Abbey" in *Preludes on Four Hymns*. Org. AFP 0800649591.

HANDBELL

Afdahl, Lee J. "Savior, Again to Thy Dear Name." 2–3 oct. NMP HB436.

Lange, Kinley. "Peaceful Reverie." 3 oct.   Ring Out! 920201703.

Young, Philip M. "Good Christian Friends, Rejoice and Sing!" 2–3 oct.   AFP 080065627X.

PRAISE ENSEMBLE

Gardner, Daniel. "My Life Is in You" in *Songs for Praise and Worship*. WRD.

Haugen, Marty. "Gather Us In." SATB, pno, gtr, ww.   GIA G-2651.

Kendrick, Graham. "Shine, Jesus, Shine" in *Maranatha! Music Praise Chorus Book. 3rd ed.*   MAR.

Ylvisaker, John. "We Shall Not Be Moved" in *Borning Cry*.   NGP.

Sunday, June 1

JUSTIN, MARTYR AT ROME, C. 165

Justin was born of pagan parents. At Ephesus he was moved by stories of early Christian martyrs and came under the influence of an elderly Christian man he met there. Justin described his conversion by saying, "Straightway a flame was kindled in my soul and a love of the prophets and those who are friends of Christ possessed me." Justin was a teacher of philosophy and engaged in debates about the truth of Christian faith. He was arrested and jailed for practicing an unauthorized religion. He refused to renounce his faith and he and six of his students, one of them a woman, were beheaded.

Justin's description of early Christian worship around the year 150 is the foundation of the church's pattern of worship, east and west. His description of it is in *With One Voice* (p. 6) and helps reveal the deep roots our contemporary shape of the liturgy has in the ancient worship of the church.

Tuesday, June 3

JOHN XXIII, BISHOP OF ROME, 1963

In his ministry as a bishop of Venice, John (then Angelo Roncalli) was well loved by his people. He visited parishes and established new ones. He had warm affection for the working class—he himself was the child of Italian peasants—and he worked at developing social action ministries. At age seventy-seven he was elected bishop of Rome. Despite the expectation that he would be a transitional pope, he had great energy and spirit. He convened the Second Vatican Council in order to open the windows of the church and "let in the fresh air of the modern world." The council brought about great changes in the church's worship, changes that have influenced Lutherans and many other protestant churches as well.

Now that representatives from the Lutheran World Federation and the Vatican have signed a Joint Declaration on the Doctrine of Justification, what are the next steps for Lutherans and Roman Catholics to take in our relations with one another?

Thursday, June 5

BONIFACE, ARCHBISHOP OF MAINZ, MISSIONARY TO GERMANY, MARTYR, 754

Boniface (his name means "good deeds") was born Wynfrith in Devonshire, England. He was a Benedictine monk who, at the age of thirty, was called to missionary work among the Vandal tribes in Germany. His first missionary attempt was unsuccessful but he returned two years later and was able to plant the gospel in an area filled with superstitious and violent practices. He led large numbers of Benedictine monks and nuns in establishing churches, schools, and seminaries. Boniface was also a reformer. He persuaded two rulers to call synods to put an end to the practice of selling church offices to the highest bidder. Boniface was preparing a group for confirmation on the eve of Pentecost when they were killed by Vandal warriors.

221

June 7, 2003

Vigil of Pentecost

INTRODUCTION

Pentecost is one of the principal festivals of the liturgical year. The tradition of night vigils precedes several of these festivals. In this night of extended prayer and silence, we anticipate being filled with the power of the Spirit, perhaps as the believers were in the second chapter of Acts (an alternate first reading this night). The Spirit gathers the church together. It is the same Spirit that enlightens us by the word, calls us in baptism, and sanctifies us with the bread of life and the cup of salvation. Come, Holy Spirit!

Today the church remembers Seattle (died 1866), chief of the Duwamish confederacy and peacemaker.

PRAYER OF THE DAY

Almighty and ever-living God, you fulfilled the promise of Easter by sending your Holy Spirit to unite the races and nations on earth and thus to proclaim your glory. Look upon your people gathered in prayer, open to receive the Spirit's flame. May it come to rest in our hearts and heal the divisions of word and tongue, that with one voice and one song we may praise your name in joy and thanksgiving; through your Son, Jesus Christ our Lord, who lives and reigns with you and the Holy Spirit, one God, now and forever.

VERSE

Alleluia. Come, Holy Spirit, fill the hearts of your faithful people; set them on fire with your love. Alleluia.

READINGS

Exodus 19:1-9

God establishes the covenant with Israel at Mt. Sinai.

or Acts 2:1-11

Psalm 33:12-22

The Lord is our help and our shield. (Ps. 33:20)

or Psalm 130

There is forgiveness with you. (Ps. 130:3)

Romans 8:14-17, 22-27

The Spirit prays for us.

John 7:37-39

Jesus nourishes believers with the living water and leads them to the Spirit of God.

COLOR Red

THE PRAYERS

Standing in the glorious light of the resurrection, let us pray for the church, the world, and all who wait for the Spirit's revealing power.

A BRIEF SILENCE.

Spirit of God, descend upon our hearts so that from them may flow rivers of living water. Empower your church to share this water with all who thirst for you. We pray:

Come, Holy Spirit.

Spirit of God, descend upon our hearts so that your people might be a holy nation and a priestly kingdom to serve you across this whole earth. We pray:

Come, Holy Spirit.

Spirit of God, descend upon our hearts with the fire of your compassion for all in need. Come to the aid of those who are weak with illness *(especially)*. We pray:

Come, Holy Spirit.

Spirit of God, descend upon our hearts so that this congregation will boldly and courageously speak about your mighty deeds of power in our lives. We pray:

Come, Holy Spirit.

HERE OTHER INTERCESSIONS MAY BE OFFERED.

Spirit of God, descend upon the hearts of all who are bowed down with grief *(especially)*. Through your eternal Spirit, may we be kept in union with Seattle and with all the beloved who have died. We pray:

Come, Holy Spirit.

Gracious God, hear our prayers and receive them for the sake of the crucified and risen one, our Savior Jesus Christ.

Amen

IMAGES FOR PREACHING

"There was no Spirit, because Jesus was not yet glorified." Difficult to imagine, no Spirit. It is even more difficult to understand, especially because some of us will confess our faith in the words of the Athanasian Creed with its eternal Spirit, and have read in the creation account in Genesis that the Spirit of God swept over the face of the waters.

But although the Holy Spirit always existed, that divine Spirit was not poured out on the whole people until the day of Pentecost according to Luke, or the day of Jesus' resurrection appearance to the eleven disciples in the Johannine account.

For John the gift of the Holy Spirit to humankind is tied to Jesus' glorification, his lifting up on the cross and his resurrection. And so when he appears to the eleven, in his glory, he bestows on them the Holy Spirit. As Acts tells it, the Spirit is poured out on the whole people—Jews, Greeks, Parthians, Medes, and all others—on the Day of Pentecost.

A religious music album entitled *Awaiting the Spirit* contains jazz arrangements of songs of the people of God, such as "Great Is Thy Faithfulness" and "Blessed Assurance." In an interview, the artist, Barry Sames, talked of having watched his mother who served as a church musician. "I wanted to do the kind of things she did. Her style influenced me, but after a while I was waiting for the Spirit to lead me in Its own direction."

Even in these days, we pray for an outpouring of God's Holy Spirit, because even though it has already been given to us at times, many times it needs to be stirred up. And we await.

WORSHIP MATTERS

Vigils always take place the night before, in anticipation of what is to come. The Vigil of Pentecost is a liturgy to anticipate the blessing and gift of God's Holy Spirit to be given tomorrow.

How might we prepare for this Spirit's day? With Christmas we have four Sundays of Advent to get ready. With Easter we have forty days of Lent and an entire Holy Week to gear up. But for Pentecost, the third great festival, we have just one night to get make sure that things are in place. What shall we do?

The scripture lessons give us some help. Gather the people, as in the first reading. Get your priorities straight and wait for the Lord, as in the psalm. With all creation, listen for the Spirit, as Paul advises. Get ready to change from thirsty seeker to overflowing spring. All of these lessons help us to get into the "spirit" of the season.

LET THE CHILDREN COME

The Vigil of Pentecost is a joyous time. People may be encouraged to dress in red. The worship space may be decorated with red flowers. Flames and candles are used and individual candles or red flower buds may be taken home as a reminder of the celebration.

HYMNS FOR WORSHIP
GATHERING
O day full of grace   LBW 161
Veni Sancte Spiritus   WOV 686

HYMN OF THE DAY
Come down, O love divine   LBW 508

COMMUNION
Spirit of God descend upon my heart   LBW 486
Like the murmur of the dove's song   WOV 685
O sacred River   OBS 107

SENDING
Now rest beneath night's shadow   LBW 282
Christ, mighty Savior   WOV 729

ADDITIONAL HYMNS AND SONGS
Holy Ghost, dispel our sadness   H82 515
Eternal light, shine in my heart   H82 465, 466
Holy Spirit, descend   TFF 107
Spirit song   TFF 105, W&P 130

MUSIC FOR THE DAY
PSALMODY
Farlee, Robert Buckley. PW C.
Inwood, Paul. "The Lord Fills the Earth with His Love" in STP 3.

CHORAL
Haas, David. "Breath of Life." U, desc, cant, cong, gtr, kybd. GIA G-5183.
Mathis, William, and Donald Livingston. "Come Down O Love Divine." SATB, org.   AFP 0800675355.
Proulx, Richard. "Christ Sends the Spirit." SAB, fl. AFP 0800652703.
Rorem, Ned. "Breathe on Me, Breath of God." SATB.   B&H B6543.
Scott, K. Lee. "Gracious Spirit, Dwell with Me." 2 pt mxd, org. AFP 0800646134.

223

CHILDREN'S CHOIRS

Callahan, Charles. "Creator Spirit, by Whose Aid." U, opt desc, org.
MSM50-5400.

White, David Ashley. "Like the Murmur of the Dove's Song."
U/2 pt, kybd.   CG CGA352.

KEYBOARD/INSTRUMENTAL

Fruhauf, Ennis. "Down Ampney" in *Ralph Vaughan Williams and the English School*. Org.   AFP 0800656873.

Hovhaness, Alan. "Prayer of St. Gregory." Org/pno, tpt.
Peer Music International 1500903.

Larsen, Libby. "Veni, Creator Spiritus" in *A New Liturgical Year*, ed.
John Ferguson. Org.   AFP 0800656717.

Sedio, Mark. "Bridegroom" in *How Blessed This Place*. Org.
AFP 0800658035.

Wold, Wayne L. "Suite on 'O Day Full of Grace.'" Org.
AFP 0800656881.

HANDBELL

Honoré, Jeffrey. "Invocation." 3–5 oct.   CPH 97-6826.

Moklebust, Cathy. "Come, Holy Spirit." 3–5 oct.   JEF MAMHB21.

PRAISE ENSEMBLE

Fragar, Russell. "I Believe the Presence" in *Hosanna! Music Songbook 11*.
INT.

Talbot, John Michael. "Send Us Out" in *Renew*.   HOP.

Saturday, June 7

SEATTLE, CHIEF OF THE DUWAMISH CONFEDERACY, 1866

Noah Seattle was chief of the Suquamish tribe and later became chief of the Duwamish Confederacy, a tribal alliance. When the tribes were faced with an increasing number of white settlers, Seattle chose to live and work peacefully with them rather than engage in wars. After Seattle became a Roman Catholic, he began the practice of morning and evening prayer in the tribe, a practice that continued after his death. On the centennial of his birth, the city of Seattle—named for him against his wishes—erected a monument over his grave.

When parish groups gather today, remember Chief Seattle and his work as a peacemaker. Consider beginning or ending parish events with a simple form of morning or evening prayer, not only today, but also as a regular part of the parish life.

June 8, 2003

The Day of Pentecost

INTRODUCTION

On Pentecost, the fiftieth day of Easter, the church prays that God would send forth the flame of the Holy Spirit and fill the church with an abundance of gifts needed to carry out its baptismal mission. We pray that the Holy Spirit would lend fire to our words and strength to our witness. We ask that God would send us forth to proclaim with boldness the wondrous work of raising Christ, who is our life and our hope.

PRAYER OF THE DAY

God, the Father of our Lord Jesus Christ, as you sent upon the disciples the promised gift of the Holy Spirit, look upon your Church and open our hearts to the power of the Spirit. Kindle in us the fire of your love, and strengthen our lives for service in your kingdom; through your Son, Jesus Christ our Lord, who lives and reigns with you in the unity of the Holy Spirit, one God, now and forever.

VERSE

Alleluia. Come, Holy Spirit, fill the hearts of your faithful people; set them on fire with your love. Alleluia.

READINGS

Acts 2:1-21

Pentecost was a Jewish harvest festival that marked the fiftieth day after Passover. In time, the festival came to celebrate the covenant made at Mount Sinai. Still later, Luke associated the outpouring of the Holy Spirit with Pentecost as the fiftieth day after the resurrection, a new covenant sealed in the body and blood of Christ.

or Ezekiel 37:1-14

The Spirit of God gives new life to those who were dead.

Psalm 104:25-35, 37 (Psalm 104:24-34, 35b [NRSV])

Alleluia. (Ps. 104:37b) or Send forth your Spirit and renew the face of the earth. (Ps. 104:31)

Romans 8:22-27

In this text, Paul speaks of the Spirit's presence in the cosmos. The entire creation groans in hope and testifies to what each Christian knows: the Spirit is the principle of new life gathering all into the harvest of hope.

or Acts 2:1-21

John 15:26-27; 16:4b-15

When speaking to his disciples before his death, Jesus referred to the Holy Spirit as "the Helper" and described the difference the Spirit would make in their lives and in the world.

COLOR Red

THE PRAYERS

Standing in the glorious light of the resurrection, let us pray for the church, the world, and all who wait for the Spirit's revealing power.

A BRIEF SILENCE.

Come to your church and inflame the hearts of your people to convey your love faithfully and boldly to the world. We pray:

Come, Holy Spirit.

Come from the four winds, O Breath of God, and breathe your peace into the hearts of every nation, that violence and war may cease in all the world. We pray:

Come, Holy Spirit.

Come and let your healing breath surround the sick *(especially)*, that they may be given new life and new health. We pray:

Come, Holy Spirit.

Come and let the new wine of your presence give us vision as we gather at your table of mercy, there to be strengthened and sent into the world empowered with your good news. We pray:

Come, Holy Spirit.

HERE OTHER INTERCESSIONS MAY BE OFFERED.

Come and intercede for those who groan in grief, that together with all your blessed saints, they might be united by your Spirit with those for whom they mourn. We pray:

Come, Holy Spirit.

Gracious God, hear our prayers and receive them for the sake of the crucified and risen one, our Savior Jesus Christ.

Amen

IMAGES FOR PREACHING

For some, the proof that one has received the gift of the Holy Spirit is speaking in tongues. All too often the Pentecost lesson from Acts is wrongly cited as evidence for that "proof." In the gospel lesson appointed for this day, the sign of having received the Advocate, the promised Holy Spirit, is in testifying on Christ's behalf. And the Advocate cannot come until Jesus goes away. The imagery is not unlike that of a tag team ministry. The Advocate, the mouthpiece, speaks for you and through you, gives you the words of Christ, because that which is of the Father is of Christ and now, is of the Spirit of truth, the Advocate.

On this day we celebrate our being clothed with the power from on high. Now comes the promised Holy Spirit poured out on all, and it is not exclusively, or even primarily, about speaking in the tongues of men and angels. The speech required of us is really quite simple. The command given to the disciples at Jesus' ascension was to proclaim repentance and forgiveness to all nations. When the Spirit of the Lord anoints us, or moves upon our hearts, we may dance like David danced or even sing like Miriam sang, but an even better response to the Spirit's anointing is to proclaim God's love through Jesus Christ. And this is duty and joy not just for the ordained pastor or called church professionals, but for every believer. Every believer needs to be about the work of sharing his or her faith.

Do we feel the Spirit's presence too faintly within us, and despair of being able to witness? Another response to outpouring of the Spirit is that of prayer, whether aloud in the assembly of God's people or alone in the privacy of one's home. So we pray, and the Spirit prays for us, and the Spirit comes to us anew.

WORSHIP MATTERS

We celebrate the gift of the Holy Spirit on the Day of Pentecost. Tongues of fire descend upon the disciples allowing them to speak in other languages "as the Spirit gave them ability." Those watching the church that day wondered what was going on. Some thought they were a little tipsy. Others probably didn't know what to think.

What do people think as they observe our Spirit-filled worship services today? Do they sense God's Spirit moving among us, or does it just seem odd to them? Do people feel like they can follow what we're doing, or does it seem like it is from another country or century?

We need to worship in ways that the Spirit leads us, but we need also to pay attention to the visitor who for the first time is catching a glimpse of God's Spirit. We may be doing things that seem perfectly normal to us but that are quite strange to newcomers; give them help to understand.

LET THE CHILDREN COME

Pentecost is a day of baptism and/or confirmation in many congregations. The emphasis can be placed on the coming of the Holy Spirit to the baptized, the confirmed, and all believers. "Come, Holy Spirit" is a simple prayer response. Hymns focus on the Holy Spirit—including some wonderful, rhythm-filled hymns from Africa. Another good musical choice for children is a song from Taizé, "Veni Sancte Spiritus" (WOV 686). Children (as well as the rest of the congregation) can be taught the ostinato either in Latin or English.

HYMNS FOR WORSHIP

GATHERING

Holy Spirit, truth divine   LBW 257

O Holy Spirit, enter in   LBW 459

I was glad   W&P 68

HYMN OF THE DAY

Gracious Spirit, heed our pleading   WOV 687, TFF 103

ALTERNATE HYMN OF THE DAY

O day full of grace   LBW 161

Song over the waters   W&P 127

COMMUNION

Breathe on me, breath of God   LBW 488

O Spirit of life   WOV 680

Holy Spirit, light divine   TFF 104

SENDING

Holy Spirit, ever dwelling   LBW 523

O Holy Spirit, root of life   WOV 688

ADDITIONAL HYMNS AND SONGS

Fill us with your spirit   DH 71

Come, O Spirit, dwell among us   PH 129

Hail this joyful day's return   H82 223, 224

Spirit of the living God   TFF 101, W&P 129
Wind of the Spirit   W&P 157

MUSIC FOR THE DAY

PSALMODY

Busarow, Donald. "Psalm for Pentecost." SATB, brass, cong.
AFP 11-04617.

Chepponis, James J. "Eastertime Psalm: Psalms for Easter, Ascension, and Pentecost." Cant, cong, opt choir, opt tpts, hb.
GIA G-3907.

Farlee, Robert Buckley. PW B.

Hopson, Hal H. "Psalm 104" in *Ten Psalms*. U, cong.
HOP HH 3930.

Kreutz, Robert E. "Lord, Send Out Your Spirit." SATB, cong, gtr, org, solo inst.   OCP 9457.

Proulx, Richard. "Psalm 104" in TP.

Saliers, Don. "Psalm 104." Cant, cong, SATB, org, hb.   OXF 94.234.

Schoenbachler, Tim. "Send Out Your Spirit" in STP 2.

Wright, Andrew. "Send Forth Your Spirit, O Lord" in PS 2.

CHORAL

Burkhardt, Michael. "Come, Holy Ghost, Our Souls Inspire." 2 pt, hb.
MSM 50-5551.

Distler, Hugo. "Creator Spirit, Heavenly Dove" in *Chantry Choirbook*.
SAB.   AFP 0800657772.

Helgen, John. "Praise the Living God Who Sings." SATB, org.
AFP 0800674618.

Jeffrey, Richard. "Wind Who Makes All Winds That Blow." SATB, fl, cello.   CPH 98-3611.

Johnson, David N. "The Lone, Wild Bird" in *To God Will I Sing*. MH voice.   AFP 0800674332. ML voice.   AFP 080067434X.

Kosche, Kenneth. "Ignite My Heart, O Holy Flame." SATB, kybd.
GIA G-4077.

Vulpius, Melchior. "O Spirit of God, Eternal Source" in *Chantry Choirbook*. SATB AFP 0800657772.

CHILDREN'S CHOIRS

Cherwien, David. "Every Time I Feel the Spirit." U.   AMSI 3020.

Hopson, Hal H. "Psalm 104" in *Ten Psalms*. U, cong.
HOP HH3930.

KEYBOARD/INSTRUMENTAL

Berthier, Jacques. "Come, Creator Spirit" in *Liturgical Meditations*.
Fl, org.   GIA-3133.

Leavitt, John. "Hyfrydol" in *Hymn Preludes for the Church Year*. Org.
AFP 0800650328.

Mann, Adrian. "O Heiliger Geist, du ewiger Gott" in *Arise and Rejoice I*. Kybd, inst.   AFP 0800674960.

Organ, Anne Krentz. "Njoo kwetu, Roho Mwema" in *Global Piano Reflections*. Pno.   AFP 0800658019.

Wold, Wayne. "Suite on 'O Day Full of Grace.'" Org.
AFP 0800656881.

HANDBELL

Afdahl, Lee J. "Spirit in the Wind." 3–5 oct, windchime/chimetree.
AFP 0800655443.

Larson, Katherine Jordahl. "O Day Full of Grace." 3–5 oct.
CPH 97-6774.

Moklebust, Cathy. "Windscape." 3–5 oct.   CPH 97-6833.

PRAISE ENSEMBLE

Baloche, Richard. "Revival Fire Fall" in *Hosanna! Music Songbook 11*.
INT.

Carter, John. "A Pentecost Meditation." SAB/2 pt mxd.   ALF 4266.

Chisum, John. "Let Your Spirit Come" in *Hosanna! Music Songbook 7*.
INT.

Joncas, Michael. "Send Forth Your Spirit." SATB, cant, cong, org, synth.   GIA G-3436.

Medema, Ken/arr. Jack Schrader and Cora Scholz. "Lord, Listen to Your Children." SSA, kybd.   SHW YS500.

Snowden, Judith. "Come into the Presence." SATB, pno, fl.
LOR CIM1000.

Monday, June 9

COLUMBA, 597; AIDAN, 651; BEDE, 735; CONFESSORS

Today we commemorate three monks from the British Isles who kept alive the light of learning and devotion during the Middle Ages. Columba founded three monasteries, including one on the island of Iona, off the coast of Scotland. That monastery was left in ruins after the reformation but today is home to an ecumenical religious community. Aidan was known for his pastoral style and ability to stir people up to charity and good works. Bede was a Bible translator and scripture scholar. He wrote a history of the English church and was the first historian to date events *anno Domini* (A.D., year of our Lord). Bede is also known for his hymns, including "A hymn of glory let us sing!" (LBW 157).

Wednesday, June 11

ST. BARNABAS, APOSTLE

The Eastern church commemorates Barnabas as one of the seventy commissioned by Jesus. Though he was not among the twelve mentioned in the gospels, the book of Acts gives him the title of apostle. His name means "son of encouragement." When Paul came to Jerusalem after his conversion, Barnabas took him in over the fears of the other apostles who doubted Paul's discipleship. Later, Paul and Barnabas traveled together on missions.

At the Council of Jerusalem, Barnabas defended the claims of Gentile Christians in relation to the law of Moses. How can his work on behalf of others and his support of other Christians serve as a model for contemporary Christians and churches?

228

Saturday, June 14

BASIL THE GREAT, BISHOP OF CAESAREA, 379; GREGORY OF NAZIANZUS, BISHOP OF CONSTANTINOPLE, C. 389; GREGORY, BISHOP OF NYSSA, C. 385

These three are known as the Cappadocian fathers and all three of them explored the mystery of the Holy Trinity. Basil was influenced by his sister Macrina to live a monastic life, and he settled near his home. Basil's *Longer Rule* and *Shorter Rule* for monastic life are the basis for Eastern monasticism to this day. In his rule, he establishes a preference for communal rather than eremetical monastic life, by making the case that Christian love and service are by nature communal. Gregory of Nazianzus was sent to preach on behalf of the orthodox faith against the Arians in Constantinople, though the Orthodox did not have a church there at the time. He defended orthodox trinitarian and christological doctrine and his preaching won over the city. Gregory of Nyssa was the younger brother of Basil the Great. He is remembered as a writer on spiritual life and the contemplation of God in worship and sacraments.

SUMMER

Jesus is our bread, blessing us through our worship

Images *of the* Season

A fond memory of many who grew up

in farming communities throughout the country was of Mother

(usually) baking homemade bread for the family.

While the rest of the family slumbered peacefully, she rose long before dawn to begin the involved, yet necessary process of breadmaking. After mixing all the essential ingredients, including just the right amount of yeast, she placed the humongous, shapeless glob of dough in an equally sizable pottery bowl and covered it with a towel. With a great deal of effort, Mother set the bowl on the warm kitchen radiator in order for the dough to rise. And rise it did! Within an hour or so, as if with a life of its own, the dough burst over the sides of the bowl ready to be kneaded. Mother repeated this process of rising and kneading several times throughout the morning until somehow she knew it was ready to be formed into individual loaves and baked in the oven. Baking this bread was nearly an all-day project, but, at least from the eaters' perspective, it was certainly worth it! The savory aroma that permeated the entire house as the bread baked and the enticing taste of warm bread formed one of those precious, indelible childhood memories.

One key to the success of the breadmaking was found in the proper temperature of that monstrous kitchen radiator upon which the dough bowl sat. And for that reason, at least in one household, Mother absolutely refused to make bread during the summer months. Much to the dismay of the rest of the family, she only made homemade bread when the heat from the furnace pushed its way through the kitchen radiator. Although summer held many seasonal delights, homemade bread was not one of them.

This summer as we hear the assigned scriptures from year B of the lectionary, however, it becomes increasingly clear that there is indeed wonderful bread in the summertime. Week after week as we gather as God's people around his word and sacrament, we are reminded that Jesus Christ is the Bread of life. Jesus is our bread in all times and all seasons as he is continually among us, with us always, incarnate, making his presence known, making his blessings available to us through our worship.

Unfortunately, because summertime provides us with the opportunity to take periodic breaks from the routine of our lives, some church members choose to observe summer as a time to take breaks from regular corporate worship. Partly as a result of that practice, many congregations cut back on worship services and discontinue programs of ministry during the summer. Sometimes, the liturgy itself is even reduced to a bare minimum during the summer. But any such practices that suggest that summer renewal doesn't need spiritual input are unfortunate. Precisely because summertime is an opportune time for renewal, refreshment, and relaxation, the church can and should provide a spiritual context. Yes, the rhythms of life may vary in this season. But in the same way that we continue with habits such as dinner, so we all still need spiritual feeding. Summertime, the long, green post-Pentecost season, can be a period of growth within the church—a time for corporate, as well as individual, renewal.

The gospels in the first part of the summer present a collage of ways in which we receive basic life from God. Through baptism into Christ, all are reborn into a life that begins now and lasts through eternity. This never-ending love is the preeminent source of security for us, even amid the storms of life. True, we are called into a life of discipleship that will take us, with Jesus, to and through the cross; like him, we will encounter opposition and even rejection because of that identity. We must never forget those who, like John the Baptist, lost their earthly life—but never their eternal one—for the sake of their witness. But as we travel with Christ, we also experience marvelous healing of body, mind, and spirit. And yes, we are fed.

The metaphor of Jesus as the Bread of life sums up all that Jesus said and did. The Bread of life, like the manna in the wilderness and like the eucharist on the altar, declares how near and involved our God actually is in our daily lives. The Bread of life reminds us once and

230

for all that we have a God who will not go away, who indeed is part of our life itself. God is present with us always, even and often especially in the midst of our summertime breaks. The God who led the Israelites out of slavery in Egypt, who provided them with daily manna in the wilderness, who faithfully nurtured his people through the centuries, is the same God we meet at the cross of Jesus and at the empty tomb and who is made continually present to us as we gather around the eucharistic table week after week.

We might not get the homemade bread or other goodies we love during certain seasons. Most of us, though, will have plenty of other delicious foods to enjoy, especially in the summer season. We participate in weekly worship all year long because we are hungry not for mere food, but for Jesus. In the weekly eucharist, Jesus is the Bread of life. In the elements of bread and wine—become his body and blood—he nurtures our faith, refreshes our spirits, and sends us out as bread for the world.

Environment *and* Art *for the* Season

Two-and-a-half months' worth of summer Sundays

lie before us. Giving the environment for worship the same quality

of attention that we have given prior seasons can seem,

231

at first, a tall order. This long stretch of the church calendar—14 Sundays—isn't even really a liturgical season, after all, at least not in the same way that Advent, Christmas, Lent, and Easter are. Each of those seasons offers its own particular, rich images from which to draw; not so for this period of numbered Sundays.

But if we look more closely, shifting our attention outward toward the natural world and the civic calendar, as well as more deeply toward the scriptures, we discover that summer is, in fact, rife with imagery.

In the natural world of the Northern Hemisphere, summer is a time of subtle shifts. From mid-May through June, late spring transitions into early summer. The fresh, clean smell of fertile earth is carried on delightful breezes that blow through the damp air. Emerging from that fertile earth are the light, fresh greens of first growth and colorful new blooms. The months of July and August bring the fullest intensity of summer heat, and in many parts of the country, the humidity creeps up as well. The light, fresh greens of early summer mature into lush, deep greens. Fruits and grains develop toward their peaks. Harvesting of some of the earth's bounty has already begun.

Alongside the unfolding natural season, in the local congregation these weeks "after Pentecost" witness the unfolding life of a dynamic community that lives and works in a world where several calendars—social, civic, and liturgical—collide. Sometimes these collisions create complementary circumstances, sometimes not. Our goal is to prepare worship that is faithful to our tradition yet at the same time speaks to the contemporary assembly in the circumstances in which it finds itself.

As the Sundays after Pentecost unfold, so do the gospels of Mark and John. They can provide some ideas for creating an environment for worship. Though we are not in a liturgical season per se, these Sundays mark our ordered progress through the scriptures, which gives them a character all their own. During these summer months, we may hear in the gospel that the harvest needs workers or that Jesus was on a boat or by the seashore, or that Jesus describes himself as the bread of life. These concrete images help make the good news real for us. Be careful, though, not to go from Sunday to Sunday illustrating particular gospel passages; instead, see if you can find a motif that spans several weeks. The best images allude to scriptural images without being too literal.

Nature's extravagant bounty surely could be brought to the assembly's place of worship during these weeks. Be sure to adorn the whole place, not just the area around the altar, with greens and flowers. Make particular use of whatever is unique to your region, and let the natural ebb and flow in your area dictate what you use, how much, and for how long. There is nothing wrong with using houseplants, provided that they do not become part of the clutter. Many varieties are not particularly interesting and lend no more to the place for worship than they do to the mall. Choose wisely, and rotate them in and out. The vessels used for greens and flowers should reflect the days as well: perhaps clay pots and planters for early summer, then glass as we get into the heart of the season. Be careful that the vessels do not call too much attention to themselves and are of good quality; plastic and bright ceramic often are not the best choices.

On the other hand, it may also feel like an appropriate time of year to keep it simple, to allow the beauty of the church's furnishings and appointments to speak for themselves. This simplicity can be refreshing (though at no time of the year, of course, should the worship environment be ignored).

It is the longest period of time in which we see green vestments. The most common school of thought on the choice of green vestments for these days says that it was chosen because it is the color that symbolizes growth. In these numbered Sundays after Pentecost, we grow in our appreciation of the gospels as we read large portions of them straight through. Another explanation is simply that green is a neutral color and thus appropriate to this stretch of ordinary Sundays. If your congregation has green vestments in a few different shades, use their variety to mirror the subtle shifts of green found in nature: from early summer's light, budding greens to the lush, deeper greens of late summer. If you have only one set, or if all of your green vestments look the same, consider making it one of the community's goals to add some varied greens. It is, after all, the most frequently prescribed color on the calendar.

One of the challenges of planning during this season is that on top of the scattering that goes along with summer getaways and other social events, people's energy sometimes wanes. A little extra effort may be needed to ensure follow-through on plans and that things don't fall through the cracks. On the positive side, with Lent, the Three Days, and the Easter season behind you, you can finally get to some of those maintenance and renovation projects that never seem to get done during the year.

Finally, take a look at the outdoor areas around the church. Outside the doors is where hospitality, and thus a sense of the season, can really begin.

Preaching *with the* Season

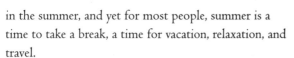

Summer means growth and harvest, fresh fruit

and vegetables. Summer means warmer weather. Summer can also

mean drought and killing heat. Many work even harder

in the summer, and yet for most people, summer is a time to take a break, a time for vacation, relaxation, and travel.

Even the observation of the church year seems, at first, to allow us a break. The conclusion of the season of Easter and the excitement of the Day of Pentecost are quickly replaced with the only feast dedicated to a doctrine of the church, the festival of the Holy Trinity. And then we mark the Sundays *after* Pentecost rather than the days leading us somewhere *to* something. Perhaps it would be more interesting if we began this liturgical season as a countdown to the feast of Christ the King and the final return of Jesus to reign once and for all time. Countdowns are much more dramatic than simply counting the Sundays after Pentecost. We are a people who like direction. We want a destination and the means to arrive at that destination quickly and without traffic! Give this summer season a destination and plot out the course to arrive there. Have patience, and remember that detours are inevitable, and may even allow us time to stop and reflect.

On our travels through the weeks of the lectionary, we begin with our old friend Nicodemus, the Pharisee who wants to see evidence of the kingdom of God. If he is to travel any roads with Jesus, he wants a glimpse of the final destination. Here is plenty of opportunity to reflect on baptism. In those waters, we all were invited into the journey of faith, the journey that begins and ends in Jesus. Soon we find ourselves on a boat with the disciples and witness again Jesus rebuking the wind and calming the sea that we might focus on the tasks at hand with a little less fear. There will be storms on our journey. How is it that some people are able to sleep through those storms? We take a detour at the request of an official of a synagogue, a man named Jairus. We visit briefly with a woman suffering from hemorrhages for twelve years—imagine!

There is a homecoming of sorts on our travels. Who has not taken a summer trip home? Jesus stops at his hometown and we share in his less-than-enthusiastic welcome there. There is horrible news on our trip: John the Baptist is dead and under bizarre circumstances. What is this journey we are on? Although we are moving in a direction, Jesus seems to never fail to stop that he might have compassion for the crowds wandering with him.

Along the way we find opportunity to celebrate the lives of fellow travelers, Peter, Paul, and Bartholomew. Be sure to spend some time visiting these familiar and not-so-familiar faces of our faith. They are our family, after all, brothers with us through the waters of baptism and fathers through the church they have passed down to us.

Propers 12 through 16 invite us to spend time with the sixth chapter of John and reflect as we journey with the Jesus who is the Bread of life. These weeks begin with a miraculous feeding but we know it means much more than full stomachs. Jesus takes a walk on the water that gives the disciples quite a start. The crowds catch up with the Jesus who has just fed them and then the conversation turns to true bread, the kind that satisfies one even into eternal life. The readings from John 6 help us to understand our weekly celebration of the eucharist, the bread of life that feeds our souls. The conversation about bread ends at a synagogue in Capernaum. Many at this point choose to not continue on the journey, but the twelve charge on. Who else could they follow? Who else can *we* follow?

The summer season ends with a lesson regarding the washing of one's hands—practical advice, to be sure, for any journey. It seems an odd transition point, a discourse on the law and the practice of it, but as always it has much broader application than it first appears.

Summer is many things to many people. For most of us, however, summer almost always goes by too quickly. Let the preacher be sure along the way to show all the sights waiting to be seen. Show some new sights. Introduce some new characters as well as spending time with old friends. Always be sure to show Jesus to the assembly. And point always to end of the journey, the day when Jesus will come again to reign for all time.

We are a people with a destination, but on the way we have a journey to enjoy.

The cross gives focus to our trip. The empty tomb provides energy. From that starting point, we venture out to explore some fascinating territory.

233

Shape *of* Worship *for the* Season

BASIC SHAPE OF THE EUCHARISTIC RITE

- Confession and Forgiveness: see alternate worship text for summer in *Sundays and Seasons* as an option to the form in the liturgy setting

GATHERING

- Greeting: see alternate worship text for summer
- Omit the Kyrie during the summer (except on the festival of the Holy Trinity and perhaps St. Peter and St. Paul, and St. Bartholomew)
- Omit or use the hymn of praise during the summer (use for the festival of the Holy Trinity and saints' days)

WORD

- Nicene Creed for Holy Trinity and saints' days; Apostles' Creed for remaining Sundays in this season
- The prayers: see the prayers in the summer section of *Sundays and Seasons*

MEAL

- Offertory prayer: see alternate worship text for summer
- Use the proper preface for Holy Trinity on the festival of the Holy Trinity, and the proper preface for Apostles on the saints' days; use the proper preface for Sundays after Pentecost for the remainder of the season
- Eucharistic prayer: in addition to four main options in *LBW*, see "Eucharistic Prayer G: Summer" in *WOV* Leaders Edition, p. 71

234

- Invitation to communion: see alternate worship text for summer
- Post-communion prayer: see alternate worship text for summer

SENDING

- Benediction: see alternate worship text for summer
- Dismissal: see alternate worship text for summer

OTHER SEASONAL POSSIBILITIES

BLESSING FOR TRAVELERS

- Use the prayer "Before Travel" in *LBW*, p. 167, before the benediction whenever groups from the congregation set out to travel. The names of those traveling may be inserted in the prayer.

FAREWELL AND GODSPEED

- See *Occasional Services*, pp. 151–52, for an order that is appropriate whenever people are transferring out of the congregation; it may be used either after the prayers or following the post-communion prayer.

Assembly Song *for the* Season

Summer is a time when many church members

reorder their lives. They spend less time and energy on school

and work, and more on vacation, recreation, and leisure.

For many, summer is a more casual season. Can the assembly's music reflect this change in the culture, and yet be worthy of use in worship? People come to our assemblies in this "casual season" with the same joys and sorrows, hopes and fears, and need to hear the clear proclamation of the gospel as they do during the rest of the year.

This year the summer season divides into two parts: June 15 to July 20, and July 27 to August 31 (when the "bread of life" passages from John make up the gospel readings for four of the Sundays). Assembly song, while following the same basic pattern for the season, could reflect this change. Be sure to sing any new songs for enough weeks that the summer "travelers" have sufficient opportunity to learn them. For the three festivals during the season—Holy Trinity; St. Peter and St. Paul, Apostles; and St. Bartholomew, Apostle—music could be somewhat more elaborate and festive.

GATHERING

- Use a simplified gathering rite, with an entrance hymn and omitting the Kyrie and hymn of praise. Be sure that the entrance hymn is of sufficient weight (and length) to gather the assembly into worship. If more singing is desired for the gathering, consider using song to replace the customary instrumental prelude. "I will sing of the mercies of the Lord" (W&P 74)—with guitar—could serve as the first song of this gathering music.
- On the three festival days, use a hymn of praise in addition to the entrance hymn.

WORD

- If the gathering rite is streamlined, use a hymn for the gospel acclamation. "Praise to you, O Christ, our Savior" (WOV 614, W&P 118) could be sung in its entirety before the gospel, or selected stanzas could be used. Alternatively, sing one or two stanzas before

and another one or two after the reading. Another choice is "Now listen, you servants of God" (LBW 11). It could also be used at the beginning of the Word portion of the liturgy to introduce all three readings.

- On the three festival days, use the appointed verse for the day. Have the assembly begin with the "alleluias" from "For all the saints" (LBW 174), then have a cantor sing the appointed verse to *LBW* psalm tone 3 (in D major), and have the assembly conclude with the "alleluias."

MEAL

- Because summer is a season of growth, when many people spend time in the garden or fields, use "As the grains of wheat" (WOV 705, W&P 10) for the offertory. Another choice is "We bring the sacrifice of praise" (W&P 150).
- Use familiar songs (or very simple, perhaps repetitive, pieces) for the distribution of communion since fewer people are present in many congregations. Sing "Eat this bread" (WOV 709) three times to replace the "Lamb of God" for the second half of the season, or use it with verses for cantor (in *Music from Taizé, vol. 2* from GIA Publications) following "Lamb of God" as the only other distribution music.

SENDING

- Use a single post-communion song. Seasonal possibilities include "You are the seed" (WOV 753, TFF 226, LLC 486) with Latin percussion, or "I received the living God" (WOV 700) with maracas. For the "bread of life" Sundays use "O living Bread from heaven" (LBW 197) or "Guide me ever, great Redeemer" (LBW 343).

235

Music *for the* Season

VERSE AND OFFERTORY

Cherwien, David. *Verses for the Season of Pentecost, set 1.* U, kybd.
MSM 80-541.

Gospel Acclamations. Cant, choir, cong, inst.   MAY 0862096324.

Powell, Robert. *Verses and Offertory Sentences, Part VI (Pentecost 10–18).*
CPH 97-5506.

Schiavone, J. *Gospel Acclamation Verses for Sundays of the Year, I, II, III.*
GIA G-2495, 2496, 2497.

Verses and Offertory Sentences, Part V (Pentecost 2–9). U/SATB, kybd.
CPH 97-5505.

CHORAL

Bisbee, Wayne. "Teach Me Your Way, O Lord." 2 pt mxd, kybd.
AFP 080065479X.

Carter, Andrew. "God Be in My Head." SATB, org.   OXF E-159.

Ferguson, John. "Lord of the Dance." SATB, org.   GAL 1.5260.

Haugen, Marty/arr. Bret Heim. "Sing Out, Earth and Skies." SATB,
fl, hb, perc.   GIA G-4495.

Jacobson, Allan S. "I Come, O Savior, to Your Table." SATB, kybd.
AFP 6000117027.

Kosche, Kenneth T. "It Is a Good Thing." SATB.
AFP 0800659635.

Leavitt, John. "Give Glory, All Creation." SATB, solo inst, perc.
CPH 98-3558.

Mendelssohn, Felix. "They That Shall Endure to the End" in *Chantry
Choirbook.* SATB.   AFP 0800657772.

Rutter, John. "For the Beauty of the Earth." SATB, kybd.
HIN HMC-550.

Schalk, Carl. "This Touch of Love." SATB, org, cong.   MSM-50-8301.

Schütz, Heinrich. "Sing to the Lord" in *Chantry Choirbook.* SATB,
kybd.   AFP 0800657772.

Scott, K. Lee. "Let the Words of My Mouth." SATB, org.
CPH 98-2963.

Telemann, G. F./arr. Ronald A. Nelson. "O Come, Holy Spirit."
U, vln, cont.   AFP 11-0314.

CHILDREN'S CHOIRS

Powell, Robert. "Treasures of the Heart." 2 pt, kybd, fl.
AFP 0800654811.

Rutter, John. "All Things Bright and Beautiful." 2 pt, kybd.
HIN HMC663.

Sleeth, Natalie. "Praise the Lord" in *Sunday Songbook.* U, kybd.
HIN HMB102.

Taylor, Jim. "A Call to Praise." U/2 pt, kybd, opt fl.   CG CGA793.

KEYBOARD/INSTRUMENTAL

Albinoni, Tomaso/ed. S. Drummond Wolff. *Albinoni for Instrument and
Keyboard.* Kybd, C/Bb inst.   CPH 97-6625.

Albrecht, Mark. *Early American Hymns and Tunes.* Pno, fl.
AFP 800656911.

Faxon, Nancy Plummer. "Prelude for Violin and Organ." Org, vln.
MSM 20-967.

Mozart, W. A. *Complete Church Sonatas.* Org, 2 vln.   Bärenreiter 4732.

Purvis, Richard. "St. Francis Suite." Org.   J. Fischer 9530-12.

HANDBELL

Afdahl, Lee. "Abbot's Leigh." 3–5 oct.   HOP 2103.

Dombrinski, Cynthia. "He Leadeth Me." 3–5 oct.   HOP 1461.

Joncas, Michael. "Drink In the Richness of God" (Psalm 34). SATB,
cong, org, cant, hb.   GIA G-4915.

Larson, Katherine J. "Holy, Holy, Holy! Lord God Almighty."
3–5 oct, opt narr tpt.   HOP 1876.

McChesney, Kevin. "Cantad al Señor." 5 oct, L3.
AFP 080065739X.

Page, Anna Laura. "I Sing the Mighty Power of God." 3–5 oct, L2.
ALF API9013.

Thompson, Martha Lynn. "Holy Manna." 3–5 oct, L2.   AG 2081.

PRAISE ENSEMBLE

Burleigh, Glenn/arr. Jack Schrader. "Order My Steps." SATB, kybd.
HOP C 5083.

Hopson, Hal H. "Amen, Sing Praises to the Lord." SATBB, solo, opt
perc.   HOP C 5057.

Kerr, Ed. "Let Your Spirit Fall Here" in *Only God for Me Songbook.*
SAT[B], kybd.   INT 15297.

McPherson, Stephen/arr. Jay Rouse. "Holy Spirit, Rain Down" in
Hillsongs Choral Collection. SATB, kybd.   INT 16996.

Pethel, Stan. "Shout for Joy." SATB, kybd.   HOP GC 888.
Cass. GC 888C.

Thomas, Andrae. "I Will Sing Praises." SATB, kybd.   CG A718.

236

Alternate Worship Texts

CONFESSION AND FORGIVENESS

In the name of the Father, and of the ✝ Son,
and of the Holy Spirit.
Amen

Let us confess our sin in the presence of God
and of one another.

Silence for reflection and self-examination.

Reconciling God,
you seek peace and unity among us,
but too often we choose walls of isolation.
You seek to be one with your creation,
but we turn away your loving Spirit.
In your forgiving love,
break down the barriers we create,
that we might see more clearly your love for us,
be reconciled with our neighbor,
and trust more deeply your promise of eternal life. Amen

We who once were far off
have been brought near to God
through the cross of Jesus Christ.
May almighty God grant you grace
to forgive one another
as God in Christ has forgiven you.
Amen

GREETING

The steadfast love of God, the life of Jesus Christ,
and the growth of the Holy Spirit be with you all.
And also with you.

PRAYERS

Growing in the soil of the Spirit, let us pray for the church,
the world, and all who seek the richness of life in God.

A brief silence.

Each petition ends:
Gracious God,
hear our prayer.

Concluding petition:
Hear us as we pray, living God,
and in your mercy give us all good things,
for the sake of Jesus Christ, our Lord and Savior.
Amen

OFFERTORY PRAYER

Gracious God,
as grains of wheat are gathered for bread,
and grapes together are poured out as wine,
so may we be united in your presence
through this sacrament of grace. Amen

INVITATION TO COMMUNION

This is the bread
that comes down from heaven
and gives life to the world.
Whoever eats this bread will live forever.

POST-COMMUNION PRAYER

O God,
we thank you for the living bread
that rains down from heaven.
From this feast of love
may we carry your eternal life
as daily food for the well-being of the world;
through Jesus Christ, our Lord.
Amen

BLESSING

May you be strengthened with the power of God,
✝ the love of Christ,
and the help of the Holy Spirit.
Amen

DISMISSAL

Go in peace to bear Christ's love to the world.
Thanks be to God.

237

June 15, 2003

The Holy Trinity
First Sunday after Pentecost

INTRODUCTION

The festival of the Holy Trinity celebrates the mystery of God, both transcendent and immanent. Though the nature of God is beyond our rational explanation, we ascribe glory to the one who is holy, whose glory fills the whole earth. Christians are born of water and the Spirit, and when we make the sign of the cross, we remember our baptism in the name of the triune God. Born anew in baptism, and nourished at the Lord's table, we now live as witnesses to God's love for us and all the world.

PRAYER OF THE DAY

Almighty God our Father, dwelling in majesty and mystery, renewing and fulfilling creation by your eternal Spirit, and revealing your glory through our Lord, Jesus Christ: Cleanse us from doubt and fear, and enable us to worship you, with your Son and the Holy Spirit, one God, living and reigning, now and forever.
or
Almighty and ever-living God, you have given us grace, by the confession of the true faith, to acknowledge the glory of the eternal Trinity and, in the power of your divine majesty, to worship the unity. Keep us steadfast in this faith and worship, and bring us at last to see you in your eternal glory, one God, now and forever.

VERSE

Alleluia. Holy, holy, holy is the LORD of hosts; the whole earth is full of his glory. Alleluia. (Isa. 6:3)

READINGS

Isaiah 6:1-8

This first reading narrates the prophet's vision of the Lord surrounded by the angelic company. They sing "Holy, holy, holy," a song the church echoes at the beginning of the great thanksgiving. In the liturgy, this text invites the church and all creation to sing in praise of God's glory. This glory is God's mercy toward sinners.

Psalm 29

Worship the LORD in the beauty of holiness. (Ps. 29:2)

Romans 8:12-17

In describing the new life of faith, Paul refers to all three persons of the Trinity: the Spirit leads us to recognize that we are children of God the Father and sisters and brothers with Christ the Son.

John 3:1-17

Jesus' miracles prompt Nicodemus to visit him in secrecy. Jesus tells him about being born of the Spirit and about the Son who has been sent by God to save.

COLOR White

THE PRAYERS

Growing in the soil of the Spirit, let us pray for the church, the world, and all who seek the richness of life in God.
A BRIEF SILENCE.
Triune God, the fullness of your identity is a mystery, and yet you reveal to the church your awesome presence. Teach us to worship you in the beauty of your holiness. Gracious God,
hear our prayer.
Be with all who care for the environment, and make us sensitive to the ways in which we can preserve our natural resources for the good of all. Gracious God,
hear our prayer.
Draw near to those whose bodies know pain and illness (*especially*). Assure them of your living presence with them, and grant them healing. Gracious God,
hear our prayer.
Help fathers to provide for the families in their care, that their service might be a sign of your love for us all. Gracious God,
hear our prayer.
Guide the work of parish worship and music leaders, and the ministry of all among us who point to your beauty and assist us as we gather in your presence. Gracious God,
hear our prayer.
HERE OTHER INTERCESSIONS MAY BE OFFERED.
Holy are you, O God; you have made us your holy

238

people. Keep us united with (names, and all) the faithful who have gone before us, and who now make their home with you. Gracious God,

hear our prayer.

Hear us as we pray, living God, and in your mercy give us all good things, for the sake of Jesus Christ, our Lord and Savior.

Amen

IMAGES FOR PREACHING

How does one see God? Do we see God "sitting on a throne, high and lofty," surrounded by winged seraphs, as in Isaiah 6:1-2? The initial question is even older than that image. Perhaps we should simply ask to see evidence of the kingdom of God, rather than actually seeing the Almighty. That seems to be the question put forth by the Pharisee named Nicodemus. Though he appears to be friendly to Jesus, he does come under the cover of darkness—after all, he had his reputation to think about. Seeing in the daylight, however, is usually easier.

A discussion ensues regarding a birth from above and a birth by the Spirit. Nicodemus is left with more questions than answers. "How can these things be?" Allow me to make it perfectly clear, Jesus responds. Do you remember the serpent on the staff in the days of Moses? The people wandering in the wilderness wanted to see God, or at least be healed. All they had to do was look up to the snake. Look up to the Son of Man hanging on a pole and there you will see, once for all time, the God you seek. One cannot help but wonder if Nicodemus left even more confused than before his nighttime visit.

We seek to see God on this Trinity Sunday. The temptation is to preach doctrine rather than Christ. Show them Jesus. Show them the one who was sent into the world, not to condemn the world but in order that the world might be saved through him. Talk of God's saving grace for the world and for each life on that world. Talk about living lives in that same grace, that others might see Jesus and God in their own lives and worlds. Make God's grace as plain as day.

WORSHIP MATTERS

In the first reading, Isaiah has a vision of God, full of glory, before whom the sinful human cannot survive. Although images of God's transcendence were typical among ancient people, much of worship today has lost that sense of awe in God's presence. Modern church architecture, which emphasized community and intimacy among the people and with the presiding minister, sometimes contributes to the loss of transcendence in worship. Cultural values of casualness and informality make their way into worship, eroding further that sense of mystery and awe before God.

Even though informality in worship style and emphasis on community and intimacy through ritual space help to express an incarnational theology, it is important to maintain a healthy tension between a transcendent and an incarnate God.

LET THE CHILDREN COME

The Voice that invites us to new birth, reassures us of our freedom, and calls us to serve also "causes the oaks to whirl, and strips the forest bare; and in his temple all say, 'Glory!' " (Ps. 29:9). Today, let the children lead the assembly in praise and awe of the triune God. Provide them with banners to hold, poles with ribbons to raise in procession, and encouragement to sing (even cry loudly) the glory of God. Contemplating God's glory involves more than our heads. Our whole bodies must be engaged in the act of worship.

HYMNS FOR WORSHIP
GATHERING
Father, we praise you   LBW 267
Come, all you people   WOV 717, TFF 138

HYMN OF THE DAY
Holy, holy, holy   LBW 165

ALTERNATE HYMN OF THE DAY
Mothering God, you gave me birth   WOV 769
Holy, holy   TFF 289, W&P 60

COMMUNION
Now the silence   LBW 205
Glory to God, we give you thanks   WOV 787
Glorify thy name   W&P 42

SENDING
Now thank we all our God   LBW 533, 534
Go, my children, with my blessing   WOV 721, TFF 161

ADDITIONAL HYMNS AND SONGS

Round the Lord in glory seated   H82 367

O sacred River   OBS 107

The Lord is in his holy temple   TFF 143

Holy ground   W&P 59

MUSIC FOR THE DAY

PSALMODY

Busarow, Donald. "It Is a Good Thing to Give Thanks." SATB, cong, hb.   CPH 98-3126.

Christiansen, David.   PW B.

Guimont, Michel. "Psalm 29: The Lord Will Bless His People" in GC.

Hopson, Hal H.   TP.

Hughes, John/arr. Hal H. Hopson. *Psalm Refrains and Tones for the Common Lectionary.* U, cong, kybd.   HOP.

Marshall, Jane. *Psalms Together II.* U.   CG CGC-21.

Smith, Geoffrey Boulton. "Give Strength to Your People, Lord" in PS I.

CHORAL

Jennings, Kenneth. "With a Voice of Singing" in *The Augsburg Choirbook.* SATB.   AFP 0800656784.

Olson, Howard, arr. "God the Father, Son and Spirit" in *Set Free.* SATB.   AFP 0806600454.

Scott, K. Lee, "Holy, Holy, Holy." SATB, org, opt cong, 2 tpt, 2 tbn, timp.   SEL 425-612.

Sedio, Mark. "Be Thankful to God." U, opt desc, kybd.   AFP 0800658701.

Tchaikovsky, Peter Ilich. "Holy, Holy, Holy" in *The New Church Anthem Book.* SATB.   OXF 0193531097.

Vaughan Williams, Ralph. "The Old 100th Psalm Tune." SATB.   OXF 42.953.

Wolff, Drummond. "Holy, Holy, Holy." SATB, org, tpt.   CPH 98-2129.

CHILDREN'S CHOIRS

Burkhardt, Michael. "From All That Dwell Below the Skies." U, kybd.   MSM 50-9415.

Glover, Rob. "Praise to the Trinity." U, kybd, opt gtr.   CG CGA668.

KEYBOARD/INSTRUMENTAL

Burkhardt, Michael. *Five Pentecost Hymn Improvisations* (Allein Gott in der Höh sei Ehr, Down Ampney, In Babilone, Den Signede Dag, Song 13). Org.   MSM 10-501.

Farlee, Robert Buckley. "Nicaea" in *Augsburg Organ Library: Easter.* Org.   AFP 0800659368.

Honoré, Jeffrey. "Nicaea" in *Classic Embellishments.* Org, inst.   AFP 0800658728.

Moore, David W. "Nicaea" in *Dona Nobis Pacem.* Pno, inst.   AFP 0800659392.

Post, Piet. "Phantasy on 'Holy, Holy, Holy.' " Org.   Ars Nova 493.

HANDBELL

Dobrinski, Cynthia. "Holy, Holy, Holy." 3–5 oct, opt narr.   AG 1905.

Moklebust, Cathy. "Festival Sanctus." 4–5 oct.   AFP 6000001185.

Moklebust, Cathy. "Nicaea" in *Hymn Stanzas for Handbells.* 4–5 oct.   AFP 0800655761. 2–3 oct.   AFP 0800657330.

Thompson, Martha Lynn. "God of Grace and God of Glory." 4–5 oct.   MSM 30-810.

PRAISE ENSEMBLE

Altrogge, Mark. "I Stand in Awe" in *Come & Worship.*   INT.

Chisum, John, and Don Moen. "I See the Lord" in *Come & Worship.* INT.

Clydesdale, David T. "Holy Is He" (Holy, Holy, Holy). SATB, orch. David C. Cook Church Ministries 3100506162.

Cull, Bob. "Open Our Eyes" in *Praise and Worship.*   MAR BK06008.

Martin, Joseph M. "Bethlehem Wind." SATB, acc.   ALF 16440.

Mohr, Jon and Randall Dennis. "More Than Anything" in *Point of Grace Songbook.* 3 pt, kybd.   WRD 3010294492.

Schutte, Dan/arr. Mark Hayes. "Here I Am, Lord." SATB, orch. GS A7101.

Saturday, June 21

ONESIMOS NESIB, TRANSLATOR, EVANGELIST, 1931

Onesimos was born in Ethiopia. He was captured by slave traders and taken from his Galla homeland to Eritrea where he was bought, freed, and educated by Swedish missionaries there. He translated the Bible into Galla and returned to his homeland to preach the gospel there. His tombstone includes a verse from Jeremiah 22:29, "O land, land, land, hear the word of the Lord!"

Does your congregation support mission work through synod or churchwide offerings, or do you have a specific missionary whom you support? Let the commemoration of Onesimos Nesib be a way for congregations to focus on missions during the summer months.

June 22, 2003

Second Sunday after Pentecost
Proper 7

INTRODUCTION

Life is sometimes like a storm that causes our hearts to fear. In today's gospel the disciples encounter a storm on the waters while Jesus is asleep. Upon waking, Jesus bids the wind to cease, and he speaks words of peace to his troubled disciples. We gather amid life's obstacles and hardships to hear words of comfort and promise, to greet one another with peace, and to celebrate Jesus' enduring presence among us at the Lord's table and in the community of faith.

PRAYER OF THE DAY

O God our defender, storms rage about us and cause us to be afraid. Rescue your people from despair, deliver your sons and daughters from fear, and preserve us all from unbelief; through your Son, Jesus Christ our Lord.

VERSE

Alleluia. Because you are children, God has sent the Spirit of his Son into your hearts, crying, "Abba! Father!" Alleluia. (Gal. 4:6)

READINGS

Job 38:1-11

Confronted with great suffering, Job attempts to prove his innocence to God. God speaks from the whirlwind, and speaks of the power of the sea and its waves. A series of ironical questions shows that Job, as a finite human, is incapable of judging the Creator.

Psalm 107:1-3, 23-32

God stilled the storm and quieted the waves of the sea. (Ps. 107:29)

2 Corinthians 6:1-13

Paul writes of the great hardships and calamities that he has faced, yet he is able to rejoice because what appears to be loss is great gain.

Mark 4:35-41

Jesus' calming of the storm on the sea reveals his power over evil, because the sea represents evil and chaos. The boat on the sea is a symbol of the church, and invites us to trust God amid life's turbulence.

SEMICONTINUOUS FIRST READING/PSALM

1 Samuel 17:[1a, 4-11, 19-23] 32-49

In this passage, the description of the soldier Goliath vividly depicts the superiority of Philistine military might. In contrast, David is armed with the name of the Lord.

or 1 Samuel 17:57—18:5, 10-16

Psalm 9:9-20

The LORD will be a refuge in time of trouble. (Ps. 9:9)

or Psalm 133

How good and pleasant it is to live together in unity. (Ps. 133:1)

COLOR Green

THE PRAYERS

Growing in the soil of the Spirit, let us pray for the church, the world, and all who seek the richness of life in God.

A BRIEF SILENCE.

Let us pray for trust in the baptismal promises we receive, that the church may face the world not in fear, but in love born of faith. Gracious God,

hear our prayer.

Let us pray for the land, planted and bringing forth growth, that those who till the soil and watch over the fields will be given strength for their labor. Gracious God,

hear our prayer.

Let us pray for all who are anxious or depressed, sick or suffering (*especially*), that they may hear the gentle stillness of Christ amid the storms of life. Gracious God,

hear our prayer.

Let us pray for those who practice a ministry of hospitality in this parish: ushers, greeters, hosts, and all who serve in the name of the Spirit who welcomes and embraces all. Gracious God,

hear our prayer.

Let us pray for the unity of the church, that all who gather in the name of the Lord would continue to strive for a deeper knowledge of Christ and his benefits. Gracious God,

hear our prayer.

HERE OTHER INTERCESSIONS MAY BE OFFERED.

Let us pray in thanksgiving for all who have died and who are now at rest in Jesus, whose Spirit keeps us united with our beloved departed. Gracious God,
hear our prayer.
Hear us as we pray, living God, and in your mercy give us all good things, for the sake of Jesus Christ, our Lord and Savior.
Amen

IMAGES FOR PREACHING

A storm rages. The boat is tossed about like a child's toy. The winds push the waves into the boat and it is swamped with water. The disciples, many of them experienced fishermen, are terrified. Surely they will all drown.

"Where is Jesus?" the disciples ask frantically. Their efforts to bail out the boat are failing miserably. Somehow Jesus, in the stern of the boat, sleeps through the storm and the cries of the disciples. On finding and rousing him, the question moves from where to what. What will you do? Do something. Do anything! The wind is rebuked with a few words, "Peace! Be still!" Now it is Jesus who gets to ask the next questions: "Why are you afraid?" "Have you no faith?" The disciples answer with still another question: "Who is this?" they wonder aloud.

Who is this? This is the only child of God who will do much more than calm wind and sea. This is the only child of God who will heal the sick, feed the hungry, welcome the sinner and outcast. This is the only child of God who will suffer death, defeat the devil, and rise again to bring everlasting life. Yes, storms rage about us, but you, O God, rescue us even from ourselves, drowning us in the waters of baptism, that we might live, truly live, in all faithfulness.

This business of faith seems to be filled with more questions than answers. Where, what, why and who; the question left for us is "When?" When is the time to respond with faith? Now is the time, Paul advises the Corinthian community (I Cor. 6:2). Not later, not tomorrow, but now is the time. Open wide your hearts to receive the one whom even the wind and sea obey.

WORSHIP MATTERS

Even though tradition might hold Lent as a season of simplifying and housecleaning, summer may serve for a more thorough review. What are the first impressions visitors, guests, or travelers receive in a congregation? Set aside what you are used to seeing, and look at the parking lot, the signs, the mailbox, the main doors, the flowers. What are the dominant smells? Then look at the greeters, the lighting, the paint, the feel of the place. What *doesn't* need to be there? What might be done better?

Take a team on a field trip to a place of hospitality with a visitor's eye: a hospital, a corporation, a resort, a restaurant, a superstore. What do they do that's worth doing (or not doing) in a church—a place of peace in a storm. In the first issue of *The Lutheran* magazine, Martin Marty gave this advice: Become interesting; God already is.

LET THE CHILDREN COME

Many of the words we say in worship also are heard in scriptures read in the liturgy. Today, we hear Jesus speak to his fearful disciples, "Peace, be still!" Peace is God's gift to us, not only to be received with gratitude but also shared with others. Passing the peace is a wonderful tactile moment, especially for children. Consider helping the entire assembly make the connection between this ritual act and the gospel text. Help adults understand that the peace-sharing is a ministry we offer and receive from others, including children who are eloquent bearers of consolation and forgiveness.

HYMNS FOR WORSHIP
GATHERING

Oh, for a thousand tongues to sing   LBW 559
Shout for joy loud and long   WOV 793

HYMN OF THE DAY

Evening and morning   LBW 465

ALTERNATE HYMN OF THE DAY

My life flows on in endless song   WOV 781
Precious Lord, take my hand   TFF 193, WOV 731

COMMUNION

We come to the hungry feast   WOV 766
Day by day   WOV 746

SENDING

O Jesus, I have promised   LBW 503

When the storms of life are raging   TFF 198

Lead me, guide me   W&P 84

ADDITIONAL HYMNS AND SONGS

I sought the Lord   H82 689

We will serve God   DH 92

Give thanks   W&P 41

MUSIC FOR THE DAY

PSALMODY

Christiansen, David. PW B.

Haas, David. "Psalm 107" in PCY 8.

Hopson, Hal H. TP.

Proulx, Richard. "Give Thanks to God" in UMH.

Stewart, Roy James. "Give Thanks to the Lord" in *Choral Refrains from Psalms for the Church Year, vol. 5.*   GIA G-3746-A.

CHORAL

Ellingboe, Bradley. "How Can I Keep from Singing." SATB, ob. KJO 8884.

Gunderson, Jerry. "We Come to the Hungry Feast." SAB, pno, inst, opt cong.   AFP 080065871X.

Honoré, Jeffrey. "How Can I Keep from Singing?" SATB, pno. CG CGA567.

Hopson, Hal H. "I Want Jesus to Walk with Me." 2 pt trbl/mxd, pno.   CG CGA 701.

Mendelssohn, Felix. "For the Lord Will Lead" in *To God Will I Sing.* MH voice.   AFP 0800674332. ML voice.   AFP 080067434X.

Nelson, Eric. "How Can I Keep from Singing?" SATB. AFP 0800657177.

Pote, Allen. "God Is Our Refuge." SATB, kybd, 2 tpt.   HOP A-583.

Schalk, Carl. "Evening and Morning." SATB, org, opt 3 tpt, 2 tb, 2 hrn, cong.   CPH 98-3314.

Viadana, Ludovico. "Sing, Ye Righteous." SATB.   PH 98-1527.

CHILDREN'S CHOIRS

Cherwien, David. "How Can I Keep From Singing?" U, pno. FP 0800658337.

Leaf, Robert. "Let the Whole Creation Cry." SA, kybd. AFP080065269X.

KEYBOARD/INSTRUMENTAL

Carlson, J. Bert. "Precious Lord" in *This Little Light of Mine.* Pno. AFP 0800659503.

Ferguson, John. "Thy Holy Wings" in *Thy Holy Wings: Three Swedish Folk Hymn Preludes.* Org.   AFP 0800647955.

Hassell, Michael. "Precious Lord" in *Jazz Spirituals.* Pno. AFP 0800674758.

Krapf, Gerhard. "Partita on 'Die güldne Sonne.'" Org. AFP 0800673727.

McKinney, Catherine and Colette Whyte. "Suaimhneas" (Peace). Fl, vln, gtr, kybd.   GIA G-4758.

Young, Jeremy. "How Can I Keep from Singing" in *At the Foot of the Cross.* Pno.   AFP 0800655397.

HANDBELL

Honoré, Jeffrey. "Aria." 3–5 oct, opt fl.   MSM 30-912.

Mathis, William H. "Let Us Talents and Tongues Employ/We Come to the Hungry Feast." 3–5 oct, opt hc, perc. AFP 0800658884.

McFadden, Jane. "How Can I Keep from Singing?" 3–5 oct. AFP 0800658124.

Page, Laura Anna. "I Sing the Mighty Power of God." 3–5 oct. AGEHR 3254521-725. L2.

Stephenson, Valerie. "The Water Is Wide." 3–5 oct, L2+. AGEHR 3265949-725.

PRAISE ENSEMBLE

Althouse, Jay. "Joyful, Joyful, Sing Praise." SATB, pno, brass, perc. ALF 16085.

Dorsey, Thomas A./arr. Artman. "Precious Lord, Take My Hand." SATB, pno, hb, fl. Also available for 2 pt.   HAL 08708841.

Gorieb, Sy, and Tim Hosman. "Peace" in *Hosanna! Music Songbook 8.* INT.

Honoré, Jeffrey. "How Can I Keep from Singing." SATB, pno. CG CGA-567.

Noblitt, Kim. "Be Still My Soul" in *Let Your Glory Fall Choral Collection.* INT.

Tuesday, June 24

THE NATIVITY OF ST. JOHN THE BAPTIST

The Nativity of St. John the Baptist is celebrated exactly six months before Christmas Eve. For Christians in the Northern Hemisphere, these two dates are deeply symbolic. John said that he must decrease as Jesus increased. John was born as the days are longest and then steadily decrease. Jesus was born as the days are shortest and then steadily increase. In many countries this day is celebrated with customs associated with the summer solstice. Mid-summer is especially popular in northern European countries that experience few hours of darkness at this time of year.

At this time of year, parishes could consider having an annual summer festival shaped by the pattern of the liturgical year. Consider a church picnic on or near this date, and use John's traditional symbols of fire and water in decorations and games.

Wednesday, June 25

PRESENTATION OF THE AUGSBURG CONFESSION, 1530; PHILIP MELANCHTHON, RENEWER OF THE CHURCH, 1560

The University of Wittenberg hired Melanchthon as its first professor of Greek and there he became a friend of Martin Luther. Melanchthon was a popular professor—even his classes at six in the morning had as many as 600 students—and was given the title "The Teacher of Germany." As a reformer he was known for his conciliatory spirit and for finding areas of agreement with fellow Christians. He was never ordained. On this day in 1530 the German and Latin editions of the Augsburg Confession were presented to Emperor Charles of the Holy Roman Empire. The Augsburg Confession was written by Melanchthon and endorsed by Luther. In 1580 when the Book of Concord was drawn up, the un-altered Augsburg Confession was included as the principal Lutheran confession.

In the spirit of Melanchthon's work, consider a summer ecumenical study group with a nearby Roman Catholic parish. Use the Augsburg Confession and the Joint Declaration on the Doctrine of Justification as study documents.

Saturday, June 28

IRENAEUS, BISHOP OF LYONS, C. 202

Irenaeus believed that the way to remain steadfast to the truth was to hold fast to the faith handed down from the apostles. He believed that only Matthew, Mark, Luke, and John were trustworthy gospels. Irenaeus was an opponent of gnosticism and its emphasis on dualism. Out of his battles with the gnostics he was one of the first to speak of the church as "catholic." By "catholic" he meant that local congregations did not exist by themselves but were linked to one another in the whole church. He also maintained that this church was not contained within any national boundaries. He argued that the church's message was for all people, in contrast to the gnostics and their emphasis on "secret knowledge."

What do we mean when we say that the church is catholic and apostolic? What are the ways that the apostolic faith is passed down through the generations?

244

June 29, 2003

St. Peter and St. Paul, Apostles

INTRODUCTION

Both Peter and Paul were put to death in the city of Rome. To the early Roman Christians, these two apostles appeared as twin founders of the Christian community, paralleling the mythical twin founders of the city itself. Peter and Paul are celebrated by the church as vigorous apostles of the risen Christ and as ardent workers in newly founded congregations throughout the ancient world. In Peter and Paul, the good news of the gospel was enfleshed. Their voices continue to be heard among us today.

PRAYER OF THE DAY

Almighty God, whose blessed apostles Peter and Paul glorified you by their martyrdom: Grant that your Church, instructed by their teaching and example, and knit together in unity by your Spirit, may ever stand firm upon the one foundation, which is Jesus Christ our Lord, who lives and reigns with you and the Holy Spirit, one God, now and forever.

VERSE

Alleluia. This Jesus God raised up, and of that all of us are witnesses. Alleluia. (Acts 2:32)

READINGS

Ezekiel 34:11-16

This reading comes from a section (ch. 33–37) that announces God's continuing care for Israel in the midst of defeat and despair. Here God is spoken of as a shepherd who offers continual guidance, nourishment, and healing for a fragile and endangered flock.

Psalm 87:1-2, 4-6 (Psalm 87:1-3, 5-7 [NRSV])

Glorious things are spoken of you, O city of our God. (Ps. 87:2)

1 Corinthians 3:16-23

Paul takes an old and well-known architectural term—temple—and says something new when he speaks of the Christian community of *persons* as a holy temple. The Spirit enlivens this living house where the treasure of God's wisdom is the crucified Christ.

Mark 8:27-35

This text is a key passage in Mark's gospel. Here the author helps the reader understand Jesus' identity. Jesus is the anointed servant of God (Peter's confession), yet a servant who does not cling to his life but, in love, shares the suffering of all humanity. His future will not be a distant throne, but the wood of the tree where the people of the earth will find shelter under God's mercy.

COLOR Red

THE PRAYERS

Growing in the soil of the Spirit, let us pray for the church, the world, and all who seek the richness of life in God.

A BRIEF SILENCE.

Loving God, ever concerned for your scattered sheep, give to your church a passion for those who need to hear the gospel, that they may experience your word of life. Gracious God,

hear our prayer.

Your persistent care for all your children overcame your apostles' hesitance and hostility and made of them great witnesses. Work your will also in and through us, that we may be faithful in our mission. Gracious God,

hear our prayer.

Give peace in the world between those are divided by lines of religion, ethnic history, or other boundaries. Gracious God,

hear our prayer.

Bring renewal and re-creation in this season to all that strives to live and grow, supporting all that is good and true. Gracious God,

hear our prayer.

Let your healing hand rest upon the brow of those who suffer from illness or injury *(especially)*. Grant them your peace and healing. Gracious God,

hear our prayer.

HERE OTHER INTERCESSIONS MAY BE OFFERED.

Your servants Peter and Paul now rest in the presence of your glory. We thank you for their lives, and pray that at

245

last we may join them in the company of *(names,* and*)* all your saints. Gracious God,
hear our prayer.
Hear us as we pray, living God, and in your mercy give us all good things, for the sake of Jesus Christ, our Lord and Savior.
Amen

IMAGES FOR PREACHING

"If any want to become my followers, let them deny themselves and take up their cross and follow me" (Mark 8:34). Bear your cross: an injunction that is easy to hear, but hard to follow.

On the feast of Saints Peter and Paul we celebrate the lives of two followers of Jesus who struggled to bear the cross. To all appearances, they were not born for this purpose. Peter began his life as Simon. He was a fisherman as was his father and, most likely, his father's father. Paul began his life as Saul. He was born into a family of means, and was expected to study and to cross the lines between Jew and Gentile. Yet these two men from different circumstances receive the call to follow Jesus of Nazareth and the way of the cross. Both men are giants of the faith but, lest we hold them in too high regard, both have their shortcomings, too. Peter has the misfortunate place in the history of the gospels as the one who rebukes and later denies Jesus. Paul admits on more than one occasion his own failings to accomplish the task at hand.

Being a rock, as Jesus describes Peter, has its advantages and disadvantages. Rocks that can be built upon can also be the source of stumbling. Rocks that are immovable, steadfast on dry land, sink quickly in water. Sometimes rocks are used against each other. Peter and Paul had their share of disagreements. And yet, these two witness to the power of Jesus and turn an empire upside down for the sake of their newfound faith.

When the way of the cross grows difficult, we need the reminder that it is God who is behind all, working God's heavenly will through, and sometimes in spite of, all of us who have been called to bear the cross. The first two readings are powerful statements of this. "I will search," "I will seek," "I will rescue." We belong to Christ, and Christ belongs to God.

WORSHIP MATTERS

The more contemporary the presider tries to be, the more tempted to abandon much of the traditional liturgy. Even though it is sometimes difficult to match old hymns to a new message without contradictions, the texts and the shape of the liturgy developed out of centuries of struggle with real issues.

"To dig to the heart of the meanings of the church's great celebrations is to probe to the heart of the gospel itself. In earliest understandings, when the church needed to hear an authentic, liberating word for itself, it developed these celebrations to remind it of the fullness of the gospel. That word is still liberating for us when we approach it, haunted by the struggles of our own time. No superficial celebrations are possible for struggling, faithful Christians" (Justo L. and Catherine G. Gonzalez, *Liberating Preaching.* Abingdon, 1980, p. 107).

LET THE CHILDREN COME

We are known by those with whom we share company. Today we remember Peter and Paul who bear us their witness as part of the great communion of saints. Giving witness always includes bearing testimony to God's faithfulness toward us. Include the testimony of children in the witness of the assembly this day. Let the prayers express thankfulness for children who show us something of God's faithful love. Including children in this way will bear witness to the rich diversity of God's faithful people. It will also deepen the mutual respect for one another as sisters and brothers in Christ.

HYMNS FOR WORSHIP
GATHERING
God, whose almighty word   LBW 400
Glories of your name are spoken   LBW 358

HYMN OF THE DAY
Lift high the cross   LBW 377

ALTERNATE HYMN OF THE DAY
The head that once was crowned with thorns   LBW 173
Rock of my salvation   W&P 161

COMMUNION

There is a balm in Gilead   WOV 737, TFF 185
In Christ there is no east or west   TFF 214

SENDING

All my hope on God is founded   WOV 782
Christ is made the sure foundation   LBW 367, WOV 747

ADDITIONAL HYMNS AND SONGS

The summons   W&P 137
Built on a rock   LBW 365
For by grace   W&P 38

MUSIC FOR THE DAY
PSALMODY

Organ, Anne Krentz.   PW A.

CHORAL

Busarow, Donald. "Lift High the Cross." 2 pt mxd/SATB, org, opt
    cong, tpt.   AFP 0800656898.
Connolly, Michael. "The Faith We Sing Was Sown." SATB, org, opt
    cong, opt 2 tpt, 2 tbn, timp.   GIA G-5358.
Haas, David. "To Be a Servant." SATB, kybd, opt cong, opt gtr, opt C
    inst.   GIA G-5185.
Kosche, Kenneth. "I Walk In Danger All the Way." SAB, fl, ob.
    CPH 98-3599.
Pelz, Walter. "Show Me Thy Ways." SATB, ob, gtr/kybd.
    AFP 0800645421.
Schalk, Carl. "Lift High the Cross." SATB, org, opt 2 tpt, 2 tb, timp.
    CPH 98-2468.

CHILDREN'S CHOIRS

Bedford, Michael. "The Lord Is My Light." U/2 pt, kybd, opt fl.
    CG CGA878.
Wagner, Douglas. "Seek Ye First." 2 pt mxd, kybd/3–5 oct hb.
    HOP C5052.

KEYBOARD/INSTRUMENTAL

Arnatt, Ronald. "Crucifer" in *Augsburg Organ Library: November*. Org.
    AFP 0800658965.
Bernthal, John. "Crucifer" in *Lift High the Cross*. Org, tpt/inst.
    AFP 0800657314.
Uehlein, Christopher. "Prelude on an Original Antiphon" in *Blue
    Cloud Abbey Organ Book*. Org.   AFP 0800653343.
Widor, Charles-Marie. "Gothic Symphony: Andante Sostenuto" in
    French Masterworks for Organ. Org.   WAR FE 09431.
Wold, Wayne L. "St. Magnus" in *A November to Remember*. Org.
    AFP 080065983X.

HANDBELL

Haugen, Marty. "Lord, You Give the Great Commission." SATB,
    cong, desc, tpt, tbn, timp, hb.   GIA G-3200.
Page, Anna Laura. "Rejoice, Ye Pure in Heart." 5 oct, L2.
    AGEHR 5957725-7253.

PRAISE ENSEMBLE

Bell, John L. "The Summons." W&P 137
Weeden, Winfield. "I Surrender All." in *Praise Hymns and Choruses, 4th
    ed.* WRD.

247

June 29, 2003

Third Sunday after Pentecost
Proper 8

INTRODUCTION

The Christian assembly gathers each Lord's day to praise God's faithfulness and steadfast love. With faith we come to hear the word and share the meal, and to know the healing that sets us free from sin and the ailments of body, mind, and soul. We go in peace to tell others of God's power to bring life from death.

PRAYER OF THE DAY

O God, you have prepared for those who love you joys beyond understanding. Pour into our hearts such love for you that, loving you above all things, we may obtain your promises, which exceed all that we can desire; through your Son, Jesus Christ our Lord.

VERSE

Alleluia. May the God of our Lord Jesus Christ enlighten the eyes of our hearts that we may know the hope to which he has called us. Alleluia. (Eph. 1:17)

READINGS

Lamentations 3:22-33

The book of Lamentations is one of our most important sources of information about the terrible conditions in Jerusalem after the Babylonian siege in 587 B.C. Though the people admit that God's judgment was just, today's reading declares a fervent trust that God will not leave them forever.

or Wisdom of Solomon 1:13-15; 2:23-24

Dating from shortly before the time of Christ, the Wisdom of Solomon is an elevated discourse in which wisdom is personified, helping to bring people closer to God. Here God is emphatically shown to be the creator and preserver of life.

Psalm 30

I will exalt you, O LORD, because you have lifted me up. (Ps. 30:1)

2 Corinthians 8:7-15

In a world where compassion burns out and people may limit their concerns to problems in their own backyards, Paul urges the Corinthian church to support the Macedonians.

Mark 5:21-43

Jairus, a respected leader, begs Jesus to heal his daughter. A woman with a hemorrhage is ritually unclean, treated as an outcast in Jewish society. Both Jairus and the unnamed woman come to Jesus in faith, believing in his power to heal and bring life out of death.

SEMICONTINUOUS FIRST READING/PSALM

2 Samuel 1:1, 17-27

This reading is a lament by David over the death of Saul. The fate of Saul illustrates the nature of power; David will also err when he turns the power he has gained toward personal ends.

Psalm 130

Out of the depths have I called to you, O LORD. (Ps. 130:1)

COLOR Green

THE PRAYERS

Growing in the soil of the Spirit, let us pray for the church, the world, and all who seek the richness of life in God.

A BRIEF SILENCE.

O God, your steadfast love never ceases and your mercies never come to an end. Bless your church with leaders whose lives will reflect the abundance of your compassionate love in their ministry. Gracious God,
hear our prayer.

O God, you bring healing to the nations and peace to all peoples. Guide our elected leaders, and all the people of our country, that we would be moved to help those who seek freedom and justice. Gracious God,
hear our prayer.

O God, you are the strength of all who seek you and the rest of all whose souls wait quietly for you. Comfort all who suffer with chronic pain and illness (*especially*), that they would know the tender touch of your healing hand. Gracious God,
hear our prayer.

O God, you are the giver of every good and perfect gift.

248

Help the members of this congregation to share from their abundance of resources, so that the needs of our community will be met equitably. Gracious God, **hear our prayer.**

HERE OTHER INTERCESSIONS MAY BE OFFERED.

O God, your children cry no cry that you do not hear and shed no tear that you do not see. Touch the lives of those who grieve losses *(especially)*, and keep us in communion with all the saints in your eternal embrace. Gracious God, **hear our prayer.**

Hear us as we pray, living God, and in your mercy give us all good things, for the sake of Jesus Christ, our Lord and Savior.

Amen

IMAGES FOR PREACHING

Jesus comes to the shore and the crowds again gather. From among them comes the plea: "My daughter is at the point of death." Jairus, a leader of the local synagogue, pleads with Jesus to bring her healing. Lay your hands on her that she may be well. Imagine a revered leader of the community begging this itinerant preacher for a miracle and in public. Then, an anonymous woman in the crowd reaches out to touch his cloak. "If I but touch his clothes, I will be made well."

We are a people in need of healing, who crave healing. We want to be healed of our aches and pains, of our diseases, of our infirmities. We need to be healed of our brokenness. Our lives are broken. Many of our relationships are broken. Evidence of a broken world is all around us. Heal us too, we plead to Jesus.

The author of Lamentations assures us that "the steadfast love of the Lord never ceases, God's mercies never come to an end" (Lam. 3:22). Paul reminds the Corinthian community, "You know the generous act of our Lord Jesus Christ . . ." (2 Cor. 8:9). Indeed, we see that generosity and mercy as Jesus not only heals the woman, but calls her "daughter." We see that generosity and mercy as Jesus raises the little girl from the sleep that is death. Such is our God, the one who calls us even out of death into life, new life in the body of Christ.

Oh, and yes, by the way, give her something to eat, Jesus tells the dumbstruck witnesses to his latest miracle. Weekly, Jesus offers us something greater than any meal, his body and blood in bread and wine that we might taste a little of what eternal life is all about.

WORSHIP MATTERS

Urban areas crave silence; intentional worship provides it. But it may take all the worship leaders' skill to instill a new habit. Some congregations seem afraid to be silent, as if it's bad that nothing is happening or being produced. God's economy is different. A silence of lament, of reflection, of expectation, of awe all deepen worship. Rubrics in *Lutheran Book of Worship* call for reflective silences after the readings, after the sermon, following the post-communion prayer. Another approach is to create silences of expectation—*before* the readings, the sermon. *LBW* calls for a long silence during confession to deepen need and anticipate the word of forgiveness. Silences during movements may heighten the action; at other times movement needs music to break tensions. What silences are called for today? How long? Is it different next week, next season? Use silences as deliberately as hymns.

LET THE CHILDREN COME

Touching has great power as evidenced in the gospel today. The sermon will not want to overlook this detail. Jesus *touches* a little girl and he *is touched by* a woman. Both have need; both are made whole. We touch many things in worship yet it is when we touch other human beings that we are drawn more deeply into human relationships. Children are especially open to giving and receiving such life-giving contact. Some adults in the assembly have not touched a child's hand for years. Let the Peace be less a handshake, and more this life-giving touch of grace.

HYMNS FOR WORSHIP
GATHERING

God, whose almighty word   LBW 400
Many and great, O God, are your works   WOV 794

HYMN OF THE DAY

If you but trust in God to guide you   LBW 453

ALTERNATE HYMN OF THE DAY

Great is thy faithfulness   WOV 771, TFF 283
Lord, my strength   W&P 9

COMMUNION

I am trusting you, Lord Jesus   LBW 460
Healer of our every ill   WOV 738

249

SENDING

Abide with us, our Savior   LBW 263

O Christ the same   WOV 778

ADDITIONAL HYMNS AND SONGS

Come, the banquet hall is ready   GS2 14

God of compassion   PH 261

Tell what God has done for us   DH 97

I'm so glad Jesus lifted me   WOV 673, TFF 191

We praise you for your glory   W&P 45

MUSIC FOR THE DAY

PSALMODY

Byrd, William/arr. Hal H. Hopson.   TP.

Christiansen, David.   PW B.

Cooney, Rory/arr. Gary Daigle. "I Will Praise You, Lord" in PCY 4.

Haas, David/arr. Jeanne Cotter. "I Will Praise You, Lord" in PCY 3.

Smith, Alan. "I Will Praise You" in PS 2.

CHORAL

Hellerman, Fred, and Fran Minkoff/arr. David Cherwien. "O Healing River" in *To God Will I Sing*. MH voice.   AFP 0800674332. ML voice.   AFP 080067434X.

Hopson, Hal H. "O Lord, Hear Me." SAB, pno.   LOR 10/2152LA.

Schütz, Heinrich. "Lift Up Your Voice" in *Chantry Choirbook*. SATB. AFP 0800657772.

Scott, K. Lee. "Open My Eyes." SATB.   CPH 98-2904.

Shute, Linda Cable. "If You Can Walk." SAB, kybd. AFP 0800659619.

Weber, Paul. "I Will Sing the Story of Your Love." SATB, org, opt cong.   AFP 0800657004.

CHILDREN'S CHOIRS

Handel, G. F. /arr. Robert J. Powell. "Then Will I Sing Jehovah's Praise." U, kybd.   CG CGA220.

Manz, Paul. "Let Us Ever Walk with Jesus." U, org.   MSM 50-9405.

KEYBOARD/INSTRUMENTAL

Berthier, Jacques. "You Are the Image and the Hope" (based on Wer nur den lieben Gott) in *Liturgical Meditations*. Fl, org. GIA G-3133.

Fieberg, Kurt. "Organ Partita on 'Wer nur den lieben Gott.' " Org. AFP 0800673700.

Gervais, Pam. "Faithfulness" in *It Is Well With My Soul*. Pno. AFP 0800674766.

Glick, Sara. "Faithfulness" in *Piano Arrangements for Worship*. Pno, opt perc, inst.   AFP 0800658809.

Rutter, John. "Toccata in Seven" in *A Second Easy Album for Organ*. Org. OXF.

Sedio, Mark. "Wer nur den lieben Gott" in *A Global Piano Tour*. Pno. AFP 0800658191.

HANDBELL

Afdahl, Lee J. "If Thou But Suffer God to Guide Thee." 3–4 oct. AFP 0800654544.

Thompson, Martha Lynn. "Great Is Thy Faithfulness." 3–5 oct. FLA HP5369.

Helman, Michael. "There Is a Balm in Gilead." 3–5 oct.   ALF 18572.

PRAISE ENSEMBLE

Dorsey, Thomas A./arr. Artmen. "Precious Lord, Take My Hand." SATB, pno, hb, fl. Also available for 2 pt.   HAL 08708841.

Elliott, John G. "Mourning into Dancing" in *I Call You To Praise*. SATB, orch.   SP 80030/1762-79434-7.

Owens, Carol. "Freely, Freely" in *The Other Song Book*. Fellowship Publications.

Runyon, William M./arr. Vaclav Nelhybel. "Great Is Thy Faithfulness." SATB, org, brass.   HOP VN109.

Underwood, Scott. "New Every Morning" in *Hosanna! Music Songbook 11*. INT.

Sunday, June 29

ST. PETER AND ST. PAUL, APOSTLES
See pages 245–47.

Monday, June 30

JOHAN OLOF WALLIN, ARCHBISHOP OF UPPSALA, HYMNWRITER, 1839

Wallin was consecrated archbishop of Uppsala and primate of the Church of Sweden two years before his death. He was considered the leading churchman of his day in Sweden, yet his lasting fame rests upon his poetry and his hymns. Of the 500 hymns in the Swedish hymnbook of 1819, 130 were written by Wallin, and approximately 200 were revised or translated by him. For more than a century the Church of Sweden made no change in the 1819 hymnbook. *Lutheran Book of Worship* contains three Wallin hymns: "All hail to you, O blessed morn!" (73), "We worship you, O God of might" (432), and "Christians, while on earth abiding" (440).

Tuesday, July 1
CATHERINE WINKWORTH, 1878;
JOHN MASON NEALE, 1866; HYMNWRITERS

Neale was an English priest associated with the movement for church renewal at Cambridge. Winkworth lived most of her life in Manchester where she was involved in promoting women's rights. These two hymnwriters translated many hymn texts into English. Catherine Winkworth devoted herself to the translation of German hymns, and John Mason Neale specialized in ancient Latin and Greek hymns. Winkworth has thirty hymns in *LBW*, and Neale has twenty-one. In addition, two texts by Neale are in *WOV*. Use the indexes at the back of both books to discover some of their most familiar translations.

July 6, 2003

Fourth Sunday after Pentecost
Proper 9

INTRODUCTION

The prophets of God speak with both conviction and compassion. Because prophetic words can threaten the security of even the most devout people, prophets are seldom popular in the church or in society as a whole. Yet in baptism, each Christian is made a prophet, one who speaks on behalf of God in this time and place. Finding strength in God's grace, we are able to offer our merciful words and actions on behalf of all those who suffer in our world.

Today the church remembers Jan Hus, a Bohemian priest and early reformer who was martyred in 1415.

PRAYER OF THE DAY

God of glory and love, peace comes from you alone. Send us as peacemakers and witnesses to your kingdom, and fill our hearts with joy in your promises of salvation; through your Son, Jesus Christ our Lord.

VERSE

Alleluia. Happy are they who hear the word, hold it fast in an honest and good heart, and bear fruit with patient endurance. Alleluia. (Luke 8:15)

READINGS

Ezekiel 2:1-5

In 597 B.C., the priest Ezekiel was removed into exile in Babylon. While there, he received a vision of God appearing majestically on a chariot throne. Today's reading recounts God's commissioning of Ezekiel during this vision. The prophet is to speak God's word to a people unwilling to hear.

Psalm 123

Our eyes look to you, O God, until you show us your mercy. (Ps. 123:3)

2 Corinthians 12:2-10

Paul uses experiences from his own life to relate his faith to the glory and pain of human existence. Visions of paradise and a mysterious "thorn in the flesh" keep him aware of the power and grace that keep him strong.

Mark 6:1-13

At home and abroad, Jesus and his disciples encounter resistance as they seek to proclaim God's word and relieve affliction.

SEMICONTINUOUS FIRST READING/PSALM

2 Samuel 5:1-5, 9-10

The rule of David over the united kingdom (northern and southern tribes) begins with these verses. Jerusalem was chosen as a political and religious center for the new combined territory.

Psalm 48

God shall be our guide forevermore. (Ps. 48:13)

COLOR Green

THE PRAYERS

Growing in the soil of the Spirit, let us pray for the church, the world, and all who seek the richness of life in God.

A BRIEF SILENCE.

O Holy One, we thank you for your message of salvation, and pray that you would continue to raise up faithful

251

leaders who will proclaim its joy to all the world. Gracious God,

hear our prayer.

Give protection and wisdom to those who serve in the military. Help them to curb tyranny and evil, that all may live in peace. Gracious God,

hear our prayer.

Come to the help of all who are in need, touching those who are weak with sickness *(especially)*, that they might sense your nearness. Gracious God,

hear our prayer.

Bless this congregation's ministries of service and outreach into the local community. May our neighborhood experience your love as we serve and welcome all people without reserve. Gracious God,

hear our prayer.

HERE OTHER INTERCESSIONS MAY BE OFFERED.

Anoint those who grieve with the healing balm of your Spirit. Keep them and all of us united with Jan Hus *(other names)* and all who have died, kindling in us the hope of the resurrection. Gracious God,

hear our prayer.

Hear us as we pray, living God, and in your mercy give us all good things, for the sake of Jesus Christ, our Lord and Savior.

Amen

IMAGES FOR PREACHING

We all have a hometown—the place where we spent time growing up, coming of age, discovering who we were meant to be. For some of us it was a wonderful experience; for others, the memories of that time and place are difficult and painful. If you left that place, you know it is never quite the same when you return. Sometimes welcomes are warm and wonderful, other returns are met with blank stares or perhaps even hostility.

"Jesus came to his hometown." People there are incredulous, even taking offense at him. Jesus invokes the old saying regarding prophets and their hometown welcomes. Because of the lack of hospitality, Jesus is unable to do much there at all. You will experience those kind of days, Jesus advises the disciples. Just shake the dust off your feet and move on.

Who would not want a visit from Jesus? Are we ready to welcome him, however and in whomever he may come to us? Are we ready with hospitality for those who

are ready to return to us, even if for the first time? God welcomes us home in the waters of baptism. God welcomes us with the outstretched arms of the Son hanging on the cross that all might be able to go home and hear that one is always welcome in the house of God.

What's that? You do not believe that you can ever go home again? Paul reminds us that God's grace is more than sufficient even for the likes of sinners (2 Cor. 12:9). Come home and discover not only who you have become but who God intends you to be, a member of the body of Christ, a child of the heavenly Father, a worker in the kingdom of God (*LBW*, p. 125).

WORSHIP MATTERS

A variety of opinions reside in any congregation on how, or whether, to express patriotism in worship. Some want a flag marched up the center aisle alongside the processional cross, some see worship as transcending nationality. Some remember "the good war," others bear the pains of Vietnam; still others have no military experience, and wonder why patriotism is so tied to war. American flag etiquette is built around the principle that the flag should never be displayed in such a way that it is not the primary symbol in a room. In church the symbols of cross, altar, font, book, and the assembly itself are primary.

It is good to acknowledge by name those in military service—and name those who serve in other community vocations too. Pray for our nation and its leaders; pray for companion synods. Pray for those who serve in global missions and tell their stories.

LET THE CHILDREN COME

Children are often made to feel that they must apologize for their weakness and inadequacy, derived from a fantasy that equates adulthood with self-sufficiency. Today we hear that God's grace is sufficient because power is made perfect in weakness. Such a truth would be powerfully heard if read by one of the so-called "weak ones." Is there a child in your congregation who might be prepared to serve this day as lector? A child serving this ministry would give powerful visibility to the spoken word.

HYMNS FOR WORSHIP
GATHERING

Let the whole creation cry   LBW 242
Lord, you give the great commission   WOV 756

252

HYMN OF THE DAY

O Christ, our light, O Radiance true   LBW 380

ALTERNATE HYMN OF THE DAY

Open your ears, O faithful people   WOV 715
Spirit, Spirit of gentleness   WOV 684

COMMUNION

Take my life, that I may be   LBW 406
One bread, one body   WOV 710, TFF 122
Fill my cup, let it overflow   TFF 127

SENDING

Sent forth by God's blessing   LBW 221
Let us talents and tongues employ   WOV 754, TFF 232

ADDITIONAL HYMNS AND SONGS

God is working his purpose out   H82 534
I believe I'll testify   TFF 225
Go, make disciples   W&P 47

MUSIC FOR THE DAY

PSALMODY

Christiansen, David. PW B.
Duffy, Philip. "Our Eyes Are on the Lord" in PS 3.
Guimont, Michel. "Psalm 123: Our Eyes Are Fixed on the Lord" in GC.
Haas, David. "Ps 123" in PCY 8.
The Psalter—Psalms & Canticles for Singing. U, cong, cant.   WJK.

CHORAL

Arnatt, Ronald. "Psalm 123." SATB, kybd, opt cong.   ECS 5405.
Bisbee, B. Wayne. "Teach Me Your Ways, O Lord." 2 pt mxd, kybd.
    AFP 080065479X.
Friedell, H. W. "Draw Us in the Spirit's Tether." SATB.
    WAR CMR 2472.
Grotenhuis, Dale. "What God Ordains Is Always Good." SATB, org,
    tpt, cong.   Northwestern Publishing House 28N6062.
Hassell, Michael. "Spirit, Spirit of Gentleness." SATB, pno, sax/cl.
    AFP 080065711X.
Hobby, Robert. "Beloved, God's Chosen" in *To God Will I Sing.* MH
    voice.   AFP 0800674332. ML voice.   AFP 0800674332.
Hobby, Robert. "Open Your Ears, O Faithful People." U, opt desc, fl,
    fc, tamb, 3 oct hb.   AFP 0800656105.
Schütz, Heinrich. "Praise God in Heaven." 2 pt.   CPH 98-3587.

CHILDREN'S CHOIRS

Brazzeal, David. "Now Paul, He Was a Servant." U/2 pt, kybd.
    CG CGA782.
Linder, Jane. "Rejoice in the Lord." U, kybd, opt fl, fc.   CG CGA844.

KEYBOARD/INSTRUMENTAL

Albrecht, Mark. "Yisrael V'Oraita" in *Three for Piano and Sax.* Pno, alto
    sax/C inst.   AFP 0800657977.
Cherwien, David. "Triptych on 'The Ash Grove.' " Org.
    AFP 0800658256.
Howells, Herbert. "Rhapsody, op. 17, no. 1" in *Three Rhapsodies for
    Organ.*   GAL 1.5244.
Kohrs, Jonathan. "Spirit" in *Four Tunes for Piano and Two Instruments.*
    Pno, 2 inst.   AFP 0800658787.

HANDBELL

Dobrinski, Cynthia. "Sing Praise to God Who Reigns Above." 3–5
    oct.   AG 2084.
Larson, Katherine Jordahl. "Be Thou My Vision." 3–4 oct, opt fl.
    AFP 0800653661.

PRAISE ENSEMBLE

Graves, Denise. "Send Me" in *Break Down the Walls.* 3 pt, kybd.
    MAR 3010133367.
Jernigan, Dennis. "You Are My All in All" in *Songs for Praise and Wor-
    ship.*   WRD.
Nystrom, Martin J. "Your Grace Is Sufficient" in *Hosanna Music Song-
    book 6.*   INT HMSB06.
Skidmore, Marsha. "Tell the World" in *Tell the World, Maranatha! Praise
    Band 5.*   MAR.

Sunday, July 6

JAN HUS, MARTYR, 1415

Jan Hus was a Bohemian priest who spoke against abuses in the church of his day in many of the same ways Luther would a century later. He spoke against the withholding of the cup at the eucharist and because of this stance was excommunicated, not for heresy but for insubordination toward his archbishop. He preached against the selling of indulgences and was particularly mortified by the indulgence trade of two rival claimants to the papacy that were raising money for war against each other. He was found guilty of heresy by the Council of Constance and burned at the stake.

253

The followers of Jan Hus became known as the Czech Brethren and later became the Moravian Church, an ecumenical partner with the Evangelical Lutheran Church in America.

Friday, July 11

BENEDICT OF NURSIA,
ABBOT OF MONTE CASSINO, C. 540

Benedict is known as the father of western monasticism. He was educated in Rome but was appalled by the decline of life around him. He went to live as a hermit and a community of monks came to gather around him. In the prologue of his rule for monasteries he wrote that his intent in drawing up his regulations was "to set down nothing harsh, nothing burdensome." It is that moderate spirit that characterizes his rule and the monastic communities that are formed by it. Benedict still encourages a generous spirit of hospitality in that visitors to Benedictine communities are to be welcomed as Christ himself.

Benedictine monasticism continues to serve a vital role in the contemporary church. A summer reading

group might choose *A Share in the Kingdom* by Benet Tvedten, OSB (Collegeville, Minn.: Liturgical Press, 1989), to learn about Benedict's Rule and hear this ancient voice speak to the church today.

Saturday, July 12

NATHAN SÖDERBLOM, ARCHBISHOP OF UPPSALA, 1931

In 1930, this Swedish theologian, ecumenist, and social activist received the Nobel Prize for peace. He saw the value of the ancient worship of the catholic church and encouraged the liturgical movement. He also valued the work of liberal protestant scholars and believed social action was a first step on the path to work for a united Christianity. He organized the Universal Christian Council on Life and Work, which was one of the organizations that, in 1948, came together to form the World Council of Churches.

As you commemorate Söderblom, discuss the ecumenical situation in the church now in this new millennium. What are some of the achievements of the past century? What hopes of Söderblom's might still wait to be achieved?

254

July 13, 2003

Fifth Sunday after Pentecost
Proper 10

INTRODUCTION

In today's gospel reading, we recognize the danger of being a prophetic voice in the world. John the Baptist denounced the intrigues of the Herodian court and eventually lost his head. Jesus criticized religious leaders who twisted life-giving practices into heavy burdens. He pointed to a justice suffused with love for all people of the earth. Jesus was put to death, as if the grave would silence him. Our worship leads us to believe just the opposite: he is alive among us, still challenging us with the vision of God's justice for this world and inspiring us to be ministers of peace.

PRAYER OF THE DAY

Almighty God, we thank you for planting in us the seed of your word. By your Holy Spirit help us to receive it with joy, live according to it, and grow in faith and hope and love; through your Son, Jesus Christ our Lord.

VERSE

Alleluia. The word is very near to you; it is in your mouth and in your heart for you to observe. Alleluia. (Deut. 30:14)

READINGS

Amos 7:7-15

Amos was not the kind of prophet attached to temples or royal courts. Rather, he was an ordinary farmer from Judah called by God to speak to Israel. God's word of judgment through Amos conflicted with the king's court prophet Amaziah, whom Amos encountered at Bethel.

Psalm 85:8-13

I will listen to what the LORD God is saying. (Ps. 85:8)

Ephesians 1:3-14

Like most of Paul's letters, the epistle to the Ephesians begins with thanksgiving and praise to God. Above all, God is blessed for the glorious grace bestowed on us in Christ.

Mark 6:14-29

As Jesus and his disciples begin to attract attention, Mark recalls the story of John the Baptist's martyrdom.

Like John, Jesus and his disciples will also suffer at the hands of those opposed to the gospel of salvation.

SEMICONTINUOUS FIRST READING/PSALM

2 Samuel 6:1-5, 12b-19

The ark, long a symbol of God's presence with the people, enters Jerusalem. David seems comfortable with the ark only insofar as it serves his needs.

Psalm 24

Lift up your heads, O gates, and the King of glory shall come in. (Ps. 24:7)

COLOR Green

THE PRAYERS

Growing in the soil of the Spirit, let us pray for the church, the world, and all who seek the richness of life in God.

A BRIEF SILENCE.

Let us pray for the church, that it would be fearless in proclaiming the word of God and faithful in celebrating the supper of the Lord. Gracious God,

hear our prayer.

Let us pray for the leaders of the nations, that they would govern the people with equity and be led in the ways of truth, justice, and peace. Gracious God,

hear our prayer.

Let us pray for the distressed and persecuted, for those living with despair and depression, and for the sick *(especially)*, that they would not be without hope. Gracious God,

hear our prayer.

Let us pray for the vacationing members of this congregation, that they would be granted safe travels, refreshing days away, and a blessed homecoming. Gracious God,

hear our prayer.

HERE OTHER INTERCESSIONS MAY BE OFFERED.

Let us pray in thanksgiving for those who have died *(especially)*, that you would keep them in communion with us until your great and glorious day to come. Gracious God,

hear our prayer.

255

Hear us as we pray, living God, and in your mercy give us all good things, for the sake of Jesus Christ, our Lord and Savior.

Amen

IMAGES FOR PREACHING

Who lost their head? Herod should never have made such a promise to Herodias. Who would have guessed that she would make such a request? No one likes to be judged and Herodias's mother was not all that happy with what John the Baptist was saying about her. Conveniently the Baptist sits in Herod's prison, convenient for Herodias the wife, anyway. "Anything?" the daughter asks. In no time at all, the Baptist's head is brought in on a platter.

Losing one's head has come to mean acting in haste or anger, without the benefit of wisdom and reason. John lost his head on a few occasions before—just ask those who came down to the river bank, especially the Pharisees and Sadducees, that "brood of vipers." No one likes to be judged, and John was rather good at pointing out the faults of others.

We know that if we want to find fault, to find sin, we need look no farther than the bathroom mirror. Sometimes we need a John the Baptist to remind us, however. Before taking on John's role ourselves, though, recall that he is most remembered not for his judgments or even his taste in clothing. John the Baptist is remembered for his pointing to Jesus. Jesus is the one who will judge and redeem us.

Herod was deeply grieved, the text tells us. Not grieved enough to do the right thing. He was more interested in saving face, or rather keeping his own head—literally if not figuratively. Grieve when you lose your head. Grieve that one lost his life because others lost their heads, blinded by fear and self-pride. But rejoice also that the one who gave his life has won for us everlasting life.

WORSHIP MATTERS

"Youth-friendly worship" does not mean singing a camp song once in a while or having young "ushers for a day." Nor does it mean every congregation needs an extravaganza every Sunday. As the ELCA's National Youth Gathering begins this week, consider some of these observations: speakers use techniques that hold attention for more than an hour; worship is full of pageantry; many leaders and servers practice and participate and move in coordinated procession.

The liturgy is highly sensory, utilizing wide, inviting, full-body gestures; ample fonts; billowing smoke; full processions; rich-tasting bread; and much more. Just perhaps, then, many youth would like more liturgy, not less. Young people are eager to participate, full of energy, and hunger for mystery and ritual. They need to be part of the planning process, even though some wild ideas may come forth. But it takes time to develop: years in a congregation, fed but not replaced by days at a Gathering.

LET THE CHILDREN COME

"I will listen to what the LORD God is saying" (Ps. 85:8). Listening is an important way through which we actively participate in worship. Young children listen best when their bodies are engaged along with their hearing. Is there need for the Bible or lectionary to be carried in the liturgy? Might a child open the book to the reading for the day? Is the gospel carried to the middle of the assembly for the people's hearing? Involving even a single child in an assisting role brings to greater alertness all the children present.

HYMNS FOR WORSHIP
GATHERING

Holy God, we praise your name   LBW 535
O God beyond all praising   WOV 797
Praise him, Jesus, blessed Savior   TFF 285

HYMN OF THE DAY

Lead on, O King eternal!   LBW 495

ALTERNATE HYMN OF THE DAY

Let justice flow like streams   WOV 763, TFF 48
Don't be worried   TFF 212

COMMUNION

Let us break bread together   LBW 212, TFF 123
We come to the hungry feast   WOV 766

SENDING

All who would valiant be   LBW 498
O Christ the same   WOV 778
Stand in the congregation   W&P 131

ADDITIONAL HYMNS AND SONGS

I sought the Lord   H82 689

Rise, O church, like Christ arisen   OBS 76, CS 63

We've come a long way, Lord   TFF 209

There is a Redeemer   W&P 140

MUSIC FOR THE DAY

PSALMODY

Berthier, Jacques. TP.

Christopherson, Dorothy. "The Lord Is My Salvation." U, fl, opt fc, movement.   AFP 0800651278.

Harbor, Rawn. "O Lord, Let Us See Your Kindness."   TFF 8.

Hopson, Hal H. *Psalm Refrains and Tones for the Common Lectionary.* U, cong.   HOP 425.

Hruby, Dolores. *Seasonal Psalms for Children.*   WLP 7102.

Makeever, Ray.   PW B.

Marcus, Mary. "Second Sunday in Advent" in *Psalm Antiphons-1.* U, hb. MSM 80-721.

Smith, Alan. "Let Us See, O Lord, Your Mercy" in PS 1.

CHORAL

Hampton, Calvin. "Fairest Lord Jesus." U, org.   GIA G-2766.

Handel, G. F. "All My Spirit Longs to Savor" in *Chantry Choirbook.* SATB, kybd.   AFP 0800657772.

Schalk, Carl. "Christ Be Our Seed." SATB, ob.   CPH 98-3602.

Scott, K. Lee. "Gracious Spirit, Dwell with Me." 2 pt mxd, org. AFP 0800646134. Also in *The Augsburg Choirbook.* AFP 0800656784.

Sedio, Mark. "The Thirsty Fields Drink In the Rain." SATB, org. AFP 0800657063.

CHILDREN'S CHOIRS

Christopherson, Dorothy. "The Lord Is My Salvation." U, fl, opt fc, movement.   AFP 0800651278.

Gieseke, Richard. "Lift Up Your Heads." U/2 pt, kybd. CPH 98-2959.

KEYBOARD/INSTRUMENTAL

Albrecht, Timothy. "Lancashire" in *Grace Notes VI.* Org. AFP 0800658264.

Bach, J. S./arr. Robert MacDonald. "Arioso." Fl, ob, hp, vc, org. MSM 20-991.

Cherwien, David. "Hungry Feast" in *O God Beyond All Praising.* Org. AFP 0800657241.

Helman, Michael. "Lancashire" in *Three for Easter: Festive Hymn Settings.* Org.   AFP 0800674790.

HANDBELL

Afdahl, Lee J. "Lancashire" in *Dear Lord - Lead On.* 3–5 oct. AFP 080065630X.

Lamb, Linda. "Canon of Grace." 2–3 oct, L2. AGEHR 3254398-725.

Stephenson, Valerie. "God's Grace." 3–5 oct.   LOR 20/1203L.

PRAISE ENSEMBLE

Cooney, Rory. "Psalm 85: Your Mercy Like Rain." SATB, cant, cong, gtr, pno, fl, sax.   GIA G-3971.

Liles, Dwight. "We Are an Offering" in SPW.

Makeever, Ray. "Dancing at the Harvest" in DH.

Tunney, Dick and Melodie Tunney/arr. Larson. "Seekers of Your Heart." SATB, orch.   GS A-6292.

Tuesday, July 15

VLADIMIR, FIRST CHRISTIAN RULER OF RUSSIA, 1015; OLGA, CONFESSOR, 969

Princess Olga became a Christian about the time that she made a visit to Constantinople, center of the Byzantine church. She had no success persuading her son or her fellow citizens to receive the gospel. Vladimir was Olga's grandson and he took the Russian throne at a ruthless time and in a bloodthirsty manner: he killed his brother for the right to rule. After Vladimir became a Christian he set aside the reminders of his earlier life, including pagan idols and temples. He built churches, monasteries, and schools, brought in Greek missionaries to educate the people, and he was generous to the poor. Together Vladimir and Olga are honored as the first Christian rulers of Russia.

The book of Colossians urges the church to give thanks to God who "has enabled you to share in the inheritance of the saints in the light." The work of Vladimir and Olga shows how that light came to the people of Russia.

257

Thursday, July 17

BARTOLOMÉ DE LAS CASAS, MISSIONARY TO THE INDIES, 1566

Bartolomé de las Casas was a Spanish priest and a missionary in the Western Hemisphere. He first came to the West while serving in the military, and he was granted a large estate that included a number of indigenous slaves. When he was ordained in 1513, he granted freedom to his servants. This act characterized much of the rest of de las Casas's ministry. Throughout the Caribbean and Central America he worked to stop the enslavement of native people, to halt the brutal treatment of women by military forces, and to promote laws that humanized the process of colonization.

In a time when churches continue to work for the right of all people we can recall the words of de las Casas: "The Indians are our brothers, and Christ has given his life for them. Why, then, do we persecute them with such inhuman savagery when they do not deserve such treatment?"

July 20, 2003

Sixth Sunday after Pentecost
Proper 11

INTRODUCTION

Built on the living foundation of the apostles and prophets, the local congregation is called to be an agent of reconciliation in a world filled with division and violence. For Christians, the ministry of peace begins and ends with Christ the shepherd, who gathers the scattered children of the world. He is the source of our life together and the center of the church's mission. To those who seek nourishment for daily life, we point to Christ who guides and feeds us on our journey.

PRAYER OF THE DAY

O Lord, pour out upon us the spirit to think and do what is right, that we, who cannot even exist without you, may have the strength to live according to your will; through your Son, Jesus Christ our Lord.

VERSE

Alleluia. My word shall accomplish that which I purpose, and succeed in the thing for which I sent it. Alleluia. (Isa. 55:11)

READINGS

Jeremiah 23:1-6

Jeremiah was a priest at Anathoth in Judah. He began his prophetic ministry well prior to the fall of Jerusalem (587 B.C.) and died in Egypt sometime after 587. Using the common metaphor of shepherd to describe the king, the prophet proclaims God's word of judgment and salvation.

Psalm 23

The LORD is my shepherd; I shall not be in want. (Ps. 23:1)

Ephesians 2:11-22

The Ephesians are urged to become an inclusive community, open to those who are near and far. They may begin by remembering that, as Gentiles, they themselves were once the outsiders.

Mark 6:30-34, 53-56

When Jesus sent his disciples out to teach and heal, they ministered among large numbers of people. Their work was motivated by Christ's desire to be among those in need.

SEMICONTINUOUS FIRST READING/PSALM

2 Samuel 7:1-14a

Instead of David building a house (temple) for the Lord, the Lord promises to establish David's house (dynasty) forever. Centuries later, after the Babylonian exile, no king sat on the throne. Even then, however, the people of Israel remembered this promise and continued to hope for a king, the messiah, the Lord's anointed.

Psalm 89:20-37

Your love, O LORD, forever will I sing. (Ps. 89:1)

258

COLOR Green

THE PRAYERS

Growing in the soil of the Spirit, let us pray for the church, the world, and all who seek the richness of life in God.

A BRIEF SILENCE.

Shepherd your people, O God, with faithful pastors and teachers who listen to your voice and proclaim your word with truth and integrity. Gracious God,

hear our prayer.

Break down the walls of hostility between the nations, O God, and bring peaceful resolution to war-torn regions of the world. Gracious God,

hear our prayer.

Gather those who are homeless and destitute, sick and powerless into your embrace of mercy, O God *(especially)*, that they may be restored to wholeness. Gracious God,

hear our prayer.

Enable the members of this parish to hear your inviting call to rest in this summer season. Give us times of refreshment in the midst of the rigorous demands of schedules and responsibilities. Gracious God,

hear our prayer.

HERE OTHER INTERCESSIONS MAY BE OFFERED.

Enfold those who are dying in your eternal arms of mercy, and comfort those who mourn with the vision of *(names, and)* all your saints, forever joined in our heavenly home. Gracious God,

hear our prayer.

Hear us as we pray, living God, and in your mercy give us all good things, for the sake of Jesus Christ, our Lord and Savior.

Amen

IMAGES FOR PREACHING

Sheep wandering about without a shepherd are a sign of the coming Day of the Lord. "I myself," [note the unprecedented emphasis in Jeremiah], God says, will shepherd the people (Jer. 23:3). Woe to those shepherds, God advises, who fail at their duty. The Day of the Lord is a day filled with both judgment and grace. And the grace will finally be recognized and appreciated after all the judgment has come to pass.

The sheep of Jesus' day seem to have no trouble at all finding him. In fact, Jesus cannot seem to lose them!

After trying to get away, Jesus is tracked down by the hurting hordes. Just to touch the fringe of his cloak would be enough for these sheep. To be in the presence of Jesus was to be healed. Have you ever had one of those days when everyone you do not want to find you, does? Despite the demands made on him, though, Jesus understands how the Day of the Lord is averted (or is that fulfilled?). Avert God's wrath with the doing of justice, the old-fashioned kind of justice: the sheltering of the homeless, the feeding of the hungry, the clothing of the naked, the healing of the sick, the welcoming of the stranger. Jesus understands that having faith in God means the doing of compassion. Indeed, as the crowds press in upon him, the text tells us "he had compassion for them."

Having compassion is not always so simple. It is tiring. It is risky. Having compassion may mean we do not get needed rest. Having compassion, however is our calling—for all Christians. As we have been shown compassion by the one who shares in our suffering, let us be passionate in our compassion with those who suffer.

WORSHIP MATTERS

The readings today are about discipleship. If summer includes a slower, more flexible period, perhaps take the opportunity to introduce and study over several weeks *Welcome to Christ* (Augsburg Fortress), resources designed to facilitate making disciples instead of just members. Although "catechumenate" may be too much of a church word for some, who wouldn't want to deepen their congregation's new member process? These resources, available now for several years, may do just that. Video and print offer much-needed guidance and focus; they support, but do not replace, the real resources—the Marys and Marthas and Lazaruses and Andrews who bring it about and say with their lives, "Come and see."

We are coming into five weeks of gospel readings on bread. Why not make it a focus on making and kneading discipleship, instead of half-baked bread?

LET THE CHILDREN COME

God's people are marked by their compassion after the manner of Jesus who gives himself to the crowds. In our prayers, the needy of the world are present with us in worship. Let our prayers name some among the world's destitute—children without families, homes, and persons to protect them—and let the children of our assemblies enact their prayers by bringing offerings of food and clothing to be shared with the vast needy. Connecting what we do in mission with what we ask God to do in prayer will impress upon children (and adults!) the deep meaning of our baptismal calling.

HYMNS FOR WORSHIP

GATHERING

Christ is made the sure foundation   LBW 367, WOV 747

All people that on earth do dwell   LBW 245

HYMN OF THE DAY

O Holy Spirit, enter in   LBW 459

ALTERNATE HYMN OF THE DAY

Oh, praise the gracious power   WOV 750

Rejoice in the mission   W&P 120

COMMUNION

Let us break bread together   LBW 212, TFF 123

One bread, one body   WOV 710, TFF 122

SENDING

Where cross the crowded ways of life   LBW 429

Father, we thank you   WOV 704

ADDITIONAL HYMNS AND SONGS

Come, bring them to the table   DH 19

My Shepherd will supply my need   CS 51, H82 664

Come to Jesus   TFF 156

Make me a servant   W&P 96

MUSIC FOR THE DAY

PSALMODY

Wold, Wayne L. PW B.

See the fourth Sunday of Easter.

CHORAL

Bach, J. S. "What God Ordains" in *Bach for All Seasons.* SATB. AFP 080065854X.

Cherwien, David. "O Holy Spirit, Enter In." U/2 pt/SATB, cong, org, 2 tpt, 2 tb, opt horn), tba, timp.   CPH 98-3484.

Kallman, Daniel. "Lord, Whose Love in Humble Service." SATB, pno.   KJO J17.

Pelz, Walter. "The King of Love My Shepherd Is." SATB, fl, org, opt cong.   AFP 0800646010.

Zimmermann, Heinz W. "Psalm 23." SATB, str bass. AFP 0800645383.

CHILDREN'S CHOIRS

Lau, Robert. "Jesus, Like a Shepherd Lead Us." U, kybd.   Jenson 423-10022.

Lutz, Deborah. "Loving Jesus, Gentle Lamb." 2 pt trbl, kybd. MSM 50-9500.

KEYBOARD/INSTRUMENTAL

Howells, Herbert. "Air No. 1" in *Two Slow Airs for Organ.* Org. NOV 01 0220.

Manz, Paul. "Wie schön leuchtet" in *A New Liturgical Year.* Org. AFP 0800656717.

Wold, Wayne L. "Christpraise Ray" in *Child of the Light.* Org. AFP 0800657993.

Wright, Searle. "Prelude on 'Brother James' Air' " in *The Oxford Book of Wedding Music.* Org.   OXF.

HANDBELL

Chepponis, James. "Called as God's Holy People." (Lord, You Give The Great Commission). SATB, cant, cong, tpt, tbn, timp, hb. GIA G-3618.

Edwards, Dan R. "The Gentle Shepherd." 3 oct.   CG CGB151.

PRAISE ENSEMBLE

Batstone, Bill, Anne Barbour, and John Barbour. "Let the Walls Fall Down" in *Maranatha! Music Praise Chorus Book, 3rd ed.*   MAR.

Bradbury, William. "Savior, Like a Shepherd Lead Us" in *Praise Worship, vol 3.*   INT HMSB03.

Funk, Billy. "By Your Blood" in *Hosanna! Music Songbook 6.*   INT.

Kingsley, Gershon/arr. Eric Knight. "Shepherd Me Lord." SAB, pno, gtr, perc.   BRN 115735. Also available in SATB, SSA, SA/TB.

Lojeski, Ed. "Amazing Grace." SATB, pno, gtr, perc.   HAL 08300531.

Pote, Allen. "The Lord Is My Shepherd." SATB, pno.   CG CGA-551.

Tuesday, July 22

ST. MARY MAGDALENE

The gospels report Mary Magdalene as one of the women of Galilee who followed Jesus. She was present at Jesus' crucifixion and his burial. When she went to the tomb on the first day of the week to anoint Jesus' body, she was the first person to whom the risen Lord appeared. She returned to the disciples with the news and has been called "the apostle to the apostles" for her proclamation of the resurrection. Because John's gospel describes Mary as weeping at the tomb, she is often portrayed in art with red eyes. Icons depict her standing by the tomb and holding a bright red egg.

This glimpse of Easter in the middle of summer invites us to keep our eyes open for the signs of Christ's resurrection and new life that is always around us.

Wednesday, July 23

BIRGITTA OF SWEDEN, 1373

Birgitta was married at age 13 and had four daughters with her husband. She was a woman of some standing who, in her early thirties, served as the chief lady-in-waiting to the Queen of Sweden. She was widowed at the age of thirty-eight, shortly after she and her husband had made a religious pilgrimage. Following the death of her husband the religious dreams and visions that had begun in her youth occurred more regularly. Her devotional commitments led her to give to the poor and needy all that she owned while she began to live a more

ascetic life. She founded an order of monks and nuns, the Order of the Holy Savior (Brigittines), whose superior was a woman. Today the Society of St. Birgitta is a laypersons' society that continues her work of prayer and charity.

Friday, July 25

ST. JAMES THE ELDER, APOSTLE

James is one of the sons of Zebedee and is counted as one of the twelve disciples. Together with his brother John they had the nickname "sons of thunder." One of the stories in the New Testament tells of their request for Jesus to grant them places of honor in the kingdom. They are also reported to have asked Jesus for permission to send down fire on a Samaritan village that had not welcomed them. Their nickname appears to be well deserved. James was the first of the twelve to suffer martyrdom and is the only apostle whose martyrdom is recorded in scripture (Acts 12:2).

James is frequently pictured with a scallop shell. It recalls his life as a fisherman, his call to fish for people, and the gift of our baptism into Christ.

261

July 27, 2003

Seventh Sunday after Pentecost
Proper 12

INTRODUCTION

The psalms speak of God as the one who feeds humanity: You open wide your hand, O God, and give us food in every season. The psalmist implies that humans have physical and spiritual hungers, hungers that will be satisfied only by God. In Christ, God satisfies our thirst with living waters and feeds us with living bread. These images speak of our desire for communion with the one who is greater than our frailty and fears. They are biblical images of Christ's presence among us in the waters of baptism and the bread and cup of the eucharist.

PRAYER OF THE DAY

O God, your ears are open always to the prayers of your servants. Open our hearts and minds to you, that we may live in harmony with your will and receive the gifts of your Spirit; through your Son, Jesus Christ our Lord.

VERSE

Alleluia. Lord, to whom shall we go? You have the words of eternal life. Alleluia. (John 6:68)

READINGS

2 Kings 4:42-44

Today's reading is part of a larger section (2 Kings 4:1—8:6) that presents the miracles of Elisha. Here the prophet asks that food be given to a hungry crowd. He trusts God, who says there shall be enough and even more.

Psalm 145:10-19 (Psalm 145:10-18 [NRSV])

You open wide your hand and satisfy the needs of every living creature. (Ps. 145:17)

Ephesians 3:14-21

Paul prays for the Christians to whom he writes, asking that God will grant them inner strength and spiritual power as they continue to grow in their understanding of the love of Christ.

John 6:1-21

In John's gospel, the miracles of Jesus are called "signs," because they reveal the true character of God. As such, they remain within the mystery of God and cannot be brought under human control.

SEMICONTINUOUS FIRST READING/PSALM

2 Samuel 11:1-15

The story of David's adulterous and ultimately murderous actions in regard to Bathsheba and her husband Uriah is one of the most infamous of the Old Testament.

Psalm 14

God is in the company of the righteous. (Ps. 14:5)

COLOR Green

THE PRAYERS

Growing in the soil of the Spirit, let us pray for the church, the world, and all who seek the richness of life in God.

A BRIEF SILENCE.

God of plenty, provide the church with faithful and generous stewards who will share of their resources to carry out your mission in the world. Gracious God,

hear our prayer.

God of fullness, help us to provide food and clothing, shelter and security for all the people of the world who live in places of famine and scarcity, that they may have enough of all they need for this life. Gracious God,

hear our prayer.

God of abundance, look with compassion on children who are living in poverty, and provide for them from the richness of your mercy, that they may be strengthened to play and grow. Gracious God,

hear our prayer.

God of good gifts, may we see your presence as we gather around tables of fellowship to enjoy friendship and the food that we eat together. Gracious God,

hear our prayer.

God of life, the riches of your glory are beyond our imagination. Hold the sick in your care *(especially)*. Grant peace to the dying and comfort to the grieving, and all for your love's sake. Gracious God,

hear our prayer.

HERE OTHER INTERCESSIONS MAY BE OFFERED.

God of eternity, around your throne saints and angels

glory in your presence. Keep us in communion with (*names,* and) all the blessed dead, both in this life and forever. Gracious God,

hear our prayer.

Hear us as we pray, living God, and in your mercy give us all good things, for the sake of Jesus Christ, our Lord and Savior.

Amen

IMAGES FOR PREACHING

Ours is a hungry world. More people do not have any bread for their stomachs than those who do. Chances are you would not have to look far to find someone who is truly hungry. They may be lingering near the door of the local convenience store, or by the bus station. It is easier for us, of course, to think about hunger in more metaphorical terms. We all know someone who hungers for meaning or truth or justice. Most likely that person looking back at you in the mirror is hungry for something. It is a good thing that we are a hungry people, for we have five weeks of readings about bread ahead of us.

The crowds who come to hear Jesus overstay their welcome. It is suppertime and the disciples are nervous at the prospect that the crowd will be hungry and, based on Near Eastern hospitality customs, expect a meal. It is Jesus who asks the question first, "Where are we to buy bread for this gathering?" There is a boy with five loaves and two fish. "But what are they among so many people?" Andrew observes. Jesus takes the loaves and fish, gives thanks and distributes them among the crowd. In the end, the baskets hold leftovers.

Yes, ours is a hungry world. Jesus comes to satisfy that hunger: the hunger for purpose and meaning and yes, the hunger in one's belly. Jesus feeds us in the holy eucharist with bread and wine, body and blood that we may be satisfied even to eternal life. Jesus gives us himself.

As we are fed so also we are invited to feed one another. Jesus, in John's account, later charges the disciples with the feeding of the sheep. "Feed my lambs" (John 20:15). A people whose hunger is satisfied know about sharing from their abundance.

WORSHIP MATTERS

The word of God models the relationship of worship to food. First fruits are brought from the fields to Elisha, the representative of God. They are not brought to just any helping organization; what is happening here is not charity—it is dedication. Elisha directs the giving so that it goes to the assembled people. Its sufficiency to feed the entire world is not at issue. The directions are repeated to emphasize the direction of the action: toward the assembly in order to let them eat. The word was fulfilled.

In John 6 the word is fulfilled by revealing Jesus. And in presenting our selves, our time, and our money in worship so that it may be given away, we too are told, "Do not be afraid." Worship already begins in the fields and is fulfilled among the poor, gathered in as one. What happens in between matters.

LET THE CHILDREN COME

In the gospel today, a boy brings his lunch and shares it with others. Everything else in this rich lection springs from this youth's forethought and willingness to share. Children easily identify with this story, and the sermon should be sensitive to this fact. Perhaps preaching from the perspective of the child is even warranted by the way the evangelist narrates the event. This Sunday is an ideal opportunity for clergy to work on being more inclusive of children in our preaching ministry.

HYMNS FOR WORSHIP
GATHERING
Evening and morning   LBW 465
Oh, sing to God above/Cantemos al Señor   WOV 726

HYMN OF THE DAY
Jesus, priceless treasure   LBW 457, 458

ALTERNATE HYMN OF THE DAY
Break now the bread of life   LBW 235
God is compassionate   DH 46

COMMUNION
O living Bread from heaven   LBW 197
You satisfy the hungry heart   WOV 711
Now in this banquet   W&P 104

SENDING
For the bread which you have broken   LBW 200
Let us talents and tongues employ   WOV 754, TFF 232

263

ADDITIONAL HYMNS AND SONGS

Bread of heaven, on thee we feed   H82 323

Just as Jesus told us   DH 29

Lord, I hear of showers of blessings   TFF 120

Here is bread   W&P 58

MUSIC FOR THE DAY

PSALMODY

Bengtson, Bruce.   PW B.

Haas, David. "I Will Praise Your Name" in PS 2.

Haugen, Marty/arr. David Haas.   PCY.

Hruby, Dolores M. *Seasonal Psalms for Children.* U.   WLP 7102.

Stewart, Roy James. "The Hand of the Lord" in PCY 5.

CHORAL

Bach, J. S. "Jesus, My Sweet Pleasure" in *Bach for All Seasons.* SATB, kybd.   AFP 080065854X.

Berger, Jean. "The Eyes of All Wait upon Thee." SATB. AFP 0800645596.

Franck, César. "O Bread of Heaven" in *To God Will I Sing.* MH voice. AFP 0800674332. ML voice.   AFP 0800674340.

Gunderson, Jerry. "We Come to the Hungry Feast." SAB, pno, C inst, opt cong.   AFP 080065871X.

CHILDREN'S CHOIRS

Albrecht, Sally. "Gather Us In." 2 pt, kybd.   ALF 18323.

Proulx, Richard. "The Eyes of All." U, org.   AFP 0800656466.

KEYBOARD/INSTRUMENTAL

Honoré, Jeffrey. "Bicentennial" in *Contemporary Hymn Settings for Organ.* Org.   AFP 0800674782.

Mathews, Peter. "Pastorale." Cl, org.   MSM 20-966.

Vierne, Louis. "Carillon" in *24 Pieces en style libré*, Livre 2. Org. DUR.

Walther, J. G. "Jesu, meine Freude" in *Orgelwerke.* Org.   Bärenreiter.

HANDBELL

Afdahl, Lee J. "Here Would I Feed Upon the Bread of God." 3–5 oct. AFP 0800657381.

Helman, Michael. "Gift of Finest Wheat." 3–5 oct, opt hc. AFP 0800657365.

McChesney, Kevin. "Holy Manna." 2–3 oct.   CG CGB143.

PRAISE ENSEMBLE

Altrogge, Mark. "How Great Is Your Love" in *Hosanna! Music Songbook* 7.   INT HMSB07.

Lovelace, Austin C. "Let Us Talents and Tongues Employ." 2 pt mxd, pno.   CG CGA619.

Paris, Twila/arr. Torrans. "We Bow Down." SAB, kybd.   Songpower ZJP7006.

Ross, Barbara. "You Who Are Thirsty" in *Songs for Praise and Worship.* WRD.

Wimber, John. "Spirit Song" in *Praise Hymns and Choruses, 4th ed.*   MAR.

Monday, July 28

JOHANN SEBASTIAN BACH, 1750; HEINRICH SCHÜTZ, 1672; GEORGE FREDERICK HANDEL, 1759; MUSICIANS

These three German composers greatly enriched the worship life of the church. Johann Sebastian Bach drew on the Lutheran tradition of hymnody and wrote over 300 cantatas, including at least two for each Sunday and festival day in the Lutheran calendar of his day. He has been called "the fifth evangelist" for the ways that he proclaimed the gospel through his music. George Frederick Handel was not primarily a church musician, but his great work, *Messiah*, is a musical proclamation of the scriptures. Heinrich Schütz wrote choral settings of biblical texts and paid special attention to ways his composition would underscore the meaning of the words.

A musical gathering might be planned to commemorate these and other great church composers. Remember to include a prayer of thanksgiving for organists, choir directors, composers, and all who make music in worship.

Tuesday, July 29

MARY, MARTHA, AND LAZARUS OF BETHANY

Mary and Martha are remembered for the hospitality and refreshment they offered Jesus in their home. Following the characterization drawn by Luke, Martha represents the active life, and Mary the contemplative. Mary is identified in the fourth gospel as the one who anointed Jesus before his passion and who was criticized for her act of devotion. Lazarus, Mary and Martha's brother, was raised from the dead by Jesus as a sign of the eternal life offered to all believers. It was over Lazarus's tomb that Jesus wept for love of his friend. Congregations might commemorate these three early witnesses to Christ by reflecting on the role of hospitality in both home and church and the blessing of friendship.

OLAF, KING OF NORWAY, MARTYR, 1030

Olaf is considered the patron saint of Norway. In his early career he engaged in war and piracy in the Baltic and in Normandy. It was there he became a Christian. He returned to Norway, declared himself king, and from then on Christianity was the dominant religion of the realm. He revised the laws of the nation and enforced them with strict impartiality, eliminating the possibility of bribes. He thereby alienated much of the aristocracy. The harshness that he sometimes resorted to in order to establish Christianity and his own law led to a rebellion. After being driven from the country and into exile, he enlisted support from Sweden to try to regain his kingdom, but he died in battle.

Olaf reminds the church of the temptation to establish Christianity by waging war, whether military or social. How might the church bear witness to the one who calls it to pray for enemies and persecutors?

August 3, 2003

Eighth Sunday after Pentecost
Proper 13

265

INTRODUCTION

Even when they grumbled and complained, God provided food for the Israelites. In today's gospel, when the disciples ask Jesus for an impressive sign, he offers them himself, the bread of life to all who truly hunger. This gift enables all believers to grow in Christ and to become one with his mission in the world. Though our hunger will always return, Christ is present to nourish us with his very life.

PRAYER OF THE DAY

Gracious Father, your blessed Son came down from heaven to be the true bread which gives life to the world. Give us this bread, that he may live in us and we in him, Jesus Christ our Lord.

VERSE

Alleluia. Jesus said, Those who love me will keep my word, and my Father will love them, and we will come to them and make our home with them. Alleluia. (John 14:23)

READINGS

Exodus 16:2-4, 9-15

Exodus 16 recounts the second of three tests for Israel in the wilderness (see also 15:22-27 and 17:1-7). In this reading, a food crisis becomes a faith crisis. The hunger of the wandering Israelites moves the people to deny God's saving work in the exodus. At least they had food when they were in Egypt! Nevertheless, God meets their need day by day.

Psalm 78:23-29

The LORD rained down manna upon them to eat. (Ps. 78:24)

Ephesians 4:1-16

In the first three chapters of Ephesians, Paul declares that, through grace, Christ reconciled all people to God and to each other. Now, he traces the specific consequences of this reconciliation for Christian communities that are diverse in their unity.

John 6:24-35

Many of the five thousand people Jesus fed in the wilderness continued to follow him throughout the countryside. Jesus challenges them to consider the real nature of their quest.

SEMICONTINUOUS FIRST READING/PSALM

2 Samuel 11:26—12:13a

God sends the prophet Nathan to rebuke David the king for his abuse of power in deceiving and killing Uriah and taking Uriah's wife.

Psalm 51:1-12

Have mercy on me, O God, according to your lovingkindness. (Ps. 51:1)

COLOR Green

THE PRAYERS

Growing in the soil of the Spirit, let us pray for the church, the world, and all who seek the richness of life in God.

A BRIEF SILENCE.

Let us pray for the church, that God would lead many to eat the bread of heaven and drink the cup of salvation, never to hunger and thirst again. Gracious God,
hear our prayer.

Let us pray for the world, that where people know scarcity of food and water they would also know a united effort to help them in their need. Gracious God,
hear our prayer.

Let us pray for those in our communities who are poor, that they would meet with compassionate assistance and opportunities for rewarding employment. Gracious God,
hear our prayer.

Let us pray for all who are hospitalized, all who are in chronic pain, and for all whose health is a concern *(especially)*. Gracious God,
hear our prayer.

Let us pray for the members of this congregation who volunteer with community food shelves, reading programs, and other forms of assistance, that they would be strengthened for service to all they reach. Gracious God,
hear our prayer.

HERE OTHER INTERCESSIONS MAY BE OFFERED.

Let us pray in thanksgiving for all who have died *(especially)*, that their memory may be blessed among us, and that their loved ones would be comforted in the hope of the resurrection. Gracious God,
hear our prayer.

Hear us as we pray, living God, and in your mercy give us all good things, for the sake of Jesus Christ, our Lord and Savior.
Amen

IMAGES FOR PREACHING

Five thousand people cross the Sea of Galilee to track down Jesus. Finding him they ask, "Rabbi, when did you come here?" At first hearing it sounds like the question of coincidence. We just happened to be in the neighborhood and what a surprise, here you are as well. So nice to see you, and by the way, we are hungry again. Jesus knows they are looking for food. They ate their fill of fish and bread and want more.

The question is a deeper one, though. Not only is it "When did you get here?" but "Where did you come from?" Perhaps it is even more the question of "Where are you going?" These are not the questions of place but of meaning. Having one's fill of food is a good thing, but the crowds want more than food this time. "Give us a sign," they ask. As God gave bread to those wandering in the wilderness, so also this God gives you bread, which gives life to the world. "Give us this bread," they ask. And Jesus responds, "I am the bread of life."

Daily in the Lord's Prayer we pray for this bread. "Give us today our daily bread." And daily we are reminded that God gives us bread, even without our asking. What is meant by daily bread? Everything that we need for daily life, as Luther pointed out in his Small Catechism. In fact, the bread offered us by Christ is even good to eternal life.

What an invitation we are offered and what an invitation we have to offer the world. "I am the bread of life. Whoever comes to me will never be hungry, and whoever believes in me will never be thirsty."

WORSHIP MATTERS

Model intercessory prayers are readily available. But they are just that: models, to help expand both the language and our expectations of God. Each congregation decides individually whether it needs printed prayers for all the worshipers. But preparing, writing, or extemporizing the Sundays' prayers can and should be a rewarding spiritual exercise. (And, by the way, it is preferable to have the prayers prepared by a lay assisting minister, with the guidance of the pastor.) How can we combine rich theological language with an immediacy that engages those who pray? How can lesser-used biblical images expand our imaginations?

LET THE CHILDREN COME

These summer Sundays feed us with gospel readings that virtually "set the table" for eucharist. What words do you use to invite the assembly to the table? When words in the liturgy are repeated in more than one place, they draw together two ideas into a common meaning. Thus, inviting worshipers to the Lord's table with Jesus' words in John 6:35 will help children connect the holy meal with the promise of Jesus as the bread of life. Let the preaching deepen our hunger and let the invitation to be fed be made to all, especially children.

HYMNS FOR WORSHIP

GATHERING
The Church's one foundation   LBW 369
God is here   WOV 719

HYMN OF THE DAY
O Bread of life from heaven   LBW 222

ALTERNATE HYMN OF THE DAY
I received the living God   WOV 700
God has spoken, bread is broken   BL 5

COMMUNION
Here, O my Lord, I see thee   LBW 211
I am the Bread of life   WOV 702
Seed, scattered and sown   W&P 121

SENDING
Blest be the tie that binds   LBW 370
Bind us together   WOV 748, TFF 217, W&P 18

ADDITIONAL HYMNS AND SONGS
This bread that we break   DH 30
Jesus, united by thy grace   UMH 561
I'm a-goin'-a eat at the welcome table   TFF 263
Broken in love   W&P 24

MUSIC FOR THE DAY

PSALMODY
Bengtson, Bruce. PW B.
Guimont, Michel. "Psalm 78: The Lord Gave Them Bread" in GC.
Haas, David. "Psalm 78" in PCY 8.
Hallock, Peter/arr. Carl Crosier. *The Ionian Psalter.* SATB/U, org.   ION.
Stewart, Roy James. "The Lord Gave Them Bread" in PCY 5.

CHORAL
Bach, J. S. "O Bread of Life from Heaven" in *Bach for All Seasons.* SATB/U, kybd.   AFP 080065854X.
Berthier, Jacques. "Eat This Bread." Mxd/equal vcs.   GIA G-2840.

Farlee, Robert Buckley. "We Are a Garden Walled Around" in *To God Will I Sing.* MH voice.   AFP 0800674332. ML voice.   AFP 0800674340.
Keesecker, Thomas. "I Am the Living Bread." SATB, sax/C inst.   AFP 6000001436.
Loli, Simon. "I Am the Bread of Life." SATB, kybd.   GIA G-4473.
McCabe, Michael. "I Am the Living Bread." SATB.   RME EC-338.

CHILDREN'S CHOIRS
Marshall, Jane. "Create in Me, O God." U antiphonal, kybd.   CG CGA750.
Pethel, Stan. "Bless This Gift." 2 pt mxd, kybd.   CG CGA761.

KEYBOARD/INSTRUMENTAL
Albrecht, Mark. "Stoneridge" in *Timeless Hymns of Faith, vol. 2.* Pno.   AFP 0800658795.
Böhm, Georg. "Praeludium in C" in *Alte Meister des Orgelspiels 1.* PET 4301a.
Carlson, J. Bert. "Christe Sanctorum" in *A New Look at the Old.* Org.   AFP 0800658760.
Miller, Aaron David. "O Welt, ich muss dich lassen" in *Improvisations for the Church Year.* Org.   AFP 0800674812.

HANDBELL
Moklebust, Cathy. "Come, Let Us Eat." 3–5 oct, opt perc.   CG CGB152.
Thompson, Martha Lynn. "Holy Manna." 3–5 oct.   JEF MHP2081.
Wagner, Douglas. "Fanfare Prelude on 'Aurelia.'" Full score.   AGEHR. 3–5 oct hb.   AG35075AG35074.   Brass, timp.   PP361.

PRAISE ENSEMBLE
Baloche, Paul and Claire Cloninger. "As Bread That Is Broken" in *Hosanna! Music Songbook 10.*   INT 08667.
Dearman, Kirk. "We Remember You" in *Songs for Praise and Worship.* WRD.
Fitts, Bob. "One God" in *Maranatha! Music Praise Chorus Book, 3rd ed.* MAR.
Knapp, Phoebe P./arr. V. Whaley and C. Clevenger. "Blessed Assurance." SATB, kybd.   PLY SHS9705.
Pote, Allen. "Many Gifts, One Spirit." SAB, kybd.   Coral Key Music 391-41417. Also available in SATB, SSA.

Friday, August 8

DOMINIC, PRIEST, FOUNDER OF THE ORDER
OF THE DOMINICANS, 1221

Dominic was a Spanish priest who preached against the Albigensians, a heretical sect that held gnostic and dualistic beliefs. Dominic believed that a stumbling block to restoring heretics to the church was the wealth of clergy, so he formed an itinerant religious order, the Order of Preachers (Dominicans) who lived in poverty, studied philosophy and theology, and preached against heresy. The method of this order was to use kindness and gentle argument, rather than harsh judgment, when bringing unorthodox Christians back to the fold. Dominic was opposed to burning Christians at the stake. Three times Dominic was offered the office of bishop, which he refused so that he could continue in his work of preaching.

August 10, 2003

Ninth Sunday after Pentecost
Proper 14

INTRODUCTION

Christ gave his flesh for the life of the world. He sustains the pilgrim people of God with the word of life and the bread of heaven. Through the holy supper, Christ comes to us so that we might find the source of our unity and follow him in the way of sacrificial love. Though we experience frustration or despair, we know that God is ever eager to nourish us back to life. We need only come to the table and receive the gift of life.

Today the church commemorates Lawrence, deacon in Rome, martyred in 258.

PRAYER OF THE DAY

Almighty and everlasting God, you are always more ready to hear than we are to pray, and to give more than we either desire or deserve. Pour upon us the abundance of your mercy, forgiving us those things of which our conscience is afraid, and giving us those good things for which we are not worthy to ask, except through the merit of your Son, Jesus Christ our Lord.

VERSE

Alleluia. Faith is the assurance of things hoped for, the conviction of things not seen. Alleluia. (Heb. 11:1)

READINGS

1 Kings 19:4-8

Chapter 18 portrays the contest between Elijah and the prophets of Baal in which God withholds and sends the fire. After the contest, Elijah orders the killing of the prophets of Baal. Angered by the deaths of her prophets, Queen Jezebel threatens to take Elijah's life. This reading finds the prophet fleeing, fatigued, and in utter despair.

Psalm 34:1-8

Taste and see that the LORD is good. (Ps. 34:8)

Ephesians 4:25—5:2

The letter to the Ephesians declares that people are reconciled with God through God's grace, not by doing good works. As these verses indicate, those who experience God's forgiveness are called upon to live as the transformed people they have become.

John 6:35, 41-51

After feeding more than five thousand people in the wilderness, Jesus teaches them regarding the true significance of this remarkable sign.

SEMICONTINUOUS FIRST READING/PSALM

2 Samuel 18:5-9, 15, 31-33

This reading begins with a report about the conflict between Absalom and his father. Even though outnumbered, David's forces secured a complete victory, scattering and killing Absalom's force.

Psalm 130

Out of the depths have I called to you, O LORD. (Ps. 130:1)

COLOR Green

THE PRAYERS

Growing in the soil of the Spirit, let us pray for the church, the world, and all who seek the richness of life in God.

A BRIEF SILENCE.

O living Bread from heaven, nourish your church with the supper of the Lord and give it boldness to invite all people to your table. Gracious God,
hear our prayer.

O God, you gave your Son to be bread for the life of the world. Watch over the fields of the earth now ripening, that many will be fed with the fruits of the harvest. Gracious God,
hear our prayer.

O Bread of life, you satisfy our every hunger. Be with all in need, and draw near to the sick who hunger for health *(especially)*. Gracious God,
hear our prayer.

O Healer of all, you raise up servants to minister to those suffering from illness. Help all nurses and doctors, therapists and caregivers to see your blessing in their work. Gracious God,
hear our prayer.

O God, you call us to imitate you as your beloved children. Bless the fruits of this congregation's ministries, that many may be drawn to you for nourishment. Gracious God,
hear our prayer.

HERE OTHER INTERCESSIONS MAY BE OFFERED.

Bread of heaven, bring us all at length to your banquet table where, in the company of Lawrence *(other names)*, and all the saints, we will dine with you for all eternity. Gracious God,
hear our prayer.

Hear us as we pray, living God, and in your mercy give us all good things, for the sake of Jesus Christ, our Lord and Savior.

IMAGES FOR PREACHING

If something is too good to be true, then it probably isn't true at all. Such is one of the lessons that life teaches us. We learn early on that all too little is what it seems to be. We learn to be skeptical, to question, to doubt. And yet, sometime in life most of us are also taught to believe, even in the face of our skepticism. When does that happen? When did you first really believe something?

The authorities complained about what Jesus was saying. He was after all, Joseph and Mary's boy. They watched him grow up, saw him learn the trade of his father Joseph. "How can he now say, 'I have come down from heaven'?" It is hard to argue with the authorities in today's reading. Are their questions not also ours?

"Do not complain," Jesus responds. It is the Father who calls you into believing. Now *there* is something hard to swallow. Believing in God is a gift from God? Martin Luther put it this way: "I believe that I cannot by my own understanding or effort believe in Jesus Christ my Lord or come to him. But the Holy Spirit has called me through the Gospel, enlightened me with his gifts, and sanctified and kept me in true faith" (Small Catechism).

We so want faith to be our work. But faith in God comes from God. We are first called to faith in the waters of baptism. Daily, that same Holy Spirit calls us back to faithfulness. Weekly in the assembly we are reminded of our calling in the faith, strengthened by the hearing of God's word and nourished with the one who is the bread of life.

"Whoever eats of this bread will live forever." Too good to be true? Not for people who eat in faith.

WORSHIP MATTERS

"In every celebration of the means of grace, God acts to show forth both the need of the world and the truth of the Gospel. In every gathering of Christians around the proclaimed Word and the holy sacraments, God acts to empower the Church for mission. Jesus Christ, who is God's living bread come down from heaven, has given his flesh to be the life of the world. . . .

"Holy Communion is that messianic banquet at which God bestows mercy and forgiveness, creates and strengthens faith for our daily work and ministry in the world, draws us to long for the day of God's manifest justice in all the world, and provides a sure and certain hope of the coming resurrection to eternal life" (*The Use of the Means of Grace*, principles 51 and 54. Evangelical Lutheran Church in America, 1997).

LET THE CHILDREN COME

How is your assembly ministered to by children? The less formal mood of summertime affords a splendid opportunity for children to assume important roles of meaningful service. With adult assistance, children can capably

269

serve as greeters and ushers. Through preparation and training, children of third and fourth grade make wonderful lectors and cantors for responsorial psalmody. Children could be invited to process the eucharistic gifts during the offertory. Using summer months to introduce children in such roles will make it easier to continue children's involvement in these ministries once the autumn months arrive.

HYMNS FOR WORSHIP
GATHERING

Praise my soul, the King of heaven   LBW 549

Here in this place   WOV 718

HYMN OF THE DAY

Soul, adorn yourself with gladness   LBW 224

ALTERNATE HYMN OF THE DAY

Eat this bread   WOV 709, TFF 125

Here would I feast/Aquí del pan partido tomaré   LLC 384

COMMUNION

We place upon your table, Lord   LBW 217

I am the Bread of life   WOV 702

SENDING

O living Bread from heaven   LBW 197

Thine the amen, thine the praise   WOV 801

ADDITIONAL HYMNS AND SONGS

O Food to pilgrims given   H82 308, 309

Jesus, we want to meet   TFF 145

Seed, scattered and sown   W&P 121

MUSIC FOR THE DAY
PSALMODY

Bengtson, Bruce.   PW B.

Eat this bread, drink this cup   WOV 706

Glynn, John. "Look Towards the Lord" in PS 2.

Harbor, Rawn. "Taste and See the Goodness of the Lord" in TFF 5.

Hobby, Robert. "I Will Bless the Lord." U, cong, org.   MSM 80-707.

Moore, James. "Taste and See." Cong, cant, acc, gtr.   GIA G-2784.

Walker, Christopher. "Taste and See" in PS 3.

Young, Jeremy. "Taste and See." U, kybd, opt 2 pt, opt cong.
    AFP 0800657608.

SUGGESTIONS FOR CHILDREN

Howard, Julie. *Sing for Joy: Psalm Settings for God's Children.*   Liturgical Press 8146-2078-7.

Hruby, Dolores. "I Will Bless the Lord at All Times." U, cong, perc. CG CGA452.

CHORAL

Isaac, Heinrich. "O Bread of Life from Heaven" in *Chantry Choirbook.* SATB.   AFP 0800657772.

Pinkham, Daniel. "This Is the Bread." 2 pt.   ECS 4447.

Scott, K. Lee. "So Art Thou to Me" in *Rejoice Now, My Spirit.* Kybd. MH voice.   AFP 0800651081. ML voice. AFP 080065109X.

Scott, K. Lee. "So Art Thou to Me." SATB, kybd.   AFP 0800674308.

Vaughan Williams, Ralph. "O Taste and See." SATB.   OXF A349.

White, David Ashley. "O Bread of Life from Heaven." 2 pt mxd, org. AFP 0800650913.

Wolff, S. Drummond. "Soul, Adorn Thyself with Gladness." SATB, kybd.   CPH 98-1906.

Young, Jeremy. "Eat This Bread, Drink This Cup." U/2 pt, cong, kybd.   AFP 0800655265.

CHILDREN'S CHOIRS

Mozart, W. A./arr. Hal H. Hopson. "I Feel the Love of God." U, kybd.   CG CGA778.

Telemann, G. P./arr. William Schoenfeld. "I Will Rejoice in the Lord." 2 pt, kybd.   CG CGA817.

KEYBOARD/INSTRUMENTAL

Biery, James. "Two Canonic Settings of 'Thine the Amen, Thine the Praise'" in *Tree of Life.* Org.   AFP 0800655370.

Cotter, Jeanne. "Eat This Bread" and "Gather Us In" in *After the Rain.* Pno.   GIA G-3390.

Kolander, Keith. "Voluntaries for Trumpet and Organ." Org, tpt. AFP 0800659406.

Miller, Aaron David. "Schmücke dich" in *Improvisations for the Church Year.* Org.   AFP 0800674812.

HANDBELL

Barnard, Mark. "Eat This Bread." 2 pt, acc, cong, hb. JEF MLC102212U.

Beard, K. "Guide Me, O Thou Great Jehovah." 4 oct. JEF MBO398899.

Helman, Michael. "Gift of Finest Wheat." 3–5 oct, opt hc. AFP 0800657365.

Helman, Michael. "Variations on 'Gather Us In.'" 3–5 oct. AFP 0800674928.

PRAISE ENSEMBLE

Baloche, Paul and Claire Cloninger. "As Bread That Is Broken" in *Hosanna! Music Songbook 10.*   INT 08667

Berthier, Jacques/ed. Brother Robert. "Eat This Bread." Cant. response.   GIA G-2840.

Lord, I Want to Be a Christian in My Heart   TFF 234

Owens, Jimmy and Carol Owens. "Make Me Like You" in *The Other Song Book.*   Fellowship Publications.

Tunney, Dick and Melodie Tunney/arr. Ed Lojeski. "O Magnify the Lord." SATB, pno.   HAL 08346681. Also available in SAB.

Ylvisaker, John. "I'll Bless the Lord Forevermore" in *Borning Cry.* NGP.

Sunday, August 10

LAWRENCE, DEACON, MARTYR, 258

Lawrence was one of seven deacons of the congregation at Rome, and like the deacons appointed in Acts, was responsible for financial matters in the church and for the care of the poor. Lawrence lived during a time of persecution under the emperor Valerian. The emperor demanded that Lawrence surrender the treasures of the church. Lawrence gathered lepers, orphans, the blind and lame. He brought them to the emperor and said, "Here is the treasure of the church." This act enraged the emperor and Lawrence was sentenced to death. Lawrence's martyrdom was one of the first to be observed by the church.

Amid the concerns for the institutional church, reflect on what we consider the treasures of the church today. If the people on the margins of life are treasured in God's eyes, consider ways a congregation can sharpen its vision for social ministry.

Wednesday, August 13

FLORENCE NIGHTINGALE, 1910; CLARA MAAS, 1901; RENEWERS OF SOCIETY

When Florence Nightingale decided she would be a nurse, her family was horrified. In the early 1800s nursing was done by people with no training and no other way to earn a living. Florence trained at Kaiserswerth, Germany, with a Lutheran order of deaconesses. She returned home and worked to reform hospitals in England. Nightingale led a group of 38 nurses to serve in the Crimean War where they worked in appalling conditions. She returned to London as a hero and resumed her work there for hospital reform. Clara Maas was born in New Jersey and served as a nurse in the Spanish-American War where she encountered the horrors of yellow fever. She later responded to a call for subjects in research on yellow fever. During the experiments, which included receiving bites from mosquitoes, she contracted the disease and died. The commemoration of these women invites the church to give thanks for all who practice the arts of healing.

271

Friday, August 15

MARY, MOTHER OF OUR LORD

The church honors Mary with the Greek title *theotokos,* meaning God-bearer. Origen first used this title in the early church and the councils of Ephesus and Chalcedon upheld it. Luther upheld this same title in his writings. The honor paid to Mary as *theotokos* and mother of our Lord goes back to biblical times when Mary herself sang, "from now on all generations will call me blessed" (Luke 1:48). Mary's life revealed the presence of God incarnate, and it revealed God's presence among the humble and poor. Mary's song, the Magnificat, speaks of reversals in the reign of God: the mighty are cast down, the lowly are lifted up, the hungry are fed, and the rich are sent away empty-handed.

Hymns to commemorate Mary as *theotokos* might include "Sing of Mary, pure and holy" (WOV 634) or a paraphrase of the Magnificat, such as "My soul proclaims your greatness" (WOV 730).

August 17, 2003

Tenth Sunday after Pentecost
Proper 15

INTRODUCTION

Wisdom sets a table and invites all to taste the wine and bread. Jesus Christ, our Wisdom, gives his life for all, inviting everyone to drink and eat. Wisdom nourishes us with the word of life and the bread from heaven. In all this hospitality, we experience the abundant grace of God. How can this congregation be gracious and welcoming to any and all who seek the Lord?

PRAYER OF THE DAY

Almighty and ever-living God, you have given great and precious promises to those who believe. Grant us the perfect faith, which overcomes all doubts, through your Son, Jesus Christ our Lord.

VERSE

Alleluia. The Word of God is living and active, sharper than any two-edged sword, able to judge the thoughts and intentions of the heart. Alleluia. (Heb. 4:12)

READINGS

Proverbs 9:1-6

Wisdom is portrayed as a woman who invites people to partake of her banquet. Just as ordinary food is necessary for physical life, Wisdom's food—insight and understanding—is necessary for fullness of life with God. Partaking of Wisdom's banquet is the way to life.

Psalm 34:9-14

Those who seek the LORD lack nothing that is good. (Ps. 34:10)

Ephesians 5:15-20

Fully aware of this world's evil, Paul still finds much for which he is grateful. Here he describes the alternative quality of life available to those who have been reconciled with God and one another.

John 6:51-58

In John's gospel, the feeding of the five thousand leads to extended teaching in which Jesus identifies himself as the true "bread of life." Finally, in these verses, he makes a connection that would not be understood until after his death, in light of the church's celebration of the eucharist.

SEMICONTINUOUS FIRST READING/PSALM

1 Kings 2:10-12; 3:3-14

This reading deals with the story of the succession of David's throne to Solomon, with the Lord's authorization of Solomon as king.

Psalm 111

The fear of the LORD is the beginning of wisdom. (Ps. 111:10)

COLOR Green

THE PRAYERS

Growing in the soil of the Spirit, let us pray for the church, the world, and all who seek the richness of life in God.

A BRIEF SILENCE.

Let us pray for the church, the community of God's love on the earth, that it may freely offer the bread of heaven and cup of salvation to all who gather at the table of the Lord. Gracious God,

hear our prayer.

Let us pray for the world, that its leaders would seek wisdom from God as they govern the nations entrusted to them, and as they lead their people in ways of justice and truth. Gracious God,

hear our prayer.

Let us pray for those in need, especially those dealing with addictions and all in recovery, that they would be given courage and patience to be made whole. Gracious God,

hear our prayer.

Let us pray for those among us who are sick *(especially)*, that they would be fed with the healing manna of life. Gracious God,

hear our prayer.

Let us pray for those who lead music in this congregation, that all will be inspired to sing psalms, hymns, and spiritual songs with joy and confidence. Gracious God,

hear our prayer.

HERE OTHER INTERCESSIONS MAY BE OFFERED.

Let us pray for those grieving losses among us *(especially)*,

272

that they would be held in communion with *(names,* and*)* all your blessed saints who are at rest in you. Gracious God, **hear our prayer.**

Hear us as we pray, living God, and in your mercy give us all good things, for the sake of Jesus Christ, our Lord and Savior.

Amen

IMAGES FOR PREACHING

We have all heard it said, "You are what you eat." In these health conscious times, we are reminded about saturated fats, sodium levels, sugars, cholesterol content and their place on the revised food pyramid. We may even have come to believe the current experts of the day. What goes in our mouths does in fact affect our health and even who we are.

The author of Proverbs reminds us that if you eat and drink of the words that wisdom has to offer then you will "walk in the way of insight." The author of the letter to the Ephesians seems quite aware of this notion. Getting drunk on wine equals "debauchery," but one's actions can positively affect who one becomes as well. Singing psalms and spiritual songs leads one into a life of thanksgiving in Christ.

Jesus was also aware that what one eats affects who one becomes. "Those who eat my flesh and drink my blood abide in me and I in them." Eating and drinking in Jesus causes God's presence to abide in one's life. Many of us claim that is our utmost desire, to abide in Christ and have Christ in us. Jesus tells us that God will indeed bring it about. Abiding in Christ and he is us means that we are ready to serve, give of our time, even sacrifice our very lives following in the way of the cross. Perhaps we need to warn those in our assemblies that partaking of the eucharist (and hearing God's word) on a regular basis is apt to lead us to Christ-like activities in daily life.

The meal is set before us. "I am the bread from heaven," Jesus announces. Let us feast that we might be more like him.

WORSHIP MATTERS

If a congregation does not regularly send servers of communion to those unable to attend, the lectionary's series on John 6 provides impetus to begin. What congregation, if asked, wouldn't volunteer to take communion to the dear people unable to be present, in response to this gospel and to the reading in which wisdom sends out the young serving women (and men)? Why not ask during a liturgy that also provides encouragement, training, demonstration, and commissioning? *Occasional Services* provides such a rite and the Sunday liturgy provides a perfect place for it.

Some of Jesus' hearers complained that an ordinary man could not give us Jesus' flesh to eat. But a congregation of lay communion servers can prove them wrong — the finite can bear the infinite in response to God's sending us to "Go in peace; serve the Lord."

LET THE CHILDREN COME

At times our worship seems principally a "head" experience. Children have a low tolerance for head-only experiences because they possess a healthy integration of the whole person as God created us. Posture and gesture invite the body to engage what the ear hears and the eye sees. Have you ever noticed a child in your congregation miming the presider's gestures in worship? The *orans* gesture for praying with outstretched hands is a ritual act once assumed by the entire assembly. Inform your congregation about this gesture and invite children to raise hands for one of the prayers of the liturgy.

HYMNS FOR WORSHIP

GATHERING

For the beauty of the earth   LBW 561

When in our music God is glorified   WOV 802

HYMN OF THE DAY

I am the Bread of life   WOV 702

ALTERNATE HYMN OF THE DAY

Come, let us eat   LBW 214, TFF 119

I'm a-goin'-a eat at the welcome table   TFF 263

COMMUNION

Let all mortal flesh keep silence   LBW 198

This is my body   WOV 707, TFF 121

Fill my cup, Lord   TFF 124

SENDING

Let all things now living   LBW 557

Father, we thank you   WOV 704

Give thanks   W&P 41

273

ADDITIONAL HYMNS AND SONGS

How deep the silence of the soul   NCH 509
My God, thy table now is spread   H82 321
Taste and see   TFF 126

MUSIC FOR THE DAY
PSALMODY

Bengtson, Bruce.   PW B.

Brown, Teresa. "The Lord Is Close to the Broken Hearted" in PS 1.

Busarow, Donald. "Proclaim with Me." SATB, cong, opt tpt.
CPH 98-3127.

Harbor, Rawn. "Taste and See the Goodness of the Lord." TFF 5.

Schalk, Carl. "Be Known to Us, Lord Jesus." SATB, cong, children.
CPH 98-3202.

CHORAL

Haugen, Marty. "Taste and See." SATB, cong, gtr, kybd, opt cant.
GIA G-3555.

Holst, Gustav. "Let All Mortal Flesh." SATB.   ECS 1.5019.

Johengen, Carl. "I Am the Living Bread." Cant, cong, org, opt SATB,
ob.   GIA G-4353.

Scott, K. Lee. "The Call" in Sing a Song of Joy: Vocal Solos for Worship. MH
voice.   AFP 0800647882. ML voice.   AFP 0800652827.

Young, Jeremy. "Eat This Bread, Drink This Cup." U, opt 2 pt, opt
cong, kybd.   AFP 0800655265.

CHILDREN'S CHOIRS

Burkhardt, Michael. "Filled with the Spirit." 3 pt canon, opt 2 oct
hb/kybd.   MSM 50-7402.

Nagy, Russell. "Song of Thanks." 2 pt, kybd.
High Street Music JH521.

KEYBOARD/INSTRUMENTAL

Bernthal, John. "I Am the Bread" in Lift High the Cross. Org, opt tpt.
AFP 0800657314.

Biery, James. "Rendez à Dieu." Org.   AFP 0800658744.

Cherwien, David. "Triptych on 'The Ash Grove.' " Org.
AFP 0800658256.

Dahl, David P. "Rendez à Dieu" in Hymn Interpretations for Organ. Org.
AFP 0800658248.

Farlee, Robert Buckley. "Rendez à Dieu" in Many and Great. Org.
AFP 0800658949.

Organ, Anne Krentz. "A va de" in Global Piano Reflections. Pno.
AFP 0800658019.

Widor, Charles Marie. "Adagio" from Symphony V, op. 42, no. 5. Org.
KAL K 04033.

HANDBELL

Edwards, Dan. "Let Us Break Bread Together." 3 oct, L2.
AGEHR 3254737-725.

McChesney, Kevin. "When Morning Gilds the Skies." Qrt.
HOP CP6067.

PRAISE ENSEMBLE

Berthier, Jacques/ed. Brother Robert. "Eat This Bread." Cant, response.   GIA G-2840.

Cloninger, Claire and Martin J. Nystrom. "Come to the Table" in
Hosanna! Music Songbook 6.   INT HMSB06.

Dearman, Kirk. "We Remember You" in Songs for Praise and Worship.
WRD.

Leech, Bryan Jeffrey/arr. Roland Tabell. "Come Share the Lord."
SATB. FB BG2053. SAB, kybd.   BG0502.

Pote, Allen. "Come to the Table." SATB, kybd.
Coral Key Music 392-41678.

Wednesday, August 20

BERNARD, ABBOT OF CLAIRVAUX, 1153

Bernard was a Cistercian monk who became an abbot of
great spiritual depth. He was a mystical writer deeply devoted to the humanity of Christ and, consequently, to
the affective dimension of medieval spirituality. He was
critical of one of the foremost theologians of the day,
Peter Abelard, because he believed Abelard's approach to
faith was too rational and did not provide sufficient
room for mystery. Bernard's devotional writings are still
read today. His sermon on the Song of Solomon treats
that Old Testament book as an allegory of Christ's love
for humanity. Bernard wrote several hymns, five of which
are in LBW. His hymn "Jesus the very thought of you"
(316) could be sung to commemorate this monk at
gatherings within the congregation today.

August 24, 2003

St. Bartholomew, Apostle

INTRODUCTION

Though little is known about this apostle, the Acts of the Apostles mentions him waiting with the other disciples for the coming of the Holy Spirit. Some scholars suggest that the Nathanael mentioned in the Gospel of John may be Bartholomew. The encounter between Jesus and Nathanael is a touching story about the call to discipleship.

PRAYER OF THE DAY

Almighty and everlasting God, who gave to your apostle Bartholomew grace truly to believe and to preach your Word: Grant that your Church may love what he believed and preach what he taught; through your Son, Jesus Christ our Lord, who lives and reigns with you and the Holy Spirit, one God, now and forever.

VERSE

Alleluia. How beautiful upon the mountains are the feet of the messenger who announces peace, who brings good news, who announces salvation. Alleluia. (Isa. 52:7)

READINGS

Exodus 19:1-6

Chapters 19–24 set forth the covenant God makes with Israel. After the former slaves arrive at Sinai, God comes to them and, in the mystery of divine wisdom, chooses them to be a holy nation. As a community publicly chosen by God, Israel is set in the midst of the world as a witness to the God who rescues the oppressed.

Psalm 12

The words of the LORD are pure. (Ps. 12:6)

1 Corinthians 12:27-31a

Paul speaks of the church, the body of Christ, formed in baptism and nourished in the eucharist. In this community, gifts are used differently than in the world. Ministries do not serve personal ambition or status, but are focused on the common good of the entire community.

John 1:43-51

Only in John's gospel do we hear of the disciple Nathanael. It has generally been assumed that he is the Bartholomew mentioned in the other gospels. Skeptical that anything good can come from a small, insignificant town, this dubious observer is transformed by Jesus' welcome and becomes a faithful follower.

COLOR Red

THE PRAYERS

Growing in the soil of the Spirit, let us pray for the church, the world, and all who seek the richness of life in God.

A BRIEF SILENCE.

O life-giving Spirit of God, you have given your words of eternal life to the church. Give us bold preachers and teachers of this word, so that many may come to believe. Gracious God,

hear our prayer.

You have given both mission and gifts to all of your children. May we, like Bartholomew, be faithful in spreading your gospel, looking not for fame but only for your blessing. Gracious God,

hear our prayer.

Give to the nations of the world your light and your peace. Grant their leaders wisdom and courage, that they may lead with compassion for all people. Gracious God,

hear our prayer.

Heal those among us who are struggling with sickness of any kind *(especially)*, that being touched by you, their sickness may be turned to health. Gracious God,

hear our prayer.

Bless those entrusted with the ministry of prayer in this congregation. Keep them alert to the needs of this community, that they may support all we do with their intercessions. Gracious God,

hear our prayer.

HERE OTHER INTERCESSIONS MAY BE OFFERED.

We remember before you those who have died, especially Bartholomew (and *names*), and ask that you would keep us in communion with them and all your saints who surround us in the great cloud of witnesses. Gracious God,

hear our prayer.

275

Hear us as we pray, living God, and in your mercy give us all good things, for the sake of Jesus Christ, our Lord and Savior.

Amen

IMAGES FOR PREACHING

Bartholomew is listed among the disciples in the synoptic gospels. In the Gospel of John, Bartholomew's alternate name seems to be Nathanael. In today's gospel, Nathanael speaks the famous line, "Can anything good come out of Nazareth?" We may defensively retort, "Can anything good come of Bartholomew?"

Apparently, the answer is yes. Tradition has Bartholomew preaching the gospel of Christ all around the ancient world. Many communities of faith trace their history to his presence among them. At least two traditions state that Bartholomew was a martyr for the faith. But as much as tradition suggests a life devoutly lived in Jesus, we simply do not know much about this disciple except that he makes the list.

Not everyone can be a Peter or James or John, a member of the inner circle. There is only one Judas, the one who would betray Jesus. Thomas occupies the unique place as the one who got caught doubting. Apart from the skepticism expressed from the mouth of Nathanael, also known as Bartholomew, nothing more is recorded about what seems to have been a rather ordinary disciple.

This feast day might best be celebrated as a day for ordinary disciples. Nothing is special here, other than a little expression of pessimism. He is also a bit too eager to believe. Maybe this feast day celebrates the likes of most of us who count ourselves among the ordinary disciples who daily confess Jesus as the Christ with a little reluctance, a little doubt, sometimes a little too zealously, but who confess nonetheless.

Paul reminds us that we, the baptized, all have our place. "Now you are the body of Christ and individually members of it." With God, all disciples have a special place and a special calling. Preach Christ in the ordinariness of your lives.

WORSHIP MATTERS

Today's second reading reminds us that in God's economy, different members of the body have different gifts. Bartholomew, apparently, was not called to be a leader of the apostles, yet he was still chosen by Christ to be one of the twelve. In our worshiping assemblies, not everyone need be drafted as a lector, an usher, an assisting minister. Perhaps one who is struggling in a given role has gifts that are better suited to another form of ministry. An evangelical procedure might be not to force people into roles for which they seem unsuited or unwilling, yet at the same time to find a place in ministry for all the baptized.

LET THE CHILDREN COME

The traditional color for the commemoration of saints is red. The color recalls the meaning of the word *martyr* as "witness." In celebration of this festive day, all might be invited to wear something red. Young children might be given a small dowel with red crepe paper streamer attached. Then, the children could process to the place of the readings and form a semicircle while the lessons are heard. In this way, visual, movement, and auditory experience come together in the hearing of scripture.

HYMNS FOR WORSHIP
GATHERING

Oh, that I had a thousand voices   LBW 560

Arise, your light has come!   WOV 652

HYMN OF THE DAY

Rejoice in God's saints   WOV 689

ALTERNATE HYMN OF THE DAY

By all your saints in warfare (stanza 17)   LBW 178

Listen, God is calling   WOV 712, TFF 130

COMMUNION

Draw us in the Spirit's tether   WOV 703

SENDING

Praise to the Lord, the Almighty   LBW 543, CS 58

Hallelujah! We sing your praises   WOV 722, TFF 158

ADDITIONAL HYMNS AND SONGS

"Come, follow me," the Savior spake   LBW 455

The summons   W&P 137

All to Jesus I surrender   TFF 235

MUSIC FOR THE DAY
PSALMODY

Organ, Anne Krentz.   PW A.

CHORAL

Carlson, J. Bert. "O Christ, Who Called the Twelve." SAB.
CPH 98-3591.

Hassell, Michael. "Beloved, God's Chosen." SATB.
AFP 0800659139.

Helvey, Howard. "Forth In Thy Name, O Lord, I Go." SATB.
LOR 10/2223R.

Hopson, Hal H. "I Want Jesus to Walk with Me." 2 pt trbl/mxd,
pno.   CGA 701.

Jennings, Kenneth. "Rise Up, O Men of God." TTBB.
AFP 0800645731.

CHILDREN'S CHOIRS

Leaf, Robert. "Let the Whole Creation Cry." SA, kybd.
AFP 080065269X.

Ziegenhals, Harriet. "Oh, Sing to the Lord" (Cantad al Señor).
U/2 pt, kybd, opt maracas.   CG CGA640.

KEYBOARD/INSTRUMENTAL

Liszt, Franz. "Adagio in D-flat" in *Liszt Orgelwerke II*. Org.   PET 3829b.

Martinson, Joel. "Postlude for a Festival Day." Org.   AUR AE 50.

Powell, Robert J. "King's Weston" in *Rejoice, Ye Pure in Heart*. Org.
AFP 0800653610.

Wold, Wayne L. "Festal Song" in *A November to Remember*. Org.
AFP 080068983X.

HANDBELL

Afdahl, Lee J. "Rejoice in God's Saints." 3–5 oct, opt perc.
AFP 0800656695.

McChesney, Kevin. "For All the Saints." 3–5 oct, org, brass, timp.
JEF 201067L.

Moklebust, Cathy. "Laudate Dominum" in *Hymn Stanzas for Handbells*.
2–3 oct.   AFP 0800657330. 4–5 oct.   AFP 0800655761.

Wagner, Douglas. "Jesu, Joy of Man's Desiring." 2 oct, org.
JEF BEHB45.

PRAISE ENSEMBLE

Burleigh, Glenn/arr. Jack Schrader. "Order My Steps." SATB, kybd.
HOP C 5083.

Thomas, Andrae. "I Will Sing Praises." SATB, kybd.   CG A718.

277

August 24, 2003

Eleventh Sunday after Pentecost
Proper 16

INTRODUCTION

In the midst of life's challenges and uncertainties we seek to understand God's words of truth and life for us. Like Joshua we make a commitment not to worship the passing gods of the day, but to serve the Lord alone. Today's reading from John includes words many of us sing before the gospel is proclaimed: "Lord, to whom shall we go? You have the words of eternal life." Our hearts yearn for the good news that sets us free and strengthens us for service.

PRAYER OF THE DAY

God of all creation, you reach out to call people of all nations to your kingdom. As you gather disciples from near and far, count us also among those who boldly confess your Son Jesus Christ as Lord.

VERSE

Alleluia. Our Savior Jesus Christ abolished death and brought life and immortality to light through the gospel. Alleluia. (2 Tim. 1:10)

READINGS

Joshua 24:1-2a, 14-18

In the Near East, *covenant* means "agreement" or "alliance." It describes relationships and is the primary word used to characterize the relationship between God and Israel. By delivering Israel, God has already begun the relationship. Joshua calls upon the people to respond.

Psalm 34:15-22

The eyes of the LORD are upon the righteous. (Ps. 34:15)

Ephesians 6:10-20

The military language in this passage calls to mind the power of the Roman Empire in the first century. Followers of Christ are to put on the armor of God and remain strong in the face of cosmic evil forces.

John 6:56-69

The "hard saying" that offends Jesus' disciples is his claim that his followers must eat his flesh and drink his blood. The followers who return to their old lives know something about how odd this sounds. Simon Peter asks the most important question: "To whom shall we go?"

SEMICONTINUOUS FIRST READING/PSALM

1 Kings 8:[1, 6, 10-11] 22-30, 41-43

The dedication of the temple concludes with the transfer of the sacred utensils and the elaborate gifts deriving from David's conquests. Now Solomon has the ark of the covenant itself brought into the temple.

Psalm 84

How dear to me is your dwelling, O Lord. (Ps. 84:1)

COLOR Green

THE PRAYERS

Growing in the soil of the Spirit, let us pray for the church, the world, and all who seek the richness of life in God.

A BRIEF SILENCE.

Generous God, you feed us with bread that will nourish us to eternal life. Keep us always faithful to the spirit and life we receive from the Bread of life. Gracious God, **hear our prayer.**

Give to the nations of the world your light and your peace. Grant their leaders wisdom and courage, that they may lead with compassion for all people. Gracious God, **hear our prayer.**

Heal those among us who are struggling with sickness of any kind *(especially)*, that being touched by you, their sickness may be turned to health. Gracious God, **hear our prayer.**

Bless those entrusted with the ministry of prayer in this congregation. Keep them alert to the needs of this community, that they may support all we do with their intercessions. Gracious God, **hear our prayer.**

HERE OTHER INTERCESSIONS MAY BE OFFERED.

We remember before you those who have died *(especially)* and ask that you would keep us in communion with them and all your saints who surround us in the great cloud of witnesses. Gracious God, **hear our prayer.**

Hear us as we pray, living God, and in your mercy give us all good things, for the sake of Jesus Christ, our Lord and Savior. **Amen**

IMAGES FOR PREACHING

The competition is stiff. Which god should we follow? We often think of the people of Israel as being steadfast in their faith in YHWH. The reading from Joshua reminds us that this was not the case. "Which god will you serve?" Joshua asks. His answer is the guide for those assembled, "As for me and my household, we will serve the Lord." Joshua's Lord is the God not only of the exodus but also the God who delivers the Hebrew people into the promised land. God provides not only an exit but an entrance as well.

Jesus' teaching about eating his body and drinking his blood is difficult for the hearers of his words. "Who can accept it?" A choice must also be made here. As disciples, can one accept in faith the words of the teacher?

As we come to the altar to receive the bread and the wine, a choice is before us as well. Do we believe the words of the teacher: this is my body, this is my blood, take and eat, take and drink, do this for the forgiveness of sins? Here is a difficult teaching. All that is required of us "is simply a believing heart" said Martin Luther in the Small Catechism. Oh, that believing was so simple. But we want desperately to believe in forgiveness for our sinfulness. For five weeks we hear that Jesus is the Bread of life. Maybe it takes five weeks for us to at least start thinking about what this bread really means for us and for our faith. Maybe it takes every week to be reminded that ours is a God who chooses us, forgives us, and loves us.

Where else could we go? Simon Peter knew the answer to this one. "Lord, to whom can we go? You have the words of eternal life."

WORSHIP MATTERS

Summer sometimes presents the problem of not having musicians for worship. High school and college musicians can accomplish a lot if given enough guidance and rehearsal time. Another idea is to teach music in harmony. It's not as hard as it sounds. Four strong voices, choir members perhaps, choose a harmonically simple hymn, or music of Taizé. Rehearse each part separately, a handbell, flute, or organ giving a note. Call and response hymns like "Come let us eat" (LBW 214) need no accompaniment. Plainsong chant can be led by a single voice, and repeated one line or one stanza at a time. Chant formulas are available for collects and other texts. Less music might also allow more time for free prayers of the people.

LET THE CHILDREN COME

The most important word spoken by the people in worship is *Amen*, which means "So be it." We assent to the prayers, express our belief, and make personal commitment all with this transliterated Hebrew verb. Children should be taught this word from their first days in the worshiping assembly. Accustomed to a more passive worship experience, adults are learning again to reclaim an active participation in the liturgy. If encouraged, children can help us all voice a hearty "Amen" in response to the prayers and affirmations of the liturgy. With just a little instruction our children will respond with enthusiasm.

HYMNS FOR WORSHIP
GATHERING
You servants of God   LBW 252
He comes to us as one unknown   WOV 768

HYMN OF THE DAY
Eternal Ruler of the ceaseless round   LBW 373

ALTERNATE HYMN OF THE DAY
Eat this bread, drink this cup   WOV 706
Some folk would rather have houses   TFF 236

COMMUNION
O God of life's great mystery   LBW 201
Mothering God, you gave me birth   WOV 769
Open our eyes, Lord   W&P 113, TFF 98

SENDING
O Jesus, I have promised   LBW 503
What a fellowship, what a joy divine   WOV 780, TFF 220
Thy word is a lamp   TFF 132

ADDITIONAL HYMNS AND SONGS
Surely it is God who saves me   H82 678, 679
Victory is mine   TFF 266
Be bold, be strong   W&P 15
The trumpets sound, the angels sing   W&P 139

MUSIC FOR THE DAY
PSALMODY
Bengtson, Bruce.   PW B.
Brown, Teresa. "The Lord Is Close to the Broken Hearted" in PS I.
Harbor, Rawn. "Taste and See the Goodness of the Lord." TFF 5.

CHORAL
Bach, J. S. "Jesu, Joy—My Joy Forever" in *Bach for All Seasons*. SATB. AFP 080065854X
Busarow, Donald. "Eternal Ruler of the Ceaseless Round." SATB, kybd, opt brass.   CPH 98-3078.
Haugen, Marty. "Halle, Halle, Halle." SATB, cant, opt cong, perc, kybd.   GIA G-3961.
Hopson, Hal H. "If You Believe and I Believe." SATB, kybd, opt perc. AFP 0800674588.
How, Martin. "Day by Day." U/2 pt/3 pt.   GIA G-4178.
Porter, Thomas J. "Let Us Be Bread." 2 pt, opt cong, gtr, kybd. GIA G-3355.

CHILDREN'S CHOIRS
Rutter, John. "For the Beauty of the Earth." 2 pt, pno.   HIN HMC-469.
Sleeth, Natalie. "Everywhere I Go." U/2 pt, kybd.   CG CGA 171.

KEYBOARD/INSTRUMENTAL
Althouse, Jay. "Let Us Break Bread Together" in *The Sacred Trumpet Soloist*. Tpt, kybd.   ALF 18923.
Farlee, Robert Buckley. "Song I" in *Gaudeamus!* Org. AFP 0800655389.
Gigout, Eugene. "Toccata." LED AH. Also in *French Masterworks for Organ*.   CLP FE 09431.
Kolander, Keith. "Munich" in *God Has Done Marvelous Things*. Org. AFP 0800659449.
Wellman, Samuel. "Munich" in *Keyboard Hymn Favorites*. Pno. AFP 0800656814.

HANDBELL
McCabe, M. "Bring Us Together, Lord." SATB, org, brass, hrn, 2 oct hb.   JEF PPMO9114.
McChesney, Kevin. "For the Beauty of the Earth." 2–3 oct, opt hc. JEF AP16463.

279

PRAISE ENSEMBLE

Chapman, Gary. "As for Me and My House" (The Family Prayer Song) in *Promise Keepers: Raise the Standard, pt 1 & 2.* MAR.

Gillard, Richard. "The Servant Song" in *Maranatha! Music Praise Chorus Book, 3rd ed.* MAR.

Gordon, Nancy and Jamie Harvill. "Because We Believe" in *Hosanna! Music Songbook 12.* INT 12906.

Medema, Ken. "Like a River That Overflows." SATB, pno. HOP GC995.

Oliver, Gary. "You Are the Holy One" in *Hosanna! Music Songbook. 6.* INT HMSB06.

Schram, Ruth Elaine. "We Come to Your Table, Lord." SATB, acc. ALF 16101.

Ylvisaker, John. "I Believe, I Do Believe" in *Borning Cry.* NGP.

Sunday, August 24

ST. BARTHOLOMEW, APOSTLE

See pages 275–77.

Thursday, August 28

AUGUSTINE, BISHOP OF HIPPO, 430

Augustine was one of the greatest theologians of the Western church. Born in North Africa, he was a philos-ophy student in Carthage, where he later became a teacher of rhetoric. Much of his young life was a debauched one. As an adult he came under the influence of Ambrose, the bishop of Milan, and through him came to see Christianity as a religion appropriate for a philosopher. Augustine was baptized by Ambrose at the Easter Vigil in 387. He was ordained four years later and made bishop of Hippo in 396. Augustine was a defender of the Christian faith and argued, against the Donatists, that the holiness of the church did not depend on the holiness of its members, particularly the clergy, but that holiness comes from Christ, the head of the church. Augustine's autobiography, *Confessions*, tells of his slow move toward faith and includes the line, "Late have I loved thee."

MOSES THE BLACK, MONK, C. 400

A man of great strength and rough character, Moses the Black was converted to Christian faith toward the close of the fourth century. Prior to his conversion he had been a thief and a leader of a gang of robbers. The story of his conversion is unknown, but eventually he became a desert monk at Skete. The habit of his monastic community was white, though Moses is reported to have said, "God knows I am black within." The change in his heart and life had a profound impact on his native Ethiopia. He was murdered when Berbers attacked his monastery.

August 31, 2003

Twelfth Sunday after Pentecost
Proper 17

INTRODUCTION

In the liturgy, we pray to God who is the giver of every good and perfect gift. We ask God to bring to fruition the word of truth sown in our hearts by Christ, so that we will live the law of love. It is this liberating law that judges all other laws of human origin. It is this gracious command that is sealed with Christ's blood. In this supper Christ forgives us and strengthens us to be communal witnesses to his love.

Today we remember John Bunyan (died 1688), who wrote the Christian spiritual classic *The Pilgrim's Progress.*

PRAYER OF THE DAY

O God, we thank you for your Son who chose the path of suffering for the sake of the world. Humble us by his example, point us to the path of obedience, and give us strength to follow his commands; through your Son, Jesus Christ our Lord.

VERSE

Alleluia. Your words became to me a joy, and the delight of my heart. Alleluia. (Jer. 15:16)

READINGS

Deuteronomy 4:1-2, 6-9

The Israelites believed the law was a divine gift that provided guidelines for living out the covenant. According to Moses, the people are to obey the law and neither add to nor subtract from it.

Psalm 15

Lord, who may dwell in your tabernacle? (Ps. 15:1)

James 1:17-27

The letter of James was intended to provide first-century Christians with instruction in godly behavior. Here, Christians are encouraged to listen carefully and to act on what they hear.

Mark 7:1-8, 14-15, 21-23

Mark's gospel depicts Jesus as challenging traditional ways in which religious people determine what is pure or impure. For Jesus, the observance of religious practices cannot become a substitute for godly words or deeds that spring from the faithful heart.

SEMICONTINUOUS FIRST READING/PSALM

Song of Solomon 2:8-13

Though using language and images of a tender love story, the Song of Solomon has long inspired the tradition of allegorical interpretation. Jewish lore sees its meaning as a depiction of the love of the Lord with the covenant people. Furthermore, Christian interpretation has often seen this work as a depiction of the love of Christ and his church.

Psalm 45:1-2, 7-10 (Psalm 45:1-2, 6-9 [NRSV])

God has anointed you with the oil of gladness. (Ps. 45:8)

COLOR Green

THE PRAYERS

Growing in the soil of the Spirit, let us pray for the church, the world, and all who seek the richness of life in God.

A BRIEF SILENCE.

Let us pray for the church, that God's word would not be crowded out by human traditions, and that right teaching would be coupled always with right living. Gracious God,

hear our prayer.

Let us pray for the world, that justice and peace might prevail over greed and violence. Gracious God,

hear our prayer.

Let us pray that the orphaned and widowed would be supported, and that God's people would respond in mercy and with compassion to all in need *(especially).* Gracious God,

hear our prayer.

Let us pray for this congregation, that it might be a beacon of hope to all in this community, offering life in abundance. Gracious God,

hear our prayer.

281

Let us pray for those in sorrow, that they will be met in the valley of their grief by the Comforter and have their hope in the resurrection restored. Gracious God,
hear our prayer.
HERE OTHER INTERCESSIONS MAY BE OFFERED.
Let us pray in thanksgiving for the lives of John Bunyan (*other names*) and all the saints, that we might be supported by their witness until we join them in paradise. Gracious God,
hear our prayer.
Hear us as we pray, living God, and in your mercy give us all good things, for the sake of Jesus Christ, our Lord and Savior.
Amen

IMAGES FOR PREACHING

Washing one's hands before eating a meal is simply good practice. It is one rule we wish to instill in our children. Laws as well as good habits help to keep us safe from harm. Laws protect us from the bad intentions of others and from ourselves. For the sake of good order, should not some laws be followed all the time, without exception?

The people of Israel believed that some laws should be a part of daily living. Give heed and observe that which is taught to you (Deut. 4:1). Jesus is born into this law. Is it unreasonable to expect him to follow that law? Surely, it is not too much to ask that Jesus should follow the most basic laws regarding good hygiene. Jesus' disciples, however, are caught with dirty hands at mealtime. "Why do your disciples eat with defiled hands?" the Pharisees and scribes ask. "Hypocrites," Jesus responds. It is not what one puts in which defiles but rather it is what comes out that defile. Twelve "evil intentions" then follow. You know the list: fornication, adultery, slander, pride, and so on.

Interestingly, Jesus conversely accused the Pharisees and the scribes of abandoning the commandment of God for their own human tradition. Perhaps it is not the last iota of the law that matters, but the intent of the law. Here is the dilemma: can absolute law, even God's law, be interpreted against the circumstance of the day? It can, Jesus asserts, when we look at the bigger picture and the greater law. We know the follow-up to that one: "And which is the greatest commandment?"

We are certain that we will break the law. But we are even more certain that God's grace is there, ready to forgive our transgression.

WORSHIP MATTERS

At this midpoint in the five-year process of Renewing Worship and twenty-fifth year of *LBW*, attention is being given to newly-developed principles for worship, and to collecting new musical and liturgical resources for the next generation. As you implement these resources, what additional steps or discussion groups need to happen to enliven worship in your community? How can you enhance the involvement, training, confidence-building, coordination, and creativity of the assembly? Creative, skillful presentation requires more than the rote leadership of a single individual. The liturgy is formed as are disciples, by "the shape of the engendering deed," as Joseph Sittler used to say.

Make use of the wisdom and discernment of the people. New resources will be helpful, but they do not guarantee better or more profound worship. Along with the churchwide planning teams, any congregation can develop its own worship planning teams. Pastors and other professional leaders may well find it affirming of their work.

LET THE CHILDREN COME

Location in worship matters greatly, especially with children. Often, parents with children choose seats near the back, fearing their restless child will distract others. In fact, children become restless because they feel remote from the action. Unable to see because of distance or obstructed sight lines, children lose interest. By sitting near the front, children are able to see well and lead with their enthusiasm. All that is needed are adults who will extend the same welcome that is offered children at any parade. Let them come to the front and all will be blessed for it.

HYMNS FOR WORSHIP
GATHERING

O Word of God incarnate   LBW 231
All my hope on God is founded   WOV 782
Stand in the congregation   W&P 131

HYMN OF THE DAY

O God, my faithful God   LBW 504

ALTERNATE HYMN OF THE DAY

Restore in us, O God   WOV 662, CS 60, 61
Lord, let my heart be good soil   WOV 713, TFF 131, W&P 52

COMMUNION

Come, my way, my truth, my life   LBW 513
Create in me a clean heart   WOV 732
Come to Jesus   TFF 156

SENDING

Oh, that the Lord would guide my ways   LBW 480
Let justice flow like streams   WOV 763, TFF 48

ADDITIONAL HYMNS AND SONGS

O God, to whom we turn   H82 681
Teach me, O Lord, your holy way   NCH 465
Have you got good religion?   TFF 113
Create in me a clean heart   W&P 34, 35

MUSIC FOR THE DAY
PSALMODY

Bengtson, Bruce.   PW B.
Gelineau, Joseph. "Psalm 15" in *RitualSong.* GIA.
Haas, David/arr. Jeanne Cotter. "They Who Do Justice" in PCY 3.
Proulx, Richard, refrain; Joseph Gelineau, tone.   TP.
Pulkingham, Betty. *Celebrate the Church Year with Selected Psalms and Canti-cles.* Cong, choir, kybd, gtr, inst.   PLY MB 94218.

CHORAL

Carter, Andrew. "God Be in My Head." SATB, org.   OXF E-159.
Fleming, Larry. "His Voice." SATB div.   AFP 0800656504.
Halloran, Jack, arr. "Witness." SSAATTBB.   Gentry JG2010.
Telemann, G. P. "Make Me Pure, O Sacred Spirit" in *To God Will I Sing.* Kybd. MH voice.   AFP 0800674332.
ML voice.   AFP 0800674340.
Willcock, Christopher. "Give Us A Pure Heart." SATB, org.   TRINITAS/OCP 4529.

CHILDREN'S CHOIRS

Honoré, Jeffrey. "All Good Gifts." U/SATB, kybd, opt 1 oct hb, opt cong.   CG CGA593.
Sleeth, Natalie. "Blessed Shall They Be." 2 pt, kybd.   AMSI 386.

KEYBOARD/INSTRUMENTAL

Albrecht, Mark. "Good Soil" in *Timeless Tunes for Piano and Solo Instru-ment, vol. 3.* Pno, inst.   AFP 0800675037.

Bach, J. S./arr. Robert Hebble. "We Thank Thee, God (Cantata no. 29)." Org.   SMP SM-60.
Burkhardt, Michael. "Praise to the Lord." Org duet.   MSM 10-725.
Johnson, David N. "Was frag ich nach der Welt" in *Wedding Music, Book 3.* Org, opt inst.   AFP 0800648943.
Powell, Robert J. "Michael" in *Sing We to Our God Above.* Org.   AFP 0800651103.

HANDBELL

Honoré, Jeffrey. "Now We Offer." 3-5 oct.   AFP 0800674898.
Leavitt, John. "All Things Bright and Beautiful." 3 oct, 2 pt, pno, tri.   JEF HLO8595443.
Robison, Kevin. "Here, O My Lord, I See Thee Face to Face." SATB, ob, org, 2 oct hb.   MSM 50310.

PRAISE ENSEMBLE

Butler, Terry. "Cry of My Heart" in *Maranatha! Music Praise Chorus Book, 3rd ed.*   MAR.
Dearman, Kirk. "We Choose the Fear of the Lord" in *Maranatha! Music Praise Chorus Book, 3rd ed.*   MAR.
Leavitt, John. "All Things Bright and Beautiful." 2 pt, pno.   HAL 08595443.
Mitchell, Tom. "All Things Bright and Beautiful." SATB, kybd.   CG CGA-492.
Ylvisaker, John. "Who Shall Live on That Holy Mountain" in *Borning Cry.* NGP.

283

Sunday, August 31

JOHN BUNYAN, TEACHER, 1688

John Bunyan had little schooling but became one of the most remarkable figures of seventeenth-century litera-ture. He was a lay preacher who made his living as a tin-ker. After the restoration in England he was ordered to stop preaching, but he refused and was jailed several times. His spiritual pilgrimage is revealed in his works, particularly *The Pilgrim's Progress.* It is an allegory of a per-son's experience from his first awareness of sin, through a personal conversion to Christ, then on to the life of faith and then finally to the "Celestial City," the true and eter-nal home. His commemoration and his own journey offer strength for people to continue their own quest for spiritual truth.

Tuesday, September 2

NIKOLAI FREDERIK SEVERIN GRUNDTVIG, BISHOP,
RENEWER OF THE CHURCH, 1872

Grundtvig was one of two principal Danish theologians of the nineteenth century; the other was Søren Kierkegaard. Grundtvig's ministry as a parish pastor had a difficult start. He was officially censured after his first sermon though he did receive approval a year later to be ordained. He served with his father for two years but was unable to receive a call for seven years after that. In 1826 he was forced to resign his parish call after he attacked the notion that Christianity was merely a philosophical idea rather than God's revelation made known to us in Christ and through word and sacrament. This belief would be a hallmark of Grundtvig's writing. He spent the last thirty-three years as a chaplain at a home for elderly women. From his university days he was convinced that poetry spoke to the human spirit better than prose and he wrote more than a thousand hymns. Eight of his hymns are in *LBW*.

Thursday, September 4

ALBERT SCHWEITZER, MISSIONARY TO AFRICA, 1965

Schweitzer was a philosopher, theologian, and an ordained Lutheran minister. He wrote *The Quest for the Historical Jesus*. He was also an organist who published a study of Johann Sebastian Bach. But he set aside careers as a university lecturer and musician, went to medical school, and became a missionary in the Gabon province of French Equatorial Africa. He believed that the solution to the world's problems was simple: have reverence for life. His primitive style of practicing medicine in the Gabon shocked some, but he was a humanitarian who served Christ by serving his neighbors in need.

Now that school is resuming in many places, parishes can hold up Schweitzer as an example of someone who used vast knowledge in service and ministry to others.

AUTUMN

Jesus Christ is our sure guide

through confusing pathways

Images *of the* Season

Even though the calendar prepares us for the arrival

of autumn, somehow it always seems to come with a degree

of surprise and suddenness. In the more northern latitudes,

the usual heat and humidity of summertime are quickly replaced with the cool, refreshing breezes of autumn. This change usually occurs on the heels of a mighty rainstorm as a clear, star-filled night brings dipping temperatures, causing one to reach for an extra blanket in bed.

Autumn is, above all else, a time of change. In addition to the changing weather, the hours of daylight shorten, curtailing or eliminating our outdoor evening activities. In many areas, nature exchanges the plush green coverings of summer for the brilliant colors of autumn. Our lifestyles often change, too. Autumn means back to the routine, back to work, back to school. Even in the church, autumn is a time of change—so much so that many members mistakenly think of September as the beginning of a new church year. After all, it is start-up time. Autumn ushers in a new year of Sunday school, the start of another catechetical year, and a new year of choir rehearsals and other programs of ministry.

We tend to be a restless people, craving frequent change. If things stay the same too long, we get restless and "itchy." Though we have favorite foods, we wouldn't want to eat the same dish all the time. We may love our home, but it's refreshing to visit different places. If we are fortunate, we find our work to be fulfilling, but we wouldn't want to do the same task endlessly. It would seem that we were created to appreciate change.

At the same time, too much change can become enervating. Psychologists warn of the ill effects of too many stressful changes within a short period of time. People often say of travel that it's good to get away, but also good to get home—back to the familiar patterns and rhythms of our daily life. So we need a balance of change and constancy.

In our relationship with God, we find that balance. Amid the fluid change that comes even with the most stable of modern lives, the love of God is faithful and steadfast. Standing in opposition to our disposable, expendable existence where little has permanence, our God

in Jesus Christ stands as a constant. As the great hymn "Abide with me" attests, "Change and decay in all around I see; O thou who changest not, abide with me." The holy God of Israel, the incarnate God of Bethlehem, the suffering God of the cross, and the triumphant God of the empty tomb is the very same God who meets us time and again, dependably, in our liturgy of word and sacrament.

As comforting as the fact of God's stability is, we dare never forget that through Christ we have met a God also of change. In our baptism, we have been made new in Christ, never to be the same again. We are now God's *new* creation. The readings of our corporate worship this autumn repeatedly remind us of God's will to transform all things in Christ. God continually brings renewal to our lives, working amazing reversals—transforming our pride into humility, our prestige into servanthood, our hatred into love, our sorrow into joy, and, ultimately, death into life. No change for the good is impossible with our God who is our life, our treasure, and our salvation. Jesus instructs the rich young man: "Go, sell what you own, and give the money to the poor, and you will have treasure in heaven; then come, follow me" (Mark 10:21).

In autumn the pace may accelerate, but we are always in a state of change, as congregations and as individual Christians. For those of us who hold dear the concept of reformation, the very idea clearly calls us to a present evolving activity in our lives, not simply to embellished memories of the past. We are called to continual renewal of the church because there is always a need for change. Yet it is not a self-directed or "flip a coin" kind of process. Rather, we rely on Jesus Christ, as revealed in the Bible, who is our sure guide through all the confusing pathways we encounter. Change is both exciting and scary, but as God's servant people, we accept the call to celebrate the gospel and to open ourselves to change, secure in the unchanging love of Christ.

Environment *and* Art *for the* Season

Autumn comes gradually, but it comes. We begin

to notice a change of season is, indeed, upon us. The world

around us is in transformation: late summer shifts into early

autumn, and despite the short bursts of summer-like weather that continue through September and October, we become aware that the steady evolution of earth's rebirth and ascending into glorious fullness has reached its peak. It is time once again to proceed through the declining side of the cycle, the slow slide from summer into winter.

In most areas, branches will soon be bare, or at the very least, plants and flowers enter into their winter hibernation. Nature's in-gathering begins; the earth retreats.

In the parish, programs are starting up again. New ones commence, familiar ones come around again, and revised ones reemerge with new purpose. There is going to be plenty to do, and plenty to be part of. This shift into high gear has an implication for those charged with keeping the environment for worship that you may not have thought of. Take a look at your entryways and vestibules. If you have bulletin boards and book racks advertising parish programs and events, see to it that they are positioned well, still sturdy and good-looking, and kept neat and tidy. These things become part of the worship environment, and beyond the entrance to the church itself, are a kind of first impression of the place. Make a good one with attractive and organized bulletin boards and racks.

Further inside the church, the changing of the season virtually demands a change of scenery in the worship environment—the lush greenery of summer will quickly feel passé. Try to make the shift from late summer to early autumn gradual but noticeable, and keep building the autumn environment so that the transition to November and its unique setting is obvious, yet seamless. The interaction of the scriptures with the seasons and the cultural calendar suggests the subtle transitions that can build one upon another into autumn's fullness.

The splendid array of what nature gives forth at this time of year easily lends its beauty to the place for worship. Take a comprehensive approach to the church's decor: not just the chancel but the whole interior as well as the outside deserve good attention and adornment. Let the natural progression in your area guide you in deciding what to use, how much, and for how long.

What makes decorating for autumn easy is that the season overflows with natural images well suited to liturgical decoration. Sheaves of corn, vines, gourds, pumpkins, leaves, and grains, placed appropriately, can look quite stunning. The clay and glass vessels you've been using might be placed into woven baskets. Cornucopia can be used in a variety of places and in a variety of ways.

As we add "stuff" to decorate for this season, keep in mind the principle that any decoration in the space for worship must be positioned well: It can never impede the assembly's movement to, from, or around the altar, font, or pulpit. A second principle to be mindful of is that decorations must be in scale with their surroundings and draw attention not to themselves but to that which they surround and accentuate. A shock or two of corn by the altar may look good—and is appropriate liturgically—but be sure to ask yourself whether the assembly is drawn to the corn itself or whether it leads them to a focus on the altar. You may find that you need to adjust how much you're using, or where exactly it is situated and how.

Eschatological images are quite appropriate for this time of year when the growing darkness can make the end of days seem closer and more real. It is tempting to shy away from these images; they can be harsh and threatening. But they can also be quite beautiful, and if done well will help us face our annual encounter with darkness boldly and faithfully. Because most eschatological images are metaphorical, banners provide a good means of visualizing the images: the Lamb with the scroll with seven seals, the tree of life, the heavenly Jerusalem, the morning star, and so on.

Putting together an arrangement of harvest plenty is easy. Gather up a nice variety of seasonal bounty:

287

apples, squash, pumpkins, gourds, and sweet potatoes can be grouped with bundles of grains and herbs, and you might add a few red, orange, or amber colored votives too. Be sure to put it all on a surface that won't be damaged if by some chance something begins to rot; it can permanently discolor marble, for instance. Put some plastic underneath the display (well-hidden, of course).

Other decorations around the space for the assembly might include corn shocks, baskets of flowers,

dried grasses, and bundles of grain. Sunflowers and asters are in season in the fall, as are marigolds and chrysanthemums.

It is possible to store some of these autumnal materials from year to year, but it must be done carefully. Indian corn lasts for several years, but most gourds do not. Whatever you store, make sure you put it in a ventilated container and that you store containers in a place where the air circulation is good and mildew does not pose a threat.

Preaching *with the* Season

In our cultural, social, and economic context,

autumn is the beginning of a significant part of the year. It is time

288

to return to "regular" schedules. In many places,

as the days shorten, it marks significant climatic change. As a new school year begins, it is clear that one more year has gone by as the relationships between children and parents undergo significant transitions. People return, fall programs begin, and the attendance in many congregations rebounds from summer doldrums. Congregational life gears up for significant education, music, and social activities.

And yet, even in the changing context, the preacher's calling is the same as it has been all summer. We are called to proclaim the word that has been given! Situated, even anchored, in our contexts we are called out to speak and proclaim this word that points to and enacts the grace that God gives to the creation. The word assigned in this season of "ordinary days," these Sundays after Pentecost, probes and disturbs, challenges and calls us out to see and hear, to be and to do. Follow me! Go! Serve! These words shape and pattern and authorize our living and doing in these autumn days.

The preacher is wise to taste and chew on this word in preparing for the weekly gathering around word and sacrament. For our lives are also caught up in the autumn days. Like those whom we serve, our relationships are enriched and stretched and broken in these days. We too enter into the shadowed places with those whom we love.

The word before us would overturn and heal our lives as well as the lives of those whom we serve.

It is a time to read again the whole Gospel according to St. Mark. Sit down and take the time to let Mark give witness to you of this event of Jesus the beloved Son of God, in whom God has torn open the heavens and come down. The brevity of Mark in comparison to the other gospels sometimes leads preachers to assume a gospel that is less complex or easier to digest than the other three. However, the readings for autumn reveal the word with such density that we might be tempted to pass over or mute its intrusion into our imaginations and our daily living. Let us remember that St. Mark is preaching to us. He seeks to convert us and bring us the new life.

The word comes to turn around our vision and our hearing. In these days the pattern and shape of what it means to follow this Jesus is revealed. We are called to faithfulness in our most intimate relationships; to prodigal sharing of our possessions; to the rearrangement of our political, economic, and social relations; and to the willingness to give away our whole lives for the sake of others. We live in the tension of this word's welcoming embrace of grace and forgiveness and its call that shatters the shallow comforts and illusions of our culture.

This word calls us to remember and to imagine. The call before us is to both receive and to go out and serve. We are not alone in this journey. The Spirit makes us one with all who have gone before us and with those now gathered with us. We preach amidst the signs of welcome and call. Here is font and table, pulpit and the gathered congregation. All announce God's welcome and the call to mission. All signal God's yes and God's no. The autumn texts work in this context to push and prod our congregational and communal lives. We all are addressed by this word and our gatherings are blessed by the promise of the Holy Spirit who comes to open our hearts and minds.

Just as the Spirit came down through the torn heavens at the baptism of Jesus, so now our God would tear open our imaginations to see a new thing! As we participate in Sunday school and confirmation, committee meetings and Bible studies, stewardship programs and the personal crises in the lives of those whom we serve let us be assured that God is active in bringing forth a new thing. We are not left to do the same old thing each fall but rather to see and participate in the new future that is promised. Let us pray that our preaching would help the baptized and those gathering at the table in their journey. May all of us dare to lean into the future that God is bringing.

Shape *of* Worship *for the* Season

289

BASIC SHAPE OF THE EUCHARISTIC RITE

- Confession and Forgiveness: see alternate worship text for autumn in *Sundays and Seasons* as an option to the text in the liturgy setting

GATHERING

- Greeting: see alternate worship text for autumn
- Omit the Kyrie during autumn (except, perhaps, for festivals)
- Omit or use the hymn of praise during autumn (use "Glory to God" or hymn equivalent for Reformation Day; also consider using "This is the feast of victory" for the festivals of the Holy Cross on September 14 and St. Matthew on September 21)

WORD

- Nicene Creed for Holy Cross, St. Matthew, and for Reformation celebration; Apostles' Creed for remaining Sundays in this season
- The prayers: see the prayers in the autumn section of *Sundays and Seasons*

MEAL

- Offertory prayer: see alternate text for autumn
- Use the proper preface for Sundays after Pentecost
- Eucharistic prayer: in addition to four main options

in *LBW*, see "Eucharistic Prayer H: Autumn" in *WOV* Leaders Edition, p. 72
- Invitation to communion: see alternate worship text for autumn
- Post-communion prayer: see alternate worship text for autumn

SENDING

- Benediction: see alternate worship text for autumn
- Dismissal: see alternate worship text for autumn

OTHER SEASONAL POSSIBILITIES

- Blessing of Teachers and Students (see seasonal rites section)
- See Recognition of Ministries in the Congregation in *Occasional Services*, pp. 143–46

DISTRIBUTION OF BIBLES

- If Bibles are publicly distributed to young readers, consider having their parents or sponsors involved in physically handing over the Bibles (as a follow-up to promises made at baptism)

HARVEST FESTIVAL OR HARVEST HOME

- Many congregations celebrate the harvest sometime each fall. Readings are appointed for the occasion of harvest in *LBW*, p. 39.

REFORMATION DAY

- Consider using the lectionary readings for proper 25 on October 26, but using the prayers of the day for both proper 25 and Reformation Day. Although much of the music and the prayers could reflect the lectionary for proper 25, one or more of the hymns could be chosen to reflect the Reformation festival. The color for the day could also be red.

SERVICE OF THE WORD FOR HEALING

- See the seasonal rites section for this order, which may be used on or near the festival of St. Luke, Evangelist (October 18).

Assembly Song *for the* Season

Three festivals occur in this autumn season,

two at the beginning (Holy Cross Day and St. Matthew,

Apostle and Evangelist) and the other at the end

(Reformation Day). In between, the gospel readings present some of Jesus' central teachings in Mark. These days and readings, if given their proper attention, keep the assembly focused on the central thing. They invite us to ask two important questions: What does our music teach/proclaim? Does our music convey the fullness of the gospel?

GATHERING

- How many settings should an assembly know and use? How frequently should the settings be alternated? Answers to these questions vary from place to place, but all assemblies need to know some music "by heart." Worshipers need a body of music they love and know so well that they can sing it with their eyes up or while walking to communion, without looking at book or worship folder. Using a single setting all the way from September through Christ the King Sunday helps an assembly to know it by heart and serves to unify the season(s). The changes made along the way (using or omitting the Kyrie, changing from "Glory to God" to "This is the feast," singing the "Holy, holy, holy Lord" strongly but simply or adorning it with instruments and choir, etc.) can help in the flow of the season and draw attention to the festival days.

WORD

- A time-honored way of singing the psalms is to use metrical paraphrases (hymn versions). Such paraphrases are found in almost all hymnbooks. For Proper 18 (Psalm 146), use "Praise the Almighty" (LBW 539). For Proper 24 (Psalm 91), use "You who dwell in the shelter of the Lord" (WOV 779). Find other such paraphrases in the scriptural index of each hymnbook. A useful tool for *LBW* and *WOV* is *Indexes for Worship Planning* (Augsburg Fortress). Another useful resource is *A New Metrical Psalter* (Christopher Webber, published by The Church Pension Fund). It contains paraphrases of almost the entire book of Psalms, plus some canticles, reprintable in service folders without charge.

MEAL

- "Let the vineyards be fruitful" is a suitable offertory song for this season of harvest. A hymn that uses the harvest as its starting point is "For the fruit of all creation" (WOV 760).
- Other stewardship hymns emphasize different aspects of the offertory. Use "Come to us, creative Spirit" (WOV 758) with its language of time and talents to balance out the usual stewardship talk of money. "Accept, O Lord, the gifts we bring" (WOV

759), and "We place upon your table, Lord" (LBW 217) connect the offertory directly to the gifts of bread and wine.

- Sing "Lamb of God" at the beginning of distribution throughout the season, as part of keeping the central focus on the cross and Christ's sacrifice.

SENDING

- Carry the processional cross to the church door on Holy Cross Day while singing a strong hymn such

as "Sing, my tongue" (LBW 118) or "Lift high the cross" (LBW 377).

- On other days, keep the sending simple by using only the post-communion canticle or a hymn while the table is cleared. "On our way rejoicing" (LBW 260), "Praise the Lord, rise up rejoicing" (LBW 196), and "Shout for joy loud and long" (WOV 793) are seasonal possibilities. All make reference to the cross of Christ, sending the assembly into the world with the central things ringing in their ears.

Music *for the* Season

VERSE AND OFFERTORY

Busarow, Donald. *Verses and Offertories (Pentecost 21–Christ the King).* AFP 0800648986.

Verses and Offertory Sentences, Part VII (Pentecost 19–Christ the King). CPH 97-5507.

CHORAL

Hampton, Keith. "My God Is an Awesome God." SATB, pno. AFP 0800659171.

Hassell, Michael. "Jesus Loves Me." SATB, pno, sop/alto sax. AFP 08006 56512.

Hassler, Hans Leo. "We Give Thanks unto Thee." SATB. CPH 98-3378.

Leaf, Robert. "Day by Day." SATB, kybd. AFP 0800649516.

Mozart, W. A. "Jubilate Deo." SATB, kybd. CPH 98-3191.

Parker, Alice. "To God, in Whom I Trust." SATB. GIA G-5085.

Praetorius, Michael/arr. Douglas E. Wagner. "We Will Praise You." 2/3 pt, kybd. CG CGA-350.

Purcell, Henry/arr. Hal H. Hopson. "Sound the Trumpet." 2 pt mxd, kybd. CFI CM8056.

Schütz, Heinrich. "Sing Praise to Our Glorious Lord." SATB. AFP 0800673646.

Sjolund, Paul. "Children of the Heavenly Father" in *The Augsburg Choirbook.* SATB, org. AFP 0800656784.

Vaughan Williams, Ralph. "At the Name of Jesus." SATB. OXF 40-100.

White, David Ashley. "O Bread of Life from Heaven" in *The Augsburg Choirbook.* 2 pt mxd, org. AFP 0800656784.

CHILDREN'S CHOIRS

Bedford, Michael. "Come Worship God This Holy Day." U, kybd, opt fl, tamb. CG CGA816.

Christopherson, Dorothy. "O Praise the Lord, Hallelujah" U/2 pt, various inst, pno 4 hands. AFP 0800654307.

Kemp, Helen. "Look Around!" U/2 pt, pno, cong. CG CGA823.

KEYBOARD/INSTRUMENTAL

Bitgood, Roberta. *Rejoice, Give Thanks.* Org, brass. HOP 333.

Burkhardt, Michael. *American Folk Hymn Suite for Organ* (Foundation, At the River and Nettleton). Org. MSM 10-835.

Held, Wilbur. *Hymn Preludes for the Autumn Festivals.* Org. CPH 97-5360.

Porter, Emily Maxson. *Five Hymn Preludes for Fall* (Dix, Kirken, Lasst uns erfreuen, Lobe den Herren, Nun danket all). Org. MSM 10-713.

HANDBELL

Cota, Sanders. "O For a Thousand Tongues." 3–5 oct. AG 2114.

Dobrinski, Cynthia. "Trust in Jesus, the Solid Rock." 3–5 oct. AG 2111.

Lamb, Linda. "Higher Ground/He Lifted Me." 2–3 oct. JEF RW8118.

Sherman, Arnold. "Fantasy No. 2 in C Minor." 3–5 oct. AG 1981.

Tucker, Sondra. "Give Me Jesus." 3 oct, L2. AMSI HB-30.

Wagner, Douglas E. "Rondo in C." 3–4 oct, L3. LAK HB 005.

PRAISE ENSEMBLE

Hampton, Keith. "Praise His Holy Name." SATB, kybd. Earthsongs.

Johnson, Ralph. "Praise the Lord (A Processional Song)." SATB, perc. Earthsongs.

Alternate Worship Texts

CONFESSION AND FORGIVENESS

In the name of the Father, and of the ✛ Son,
and of the Holy Spirit.
Amen

Calling to mind the frailty of our human condition,
let us confess our sin to God.

Silence for reflection and self-examination.

Good and loving God,
you made your abundant creation
for the use and enjoyment of all people.
We confess that we hold
the things you give us too closely,
and do not share freely with all in need.
Forgive our selfishness,
and help us to receive your gracious word
and to practice generosity in our daily lives. Amen

God calls us to seek good
and to turn away from evil.
To those who believe in Jesus Christ,
God grants forgiveness of sin,
strength in weakness,
and the promise of eternal salvation.
Amen

GREETING

The rich presence of God,
the beginning and end of all that is good,
be with you now and always.
And also with you.

PRAYERS

As we await the full harvest of the Spirit,
let us offer our prayers to God
who is abundant in every good gift.

A brief silence.

Each petition ends:
Hear us, O God;
your mercy is great.

Concluding petition:
Teach us to pray, O God, and grant us wisdom in our asking,
in the name of Jesus Christ our Lord.
Amen

OFFERTORY PRAYER

Kind and gracious God,
by Christ's death on the cross
you gave new life to us.
Receive these gifts as signs of our love for you,
that we might give thanks for the fullness of your salvation
in Jesus Christ our Lord. Amen

INVITATION TO COMMUNION

Let all who seek the gifts of Christ
receive the bounty of this meal.

POST-COMMUNION PRAYER

Gracious God,
through the gift of this meal
you heal our brokenness
and strengthen our spirits.
Increase our faith in you,
that the power of this holy sacrament
might bring us to new life
in Jesus Christ our Lord.
Amen

BLESSING

May the gracious gifts of the Lord God be upon you,
and increase the work of your hands.
Almighty God, Father, ✛ Son, and Holy Spirit,
bless you now and forever.
Amen

DISMISSAL

Go in peace.
Welcome others as Christ has welcomed you.
Thanks be to God.

292

Seasonal Rites

Blessing of Teachers and Students

HYMN
Earth and all stars!   LBW 558

If used on a Sunday morning the following prayer may be used during or following the prayers.

Let us pray for all who are beginning a new school year, that both students and teachers will be blessed in their academic endeavors.

Almighty God, you give wisdom and knowledge. Grant teachers the gift of joy and insight, and students the gift of diligence and openness, that all may grow in what is good and honest and true. Support all who teach and all who learn, that together we may know and follow your ways; through Jesus Christ our Lord. Amen

Service of the Word for Healing

This service may be celebrated at any time. It may be especially appropriate on or near the festival of St. Luke, Evangelist (October 18), who was a physician.

HYMN
O Christ, the healer, we have come   LBW 360
Word of God, come down on earth   WOV 716
Heal me, O Lord   TFF 189

GREETING AND WELCOME
The grace of our Lord Jesus Christ, the love of God, and the communion of the Holy Spirit be with you all.
And also with you.

We gather to hear the word of God, pray for those in need, and ask God's blessing on those who seek healing and wholeness through Christ our Lord.

PRAYER OF THE DAY

The proper prayer of the day may be used, or the prayer for St. Luke (October 18), LBW p. 35, or the following:

Great God, our healer, by your power the Lord Jesus healed the sick and gave hope to the hopeless. As we gather in his name, look upon us with mercy, and bless us with your healing Spirit. Bring us comfort in the midst of pain, strength to transform our

weakness, and light to illuminate our darkness. We ask this in the name of Jesus Christ, our crucified and risen Lord, who lives and reigns with you and the Holy Spirit, one God, now and forever. Amen

READINGS

These readings, the readings listed for St. Luke, Evangelist (LBW p. 35), or the readings listed on pp. 96–97 of Occasional Services may be used.

Isaiah 61:1-3a
Psalm 23
The Lord is my shepherd; I shall not be in want. (Ps. 23:1)
Luke 17:11-19

SERMON

HYMN
Lord, whose love in humble service   LBW 423
Healer of our every ill   WOV 738
Bless the Lord, O my soul   WOV 798
Come, ye disconsolate   TFF 186

THE PRAYERS

This litany or the prayers in Occasional Services (pp. 91–93) may be used.

God the Father, you desire the health and salvation of all people.
We praise you and thank you, O Lord.
God the Son, you came that we might have life
and might have it more abundantly.
We praise you and thank you, O Lord.
God the Holy Spirit,
you make our bodies the temples of your presence.
We praise you and thank you, O Lord.
Holy Trinity, one God,
in you we live and move and have our being.
We praise you and thank you, O Lord.
Lord, grant your healing grace to all who are sick, injured, or disabled, that they may be made whole;
hear us, O Lord of life.
Grant to all who are lonely, anxious, or despondent the awareness of your presence;
hear us, O Lord of life.
Mend broken relationships,
and restore those in emotional distress
to soundness of mind and serenity of spirit;
hear us, O Lord of life.

293

Bless physicians, nurses, and all others who minister
to the suffering; grant them wisdom and skill,
sympathy and patience;
hear us, O Lord of life.
Grant to the dying a peaceful, holy death,
and with your grace strengthen those who mourn;
hear us, O Lord of life.
Restore to wholeness whatever is broken in our lives,
in this nation, and in the world;
hear us, O Lord of life.
Turn your ear to us, O God:
heal us, and make us whole.

Gracious God, in baptism you anointed us with the oil of salvation, and joined us to the death and resurrection of your Son. Bless all who seek your healing presence in their lives. In their suffering draw them more deeply into the mystery of your love, that following Christ in the way of the cross, they may know the power of his resurrection; who lives and reigns with you and the Holy Spirit, one God, now and forever.
Amen

LAYING ON OF HANDS AND ANOINTING

Those who wish to receive the laying on of hands (and anointing) come to the altar and, if possible, kneel. The minister lays both hands on each person's head in silence, after which he or she may dip a thumb in the oil and make the sign of the cross on the person's forehead, saying:

(Through this holy anointing) may God's love and mercy uphold you by the grace and power of the Holy Spirit.
Amen

During the anointing, the assembly may sing various hymns and songs, instrumental music may be played, or a simple interval of silence may be observed.

294

PRAYER

After all have returned to their places, the minister may say:

As you are anointed with this oil, may God bless you with the healing power of the Holy Spirit. May God forgive you your sins, release you from suffering, and restore you to wholeness and strength. May God deliver you from all evil, preserve you in all goodness, and bring you to everlasting life, through Jesus Christ our Lord. Amen

THE LORD'S PRAYER

BLESSING AND DISMISSAL

HYMN
Abide with us, our Savior   LBW 263
Go, my children, with my blessing   WOV 721, TFF 161
There is a balm in Gilead   WOV 737, TFF 185

September 7, 2003

Thirteenth Sunday after Pentecost
Proper 18

INTRODUCTION

In today's gospel Jesus heals a deaf and mute man using the word *ephphatha*, which means "be opened." The author of James exhorts the community of faith to guard against favoritism among its members. In baptism we died to any distinctions that would separate us from each other. Likewise, in the eucharist each one receives the free gift of Christ equally and without discrimination. Through word and sacrament God opens our minds and hearts to the healing and liberating gospel of Christ.

PRAYER OF THE DAY

Almighty and eternal God, you know our problems and our weaknesses better than we ourselves. In your love and by your power help us in our confusion and, in spite of our weakness, make us firm in faith; through your Son, Jesus Christ our Lord.

VERSE

Alleluia. Rejoice in the Lord always; again I will say, Rejoice. Alleluia. (Phil. 4:4)

READINGS

Isaiah 35:4-7a

These verses arise as a word of hope to the exiles in Babylon. Chapter 34 portrays God's vengeance on Edom, Israel's age-old enemy, which makes the path from Babylon to Zion safe for the exiles' return. This chapter concludes with a description of the highway home, the holy way of God's people, blossoming with God's glory.

Psalm 146

I will praise the LORD as long as I live. (Ps. 146:1)

James 2:1-10 [11-13] 14-17

The epistle of James is written to Christians who may have misunderstood the teaching that salvation comes by faith rather than by doing good works. James insists that true faith shows itself in action.

Mark 7:24-37

In Mark's gospel, encounters with women usually signify turning points in Jesus' ministry. Here, a conversation with a Syrophoenician woman marks the beginning of his mission to the Gentiles.

SEMICONTINUOUS FIRST READING/PSALM

Proverbs 22:1-2, 8-9, 22-23

This section of material from Proverbs deals with the binary sets of rich and poor, wealth and poverty. The wisdom imparted from these particular verses is that those who are blessed by God will honor the poor, for they are within God's special care.

Psalm 125

Those who trust in the LORD stand fast forever. (Ps. 125:1)

COLOR Green

THE PRAYERS

As we await the full harvest of the Spirit, let us offer our prayers to God who is abundant in every good gift.
A BRIEF SILENCE.

Let us pray that all people be welcomed without reserve to the community of faith gathered around word and sacrament. Hear us, O God;
your mercy is great.

Let us pray that God's inclusive love might be the standard by which the needs of all people are addressed. Hear us, O God;
your mercy is great.

Let us pray that all who labor might receive a fair wage, and that those who are unemployed or underemployed might soon find fulfilling work. Hear us, O God;
your mercy is great.

Let us pray that those who plan and prepare for the start of fall ministries in our congregation might be encouraged and strengthened in their efforts. Hear us, O God;
your mercy is great.

Let us pray that those suffering from any sickness or adversity *(especially)* would find comfort and healing. Hear us, O God;
your mercy is great.

HERE OTHER INTERCESSIONS MAY BE OFFERED.

295

Let us pray that we may be kept in communion with those who have died and who now rest from their labors in your own eternal peace *(especially)*. Hear us, O God; **your mercy is great.**

Teach us to pray, O God, and grant us wisdom in our asking, in the name of Jesus Christ our Lord. **Amen**

IMAGES FOR PREACHING

Miracle stories are problematic. For many of us they are too primitive, too raw, even too unclean. They tread in arenas or dimensions of life that are outside of our control and powers of explanation. Miracle stories deal with events that violate our systems of thought and the way we understand the world. We are cautious with these stories, because they are not easily pressed into our categories of explanation or thought.

When preaching upon such text we must take care that the first move we make is not to move on—either explaining them away or moving too quickly into symbolic meanings. First let us encounter these outsiders pounding at the door and heart of God; first let us encounter fingers in ears, bodily fluids, and a strange word from an ancient tongue spoken in a groan that bridges the distance between heaven and earth.

Today we hear a mother's plea and the begging by a blind man's acquaintances. Sitting in hospital or hospice rooms we know of these prayers and have uttered them ourselves. These stories honor and affirm our human cries for the new and unexpected. These stories situate hearers in familiar places where futures are bound and determined by the "way things happen." These stories then break open imaginations and lives that are closed in by "reality" and offer us a God who comes near to touch and heal, to save and embrace.

Ephphatha! With this word and this touch, this miracle story opens us up to move into textures and layers of meaning that are beyond the event itself. As we move deeper into Jesus' story in the coming weeks, we shall encounter disciples and religious leaders and crowds struggling with spiritual hearing and sight. As we begin fall schedules and programs, this word seeks to enact miracles that would open up congregations and the baptized of God to the future promised by this Jesus. *Ephphatha!* Be opened. Open to God, to one another, to strangers, neighbors, and enemies. Open to the orphan and the

296

widow, to the Syrophoenicians and people of the Decapolis in our midst—the "those people" we have excluded for so long.

WORSHIP MATTERS

Healings by Jesus and consideration for the poor or those in need invite us to think about something as basic as physical arrangements for worship. If we sit in fixed pews, do those who come first sit on the aisles and make people less than welcome by the physical barrier of their bodies? Is the congregation even aware of its seating configuration with the empty seats in the middle of such barriers?

How are the physically disabled communed? Could they be accommodated smoothly as part of a regular table just as easily as being singled out to be served first or last? Do people unable to hear well have to ask only a special person for hearing devices, or do ushers quietly provide them without fanfare? Are large print materials provided and people encouraged to sit with them where the light is best? As Jesus gives preference to the poor and those with disabilities, the worshiping community can make certain that their participation is valued at least equally to others.

LET THE CHILDREN COME

The texts for the day are rich with images and actions: growing, praising, opening our eyes, reaching out, and healing. Children can do all of these things. On this Sunday, as people begin to return from summer vacations, ready to begin fall programs in the church, allow children to help welcome them back. Let them greet along with adults. Perhaps they could hand out a small "welcome back" gift to each person as they arrive or an invitation asking all ages to come and grow in God's word. It is often hard to resist a child's bright eyes and smile!

HYMNS FOR WORSHIP
GATHERING

Oh, for a thousand tongues to sing   LBW 559
O God beyond all praising   WOV 797

HYMN OF THE DAY

Word of God, come down on earth   WOV 716

ALTERNATE HYMN OF THE DAY

How sweet the name of Jesus sounds   LBW 345

Sing unto the Lord   DH 47

COMMUNION

Draw near and take the body of the Lord   LBW 226

Healer of our every ill   WOV 738

Here is bread   W&P 58

SENDING

On our way rejoicing   LBW 260

We all are one in mission   WOV 755

The blood that Jesus shed for me   TFF 201

ADDITIONAL HYMNS AND SONGS

Someone in need of your love   DH 94

O love that casts out fear   H82 700

O Lord, open my eyes   TFF 134

He who began a good work in you   W&P 56

MUSIC FOR THE DAY
PSALMODY

Comer, Marilyn.   PW B.

Cooney, Rory and Gary Daigle. "Praise the Lord, My Soul" in PCY 4.

Dobry, Wallace. "A Trio of Psalms." U/2pt, cong, kybd.
MSM 80-706.

Haugen, Marty. "Lord, Come and Save Us" in PCY 2.

Oh, praise the Lord, my soul   LBW 538

Praise the Almighty   LBW 539

Stewart, Roy James. "Praise the Lord" in PCY 5.

Wellicome, Paul. "Maranatha, Alleluia!" in PS 2.

CHORAL

Brahms, Johannes. "Let Grief Not Overwhelm You" in *Chantry Choirbook*. SATB, org.   AFP 0800657772.

Ferguson, John. "God Is Here." SATB, org, brass.   HOP DFW 214.
Inst pt.   DFW 214B.

Fleming, Larry L. "Azmon" in *Embellishments for Choir*. SATB.
AFP 080065529X.

Haugen, Marty. "Healer of Our Every Ill." 2 pt, C inst, pno.
GIA G-3478.

Kallman, Daniel. "What a Friend We Have in Jesus." SATB, pno.
MSM 50-9065.

Scott, K. Lee. "Gracious Spirit, Dwell with Me" in *The Augsburg Choirbook*. 2 pt mxd, org.   AFP 0800656784.

Zimmermann, Heinz W. "Those Who Trust in the Lord." SATB.
CPH 98-2178.

CHILDREN'S CHOIRS

Collins, Dori Erwin. "God Will Always Be with Me." U, kybd, opt fl.
AFP 0800675193.

Kerrick, Mary Ellen. "It Is Good to Sing Praise." 2 pt, kybd.
CG CGA829.

Wold, Wayne L. "Build New Bridges." U/2 pt, kybd.
AFP 0800657438.

KEYBOARD/INSTRUMENTAL

Albrecht, Timothy. "St. Peter" in *Grace Notes, vol. 8*. Org.
AFP 0800657233.

Cherwien, David. "Azmon" in *Groundings: Five New Organ Settings*. Org.
AFP 0800659805.

Frahn, Frederick. "Liebster Jesu, wir sind hier" in *Augsburg Organ Library: Epiphany*. Org.   AFP 0800659341.

Johnson, David N. "Trumpet Tune in D Major" and other keys in *Trumpet Tunes for Organ*. Org.   AFP 0800645499.

Keesecker, Thomas. "Lullaby on 'Kuortane' " in *Come Away to the Skies*.
Pno.   AFP 0800656555.

Oliver, Curt. "Liebster Jesu, wir sind hier" in *Built on a Rock*. Pno.
AFP 080065496X.

Smith, Mark Brampton. "Azmon" (Partita). Org.   MSM 10-718.

HANDBELL

Frier, Louise. "Hyfrydol." Bell tree, 6-in-hand, kybd, hc, 3 oct.
JEF PS BP05.

Maggs, Charles. "Lord Jesus, I Love Thee." Qrt.   JEF CA CP6027.

Moklebust, Cathy. "Azmon" in *Hymn Stanzas for Handbells*.
2–3 oct.   AFP 0800657330.   4–5 oct.   AFP 0800655761.

PRAISE ENSEMBLE

Baloche, Paul. "Open the Eyes of My Heart" in *First Love Songbook*.
3 pt, kybd, gtr. INT.

Founds, Rick/arr. Rhodes. "Lord, I Lift Your Name on High."
SATB, kybd.   WRD 301 0805 1660.

297

Tuesday, September 9

PETER CLAVER, PRIEST, MISSIONARY TO COLOMBIA, 1654

Peter Claver was born into Spanish nobility and was persuaded to become a Jesuit missionary. He served in Cartagena (in what is now Colombia) by teaching and caring for the slaves. The slaves arrived in ships where they had been confined in dehumanizing conditions. Claver met and supplied them with medicine, food, clothing, and brandy. He learned their dialects and taught them Christianity. He called himself "the slave of the slaves forever." Claver also ministered to the locals of Cartagena who were in prison and facing death.

Claver's advocacy on behalf of the rights of slaves is a witness to a gospel that is for all people. Pray for contemporary ministries and for persons who offer care and compassion to people living in substandard living conditions.

Saturday, September 13

JOHN CHRYSOSTOM, BISHOP OF CONSTANTINOPLE, 407

John was a priest in Antioch and an outstanding preacher. His eloquence earned him the nickname "Chrysostom" (golden mouth) but it also got him into trouble. As bishop of Constantinople he preached against corruption among the royal court. The empress, who had been his supporter, sent him into exile. His preaching style emphasized the literal meaning of scripture and its practical application. This interpretation stood in contrast to the common style at the time, which emphasized the allegorical meaning of the text.

Chrysostom's skill in the pulpit resulted in the description of him as the patron of preachers. This week at gatherings of parish groups include prayers for pastors and all who proclaim the gospel through preaching.

298

September 14, 2003

Holy Cross Day

INTRODUCTION

The festival of the Holy Cross began in Jerusalem in the early fourth century when a church was built over the place of the crucifixion. The forty-day period between August 6 (Transfiguration) and September 14 became a special season to honor the central symbol of the Christian faith. This day turns the church toward the crucified Lord who became one with the poor, the outcast, the little ones of this world. Marked by the holy cross in baptism, throughout our lives we acclaim the cross as the sign of the world's salvation.

PRAYER OF THE DAY

Almighty God, your Son Jesus Christ was lifted high upon the cross so that he might draw the whole world to himself. Grant that we who glory in his death for our salvation may also glory in his call to take up our cross and follow him; through your Son, Jesus Christ our Lord, who lives and reigns with you and the Holy Spirit, one God, now and forever.

VERSE

Alleluia. May I never boast of anything except the cross of our Lord Jesus Christ. Alleluia. (Gal. 6:14)

READINGS

Numbers 21:4b-9

This story is one of many describing the journey of the Israelites from Mount Sinai to Moab. The symbol of the snake, common in Canaan at this time, becomes a sign of God's judgment and healing.

Psalm 98:1-5 (Psalm 98:1-4 [NRSV])

The LORD has done marvelous things. (Ps. 98:1)

or Psalm 78:1-2, 34-38

God was their rock and the Most High God their redeemer. (Ps. 78:35)

1 Corinthians 1:18-24

In this letter, Paul makes clear his purpose to preach Christ and the wisdom of the cross. This "wisdom" confounds common perceptions of God: Christ crucified reveals God as the One who suffers with humankind.

John 3:13-17

After explaining to Nicodemus that one must be born of water and the Spirit, Jesus speaks of being lifted up on the cross with reference to the bronze serpent lifted up by Moses in the desert. Here the Son of God is revealed as the source of healing.

COLOR Red

THE PRAYERS

As we await the full harvest of the Spirit, let us offer our prayers to God who is abundant in every good gift.

A BRIEF SILENCE.

God of our salvation, as the Son of Man was lifted up on the cross, so may we be lifted up with him, sharing in his death that we may also share in his resurrection. Hear us, O God;

your mercy is great.

We pray for the leaders of the world, that in their dealings with one another they may be gentle of speech and wise in heart. Hear us, O God;

your mercy is great.

We pray for those who bear the foolish word of the cross to the world. Encourage them in their witness, and assure them that through their work, your own power is being brought to many. Hear us, O God;

your mercy is great.

We pray for those struggling with ill health *(especially)*, that they would know your healing strength. Hear us, O God;

your mercy is great.

We pray for all who teach in this congregation, that they would be strengthened in your word, and that their efforts would be used to sustain the weary and instruct the wise. Hear us, O God;

your mercy is great.

We pray for those whose hearts are heavy with sorrow *(especially)*, that they may know the consolation of your love and the hope of heaven. Hear us, O God;

your mercy is great.

HERE OTHER INTERCESSIONS MAY BE OFFERED.

We give thanks for all the saints who, through the ages, followed in the way of the holy cross. Keep us in fellowship with them, now and to eternity. Hear us, O God;

your mercy is great.

Teach us to pray, O God, and grant us wisdom in our asking, in the name of Jesus Christ our Lord.

Amen

IMAGES FOR PREACHING

It seems an odd thing to set aside a day for the cross. Good Friday at least has a historical referent while we have long forgotten the antecedents of Holy Cross Day in the dedication of Constantine's basilica in Jerusalem in A.D. 335 on September 14. Even in that history we have the mixture of emperor and gospel—worldly power and the foolishness of God intertwined in the balance of church and state.

In a time when the church seems to be seeking user-friendly symbols, we might ask: How shall a church, a congregation, seeking to build itself up with the excitement of fall schedule, celebrate this day? How shall the preacher preach this stumbling block of foolishness? Shall we speak of the light without the shadows; can we point to the gift of life without the journey through death? Can we hear the beloved word "gave his only Son" without seeing him hanging on a cross?

Can we, rather, begin to strip away the varnish and lacquer that seems to cover such phrases as "Jesus died for me" and "for God so loved the world" so that they bring their power into the lives of our congregation and communities? Can we point to the cross and the font and table as events of this love of God—where God enters in to reconcile the whole creation?

Despite our pretty jewelry and pretty language, a focus on the cross still stings and disturbs even after all these years. It disorients and overturns settled worlds where the gravitational pull of power and wealth control the orbits of our attention and hope. We look for other symbols and signs to guide us; ever-present corporate logos signal our allegiance to the wisdom and seductions of the age. Paying attention to this holy cross will help us orient our way in this world that God loves.

WORSHIP MATTERS

This observance is a natural time to pay attention to the presence of the cross in the worship space. As the central symbol of those who follow Jesus Christ, it should, of course, have a prominent place. In the Lutheran tradition, both plain crosses and crucifixes are used, as well as the Christus Rex, or triumphant Christ reigning from the

299

cross. Processional crosses can lead the people of God into and out of worship, and also keep a consistent focus for gospel and offertory processions. Some parishes have more than one processional cross for use in festive, solemn, or ordinary times.

Be aware, though, that too many crosses in a space can detract from the focus, making the cross merely another decorative element.

LET THE CHILDREN COME

Children, as they grow, begin to realize that the symbol of the cross has a special meaning, related to what they see and hear in worship and Sunday school. On this day, encourage them to look for crosses in the sanctuary. A special activity sheet could be given to them, encouraging them to draw what they see. "Lift high the cross" (LBW 377) could be sung—children could at least sing the first four words of the refrain. Give children gold paper crosses to be raised up as they sing. Ask members of all ages to wear crosses that day, allowing children to have a full visual experience.

HYMNS FOR WORSHIP
GATHERING
Lift high the cross   LBW 377
Shout for joy loud and long   WOV 793

HYMN OF THE DAY
Sing, my tongue   LBW 118, CS 66

ALTERNATE HYMN OF THE DAY
In the cross of Christ I glory   LBW 104
Oh, sing to the Lord/Cantad al Señor   WOV 795, LLC 598

COMMUNION
When I survey the wondrous cross   LBW 382, CS 88
You satisfy the hungry heart   WOV 711

SENDING
Oh, praise the gracious power   WOV 750
By grace we have been saved   W&P 25

ADDITIONAL HYMNS AND SONGS
There in God's garden   WOV 668
For God so loved   W&P 39
Must Jesus bear the cross alone   TFF 237

MUSIC FOR THE DAY
PSALMODY
Organ, Anne Krentz.   PW C.

CHORAL
Busarow, Donald. "Lift High the Cross." 2 pt/SATB, opt tpt.
AFP 0800645898.
Ferguson, John. "Let All Mortal Flesh." SATB, hb.   AFP 0800646681.
Glover, Rob. "Embrace My Way and Cross." U, cong, org, pno.
GIA G-4594.
Scott, K. Lee. "The Glory of Christ." SATB, hb, brass.
CPH 98-2982.
Smith, Lani. "Take Up Your Cross." SATB, kybd.   LOR 1783L.

CHILDREN'S CHOIRS
Carter, John. "We Praise You, Lord!" in *Sing a New Song!* 2 pt, kybd.
HOP 1054.
Marshall, Jane, arr. "Dear Lord, Lead Me Day by Day." U, kybd, opt fl.   CG CGA637.

KEYBOARD/INSTRUMENTAL
Bernthal, John. "Crucifer" in *Lift High the Cross*. Org, tpt/inst.
AFP 0800657314.
Callahan, Charles. "Partita on 'Crucifer.'" Org.   CPH 97-6456.
Carter, John. "Picardy" in *Contemplative Folk Tunes for Piano*. Pno.
AFP 0800659775.
Cherwien, David. "Toccata on 'In the Cross of Christ I Glory'" in *Augsburg Organ Library: Lent*. Org.   AFP 0800658973.
Hyslop, Scott. "Picardy" in *Six Chorale Fantasias for Solo Instrument and Piano*. Pno, sax, cello/solo inst.   AFP 0800656601.
Mathias, William. "Processional" in *Modern Organ Music, book 1*. Org. OXF.
Organ, Anne Krentz. "Picardy" in *Reflections on Hymn Tunes for Holy Communion*. Kybd.   AFP 0800654978.
Young, Jeremy. "Picardy" in *Gathering Music for Advent*. Kybd, 2 inst.
AFP 0800656598.

HANDBELL
Anderson, Christine D./arr. Joseph M. Martin. "Soldiers of the Cross." Hb solo, pno.   AG 2102.
Dobrinski, Cynthia. "Lift High the Cross." 3–5 oct.   HOP 1491.

PRAISE ENSEMBLE
Founds, Rick/arr. Rhodes. "Lord, I Lift Your Name on High." SATB, kybd. WRD 301 0805 1660.

300

September 14, 2003

Fourteenth Sunday after Pentecost
Proper 19

INTRODUCTION

Those who confess Jesus as Messiah are called to deny themselves, take up their cross, and follow Christ. As we face the suffering of the world and the brokenness of our own lives, we learn the meaning of losing our lives for the sake of the gospel. Each time we make the sign of the cross, and share the broken bread and the cup of salvation, we remember the good news that our baptism into Christ's death is also the promise of the resurrection.

PRAYER OF THE DAY

O God, you declare your almighty power chiefly in showing mercy and pity. Grant us the fullness of your grace, that, pursuing what you have promised, we may share your heavenly glory; through your Son, Jesus Christ our Lord.

VERSE

Alleluia. Whatever was written in former days was written for our instruction, so that by steadfastness and by the encouragement of the scriptures we might have hope. Alleluia. (Rom. 15:4)

READINGS

Isaiah 50:4-9a

This reading gives good advice to sufferers: trust in God even (and especially) in the midst of pain. The servant remains faithful throughout trials, knowing that God is with and for the sufferer in the midst of pain.

Psalm 116:1-8 (Psalm 116:1-9 [NRSV])

I will walk in the presence of the LORD. (Ps. 116:8)

James 3:1-12

The author of James warns against the power of human speech and the difficulties of controlling the tongue. With our mouths we have the capacity both to bless God and to curse.

Mark 8:27-38

This story provides the turning point in the Markan gospel. Peter is the first human being in the narrative to acknowledge Jesus as the Messiah, but he cannot accept that, as the Messiah, Jesus will have to suffer. Moreover, Jesus issues a strong challenge to all by connecting discipleship and the cross.

SEMICONTINUOUS FIRST READING/PSALM

Proverbs 1:20-33

In these verses Wisdom is personified as a woman. Here wisdom is a gift of the Lord, rather than human achievement. Though Wisdom offers her hand to those who scoff at her, they have spurned all such counsel. That they come to ruin is predictable.

Psalm 19

The statutes of the LORD are just and rejoice the heart. (Ps. 19:8)

or Wisdom of Solomon 7:26—8:1

God loves nothing so much as the person who lives with wisdom. (Wis. of Sol. 7:28)

COLOR Green

THE PRAYERS

As we await the full harvest of the Spirit, let us offer our prayers to God who is abundant in every good gift.
A BRIEF SILENCE.

Let us pray that children and adults alike might be drawn to love God's word and holy supper as they are proclaimed by faithful teachers and leaders in our congregation. Hear us, O God;
your mercy is great.

Let us pray for the leaders of the world, that in their dealings with one another they may be gentle of speech and wise in heart. Hear us, O God;
your mercy is great.

Let us pray for those who have been verbally or emotionally abused, that they may be healed from the evil words that have broken their spirits. Hear us, O God;
your mercy is great.

Let us pray for those struggling with ill health (*especially*), that they would know God's healing strength. Hear us, O God;
your mercy is great.

301

Let us pray for all who teach in this congregation, that they would be strengthened in God's word, and that their efforts would be used to sustain the weary and instruct the wise. Hear us, O God;
your mercy is great.
HERE OTHER INTERCESSIONS MAY BE OFFERED.
Let us pray for those whose hearts are heavy with sorrow (*especially*), that they may know the consolation of God's love and the hope of heaven. Hear us, O God;
your mercy is great.
Teach us to pray, O God, and grant us wisdom in our asking, in the name of Jesus Christ our Lord.
Amen

IMAGES FOR PREACHING

At noon, a school principal noticed on the first day of school that a first grader was outside with his backpack on at the bus-loading zone. He went out and asked the boy why he wasn't in class. The child answered that it was time to go home. The principal told him that now that he was in first grade, he would be staying at school all day instead of a half day. The boy then exclaimed, "Who signed me up for this?!"

Upon hearing the word this day, we who have always been attracted to a "baby in a manger, meek and mild" and to a "Jesus loves me, this I know" might just also ask "Who signed me up for this?" We who bring our children to be nurtured and cared for might wonder what kind of dangerous journey we are setting them on.

This word pushes us to answer the question as to who we think this Jesus is and where he might be leading us. Is he the one who simply forgives and comforts or does he also challenge and overturn imaginations and expectations and the way we live? Where will he lead us when he calls on us to let go as well as to receive? Can we hear his command to get behind him and follow, when we seek to get out in front and slow down the procession of grace? Are we able to trust that more things remain for us to learn from him than just those things that we learned in kindergarten?

WORSHIP MATTERS

It is easy to overlook the physical signs of our reverence for God in worship. Making people feel comfortable is important, but so is making sure we say this Lord Jesus is Messiah, the Son of God, God incarnate. By our reverent motions in worship, different from those of inter-

personal interaction, we underline with our bodies this identity of Jesus.

Worship leaders—acolytes, ushers, assisting ministers—speak eloquently when they address the altar with a profound bow, handle the elements with reverence and awe, attend to the current actions of worship with their whole bodies. Consider reminding worship leaders not to move into position during prayers or readings but rather to model participation by their own attentive conduct.

LET THE CHILDREN COME

The Isaiah text for the day contains two insights that relate to children and communication. The writer speaks of words that give strength and of having ears opened. Children are remarkable with words. What renews weary hearts better than a child's simple, "I love you"? Yet we are often too busy to listen, to "open our ears." We are too much of a grown-up to realize that the words of a child are many times closer to the simple message of our God: "I love you." Listen to the voices in worship. When and how are the children heard?

HYMNS FOR WORSHIP
GATHERING
Give to our God immortal praise!　LBW 520
I, the Lord of sea and sky　WOV 752, TFF 230

HYMN OF THE DAY
O Jesus, king most wonderful　LBW 537

ALTERNATE HYMN OF THE DAY
Once he came in blessing　LBW 312
Strengthen for service, Lord　LBW 218, CS 69, HFW

COMMUNION
Come, let us eat　LBW 214, TFF 119
In the morning when I rise　WOV 777, TFF 165
Have thine own way, Lord　TFF 152

SENDING
Sent forth by God's blessing　LBW 221
What a fellowship, what a joy divine　WOV 780, TFF 220
I will sing of the mercies of the Lord　W&P 74

ADDITIONAL HYMNS AND SONGS
I call on thee, Lord Jesus Christ　H82 634

302

In you, O Lord, I put my trust   CW 448
Must Jesus bear the cross alone   TFF 237
The Summons   W&P 137

MUSIC FOR THE DAY
PSALMODY

Brown, Teresa. "The Blessing Cup" in PS 2.

Comer, Marilyn.   PW B.

Daigle, Gary and Rory Cooney. "Psalm 116: I Will Walk in the Presence of God" in GC.

Fabing, Bob. "Be Like the Sun" in *Rise Up and Sing*. U.   OCP 9391.

Glynn, John. "Lord, How Can I Repay" in PS 2.

Mahnke, Allan. *Psalms for Cantor and Congregation.*   CPH 97-6093.

Roberts, Leon C. "I Will Call upon the Name of the Lord." TFF 14.

Schalk, Carl. "Ps 116" in *Sing Out! A Children's Psalter*.   WLP 7191.

Stewart, Roy James. "I Will Walk in the Presence of God" in PCY 5.

CHORAL

Bouman, Paul. "O God of Mercy" in *To God Will I Sing*. Kybd.   MH voice.   AFP 0800674332. ML voice.   AFP 0800674340.

Collins, Dori Erwin. "Offering." SATB, pno, fl, opt hb, U.   AFP 0800659694.

Gehring, Philip. "Those Who Observe the Day." SATB.   CPH 98-3585.

Haugen, Marty. "I Will Walk in the Presence of God." 3 pt, cant, cong, gtr, 2 ww.   GIA G-4282. Inst pt.   G-4282INST.

Hobby, Robert. "Take My Life, That I May Be." SATB, fl.   MSM 50-8820.

Keesecker, Thomas. "I Am the Living Bread." SATB, kybd, opt cong, opt sop sax/C inst.   AFP 6000001436.

Mendelssohn, Felix. "On God Alone My Hope I Build" in *Chantry Choirbook*.   AFP 0800657772. SATB, kybd.

Sedio, Mark. "Once He Came in Blessing." 2 pt mxd, org, fl.   AFP 080065241X.

Smith, Lani. "Take Up Your Cross." SATB, kybd.   LOR 1783L.

Young, Ovid, arr. "Here I Am, Lord." SATB, kybd.   AFP 0800656059.

CHILDREN'S CHOIRS

Daigle, Gary and Rory Cooney. "Psalm 116: I Will Walk in the Presence of God." U.   GC.

Sleeth, Natalie. "The Kingdom of the Lord." 2 pt, kybd, fl.   AMSI 301.

KEYBOARD/INSTRUMENTAL

Albrecht, Mark. "Here I Am, Lord" in *Timeless Tunes for Piano and Solo Instrument, vol. 3*. Pno, inst.   AFP 0800675037.

Farlee, Robert Buckley. "Here I Am, Lord" in *Many and Great*. Org.   AFP 0800658949.

Howells, Herbert. "Intrada No. 2" in *Three Pieces for Organ*. Org.   NOV 01 0222.

Kohrs, Jonathan. "Here I Am, Lord" in *Four Tunes for Piano and Two Instruments*." Pno, 2 inst.   AFP 0800658787.

Leavitt, John. "Gottes Sohn ist kommen" in *Christmas Suite*. Org.   AFP 0800657217.

Mulet, Henry. "Tu es Petra" (You are the Rock). Org.   LED AL21309.

HANDBELL

McChesney, Kevin. "Jesus, Keep Me Near the Cross." 3 oct, opt hc.   JEF JHS9251.

Sherman, Arnold. "Here I Am, Lord." 3–5 oct.   AG 2140.

Vivaldi, Antonio/arr Susan T. Nelson. "Largo." 3 oct, opt inst.   AFP 0800654366.

PRAISE ENSEMBLE

Bell, John L. "The Summons." W&P 137

Weeden, Winfield. "I Surrender All." in *Praise Hymns and Choruses, 4th ed.*   MAR.

303

Sunday, September 14

HOLY CROSS DAY

See pages 298–300.

Tuesday, September 16

CYPRIAN, BISHOP OF CARTHAGE, MARTYR, C. 258

Cyprian worked for the unity of the church and cared for his flock in North Africa during a time of great persecution. During Cyprian's time as bishop many people denied the faith under duress. In contrast to some who held the belief that the church should not receive these people back, Cyprian believed they ought to be welcomed into full communion after a period of penance. Cyprian insisted on the need for compassion in order to preserve the unity of the church. His essay, *On the Unity of the Catholic Church*, stressed the role of bishops in guaranteeing the visible, concrete unity of the church. Cyprian was also concerned for the physical well-being of the people under his care. He organized a program of medical care for the sick during a severe epidemic in Carthage.

Thursday, September 18

DAG HAMMARSKJÖLD, PEACEMAKER, 1961

Dag Hammarskjöld was a Swedish diplomat and humanitarian who served as Secretary General of the United Nations. He was killed in a plane crash on this day in 1961 in what is now Zambia while on his way to negotiate a cease-fire between the United Nations and the Katanga forces. For years Hammarskjöld kept a private journal and it was not until that journal was published as *Markings* that the depth of his Christian faith was known. The book revealed that his life was a combination of diplomatic service with personal spirituality, a combination of contemplation on the meaning of Christ in his life and action in the world.

304

To commemorate Hammarskjöld, pray for the work of the United Nations and for all peacemakers. Here is an example of a person whose quiet contemplation led to visible action in the world.

Saturday, September 20

NELSON WESLEY TROUT, BISHOP, 1996

Trout was born in Columbus, Ohio, and attended the Evangelical Lutheran Theological Seminary in Columbus. Ordained in 1952, he served parishes in Montgomery, Alabama; Los Angeles, California; and Eau Claire, Wisconsin. Trout also served in staff positions with the American Lutheran Church, Lutheran Social Services of Dayton, and the Columbus seminary. In 1983 Trout was elected bishop of the South Pacific District of the American Lutheran Church, the first African American to serve in such a capacity.

September 21, 2003

St. Matthew, Apostle and Evangelist

INTRODUCTION

In the time of Jesus, tax collectors were social outcasts. Many were known for being dishonest and brutal in their collection of taxes. Jesus called Matthew to be his disciple and willingly shared a meal with this seemingly unsavory fellow. To his critics, Jesus said, I did not come to call the virtuous, but sinners. Here is the source of our hope: Jesus has no desire to condemn us, but to forgive and heal us.

PRAYER OF THE DAY

Almighty God, your Son our Savior called a despised collector of taxes to become one of his apostles. Help us, like Matthew, to respond to the transforming call of your Son, Jesus Christ our Lord, who lives and reigns with you and the Holy Spirit, one God, now and forever.

VERSE

Alleluia. You will be my witnesses in Jerusalem, in all Judea and Samaria, and to the ends of the earth. Alleluia. (Acts 1:8)

READINGS

Ezekiel 2:8—3:11

Following the call of the prophet to speak the word of God, this passage relates in vivid imagery the need to consume the word until it is fully assimilated by the prophet.

Psalm 119:33-40

Teach me, O LORD, the way of your statutes. (Ps. 119:33)

Ephesians 2:4-10

The author of this letter is eager to show God's love for sinners. God reaches into the deathly snare of sin and death in order to draw us out into life with Christ. This act is nothing less than the gift of God's mercy.

Order next year's resources now!

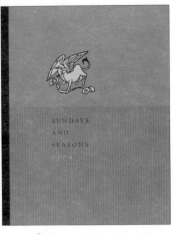

Sundays and Seasons 2004
YEAR C

Make worship planning easy with this new comprehensive resource! Based on the ecumenical lectionary and church year, this guide will provide you with the materials needed to prepare worship for Sundays and seasons of the church year. This annual guide is organized around the three major cycles: Advent, Christmas, and Epiphany; Lent, Holy Week, and Easter; and Time of the Church: Summer, Autumn, and November.

ISBN 0-8066-4543-1 $35.00
Three or more $29.00 each

Worship Planning Calendar 2004
YEAR C

Order next year's copy today! It's the perfect complement to *Sundays and Seasons*. Use this worship planning guide, daily devotional, and appointment calendar as your workbook.

ISBN 0-8066-4545-8 $20.00

Words for Worship 2004 CD-ROM YEAR C

This CD-ROM contains resources for use with the Revised Common Lectionary, Cycle C. These easy-to-use text and graphic files are organized by calendar date. Includes readings, prayers, introductions to the day, psalm refrains and tones, seasonal rites and texts, and the *LBW* Symbol font.

CD-ROM AND COPYRIGHT LICENSE ·
ISBN 0-8066-4285-8 $139.00

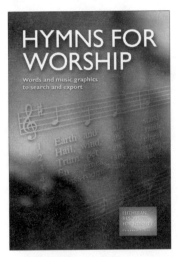

0-8066-4074-X $329.00

Hymns for Worship

Hymn graphics on CD-ROM! More than 1,200 hymns and songs from *LBW, With One Voice, This Far by Faith, Worship and Praise* and other sources make this a must have addition. A Playback feature allows you to hear the melodies you've selected and an easy to use search engine will quickly locate the hymns and songs you have in mind. Printing or downloading any hymn requiring copyright permission automatically generates the necessary information and paperwork for submission to the publisher.

Kids Celebrate
Bulletins Year C Luke

Worship Bulletins for Children Contains 60 **reproducible** children's worship bulletins, this every Sunday (plus festivals) worship bulletin is developed for lower elementary children as well. 136 pages, perfect bound and perforated.

0-8066-4549-0 $39.99

Order Form
Worship Planning Resources 2004, Year C

Just complete this order card, affix postage, and drop it in the mail.
To order by phone: 1-800-328-4648 By fax: 1-800-722-7766

Send to: _____
Address: _____
City: _____ State: _____ Zip: _____
Phone: _____

Bill to: _____
Address: _____
City: _____ State: _____ Zip: _____

Method of Payment *(check one)*
❑ Augsburg Fortress Acct # _____
❑ Credit Card # _____
Exp. Date: _____
   (Must be valid for Sept. 2003. Products ship August 2003.)
Signature: _____
   (Required on all credit card orders.)
❑ Check *(Place check and order card in envelope and mail to address on reverse. Include proper shipping charges and sales tax.)*

Qty.	Title	ISBN	Price
____	Sundays and Seasons 2004 0-8066-4543-1		$35.00
____	Worship Planning Calendar 2004 0-8066-4545-8		$20.00
____	Word for Worship CD-ROM 2004 0-8066-4544-X		$139.00
____	Hymns for Worship 2004 0-8066-4074-X		$329.00
____	Kids Celebrate Bulletins Year C Luke 0-8066-4549-0		$39.99
____	Calendar of Word and Season 2004 w/o imprint 0-8066-4546-6		$9.95
____	Church Year Calendar 2004 Year C 0-8066-4548-2		$1.95

Augsburg Fortress

Thank you for your order.
Prices valid through April 15, 2003.

Augsburg Fortress

Calendar of Word and Season 2004
YEAR C

This beautiful full-color wall calendar will keep you on track at a glance. Identifies church festivals, and U.S. and Canadian holidays. Large date blocks note Bible readings from the Revised Common Lectionary for Sundays and church festivals and identify the seasonal or festival color. Makes a great gift with custom imprinting available. Create a reference tool for each household, or staff and committee members! 10⅞ x 8⅜". Spiral bound, punched for hanging, 28 pages.
Call for details regarding custom imprinting.

ISBN 0-8066-4546-6 $9.95

Church Year Calendar 2004
YEAR C

This simple sheet is a useful tool for anyone in your church: committee members, choir members, worship planners, the altar guild, teachers, and pastors. The full-color calendar gives dates, Bible readings, hymn of the day, and liturgical color for each Sunday and festival of the church year.
Two sides 11 x 8½

ISBN 0-8066-4548-2 $1.95

Quantity pricing available! Please Call!

520850-202
Keycode: AI1005

Place Stamp Here

AUGSBURG FORTRESS PUBLISHERS
ATTN MAILING CENTER
PO BOX 59303
MINNEAPOLIS, MN 55459-0303

Matthew 9:9-13

Regarded as a traitor to his people and an oppressor of the poor, this tax collector follows Jesus and then offers him hospitality. In the sharing of a meal Jesus reveals his mission: to serve God's mercy.

COLOR Red

THE PRAYERS

As we await the full harvest of the Spirit, let us offer our prayers to God who is abundant in every good gift.
A BRIEF SILENCE.

God of grace, through your Son you called Matthew along with many sinners to share in your mercy. Welcome us sinners also, through the merits of our Savior. Hear us, O God;
your mercy is great.

God of love, you created us for good works. Fill us with a desire to reflect to the world your lovingkindness. Hear us, O God;
your mercy is great.

God of peace, conflicts and disputes are many among the nations of the world. In places of turmoil and terror, bring a harvest of righteousness and reconciliation, sown in justice and peace. Hear us, O God;
your mercy is great.

God of hope, all the woes of those in need are completely known by you. Let your compassion rest on those who are terminally ill, and on all who are sick who look for your healing *(especially)*. Hear us, O God;
your mercy is great.

God of comfort, be near to all who grieve *(especially)*. Strengthen all of us to commend our beloved dead to your eternal and loving home. Hear us, O God;
your mercy is great.
HERE OTHER INTERCESSIONS MAY BE OFFERED.

God of life, your throne is surrounded by saints who, like Matthew, were welcomed by your great love. We give thanks for their lives and witness, and ask that we may faithfully follow their example. Hear us, O God;
your mercy is great.

Teach us to pray, O God, and grant us wisdom in our asking, in the name of Jesus Christ our Lord.
Amen

IMAGES FOR PREACHING

In the midst of a simple phrase, a profound drama is enacted. "Follow me," says Jesus to Matthew sitting at the tax booth. With a phrase, Jesus overturns psychological, social, political, economic, and theological categories. So often, we think of the offense of this call to the Pharisee and other leaders of the day. However, not only are religious leaders and categories challenged by this audacious call of Jesus, but so is Matthew.

Will he follow this Jesus who has called him out? Will he leave his life behind for the new and unknown? Will he leave a life patterned with the familiar for the unsettled journey following this Jesus? Following this Jesus will overturn the patterns of relationships and status that ordered his whole life. This invitation is not simply to climb up the ladder of success as he knows it or to simply to change status positions in a familiar structure. Rather, Matthew is called to new categories of human dynamics and interactions. This call threatens him as much as it threatens the religious leaders who murmur and ask questions concerning the behavior of Jesus at dinner.

The gift and call of grace also overturn and unsettle *our* lives. It is a call to let go as well as to receive a gift that makes its home in our hearts and minds and imaginations in order to shape our living as Christ's body in the world. On this day, living in this world, where so often we are in need of examples, we give thanks that Matthew got up and followed.

WORSHIP MATTERS

The traditional symbol for Matthew is the winged man, one example out of a vocabulary of symbols accumulated by the church over the centuries. In less literate times, such visual clues helped remind worshipers of some of the central truths of the faith. Today, ironically, they may function in the opposite manner, puzzling those who see them, or just cluttering up the scene, which is not to suggest that we do as the sixteenth-century iconoclasts did, and tear down all the symbols in our churches. Especially in more traditionally styled buildings, visual symbolism adds richness to the architecture. But how can we help those who come to the church to understand the meanings of these symbols? Perhaps we could, by consulting with reference books or religious artists, produce a pamphlet explaining what the designs in our space signify. (As a starter, the symbols for Matthew and the other evangelists come from Rev. 4:6b-7.)

305

LET THE CHILDREN COME

As we celebrate Matthew on this day, it is good to remember that his name means "gift of the Lord." Notice the children in worship. How is each a gift? What talents and interests can they share to strengthen the congregation's mission? How well do we know our children? Perhaps it is time to learn more about them. Another idea would be to have "Matthew" visit, either for a children's sermon or in the classroom. His story teaches us that we are all of value, a lesson we sometimes ignore or forget when it comes to children and worship.

HYMNS FOR WORSHIP

GATHERING

"Come, follow me," the Savior spake   LBW 455

Be thou my vision   WOV 776

HYMN OF THE DAY

How blest are they who hear God's Word   LBW 227

ALTERNATE HYMN OF THE DAY

One there is, above all others   LBW 298

Praise to you, O Christ, our Savior   W&P 119, WOV 614

COMMUNION

Let us break bread together   LBW 212, TFF 123

Come, thou fount of every blessing   LBW 499, TFF 108

I received the living God   WOV 700

SENDING

Sent forth by God's blessing   LBW 221

We all are one in mission   WOV 755

ADDITIONAL HYMNS AND SONGS

For by grace   W&P 38

The Summons   W&P 137

I'd rather have Jesus   TFF 233

MUSIC FOR THE DAY

PSALMODY

Nelson, Ronald A. PW A.

Organ, Anne Krentz. PW C.

CHORAL

Batastini, Robert. "To Be Your Presence." SATB, org, opt cong, opt 1 or 2 tpt.   GIA G-5413.

Bisbee, B. Wayne. "Teach Me Your Way, O Lord." 2 pt mxd, kybd.   AFP 080065479X.

Ferguson, John. "Be Thou My Vision." SATB, org.   AFP 0800657934.

Shute, Linda Cable. "Who Are These Like Stars Appearing." SATB.   AFP 0800659678.

Sweelinck, Jan Pieterszoon. "Sing to the Lord, New Songs Be Raising" in *Chantry Choirbook.* SATB.   AFP 0800657772.

Valentine, Timothy. "Here Am I, Lord." SATB, opt cong, kybd, opt gtr.   GIA G-4813.

CHILDREN'S CHOIRS

Jothen, Michael. "We Are Children of Our God." U/2 pt, kybd, opt fl/vln, opt 3 oct hb, opt cong.   CG CGA731.

Sleeth, Natalie. "Praise the Lord" in *Sunday Songbook.* U, kybd.   HIN HMB102.

KEYBOARD/INSTRUMENTAL

Albrecht, Mark. "In This Very Room" in *Timeless Tunes for Piano and Solo Instrument, vol. 3.* Pno, inst.   AFP 0800675037.

Callahan, Charles. "Canticle." Eng hrn, org.   CPH 97-6115.

Hassell, Michael. "Machs mit mir Gott" in *Traveling Tunes.* Kybd, solo inst.   AFP 0800656199.

Hovland, Egil. "Nu La Oss Takke Gud." Org.   Norsk Musikvorlag 8822.

Johnson, David N. "St. Catherine" in *Hymn Settings for Organ.* Org.   AFP 0800674987.

Neswick, Bruce. "Partita on Winchester New." Org.   AFP 0800674995.

Wasson, Laura E. "Make Me a Channel of Your Peace" in *A Piano Tapestry, vol. 2.* Pno.   AFP 0800658183.

HANDBELL

Campbell, Rosemary Corrigan. "Litany of the Saints." Hb/kybd, cant. cong.   GIA (5-E) G5250.

Cota, Patricia. "Change My Heart." 3-5 oct.   AG 2136

PRAISE ENSEMBLE

Founds, Rick. "I Love Your Grace" in *Praise Band Songbook 3.*   MAR.

September 21, 2003

Fifteenth Sunday after Pentecost
Proper 20

INTRODUCTION

In worship we learn the reversals in the kingdom of God: greatness is not defined by wealth, power, or prestige. Rather, all people are welcomed in the name of Christ. The children in our midst are a sign of the hospitality that God offers to all persons regardless of their status in the world. We go forth from the liturgy to be servants who find greatness in humble service on behalf of those who are often forgotten or rejected in society.

PRAYER OF THE DAY

Lord God, you call us to work in your vineyard and leave no one standing idle. Set us to our tasks in the work of your kingdom, and help us to order our lives by your wisdom; through your Son, Jesus Christ our Lord.

VERSE

Alleluia. Live your life in a manner worthy of the gospel of Christ; strive side by side for the faith of the Gospel. Alleluia. (Phil. 1:27)

READINGS

Jeremiah 11:18-20

Today's reading tells of the suffering of a just man, the prophet Jeremiah, who announced God's message of impending doom only to receive opposition. The common idea of the just sufferer seems to have influenced the early Christians as they sought to understand the sufferings and death of Jesus.

or Wisdom of Solomon 1:16—2:1, 12-22

This reading from a wisdom book written shortly before Jesus' birth portrays the ungodly scheming the downfall of the righteous person. Their plot includes the shameful death of the righteous one, to see whether God will help him.

Psalm 54

God is my helper; it is the Lord who sustains my life. (Ps. 54:4)

James 3:13—4:3, 7-8a

James contrasts the wisdom from above, with all its good characteristics, with the desire to "have things," which leads to conflicts and disputes in the community. Meaning in life does not come from cravings for possessions or pleasure, which only breed competition.

Mark 9:30-37

Jesus' teaching and action in this text are directed to the church whenever it is seduced by the world's definition of greatness: prestige, power, influence, and money. The antidote to such a concern for greatness is servanthood.

SEMICONTINUOUS FIRST READING/PSALM

Proverbs 31:10-31

The good wife portrayed in these verses provides a view of someone who is equally diligent in household matters as well as those of the commercial arena. Not only does she care for the needs of her family, but she also reaches out to the poor.

Psalm 1

Their delight is in the law of the Lord. (Ps. 1:2)

COLOR Green

THE PRAYERS

As we await the full harvest of the Spirit, let us offer our prayers to God who is abundant in every good gift.
A BRIEF SILENCE.

God of love, give to your church such a spirit of servanthood that our fears would give way to childlike trust and gentle regard for all people. Hear us, O God;
your mercy is great.

God of peace, conflicts and disputes are many among the nations of the world. In places of turmoil and terror, bring a harvest of righteousness and reconciliation, sown in justice and peace. Hear us, O God;
your mercy is great.

God of hope, all the woes of those in need are completely known by you. Let your compassion rest on those who are terminally ill, and on all who are sick and look for your healing (especially). Hear us, O God;
your mercy is great.

God of grace, bless the children of our congregation and all who minister among them, that we would seek to pat-

tern our faith after their simple trust in you. Hear us, O God;
your mercy is great.

HERE OTHER INTERCESSIONS MAY BE OFFERED.

God of comfort, be near to all who grieve *(especially)*. Strengthen all of us to commend our beloved dead to your eternal and loving home. Hear us, O God;
your mercy is great.

Teach us to pray, O God, and grant us wisdom in our asking, in the name of Jesus Christ our Lord.
Amen

IMAGES FOR PREACHING

Like the blind man in Mark 8, who when first asked by Jesus what he sees, can only answer "I can see people but they look like trees walking," the vision of the disciples takes time to open (all the way to Pentecost). They just don't get it in Mark's gospel. First Peter, and now the rest of them seem to miss the point. Jesus predicts his dying and rising and instead of attending to the word, the disciples change the subject. They wonder who is the greatest among them.

Obviously, they do sense something is afoot here in this event of Jesus. They left their families and homes, after all. For them and us, though, the shadow of cross and suffering, service and welcome is confounding. Like us, their sight seems distorted. They are looking at the right place but they don't see clearly. They want to know how the social ladder will be structured in the community of Jesus. They want to know who shall be the greatest. In a world of status and net worth, they wonder who will end up on top.

Jesus takes a little child in his arms to show them. As tall as their kneecaps, limited vocabulary, unemployed, zero net worth, nobody in their world, and yet here a sign of the way God organizes community. Did the scales fall from their eyes? How about ours? However we choose to organize our lives, we have this little child in the arms of Jesus to remind us that God organizes things differently. In the topsy-turvy vision of God's imagination, we may safely ignore no one—they just might turn out to be the greatest.

WORSHIP MATTERS

Sometimes liturgical leaders, whether choirs, assisting ministers, or pastors, feel they must dictate the pace of

congregational readings. But excessive urges of leadership change the voice of the people into the murmuring of the masses prodded through their paces by the strongest voices.

Suggest that the more prominent voices in leadership treat the congregation as an instrument. For example, if the choir were singing an anthem, the choir would not race ahead of the organ and hopefully would not drag behind it. The singers take their cue from the instrument's pace as well as the direction. In congregational readings and recitations, let the pace come from the particular group worshiping that day during that service. As each listens for the voice of the entire body, the rhythm of worship reflects the care for each other. By neither rushing nor dragging, the congregational readings fall into place with great beauty and a renewed sense of unity.

LET THE CHILDREN COME

A child is held lovingly in the arms of Christ. A baby is held close in the arms of a pastor. Disciples must be taught how and why to welcome the little one. Our congregations hear the same instructions. Then, as now, we struggle with how to fulfill Jesus' words. How do we give children the importance they are due? How well do we "hold them close"? Or are they kept more at arm's length? Worship planners must continually wrestle with these questions—creatively and carefully—and develop ways to include and uplift children in worship practices.

HYMNS FOR WORSHIP
GATHERING

Glories of your name are spoken   LBW 358
God is here!   WOV 719

HYMN OF THE DAY

Lord, whose love in humble service   LBW 423

ALTERNATE HYMN OF THE DAY

Children of the heavenly Father   WOV 474
Loving Spirit   WOV 683

COMMUNION

Draw near and take the body of the Lord   LBW 226
Thy holy wings   WOV 741
Here is bread   W&P 58

SENDING

O Master, let me walk with you   LBW 492

Thine the amen, thine the praise   WOV 801

Pass me not, O gentle Savior   TFF 150

ADDITIONAL HYMNS AND SONGS

How deep the silence of the soul   NCH 509

Jesus, our mighty Lord   H82 478

Come by here, my Lord   TFF 42, 43

For God so loved   W&P 39

MUSIC FOR THE DAY

PSALMODY

Comer, Marilyn.   PW B.

Guimont, Michel. "Psalm 54: The Lord Upholds My Life" in GC.

Haas, David. "The Lord Upholds My Life" in PCY 3.

CHORAL

Fleming, Larry. "Humble Service." SATB.   AFP 0800646223.

Nelson, Ronald A. "Whoever Would Be Great Among You." SAB, gtr/kybd.   AFP 0800645804.

Scholz, Robert. "Children of the Heavenly Father." SATB.   AFP 0800659112.

Sjolund, Paul. "Children of the Heavenly Father" in *The Augsburg Choirbook.* SATB, kybd. AFP 0800656784.

Telemann, G. P. "Make Me Pure, O Sacred Spirit" in *To God Will I Sing.* Kybd, MH voice.   AFP 0800674332.
ML voice.   AFP 0800674340.

CHILDREN'S CHOIRS

Ferguson, John. "Children of the Heavenly Father." U, kybd.   AFP 0800647620.

Hruby, Dolores. "Help Us Accept Each Other." U, kybd, opt fl, opt gtr.   CG CGA713.

Scott, K. Lee. "Best of All Friends." 2 pt, pno.   MSM 50-9003.

KEYBOARD/INSTRUMENTAL

Ferguson, John. "Children of the Heavenly Father" in *Thy Holy Wings: Three Swedish Folk Hymn Preludes.* Org.   AFP 0800647955.

Mathews, Peter. "The Last Song of Summer." Org, vc.   MSM 20-960.

Miller, Aaron David. "Tryggare kan ingen vara" in *Improvisations for the Church Year.* Org.   AFP 0800674812.

Organ, Anne Krentz. "Beach Spring" in *Woven Together.* Pno, inst.   AFP 0800658167.

Various. "Beach Spring" in *Augsburg Organ Library: Lent.* Org.   AFP 0800658973.

HANDBELL

Behnke, John. "When Morning Gilds the Skies." 3–5 oct.   AFP 0800674863.

McChesney, Kevin. "Beach Spring." 2–3 oct.   AFP 080065885X.

Thompson, Martha Lynn. "Thy Holy Wings." 3–5 oct, opt hc, narr, wind chime.   JEF AP19005.

PRAISE ENSEMBLE

Bullock, Geoff/arr. Williamson. "I Will Never Be (The Same Again)." SATB, pno, gtr. WRD 0 80689 82027 4.

Butler, Terry. "Cry of My Heart" in *Praise Band Songbook 4.*   MAR.

Gardner, Daniel/arr. Tom Fettke. "My Life Is in You, Lord." SATB, kybd.   LIL AN-8102.

Sunday, September 21

ST. MATTHEW, APOSTLE AND EVANGELIST

See pages 304–306.

Thursday, September 25

SERGIUS OF RADONEZH, ABBOT OF HOLY TRINITY, MOSCOW, 1392

The people of Russia honor Sergius as the most beloved of all their saints and a model of Russian spiritual life at its best. At the age of twenty he began to live as a hermit and others joined him. From their monastery in the forest, Sergius led the renewal of Russian monastic life. His monastery, the Monastery of the Holy Trinity, was a center for pilgrimage where people came to worship and receive spiritual support. Sergius was also a peacemaker whose influence stopped four civil wars between Russian princes. Sergius left no writings, but his disciples founded seventy-five monasteries and spread his teachings.

The commemoration of Sergius is an opportunity to consider the Russian church and the traditions of Russian Orthodoxy. For example, a discussion could begin about the place of icons in orthodox spirituality and in what ways icons can find a home among Lutherans.

September 28, 2003

Sixteenth Sunday after Pentecost
Proper 21

INTRODUCTION

The disciples ask Jesus how to deal with those who are doing good in his name, but are not a part of their company. The Lord's response assures them that the reign of God can be served in many and diverse ways. Such words invite the contemporary church to be attentive to those who serve Christ in new or unexpected ministries. Even as Jesus encourages us to be seasoned with salt and to be at peace with one another, James urges us to confess our sins and to pray for the healing of all who are sick.

The church remembers today Jehu Jones, the Lutheran church's first African American pastor, who died in 1852.

PRAYER OF THE DAY

God of love, you know our frailties and failings. Give us your grace to overcome them; keep us from those things that harm us; and guide us in the way of salvation; through your Son, Jesus Christ our Lord.

VERSE

Alleluia. At the name of Jesus every knee should bend, and every tongue should confess that Jesus Christ is Lord, to the glory of God the Father. Alleluia. (Phil. 2:10-11)

READINGS

Numbers 11:4-6, 10-16, 24-29

What constitutes legitimate need and legitimate leadership is the focus of this reading. God provides sustenance as manna to the people in the desert, yet the people crave meat. What is truly needful? God bestows the spirit on seventy elders in order to provide leadership for the people, yet complaints are heard when two men not designated as leaders prophesy in the power of God's spirit. What constitutes real leadership?

Psalm 19:7-14

The commandment of the LORD gives light to the eyes. (Ps. 19:8)

James 5:13-20

The epistle of James is a letter offering advice to the church concerning a variety of common problems. In these verses, however, the author concludes with an uplifting picture of what the church can be: a community of prayer and praise, restoration and healing.

Mark 9:38-50

On the way to Jerusalem, Jesus teaches his disciples about ministry that involves service and sacrifice. His disciples are slow to realize these words apply to them as well as to others.

SEMICONTINUOUS FIRST READING/PSALM

Esther 7:1-6, 9-10; 9:20-22

As the book of Esther demonstrates, the Persian king, Ahasuerus, enjoyed banquets and courtly ceremony. A Jewish woman named Esther won the king's favor and was crowned queen. Though the king subsequently decreed that all Jews should die, Esther succeeded in convincing the king not to carry out the decree, thereby marking the occasion for even more feasting.

Psalm 124

We have escaped like a bird from the snare of the fowler. (Ps. 124:7)

COLOR Green

THE PRAYERS

As we await the full harvest of the Spirit, let us offer our prayers to God who is abundant in every good gift.
A BRIEF SILENCE.

Let us pray that the church would be seasoned with the Spirit, and that all the baptized would proclaim God's promises to the world. Hear us, O God;
your mercy is great.

Let us pray that the world's fields would yield an abundant harvest, and that many would be fed by the produce of the land God has blessed. Hear us, O God;
your mercy is great.

Let us pray that those who are sick and suffering (*especially*) will be anointed with the healing oil of God's presence, that they may be restored to wholeness. Hear us, O God;
your mercy is great.

Let us pray that the diversity of spiritual gifts in this congregation would be celebrated, and that each gift would be embraced by this community in humility and thankfulness. Hear us, O God;
your mercy is great.
HERE OTHER INTERCESSIONS MAY BE OFFERED.

Let us pray that our memories would be blessed by the living testimonies of all God's saints (especially Jehu Jones *and other names*), and that we would be held in communion with them until we are called to join them in eternal light. Hear us, O God;
your mercy is great.
Teach us to pray, O God, and grant us wisdom in our asking, in the name of Jesus Christ our Lord.
Amen

IMAGES FOR PREACHING

The metaphors and hyperboles come rushing at us in this gospel. It is difficult even to call it gospel. Cut it off? Good news? So many texts in these autumn days seem so hard to preach to a people whom we are just thankful are still showing up. So many are searching for a word that comforts and yet here is a word that cuts into our dulled sensibilities. It is almost as if Jesus believes that this is all a matter of life and death. And so it is.

We are not simply learning about body parts here; we are hearing of the dangers of keeping someone from a relationship with our Lord. We are hearing a warning to the organized faithful of being too organized or rigid. We are led to wonder whom we might be keeping from speaking or enacting God's word outside the camp or even in our midst. Are we a living, organic body of Christ or a calcified institution more jealous for our status positions than jealous for the gospel? Have we cut others off from the gift of God's embrace?

We encounter the passion and strong will of Jesus to open up categories of "us and them" so that our loyalties and our imaginations and actions instead seek to join the journey through death to life. On this day the word points to those providing cups of water to the thirsty and to those speaking and acting for life outside of camp or even out of turn. It even commends risking limb and breath so that others may see, walk, hear, and taste that God is good—all for the sake of God's will for life and for a future of shalom.

WORSHIP MATTERS

The reading from James gives us a wonderful opportunity to hold a corporate service of healing. For this service we have many resources, from the Eastern Orthodox tradition, the ecumenical liturgies used in places such as hospitals and nursing homes, the *LBW's Occasional Services* companion, and from other denominations. Using this time to anoint with oil those in need of healing in the community acts out the faithful use of the scripture.

If the congregation always kneels for communion, encourage those communing next to people who must stand, also to remain standing with them. In this way they show oneness with that person and openness to alternatives that can accommodate more worshipers.

LET THE CHILDREN COME

Parents often struggle with bringing children to worship. What if they don't behave? Moses, in today's first lesson, feels some of that parenting hardship as he deals with a "family" that demands attention. Within our congregations we need to reach out and minister to these persons. Special parenting sessions that explore the issue of children and worship can be helpful and supportive. Placed in the narthex, baskets that hold user-friendly books and toys for young children to borrow during worship provide a sign of welcome and assistance. We can help make easier the way toward a full worship life.

HYMNS FOR WORSHIP
GATHERING

Father, we praise you   LBW 267
Glory to God, we give you thanks and praise   WOV 787
We have come into his house   TFF 136

HYMN OF THE DAY

Where cross the crowded ways of life   LBW 429

ALTERNATE HYMN OF THE DAY

You are the seed/Sois la semilla   WOV 753, LLC 486
Now we remain   W&P 106

COMMUNION

Let us ever walk with Jesus   LBW 487
Spirit, Spirit of gentleness   WOV 684

311

SENDING

On what has now been sown   LBW 261
The Spirit sends us forth to serve   WOV 723
Rock of my salvation   W&P 161

ADDITIONAL HYMNS AND SONGS

All creatures, worship God most high!   CS 8
Come, labor on   H82 541
Every time I feel the spirit   TFF 241
Bring forth the kingdom   W&P 22

MUSIC FOR THE DAY

PSALMODY

Bell, John L. *Psalms of Patience, Protest and Praise.* GIA G-4047. U.

Comer, Marilyn. PW B.

Dohms, Ann Celeen. "Psalm 19" in *Sing Out! A Children's Psalter.*
   WLP 7191.

Haas, David. "Psalm 19: Lord, You Have the Words" in GC.

Hruby, Dolores M. *Seasonal Psalms for Children.* U.   WLP 7102.

Walker, Christopher. "Your Law, O God" in *Rise Up and Sing.* U.
   OCP 939. Acc book.   9391GC.

CHORAL

Hassler, H. L. "Cantate Domino" in *Chantry Choirbook.* SATB.
   AFP 0800657772.

Kallman, Daniel. "Lord, Whose Love in Humble Service." SATB,
   pno.   KJO J17.

Landrey, Carey and Larry Theiss. "Feed Us, Lord." 2 pt, kybd, cong,
   rec.   OCP 10665.

Mathis, William. "Come Down, O Love Divine." SATB, org.
   AFP 0800675355.

Proulx, Richard. "Christ Has Called Us to New Visions." SATB,
   brass qnt, timp.   GIA G-4220.

Rutter, John. "Open Thou Mine Eyes." SATB.   HIN HMC-467.

Schütz, Heinrich. "We Offer Our Thanks" in *Chantry Choirbook.*
   SATB, kybd. AFP 0800657772.

CHILDREN'S CHOIRS

Lovelace, Austin. "Let Us Talents and Tongues Employ." 2 pt mxd,
   kybd, opt gtr, opt bng.   CG CGA619.

Marshall, Jane. "For Hard Things." U, 2 pt mxd/SAB, kybd.
   CG CGA618.

KEYBOARD/INSTRUMENTAL

Albrecht, Timothy. "Walton" in *Grace Notes, vol. 8.* Org.
   AFP 0800658264.

Hassell, Michael. "De colores" in *Folkways.* Pno, inst.
   AFP 0800656903.

Peeters, Flor. "Toccata" in *Suite Modale,* op. 43. Org.   LEM 23673 HL.

Petersen, Lynn. "Darwall's 148th" in *Abide with Me.* Org.
   AFP 0800659465.

Stoldt, Frank. "Come Down, O Love Divine." Org, vc/inst.
   MSM 20-441.

Wold, Wayne L. "Prelude, Meditation and Finale on 'Darwall's
   148th.' " Org.   AFP 0800656709.

HANDBELL

Honoré, Jeffrey. "Now We Offer." 2–3 oct.   AFP 0800674898.

Hornibrook, W. "Psalm XIX." 3–5 oct.   Prism 49442014.

McChesney, Kevin. "Praise God. Praise Him." 2–3 oct, opt perc.
   AFP 0800655060.

Page, Anna Laura. "God of Grace and God of Glory." 3–5 oct.
   AG 35104.

Tucker, Sondra. "Thorncrown Chapel Portrait." 3–5 oct.
   AFP 0800658922.

PRAISE ENSEMBLE

DeShazo, Lynn/arr. Stan Pethel. "More Precious than Silver." 2 pt,
   kybd.   HAL 08742547.

Haugen, Marty. "Bring Forth the Kingdom."   W&P 22

Manley, James/arr. Hassell, Michael "Spirit, Spirit of Gentleness."
   SATB, pno, sax or clar.   AFP 0800657711X.

Muchow, Rick. "All about Love." U, pno, gtr, orch.
   Encouraging Music.

Sunday, September 28

JEHU JONES, MISSIONARY, 1852

A native of Charleston, South Carolina, Jones was ordained by the New York Ministerium in 1832, the
Lutheran church's first African American pastor. Upon
returning to South Carolina he was arrested under a law
prohibiting free blacks from reentering the state, and so
was unable to join the group of Charlestonians he had
been commissioned to accompany to Liberia. For nearly
twenty years Jones carried out missionary work in
Philadelphia in the face of many difficulties. There he
led in the formation of the first African American
Lutheran congregation, St. Paul's, and the construction
of its church building.

Monday, September 29

ST. MICHAEL AND ALL ANGELS

On this festival day we ponder the richness and variety of God's created order and the limits of our knowledge of it. The scriptures speak of angels who worship God in heaven, and in both testaments angels are God's messengers on earth. They are remembered most vividly as they appear to the shepherds and announce the birth of the savior. Michael is an angel whose name appears in Daniel as the heavenly being who leads the faithful dead to God's throne on the day of resurrection. In Revelation, Michael fights in a cosmic battle against Satan.

The hymn "Ye watchers and ye holy ones" (LBW 175) delights in the presence of the whole heavenly host of seraphs, cherubim, thrones, archangels, virtues, and angel choirs all led in praise of God by Mary, the "bearer of the eternal Word."

Tuesday, September 30

JEROME, TRANSLATOR, TEACHER, 420

Jerome is remembered as a biblical scholar and translator. Rather than choosing classical Latin as the basis of his work, he translated the scriptures into the Latin that was spoken and written by the majority of the persons in his day. His translation is known as the Vulgate, which comes from the Latin word for common. Even though Jerome is remembered as a saint, he could be anything but saintly. He was well known for his short temper and his arrogance, but he was also quick to admit to his personal faults.

Thanks to the work of Jerome, many people received the word in their own language and lived a life of faith and service to those in need.

Saturday, October 4

FRANCIS OF ASSISI, RENEWER OF THE CHURCH, 1226

Francis was the son of a wealthy cloth merchant. In a public confrontation with his father he renounced his wealth and future inheritance and devoted himself to serving the poor. Francis described this act as being "wedded to Lady Poverty." Under his leadership the Order of Friars Minor (Franciscans) was formed, and they understood literally Jesus' words to his disciples that they should take nothing on their journey and receive no payment for their work. Their task in preaching was to "use words if necessary." Francis had a spirit of gladness and gratitude for all of God's creation. This commemoration has been a traditional time to bless pets and animals, creatures Francis called his brothers and sisters. A prayer attributed to St. Francis is included in *LBW* (p. 48) and could be used at gatherings in the congregation today.

THEODORE FLIEDNER, RENEWER OF SOCIETY, 1864

Fliedner's work was instrumental in the revival of deaconesses among Lutherans. He was a pastor in Kaiserswerth, Germany, and ministered to prisoners in Düsseldorf. Through his ministry to prisoners he came in contact with Moravian deaconesses, and through this Moravian influence he was convinced that the ministry of deaconesses had a place among Lutherans. His work and writing encouraged women to care for the sick, the poor, and the imprisoned. Fliedner's deaconess motherhouse in Kaiserswerth inspired Lutherans all over the world to commission deaconesses to serve in parishes, schools, prisons, and hospitals. At this motherhouse in Kaiserswerth Florence Nightingale received her training as a nurse (see August 13).

313

October 5, 2003

Seventeenth Sunday after Pentecost
Proper 22

INTRODUCTION

The psalmist sings that human beings are the crown of God's creation. Our loving human relationships, though marred by sin, are a sign of the kingdom of God among us. In their mutual respect and love, they symbolize the wholeness intended for all life. Yet neither husband nor wife nor the creation itself is the property of humans to do with as they will. The world, and all that lives within it, belongs to God, who transforms all things through Christ.

PRAYER OF THE DAY

Our Lord Jesus, you have endured the doubts and foolish questions of every generation. Forgive us for trying to be judge over you, and grant us the confident faith to acknowledge you as Lord.

VERSE

Alleluia. I will proclaim your name to my brothers and sisters; in the midst of the congregation I will praise you. Alleluia. (Heb. 2:12)

READINGS

Genesis 2:18-24

Genesis 2 stresses that people are not meant to live in isolation but in relationship. While speaking of the unity of a man and a woman, the focus of this reading is on human community more broadly considered. Ultimately what unites the man and the woman is their common humanity.

Psalm 8

You adorn us with glory and honor. (Ps. 8:6)

Hebrews 1:1-4; 2:5-12

Hebrews, an early Christian sermon, emphasizes that Jesus became so fully human that he shared our experience of death. The one through whom all things exist is the one who calls us brother and sister.

Mark 10:2-16

Jesus announced and enacted in history the new reality of God's surprising activity. These two Markan stories demonstrate this new reality: women and children are accepted and valued, not dismissed as inferior to adult men.

SEMICONTINUOUS FIRST READING/PSALM

Job 1:1; 2:1-10

Job was a man of wealth and status who came upon horrible reversals of fortune without complaint. No matter the calamity, Job remains the picture of profound faith in God.

Psalm 26

Your love is before my eyes; I have walked faithfully with you. (Ps. 26:3)

COLOR Green

THE PRAYERS

As we await the full harvest of the Spirit, let us offer our prayers to God who is abundant in every good gift.
A BRIEF SILENCE.

Faithful God, guide your church in the ways of childlike faithfulness and deep trust, that we may put aside division born of fear. Hear us, O God;
your mercy is great.

All powers and dominions are under your subjection, mighty God. Grant that the leaders of the nations would rule justly and deal wisely in all their governing. Hear us, O God;
your mercy is great.

Our joys and sorrows are fully known to you, God of compassion. Heal those who have experienced broken relationships, or who stand in need of physical healing *(especially)*. Hear us, O God;
your mercy is great.

Watch over the young people from this congregation who are away from home at school or in military service. Guide them and keep them in your care. Hear us, O God;
your mercy is great.

Comfort those grieving the loss of loved ones *(especially)*, that they may be consoled in your tender and merciful arms. Hear us, O God;
your mercy is great.

HERE OTHER INTERCESSIONS MAY BE OFFERED.

Keep us in union with *(names, and)* all your saints, until

we are united in our eternal home. Hear us, O God;
your mercy is great.
Teach us to pray, O God, and grant us wisdom in our asking, in the name of Jesus Christ our Lord.
Amen

IMAGES FOR PREACHING

The preacher stands in the pulpit and knows the fractured and broken relationships that are part of his or her life. The preacher looks at the beloved ones of the congregation who have shed tears and spoken of the anguish, shame, and anger that welled up within them at the death of a relationship that had been enacted in public promises before family and friends. This text cuts close to almost all who have gathered for hope this week. There seems to be no one on whom to set your eyes who has not been touched in some fashion, as child or adult, by the force of this word.

The word before us is not to be talked about or around or finessed. This word addresses all of us with the seriousness of God's passion for faithfulness. The promises we make imagine and enact a future. Promises broken unsettle and disturb the present and call tomorrow into question. So it is that the creator of the universe, who sustains all things by a powerful word of promise, would command faithfulness and promise-keeping. So it is that the ruler of the universe would not desire the suffering that comes when relationships break in the lives of God's beloved creatures.

What is amazing is the faithfulness of this God in the face of our promise-breaking. Whether it is the people Israel or the disciples and the church, this God keeps speaking a word to sustain life. Whether it be worshipers of a golden calf, an adulterous King David, disciples who flee or deny, or a church that is more faithful to a consumer culture than a gospel vision, this God is steadfast in keeping the promise of forgiveness and with grace intruding into our lives.

WORSHIP MATTERS

It is important to resist the temptation to avoid preaching on difficult texts. People struggle with "hard sayings" such as Jesus' words on divorce, and appreciate knowing that the preacher, too, struggles.

Consider starting a feedback leadership group for worship. Let six people serve for six weeks each, staggered in two-week overlaps. After worship, let them talk about the texts, the sermon, logistics for communion, whatever was hard about worship that day as the central focus. As they work together thinking about the difficulty of texts, of logistical matters in community worship, and do so freshly nourished and fed, the worship committee will find it easier to deal with planning for the seasons ahead.

LET THE CHILDREN COME

Communion offers us a valuable moment with children. How can we not think of Jesus, laying his hands on children, blessing them, as we reach out to do likewise? Children are no longer left behind in pews. Even if they don't yet receive communion, they are now invited to come to the Lord's table, and their presence is a joy. What a humble yet wonderful feeling to place your hand on a child's head and look fully into their eyes. "Blessed and loved are you, child of God!" It is a moment full of grace.

HYMNS FOR WORSHIP
GATHERING

O Jesus, joy of loving hearts   LBW 356
Oh, praise the gracious power   WOV 750

HYMN OF THE DAY

Our Father, by whose name   LBW 357

ALTERNATE HYMN OF THE DAY

When love is found   WOV 749
Bring the children   DH 74

COMMUNION

Now we join in celebration   LBW 203
Draw us in the Spirit's tether   WOV 703

SENDING

For the beauty of the earth   LBW 561
Bind us together   WOV 748, TFF 217, W&P 18

ADDITIONAL HYMNS AND SONGS

Book of books   H82 631
When Jesus left his Father's throne   H82 480
We are all one in Christ   TFF 221
Beauty for brokenness   W&P 17

315

MUSIC FOR THE DAY

PSALMODY

Bell, John L. *Psalms of Patience, Protest and Praise.* GIA G-4047.

Comer, Marilyn. PW B.

Cooney, Rory/arr. Gary Daigle. "How Glorious Is Your Name" in PCY.

Dykes, J. B./arr. Hal H. Hopson. *Eighteen Psalms for the Church Year.* HOP HH-3941.

Geary, Patrick. "Your Name Is Praised" in PS 3.

Pulkingham, Betty. *Celebrate the Church Year with Selected Psalms and Canticles.* Cong, choir, kybd, inst. PLY MB94218.

CHORAL

Carnahan, Craig. "Come and Be Fed." 2 pt mxd, kybd, opt hb. AFP 0800674065.

Gehring, Philip. "Taste and See." SATB. CPH 98-3585.

Haugen, Marty. "Unless You Learn." SATB, solo, children's choir, opt ob/vc/synth. GIA G-5174.

Hillert, Richard. "How Great Is Your Name." SATB/U, brass qrt, timp. GIA G-3187.

Nygard, Carl J. Jr. "Grateful Praise." 2 pt, kybd. AFP 0800675185.

Rutter, John. "For the Beauty of the Earth." SATB, kybd. HIN HMC-550. SA. HMC-469.

Shepperd, Mark. "Bless His Holy Name." SATB, kybd, opt U, hb, cong. AFP 0800674030.

CHILDREN'S CHOIRS

Cox, Joe. "Blessed to Be a Blessing." U/2 pt, pno. MSM 50-9409.

Handel, G. F./arr. Stephen Andrews. "I Will Praise Forever." U/2 pt, kybd, fl. LOR 10/1443K.

Pearson, Brian and Sherry Pearson. "Life Together." U/2pt, kybd, opt perc, alto sax, tpt, trb, bass. AFP 0800674197.

KEYBOARD/INSTRUMENTAL

Albrecht, Mark. "O Waly Waly" in *Three for Piano and Sax.* Pno, sax/inst. AFP 0800657977.

Cherwien, David. "O Waly Waly" in *Eight for Eighty-Eight.* Pno, opt inst. AFP 0800657322.

Diemer, Emma Lou. "O Waly Waly" in *Eight Hymn Preludes for Organ.* Org. AFP 0800651863.

Miller, Aaron David. "O Waly Waly" in *Improvisations for the Church Year.* Org. AFP 0800674812.

Vaughan Williams, Ralph. "Rhosymedre" in *Augsburg Organ Library: Lent.* Org. AFP 0800658973.

Willan, Healey. "Matins" in *Two Pieces for Organ.* Org. CFP 6358.

HANDBELL

Behnke, John. "O Waly Waly." 2–3 oct, opt fl. AFP 0800657403.

Engle, M. "For the Beauty of the Earth." 4 oct. NMP HB212.

Waldrop, Tammy. "How Excellent Is Thy Name." 3–5 oct. JEF RW 8031.

PRAISE ENSEMBLE

Espinosa, Eddie. "Change My Heart, Oh God." in *Praise Hymns and Choruses, 4th ed.* MAR.

Gillman, Bob. "Bind Us Together." WOV 748

Sabolick, Joseph/arr. Richard Kingsmore. "Come Just As You Are." SATB, pno, gtr. WRD 301 0906 161.

Zschech, Darlene/arr. Mark Cole. "All Things Are Possible." 3 pt, pno, gtr, orch. Praise Charts.

Monday, October 6

WILLIAM TYNDALE, TRANSLATOR, MARTYR, 1536

William Tyndale was ordained in 1521, and his life's desire was to translate the scriptures into English. When his plan met opposition from Henry VIII, Tyndale fled to Germany where he traveled from city to city and lived in poverty and constant danger. He was able to produce a New Testament in 1525. Nine years later he revised it and began work on the Old Testament, which he was unable to complete. He was tried for heresy and burned at the stake. Miles Coverdale completed Tyndale's work; the Tyndale-Coverdale version was published as the "Matthew Bible" in 1537. The style of this translation has influenced English versions of the Bible such as the King James (Authorized Version) and the New Revised Standard Version for four centuries.

Tuesday, October 7

HENRY MELCHIOR MUHLENBERG, MISSIONARY TO NORTH AMERICA, 1787

Muhlenberg was prominent in setting the course for Lutheranism in this country. He helped Lutheran churches make the transition from the state churches of Europe to independent churches of America. Among other things, he established the first Lutheran synod in America and developed an American Lutheran liturgy. His liturgical principles became the basis for the Common Service of 1888, used in many North American service books for a majority of the past century. *Lutheran Book of Worship* was an attempt to produce Muhlenberg's dream of a common service book for Lutherans in North America. That Muhlenberg and his work are remembered today was anticipated at his death. The inscription on his grave reads in Latin, "Who and what he was, future ages will know without a stone."

The commemoration of Muhlenberg invites congregations to look back on what shaped their identity, worship, and mission in the past and to look ahead to what might shape it in the future.

October 12, 2003

Eighteenth Sunday after Pentecost
Proper 23

INTRODUCTION

Jesus knows our weaknesses, especially the weakness of clinging to those things that could be given away or shared for the good of others. In the gospel reading, Jesus states that it will be difficult for those who pursue wealth to enter the reign of God. Living in a culture that seems driven by the pursuit of money and comfort, we may find these words difficult to hear. Yet Jesus announces that nothing is impossible with God who is our life, our treasure, and our salvation.

PRAYER OF THE DAY

Almighty God, source of every blessing, your generous goodness comes to us anew every day. By the work of your Spirit lead us to acknowledge your goodness, give thanks for your benefits, and serve you in willing obedience; through your Son, Jesus Christ our Lord.

VERSE

Alleluia. This is the LORD for whom we have waited; let us be glad and rejoice in his salvation. Alleluia. (Isa. 25:9)

READINGS

Amos 5:6-7, 10-15

Amos was a herdsman by profession and a prophet by

Friday, October 10

MASSIE L. KENNARD, RENEWER OF THE CHURCH, 1996

Massie L. Kennard was a native of Chicago, Illinois. He was a major figure in supporting and working toward ethnic and racial inclusiveness in the former Lutheran Church in America. Ordained in 1958, he served the church in various staff positions, including work as the director for Minority Concerns of the Division for Mission in North America.

Kennard's commemoration invites the church to re-examine his work for inclusiveness and consider what continues to stand in the way of a full expression of our baptismal unity in which we are all one in Christ Jesus.

317

God's call. During a time of great prosperity in the Northern Kingdom, the prophet speaks of poverty, corruption, and oppression to the wealthy upper class. He warns his listeners that fulfilling God's demand for justice brings blessing, while corruption and evil bring curse.

Psalm 90:12-17

So teach us to number our days that we may apply our hearts to wisdom. (Ps. 90:12)

Hebrews 4:12-16

The letter to the Hebrews teaches that God knows all our failings and understands our struggles. Christ reveals to us that we need not hide from God in shame. We can draw near to receive mercy.

Mark 10:17-31

Jesus has been teaching his disciples about what is most valued in God's eyes. Now, a conversation with a rich man brings his message home to the disciples in a way that is surprising but unforgettable.

SEMICONTINUOUS FIRST READING/PSALM

Job 23:1-9, 16-17

Having experienced much personal loss and tragedy, Job expressed his anger about God, even though he was unable to locate God directly. Yet through it all, Job did not doubt God's existence.

Psalm 22:1-15

My God, my God, why have you forsaken me? (Ps. 22:1)

COLOR Green

THE PRAYERS

As we await the full harvest of the Spirit, let us offer our prayers to God who is abundant in every good gift.
A BRIEF SILENCE.

Let us pray for the church, and especially for all mission congregations and their pastor-developers, that the gospel would be firmly planted in all communities. Hear us, O God;
your mercy is great.

Let us pray for a fruitful harvest of grain from the fields and for a healthy global economy, that a fair and just distribution of the world's goods would be accomplished. Hear us, O God;
your mercy is great.

Let us pray for justice to prevail in our community, that those in need would be cared for, the oppressed be freed from abuse, and the courts be governed with truth. Hear us, O God;
your mercy is great.

Let us pray for the healing of all who suffer with pain and illness *(especially)*, that they may be restored to good health and well-being. Hear us, O God;
your mercy is great.

Let us pray for those who are on the fringes of this congregation and have many questions of faith. May they find a hospitable welcome and experience your presence in their inquiry. Hear us, O God;
your mercy is great.
HERE OTHER INTERCESSIONS MAY BE OFFERED.

Let us pray in thanksgiving for *(names, and all)* the faithful departed, that we might be inspired by their love and faithfulness, and remain united with them in God's eternal community. Hear us, O God;
your mercy is great.

Teach us to pray, O God, and grant us wisdom in our asking, in the name of Jesus Christ our Lord.
Amen

IMAGES FOR PREACHING

Go! Sell! Give! Come! Follow! This word truly is a sword, dividing not only joints from marrow, soul from spirit, but wallets from pockets. These verbs of flint resist our efforts to temporize or qualify or mute their force. "Go, sell all that you have and give it to the poor, then come, follow me." How do we dare read and hear this word and then go and continue to live as we have become accustomed? Hearing this word, can we continue to live comfortably in this culture and economy? What does this word say to the decent, faithful, religious folk in our midst who try and live as "good" people? Here is a decent, faithful, religious man who lives a *good* life and yet Jesus calls him out to a *new* life.

We live in a society where we are consumed by possessions. In the turning of everything into a commodity we discover that we too are no longer *homo sapiens* but *homo consumerus.* Our lives are summed up not only in actuary tables but in cost/benefit analyses of the risks of pollution and determinations of how safe to make cars or regulate drugs. In church life, we now talk of growth, markets, entrepreneurs, and determining and meeting the needs of "our" customer.

How shall we who have not left family, home, or possessions respond to this word? Perhaps we can only cling to the phrases; "Jesus, looking at him, loved him" and "for mortals it is impossible, but not for God; for God all things are possible." Cling to these phrases and pray that we might have the courage to let go and become last so that others might be first.

WORSHIP MATTERS

The matters of worship often have to do with how we, as leaders, actually live the worship life, knowing that we always want to do one thing more to make our worship perfect. Whatever it is that we ask of others in worship, we ask doubly of ourselves.

Worship leadership can actually be quite detrimental to the worship of the leader. Therefore, maintaining a good rotation of worship assistants of all kinds helps the spiritual health of all. Encourage leaders to spend time in worship especially when they are not leading that day, to help keep focus on the important things—the prayer and shared worship of the community of God. Pastors in particular need to take their Sundays off not to supply elsewhere but to be a simple worshiper in as many different settings as possible.

LET THE CHILDREN COME

Possessions often give us trouble. We know we have too much, but it is hard to stop possessing. Fortunately, that's true even for God, who didn't want to give us up.

Our children learn about "having stuff" from us. They can unlearn this concept of needing more through good and caring stewardship experiences. Consider asking older children to donate one of their possessions still in good condition to the younger members of the congregation. It could be a toy for the nursery or a book with a religious theme to be looked at by a small child during worship. Young people can learn to "give up" in God's name.

HYMNS FOR WORSHIP
GATHERING
Praise and thanksgiving   LBW 409
All my hope on God is founded   WOV 782

HYMN OF THE DAY
Son of God, eternal Savior   LBW 364

ALTERNATE HYMN OF THE DAY
God, whose giving knows no ending   LBW 364
Seek ye first   WOV 783, TFF 149, W&P 122

COMMUNION
Now the silence   LBW 205
Father, we thank you   WOV 704

SENDING
The Church of Christ, in every age   LBW 433
Great is thy faithfulness   WOV 771, TFF 283
Lead me, guide me   TFF 70, W&P 84

ADDITIONAL HYMNS AND SONGS
Give it away   DH 96
Word of God, come down on earth   H82 633
Some folk would rather have houses   TFF 236
The church song   W&P 135

MUSIC FOR THE DAY
PSALMODY
Comer, Marilyn.   PW B.
Hallock, Peter/arr. Carl Crosier. *The Ionian Psalter.* U/SATB, org.   ION.
O God, our help in ages past   LBW 320
Stewart, Roy James. "Psalm 90: Fill Us with Your Love, O Lord" in GC.
Walker, Christopher. "Fill Us, Lord, with Your Love" in PS 3.

CHORAL
Armstrong, Matthew. "Take My Life and Let It Be." SATB, kybd.   CPH 98-3455.

Bell, John L. "Lord, You Have Been Our Refuge." SATB, desc.   GIA G-4297.
Bouman, Paul. "Son of God, Eternal Savior." SATB, org, cong, tpt.   CPH 98-2818.
Buxtehude, Dieterich. "Everything You Do" in *Chantry Choirbook.* SATB, org.   AFP 0800657772.
Ferguson, John. "Be Thou My Vision." SATB, org.   AFP 0800657934.
Scott, K. Lee. "Teach Me, My God and King." SATB, org.   AFP 0800659732.
Sedio, Mark. "Take My Life That I May Be" (Toma, oh Dios, mi voluntad). SAB, kybd.   AFP 0800658299.
Traditional/arr. Shaw-Parker. "My God Is a Rock." SATB.   LAW 51107.

CHILDREN'S CHOIRS
Bedford, Michael, arr. "I Sing the Mighty Power of God." U/2 pt, cong, fl, org, opt hb.   CG CGA884.
Hopson, Hal H. "O Lord, You Know Me Completely." U/2 pt, kybd.   CG CGA833.

KEYBOARD/INSTRUMENTAL
Albrecht, Mark. "Lafferty" in *Timeless Hymns of Faith, vol. 2.* Pno.   AFP 0800658795.
Haan, Raymond H. "Variations on 'In Babilone.'" Org.   FLA HH-5035.
Leavitt, John. "In Babilone" in *Hymn Preludes for the Church Year.* Org.   AFP 0800650328.
Lefébure-Wely, Louis. "March" in *The Oxford Book of Wedding Music.* Org.   OXF.
Lindberg, Oskar. "Gammal fäbodpsalm" in *Augsburg Organ Library: Epiphany.* Org.   AFP 0800659341.
Wasson, Laura E. "Lafferty" in *A Piano Tapestry, vol. 2.* Pno.   AFP 0800658183.

HANDBELL
Linker, Janet. "Morning Has Broken." 3 oct hb, org/kybd/5 oct hb.   AFP 0800654323.
McKechnie, Linda D. "O God, Our Help in Ages Past." 3–5 oct, kybd, opt tpt, cong. Genevox GVX 3197-12.
Ives, Charles/arr. G. Smith. "Psalm 90." 3+ oct, SATB, org.   JEF TP 34240021.

PRAISE ENSEMBLE
Beech, Jay. "The Church Song." W&P 135
Helming, Brent. "Come As You Are" in *Come As You Are Songbook.*   MAR.
Lafferty, Karen. "Seek Ye First." WOV 783
Paris, Twila/arr. Allen. "We Will Glorify" in *Celebration Hymnal.* WRD.

319

October 13, 2003

Day of Thanksgiving (Canada)

INTRODUCTION

As winter darkness crosses the land, the nation takes time to offer thanks for the harvest and the abundant resources of this land. Even though this holiday witnesses many households gathering for a festive meal, Christians recognize that the source of all good things is the God who feeds the birds and clothes the grass of the field. Gathered at Christ's supper, we offer thanksgiving for the bread of life and the cup of blessing. And here, as we share these gifts, we are knit together into a community whose mission is among the poor and those in need. We offer thanks to God for the bounty of the land and seek to share these riches with all in need.

PRAYER OF THE DAY

Almighty God our Father, your generous goodness comes to us new every day. By the work of your Spirit lead us to acknowledge your goodness, give thanks for your benefits, and serve you in willing obedience; through your Son, Jesus Christ our Lord.

VERSE

Alleluia. God is able to provide you with every blessing in abundance, so that by always having enough of everything, you may share abundantly in every good work. Alleluia. (2 Cor. 9:8)

READINGS

Joel 2:21-27

The prophecy of Joel comes from the period of 500 to 350 B.C. He views a locust plague that ravaged the country as God's judgment on the people, whom he then calls to repentance. Today's reading points beyond the judgment of the Day of the Lord, when the Lord will repay "the years that the swarming locust has eaten."

Psalm 126

The LORD has done great things for us, and we are glad indeed. (Ps. 126:4)

1 Timothy 2:1-7

The letter to Timothy was written at a time when kings and rulers persecuted those who believed in Christ. Still, the writer calls upon Christians to pray for these rulers and offer thanksgiving on their behalf.

Matthew 6:25-33

In the Sermon on the Mount, Jesus taught his disciples about the providence of God so that they would regard life with thanksgiving and trust rather than anxiety.

COLOR White

THE PRAYERS

As we await the full harvest of the Spirit, let us offer our prayers to God who is abundant in every good gift.
A BRIEF SILENCE.

We give you thanks, O God, for your church and for the wondrous ways in which you have dealt with your people. Continue to inspire the church to be a blessing in our communities and in the society at large. Lord, in your mercy,
hear our prayer.

We give you thanks, O God, for the diversity of the world's people, for all nations and their leaders. Grant to all your wisdom and grace, that a quiet and peaceable life would be possible for all people. Lord, in your mercy,
hear our prayer.

We give you thanks, O God, for your abundant blessings to us and for the bounty of the world's resources. Help us to share of our plenty with those in need. Lord, in your mercy,
hear our prayer.

We give you thanks, O God, for this congregation and for the praises you have put in our mouths and in our hearts. Help us work to insure that people in our community have sufficient food, clothing, and shelter. Lord, in your mercy,
hear our prayer.

HERE OTHER INTERCESSIONS MAY BE OFFERED.

We give you thanks, O God, for bringing the promise of comfort to those who grieve. We remember with praise and thanksgiving all who have died and who now rest at peace in your eternal harvest home. Lord, in your mercy,
hear our prayer.

Teach us to pray, O God, and grant us wisdom in our asking, in the name of Jesus Christ our Lord.
Amen

320

IMAGES FOR PREACHING

Feasting and gathering family and friends is a wonderfully human thing to do. The images in scripture of the heavenly banquet are a promise that resonates deep within the human spirit. Thanksgiving Day at its best connects with our need to gather and celebrate and to give thanks. Thanksgiving Day in North America is all of these things, but it is also a day layered with distortions and tensions.

The very act of giving thanks assumes that one is thanking another. We in the church give witness that it is God who has given us the gifts of food and family and community. We point to this God as the creator of the wonderful diversity of the cosmos; it is this God whom we thank this day. But our witness also proclaims these gifts as gifts for all, and here we sense the bite. We know of our use and abuse of these gifts and the reality that many do not share in them. We are aware of the ways in which we squander and hoard even as we see that the pattern of giving away is what brings life.

The response to this tension, however, ought not to be that of calling off the feast but rather going deeper into it. Let us seek to open our eyes and ears to this creator of all things. Open our imaginations to God's rich and passionate regard for life. Affirm that all that we have comes from God who gives it away and would teach us that path of stewardship and living. On this day, we open our eyes in thanksgiving to all our fellow humans and creatures and the earth itself and pray that this vision remain before us in the days ahead.

WORSHIP MATTERS

It is a day for warmth and comfort in our worship. Yes, we may want to challenge assumptions that everyone is well off as we are, and any good sermon will include law as well as gospel. But the overall theme, properly, is simple thanksgiving for God's blessings. Familiar hymns will be welcome, perhaps some harvest decorations, even an element or two that is borderline kitschy. It isn't that we feel we must pander to those who complain about anything difficult in worship. Rather, we recognize that, at times, it is healthy not to have to think too hard about the darker side of life and of our relationship with God and neighbor, but simply open ourselves in grateful praise.

LET THE CHILDREN COME

As the church celebrates this time of giving thanks, children can help provide ways of recalling for us all we have been given. A thanksgiving banner could be made ahead of time by a Sunday School class and used during this service. A table in the narthex could display objects or pictures chosen or drawn by children to show things for which they are thankful. These may serve as visual reminders of gifts that we as adults take for granted. Consider having a young person participate in the prayers. Thanking God is an inclusive act!

HYMNS FOR WORSHIP

GATHERING

We praise you, O God   LBW 241
O God beyond all praising   WOV 797

HYMN OF THE DAY

For the fruit of all creation   WOV 760

ALTERNATE HYMN OF THE DAY

Praise to the Lord, the Almighty   LBW 543, CS 58
Sing praise to God, who has shaped   CS 67
Glory and praise to our God   W&P 43

COMMUNION

Praise and thanksgiving   LBW 409
As the grains of wheat   WOV 705

SENDING

The day you gave us, Lord, has ended   LBW 274
Great is thy faithfulness   WOV 771

ADDITIONAL HYMNS AND SONGS

O praise ye the Lord!   H82 432
In sacred manner   OBS 64
Thank you, Lord   TFF 293
I will sing, I will sing   W&P 73

MUSIC FOR THE DAY

PSALMODY

Beckstrand, William.   PW B.
Foley, John. "Psalm 126" in PCY 7.
Haas, David. "Psalm 126" in PCY 8.
Roff, Joseph. "Psalm 126" in PCY 3.
Smith, Alan. "The Lord Has Done Great Things" in PS 1.

321

CHORAL

Bach, J. S. "Now Thank We All Our God" in *Bach for All Seasons*.
SATB. AFP 080065854X.

Ferguson, John. "A Song of Thanksgiving." SATB, org.
AFP 0800653858.

How, Martin. "Praise, O Praise" in *The New Church Anthem Book*.
2 pt, org. OXF 0193531097.

Jennings, Carolyn. "We Praise You, O God." SATB, org, opt tpt.
AFP 0800658485.

Kosche, Kenneth. "It Is a Good Thing." SATB. AFP 0800659635.

Porter, Emily. "Many and Great, O God." SATB, fl, drm.
Calfaria Music 00-104.

CHILDREN'S CHOIRS

Beebe, Hank. "The Earth is the Lord's" from *The Twenty-fourth Psalm:
A Suite for Choirs*. U, kybd. CFI PCI004.

Farrar, Sue. "Song of Thanksgiving." 2 pt, kybd. BEC BP1291.

Patterson, Mark. "Let Praise Be the First Word." 2 pt, kybd.
AFP 0800675347.

KEYBOARD/INSTRUMENTAL

Albrecht, Mark. "Ar hyd y nos" in *Timeless Hymns of Faith, vol. 2*. Pno.
AFP 0800658795.

Callahan, Charles. "A Gaelic Improvisation" (Bunessan) in *Thanksgiving
Suite*. Org. MSM 10-600.

Cherwien, David. "Now Thank We All Our God" in *Postludes on Well-
Known Hymns*. Org. AFP 800656563.

Peeters, Flor. "Kremser" in *Augsburg Organ Library: November*. Org.
AFP 0800659865.

Various. "Lobe den Herren" in *Augsburg Organ Library: November*. Org.
AFP 0800659865.

HANDBELL

Honoré, Jeffrey. "Now We Offer." 3–5 oct. AFP 0800674898.

Kunda, Keith. "Thanksgiving Medley." 3 oct. JEF LWHB207.

Linker, Janet and Jane McFadden. "Come, Ye Thankful People,
Come." 3–5 oct. BEC BEHB95.

Moklebust, Cathy and David Moklebust. "Praise to the Lord, the
Almighty." 4–5 oct, org, opt cong. AFP 0800659333.

PRAISE ENSEMBLE

Landgrave, Phillip. "Come with Thanksgiving." SATB, pno.
Church Street Music 0-7673-9691-X.

Rutter, John. "All Things Bright and Beautiful." 2 pt, kybd.
HIN HMC-663.

Schwartz, Stephen/arr. Richard Walters. "All Good Gifts." SATB,
pno. HAL 08656516.

Smith, Henry/arr. John F. Wilson. "Give Thanks." SAB, kybd.
HOP GC972.

Wednesday, October 15

TERESA DE JESÚS, TEACHER,
RENEWER OF THE CHURCH, 1582

Teresa de Jesús is also known as Teresa of Avila. She is commemorated with John of the Cross on December 14. Teresa chose the life of a Carmelite nun after reading the letters of Jerome. She was frequently sick during her early years as a nun and found that when she was sick her prayer life flowered, but when she was well it withered. Steadily her life of faith and prayer deepened and she grew to have a lively sense of God's presence with her. She worked to reform her monastic community in Avila, Spain, which she believed had strayed from their original purpose and intent. Her reforms asked nuns to maintain life in the monastic enclosure without leaving it, and also to identify with the poor by not wearing shoes. Teresa's writings on devotional life are widely read by members of various denominations.

Friday, October 17

IGNATIUS, BISHOP OF ANTIOCH, MARTYR, C. 115

Ignatius was the second bishop of Antioch in Syria. It was there that the name Christian was first used to describe the followers of Jesus. Ignatius remains known to us through his letters. In them he encouraged Christians to live in unity sustained with love while standing firm on sound doctrine. Ignatius believed Christian martyrdom was a privilege. When his own martyrdom approached, he wrote in one of his letters, "I prefer death in Christ Jesus to power over the farthest limits of the earth.... Do not stand in the way of my birth to real life." Ignatius and all martyrs are a reminder that even today Christians face death because of their faith in Jesus.

322

Saturday, October 18

ST. LUKE, EVANGELIST

Luke is identified as the author of both Luke and Acts. Luke's gospel is careful to place the events of Jesus' life in both their social and religious contexts. Some of the most loved parables are found only in this gospel, including the good Samaritan and the prodigal son. Luke's gospel has also given the church some of its most beautiful songs: the Benedictus sung at morning prayer, the Magnificat sung at evening prayer, and the Nunc dimittis sung at the close of the day. These songs are powerful witnesses to the message of Jesus Christ.

Paul calls Luke the "beloved physician," and some congregations use the day of St. Luke to remember and pray for those in healing professions. The Service of the Word for Healing in *Occasional Services* may be used, or that on pages 293–94 of this resource. Prayer for healing in this service would include the emotional, spiritual, and physical dimensions of our lives.

October 19, 2003

Nineteenth Sunday after Pentecost
Proper 24

INTRODUCTION

Baptism into Christ is our entrance into the Lord's mission. This calling is made abundantly clear at the end of the liturgy when the assembly is charged to go in peace and serve the Lord. Such service cannot avoid the cup of suffering. Indeed, the good news is that, in Christ, God embraces us in love where we are most weak and frail. How shall we do the same for each other and for those in need?

PRAYER OF THE DAY

Almighty and everlasting God, in Christ you have revealed your glory among the nations. Preserve the works of your mercy, that your church throughout the world may persevere with steadfast faith in the confession of your name; through your Son, Jesus Christ our Lord.

VERSE

Alleluia. In fulfillment of his own purpose God gave us birth by the word of truth, so that we would become a kind of first fruits of his creatures. Alleluia. (James 1:18)

READINGS

Isaiah 53:4-12

This reading is a section from the last of four passages in Isaiah that are often called "servant songs." Christians are most familiar with the various New Testament interpretations of this passage. In light of Christian faith, the servant's healing ministry and redemptive suffering are brought to fullness in the life and death of Christ.

Psalm 91:9-16

You have made the LORD your refuge, and the Most High your habitation. (Ps. 91:9)

Hebrews 5:1-10

Using imagery borrowed from Jewish worship, the letter to the Hebrews describes Jesus as a great high priest who offers himself as a sacrifice for our sins.

Mark 10:35-45

On the way to Jerusalem, the disciples ask Jesus to grant them seats of honor. Jesus responds by announcing that he and his followers will "rule" through self-giving service.

SEMICONTINUOUS FIRST READING/PSALM

Job 38:1-7 [34-41]

Confronted with great suffering, Job attempts to prove his innocence to God. God speaks from the whirlwind, and speaks of the power of the sea and its waves. A series of ironical questions shows that Job, as a finite human, is incapable of judging the Creator.

Psalm 104:1-9, 25, 37 (Psalm 104:1-9, 24, 35c [NRSV])

O LORD, how manifold are your works! In wisdom you have made them all. (Ps. 104:25)

COLOR Green

323

THE PRAYERS

As we await the full harvest of the Spirit, let us offer our prayers to God who is abundant in every good gift.

A BRIEF SILENCE.

God of suffering service, grant to your church faithful leaders who have the hearts of servants, and who will gently lead your people into love for you and service to their neighbors. Hear us, O God;

your mercy is great.

God of gentle justice, raise up righteous leaders in every nation who will govern with truth and guide their people with fairness and equity. Hear us, O God;

your mercy is great.

God of tender compassion, hear the cries of all who suffer and who are contending with sickness and disease *(especially)*. Lay upon them your gentle hand of healing. Hear us, O God;

your mercy is great.

God of all goodness, guide the work of the congregation council and committees of this parish, that a unity of purpose would prevail over all their decision making. Hear us, O God;

your mercy is great.

HERE OTHER INTERCESSIONS MAY BE OFFERED.

God of comforting hope, tend to those who are grieving, that their mourning may be tempered with joy. Bring us at length, with *(names, and)* all our blessed dead, to the joy of your heavenly realm. Hear us, O God;

your mercy is great.

Teach us to pray, O God, and grant us wisdom in our asking, in the name of Jesus Christ our Lord.

Amen

IMAGES FOR PREACHING

Firefighters, police officers, and rescue teams who rushed up the World Trade Center towers two years ago in order to serve and save rightfully became our models of the heroic. On a day that exhibited the worst of human activity, they and others revealed the best. Watching from afar, many of us wondered whether we would be able to muster up such courage and devotion to strangers.

Jesus, on this day, invites his followers to let such patterns of self-giving and serving be a model of the normal, daily living of his people. He invites us to find our way in the shape and pattern of his suffering, death, and resurrection. He would have us open our eyes and ears to those with whom we gather around the table: those with whom we share in common a Creator and a Savior; those who like us, come with open hands and hungry hearts to receive a gift that gives life as it is given away.

Jesus would have us go out and serve those who haven't yet come to the font or this table. To be witnesses of God's life-giving Yes in a world full of shadows and Nos. To be those whose living points to the one who gave his life as a ransom for the creation.

Jesus seeks out a community, a body, which will serve and give itself away. Some of that activity will be dramatic and powerful; some will be found in quiet acts of grace and mercy. For all of us it means we are invited to become last so that others might be first.

WORSHIP MATTERS

The Blessing of the Lectors, a short liturgical rite in *This Far by Faith*, is a simple, visible acting out of the way worship leadership is envisioned. On Sunday morning the ability to read for worship comes less from technique and innate gifts than by preparation and prayer. If a lector reads and prays the text two weeks in advance, then that reader is apt to be well prepared.

The ritual of setting apart the lector by laying on of hands and prayer during worship can be quite moving, because the person reading knows they are blessed to serve the worshiping body. Representatives of the congregation have blessed the serving and in that blessing the entire congregation is strengthened spiritually. Similar blessings could also be extended to others who serve: choirs, acolytes, those who deliver service tapes to homebound members, and many others.

LET THE CHILDREN COME

Today's gospel text closes with words on serving. We are called to a servant ministry. Children's hearts and hands are wonderful tools for doing God's work. When invited, children are often more than willing to help—we just need to ask. Consider having several children work with the altar guild to ready the church for Sunday's worship. Others could make sure that pew racks are well supplied and neat. A children's choir could sing a service-related anthem from *LifeSongs*. Perhaps they could help deliver the flowers afterwards. Serving in the Lord's name is a job for all ages!

324

HYMNS FOR WORSHIP

GATHERING

You servants of God   LBW 252

Many and great, O God, are your works   WOV 794

HYMN OF THE DAY

The Church of Christ, in every age   LBW 433

ALTERNATE HYMN OF THE DAY

Weary of all trumpeting   WOV 785

Praise God. Praise him   LBW 529

COMMUNION

O God of life's great mystery   LBW 201

In the morning when I rise   WOV 777, TFF 165

A song of unity   W&P 1

SENDING

God the omnipotent!   LBW 462

What a fellowship, what a joy divine   WOV 780, TFF 220

ADDITIONAL HYMNS AND SONGS

Rise, O church, like Christ arisen   OBS 76, CS 63

Cross of Jesus, cross of sorrow   H82 160

If when you give the best of your service   TFF 172

Sing out, earth and skies   W&P 126

MUSIC FOR THE DAY

PSALMODY

Bell, John L. *Psalms of Patience, Protest and Praise.* U/SATB.   GIA G-4047.

Comer, Marilyn.   PW B.

Glynn, John. "Song of Blessing" in PS 2.

Haugen, Marty/arr. David Haas.   PCY.

Marshall, Jane. "Psalm 91" in *Psalms Together II.* U, cong.   CG CGC21.

You who dwell in the shelter of the Lord   WOV 779, W&P 110

CHORAL

Busarow, Donald. "The Church of Christ in Every Age." SATB, org, opt cong, 2 tpt, 2 tbn.   AFP 0800652118.

Gehring, Philip. "The Cup of Blessing." SATB.   CPH 98-3585.

Kallman, Daniel. "Lord, Whose Love in Humble Service." SATB, pno.   KJO J17.

Nelson, Ronald A. "Whoever Would Be Great among You" in *The Augsburg Choirbook.*   AFP 0800656784. SAB, gtr/kybd. AFP 0800645804.

Proulx, Richard. "Weary of All Trumpeting." SAB, brass qrt. AFP 0800657632.

CHILDREN'S CHOIRS

Nystedt, Knut. "Teach Me, O Lord." 2 pt, pno, opt perc.   MSM 50-9400.

Schoenfeld, William. "The Prayer of St. Patrick." U, kybd. CG CGA462.

KEYBOARD/INSTRUMENTAL

Bender, Jan. "Variations on a Theme by Hugo Distler." Org. AFP 0800673697.

Carlson, J. Bert. "Wareham" in *Blessed Assurance: Hymn Preludes for Organ.* Org.   AFP 0800674774.

Diemer, Emma Lou. "Lac qui parle" in *Eight Hymn Preludes for Organ.* Org.   AFP 0800651863.

Farlee, Robert Buckley. "Lac qui parle" in *Many and Great.* Org. AFP 0800658949.

Johnson, David N. "Lac qui parle" in *Hymn Settings for Organ.* Org. AFP 0800674987.

Keesecker, Thomas. "Lac qui parle" in *Together Again.* Pno. AFP 0800655710.

Manz, Paul. "Praise God, Praise Him" in *Three Hymns for Flute, Oboe and Organ.* Fl, ob, org.   MSM 20-871.

Purcell, Henry/ed. E. Power Biggs. "Voluntary on the Doxology, Old Hundredth" in *Ceremonial Music for Organ.* Org, opt tpt. PRE 4534-00090.

HANDBELL

Afdahl, Lee J. "Two Spanish Tunes for Handbells." 3–5 oct, opt perc, hc.   AFP 0800657381.

Berns, Susan. "Psalm 91" (Naoma's Theme). 3 oct hb/hc. JEF TH1H708952.

Edwards, Dan. "On Eagle's Wings." 3 oct.   CG CGB165.

Honoré, Jeffrey. "Marching to Zion." 3–5 oct.   AFP 080067488X.

PRAISE ENSEMBLE

Beech, Jay. "Here, in the Kingdom." 3 pt, pno.   Baytone Music.

Foote, Billy James. "You Are My King" in *Worship Together Songbook 2.* U, pno, gtr. Worship Together.

Joncas, Michael/arr. M. Hayes. "On Eagle's Wings." SATB, pno. ALF 16104.

Ylvisaker, John/arr. John Helgen. "I Was There to Hear Your Borning Cry." SAATB, pno, rec/fl.   KJO 8826.

Thursday, October 23

JAMES OF JERUSALEM, MARTYR

James became an early leader of the church in Jerusalem. He is described in the New Testament as the brother of Jesus, and secular historian Josephus calls James, the brother of Jesus "the so-called Christ." Little is known about him, but Josephus reported that the Pharisees respected James for his piety and observance of the law. His enemies had him put to death.

Was James a blood brother of the Lord? It is difficult to answer that question because the Aramaic word for brother can also mean cousin. Jesus also said, "Whoever does the will of God is my brother and sister and mother." The commemoration of James and his connection to Jesus as "brother" can spark further discussion about how we all share Christ as our brother through baptism into his death and resurrection.

October 26, 2003

Reformation Sunday

INTRODUCTION

By the end of the seventeenth century, many Lutheran churches celebrated a festival commemorating Martin Luther's posting of the Ninety-five Theses, a summary of abuses in the church of his time. At the heart of the reform movement was the gospel, the good news that by grace through faith we are justified and set free. As we observe the Reformation today the church prays for renewal and reconciliation among all Christians, that we may more faithfully witness to the world.

Today the church commemorates three important German hymnwriters of the sixteenth and seventeenth centuries: Philipp Nicolai (died 1608), Johann Heermann (1647), and Paul Gerhardt (1676).

PRAYER OF THE DAY

Almighty God, gracious Lord, pour out your Holy Spirit upon your faithful people. Keep them steadfast in your Word, protect and comfort them in all temptations, defend them against all enemies, and bestow on the church your saving peace; through your Son, Jesus Christ our Lord, who lives and reigns with you and the Holy Spirit, one God, now and forever.

VERSE

Alleluia. If you continue in my word, you are truly my disciples, and you will know the truth, and the truth will make you free. Alleluia. (John 8:31-32)

READINGS

Jeremiah 31:31-34

After the fall of Jerusalem to the Babylonian army, Jeremiah's message changes from doom to comfort. This reading presents the prophet's vision of the restored community of Israel. The new covenant will fulfill the original intention of the covenant with Moses—God and humanity living in harmonious relationship. The difference between then and now is that the people's response to the liberating God will come naturally.

Psalm 46

The Lord of hosts is with us; the God of Jacob is our stronghold. (Ps. 46:4)

Romans 3:19-28

Martin Luther and other leaders of the Reformation believed the heart of the gospel was found in these words of Paul written to the Romans. All people have sinned, but God offers forgiveness through Christ Jesus. We are justified, or put right with God, by grace through faith in Jesus.

John 8:31-36

Here Jesus promises that true freedom—the freedom to serve our loving God—comes through the truth of the gospel. It is this truth that is revealed in the life of the Lord Jesus.

COLOR Red

THE PRAYERS

As we await the full harvest of the Spirit, let us offer our prayers to God who is abundant in every good gift.

A BRIEF SILENCE.

O mighty God, give your church an unswerving trust in the great heritage of your word, that it may boldly and freely proclaim the forgiveness of sins with joy. Hear us, O God;

your mercy is great.

O God of all, strengthen those who bring in the abundance of fruit and grain from the fields, that the work of their hands will feed many who hunger for physical nourishment. Hear us, O God;

your mercy is great.

O God our shield, be the protector of the powerless and the hope for those on the margins of society. Touch those who are sick with your tender, healing hand (*especially*). Hear us, O God;

your mercy is great.

O God our rock, let your sure grace have free course in this congregation, that we would be strong in faith and bold to give witness to the great heritage passed on to us. Hear us, O God;

your mercy is great.

HERE OTHER INTERCESSIONS MAY BE OFFERED.

O God our redeemer, you are our heritage from one generation to another. We praise you for Philipp Nicolai, Johann Heermann, and Paul Gerhardt, and for all the saints and reformers who have paved the way for us, and who cheer us on toward our eternal home. Hear us, O God;

your mercy is great.

Teach us to pray, O God, and grant us wisdom in our asking, in the name of Jesus Christ our Lord.

Amen

IMAGES FOR PREACHING

One of the significant ironies of this twenty-first century is that with all of our technological marvels such as cell phones, e-mails, faxes, and the Internet, all advertised as the means to more freedom, we feel less free. We proclaim our allegiance to freedom but yet we take our cell phones on vacation and to the golf course and the fishing hole. We have our phones near us out in the flower garden just in case a friend calls us. Always available, we are never free.

Jesus asserts that the truth shall make us free. What truth? Scientific? Philosophical? Political? Sociological?

Psychological? Economic? No! Rather, a truth concerning who creates and gives life. This truth concerns the God who enables and sustains community and life. The life-giver, the reconciler, the one who imagines and creates a future where shalom—wholeness—is enacted and celebrated.

The days are surely coming when God's reconciliation with the creation will be revealed. The days are surely coming, so let us live as if they were fulfilled now. Let us be free to love neighbor, stranger, and enemy. Let us be free to sell all that we have and give to the poor. Let us be free to turn the other cheek and give away our lives. Let us be free to dance with Miriam and feast with Zacchaeus. Let us be free to welcome the alien and the sojourner. Let us be free to be our brothers' and sisters' keeper. Let us be free to feast at the meal where all are welcome. Let us be free to embrace the gift of creation as creatures and not as dominators. Let us be free to hope and enjoy the grace and shalom of God.

327

WORSHIP MATTERS

Processions add a festive touch to celebrations such as Reformation Sunday. They not only get large numbers of people into place but also provide color, possibly liturgical dance, and of course movement. Including specific banners can help to highlight the particular day. When banners are carried in procession, they should preferably be large and the symbols easy to see. Banners are not signboards: the fewer words, the better. After processing in, stand banners where they can be seen by people as they move to and from the altar for communion. Keep banners in good repair and discard any that are frayed, faded, or damaged.

LET THE CHILDREN COME

Martin Luther realized the transforming power of learning about and living within the context of God's word. This importance is not lost on children. Therefore, this Sunday may be an appropriate day to present Bibles to young people. Presentations within the worship setting remind the gathered community of the baptismal promise, made by a child's parents, to "place in their hands the Holy Scriptures." Biblical words and insights have inspired many to work for reforming change. We need to help children realize that they, too, can understand and live these words to bring about change for the better.

HYMNS FOR WORSHIP

GATHERING

A mighty fortress is our God   LBW 228, 229, CS 1, 2
Oh, praise the gracious power   WOV 750

HYMN OF THE DAY

Built on a rock   LBW 365

ALTERNATE HYMN OF THE DAY

O God, O Lord of heaven and earth   LBW 396
For by grace   W&P 38

COMMUNION

Lord Jesus Christ, we humbly pray   LBW 225
O Spirit of life   WOV 680

SENDING

Lord, keep us steadfast   LBW 230
We all are one in mission   WOV 755
Praised be the rock   TFF 290

ADDITIONAL HYMNS AND SONGS

We've come this far by faith   TFF 197
Rock of my salvation   W&P 161
What a mighty word   W&P 155
That priceless grace   TFF 68

MUSIC FOR THE DAY

PSALMODY

Burkhardt, Michael. *Three Psalm Settings.* U, cong, opt inst.
   MSM 80-705.
Cherwien, David. "Psalm 46: God Is Our Refuge." U, cong, org.
   MSM 80-800.
Folkening, John. *Six Psalm Settings with Antiphons.* U, SATB, cong, kybd.
   MSM 80-700.
Hallock, Peter/arr. Carl Crosier. *The Ionian Psalter.* U, org.   ION.
Harbor, Rawn. "The Lord of Hosts Is with Us." TFF 6.
Wood, Dale.   PW B.

CHORAL

Bach, J. S. "Ein feste Burg" in *Bach for All Seasons.* SATB.
   AFP 080065854X.
Bertalot, John. "Thy Word Is a Lantern." SATB div, org, opt brass
   qrt, perc. AFP 0800674251.
Cherwien, David, arr. "Lord, Keep Us Steadfast." SATB, tpt.
   CPH 98-3640.

Ferguson, John. "The Church's One Foundation." SATB, opt cong,
   brass, org.   AFP 0800658310.
Ferguson, John. "Psalm 46." SATB, org.   AFP 0800656067.
Hassler, Hans Leo. "A Mighty Fortress Is Our God" in *Chantry Choirbook.*   AFP 0800657772.
Hayes, Mark. "Let the Word Go Forth." SATB, org.
   AFP 0800674189.
Mendelssohn, Felix. "On God Alone My Hope" in *Chantry Choirbook.*
   SATB, AFP 0800657772.
Pote, Allen. "God Is Our Refuge." SATB, pno, 2 tpt.   HOP A 583.
Sadowski, Kevin. "A Mighty Fortress Is Our God." SATB, 2 tpt,
   2 tbn.   CPH 98-2830.

CHILDREN'S CHOIRS

Bertalot, John. "God Is Our Hope." 2 pt, kybd.   CG CGA444.
Drexler, Richard, and Rusty Edwards. "Simple Song." U, kybd, opt
   inst.   AFP 0800674219.
Larson, Lloyd. "Take Up the Tambourine." U/2 pt, kybd.
   CG CGA819.

KEYBOARD/INSTRUMENTAL

Alain, Jehan. "Litanies" in *Livre d'orgue de Jehan Alain, Tome II.* Org.
   LED.
Albrecht, Mark. "Eden Church" in *Early American Hymns and Tunes for
   Flute and Piano.* Pno, inst.   AFP 0800658911.
Bach, J. S. "Ein feste Burg" in *Orgelwerke.* Org.   Various ed.
Behnke, John. "Kirken den er et gammelt Hus" in *Variations for Seven
   Familiar Hymns.* Org.   AFP 0800655605.
Cherwien, David. "Amazing Grace" in *Amazing Grace: Four for Piano.*
   Pno.   AFP 0800659031.
Harbach, Barbara. "Suite on German Chorales." Org.
   AFP 0800675010.
Hobby, Robert. "Ein feste Burg" in *Hymn Preludes for Funerals and
   Memorials.* Org.   AFP 0800675371.
Pelz, Walter L. "Fanfare for Reformation." Org.   MSM 10-802.
Walcha, Helmut. "Ein feste Burg" in *A New Liturgical Year.* Org.
   AFP 0800656717.
Various. "Ein feste Burg" in *Augsburg Organ Library: November.* Org.
   AFP 0800658965.

HANDBELL

Fedak, Alfred. "Built on the Rock." 2–3 oct, 2 pt, kybd, opt cong.
   JEF MSL241503.
Linker, Janet. "Built on a Rock." 3 oct, cong, opt tpt, org, SATB.
   AFP 0800655680.
Page, Anna Laura. "A Mighty Fortress Is Our God." 3–5 oct, opt hc.
   AFP 0800658841.

Rogers, Sharon Elery. "Songs of Hope and Strength." 2–3 oct (medley). JEF MRW8083.

Waldrop, Tammy. "Ein feste Burg." 3–5 oct, opt org, brass. JEF MJHS9173.

PRAISE ENSEMBLE

Baloche, Rita. "Rock of Ages" in *Praise Band Songbook* 7. 3 pt, pno, gtr. MAR.

Beech, Jay. "Freedom Has Come" in *The Rock Hymnal, vol. 2.* Baytone Music.

Cook, Steve and Vicki Cook/arr. Christopher. "We Rejoice in the Grace of God." SATB, pno. WRD 3010770162.

Luther, Martin/arr. Tommy Walker. "A Mighty Fortress" in *Praise Hymns and Choruses, 4th ed.* MAR.

Muller, Teresa. "Rock of My Salvation." W&P 161

October 26, 2003

Twentieth Sunday after Pentecost
Proper 25

INTRODUCTION

Bartimaeus, a blind beggar, beseeches Jesus with these words, "Son of David, have mercy on me." We too seek God's mercy on behalf of the world, the church, and all those in need. In the words of the ancient Kyrie, we sing, "Lord, have mercy." Gathered as God's people, we pray for a faith that will enable us to see the signs of God's merciful presence among us even as we become signs of healing in the world.

Today the church commemorates three important German hymnwriters of the sixteenth and seventeenth centuries: Philipp Nicolai (died 1608), Johann Heermann (1647), and Paul Gerhardt (1676).

PRAYER OF THE DAY

Almighty and everlasting God, increase in us the gifts of faith, hope, and charity; and, that we may obtain what you promise, make us love what you command; through your Son, Jesus Christ our Lord.

VERSE

Alleluia. The Lord will rescue me from every evil attack and save me for his heavenly kingdom. Alleluia. (2 Tim. 4:18)

READINGS

Jeremiah 31:7-9

Part of a poem celebrating the return from exile, this passage makes it clear that those who are blind and lame are among those who receive God's gracious consolation.

Psalm 126

Those who sowed with tears will reap with songs of joy. (Ps. 126:6)

Hebrews 7:23-28

Jesus is our great high priest, who not only offers us salvation through his sacrificial death, but lives to make intercession on our behalf.

Mark 10:46-52

In contrast to the disciples who seek after glory in last Sunday's gospel, Bartimaeus comes to Jesus with faith, asking that he might see again. Recognizing Jesus' identity, Bartimaeus is the first person to call him "Son of David" in the Gospel of Mark.

SEMICONTINUOUS FIRST READING/PSALM

Job 42:1-6, 10-17

In these verses we read of Job's period of prolonged suffering coming to an end. Though the end of the book sees Job's fortunes restored to an even greater level than before his string of adversities, the overarching message of the book is that the righteous are not always prosperous.

Psalm 34:1-8 [19-22]

Taste and see that the LORD is good. (Ps.34:8)

COLOR Green

THE PRAYERS

As we await the full harvest of the Spirit, let us offer our prayers to God who is abundant in every good gift.

329

A BRIEF SILENCE.

Let us pray for the church, that its leaders would see God's vision and would encourage the faithful to proceed without fear into the uncertainties of the future. Hear us, O God;

your mercy is great.

Let us pray for the nations of the world and for our own country, that God's peace-giving Spirit would rest upon all who govern and guide us. Hear us, O God;

your mercy is great.

Let us pray for those in need, especially expectant mothers, that their pregnancy would be without complication, and the day they deliver one of rejoicing. Hear us, O God;

your mercy is great.

Let us pray for those who are sick *(especially)*, that they might be touched by God's tender, healing hand. Hear us, O God;

your mercy is great.

Let us pray for all who are dying, and all who mourn. Grant your comfort to all who grieve. Hear us, O God;

your mercy is great.

HERE OTHER INTERCESSIONS MAY BE OFFERED.

Let us pray in thanksgiving for all who have finished the race and now rest in God's eternal presence, especially Philipp Nicolai, Johann Heermann, and Paul Gerhardt (and *names*). Bring us at last to that same blessed place. Hear us, O God;

your mercy is great.

Teach us to pray, O God, and grant us wisdom in our asking, in the name of Jesus Christ our Lord.

Amen

IMAGES FOR PREACHING

The Brief Order for Confession and Forgiveness with which we often prepare ourselves for worship is interestingly named. "Brief" of course is used to compare it to a longer order of confession available. Yet that word might lead us to wonder if, proportionate to our sin, we should spend more time in this rite where we depend on our great high priest Jesus making intercession for us. "Order" is the other word that is of interest. Confession and forgiveness seem both to be occasions where the reserved proper "order" is not proportional either to the sin or the event of forgiveness.

Bartimaeus, son of Timaeus, began and apparently continued to shout out and say "Jesus, Son of David, have mercy on me." Neither brief nor orderly, it seems, and therefore many folk sternly ordered him to be quiet. But he would have none of this desire for decorum or brevity or order; and knowing his need, he cried out even more loudly.

Perhaps we might assume his posture on this day in regard to our need for an intercessor. Perhaps we might also cry out for the sake of this shadowed creation, *Kyrie eleison*—Lord, have mercy! What if the church were more insistent in its praying and its pleas? Would that we would be more like Bartimaeus in passionately knowing our need and less like the "many" who would seek to silence those unable to be brief and orderly in their praying and need. Let us not be surprised when Jesus turns aside to engage those who embarrass our structured and ordered ways. Instead, let us demandingly shout out as well, seeking vision and hearing for the work of leaning into the future that our God offers in the gift of the beloved Son.

WORSHIP MATTERS

Often certain parts of the ordinary in the liturgy can be highlighted on appropriate Sundays. The creed is one section that is frequently taken for granted—just mumbled through on the way from the hymn of the day to the prayers. But it is, perhaps more than any other part, the great celebration of our unity in Christ. And we are united not only within this congregation but, by use of the ecumenical creeds, with the great catholic church. "I believe," and so have uncounted other worshipers of all times and places. As promised, God is bringing us together from the farthest parts of the earth. Help the people to see the grandeur of this seemingly humble moment, and encourage them to speak it out accordingly.

LET THE CHILDREN COME

The lessons for this day weave together the themes of celebration and thanksgiving for gifts of home, harvest, and healing. As we look around our worship settings, what would children see that celebrates the blessings of God? What would they hear? Where would their voices fit in? When it comes to the gift of healing, how can children relate to the wonderful story of Bartimaeus? One way would be to include, in prayers for those to be healed, names that children might want to offer. Their requests, joined with those of adults, proclaim the strength of God's healing power.

330

HYMNS FOR WORSHIP

GATHERING

Oh, for a thousand tongues to sing   LBW 559

Each morning brings us   WOV 800

HYMN OF THE DAY

God, whose almighty word   LBW 400

ALTERNATE HYMN OF THE DAY

Here in this place   WOV 718

Your hand, O Lord, in days of old   LBW 431

COMMUNION

Amazing grace   LBW 448

We come to the hungry feast   WOV 766

SENDING

Praise, my soul, the King of heaven   LBW 549

I'm so glad Jesus lifted me   WOV 673, TFF 191

Give thanks   TFF 292, W&P 41

ADDITIONAL HYMNS AND SONGS

O very God of very God   H82 672

O Lord, open my eyes   TFF 134

I will sing of the mercies of the Lord   W&P 74

MUSIC FOR THE DAY

PSALMODY

Beckstrand, William.   PW B.

Smith, Alan. "The Lord Has Done Great Things." PS 1.

CHORAL

Bertalot, John. "Amazing Grace." SATB, org.   AFP 0800649141.
   Also in *The Augsburg Choirbook.* AFP 0800656784.

Copland, Aaron. "Help Us, O Lord." SATB.   B&H OCTB6018.

Haugen, Marty. "Healer of Our Every Ill." 2 pt, C inst, pno.
   GIA G-3478.

Hopson, Hal H. "Sing Aloud to God." SATB, org, opt tpt.
   AFP 0800674642.

Wienhorst, Richard. "Amazing Grace." SATB, 2 fl.   MF MF2010.

CHILDREN'S CHOIRS

Carter, John. "We Are Gathered Here to Praise the Lord" in *Sing a New Song!* U, desc. kybd.   HOP 1054.

Jothen, Michael. "We Are Children of Our God." U/2 pt, kybd, opt fl/vln, opt 3 oct hb, opt. cong.   CG CGA731.

KEYBOARD/INSTRUMENTAL

Cotter, Jeanne. "Gather Us In" in *After the Rain.* Pno.   GIA G-3390.

Lübeck, Vincent. "Praeludium in E" in *Organ Works.* Org.
   KAL 9086.

HANDBELL

Geschke, Susan. "Just As I Am." 3 oct.   JEF LC201185L.

McKechnie, Linda. "Amazing Grace." 3–5 oct, org, opt tpt.
   JEF JHS9101.

PRAISE ENSEMBLE

Baloche, Paul. "Open the Eyes of My Heart" in *First Love Songbook.*
   3 pt, kybd, gtr. INT.

Falson, Chris. "I Walk by Faith" in *Praise Band Songbook 8.* 3 pt, pno,
   gtr.   INT.

Morgan, Reuben/arr. Cole. "What the Lord Has Done in Me."
   3 pt, pno, gtr, orch.   Praise Charts.

Nuzum, Eric. "God Is Now Reviving His People" in *Smithton Outpouring Songbook.* 3 pt, pno, gtr.   INT.

Paris, Twila/arr. Rhodes. "Lamb of God." SATB, pno.
   WRD 301 0924 16X.

331

Sunday, October 26

PHILIPP NICOLAI, 1608; JOHANN HEERMANN, 1647; PAUL GERHARDT, 1676; HYMNWRITERS

These three outstanding hymnwriters all worked in Germany in the seventeenth century during times of war and plague. When Philipp Nicolai was a pastor in Westphalia, the plague killed 1,300 of his parishioners. One hundred seventy people died in one week. His hymns "Wake, awake for night is flying" (LBW 31) and "O Morning Star, how fair, how bright" (LBW 76) were included in a series of meditations he wrote to comfort his parishioners during the plague. The style of Johann Heermann's hymns moved away from the more objective style of Reformation hymnody toward expressing the emotions of faith. Three of his hymns are in *LBW* including his plaintive text, "Ah, holy Jesus" (123). Paul Gerhardt lost a preaching position at St. Nicholas's Church in Berlin because he refused to sign a document stating he would not make theological arguments in his sermons. Some have called him the greatest of Lutheran hymnwriters.

Tuesday, October 28

ST. SIMON AND ST. JUDE, APOSTLES

We know little about Simon and Jude. In New Testament lists of the apostles, Simon the "zealot" or Cananean is mentioned, but he is never mentioned apart from these lists. Jude, sometimes called Thaddeus, is also mentioned in lists of the twelve. At the last supper Jude asked Jesus why he had chosen to reveal himself to the disciples but not to the world. A traditional story about Simon and Jude says that they traveled together on a missionary journey to Persia and were both martyred there.

The prayer of the day for this lesser festival asks that as Simon and Jude "were faithful and zealous in their mission, so we may with ardent devotion make known the love and mercy of our Lord and Savior Jesus Christ."

Friday, October 31

REFORMATION DAY

By the end of the seventeenth century, many Lutheran churches celebrated a festival commemorating Martin Luther's posting of the Ninety-five Theses, a summary of the abuses in the church of his time. At the heart of the reform movement was the gospel, the good news that it is by grace through faith that we are justified and set free.

With the 1999 signing of the Joint Declaration on the Doctrine of Justification on this very date, the question of how the reformation might be celebrated appropriately is a lively question. If Lutherans and Roman Catholics agree on the basic nature of the gospel, now what? This commemoration is less a victory day for Lutherans than it is an opportunity to be reminded of the reformers' belief that the church would always stand in need of reformation.

NOVEMBER

The church celebrates Christ

as the gateway to eternal life

Images *of the* Season

The month of November often takes on a somewhat

mysterious aura. In the Northern Hemisphere, the days grow

noticeably shorter. In many areas, the trees are bare. The crops

are mostly harvested, the garden greenery mulched or composted. The weather cools down, although warm spells may bring in fog. All of that loss of summer's vitality makes it a natural time for those attuned to the earth to meditate on the passing of life.

The church "season" of November is one that people seem to understand on a visceral level, needing little theological rationale. We somehow realize intuitively that we need to take the time to contemplate the transitory nature of earthly life, to remember those who have died before us, to meditate on our own mortality, and to look to the eternal life that awaits us around the throne of God.

We may recall the resonant words from the Ash Wednesday liturgy: "Remember that you are dust, and to dust you shall return." Other times and cultures needed less help in remembering that truth. Throughout Europe, in medieval churches one can see skulls in stonework, in paintings—signs of the all-too-obvious reality of death, which could and did come in plague, in accident, in childbirth, and was readily acknowledged. By contrast, today death takes place in carefully controlled surroundings; or if that can't be arranged, as in the case of an accident, then it is tidied up and whisked away as quickly as possible. Death, outside of generalities, is not a subject for polite conversation. Among other things, it interferes with the "selling" of life.

And yet, to paraphrase the infamous bumper sticker, death happens. We may take extreme steps to hide it, but barring the second coming of Christ in the near future, all of us, and all of our loved ones, will die—whether we are ready or not. So the instinct to come to grips with death and prepare ourselves for its arrival serves us well, and the church does well to help people broach the topic.

Of course, the church has always had a love/hate relationship with death—usually more hate than love. Partly because death is one of those liminal areas—somewhat scary, little known—in which we are vulnerable to all sorts of religious and quasi-religious hocus-pocus. And the church is rightly wary of being associated with

that. But theological reasons affect the ambivalence as well. Christ is the Lord of life, and has won the victory over death. St. Paul is eloquent in 1 Corinthians 15 about death as the final enemy. At the same time, of course, death is a present reality and must be seen, to some extent, as a good part of God's creation. Death feeds further life, as Jesus alluded to in his teaching: "Unless a grain of wheat falls into the earth and dies, it remains just a single grain; but if it dies, it bears much fruit" (John 12:24). What's more, if death, though still with us, has lost its sting, its ultimate authority, then St. Francis of Assisi was on target in addressing it as sister, like us a servant of God. Death ushers most of us into the heavenly presence of God, and so it is that most saints are commemorated not on their birthday, but their death day.

Clearly, then, November bears a rich cargo of meaning, both spoken and not. And while the church need not dwell morbidly on death throughout the month, it finds opportunities to interweave our worship with the natural tendency to think on death and the eternal life beyond. It begins with All Saints Day, which many congregations observe on the first Sunday of every November, and which leads us into a remembrance of those well-known and little-known people who have died in the faith. At the other end of the month, we have the festival of Christ the King, with its strong eschatological emphasis. Christ, who died, who is risen, this same Christ will come again to gather his kingdom to himself and deliver it to God. Then we, together with all who have died, will be reunited in eternal life. The two Sundays in between also provide openings for thoughts on death and the end times: a woman saved from starvation, another who gave up her last life's savings, Daniel's prophecy of the resurrection of the dead, Jesus' apocalyptic message.

Some fear that talk of death is too gloomy for church, but it need not be. It is a topic that is on people's minds anyway. Take the opportunity to lift it out of the shadows of fear and the hokum of the charlatan, and bring it into the brilliant light of the risen Christ.

334

Environment *and* Art *for the* Season

All around us, the natural world is in decline.

The days noticeably shorten. Flowers and plants fade.

The cooler temperatures, bare trees, gray skies,

and harvested fields whose ground is slowly hardening to the cold remind us it is the annual time for remembering our beloved dead, being conscious of our own inevitable death, and giving thanks for family, friends, and the glorious bounty the earth brings forth. We take time to decorate the graves of those who have gone before us, and Americans begin to plan the Thanksgiving feast.

But for those of us entrusted with caring for the worship environment of our church community, November is marked by the month-long celebration of the communion of saints, of remembering our beloved dead, and of heightened focus on Christ's eventual second coming at the end of time. Each of these themes contributes to complementary liturgical moods.

The best place to start in decorating for the month of November is with harvest motifs. Thematically, All Saints Day is undeniably tied to the harvest, an intense image of the paschal mystery that the Scriptures use repeatedly as a sign of the kingdom to come, the time when all things will be made new. This feast sets the tone for the entire month, and if done well, the environment for this day requires only few, if any, modifications between now and Christ the King. It may take a bit of work to get people thinking this way, but it is worth pursuing: Something about All Saints flows into our giving thanks for the harvest, and something about our appreciation of the bountiful earth and the many blessings in our lives that leads us to remembrance of the dead.

During November, many congregations set up a memorial to those gone before us whose focal point is the community's beautifully bound book of the names of the dead. The memorial may simply be a place to lovingly display this blank book in which people can write the names of their deceased loved ones, or it could be more elaborate, including photos and other mementos. A more elaborate memorial might fit in the space for the baptismal font, but it would also be appropriately placed in an alcove or some other place where people can both find it easily as well as spend time in quiet reflection. But

choose only one site: putting the book of the names of the dead by the font and paschal candle is highly appropriate symbolically, but creating a second space for photos and other mementos is disjointed.

Whatever site is chosen, consider a few important things, including how the book will be used. If people will be invited to write in names themselves, the space where it is displayed should be fully accessible (no steps leading to or from it, for example), and the book should be unencumbered (not surrounded by flowers, candles, and so forth, on all sides). You will also need to keep pens handy; choose a couple inexpensive yet good-looking ones, worthy of being placed next to so fine a book. It is probably better to have people write the names in the book themselves than to have a calligrapher do it. Although folks may not look back to see what they wrote in last year and write in the same names again, this is not bad—it may be an annual ritual to come forward to the book and call to mind all those whose presence is missed.

If you have a memorial that allows people to bring photos, mementos, votive candles, and so forth, you will need to decide how those items are handled. Allowing people to add to the display freely lends one kind of feel; collecting these items and having someone be in charge of artfully arranging them lend another. Decide what is best based on the location of the memorial and the degree of use. Either way, someone will still need to keep an eye on the space to keep it neat and looking good. Don't forget to include some harvest imagery around the memorial to the dead to tie together harvest, the dead, and All Saints in the way described earlier.

Whatever your memorial to the faithful departed looks like—as well as the rest of the worship space— keep the following in mind: The liturgical calendar gives the church, in the month of November, an unparalleled opportunity to create an environment in which we can acknowledge and reflect on death, loss, grief, and the hope that we are assured of through Christ. From a pastoral perspective, what we are able to do in this month is

335

allow people to sort through whatever wide variety of feelings they may carry with them on a subject that touches us all.

Taking care of cemeteries and gravesites is a sign of respect not only to the dead but also to all those who visit. If your parish has a cemetery, consider decorating the entrance to it and taking special care of its maintenance this month. A simple arrangement of sturdy fabrics in autumn colors can communicate the connection between All Saints, the harvest, and the kingdom that will one day come. A grapevine wreath is another fine symbol, an emblem of victory and of God's eternal reign.

Preaching *with the* Season

The environments of time and space intensify their presence in our November lives. The change from daylight time to standard time brings an earlier shadowed evening,

336

and the farther north one journeys, the more the landscape reveals the decay and death that must precede life. In November, the anxiety over the shadows in our existence begins to build in many hearts as many thoughts turn to mortality. And so we gather to be addressed by a word that would offer us hope and life even as we journey in these November days.

It is important to note the nature of utterance and speech that occurs in worship and that leads to the shaping and patterning of the community of faith. Many of the words spoken in worship come in the form of address, where we hear a word spoken to us from outside of ourselves. The one who speaks is the one whom we confess spoke the world into being with a passionate address that exclaimed "Let there be!" For "in the beginning was the Word and the Word was with God. . . . All things came into being through him." It is the continued speaking of God that sustains life—as we are addressed by God, we are given life. The community that gathers for worship, then, is a listening community. The liturgy of the church brings us to the font, table, and pulpit so that God might address us. We come together to listen to God's address to creation.

In November, the word speaks to the realities of limit and endings, both of individual lives and of the cosmos. As the weight of increasing November darkness bears in on us, we become aware of our mortality and of our limits as humans. At gatherings to celebrate All

Saints and even Thanksgiving, we are aware of our losses and of the absence of those who have died. The texts that end the church year speak of the end of all things.

While we are intellectually aware of the truth of mortality and perhaps even the universe, we spend much of our time living with the illusions of immortality. A culture of consuming shapes our imaginations and expectations and impinges on our social, cultural, and economic journeys in November. One of the clear signs of this consumer focus is the ever-earlier rush to fend off the darkness and to bring meaning to the approaching holidays through purchasing. We live in a culture where many seek to hide their mortality. Too often we leave talk of the end times to fundamentalists and millennialists even as we confess each week that Christ shall come again to judge the living and the dead. November is a good month to explore death as a promise rather than a primitive threat. It is a good month to preach on mortality and to lead adult forums on issues of death and dying. It is one of the gifts of the church that we do have something to say. Despite our culture's great fear, people are thirsting to engage these issues.

In worship we hear the call to face the truth concerning the End. Our texts, our liturgies, our creeds, and our hymnody contain wonderful resources a preacher can use and learn from. Like cosmologists and physicists, we give witness to endings and limit. The gathered community for worship will find itself addressed with a word that is brutally honest about the reality of limit and end and death. But it is also in worship that hope is born in the proclamation of God's entering into the creation and into the end. In worship we are addressed by our God who comes from the outside to enter in. This God also then promises to continue to speak life to us. It is this word upon which we live and depend.

However, even as God speaks life to us, we note that this address not only gives us life but also calls us into a life. We are called into a life of service in the creation.

Go! Love your neighbor as yourself. Forgive one another as I have forgiven you. Make disciples. Baptize. God addresses us *for the sake of* the cosmos, not so that we might escape from it.

November is a time, then, to speak of the congregation's ministry and mission to a world both wonderfully created by God's "Let there be!" and shadowed as well by sin. It is the time to proclaim that our beginnings and endings are held close in the embrace of this lover of the cosmos who is the Alpha and the Omega.

Shape *of* Worship *for the* Season

BASIC SHAPE OF THE EUCHARISTIC RITE

- Confession and Forgiveness: see alternate worship text for November in *Sundays and Seasons* as an option to the text in the liturgy setting

GATHERING

- Greeting: see alternate worship text for November
- Omit the Kyrie during November (except on the festivals of All Saints and Christ the King)
- Use the hymn of praise throughout November (or use "This is the feast of victory" just for the festivals of All Saints and Christ the King)

WORD

- Use the Nicene Creed for the festivals of All Saints and Christ the King, use the Apostles' Creed for the remainder of the month
- The prayers: see the prayers in the November section of Sundays and Seasons
- Incorporate the names of those who have died into one of the prayer petitions on All Saints Sunday

BAPTISM

- Consider observing All Saints Sunday (November 2) as a baptismal festival

MEAL

- Offertory prayer: see alternate worship text for November
- Use the proper preface for Sundays after Pentecost; for the festival of All Saints, use the proper preface for All Saints; *WOV* Leaders Edition provides a proper preface for Christ the King
- Eucharistic prayer: in addition to four main options in *LBW*, see "Eucharistic Prayer I: November" in *WOV* Leaders Edition, p. 73
- Invitation to communion: see alternate worship text for November
- Post-communion prayer: see alternate worship text for November

SENDING

- Benediction: see alternate worship text for November
- Dismissal: see alternate worship text for November

337

Assembly Song *for the* Season

"Let us rejoice and exult and give God the glory,

for the marriage of the Lamb has come, and his Bride has made

herself ready" (Rev. 19:7, Offertory for All Saints' Day).

November brings the church year to a stirring conclusion. What was begun a year ago in Advent now erupts in music that rejoices, exults, and gives God the glory. Framed by All Saints Day and Christ the King, this month would have us focus on the great feast that is to come. And the surprise as we celebrate Christ the King is that we are once again prepared for Advent. Our cycle begins again; the Alpha is the Omega is the Alpha . . .

GATHERING

- Begin each liturgy with a festive entrance hymn, calling the people to the feast and inviting God into the assembly.
- The Te Deum is one of the most ancient and glorious of the hymns of the church. Historically it has been associated with Morning Prayer, but use it each Sunday this month for the hymn of praise. Have the choir sing one of the many and varied choral arrangements that are readily available. Or have the assembly sing it, using "Holy God, we praise your name" (LBW 535, a hymn paraphrase), the Te Deum from the paschal blessing of Morning Prayer (*LBW* p. 139), or "You are God; we praise you" (LBW 3). One possible scheme would be to use a festive setting on All Saints' Day and Christ the King, and the simple chant setting at LBW 3 on the intervening Sundays. Accompany the latter with handbells, and use alternation.
- Add the Kyrie to the gathering rite on Christ the King Sunday.

WORD

- Use the first stanza of "Soon and very soon" (WOV 744, TFF 38, W&P 128) for a seasonal psalm refrain. Sing it just at the beginning and end of each psalm, and have the choir do the psalm verses. Use *LBW* tone 9 transposed to F (an accompaniment is found at TFF 6); if the psalm has an odd number of verses, repeat the second half of the tone for the final verse.

- Have the choir sing the proper verse in one of the published settings that are available, or use the "alleluias" from "For all the saints" (LBW 174) as a frame for the verse chanted by the choir; use *LBW* tone 3 in G major (which will give it a very bright sound) accompanied by G, A, B, and D handbells.

MEAL

- "Let the vineyards be fruitful" is appropriate for the offertory song as the harvest season continues. As an alternative, if the Te Deum served as the hymn of praise, use "This is the feast" as offertory. It could also be sung as the first music during the distribution of communion.
- If you continue to use the liturgical setting from autumn, dress up the Sanctus with instruments and choir. Use a eucharistic prayer that calls for the "Through him, with him" musical response. "Holy, holy, holy Lord" and "Acclamations and Amen" set to LAND OF REST (WOV 616a and 616b) work well during this season also, especially if the assembly knows the hymn "Jerusalem, my happy home" (LBW 331).
- Sing some hymns that paint the vision of the great heavenly banquet, the feast at which all the saints and angels sing praise to Christ the King. Some examples are "Let all mortal flesh keep silence" (LBW 198), "At the Lamb's high feast we sing" (LBW 210), "Love divine, all loves excelling" (LBW 315), and "Oh, what their joy" (LBW 337).

SENDING

- If you used one of the "alleluias" for the gospel acclamation in Easter (such as WOV 609, 610, 612, 613; LLC 203, 204; TFF 25, 26, 27) use it again for the post-communion canticle as the table is cleared.
- Sing a seasonal sending hymn, such as "Father, we thank you" (WOV 704) or "Thine the amen, thine the praise" (WOV 801).

Music *for the* Season

VERSE AND OFFERTORY

Hobby, Robert. "Offertory for All Saints Day." 2 pt mxd.
　　MSM 80-811.

Hobby, Robert. "Verse for All Saints Day." 2 pt mxd.　MSM 80-810.

See also Music for the Season of Autumn.

CHORAL

Bach, J. S. "Now Thank We All Our God" in *Bach for All
　　Seasons*. SATB, kybd.　AFP 080065854X.

Berger, Jean. "The Eyes of All Wait Upon Thee." SATB.
　　AFP 0800645596. Also in *The Augsburg Choirbook*.
　　AFP 0800656784.

Brahms, Johannes. "How Lovely Is Thy Dwellingplace" in *Chantry
　　Choirbook*. SATB, org.　AFP 0800657772.

Campbell, Sidney. "Sing We Merrily Unto God Our Strength."
　　SATB, org.　NOV 29 0253.

Copland, Aaron. "At the River" SATB (or other voicings), pno.
　　B&H 5513.

Forsberg, Charles. "Fairest Lord Jesus." SATB, pno.
　　AFP 0800656962.

Handel, G. F. "The Trumpet Shall Sound" in *Messiah*. baritone solo,
　　kybd, opt tpt.　Various ed.

Hobby, Robert. "Lord, Let Us Listen." 2 pt trbl, pno.
　　AFP 0800659236.

Johnson, Ralph M. "Be Thou a Smooth Way." SATB, pno.
　　AFP 0800659325.

Kosche, Kenneth T. "Bring Us, O Lord God." SATB.　MSM 50-8103.

Lovelace, Austin C. "How Lovely Is Thy Dwelling Place." SATB, org.
　　AFP 0800650948.

Manz, Paul. "E'en So, Lord Jesus, Quickly Come." SATB.
　　MSM 50-900.

Martinson, Joel. "By All Your Saints." 2 pt, mxd, org.
　　AFP 080065160X.

Parker, Alice. "Hark, I Hear the Harps Eternal." SATB.　LAW 51331.

Schalk, Carl. "I Saw a New Heaven and a New Earth." SATB.
　　AFP 0800656644. Also in *The Augsburg Choirbook*.
　　AFP 0800656784.

Shute, Linda Cable. "Who Are These like Stars Appearing." SATB,
　　org.　AFP 0800658507.

White, Nicholas. "Steal Away." SATB.　AFP 0800653866.

CHILDREN'S CHOIRS

McIver, Robert. "Shall We Gather at the River?" Combined U, SATB,
　　pno, opt trbl inst.　CG CGA688.

Pooler, Marie. "Sing to the Lord of Harvest" in *Unison and Two-Part
　　Anthems*. U/2 pt, kybd.　AFP 0800648919.

Powell, Robert J. "We Give Thee Thanks Today." 2 pt, kybd.
　　AFP 6000102666.

Wood, Dale. "Jubilate Deo." SA, org, opt perc.　AFP 0800645812.

KEYBOARD/INSTRUMENTAL

Augsburg Organ Library: November. Org.　AFP 0800658965.

Bach, J. S./arr. Hyslop. *Now Thank We All Our God* (Cantata 79).
　　Brass qrt, org.　GIA 4765.

Ferguson, John. "Softly and Tenderly Jesus Is Calling" in *Three Nine-
　　teenth Century Revival Hymns*. Org.　AFP 0800658205.

Hobby, Robert. "Variations on 'Jerusalem, My Happy Home.' " Org.
　　MSM 10-807.

Peeters, Flor. "Aria." Org.　PRE EH 265.

West, John. "Fanfare on 'Sine Nomine.'" Org.　AFP 0800659473.

Wold, Wayne L. *A November to Remember*. Org.　AFP 080065983X.

HANDBELL

Giardini, Felice de/arr. Page. "Come Thou Almighty King." 2–3 oct.
　　ALF 18577.

Handel, G. F./arr. J. Wilson. "Thanks Be to Thee." 2–4 oct, opt C
　　inst.　JEF HP1396.

Kinyon, Barbara. "Blessed Assurance." 2–3 oct, hc.　AG 2087.

McChesney, Kevin. "Ring Together Church Year." 2–3 oct, L1+.
　　JEF JHS 9241.

McFadden, Jane. "In Heaven Above." 3–5 oct.　AFP 0800659929.

Morris, Hart. "In Praise of Life." 3–5 oct, fl, cl/hc.　AG 35194J.

Wagner, Douglas. "Make Me a Channel of Your Peace." 3–5 oct,
　　SATB, kybd.　AG 2064.

Wagner, H. Dean. "Fantasy on 'Kingsfold.' " 3–5 oct, opt hc.
　　AG 2134.

PRAISE ENSEMBLE

Joncas, Michael/arr. Mark Hayes. "On Eagle's Wings." SATB, orch.
　　ALF 16104.

Mollicone, Henry. "Hear Me, Redeemer." SATB, solo, pno.　ECS.

339

Alternate Worship Texts

CONFESSION AND FORGIVENESS

In the name of the Father, and of the ✙ Son,
and of the Holy Spirit.
Amen

Let us approach God with a true heart,
in full assurance of God's power
to heal and to forgive sins.

Silence for reflection and self-examination.

Merciful God,
**you have loved your people
from the beginning of time,
desiring that we also love you
and our neighbor with fullness of heart.
We confess that we often seek wealth
or security for ourselves,
without acting generously toward others.
Forgive us and point us in your ways,
that we might reflect your will
for us and your creation. Amen**

God promised that everyone who calls
on the name of the Lord shall be saved.
As an ordained minister of the church of Christ,
and by his authority, I declare to you pardon
and forgiveness of all your sins.
Amen

GREETING

The grace of eternal God, the holy and living One,
Father, Son, and Holy Spirit, be with you all.
And also with you.

PRAYERS

In communion with all the saints,
let us pray to God who is our eternal home.

A brief silence.

Each petition ends:
Lord, in your mercy,
hear our prayer.

Concluding petition:
Your reign, O God, endures forever,
and in Christ we are free to be your saints and servants.
Hear our prayers for the sake of him who died and rose again,
and lives with you in the company of all your saints in light.
Amen

OFFERTORY PRAYER

Generous God,
**your jar of meal will not be emptied,
and your heavenly banquet will last for eternity.
Through your gift of this sacrament,
transform us to be servants
of your humble and eternal reign. Amen**

INVITATION TO COMMUNION

The Lord of hosts makes for all peoples
a feast of rich food, a feast of well-aged wines.
Come and rejoice in God's salvation.

POST-COMMUNION PRAYER

By your word and sacraments, O God,
you give us a foretaste
of the new heaven and new earth
that will be ours forever.
Strengthen us in this vision
that we might draw others to believe
in the hope that is ours,
through Jesus Christ our Lord.
Amen

BLESSING

May almighty God,
who makes all things new in Jesus Christ,
uphold you by the Spirit in times of trial
and ✙ bring you at last to the heavenly Jerusalem.
Amen

DISMISSAL

Go in peace to love God and serve your neighbor.
Thanks be to God.

340

Seasonal Rites

Vigil of All Saints

This order of worship may be used on All Hallows Eve, October 31, or the evening before All Saints Sunday.

SERVICE OF LIGHT
PROCESSION

All stand as the lighted paschal candle is carried in procession to its stand in front of the assembly. The people may light hand-held candles from its flame.

In the new Jerusalem there will be no need of | sun or moon,
for the glory of God will be its | light.
Before the Lamb is a multitude from | every nation,
and they worship God night and | day.
Surely he is | coming soon.
Amen. Come, Lord | Jesus.

HYMN OF LIGHT

As this hymn is sung, the candles on and near the altar are lighted from the flame of the paschal candle.

Joyous light of glory:
of the immortal Father;
heavenly, holy, blessed Jesus Christ.
We have come to the setting of the sun,
and we look to the evening light.
We sing to God, the Father, Son, and Holy Spirit:
You are worthy of being praised
with pure voices forever.
O Son of God, O Giver of light:
The universe proclaims your glory.

THANKSGIVING FOR LIGHT
The Lord be with you.
And also with you.
Let us give thanks to the Lord our God.
It is right to give our thanks and praise.
Blessed are you, O Lord our God, king of the universe,
who led your people Israel by a pillar of cloud by day
and a pillar of fire by night:
Enlighten our darkness by the light of your Christ;
may his Word be a lamp to our feet and a light to our path;
for you are merciful, and you love your whole creation,
and we, your creatures, glorify you, Father, Son, and Holy Spirit.
Amen

LITURGY OF THE WORD
FIRST READING
Genesis 12:1-8
Psalm 113

SECOND READING
Daniel 6:[1-15] 16-23
Psalm 116

THIRD READING
Hebrews 11:32—12:2
Psalm 149

FOURTH READING
Revelation 7:2-4, 9-17

CANTICLE
This is the feast of victory

GOSPEL
Matthew 5:1-12

SERMON

HYMN OF THE DAY

THANKSGIVING FOR BAPTISM

If possible, the people may gather around the font. After the prayer each person may dip a hand in the water and make the sign of the cross in remembrance of baptism.

The Lord be with you.
And also with you.
Let us give thanks to the Lord our God.
It is right to give our thanks and praise.
Holy God and mighty Lord, we give you thanks,
for you nourish and sustain us and all living things
with the gift of water.
In the beginning your Spirit moved over the waters,
and you created heaven and earth.
By the waters of the flood you saved Noah and his family.
You led Israel through the sea out of slavery
into the promised land.
In the waters of the Jordan
your Son was baptized by John and anointed with the Spirit.
By the baptism of his death and resurrection
your Son set us free from sin and death
and opened the way to everlasting life.
We give you thanks, O God,
that you have given us new life in the water of baptism.

341

Buried with Christ in his death,
you raise us to share in his resurrection
by the power of the Holy Spirit.
Through it we are united to your saints
of every time and place
who proclaim your reign
and surround our steps as we journey
toward the new and eternal Jerusalem.
May all who have passed through the waters of baptism
continue in the risen life of our Savior.
To you be all honor and glory, now and forever.
Amen

LITURGY OF THE EUCHARIST

*After all have returned to their places, the liturgy continues with
the preparation of the altar and the presentation of the gifts.*

342

NOTES ON THE SERVICE:
*- The opening verses in the procession of the paschal candle
may be sung using the musical setting found in LBW, p. 142.
- The hymn of light is found in LBW, p. 143. An alternate hymn
is "O Light whose splendor thrills" (WOV 728).
- The thanksgiving for light (LBW, p. 144) may be sung or spoken
by the leader.
- The psalm responses to the readings may be sung or spoken
by the assembly.
- The canticle is sung using one of the available musical settings
of this text.
- For the hymn of the day, one of the following hymns is suggested: "Sing with all the saints in glory" (WOV 691) or "Who is
this host arrayed in white" (LBW 314 or CS 13).
- If the people cannot gather at the font, the worship leaders
may process there during the singing of the hymn of the day.*

Saturday, November 1

ALL SAINTS DAY

The custom of commemorating all of the saints of the church on a single day goes back at least to the third century. Our All Saints Day celebrates the baptized people of God, living and dead, who make up the body of Christ. Today, or on tomorrow's All Saints Sunday, many congregations will remember the faithful who have died during the past year.

November 2, 2003

All Saints Sunday

INTRODUCTION

All Saints Sunday celebrates the baptized people of God, living and dead, who make up the body of Christ. With thanksgiving we remember all the faithful departed, especially those most dear to us who have died. Today's readings are filled with rich images of the eternal life promised to all the saints. The holy meal is a foretaste of that great and promised feast where death or pain will be no more. Even in the midst of loss and grief God wipes away the tears from our eyes and makes all things new.

PRAYER OF THE DAY

Almighty God, whose people are knit together in one holy Church, the body of Christ our Lord: Grant us grace to follow your blessed saints in lives of faith and commitment, and to know the inexpressible joys you have prepared for those who love you; through your Son, Jesus Christ our Lord, who lives and reigns with you and Holy Spirit, one God, now and forever.

VERSE

Alleluia. They are before the throne of God, and the one seated on the throne will shelter them. Alleluia. (Rev. 7:15)

READINGS

Isaiah 25:6-9

This reading focuses on the future day when the Lord will fully manifest sovereignty over the universe. On that

Our liturgy abounds with references to the saints and to our continual relationship with them. The preface for All Saints describes the relationship this way: "that moved by their witness and supported by their fellowship, we may run with perseverance the race that is set before us and with them receive the unfading crown of glory." Today and this week invite people to reflect on others—living and dead—who have moved and supported others by their lives of faith.

day, the Lord will host a banquet for God's faithful subjects. This banquet symbolizes the establishment of the Lord's dominion on earth. It symbolizes the joy, companionship, and prosperity that will characterize the Lord's reign.

or Wisdom of Solomon 3:1-9

The writer of this highly respected wisdom volume offers a glorious vision of the righteous resting at peace in the hand of God.

Psalm 24

They shall receive a blessing from the God of their salvation. (Ps. 24:5)

Revelation 21:1-6a

In the book of Revelation, John describes his vision of heaven, where the saints of God will live in light and glory. Of all the blessings found there, none will exceed that of simply being with God.

John 11:32-44

Through the raising of Lazarus, Jesus offers the world a vision of the life to come, when death and weeping will be no more.

COLOR White

THE PRAYERS

In communion with all the saints, let us pray to God who is our eternal home.

A BRIEF SILENCE.

343

O God our Alpha and our Omega, empower your church to remain faithful to you and to proclaim your salvation from day to day. Lord, in your mercy,
hear our prayer.
O Ruler of earth and heaven, strengthen all who seek to serve in offices of government, and guide all citizens who participate in the political process. Lord, in your mercy,
hear our prayer.
O Comforter of priceless worth, bless those who look to you for comfort in time of illness *(especially)*. Lord, in your mercy,
hear our prayer.
O Lover of our souls, we remember all those who are at rest in your great love and whose names we call to mind in this moment *(names of those who have recently died are mentioned)*. As they blessed us in life, we give you thanks for the blessing of their memory in death. Lord, in your mercy,
hear our prayer.
HERE OTHER INTERCESSIONS MAY BE OFFERED.
O Hope of the world to come, strengthen our hope that one day we will dwell with you in that new Jerusalem, where our every tear will be dried and our mourning will be turned into dancing. Lord, in your mercy,
hear our prayer.
Your reign, O God, endures forever, and in Christ we are free to be your saints and servants. Hear our prayers for the sake of him who died and rose again, and lives with you in the company of all your saints in light.
Amen

IMAGES FOR PREACHING

The richness of the texts appointed for this day is overwhelming. These texts focus our attention on the saints who have gone before us. As the daylight hours continue to shorten, these texts, combined with the powerful liturgical images and the remembrance rites in many congregations, present the preacher with many opportunities to engage significant issues of life and death and resurrection. Many congregations provide opportunities on this day to light candles in memory and honor of those saints who have given witness to faith and life, as well as those who have been baptized over the past twelve months. The preacher may be surrounded by the light of these flickering candles as a sign of the witness of those who have gone before us.

The flickering lights represent the stories of life and death that have touched those who come now to hear a word of good news. The flames are signs of the aching hearts and the tears of those present who know of the shroud of death that is cast over all peoples. It is a shroud we share with each other and all living things. It is the shroud where much ministry takes place in any worshiping community. It is the shroud the preacher knows of in her or his own life. It is the shroud we share with Jesus of Nazareth, the Son of the living God.

Hearers on this day need to know that God knows and honors their aching hearts, their memories, and their tears. They need to hear the truth spoken regarding death as well as new life. They need to hear the promise that the Alpha and Omega also weeps for Lazarus. This same promised one bends to wipe away all the tears shed in the shadows of death and bring us to the feast of all time and beyond time. On this day, we gather with all the saints around the foretaste of that feast, trusting that the death of Jesus has taken the disgrace of God's people from all the earth.

WORSHIP MATTERS

For many congregations, this day includes a reading of the names of those who have died in the past year, possibly the lighting of candles, the tolling of a bell. But the living baptized who joined the congregation in the last year are as much saints as those who died. Consider including some way to remind people that it is through baptism that we receive the promises fully fulfilled at our death.

The createdness of time and God's transcendence of it open people's eyes. Enabling long vistas this day helps bring us out of our own mournful memories and glimpse eternity. Use the entire worship area as much as possible for different parts of the liturgy. Moving to the perimeters and returning to the center during worship gives a physical representation of the ebb and flow of our physical lives in relationship with others whom we miss. Be creative in your use of space and in where readings are done, psalms intoned, or other worship acts assisted.

LET THE CHILDREN COME

Children are continuing stories. Sealed with the sign of the cross, they join the communion of saints, part of the ongoing narrative of God's love through the ages. On this Sunday we remember with thanksgiving those who have gone before us. Our children need this connection to the past, for it is part of who they are now and will be in the future. Candles could be lit at home for family members who have died, with prayers offered thanking God for their lives. Families could talk about spiritual legacies left behind to strengthen and guide the present generation.

HYMNS FOR WORSHIP

GATHERING

Ye watchers and ye holy ones   LBW 175
Shall we gather at the river   WOV 690, TFF 179

HYMN OF THE DAY

For all the saints   LBW 174

ALTERNATE HYMN OF THE DAY

I know that my Redeemer lives!   LBW 352
No longer strangers   W&P 102

COMMUNION

In heaven above   LBW 330
I am the Bread of life   WOV 702

SENDING

Rejoice, O pilgrim throng!   LBW 553
Thine the amen, thine the praise   WOV 801

ADDITIONAL HYMNS AND SONGS

Behold a host   CS 13
Sing with all the saints in glory   WOV 691, CS 68
Oh, when the saints go marching in   TFF 180
The trumpets sound, the angels sing   W&P 139

MUSIC FOR THE DAY

PSALMODY

Comer, Marilyn. PW B.
Gieseke, Richard. "Lift Up Your Heads." U/2pt, cong.
   CPH 98-2959.
Harbor, Rawn. "Lift Up Your Heads." TFF 4.
Lift up your heads, O gates   WOV 631
Mahnke, Allen. "Fling Wide the Gates." U, cong.   CPH 98-2983.
Smith, Geoffrey Boulton. "Stretch towards Heaven" in PS 1.

CHORAL

Bach, Johann Christoph Friedrich. "In the Resurrection Glorious" in
   Chantry Choirbook. SATB, org.   AFP 0800657772.

Bell, John L. "In Zion." SATB.   GIA G-4541.
Fleming, Larry. "Blessed Are They." SATB div, cong, opt inst/hb.
   MSM 50-8106.
Haan, Raymond. "They Shall Shine as the Stars." SATB, org, opt hb.
   AFP 0800674014.
Schultz, Donna Gartman. "Shall We Gather at the River." SATB, pno.
   AFP 0800659376.
Schulz-Widmar, Russell. "Give Rest, O Christ." SATB.   GIA G-3819.
Young, Jeremy. "Taste and See." 2 pt, kybd, opt cong.
   AFP 0800657608.

CHILDREN'S CHOIRS

Exner, Max. "Saints of God." U, kybd.   AFP 0800646282.
Hassell, Michael. "I Sing a Song of the Saints of God." 2 pt, kybd, fl.
   AFP 0800658515.

KEYBOARD/INSTRUMENTAL

Biery, Marilyn. "Lazarus" in *Meditations on the Love of God*. Org.
   MSM 10-949.
Cherwien, David. "For All the Saints" in *Postludes on Well-Known
   Hymns*. Org.   AFP 0800656563.
Ferguson, John. "Shall We Gather at the River." Org.
   AFP 0800656857.
Kolander, Keith. "Trio on 'Blest Are They' " in *Laudate, vol. 2*. Org.
   CPH 97-6508.
Proulx, Richard. "Variations on 'Sine Nomine.' " Org.   MSM 10-810.
West, John. "Fanfare on 'Sine Nomine.' " Org.   AFP 0800659473.

HANDBELL

Afdahl, Lee. "Rejoice in God's Saints." 3–5 oct, opt perc.
   AFP 0800656695.
McChesney, Kevin. "For All the Saints." 3–5 oct, org, opt brass, timp.
   JEF MLC201067L.
Stephenson, Valerie. "When the Saints Go Marching In." 2–3 oct.
   JEF MCEGP2009.
Young, Philip M. "Shall We Gather at the River." 3–5 oct.
   AFP 0800655095.

PRAISE ENSEMBLE

Beech, Jay. "The Presence of God." 2 pt, pno, gtr.   Baytone Music.
Crouch, Andraé/arr. John Helgen. "Soon and Very Soon." SATB,
   solo, pno.   KJO 8889.
South African. "We Are Marching in the Light of God."   WOV 650
Toolan, Suzanne. "I Am the Bread of Life." WOV 702
Walker, Tommy. "Lift Up Your Heads." in *I Will Sing Songbook*.   INT.

345

November 2, 2002

Twenty-first Sunday after Pentecost
Proper 26

INTRODUCTION

In today's gospel Jesus speaks of the two great commandments—love of God, and love of neighbor—yet how difficult it is to observe them diligently. A well-known prayer of confession includes these words: "We have not loved you with our whole heart; we have not loved our neighbors as ourselves." As we hear the word and share the meal we receive the forgiveness, strength, and courage to offer our lives in God's service, loving God through our gracious acts of mercy and kindness.

PRAYER OF THE DAY

Stir up, O Lord, the wills of your faithful people to seek more eagerly the help you offer, that, at the last, they may enjoy the fruit of salvation; through our Lord Jesus Christ.

VERSE

Alleluia. Let the word of the Lord spread rapidly and be glorified everywhere, for the Lord is faithful and will strengthen you. Alleluia. (2 Thess. 3:1, 3)

READINGS

Deuteronomy 6:1-9

As Israel enters the promised land, the people are bid to keep the Law in future generations. Verses 4-5 are called the Shema, which is used in Jewish daily prayer.

Psalm 119:1-8

Happy are they who seek the LORD with all their hearts. (Ps. 119:2)

Hebrews 9:11-14

The sacrifice of Christ, the high priest, not only cleanses from ritual impurity, but brings about forgiveness and thus the worship of the living God.

Mark 12:28-34

When a scribe asks Jesus which commandment is first of all, Jesus answers that love of God and love of neighbor are interconnected and define the heart of the kingdom of God.

SEMICONTINUOUS FIRST READING/PSALM

Ruth 1:1-18

In this reading, Ruth, a foreign (Moabite) woman, goes beyond duty to stay with her Israelite mother-in-law and expose herself to life in a strange land by accompanying Naomi to live in Bethlehem.

Psalm 146

The LORD lifts up those who are bowed down. (Ps. 146:7)

COLOR Green

THE PRAYERS

In communion with all the saints, let us pray to God who is our eternal home.

A BRIEF SILENCE.

Guide your church, O God, and give us courage to love you with all our hearts, and to proclaim your gospel in a culture of change and doubt. Lord, in your mercy,

hear our prayer.

Watch over this troubled world. Bring peace to areas torn by strife, justice where it is lacking, and food and shelter to those in need of it, and lead us to be your agents in that work. Lord, in your mercy,

hear our prayer.

Care for those who are overlooked, have compassion on those who are forgotten, and grant your gift of healing to all who struggle with ill health *(especially)*. Lord, in your mercy,

hear our prayer.

Guide those who are making inquiry into the faith, and all who wish to explore the baptized life among us. Give them strength in their exploration, and keep them in the nurture of this community. Lord, in your mercy,

hear our prayer.

HERE OTHER INTERCESSIONS MAY BE OFFERED.

Sanctify the memory of all your saints, and especially those who have recently died. Keep us in fellowship with them always in your eternal love. Lord, in your mercy,

hear our prayer.

Your reign, O God, endures forever, and in Christ we are free to be your saints and servants. Hear our prayers for

346

the sake of him who died and rose again, and lives with you in the company of all your saints in light.
Amen

IMAGES FOR PREACHING

Preaching on familiar texts is perhaps the most difficult, especially one that is so straightforward. The commandments before us in the gospel are clear and concise. "Love the Lord your God and your neighbor as yourself." It is how we often summarize these two commands. Note also that the text seeks to make us even more familiar with this word. Echoing the Shema of Deuteronomy 6, we are to love the Lord our God with all of our heart, and with all of our soul, and with all of our mind, and with all of our strength. Deuteronomy goes on to command us to teach this diligently to our children and to make it a centerpiece of every part of our daily living.

Familiarity does not breed contempt here. These commandments are to orient our every moment. They are the compass, the horizon, and the anchor of our daily living. They contextualize the decisions we make and the directions we take each day. If God is one, what does the direction I am taking reveal about whom or what I worship? Loving this One whose image I share as creature, how shall I live with others who also bear the image of the Creator? Familiar though the commandments are, their application is full of the nuance and diversity of life.

We in the church are those people who see mission and ministry called forth in these commandments. Commanding us to be neighbors to those both far and near who are in need, the word this day pulls us to the center of our gathering. The God who is one, whom we are to love with all our being, is the God whose holiness is emptied out in the gift of this Jesus. From this gathering, held in this love for us, we are sent out to be for the other.

WORSHIP MATTERS

These pericopes remind us that it is not the peripheral matters of our worship that are pleasing to God, but how we live out our faith. Burnt offerings were central to worship in biblical times, but even they are not what is necessary. Can we change our practice for the benefit of the body of Christ, when that is called for? Providing the history and rationale of worship choices in a weekly bul-

letin note helps a congregation understand the origins and helps open them to those enhancements that are not mere gimmicks. And it is important for worship planners to consider the full range of options, which is one of the goals of this resource. Not all will work for a given community, but some changes are beneficial.

LET THE CHILDREN COME

We are called to pass on God's story from generation to generation. Children are part of this telling. It is a story of love—God loves them, they love others. "You shall love your neighbor as yourself" the gospel text tells us. Children need to learn that these words come alive through actions and deeds. Encourage them to think of something kind that they can do for a "neighbor." Consider having them, or a parent, write what that is on a small piece of paper. These can be placed along with the offering and lifted up as gifts to God.

HYMNS FOR WORSHIP
GATHERING
Joyful, joyful we adore thee   LBW 551
O day of peace   WOV 762
In Christ there is no east or west   TFF 214

HYMN OF THE DAY
O God beyond all praising   WOV 797

ALTERNATE HYMN OF THE DAY
Lord, thee I love with all my heart   LBW 325
With all your heart   DH 95

COMMUNION
Spirit of God, descend upon my heart   LBW 486
Draw us in the Spirit's tether   WOV 703

SENDING
Oh, that the Lord would guide my ways   LBW 480
Bind us together   WOV 748, TFF 217, W&P 18

ADDITIONAL HYMNS AND SONGS
Around the great commandment   DH 93
My God, accept my heart this day   H82 697
Help me, Jesus   TFF 224
I love you, Lord   W&P 67

347

MUSIC FOR THE DAY

PSALMODY

Beckstrand, William.   PW B.

Walker, Christopher. "Teach Me, O God" in PS 3.

CHORAL

Colvin, Tom/arr. Carlton Young. "Fill Us with Your Love." SATB, kybd.   AG AG7256.

Emerson, Roger, arr. "O Sifuni Mungu." SATB, perc. HAL 40326302.

Erickson, Richard. "Where Charity and Love Prevail." 2 pt mxd/SAB/STB, kybd, opt perc.   KJO 6306.

Nicholson, Paul A. "Jerusalem." SATB, opt tpt, cong, brass sextet.   AFP 0800653815.

Stanford, Charles. "Beati quorum via." SSATBB.   B&H OCT5318.

White, David Ashley. "O Bread of Life from Heaven" in *The Augsburg Choirbook.* 2 pt, mxd, org.   AFP 0800656784.

Young, Jeremy. "Nothing Can Come between Us." SAB, kybd, opt cong.   AFP 0800657098.

CHILDREN'S CHOIRS

Davis, Sid. "Love Divine, All Loves Excelling." SA, kybd. MSM 50-9408.

Reeves, Jeff. "Create in Me a Clean Heart." U/2 pt, pno. CG CGA879.

KEYBOARD/INSTRUMENTAL

Albrecht, Mark. "Thaxted" in *Timeless Tunes for Flute and Piano.* Pno, inst.   AFP 0800659074.

Callahan, Charles. "Partita on 'Hyfrydol.'" Org.   CPH 97-5940.

Cherwien, David. "Joyful, Joyful We Adore Thee" in *Postludes on Well-Known Hymns.* Org.   AFP 0800656563.

HANDBELL

Afdahl, Lee. "Thaxted." 3–5 oct, opt brass, timp. AFP 0800658140.

Hentz, Phyllis Treby. "Meditation on 'Morecambe.'" 4–6 oct, opt 3 oct.   MSM 30-801.

Mager, Stephen. "Pavane." 3 oct, opt fl.   MSM 30-813.

PRAISE ENSEMBLE

Batstone, Bill and Morris Chapman. "With All of My Heart" in *Praise Hymns and Choruses, 4th ed.* MAR.

Klein, Laurie. " I Love You, Lord."   W&P 67

Muchow, Rick. "All about Love." U, pno, gtr, orch. Encouraging Music.

Monday, November 3

MARTÍN DE PORRES, RENEWER OF SOCIETY, 1639

Martín was the illegitimate son of a Spanish knight and Ana Velázquez, a freed black slave from Panama. Martín apprenticed himself to a barber-surgeon in Lima, Peru, and was known for his work as a healer. Martín was a lay brother in the Order of Preachers (Dominicans) and engaged in many charitable works. He was a gardener as well as a counselor to those who sought him out. He was noted for his care of all the poor, regardless of race. His own religious community described him as the "father of charity." His work included the founding of an orphanage, a hospital, and a clinic for dogs and cats. He is recognized as an advocate for Christian charity and interracial justice.

Friday, November 7

JOHN CHRISTIAN FREDERICK HEYER, MISSIONARY TO INDIA, 1873

Heyer was the first missionary sent out by American Lutherans. He was born in Germany and came to the United States after his confirmation. He was ordained in 1820, established Sunday schools, and taught at Gettysburg College and Seminary. Heyer became a missionary in the Andhra region of India. During a break in his mission work he received the M.D. degree from what would later be Johns Hopkins University. He later served as chaplain of the Lutheran seminary at Philadelphia until his death.

Because of Heyer's work as a pastor, missionary, and a medical doctor, his commemoration can lead us to be mindful of all who work for healing of both body and spirit.

November 9, 2003

Twenty-second Sunday after Pentecost
Proper 27

INTRODUCTION

All that we have—our lives, families, possessions, labor, and talents—comes from God and belongs to God. From the Christian perspective, we are not owners but stewards of all that the Creator has given us. And all that we have is given to us for the good of others. The divine economy works with equity for all, a hand always open to the poor, the outcast, and the forgotten ones. God's bounty gives us the grace to hold nothing back in serving God.

PRAYER OF THE DAY

Lord, when the day of wrath comes we have no hope except in your grace. Make us so to watch for the last days that the consummation of our hope may be the joy of the marriage feast of your Son, Jesus Christ our Lord.

VERSE

Alleluia. Keep awake therefore, for you do not know on what day your Lord is coming. Alleluia. (Matt. 24:42)

READINGS

1 Kings 17:8-16

The books of Joshua, Judges, Samuel, and Kings present a theological perspective derived from the book of Deuteronomy. One of the basic themes of this theological perspective is that faithful obedience to God's Law brings blessing while disobedience brings curse. Today's reading dramatizes God's power over nature to reward obedience to the Law (survival) and to punish disobedience (drought).

Psalm 146

The LORD lifts up those who are bowed down. (Ps. 146:7)

Hebrews 9:24-28

The letter to the Hebrews describes Christ as a high priest who offers himself as a sacrifice for our sin. Christ does not die again and again each year. He died once, is alive with God, and will reveal himself on the last day.

Mark 12:38-44

After engaging in a series of public arguments with religious leaders in the temple, Jesus contrasts the proud and evil ways of those leaders with the sacrificial humility and poverty of the widow.

SEMICONTINUOUS FIRST READING/PSALM

Ruth 3:1-5; 4:13-17

Naomi, who lost her husband and both her sons, still has the support of her widowed daughter-in-law Ruth. Naomi is resourceful in arranging the marriage of Ruth to a wealthy kinsman who, in marrying Ruth, also "redeems" by purchasing a small plot of land that belonged to Naomi's husband.

Psalm 127

Children are a heritage from the LORD. (Ps. 127:4)

COLOR Green

THE PRAYERS

In communion with all the saints, let us pray to God who is our eternal home.

A BRIEF SILENCE.

Let us pray for the church, that it would always seek to welcome those disregarded or misunderstood by society at large. Lord, in your mercy,

hear our prayer.

Let us pray for the world, that leaders of the nations would be diligent in making policy that honors those who are poor and in need. Lord, in your mercy,

hear our prayer.

Let us pray for those whose spouses have died and whose income is limited. May they be provided for by caring family, friends, and neighbors. Lord, in your mercy,

hear our prayer.

Let us pray for those who are ill *(especially)*, that they would know God's love in the midst of their sickness, and that healing strength would be theirs. Lord, in your mercy,

hear our prayer.

Let us pray for all who give of their abundance of resources in this congregation, that they might be blessed in their giving and our congregation's mission be extended. Lord, in your mercy,

hear our prayer.

HERE OTHER INTERCESSIONS MAY BE OFFERED.

Let us remember the faithful departed and those who mourn their absence *(especially)*, that the comfort of the

Spirit would keep them in the resurrection's hope. Lord, in your mercy,

hear our prayer.

Your reign, O God, endures forever, and in Christ we are free to be your saints and servants. Hear our prayers for the sake of him who died and rose again, and lives with you in the company of all your saints in light.

Amen

IMAGES FOR PREACHING

A story always seems to be useful for "Stewardship Sunday" this time of the year. This story must be the one for November this year. No doubt, giving all that one has is a powerful stewardship message. But this story holds so much more. It is a dangerous story as well. It unsettles and disturbs and no amount of exhortation to support the mission and ministry of our particular congregation will cover up the sting of this story for most of our folk. The widow gives her all. Foreshadowing the self-giving of Jesus on the cross, she lets go of all that she has.

Barbara Brown Taylor suggested that the most amazing part of the story is that Jesus was watching this woman instead of the rich and wealthy. Taylor says it's something about "it takes one to know one." This self-giving withholds nothing from God. By pointing her out, Jesus seems to be saying once again that gaining one's life comes in the letting go instead of the grasping.

Whom do we watch? Look at our tabloids, our magazines, our newspapers, and our televisions. We are enamored with those who have and are getting more. Occasionally we lift up those who give away their lives, but we keep this behavior at a distance so as not to confound our daily living. We treat those who give of themselves (World Trade Center firefighters, Mother Teresa) as heroic but not as normative models for those who follow Jesus.

The woman is worth watching. Ironically, in her giving all to God, she reminds us that all that we have is God's. In watching her, we can see the gift of life and grace that God provides for us and the whole creation. In this gift we receive all that we need and are freed so that we might give of ourselves to God and to others.

WORSHIP MATTERS

Gathering the offering is "down time" in many congregations, rather than a central worship act. Make the giving as visible as the receiving. Even the vested worship leaders—pastor, assisting ministers, acolytes—can put their offerings into the collection basket when it arrives at the altar, modeling at the same time individual giving as well as receiving the offerings on behalf of the body of Christ. Children can receive small offering envelope boxes of their own, the cost considered as much a part of the worship as the candles. For those who may give monthly, on days when money is not put into the offering, enclosing a note instead about service in God's name will make the offering of one's time and skill more visible. Money is merely frozen time and action, so teaching to give both gifts at the time of the collection symbolizes much more when both are encouraged.

LET THE CHILDREN COME

The story of the widow giving all she had, despite her poverty, is a powerful one. Children, though often having little money of their own, can be encouraged to give from the heart. Perhaps there could be a special children's offering taken this day. The money would come from the children (maybe earned by doing special jobs) and collected separately from the regular offering. Children could serve as ushers for this collection and participate in an offertory prayer that they helped write. Monies collected could be donated to an organization that assists those living in poverty.

HYMNS FOR WORSHIP
GATHERING

God is truly present   CS 32, LBW 249

For the fruit of all creation   WOV 760

HYMN OF THE DAY

Take my life, that I may be   LBW 406

ALTERNATE HYMN OF THE DAY

Day by day   WOV 746

All that we have   W&P 5

COMMUNION

O Bread of life from heaven   LBW 222

Now we offer   WOV 761

SENDING

Lord of all good   LBW 411

Blessed assurance   WOV 699, TFF 118

ADDITIONAL HYMNS AND SONGS

Blest are the pure in heart   H82 656
As saints of old   CS 12
I'd rather have Jesus   TFF 233
We are an offering   W&P 146

MUSIC FOR THE DAY

PSALMODY

Beckstrand, William.   PW B

Cooney/arr. Daigle. "Praise the Lord, My Soul" in PCY 4.

Praise the Almighty   LBW 539

Stewart, Roy James. "Praise the Lord" in PCY 5.

Wellicome, Paul. "Maranatha, Alleluia!" in PS 1.

CHORAL

Christiansen, F. Melius. "Psalm 50: Offer unto God" in *The Augsburg Choirbook*. SATB div.   AFP 0800656784.

Collins, Dori Erwin. "Offering." SATB, pno, fl, opt hb.
   AFP 0800659694.

Ellingboe, Bradley, arr. "Tandi Tanga Jesus." SATB, perc.
   AFP 0800654781.

Erickson, Karle. "Three Swedish Hymns." SATB, kybd, 2 fl.
   AFP 0800649834.

Hayes, Mark. "Day by Day." SATB, pno.   AFP 0800658345.

Svedlund, Karl-Erik/ed. Bruce Bengtson. "There'll Be Something in Heaven." SATB.   AFP 0800657616.

CHILDREN'S CHOIRS

Kosche, Kenneth. "God's Angels." 2 pt, kybd.   MSM 50-9401.

Wold, Wayne L. "God's Loving Call." U, kybd.   CG CGA649.

KEYBOARD/INSTRUMENTAL

Mathews, Peter. "Autumn Nocturne." Vc, org.   MSM 20-959.

Petersen, Lynn. "Blott en dag" in *Abide with Me*. Org.
   AFP 0800659465.

Porter, Rachel Trelstad. "Blott en dag" in *Day By Day*. Pno.
   AFP 0800656326.

Stoldt, Frank. "Ar hyd y nos" in *Augsburg Organ Library: November*. Org.
   AFP 0800658965.

HANDBELL

Lorenz, Ellen Jane. "Shaker Tune." 3 oct, fl.   AMSI HB-2.

McChesney, Kevin. "Day by Day." 3 oct.   JEF JHS9182.

McFadden, Jane. "Two More Swedish Melodies." 3–4 oct, opt hc.
   AFP 0800657357.

Powell, Robert. "Psalm 146." 2 oct, 2 pt.   GIA G2089.

PRAISE ENSEMBLE

Ash, Mike. "I Will Rise Up" in *Praise Band Songbook 9*. 3 pt, pno, gtr.
   MAR.

Blanchard, Michael/arr. Greer. "Be Ye Glad." SATB, pno.
   Allegis AG-1006.

Underwood, Scott. "Take My Life." in *Holiness Songbook*.
   Vineyard Music.

Tuesday, November 11

MARTIN, BISHOP OF TOURS, 397

Martin's pagan father enlisted him in the army at age fifteen. One winter day, a beggar approached Martin for aid and he cut his cloak in half and gave a portion to the beggar. Later, Martin understood that he had seen the presence of Christ in that beggar and this ended his uncertainty about Christianity. He soon asked for his release from his military duties, but he was imprisoned instead. After his release from prison he began preaching, particularly against the Arians. In 371 he was elected bishop of Tours. As bishop he developed a reputation for intervening on behalf of prisoners and heretics who had been sentenced to death.

Today, at the same time as we remember this soldier turned peacemaker, the United States remembers the end of World War I and veterans of all U.S. wars. Let these commemorations together move us to pray and work for peace in our families, congregations, and nation.

SØREN KIERKEGAARD, TEACHER, 1855

Kierkegaard, a nineteenth-century Danish theologian whose writings reflect his Lutheran heritage, was the founder of modern existentialism. Though he was engaged to a woman he deeply loved, he ended the relationship because he believed he was called to search the hidden side of life. Many of his works were published under a variety of names, so that he could reply to arguments from his own previous works. Kierkegaard's work attacked the established church of his day. He attacked the church's complacency, its tendency to intellectualize faith, and its desire to be accepted by polite society.

Kierkegaard's work makes room for doubt in the life of faith. He also served as a prophetic challenge to churches that may want to set aside paradox for an easy faith and the gospel for cultural acceptability.

351

November 16, 2003

Twenty-third Sunday after Pentecost
Proper 28

INTRODUCTION

During November the lectionary leads the worshiping assembly to visions of the last day, to a reflection on the resurrection of the body and life everlasting. Some religious people see only panic and doom in the future. They dwell in the land of fear. The conclusion to the Lord's Prayer offers another view: the kingdom, the power, and the glory are yours, now and forever. It is a bold confession of faith in God, who is our refuge and our strength. Such a hope, according to Hebrews, leads us to encourage one another in love and good deeds.

PRAYER OF THE DAY

Lord God, so rule and govern our hearts and minds by your Holy Spirit that, always keeping in mind the end of all things and the day of judgment, we may be stirred up to holiness of life here and may live with you forever in the world to come, through your Son, Jesus Christ our Lord.

VERSE

Alleluia. The Lord says, "Surely I am coming soon." Amen. Come, Lord Jesus! Alleluia. (Rev. 22:20)

READINGS

Daniel 12:1-3

The book of Daniel represents a kind of literature called "apocalyptic," which is full of bizarre visions, strange symbolism, and supernatural happenings. Arising during times of great persecution, apocalyptic literature employs a vivid language that prevents outsiders to the faith from understanding its content. Overall, it is concerned with God's revelation about the end-time and the coming kingdom of God, when God will vindicate the righteous who have been persecuted.

Psalm 16

My heart is glad and my spirit rejoices; my body shall rest in hope. (Ps. 16:9)

Hebrews 10:11-14 [15-18] 19-25

The letter to the Hebrews presents an extended discussion of how Christ offered himself as a sacrifice so that sinners, cleansed by his blood, might have life. Therefore, the writer concludes, our life together should be marked by confidence, assurance, hope, and encouragement.

Mark 13:1-8

In the last week of his life, Jesus warned his disciples concerning trials that were to come upon them and upon the world. He exhorts the listener: Do not be alarmed.

SEMICONTINUOUS FIRST READING/PSALM

1 Samuel 1:4-20

This story explains the circumstances leading to the birth of Samuel in a pious Israelite family. It exhibits the familiar Israelite motif of the devout barren wife who eventually conceives a son with the help of God.

1 Samuel 2:1-10

My heart exults in the LORD; my strength is exalted in my God. (1 Sam. 2:2)

COLOR Green

THE PRAYERS

In communion with all the saints, let us pray to God who is our eternal home.
A BRIEF SILENCE.
Almighty God, keep your church expectant and ready for that day when you will bring to completion your plan for earth and heaven, making all things new. Lord, in your mercy,
hear our prayer.
Lord of the nations, violence and war threaten to devour the well-being of your people throughout the world. Come to the assistance of all who seek to bring an end to fighting and unrest. Lord, in your mercy,
hear our prayer.
God of the lowly, draw near to all who are imprisoned in body or mind. Restore them to wholeness, and bring to health all who struggle with sickness (*especially*). Lord, in your mercy,
hear our prayer.
God of grace, help the worship of this congregation to provide nourishment to all, that we might serve you to-

gether in the confession of our faith without wavering.
Lord, in your mercy,

hear our prayer.

HERE OTHER INTERCESSIONS MAY BE OFFERED.

Holy God, give us joy as we remember the loved ones
who are now at rest in your blessed peace *(especially)*.
Bring us one day to be reunited with them in your new
Jerusalem. Lord, in your mercy,

hear our prayer.

Your reign, O God, endures forever, and in Christ we are
free to be your saints and servants. Hear our prayers for
the sake of him who died and rose again, and lives with
you in the company of all your saints in light.

Amen

IMAGES FOR PREACHING

The end of all things is not a concept or idea limited to
religious communities. It is a significant part of the discussion in the sciences of physics and cosmology.
Known as the necrotic principle, it seems a "fact" that
the end of the universe shall come. Just as scientists
know that death is necessary to the continuation of life,
their formulas and observations indicate that either the
universe shall collapse back upon itself or will eventually
spin apart. The book *The End of the World and The Ends of
God* contains many interesting essays that provide a window to this discussion.

Christian worship is one place in our society and culture where every week witness is given to the end of
things. Witness is given to a view of time that is at odds
with the *chronos* of the world. In worship, the end of this
world is proclaimed, confessed, sung, and prayed for. We
are given stories and metaphors, songs and liturgies that
enact this conversation and speak of God's participation
in this process of ending. In such a gathering, in such a
community, the insights of the community of scientists
concerning the end of the cosmos can find a place and be
welcomed as the community seeks orientation and integration for life in the world and for the new life to come.

Our congregations benefit when we speak the
promise of the end. Such proclamation not only destabi-
lizes structures and institutions that claim ultimate alle-
giances, but also provides hope for all seeking light in
these shadowed days. For unlike the scientist, we are able
to give a witness that the endings are but the beginning
of birth pangs that usher in life eternal.

WORSHIP MATTERS

Contemporary messianic imposters and awareness of the
end times make November a time of sober contemplation even without today's readings. However, sometimes
we overlook the people's terror in hearing these scriptures at a time when the secular world wants the focus to
be on the holidays and their attendant consumer spending. Benefit November worship by surrounding the readings with the music that emphasizes the beauty of a
minor key. Ask the children of the congregation or
adults who can sketch to draw in black and white a
world preparing for winter and a church aware of tough,
even frightening times. Use some of the drawings to illustrate a bulletin inside or out. Acknowledge darker
times by reduced lighting if possible during some parts
of the worship experience, but end on a note of jubila-
tion with the promised light coming forth.

LET THE CHILDREN COME

The text from Hebrews encourages people to gather together and build up the community through "love and
good deeds." Today we still need to remind congregations of the importance of consistent worship attendance. For families with children, worshiping regularly is
a valuable and needed priority in lives that are frag-
mented and pulled in many directions. Children can
learn early on that worship is a special place where they
are welcomed, where they can praise and pray, where they
can share the peace with all kinds of people, and where
they can wait in hope for what is to come.

HYMNS FOR WORSHIP

GATHERING

Christ is made the sure foundation   LBW 367, WOV 747
Come, we that love the Lord   WOV 742, TFF 135

HYMN OF THE DAY

Through the night of doubt and sorrow   LBW 355

ALTERNATE HYMN OF THE DAY

Judge eternal, throned in splendor   LBW 418
Fear not for tomorrow   HFW

COMMUNION

Spirit of God, descend upon my heart   LBW 486
I am the Bread of life   WOV 702

353

SENDING

With God as our friend   LBW 371

Soon and very soon   WOV 744, TFF 38, W&P 128

ADDITIONAL HYMNS AND SONGS

For to this end   DH 104

O day of God, draw nigh   H82 600, 601

Deep river   TFF 174

Blessing, honor, and glory   W&P 21

MUSIC FOR THE DAY

PSALMODY

Beckstrand, William.   PW B.

Foley, John. "Psalm 16" in PCY 7.

Haas, David. "Psalm 16" in PCY 8.

Howard, Julie. *Sing for Joy: Psalm Settings for God's Children.* Liturgical Press 81462078-7.

Inwood, Paul. "Centre of My Life" in PS 2.

Marshall, Jane. *Psalms Together.* U, cong.   CG CGC 18.

CHORAL

Bach, J. S. "O Jesus Christ, My Life, My Light" in *Bach for All Seasons.* SATB, org. AFP 080065854X.

Fleming, Larry. "Blessed Are They." SATB, hb.   MSM 50-8106

Haan, Raymond. "They Shall Shine As the Stars." SATB, org, opt hb. AFP 0800674014.

Hurd, David. "Love Bade Me Welcome." SATB.   Selah 418-610.

Johnson, Ralph. "Be Still and Know That I Am God." SATB, pno. KJO 8961.

Keesecker, Thomas. "Remember." SATB, kybd, 2 trbl inst, opt cong. AFP 0800656016.

Schrader, Jack. "Soon and Very Soon." SATB, pno.   HOP GC 952.

CHILDREN'S CHOIRS

Lindh, Jody. "Praise the Lord Who Reigns Above." U, pno, opt Orff inst, 3 oct hb, tamb, bass.   CG CGA583.

Marshall, Jane. "Psalm 16" in *Psalms Together.* U antiphonal, kybd. CG CGA18.

KEYBOARD/INSTRUMENTAL

Henkelman, Brian. "Let All Mortal Flesh Keep Silence" in *Communion Meditations.* Org, opt vc.   CPH 97-6535.

Kerr, J. Wayne. "Ebenezer" in *Christ Is Alive!* Org.   AFP 0800658027.

Leupold, Anton Wilhelm. "Jesus, meine Zuversicht" in *Augsburg Organ Library: Easter.* Org.   AFP 0800639368.

Martinson, Joel. "Festival Intrada." Org, tpt.   CPH 97-6193.

HANDBELL

Anderson, C. "It Is Well with My Soul." 3–4 oct, hb solo, duet, pno. JEF HP1439.

Hall, J. "I Am the Bread of Life." 3–5 oct, opt hc.   JEF CO976659.

Honoré, Jeffrey. "Marching to Zion." 3–5 oct.   AFP 080067488X.

Young, Philip. "Deep River." 3–5 oct.   FLA HP5371.

PRAISE ENSEMBLE

Baloche, Rita. "Rock of Ages" in *Praise Band Songbook 7.* 3 pt, pno, gtr. MAR.

Croft, William/arr. Tommy Walker. "O God, Our Help in Ages Past." in *Live a Legacy Songbook.*   MAR.

Moen, Don. "I Will Sing" in *I Will Sing Songbook.* 3 pt, pno, gtr.   INT.

Muller, Teresa. "Rock of My Salvation."   W&P 161

Monday, November 17

ELIZABETH OF THURINGIA, PRINCESS OF HUNGARY, 1231

This Hungarian princess gave away large sums of money, including her dowry, for relief of the poor and sick. She founded hospitals, cared for orphans, and used the royal food supplies to feed the hungry. Though she had the support of her husband, her generosity and charity did not earn her friends within the royal court. At the death of her husband, she was driven out. She joined a Franciscan order and continued her charitable work, though she suffered abuse at the hands of her confessor and spiritual guide. Her lifetime of charity is particularly remarkable when one remembers that she died at the age of twenty-four. She founded two hospitals and many more are named for her.

November 23, 2003

Christ the King
Proper 29

INTRODUCTION

We proclaim Christ our king as he goes to the throne of the cross. We acclaim him our ruler as he sheds his blood. We acknowledge him as our Lord as he gives himself to us in bread and cup. Christ is our king as he reigns from the tree, sharing our fears and experiencing our frailties. In the reign of God, the powerful one does not intimidate the weak, but cares for them. In the reign of God, the person of authority does not use others, but seeks them out and crowns them with mercy.

On this date, the church commemorates Clement, the third bishop of Rome (died 100) as well as Miguel Augustín Pro, a priest who was martyred in 1927 for his support of poor people in Mexico.

PRAYER OF THE DAY

Almighty and everlasting God, whose will it is to restore all things to your beloved Son, whom you anointed priest forever and king of all creation: Grant that all the people of the earth, now divided by the power of sin, may be united under the glorious and gentle rule of your Son, our Lord Jesus Christ, who lives and reigns with you and the Holy Spirit, one God, now and forever.

VERSE

Alleluia. I am the Alpha and the Omega, the first and the last, the beginning and the end. Alleluia. (Rev. 22:13)

READINGS

Daniel 7:9-10, 13-14

To the community for whom this passage was written, it seemed as though the oppression God's people were experiencing would never end. Daniel's message is: Indeed, it shall end. The Ancient One who is judge will call all nations to account and will give dominion to God's people who are represented by "one like a human being."

Psalm 93

Ever since the world began, your throne has been established. (Ps. 93:3)

Revelation 1:4b-8

The book of Revelation begins with a series of messages addressed to seven churches. John's greeting to these churches extols God as one who controls their past, present, and future.

John 18:33-37

In John's gospel, the story of Jesus and Pilate presents two different ways of exercising power: through force or with love.

SEMICONTINUOUS FIRST READING/PSALM

2 Samuel 23:1-7

This passage is a song that aims to give theological and moral legitimacy to the ongoing dynasty of David that endured over four hundred years until the destruction of Jerusalem in 587 B.C.

Psalm 132:1-13 [14-19] (Psalm 132:1-12 [13-18] [NRSV])

Let your faithful people sing with joy. (Ps. 132:9)

COLOR White

THE PRAYERS

In communion with all the saints, let us pray to God who is our eternal home.

A BRIEF SILENCE.

Let us pray that the church would always lift high the cross from which Christ our king rules and reigns. Lord, in your mercy,

hear our prayer.

Let us pray that all people, nations, and languages would be brought into the peace of Christ's eternal dominion of love. Lord, in your mercy,

hear our prayer.

Let us pray that all who have been victims and all who have been mistreated by injustice would be comforted by the one who endured the shame of the cross. Lord, in your mercy,

hear our prayer.

Let us pray that this congregation would identify with the suffering, the sorrowing, and the sick of the community *(especially)*. May we always seek avenues to reach out in tangible and loving ways. Lord, in your mercy,

hear our prayer.

HERE OTHER INTERCESSIONS MAY BE OFFERED.

Let us pray in thanksgiving for those who have died *(es-*

355

pecially), that we, with all your saints, will be brought one day to rejoice in your eternal kingdom, there to sing your praises for all eternity. Lord, in your mercy,
hear our prayer.

Your reign, O God, endures forever, and in Christ we are free to be your saints and servants. Hear our prayers for the sake of him who died and rose again, and lives with you in the company of all your saints in light.
Amen

IMAGES FOR PREACHING

"Who is this king of glory?" What kind of king; what kind of glory? It is a glory and kingship revealed on a cross. It is a life revealed in service. This title "king" sits on Christ's head uncomfortably like a crown of thorns, and so our imaginations are stirred. His actions and words mess with our tidy definitions. Even though we no longer like kings and queens in our public life except as quaint relics of other nations, we do want someone with power and might.

But this Jesus will not play our game in which we determine how and where that power is exercised. He speaks of power in weakness, strength in loss, and life in giving it away. Yet we also long for that time, foreshadowed in the night visions, when he shall come and all creation will serve him.

On this day, we proclaim the assurance that one who is Alpha and Omega also is the one who weeps at the tomb of Lazarus and who bids us come unto him as children to whom the dominion of God belongs. On this day, we proclaim his truth that the first shall be last and the last first. On this day, we claim that in the midst of all the transitory powers and principalities of this earth, this one is steadfast and true in the giving of God's mercy and forgiveness.

Despite the claims of the world, this day is a shout to all that true power belongs to God. On this day we give witness to our trust that God's power has been offered on behalf of the powerless and the vulnerable. This day is a confession and a claim that God is fashioning a new kingdom where all peoples and nations and languages will be as one.

WORSHIP MATTERS

The readings for today remind us that God, even in Christ, is to a large extent beyond our understanding. The mysteries of Daniel and Revelation lead us to Jesus

saying that his kingdom is not of this world. Today, especially, our approach in worship should be filled with awe. Many who attend Eastern Orthodox worship emerge with the sense that those liturgies may not be immediately accessible to visitors, but they do capture something missing in many Western services. The combination of visual splendor, chanted music, and great reverence gives witness to a God, and a salvation, utterly beyond our comprehension. We might not want to move as far in that direction, but how can we help people leave our services with the awareness that they have encountered the Almighty?

LET THE CHILDREN COME

The concept of a king whose power is stretched out on the arms of a cross is a difficult one for many children to understand. Yet they can begin to realize that Christ is like no other king. Fairy tales have given generations of children images of ermine-robed kings, sitting on majestic thrones, surrounded by opulence—kings who often ruled self-centeredly. Christ the King presents a totally different image. We have the opportunity on this Sunday to introduce our children to one who rules with justice, dignity, and selfless love—a king for real life.

HYMNS FOR WORSHIP
GATHERING

Crown him with many crowns   LBW 179
Glory to God, we give you thanks   WOV 787

HYMN OF THE DAY

At the name of Jesus   LBW 179

ALTERNATE HYMN OF THE DAY

O Christ, our king, creator, Lord   LBW 101
Soon and very soon   WOV 744, TFF 38, W&P 128

COMMUNION

Let all mortal flesh keep silence   LBW 198
Jesus, remember me   WOV 740

SENDING

Beauiful Savior   LBW 518
Lift up your heads, O gates   WOV 631
Jesus, name above all names   W&P 77, TFF 268

ADDITIONAL HYMNS AND SONGS

Blessing be and glory   OBS 50

Christ is the world's true Light   H82 542

All hail the power of Jesus' name   TFF 267

Lift up your heads   W&P 88

MUSIC FOR THE DAY

PSALMODY

Beckstrand, William.   PW B.

Bridges. "O Come and Sing unto the Lord." U, hb.   CPH 98-2927.

Hopson, Hal H. *Psalm Refrains and Tones for the Common Lectionary.*
U, cong.   HOP 425.

Wellicome, Paul. "The Lord Is King" in PS 2.

CHORAL

Clausen, René. "At the Name of Jesus." SATB, org, opt tpt/tbn/tba.
Mark Foster MF-2052.

Rameau, Jean Philippe. "Come, Thou Long-Expected Jesus" in *To God
Will I Sing.* Kybd, opt Orff inst, MH voice. AFP 0800674332.
ML voice. AFP 0800674340.

Rorem, Ned. "Sing, My Soul." SATB.   PET 6386.

Sirett, Mark. "Thou Shalt Know Him When He Comes."
SATB.   AFP 0800655206. SSAA.   AFP 0800675304.

Vaughan Williams, Ralph. "Antiphon." SATB.   ECS 1.5028.

Wood, Dale. "Jubilate Deo" in *The Augsburg Choirbook,* 2 pt mxd, org.
AFP 0800656784. Also available in SATB, org, 3 tpt, 2 hrn, perc.

CHILDREN'S CHOIRS

Carter, John/Mary Kay Beall. "How Excellent Is Your Name." 2 pt,
kybd.   AFP 0800674553.

Leaf, Robert. "To the Glory of Our King." U, kybd.   CG CGA173.

Mathews, Peter. "Praise the Lord, His Glories Show." U, pno.
CG CGA864.

KEYBOARD/INSTRUMENTAL

Carter, John. "Picardy" in *Contemplative Folk Tunes for Piano.* Pno.
AFP 0800659775.

Fields, Tim. "All Hail the Power of Jesus' Name." Org.
AFP 0800658736.

Hyslop, Scott. "Picardy" in *Six Chorale Fantasias for Solo Instrument and
Keyboard.* Kybd, solo inst.   AFP 0800656601.

Kerr, J. Wayne. "Woodlands" in *Christ Is Born!* Org.
AFP 0800658981.

Matthias, William. "Processional" in *Modern Organ Music, book 1.* Org.
OXF.

Young, Jeremy. "Picardy" in *Gathering Music for Advent.* Kybd, 2 inst.
AFP 0800656598.

HANDBELL

Burkhardt, Michael. "Lift High the Cross." 3 oct, SATB, org, brass,
timp. MSM 60-6001.

Kinyon, Barbara. "Rejoice the Lord Is King." 3–6 oct.   JEF HP1931.

Wagner, Douglas. "Crown Him with Many Crowns." 2–4 oct.
JEF HP1268.

PRAISE ENSEMBLE

Boschman, Lamar and Tyrone Williams/arr. Clydesdale. "Thine Is the
Kingdom." SATB, pno.   WRD 0 80689 72227 1.

Crouch, Andraé/arr. John Helgen. "Soon and Very Soon." SATB,
solo, pno.   KJO 8889.

Holden, Oliver/arr. Baloche. "All Hail the Power of Jesus' Name" in
Praise Band Songbook 7. 3 pt, pno, gtr.   MAR.

Sunday, November 23

CLEMENT, BISHOP OF ROME, C. 100

Clement was the third bishop of Rome and served at the
end of the first century. He is best remembered for a letter he wrote to the Corinthian congregation still having
difficulty with divisions in spite of Paul's canonical letters. Clement reminded the Corinthians of the value of
Christian love and the importance of unity within the
church. His writing echoes Paul's. "Love . . . has no limits
to its endurance, bears everything patiently. Love is neither servile nor arrogant. It does not provoke schisms or
form cliques, but always acts in harmony with others."
Clement's letter is also a witness to early understandings
of church government and the way each office in the
church works for the good of the whole.

Clement's letter reminds us that divisions within the
church are a sad part of our history and that pastoral
love for people must be present amid our differing views
of authority, scripture, and ministry.

MIGUEL AGUSTÍN PRO, PRIEST, MARTYR, 1927

Miguel Pro grew up among oppression in Mexico where
revolutionaries accused the church of siding with the
rich. He was a Jesuit priest who served during a time of
intense anticlericalism, and therefore he carried out
much of his ministry in private settings. He worked on
behalf of the poor and homeless. Miguel and his two
brothers were arrested, falsely accused of throwing a
bomb at the car of a government official, and assassinated by a firing squad. Just before the guns fired he

357

yelled, "Viva Christo Rey!" which means "Long live Christ the king!"

Make plans for work that can be done on behalf of the poor in the upcoming weeks. Raise questions of what long-term solutions may bridge the gap between rich and poor.

Tuesday, November 25

ISAAC WATTS, HYMNWRITER, 1748

Watts was born in England to a nonconformist family, people who thought the Church of England had not carried its reforms far enough. As a youth, Watts com-plained to his father about the quality of hymnody in the metrical psalter of his day. That was the start of his hymnwriting career. He wrote about 600 hymns, many of them during a two-year period that began when he was twenty years old. Some of Watt's hymns are based on psalms, a nonconformist tradition, but others are not. When he was criticized for writing hymns not taken from scripture he responded that if we can pray prayers that are not from scripture but written by us, then surely we can sing hymns that we have made up ourselves.

Thirteen of Watts's hymns are in *LBW*. "From all that dwell below the skies" (550) is set to a familiar tune and could be sung without accompaniment at gatherings today.

358 November 27, 2003

Day of Thanksgiving (U.S.A.)

INTRODUCTION

As winter darkness crosses the land, the nation takes time to offer thanks for the harvest and the abundant resources of this land. Even though this holiday witnesses many households gathering for a festive meal, Christians recognize that the source of all good things is the God who feeds the birds and clothes the grass of the field. Gathered at Christ's supper, we offer thanksgiving for the bread of life and the cup of blessing. And here, as we share these gifts, we are knit together into a community whose mission is among the poor and those in need. We offer thanks to God for the bounty of the land and seek to share these riches with all in need.

PRAYER OF THE DAY

Almighty God our Father, your generous goodness comes to us new every day. By the work of your Spirit lead us to acknowledge your goodness, give thanks for your benefits, and serve you in willing obedience; through your Son, Jesus Christ our Lord.

VERSE

Alleluia. God is able to provide you with every blessing in abundance, so that by always having enough of every-thing, you may share abundantly in every good work. Alleluia. (2 Cor. 9:8)

READINGS

Joel 2:21-27

The prophecy of Joel comes from the period of 500 to 350 B.C. He views a locust plague that ravaged the country as God's judgment on the people, whom he then calls to repentance. Today's reading points beyond the judgment of the Day of the Lord, when the Lord will repay "the years that the swarming locust has eaten."

Psalm 126

The LORD has done great things for us, and we are glad indeed. (Ps. 126:4)

1 Timothy 2:1-7

The letter to Timothy was written at a time when kings and rulers persecuted those who believed in Christ. Still, the writer calls upon Christians to pray for these rulers and offer thanksgiving on their behalf.

Matthew 6:25-33

In the Sermon on the Mount, Jesus taught his disciples about the providence of God so that they would regard life with thanksgiving and trust rather than anxiety.

COLOR White

THE PRAYERS

In communion with all the saints, let us pray to God who is our eternal home.

A BRIEF SILENCE.

We give you thanks, O God, for your church and for the wondrous ways in which you have dealt with your people. Continue to inspire the church to be a blessing in our communities and in the society at large. Lord, in your mercy,

hear our prayer.

We give you thanks, O God, for the diversity of the world's people, for all nations and their leaders. Grant to all your wisdom and grace, that a quiet and peaceable life would be possible for all people. Lord, in your mercy,

hear our prayer.

We give you thanks, O God, for your abundant blessings to us and for the bounty of the world's resources. Help us to share of our plenty with those in need. Lord, in your mercy,

hear our prayer.

We give you thanks, O God, for this congregation and for the praises you have put in our mouths and in our hearts. Help us work to insure that people in our community have sufficient food, clothing, and shelter. Lord, in your mercy,

hear our prayer.

HERE OTHER INTERCESSIONS MAY BE OFFERED.

We give you thanks, O God, for bringing the promise of comfort to those who grieve. We remember with praise and thanksgiving all who have died and who now rest at peace in your eternal harvest home. Lord, in your mercy,

hear our prayer.

Your reign, O God, endures forever, and in Christ we are free to be your saints and servants. Hear our prayers for the sake of him who died and rose again, and lives with you in the company of all your saints in light.

Amen

IMAGES FOR PREACHING

Feasting and gathering family and friends is a wonderfully human thing to do. The images in scripture of the heavenly banquet are a promise that resonates deep within the human spirit. Thanksgiving Day at its best connects with our need to gather and celebrate and to give thanks. Thanksgiving Day in North America is all

of these things, but it is also a day layered with distortions and tensions.

The very act of giving thanks assumes that one is thanking another. We in the church give witness that it is God who has given us the gifts of food and family and community. We point to this God as the creator of the wonderful diversity of the cosmos; it is this God whom we thank this day. But our witness also proclaims these gifts as gifts for all, and here we sense the bite. We know of our use and abuse of these gifts and the reality that many do not share in them. We are aware of the ways in which we squander and hoard even as we see that the pattern of giving away is what brings life.

The response to this tension, however, ought not to be that of calling off the feast but rather going deeper into it. Let us seek to open our eyes and ears to this creator of all things. Open our imaginations to God's rich and passionate regard for life. Affirm that all that we have comes from God who gives it away and would teach us that path of stewardship and living. On this day, we open our eyes in thanksgiving to all our fellow humans and creatures and the earth itself and pray that this vision remain before us in the days ahead.

WORSHIP MATTERS

It is a day for warmth and comfort in our worship. Yes, we may want to challenge assumptions that everyone is well off as we are, and any good sermon will include law as well as gospel. But the overall theme, properly, is simple thanksgiving for God's blessings. Familiar hymns will be welcome, perhaps some harvest decorations, even an element or two that is borderline kitschy. It isn't that we feel we must pander to those who complain about anything difficult in worship. Rather, we recognize that, at times, it is healthy not to have to think too hard about the darker side of life and of our relationship with God and neighbor, but simply open ourselves in grateful praise.

LET THE CHILDREN COME

As the church celebrates this time of giving thanks, children can help provide ways of recalling for us all we have been given. A thanksgiving banner could be made ahead of time by a Sunday School class and used during this service. A table in the narthex could display objects or pictures chosen or drawn by children to show things for which they are thankful. These may serve as visual

359

reminders of gifts that we as adults take for granted. Consider having a young person participate in the prayers. Thanking God is an inclusive act!

HYMNS FOR WORSHIP

GATHERING

We praise you, O God   LBW 241

O God beyond all praising   WOV 797

HYMN OF THE DAY

For the fruit of all creation   WOV 760

ALTERNATE HYMN OF THE DAY

Praise to the Lord, the Almighty   LBW 543, CS 58

Sing praise to God, who has shaped   CS 67

Glory and praise to our God   W&P 43

COMMUNION

Praise and thanksgiving   LBW 409

As the grains of wheat   WOV 705

SENDING

The day you gave us, Lord, has ended   LBW 274

Great is thy faithfulness   WOV 771

ADDITIONAL HYMNS AND SONGS

O praise ye the Lord!   H82 432

In sacred manner   OBS 64

Thank you, Lord   TFF 293

I will sing, I will sing   W&P 73

MUSIC FOR THE DAY

PSALMODY

Beckstrand, William.   PW B.

Foley, John. "Psalm 126" in PCY 7.

Haas, David. "Psalm 126" in PCY 8.

Roff, Joseph. "Psalm 126" in PCY 3.

Smith, Alan. "The Lord Has Done Great Things" in PS 1.

CHORAL

Bach, J. S. "Now Thank We All Our God" in *Bach for All Seasons*. SATB.   AFP 080065854X.

Ferguson, John. "A Song of Thanksgiving." SATB, org. AFP 0800653858.

How, Martin. "Praise, O Praise" in *The New Church Anthem Book*. 2 pt, org.   OXF 0193531097.

Jennings, Carolyn. "We Praise You, O God." SATB, org, opt tpt. AFP 0800658485.

Kosche, Kenneth. "It Is a Good Thing." SATB.   AFP 0800659635.

Porter, Emily. "Many and Great, O God." SATB, fl, drm. Calfaria Music 00-104.

CHILDREN'S CHOIRS

Beebe, Hank. "The Earth is the Lord's" from *The Twenty-fourth Psalm: A Suite for Choirs*. U, kybd.   CFI PC1004.

Farrar, Sue. "Song of Thanksgiving." 2 pt, kybd. BEC BP1291.

Patterson, Mark. "Let Praise Be the First Word." 2 pt, kybd. AFP 0800675347.

KEYBOARD/INSTRUMENTAL

Albrecht, Mark. "Ar hyd y nos" in *Timeless Hymns of Faith, vol. 2*. Pno. AFP 0800658795.

Callahan, Charles. "A Gaelic Improvisation" (Bunessan) in *Thanksgiving Suite*. Org.   MSM 10-600.

Cherwien, David. "Now Thank We All Our God" in *Postludes on Well-Known Hymns*. Org.   AFP 800656563.

Peeters, Flor. "Kremser" in *Augsburg Organ Library: November*. Org. AFP 0800659865.

Various. "Lobe den Herren" in *Augsburg Organ Library: November*. Org. AFP 0800659865.

HANDBELL

Honoré, Jeffrey. "Now We Offer." 3–5 oct.   AFP 0800674898.

Kunda, Keith. "Thanksgiving Medley." 3 oct.   JEF LWHB207.

Linker, Janet and Jane McFadden. "Come, Ye Thankful People, Come." 3–5 oct.   BEC BEHB95.

Moklebust, Cathy and David Moklebust. "Praise to the Lord, the Almighty." 4–5 oct, org, opt cong.   AFP 0800659333.

PRAISE ENSEMBLE

Landgrave, Phillip. "Come with Thanksgiving." SATB, pno. Church Street Music 0-7673-9691-X.

Rutter, John. "All Things Bright and Beautiful." 2 pt, kybd. HIN HMC-663.

Schwartz, Stephen/arr. Richard Walters. "All Good Gifts." SATB, pno.   HAL 08656516.

Smith, Henry/arr. John F. Wilson. "Give Thanks." SAB, kybd. HOP GC972.

360

Sunday, November 30

ST. ANDREW, APOSTLE

Andrew was the first of the twelve. He is known as a fisherman who left his net to follow Jesus. As a part of his calling, he brought other people including Simon Peter to meet Jesus. The Byzantine church honors Andrew as its patron and points out that because he was the first of Jesus' followers he was, in the words of John Chrysostom, "the Peter before Peter." Together with Philip, Andrew leads a number of Greeks to speak with Jesus. It is Andrew who shows Jesus a boy with five barley loaves and two fish. Andrew is said to have died on a cross saltire, an "X" shaped cross.

We too are called to invite others to the life of Christ that we will soon celebrate during Advent and Christmas. In what ways will the hope people have in the upcoming weeks be found in the church that bears the light of Christ?

Bibliography

CHOIRBOOKS

Augsburg Choirbook, The. Minneapolis: Augsburg Fortress, 1998. Kenneth Jennings, ed. Sixty-seven anthems primarily from twentieth-century North American composers.

Bach for All Seasons. Minneapolis: Augsburg Fortress, 1999. Richard Erickson and Mark Bighley, eds. Offers movements from cantatas and oratorios presented with carefully reconstructed keyboard parts and fresh English texts. Instrumental parts available.

Chantry Choirbook. Minneapolis: Augsburg Fortress, 2000. Choral masterworks of European composers spanning five centuries, many with new English translations, and indexed for use in the liturgical assembly throughout the year.

100 Carols for Choirs. Oxford and New York: Oxford University Press, 1987. David Willcocks and John Rutter, eds. One hundred classic choral settings of traditional Christmas carols.

COMPUTER RESOURCES

Icon: Visual Images for Every Sunday. Minneapolis: Augsburg Fortress, 2000. More than 600 images by liturgical artist Tanja Butler that are based on the church year and lectionary gospel readings for use in congregational bulletins and other self-published materials.

Lutheran Resources for Worship Computer Series. *Lutheran Book of Worship Liturgies; With One Voice Liturgies; Words for Worship: 2003*, Year B; *Graphics for Worship; Hymns for Worship*. Minneapolis: Augsburg Fortress, 1997–2001. *Hymns for Worship* contains more than 1,400 hymn texts and music graphics with multiple search functions.

DAILY PRAYER RESOURCES

Book of Common Worship: Daily Prayer. Louisville, Ky.: Westminster John Knox Press, 1993. Presbyterian.

Cherwien, David. *Stay with Us, Lord: Liturgies for Evening*. Minneapolis: Augsburg Fortress, 2001. Settings for Evening Prayer and Holy Communion, available in full music and congregational editions.

For All the Saints. 4 vols. Frederick Schumacher, ed. Delhi, N.Y.: American Lutheran Publicity Bureau, 1994.

Haugen, Marty. *Holden Evening Prayer*. Chicago: GIA Publications, Inc., 1990.

Makeever, Ray. *Joyous Light Evening Prayer*. Minneapolis: Augsburg Fortress, 2000.

Ramshaw, Gail. *Between Sundays: Daily Bible Readings Based on the Revised Common Lectionary*. Minneapolis: Augsburg Fortress, 1997. Readings, indexes, and other helps for daily prayer.

Weber, Paul. *Music for Morning Prayer*. Minneapolis: Augsburg Fortress, 1999. Setting of liturgical music for morning prayer.

Welcome Home: Year of Mark. Minneapolis: Augsburg Fortress, 1996. Scripture, prayers, and blessings for the household.

ENVIRONMENT AND ART

Chinn, Nancy. *Spaces for Spirit: Adorning the Church*. Chicago: Liturgy Training Publications, 1998. Imaginative thinking about ways to treat visual elements in the worship space.

Clothed in Glory: Vesting the Church. David Philippart, ed. Chicago: Liturgy Training Publications, 1997. Photos and essays about liturgical paraments and vestments.

Huffman, Walter C., S. Anita Stauffer, and Ralph R. Van Loon. *Where We Worship*. Minneapolis: Augsburg Publishing House, 1987. Written by three Lutheran worship leaders, this volume sets forth the central principles for understanding and organizing space for worship. Study book and leader guide.

Mauck, Marchita. *Shaping a House for the Church*. Chicago: Liturgy Training Publications, 1990. The author presents basic design principles for worship space and the ways in which the worship space both forms and expresses the faith of the worshiping assembly.

Mazar, Peter. *To Crown the Year: Decorating the Church through the Seasons*. Chicago: Liturgy Training Publications, 1995. A contemporary guide for decorating the worship space throughout the seasons of the year.

Stauffer, S. Anita. *Altar Guild and Sacristy Handbook*. Minneapolis: Augsburg Fortress, 2000. Revised and expanded edition of this classic on preparing the table and the worship environment.

HYMN AND SONG COLLECTIONS

As Sunshine to a Garden: Hymns and Songs. Rusty Edwards. Minneapolis: Augsburg Fortress, 1999. Forty-six collected hymns from the author of "We all are one in mission."

Bread of Life: Mass and Songs for the Assembly. Minneapolis: Augsburg Fortress, 2000. Jeremy Young's complete eucharistic music based on *With One Voice* settings 5 and 12 of his worship songs.

Congregational Song: Proposals for Renewal (Renewing Worship I). Chicago: Evangelical Lutheran Church in America, 2001. Almost 100 hymns and songs demonstrating possible strategies for revision of present collections.

Dancing at the Harvest: Songs by Ray Makeever. Minneapolis: Augsburg Fortress, 1997. More than 100 songs and service music items.

362

O Blessed Spring: Hymns of Susan Palo Cherwien. Minneapolis: Augsburg Fortress, 1997. New hymn texts set to both new and familiar hymn tunes.

Worship & Praise. Minneapolis: Augsburg Fortress, 1999. A collection of songs in various contemporary and popular styles, with helps for using them in Lutheran worship.

LEADING WORSHIP

Adams, William Seth. *Shaped by Images: One Who Presides.* New York: Church Hymnal Corporation, 1995. An excellent review of the ministry of presiding at worship.

Hovda, Robert. *Strong, Loving and Wise: Presiding in Liturgy.* Collegeville, Mn.: The Liturgical Press, 1981. Sound, practical advice for the worship leader from a beloved advocate of social justice and liturgical renewal.

Huck, Gabe. *Liturgy with Style and Grace,* rev. ed. Chicago: Liturgy Training Publications, 1984. The first three chapters offer a practical, well-written overview of the purpose of worship, the elements of worship, and liturgical leadership.

Huffman, Walter C. *Prayer of the Faithful: Understanding and Creatively Leading Corporate Intercessory Prayer,* rev. ed. Minneapolis: Augsburg Fortress, 1992. A helpful treatment of communal prayer, the Lord's Prayer, and the prayers of the people.

Singing the Liturgy: Building Confidence for Worship Leaders. Chicago: Evangelical Lutheran Church in America, 1996. A demonstration recording of the chants assigned to leaders in *LBW* and *WOV*.

See also Worship Handbook Series under Worship Studies.

LECTIONARIES

Lectionary for Worship (B). Minneapolis: Augsburg Fortress, 1996. The Revised Common Lectionary. Includes first reading, psalm citation, second reading, and gospel for each Sunday and lesser festival. Each reading is "sense-lined" for clearer proclamation of the scriptural texts. New Revised Standard Version.

Lectionary for Worship, Ritual Edition. Minneapolis: Augsburg Fortress, 1996. Large print, illustrated, hardbound edition that includes the complete three-year Revised Common Lectionary and lesser festival scriptural readings.

Readings and Prayers: The Revised Common Lectionary. Minneapolis: Augsburg Fortress, 1995. Scripture citations for the Revised Common Lectionary in use within the Evangelical Lutheran Church in America.

Readings for the Assembly (B). Gordon Lathrop and Gail Ramshaw, eds. Minneapolis: Augsburg Fortress, 1996. The Revised Common Lectionary. Emended NRSV with inclusive language.

LECTIONARY-BASED RESOURCES

Life Together. Minneapolis: Augsburg Fortress. A comprehensive series of Revised Common Lectionary resources that integrates the primary activities of congregational life: worship, proclamation, and learning.

Kids Celebrate. Reproducible children's bulletins.

LifeSongs (children's songbook, leader book, and audio cds). A well-rounded selection of age-appropriate songs, hymns, and liturgical music that builds a foundation for a lifetime of singing the faith.

Life Together: Faith Nurturing Resources for Children. Quarterly teaching and learning resources for three age levels: pre-elementary, lower elementary, upper elementary.

Living and Learning. A quarterly (except summer) guide for educational planning using the resources of *Life Together.*

Word of Life. Weekly devotional studies for adults based on the lectionary texts.

Share Your Bread: World Hunger and Worship. A Lectionary-Based Planning Guide. Chicago: Evangelical Lutheran Church in America, 2000. Worship materials, activity ideas, and devotional reflections that relate worship and the three-year lectionary to the church's mission in the areas of world hunger and social justice.

PERIODICALS

Assembly. Notre Dame Center for Pastoral Liturgy. Chicago: Liturgy Training Publications. Published five times a year. Each issue examines a particular aspect of worship. (800) 933-1800.

Catechumenate: A Journal of Christian Initiation. Chicago: Liturgy Training Publications. Published bimonthly with articles on congregational preparation of older children and adults for the celebration of baptism and eucharist. (800) 933-1800.

CrossAccent. Journal of the Association of Lutheran Church Musicians. Publication for church musicians and worship leaders in North America. (800) 624-ALCM.

Faith & Form. Journal of the Interfaith Forum on Religion, Art and Architecture. Editorial office. (617) 965-3018.

Grace Notes. Newsletter of the Association of Lutheran Church Musicians. (800) 624-ALCM.

Liturgy. Quarterly journal of The Liturgical Conference, Washington, D.C. Each issue explores a worship-related issue from an ecumenical perspective. (800) 394-0885.

Plenty Good Room. Chicago: Liturgy Training Publications. Published bimonthly. A magazine devoted to African American worship within a Roman Catholic context. Helpful articles on the enculturation of worship. (800) 933-1800.

363

Procession. Published periodically by the Office of Worship of the Evangelical Lutheran Church in America. Articles and annotated bibliographies on a range of worship topics. (800) 638-3522.

Worship. Collegeville, Mn: The Order of St. Benedict, published through The Liturgical Press six times a year. Since the early decades of this century, the primary promoter of liturgical renewal among the churches. (800) 858-5450.

PLANNING TOOLS

Calendar of Word and Season 2003: Liturgical Wall Calendar. Minneapolis: Augsburg Fortress, 2002. Date blocks note Revised Common Lectionary readings for Sundays and festivals and identify seasonal or festival color. A reference tool for home, sacristy, office.

Church Year Calendar 2003. Minneapolis: Augsburg Fortress, 2002. A one-sheet calendar of lectionary citations and liturgical colors for each Sunday and festival of the liturgical year. Appropriate for bulk purchase and distribution.

Choosing Contemporary Music: Seasonal, Topical, Lectionary Indexes. Minneapolis: Augsburg Fortress, 2000. Provides references to multiple collections of contemporary praise and liturgical songs. Includes extensive scripture and topic indexes.

Indexes for Worship Planning: Revised Common Lectionary, Lutheran Book of Worship, With One Voice. Minneapolis: Augsburg Fortress, 1996. Indexes the hymns and songs in *Lutheran Book of Worship* and *With One Voice.* Includes extensive scripture and topic indexes.

Worship Planning Calendar 2003. Minneapolis: Augsburg Fortress, 2002. A two-page per week calendar helpful for worship planners, with space to record appointments and notes for each day. Specially designed to complement *Sundays and Seasons.*

PREPARING MUSIC FOR WORSHIP

Cherwien, David. *Let the People Sing! A Keyboardist's Creative and Practical Guide to Engaging God's People in Meaningful Song.* St. Louis: Concordia Publishing House, 1997. Emphasis on the organ.

Cotter, Jeanne. *Keyboard Improvisation for the Liturgical Musician.* Chicago: GIA Publications, Inc., 1993. Practical tips for keyboard improvisation.

Farlee, Robert Buckley, gen. ed. *Leading the Church's Song.* Minneapolis: Augsburg Fortress, 1998. Articles by various contributors, with musical examples and audio CD, giving guidance on the interpretation and leadership of various genres of congregational song.

Handbells in the Liturgy: A Practical Guide for the Use of Handbells in Liturgical Worship Traditions. St. Louis: Concordia Publishing House, 1996.

Haugen, Marty. *Instrumentation and the Liturgical Ensemble.* Chicago: GIA Publications, Inc., 1991.

Hopson, Hal H. *The Creative Use of Handbells in Worship; The Creative Use of Choir in Worship; The Creative Use of Instruments in Worship; The Creative Use of Descants in Worship; The Creative Use of Organ in Worship.* Carol Stream: Hope Publishing Co.

Let It Rip! at the Piano and *Pull Out the Stops.* Minneapolis: Augsburg Fortress, 2000–2001. Collections for piano and organ respectively, each containing introductions and varied musical accompaniments by various composers for more than 100 widely used hymns and songs. Emphasis on current musical styles including blues, gospel, new age, jazz, and rolling contemporary.

Rotermund, Donald. *Intonations and Alternative Accompaniments for Psalm Tones.* St. Louis: Concordia Publishing House, 1997. (*LBW* and *LW* versions available separately.)

Weidler, Scott, and Dori Collins. *Sound Decisions.* Chicago: Evangelical Lutheran Church in America, 1997. Theological principles for the evaluation of contemporary worship music.

Westermeyer, Paul. *The Church Musician,* rev. ed. Minneapolis: Augsburg Fortress, 1997. Foundational introduction to the role and task of the church musician as the leader of the people's song.

———. *Te Deum: The Church and Music.* Minneapolis: Fortress Press, 1998. A historical and theological introduction to the music of the church.

Wilson-Dickson, Andrew. *The Story of Christian Music.* Minneapolis: Fortress Press, 1996. An illustrated guide to the major traditions of music in worship.

Wold, Wayne. *Tune My Heart to Sing.* Minneapolis: Augsburg Fortress, 1997. Devotions for choirs based on the lectionary.

PROCLAIMING THE WORD

Brueggemann, Walter, et al. *Texts for Preaching: A Lectionary Commentary Based on the NRSV.* Cycles A, B, C. Louisville, Ky.: Westminster John Knox Press, 1993–95.

Craddock, Fred, et al. *Preaching through the Christian Year.* Three volumes for Cycles A, B, C. Valley Forge, Pa.: Trinity Press International, 1992, 1993. In three volumes, various authors comment on the Sunday readings and psalms as well as various festival readings.

Days of the Lord: The Liturgical Year. 7 vols. Collegeville, Mn.: The Liturgical Press, 1991–94. Written by French biblical and liturgical experts, this series provides helpful commentary useful also with the Revised Common Lectionary.

Homily Service: An Ecumenical Resource for Sharing the Word. Silver Spring, Md.: The Liturgical Conference. A monthly publication with commentary on Sunday readings (exegesis, ideas and illustrations, healing aspects of the word, a preacher's reflection on the readings).

New Proclamation, Year B. Minneapolis: Augsubrg Fortress, 2002–2003. Various authors. A sound and useful series of commentaries on year B readings. In two volumes, Advent–Holy Week and Easter–Pentecost.

See also Worship Handbook Series under Worship Studies.

PSALM COLLECTIONS

Anglican Chant Psalter, The. Alec Wyton, ed. New York: Church Hymnal Corporation, 1987.

Daw, Carl P., and Kevin R. Hackett. *A Hymn Tune Psalter.* New York: Church Publishing, 1999.

Grail Gelineau Psalter, The. Chicago: GIA Publications, Inc., 1972. 150 psalms and eighteen canticles.

Plainsong Psalter, The. James Litton, ed. New York: Church Hymnal Corporation, 1988.

Psalm Songs. David Ogden and Alan Smith, eds. Minneapolis: Augsburg Fortress, 1998. Three volumes of responsorial psalm settings by various composers.

Psalms for the Church Year. Various volumes by different composers. Chicago: GIA Publications, Inc., 1983–present.

Psalter, The. International Commission on English in the Liturgy (ICEL). Chicago: Liturgy Training Publications, 1995.

Psalter for Worship (A, B, C). Martin Seltz, ed. Minneapolis: Augsburg Fortress, 1995–97. Settings of psalm antiphons by various composers with *LBW* and other psalm tones. Psalm texts included. Revised Common Lectionary. Volume C includes all lesser festivals.

The Psalter: Psalms and Canticles for Singing. Louisville, Ky.: Westminster John Knox Press, 1993. Various composers.

Singing the Psalms. Various volumes with various composers represented. Portland: Oregon Catholic Press, 1995–present.

REFERENCE WORKS

Concordance to Hymn Texts: Lutheran Book of Worship. Robbin Hough, compiler. Minneapolis: Augsburg Publishing House, 1985.

Foley, Edward. *Worship Music: A Concise Dictionary.* Collegeville, Minn.: The Liturgical Press, 2000.

New Dictionary of Sacramental Worship, The. Peter Fink, ed. Collegeville, Mn.: Michael Glazier/Liturgical Press, 1990.

Praying Together. English Language Liturgical Consultation. Nashville: Abingdon Press, 1988. Core ecumenical liturgical texts with annotation and commentary.

Pfatteicher, Philip. *Festivals and Commemorations.* Minneapolis: Augsburg Publishing House, 1980.

———. *Commentary on Occasional Services.* Philadelphia: Fortress Press, 1983.

———. *Commentary on Lutheran Book of Worship.* Minneapolis: Augsburg Fortress, 1990.

Pfatteicher, Philip, and Carlos Messerli. *Manual on the Liturgy: Lutheran Book of Worship.* Minneapolis: Augsburg Publishing House, 1979.

Stulken, Marilyn Kay. *Hymnal Companion to the Lutheran Book of Worship.* Philadelphia: Fortress Press, 1981.

———. *With One Voice Reference Companion.* Minneapolis: Augsburg Fortress, 2000.

Van Loon, Ralph, and S. Anita Stauffer. *Worship Wordbook.* Minneapolis: Augsburg Fortress, 1995.

SEASONS AND LITURGICAL YEAR

Huck, Gabe. *The Three Days: Parish Prayer in the Paschal Triduum,* rev. ed. Chicago: Liturgy Training Publications, 1992. For worship committees, it is an excellent introduction to worship during the Three Days: Maundy Thursday, Good Friday, and Holy Saturday/Easter Sunday.

Hynes, Mary Ellen. *Companion to the Calendar.* Chicago: Liturgy Training Publications, 1993. An excellent overview of the seasons, festivals and lesser festivals, and many commemorations. Written from an ecumenical/Roman Catholic perspective, including commemorations unique to the Lutheran calendar.

WORSHIP BOOKS

Libro de Liturgia y Cántico. Minneapolis: Augsburg Fortress, 1998. A complete Spanish-language worship resource including liturgies and hymns, some with English translations. Leader edition (2001) with complete psalter.

Lutheran Book of Worship. Minneapolis: Augsburg Publishing House; Philadelphia: Board of Publication, Lutheran Church in America, 1978.

Occasional Services: A Companion to Lutheran Book of Worship. Minneapolis: Augsburg Publishing House; Philadelphia: Board of Publication, Lutheran Church in America, 1982.

Ritos Ocasionales. Minneapolis: Augsburg Fortress, 2000. Spanish language translation of rites from *Occasional Services.*

This Far by Faith: An African American Resource for Worship. Minneapolis: Augsburg Fortress, 1999. A supplement of worship orders, psalms, service music, and hymns representing African American traditions and developed by African American Lutherans.

With One Voice: A Lutheran Resource for Worship. Minneapolis: Augsburg Fortress, 1995. Pew, leader, and accompaniment editions; instrumental parts, organ accompaniment for the liturgy, cassette/CD (selections).

WORSHIP STUDIES

Foley, Edward. *From Age to Age: How Christians Have Celebrated the Eucharist.* Chicago: Liturgy Training Publications, 1991. A survey of Christian worship, music, environment, and theological concerns.

Gathered and Sent: An Introduction to Worship. Participant book by Karen Bockelman. Leader guide by Roger Prehn. Minneapolis: Augsburg Fortress, 1999. Basic worship study course for inquirers and general adult instruction in congregations.

Inside Out: Worship in an Age of Mission. Thomas Schattauer, gen. ed. Minneapolis: Fortress Press, 1999. Lutheran seminary teachers address the mission of the church as it pertains to various aspects of worship.

Open Questions in Worship. Gordon Lathrop, gen. ed. Minneapolis: Augsburg Fortress, 1994–96. Eight volumes on matters of current conversation and concern regarding Christian worship.

What are the essentials of Christian worship? vol. 1 (1994).

What is "contemporary" worship? vol. 2 (1995).

How does worship evangelize? vol. 3 (1995).

What is changing in baptismal practice? vol. 4 (1995).

What is changing in eucharistic practice? vol. 5 (1995).

What are the ethical implications of worship? vol. 6 (1996).

What does "multicultural" worship look like? vol. 7 (1996).

How does the liturgy speak of God? vol. 8 (1996).

Ramshaw, Gail. *Every Day and Sunday, Too.* Minneapolis: Augsburg Fortress, 1996. An illustrated book for parents and children. Daily life is related to the central actions of the liturgy.

————. *1-2-3 Church.* Minneapolis: Augsburg Fortress, 1996. An illustrated rhyming primer and number book. For parents with young children, this book presents the fundamental actions of worship through numbered rhymes. A song for singing at home or in church school is included.

————. *Sunday Morning.* Chicago: Liturgy Training Publications, 1993. A book for children and adults on the primary words of Sunday worship.

Renewing Worship. Minneapolis: Augsburg Fortress, 2001–. A continuing series of provisional resources prepared by the Evangelical Lutheran Church in America.

Congregational Song: Proposals for Renewal (2001).

Holy Baptism and Related Rites (2002).

Principles for Worship (2002).

Revised Common Lectionary Prayers. Proposed by the Consultation on Common Texts. Minneapolis: Augsburg Fortress, 2002. Thematic, intercessory, and scripture prayers for each Sunday and holy day in the three-year cycle.

Senn, Frank. *Christian Liturgy: Catholic and Evangelical.* Minneapolis: Fortress Press, 1997. A comprehensive historical introduction to the liturgy of the Western church with particular emphasis on the Lutheran traditions.

Use of the Means of Grace: A Statement on the Practice of Word and Sacrament, The. Chicago: Evangelical Lutheran Church in America, 1997. Also available in Spanish and Mandarin versions.

Welcome to Christ: A Lutheran Catechetical Guide. Minneapolis: Augsburg Fortress, 1997.

Welcome to Christ: A Lutheran Introduction to the Catechumenate. Minneapolis: Augsburg Fortress, 1997.

Welcome to Christ: Lutheran Rites for the Catechumenate. Minneapolis: Augsburg Fortress, 1997.

What Do You Seek? Welcoming the Adult Inquirer. Minneapolis: Augsburg Fortress, 2000. An introduction to a congregational process for welcoming Christians through affirmation of their baptism.

Worship Handbook Series. Minneapolis: Augsburg Fortress, 2001–. Brief guides to liturgical ministries and celebrations for those who lead and participate in worship.

Acolytes and Servers. Gerald Spice. A guide for acolytes and servers as they prepare the worship space, participate in processions, and carry out other worship leadership roles.

Assisting Ministers and Readers. Gerald Spice. A guide for those who read the scriptures, offer prayer, and carry out other roles of assisting ministers in worship.

Christian Burial. Karen Bockelman. An invitation into the funeral liturgy, written to those preparing for worship in the time of death.

Marriage. Karen Bockelman. An invitation into the marriage liturgy, written to those planning for a wedding or the renewal of marriage vows.

Ministers of Communion from the Assembly. Donald Luther. Encouragement and practical helps for the ministry of carrying communion to those who are sick or otherwise absent from the worshiping assembly.

Musicians in the Assembly. Robert Buckley Farlee. Essentials of making music for worship, written for those who inspire congregational song and lead ensembles of voices or instruments in a variety of styles.

Preparing the Assembly's Worship. Craig Mueller. An overview of the work of the worship committee or other group that organizes and leads the congregation in a vibrant worship life.

Preparing the Worship Folder. Techniques for building a hospitable and effective aid to assembly participation in worship (2003).

Presiding in the Assembly. Essentials of presiding and preaching within the assembly gathered around word and sacrament (2003).

Sponsors and Baptism. Elaine Ramshaw. Encouragement and suggestions for those who serve as sponsors or godparents (especially for children) in the baptismal liturgy and in the ongoing life of the baptized.

Ushers and Greeters. Gerald Spice. Introduction to ministries of hospitality.

Welcome to Worship. Karen Bockelman. In leaflet form for pew or tract rack, a brief and very basic introduction to the essential pattern of worship.

The Art

Sundays and Seasons presents image selections from *Icon: Visual Images for Every Sunday,* an electronic library of illustrations for all three cycles of the liturgical year. The Icon artwork, sampled here, is a series of papercuttings, a technique associated with folk art that employs incisive lines and bold contrasts.

Tanja Butler is a painter and printmaker whose work has been displayed in many solo and group exhibitions across the United States. Her artwork is included in the collection of the Vatican Museum of Contemporary Religious Art and the Armand Hammer Collection of Art. Her illustrations have been published in a variety of publications and worship resource materials. She currently teaches art at Gordon College in Wenham, Massachusetts, and lives in Lynn, Massachusetts, and Averill Park, New York.

The Design

The design elements of *Sundays and Seasons* are elemental in form and structure, expressing a simplicity of means. Silver metallic ink, chosen to fill the intimately sized icons, reflects the precious nature of both image and word. The cover's striped and solid fields of color provide a sense of serenity and order. The typeface Centaur, modeled on letters cut by the fifteenth-century printer Nicolas Jenson, expresses a beauty of line and proportion that has been widely acclaimed since its release in 1929. The book's contents use a combination of the typefaces Centaur (body text) and Univers (subtexts).

The Kantor Group, based in Minneapolis, provides communication design solutions to its clients nationwide.